KU-484-972

Growth Hormone Deficiency in Adults

10 Years of KIMS

Edited by Roger Abs and Ulla Feldt-Rasmussen

Growth Hormone Deficiency in Adults

10 Years of KIMS

Edited by Roger Abs and Ulla Feldt-Rasmussen

Contributions by
Pascale Abrams, Roger Abs, Gianluca Aimaretti, Andre Aleman, Lars Anker, Anne Barlier, Gerhard Baumann, Albert Beckers, Bengt-Åke Bengtsson, Greet Van den Berghe, Hugo R Boquete, Antonia M Brooke, Thierry Brue, Felipe F Casanueva, Ginevra Corneli, P Sytze van Dam, Carlos Dieguez, William M Drake, Alain Enjalbert, Rudolf Fahlbusch, Ulla Feldt-Rasmussen, Hugo L Fideleff, Rolf-Christian Gaillard, Valentina Gasco, Ezio Ghigo, James Gibney, Vittorio Giusti, Miklós I Góth, Silvia Grottoli, Edward HF de Haan, Václav Hána, Hans Herlitz, Erika Hubina, Olle GP Isaksson, Joop AMJL Janssen, John-Olov Jansson, Gudmundur Johannsson, Peter H Kann, Fahrettin Keleştimur, Pat Kendall-Taylor, Paul Kind, Maria Kołtowska-Häggström, Hans PF Koppeschaar, Márta Korbonits, Harald Kotzmann, Alfonso Leal, Aart Jan van der Lely, Anton Luger, Dominique Maiter, Henriette Mersebach, John P Monson, Annice Mukherjee, Claes Ohlsson, Patrick Petrossians, Manuel Pombo, Vera Popovic, Åse K Rasmussen, Aled Rees, Rachel Reynaud, Michaela Riedl, Alexandre Saveanu, Maurice Scanlon, Stephen M Shalet, Klara Sjögren, Johan Svensson, Andrew A Toogood, Mary Lee Vance, Johan Verhelst, Frank Weekers, Patrick Wilton

Oxford PharmaGenesis™ Ltd

Professor Roger Abs
Department of Endocrinology, University of Antwerp, Antwerp, Belgium

Professor Ulla Feldt-Rasmussen
Department of Endocrinology, Copenhagen University Hospital, Copenhagen, Denmark

IBSN 1-903539-02-1

British Library Cataloguing-in Publication Data

A catalogue record for this book is available from the British Library.

The publisher has made every effort to ensure that the information contained in this publication is accurate at the time of printing. No responsibility for loss occasioned to any person acting or refraining from acting as a result of the material in this publication can be accepted by the authors, publisher or sponsor.

Published by Oxford PharmaGenesis™ Ltd, 1 Tubney Warren Barns, Tubney, Oxford OX13 5QJ, UK.

Printed and bound in the UK by Biddles Ltd, England.

The opinions expressed in this publication are those of the authors and do not necessarily reflect the opinions or recommendations of the publisher. The dosages, indications and methods of use for the products referred to by the authors are not necessarily the same as indicated in the package inserts for these products and may reflect the clinical experience of the authors or may be derived from the professional literature or other clinical sources.

The publisher can give no guarantee for information about drug dosage and application thereof contained in this publication. In every individual case, the respective user must check its accuracy by consulting other pharmaceutical literature.

Cover illustration: Human growth hormone.
Image from the CD-ROM: *Adult Growth Hormone Deficiency 2003* by A Beckers and Graphmed. 1) Chantalat L, Chirgadze NY, Jones N, Korber F, Navaza J, Pavlovsky AG, Wlodawer A. The crystal structure of wild-type growth hormone at 2.5 Å resolution. Protein and Peptide Letters 1995;2:333 (PDB ID: 1HGU). 2) Berman HM, Westbrook J, Feng Z, Gilliland G, Bhat TN, Wessig H, Shindyalov IN, Bourne PE. The protein data bank. Nucleic Acids Res 2000;28:235–42.

Foreword

Ulla Feldt-Rasmussen[1] and Roger Abs[2]

[1]*Department of Endocrinology, Copenhagen University Hospital, Copenhagen, Denmark and* [2]*Department of Endocrinology, University of Antwerp, Antwerp, Belgium*

KIMS – Pfizer International Metabolic Database – is the world's largest and most comprehensive pharmacoepidemiological survey on growth hormone (GH) therapy in adults, containing data on approximately 9000 patients for almost 30 000 patient treatment years. It was initiated in 1994 mainly as a result of experience from KIGS – Pfizer International Growth Database – with the aim of monitoring the safety and outcome of long-term treatment of adult GH-deficient patients with Genotropin (somatropin, rbe). Over the past 10 years, KIMS has provided the evidence base necessary to optimize GH replacement therapy in adults, and has vastly increased our understanding of the consequences of GH deficiency (GHD).

Throughout the 10 years of its existence, the scientific, ethical and policy decisions relating to the use of data from KIMS have been made as a result of close collaboration between the pharmaceutical company and participating physicians. The success of this partnership has been made possible thanks to the mutual respect and trust between the company and the participating physicians who form the International KIMS Board, the latter representing the National KIMS Boards and thus all participating physicians. In this way, the quality of the data collected, the validity of the analyses carried out and the surveillance of quality control systems related to the database are optimized. Although the database is potentially open to dilution by the inclusion of patients treated outside the formal indication for GH treatment, the strict scientific attitude of the KIMS scientific community and company representatives has prevented this from happening.

The validity of the database and the rigour of the analyses have been proven by several peer-reviewed publications. Examples of the many publications based on data from KIMS appear in the reference list of the first chapter in this book. The power of databases such as KIMS compared with randomized controlled clinical trials is derived from the quantity of data that can be obtained, and the inclusion of large numbers of relatively rare cases, which could not have been evaluated separately in controlled trials. For example, data have been published on GHD and GH replacement therapy in elderly GH-deficient patients, and in patients with isolated GHD, Sheehan's syndrome, Cushing's syndrome and acromegaly. The database has also been useful for gaining rapid access to information, such as when there were concerns over the possible development of diabetes mellitus during GH therapy; fortunately, this did not appear to be the case. Information from KIMS was also useful when the UK National Institute for Clinical Excellence was in the process of evaluating the adult indication for GH therapy.

This book, comprising thirty chapters, is intended to provide a compendium of available information on GHD and GH replacement, including, where appropriate, analyses of data from the first 10 years of KIMS. The opening chapter of the book summarizes the structure and accomplishments of KIMS. Following this, three separate chapters discuss basic information on the physiology of the GH/IGF axis, including effectors of the GH axis (e.g. lipids, bone, carbohydrate), differential effects of IGF-I and the interaction of the GH/IGF axis with other hormone axes. A general overview of GHD in adults is then presented, followed by more specific detailed chapters addressing a range of topics. These include assessments of cardiovascular risk and mortality in patients with GHD, demography and aetiology of GHD, genetics of

GHD, biochemical diagnosis of GHD, and dosing and individual responsiveness to GH replacement therapy. Also covered in individual chapters are the relationship of GH with body composition, lipids, bone, cardiovascular function, coagulation and inflammation, renal function and cognitive function. Two chapters are devoted to quality of life, one providing a critique of the methodology used, and the second providing a more specific description of the impact of GHD and GH replacement on quality of life. Further chapters cover such topics as the transition of GH-deficient patients from paediatric to adult endocrinologists, GHD and GH replacement in the elderly, advanced pituitary surgery, GH-deficient patients with craniopharyngioma, and the association between radiotherapy and GHD. Then follows a description of conditions with a high risk of GHD in adulthood; the classic Sheehan's syndrome, which is rare in some countries but still prevalent in others, GH and the metabolic syndrome, and the catabolic syndrome of prolonged critical illness. Safety during GH replacement is covered in the penultimate chapter, and the final chapter tries to envisage possible future areas of research in the field of adult GHD and GH replacement.

In most of the KIMS analyses performed, as well as in the published controlled clinical trials, dramatic changes have been demonstrated in patients with GHD after commencement of GH therapy, including marked improvements in quality of life and body composition. It must be foreseen that such improvements will probably not be observed in the future – or at least they should not be – as individuals with GHD will hopefully be diagnosed and treated at an earlier stage, before the development of the full-blown syndrome. Safety, however, will remain a key issue in KIMS. Time will show whether any concern over the recurrence of pituitary adenomas, or the development of diabetes mellitus or cancer can be alleviated. Future long-term analyses of the database will also demonstrate whether the number of cardiovascular-related deaths in patients with GHD can be normalized as a result of GH therapy. Evaluation of data from databases such as KIMS has therefore been extremely useful to those involved in the clinical care of patients with GHD and will continue to be so in the foreseeable future.

We would like to acknowledge everyone who has contributed to the contents of this book and to the achievements of KIMS. We would like to thank the authors for their excellent contributions, the KIMS team in Stockholm, including all present and past members, our present and past physician colleagues in the Strategic Committee and the KIMS International Board, all other participating KIMS physicians – and, particularly, patients with GHD.

Contents

List of abbreviations

ACAT	Acylcoenzyme A:cholesterol acyltransferase
ACTH	Adrenocorticotrophin
ADH	Antidiuretic hormone
ALS	Acid-labile subunit
ANP	Atrial natriuretic peptide
AO	Adult-onset
apo	Apolipoprotein
ARF	Acute renal failure
ARG	Arginine
BAP	Bone-specific alkaline phosphatase
BI	Bioelectrical impedance
BMC	Bone mineral content
BMD	Bone mineral density
BMI	Body mass index
CETP	Cholesteryl transfer protein
CI	Confidence interval
CMI	Cardiac mass index
CNS	Central nervous system
CO	Childhood-onset
CRF	Chronic renal failure
CRP	C-reactive protein
CSF	Cerebrospinal fluid
CT	Computed tomography
DXA	Dual-energy X-ray absorptiometry
ECV	Extracellular volume
ECW	Extracellular water
ESRF	End-stage renal failure
FFA	Free fatty acid
FFM	Fat-free mass
FM	Fat mass
FMD	Flow-mediated endothelium-derived dilatation
FSH	Follicle-stimulating hormone
GFR	Glomerular filtration rate
GH	Growth hormone
GHBP	GH-binding protein
GHD	GH deficiency
GHR	GH receptor
GHRH	GH-releasing hormone
GHRHR	GHRH receptor
GHRP-6	GH-releasing peptide-6
GHS	GH secretagogue
GHS-R	GHS receptor
GnRH	Gonadotrophin-releasing hormone
Gy	Gray
HbA_{1C}	Glycosylated haemoglobin

HDL	High-density lipoprotein
HPA	Hypothalamic–pituitary–adrenal
HrQoL	Health-related quality of life
11β-HSD	11β-hydroxysteroid dehydrogenase
ICAM-1	Intercellular adhesion molecule-1
IFN	Interferon
IGF	Insulin-like growth factor
IGFBP	IGF-binding protein
IGHD	Isolated GH deficiency
IL	Interleukin
IMT	Intima–media thickness
ITT	Insulin tolerance test
JAK	Janus kinase
LBM	Lean body mass
LDL	Low-density lipoprotein
LPL	Lipoprotein lipase
LH	Luteinizing hormone
LV	Left ventricular
LVEF	LV ejection fraction
MBL	Mannan binding lectin
MPHD	Multiple pituitary hormone deficiency
MRI	Magnetic resonance imaging
NFPA	Non-functioning pituitary adenoma
NHP	Nottingham Health Profile
NK	Natural killer
NO	Nitric oxide
PAH	Para-aminohippurate
PAI-1	Plasminogen activator inhibitor type 1
PBM	Peak bone mass
PGWB	Psychological General Well-Being
PI3K	Phosphatidylinositol-3-kinase
PitAb	Autoantibody against the pituitary
PLSF	Patient Life Situation Form
PRA	Plasma renin activity
PRO	Patient-reported outcomes
QALY	Quality-adjusted life year
QoL	Quality of life
QoL-AGHDA	Quality of Life Assessment of GHD in Adults
RAAS	Renin–angiotensin–aldosterone system
ROC	Receiver operating characteristics
RPF	Renal plasma flow
RR	Relative risk
SCRT	Stereotactic conformal radiotherapy
SD	Standard deviation
SDS	SD score
SMR	Standardized mortality ratio
SOCS	Supressors of cytokine signalling
SRS	Stereotactic radiosurgery

STAT	Signal transducers and activators of transcription
T_3	Tri-iodothyronine
T_4	Thyroxine
TBF	Total body fat
TNF	Tumour necrosis factor
t-PA	Tissue-type plasminogen activator
TRH	Thyrotrophin-releasing hormone
TSH	Thyrotrophin
VLDL	Very low-density lipoprotein
vWF	von Willebrand factor
WHR	Waist/hip ratio

KIMS – its rationale and contribution to progress in managing growth hormone-related disorders

Maria Kołtowska-Häggström and Patrick Wilton
KIGS/KIMS Outcomes Research, Endocrine Care, Pfizer, Stockholm, Sweden

Summary

KIMS – Pfizer International Metabolic Database – is one of two large, global pharmacoepidemiological surveys conducted by KIGS/KIMS Outcomes Research. Initiated in 1994, the principal aim of KIMS is to monitor the long-term outcomes and safety of growth hormone (GH) replacement therapy in adult hypopituitary patients with GH deficiency (GHD). Over the past 10 years, KIMS has developed into a unique source of clinical data on the aetiologies and treatment of a variety of GH disorders. In addition to facilitating improvements in clinical practice, KIMS has sought to gain new insights into the pathology of GH disorders, to contribute to continuing education and communication and to facilitate international collaboration among the participating physicians. KIMS now includes some 9000 patients with almost 30 000 patient years of follow-up. The large numbers of patients, long duration of follow-up and wide range of variables recorded in the database enable KIMS analyses to complement and extend the information obtained from randomized controlled clinical trials. KIMS has thus evolved into an important tool within evidence-based medicine, and will continue to make a substantial contribution to scientific development and progress in the management of hypopituitarism.

Introduction

One of the fundamental features of human beings is the willingness to learn more and to have a better understanding of the world. As Aristotle said, "*All men by nature desire knowledge*". This quest for knowledge underlies the continuous progress and development of humanity and obviously applies to all areas of research, including medicine. Knowledge is an essential part of human heritage, and is built from the accumulation of information over many generations. In any area of research, information must be collected, stored, organized, analysed, interpreted and disseminated. Basic laboratory research, animal-based studies and non-experimental studies are all equally important sources of information in medicine. Among the latter category, outcomes research has a well-established and recognized place. Outcomes research collects information using large observational surveys and creates databases in which data are stored and organized. The information may then be analysed and interpreted, providing the basis for evidence-based medicine. KIGS/KIMS Outcomes Research with its large, global pharmacoepidemiological surveys – KIGS (Pfizer International Growth Database) and KIMS (Pfizer International Metabolic Database) – is a good example of how outcomes research contributes to scientific development and progress in medicine, specifically in the management of growth hormone (GH)-related disorders.

Before taking a closer look at the organization and rationale of KIMS, the strengths and limitations of this type of open survey should be outlined. The principle of such surveys is to collect data on only certain parameters, accepting measurements recorded by individual investigators [1], with no restrictions regarding the number of patients enrolled, or the duration of follow-up. They do not follow precisely designed protocols or incorporate strict inclusion/exclusion criteria. On the contrary, such surveys aim to collect information as it is recorded by the clinician, from any patient with a given condition who meets the criteria for a study. In other words, the rule of such surveys is not to interfere with routine clinical practice.

Not surprisingly, a large number of patients and corresponding extensive, longitudinal, long-term observations, as well as documentation of everyday clinical practice based in 'real life' are the characteristics of this kind of survey. These properties provide the opportunity to detect rare adverse events and unexpected treatment responses, and also allow therapy to be monitored in unselected patients. In addition, they give new insights into atypical or very specific patient subgroups that otherwise would be very difficult to investigate in a traditional clinical trial. For example, KIMS has contributed significantly to research on GH deficiency (GHD) caused by previous Cushing's disease and acromegaly [2]. Interestingly, as of February 2004, 153 patients in KIMS with GHD after previously treated acromegaly have been successfully treated with GH, and there has been no recurrence of signs or symptoms of acromegaly. Additionally, as data are collected from all over the world, such surveys incorporate a global spectrum of therapeutic routines. In this way, current medical practice and the changes it undergoes over time are also documented, and valuable information, with regard to different treatment regimens, can be accumulated. Despite all these advantages, certain aspects of these surveys, such as the limited number of controls, different methodologies and their optional nature are inherent limitations [3].

Data from observational surveys, therefore, do not replace conventional randomized controlled trials, but complement and extend the information that can be obtained from these studies.

"*Let us suppose that an ichthyologist is exploring the life of the ocean. He casts a net into the water and brings up a fishy assortment. Surveying his catch, he proceeds in the usual manner of a scientist to systematise what it reveals. He arrives at two generalisations:*
1. No sea-creature is less than two inches long
2. All sea-creatures have gills."

Sir Arthur Eddington

As in Sir Arthur Eddington's story, it is worth remembering that "*There are plenty of sea-creatures under two inches long, only your net is not adapted to catch them*", and therefore we should not reject additional sources for gaining information. In conclusion, the large number of patients included in these surveys, the extensive duration of follow-up (almost 50 000 patients with more than 100 000 patient years, and 9000 patients with almost 30 000 patient years in KIGS and KIMS, respectively) and the range of variables available for analysis, have particular importance in terms of evidence-based medicine. Providing that the data obtained are appropriately analysed and interpreted, bearing in mind all the strengths and limitations, such surveys will continue to provide outcome information that could not be derived from other sources [4].

History of KIMS

KIMS was initiated in 1994 at the request of clinical endocrinologists and as a logical extension of KIGS – a similar database collecting data on children with growth disorders. The first informal meeting to discuss the structure and concept of KIMS took place in 1993. Initial efforts were focussed on designing Case Report Forms that were simple and, at the same time, reflected the key features of GHD in a comprehensive way. This fundamental work, which still underpins the existing database, was carried out by endocrinologists from Belgium (Roger Abs), France (Jean-Pierre Tauber), Germany (Christian Wüster), Sweden (Bengt-Åke Bengtsson) and the UK (John Monson) together with representatives from Endocrine Care at Pharmacia.

Analyses from KIMS were presented for the first time at a KIMS Highlights session during the 22nd International Symposium on Growth Hormone and Growth Factors in Endocrinology and Metabolism, held in Vienna in October 1996. Jean-Pierre Tauber presented the demographic characteristics of patients enrolled in KIMS, and the clinical characteristics were discussed by Christian Wüster. John Monson talked about dose titration and Roger Abs described the effects of GH replacement and Bengt-Åke Bengtsson discussed safety aspects (Fig. 1). The first KIMS paper published in *Clinical Endocrinology* [5] was based on these data (Fig. 2). The organization and structure of KIMS was also inaugurated during this meeting, when the KIMS International Board met for the first time. The KIMS International Board in Vienna decided to establish the first KIMS Strategic Committee consisting of the pioneers. Over the years the national representatives from Denmark (Ulla Feldt-Rasmussen) and Hungary (Miklós Góth) joined the group.

The fruitful working relationship between participating endocrinologists and the company resulted in annual KIMS Highlights sessions, presenting updated analyses of the database, as

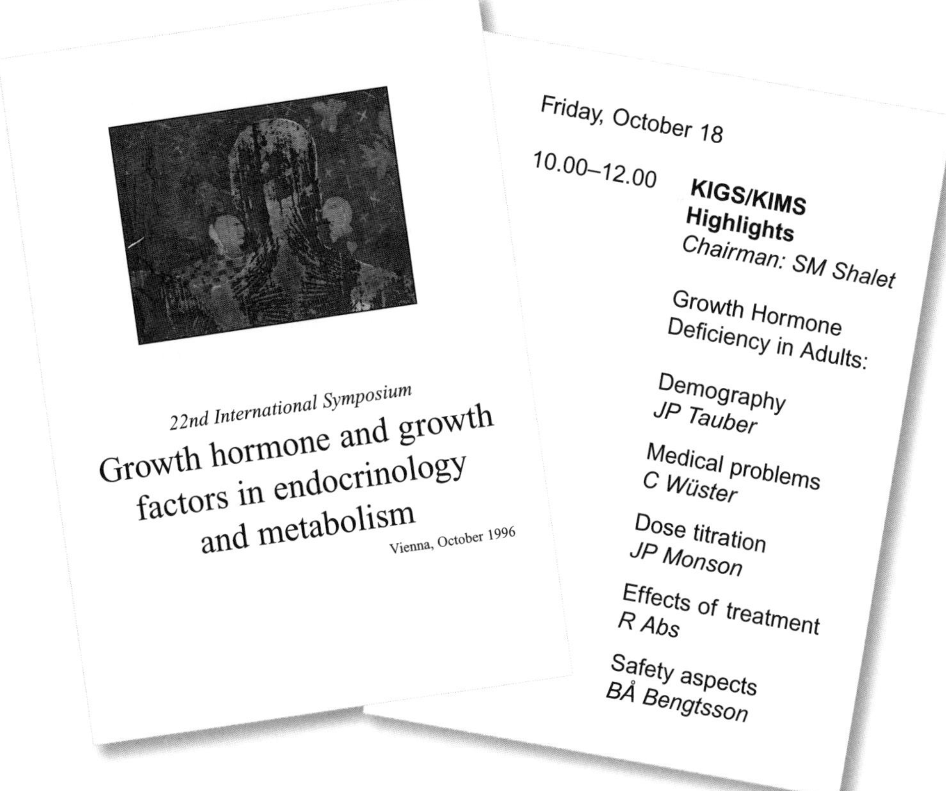

Figure 1. *The first KIMS Highlights session held during the 22nd International Symposium on Growth Hormone and Growth Factors in Endocrinology and Metabolism, held in Vienna in October 1996.*

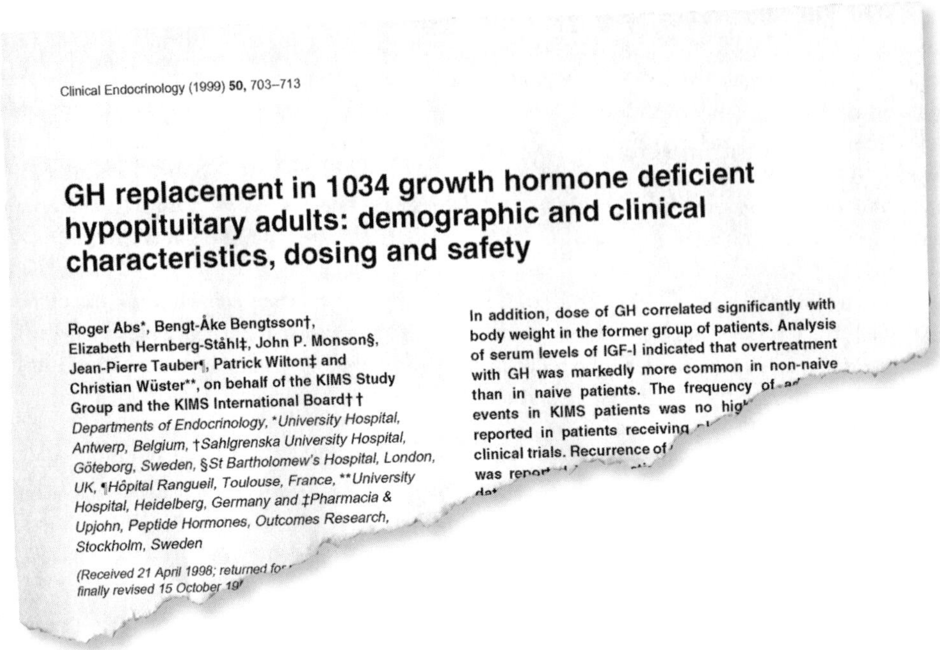

Clinical Endocrinology (1999) **50**, 703–713

GH replacement in 1034 growth hormone deficient hypopituitary adults: demographic and clinical characteristics, dosing and safety

Roger Abs*, Bengt-Åke Bengtsson†, Elizabeth Hernberg-Ståhl‡, John P. Monson§, Jean-Pierre Tauber¶, Patrick Wilton‡ and Christian Wüster, on behalf of the KIMS Study Group and the KIMS International Board††**
*Departments of Endocrinology, *University Hospital, Antwerp, Belgium, †Sahlgrenska University Hospital, Göteborg, Sweden, §St Bartholomew's Hospital, London, UK, ¶Hôpital Rangueil, Toulouse, France, **University Hospital, Heidelberg, Germany and ‡Pharmacia & Upjohn, Peptide Hormones, Outcomes Research, Stockholm, Sweden*

(Received 21 April 1998; returned for … finally revised 15 October 19…

In addition, dose of GH correlated significantly with body weight in the former group of patients. Analysis of serum levels of IGF-I indicated that overtreatment with GH was markedly more common in non-naive than in naive patients. The frequency of … events in KIMS patients was no hig… reported in patients receiving … clinical trials. Recurrence of … was repor…

Figure 2. The first paper published using data from KIMS. Reproduced from [5] with permission from Blackwell Publishing.

well as the creation of numerous project units devoted to specific areas of research. This dual approach has contributed to our increased understanding of GHD in adults, as demonstrated in the many peer-reviewed publications based on KIMS analyses [2, 5–15]. By the end of 1995, data on 500 patients from 10 countries were collected. By 1998, more than 3000 patients and 21 countries were part of the KIMS database. To date, there are 28 countries worldwide, 9000 patients and almost 30 000 patient-years of data (Fig. 3).

The principal aim of the KIMS survey is to monitor the long-term outcomes and safety of GH replacement therapy in adult hypopituitary patients with GHD [16]. Other objectives include optimizing the use of GH replacement throughout life, and increasing knowledge and improving understanding of the consequences of GHD. Over the years, KIMS has become a unique source of in-depth information on the various aspects of GH disorders associated with different aetiologies in adults. The philosophy behind KIMS is based on four cornerstones, namely improving clinical practice, gaining new insights, contributing to continuing education and communication, and facilitating international collaboration. All of these play an important role in providing outcomes research and thus meeting the goals of KIMS.

Improving clinical practice

Physicians participating in KIMS are offered a number of services to enhance patient management.

Centralized analysis of serum insulin-like growth factor I (IGF-I)

As IGF-I plays an important role in dose titration and in monitoring safety, a reliable and standardized method of analysing IGF-I is crucial in patient management [6]. It has been shown that an optimal GH dose results in IGF-I levels that are maintained in the middle-to-high region of the sex- and age-adjusted normal range throughout treatment [5], therefore dose titration against

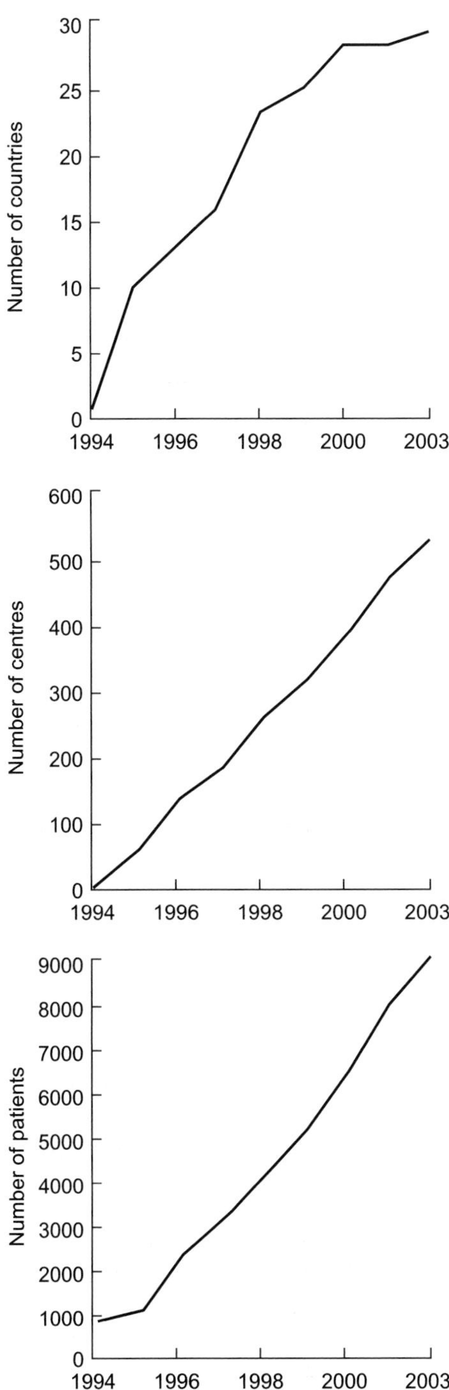

Figure 3. *Growth of KIMS between 1994 and 2003. KIMS now includes data on almost 30 000 treatment years from more than 9000 patients from over 500 centres in 28 countries worldwide.*

serum IGF-I has become the standard practice [17]. At the same time, the centralized analysis of IGF-I makes it possible to pool data from different clinics and to conduct studies on IGF-I in relation to different aspects of GHD and GH replacement therapy. Data analysis carried out by KIMS has provided normative data that are reliable and widely recognized [7]. In KIMS, serum samples are transported by courier to the central laboratory. Results, in the form of tables and graphic representations plotted on sex- and age-adjusted reference ranges, are returned to the clinic within 2 weeks. The charts not only present the most recent results for the patient, but also all previously analysed values for that patient for comparison purposes (Fig. 4).

Lipid analysis

It has been clearly demonstrated that the increased risk of cardiovascular disease observed in patients with GHD [18, 19] can be reversed by GH replacement therapy [20]. KIMS therefore provides a service for measuring cardiovascular risk factors, such as the lipid profile (triglycerides, total cholesterol, high-density lipoprotein cholesterol and low-density lipoprotein cholesterol) [21–24]. The results from these analyses are also returned to individual clinics in the form of lipid reports (Fig. 5).

To date almost 40 000 IGF-I and 20 000 lipid serum samples have been analysed within KIMS.

Patient Feedback Report

A Patient Feedback Report, which provides a general overview of the progress of an individual patient under treatment, is generated automatically each time any new clinical information is entered into the main database, and sent back to the clinic. This provides a graphical and tabular summary of relevant clinical characteristics (for example, profile of GH doses and IGF-I responses, lipid profile, body composition parameters, changes in quality of life [QoL] and patient-reported outcomes), as well as concomitant medications and adverse events. Patient Feedback Reports help physicians follow patient responses to treatment and can be used in

Serum IGF-I analysis report

Country: *Centre No:* *Patient No:*

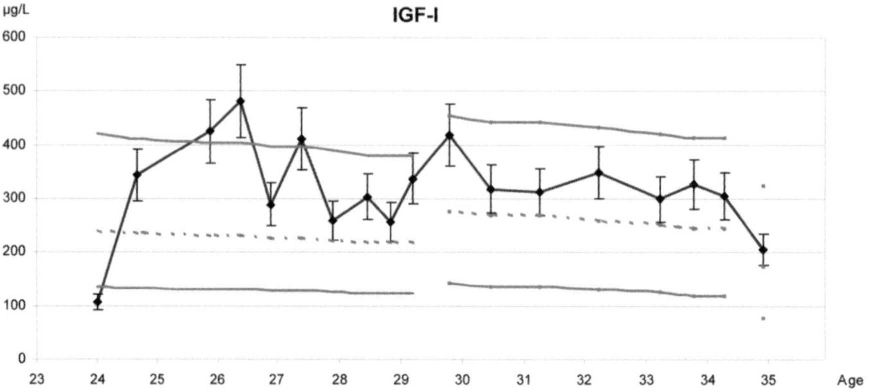

IGF-I

µg/L
600
500
400
300
200
100
0
23 24 25 26 27 28 29 30 31 32 33 34 35 Age

Date and time of sample year-month-day	 hour:minute	IGF-I Concentration nmol/L	 µg/L	SDS	Reference Range LRL	 URL µg/L
▲ *2003-05-09*	*10:00*	*26,9*	*206*	*0,5*	*77*	*323*
◄ *2002-09-17*	*11:10*	*39,9*	*305*	*0,8*	*119*	*413*
◄ *2002-03-19*	*10:58*	*42,8*	*327*	*1,0*	*119*	*413*
◄ *2001-08-29*	*09:30*	*39,1*	*299*	*0,6*	*125*	*422*
◄ *2000-08-29*	*10:15*	*45,6*	*349*	*1,1*	*130*	*432*
◄ *1999-09-06*	*10:30*	*40,7*	*311*	*0,6*	*136*	*443*
◄ *1998-11-23*	*10:15*	*41,6*	*318*	*0,6*	*136*	*443*
◄ *1998-03-25*	*10:45*	*54,6*	*418*	*1,6*	*143*	*455*
▼ *1997-08-18*		*44,1*	*337*	*1,6*	*123*	*381*
▼ *1997-04-08*		*33,6*	*257*	*0,6*	*123*	*381*
▼ *1996-11-25*		*39,6*	*303*	*1,2*	*123*	*381*
▼ *1996-04-29*		*33,7*	*258*	*0,5*	*126*	*389*
▼ *1995-10-30*		*53,9*	*412*	*2,2*	*128*	*396*
▼ *1995-04-27*		*37,8*	*289*	*0,9*	*128*	*396*
▼ *1994-10-25*		*63,0*	*482*	*2,7*	*131*	*404*

References

Method

▲ *2002-11-18 to date*

Chemiluminescence immunoassay.
[Nichols Advantage System]
Reference values based on Brabant G. et al. Hormone Research 2003; 60: 53 - 60.

◄ *1997-10-01 to 2002-11-17*

IGF-I by extraction, RIA Kit from Nichols Institute Diagnostics, San Juan Capistrano, CA 92675 USA. (Cat. No. 40-2100).

▼ *1994 to 1997-09-30*

Kabi Pharmacia. Quantification of IGF-I, Insuline like growth factor I, in serum by means of radioimmunoassay. Document I 600-02 (Confidential)
Underwood L E, Murphy M G. Radioimmunoassay of the Somatomedins/Insulin-like growth factors. In Patrano C and Peskar B A (eds.) Radioimmunoassay in Basic and Clinical Pharmacology. Springer-Verlag Berlin, 561-574 (1987).

Legends

IGF-I value *±2SD based on method reproducibility*

Reference population

-------- *Mean*

________ *±2SD*

Information Service, KIGS/KIMS Outcomes Research, Pharmacia AB, Stockholm, Sweden 2004-01-12 *Edition 0304*

Figure 4. *Example of the results of the analysis of serum IGF-I values provided by KIMS. The charts present individual patient data plotted against reference values.*

Serum Lipids analysis report

Country: *Centre No:* *Patient No:*

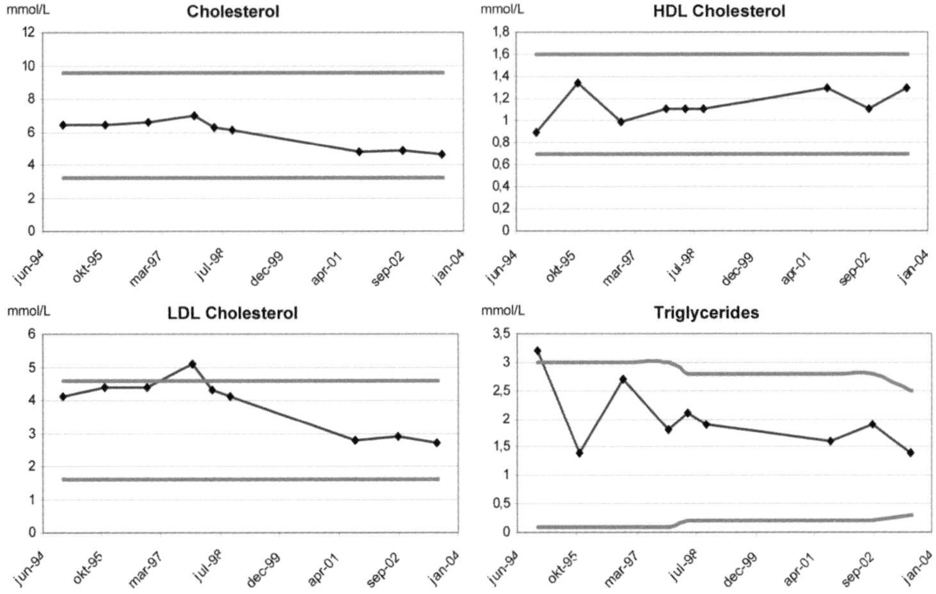

Cholesterol (mmol/L)

HDL Cholesterol (mmol/L)

LDL Cholesterol (mmol/L)

Triglycerides (mmol/L)

Date and time of sample year-month-day	hour:minute	Cholesterol mmol/L Total	HDL	LDL	Triglycerides mmol/L
2003-07-15	*11:15*	*4,6*	*1,3*	*2,7*	*1,4*
2002-08-29	*10:45*	*4,9*	*1,1*	*2,9*	*1,9*
2001-08-28	*10:00*	*4,8*	*1,3*	*2,8*	*1,6*
1998-10-13		*6,1*	*1,1*	*4,1*	*1,9*
1998-05-14		*6,3*	*1,1*	*4,3*	*2,1*
1997-12-01		*7,0*	*1,1*	*5,1*	*1,8*
1996-11-18		*6,6*	*0,99*	*4,4*	*2,7*
1995-11-20		*6,4*	*1,3*	*4,4*	*1,4*
1994-12-01		*6,4*	*0,90*	*4,1*	*3,2*

References

Cholesterol method

Roche/Hitachi product sheet No 1491458, July 2000

Reference values

Carlsson A L, Lindstedt S. The Stockholm Prospective Study 1, 1968; 48-49
Expert panel on Detection, Evaluation, and Treatment of High Blood Cholesterol in Adults. JAMA 2001, 285; 2486-2497

HDL-Cholesterol method

Roche/Hitachi product sheet No 3045935, June 2001

Reference values

Burtis & Ashwood. Tietz Textbook of Clinical Chemistry 2nd ed., 1994; 1024 -1054
Expert panel on Detection, Evaluation, and Treatment of High Blood Cholesterol in Adults. JAMA 2001, 285; 2486-2497

LDL-Cholesterol method

Friedewald W T et al. Clin.Chem. (18), No 6, 1972; 499 - 502

Reference values

Expert panel on Detection, Evaluation, and Treatment of High Blood Cholesterol in Adults. JAMA 2001, 285; 2486-2497

Triglycerides method

Roche/Hitachi product sheet No 1730711, August 2000

Reference values

Carlsson A L, Lindstedt S. The Stockholm Prospective Study 1, 1968; 48-49
Expert panel on Detection, Evaluation, and Treatment of High Blood Cholesterol in Adults. JAMA 2001, 285; 2486-2497

Information Service, KIGS/KIMS Outcomes Research, Pharmacia, Stockholm AB, Sweden 2004-01-12 *Edition 0304*

Figure 5. *Lipid analysis report produced by the KIMS lipid analysis service.*

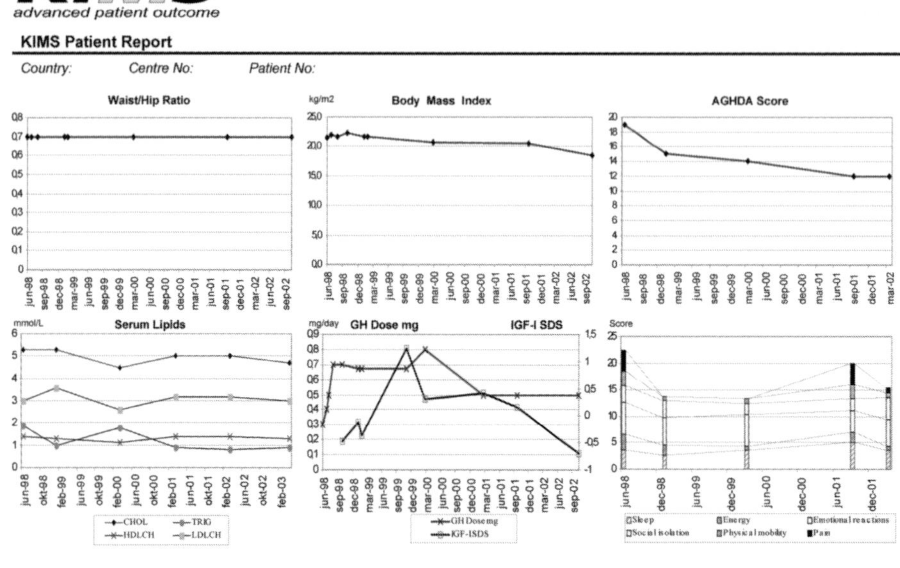

Figure 6. *Patient Feedback Reports, which help physicians to follow patient performance.*

discussions with the individuals concerned to illustrate and explain their progress (Fig. 6).

QoL and patient-reported outcomes

Impairment of QoL is another well-recognized clinical feature of GHD (see Chapter 19). Lack of energy, fatigue, social isolation and problems with sexual relationships [25], as well as lapses of memory, difficulty in concentration and forgetfulness [26], are the most commonly reported complaints. Therefore, objective, robust and validated instruments that capture all of these changes are required. KIMS collects QoL data using three different measures, two of which are generic (Nottingham Health Profile [NHP] and Psychological General Well-Being [PGWB] schedule [see Appendix A]) and one that is specific for this patient category – Quality of Life Assessment of GHD in Adults (QoL-AGHDA, see Appendix B) [27]. The QoL-AGHDA was developed through in-depth interviews with hypopituitary adults, then validated and adopted for cross-cultural use [28]. There are a number of multicentre studies ongoing within KIMS to gain further insights into QoL and patient-reported outcomes (PRO).

The burden and the cost of hypopituitary disease have been the subject of many studies. These have shown that healthcare utilization is highest in hypopituitary adults receiving routine replacement but not receiving GH [29, 30]. Collected in KIMS, and widely used in different studies, information on each patient's personal situation, social functioning and healthcare consumption broadens our understanding of the consequences of GHD and confirms the additional benefits of GH treatment [8]. For this purpose a specific, Patient Life Situation Form (PLSF) has been designed and validated (see Appendix C).

KIMS data were also used in pharmacoeconomic evaluations to estimate health utility of treatment in adults with GHD [14].

The KIMS patient management systems

KIMS provides computerized patient management systems that have been constructed to facilitate the monitoring of patients with any pituitary disorder and to help in KIMS data entry.

Questions to the KIMS database

Information collected in the KIMS database is accessible to all participating physicians, and can be accessed by posing questions to the database. This KIMS service is frequently used, and a wide range of problems related to safety, adverse events, tolerability, efficacy and atypical patient groups have been addressed. Answers for personal use in daily clinical practice are provided within 4 weeks.

Gaining new insights

Although there are many questions in the field of GH disorders that have already been answered, there are still a lot of issues that need to be addressed. KIMS is continually undertaking new studies and maintaining its contribution to the progress of endocrinology. Long-term efficacy, measured as changes in body composition, lipid profiles, bone metabolism and QoL, as well as safety, are without doubt the focus of research within KIMS. In addition, KIMS continues to broaden our knowledge of underlying pathology, providing information on new conditions that could result in acquired GHD. Examples of ongoing projects include GHD in craniopharyngioma [31, 32], Sheehan's syndrome [33] and traumatic brain injury [34], and GHD due to irradiation [35].

Research based on data from the KIMS database has contributed not only to our understanding of demographic and clinical characteristics of adult patients with GHD and to optimizing dosing, but has also revealed that the principal determinant of IGF-I SD score (SDS) was age at onset of pituitary disease. In other words, patients who acquire GHD in childhood have a greater IGF-I deficit [10]. This finding highlights the need for higher doses of GH in patients with childhood-onset GHD, as pre-treatment IGF-I is a major determinant of GH dosage in adult patients with GHD [36].

Long-term outcomes

The first large-scale analysis to show that there is an increased fracture risk in hypopituitary adults with GHD was based on KIMS data [9]. Similarly, the beneficial effects of GH treatment on QoL, in parallel with a decrease in healthcare utilization, were the main conclusions of another study undertaken using the KIMS database. This study is being continued, and it has been demonstrated that the same findings are observed in country-specific cohorts and have been maintained over a period of up to 3 years [8, 37–39].

Long-term safety

Long-term safety data from KIMS have been presented at various international meetings, including as oral communications at the Endocrine Society Meetings in 2001 and 2003, and have been published frequently in peer-reviewed journals [40] (see Chapter 29). KIMS, with its almost 30 000 patient-years of follow-up, is a remarkable contributor to safety research. During the last few years, KIMS analyses have shown no real indication of an increased risk of neoplasm or diabetes mellitus during GH replacement [11, 41], although it should be noted that the prevalence of diabetes mellitus at baseline is higher in GH-deficient patients than in the general population [42]. The first analysis of mortality rates in KIMS, published in 1999, was based on 1903 patients (2334 patient-years) and indicated that GH replacement in adults with GHD was not associated with an increased mortality [12]. The continuing analyses of mortality rates in KIMS, which are performed on an annual basis, still demonstrate standardized mortality ratios (SMRs) that are indistinguishable from country-adjusted background rates [17], in contrast to the increased SMR demonstrated in epidemiological studies of hypopituitary, GH-deficient adults.

Another aspect of safety in the treatment of GH-related disorders was thoroughly discussed in the recently published paper by Mukherjee *et al.* [15]. This is the first study to address and define the concept of risk of functional GHD during the therapy of such abnormalities. According to the authors, functional GHD can result from overtreatment of acromegaly, or insufficient replacement of GHD, and is defined by low levels of IGF-I, regardless of GH status. The study used KIMS baseline data on patients with severe GHD to determine age- and sex-related risk estimates, expressed as IGF-I SDS, for functional GHD. These estimates, together with clinical parameters, may be employed to aid dose titration of medical therapies for GH disorders in adulthood.

Treatment throughout life

In addition to studies on specific patient subgroups, as already mentioned with Cushing's disease or acromegaly, different age-groups have been another focus of interest for KIMS researchers. In one study, John Monson and colleagues [13] compared patients with GHD aged above 65 years with younger patients and concluded that both the consequences of deficiency, and the benefits of therapy, are broadly similar in older and younger patients, particularly in relation to QoL. Currently there is a project unit working on adolescent patients with GHD, which includes the issues and problems associated with transition from paediatric to adult endocrine care.

Contributing to continuing education and communication

Despite the fact that GHD in adults is now well documented and established as a distinct clinical condition, there is still a need for education about GHD in adulthood and its treatment. KIMS aims to provide endocrinologists and general practitioners, as well as health authorities, with objective and valuable information based on a large amount of detailed data. In addition to the results presented at scientific meetings/ congresses and published in peer-reviewed journals, KIMS publishes the following periodicals: KIMS Annual Reports, KIMS Abstract Books and KIMS News. The KIMS Website plays an important role in the communication of this information (Fig. 7).

KIMS Annual Reports provide physicians with an update of demographic and safety data from the database. Since 2001, KIMS Annual Reports have included QoL and PRO analyses, and discussed specific aspects related to GHD, for example bone metabolism or the effect of GH on lipid profile, and other topics of current high interest among GH specialists.

KIMS Abstract Books, published yearly, contain all the KIMS communications presented at different forums during the year, thus providing a comprehensive overview of areas of interest and research. The steadily growing volume of the KIMS Abstract Books compared with the first edition, published in 2000, highlights the increasing value of KIMS as a tool for clinical research.

KIMS News is a newsletter, which informs readers about what is happening in KIMS worldwide. Apart from presenting a summary of recent KIMS analyses, it visits KIMS centres in different countries, shows people working there, their enthusiasm and commitments. Articles about concepts such as outcomes research, pharmaco-economics or evidence-based medicine help to keep readers up to date with developments in clinical practice and to understand the difference between outcomes research and clinical trials. The newsletter always includes a short guide to upcoming scientific meetings

The KIMS Website (http://kims.pnu.com) is built around three main areas – one for patients, one for doctors and one for dedicated KIMS physicians. The Doctor and Patient areas are open to everyone; however, access to the KIMS Physician Center is restricted to participating doctors. The KIMS Website also includes an extensive library and regularly updated meeting list.

Facilitating international collaboration – KIMS structure and scientific governance

Much of the scientific work of KIGS and KIMS is carried out in small Project Units. Any participating physician can suggest a topic to study and, if approved by the International Board, a Project Unit will be established to undertake

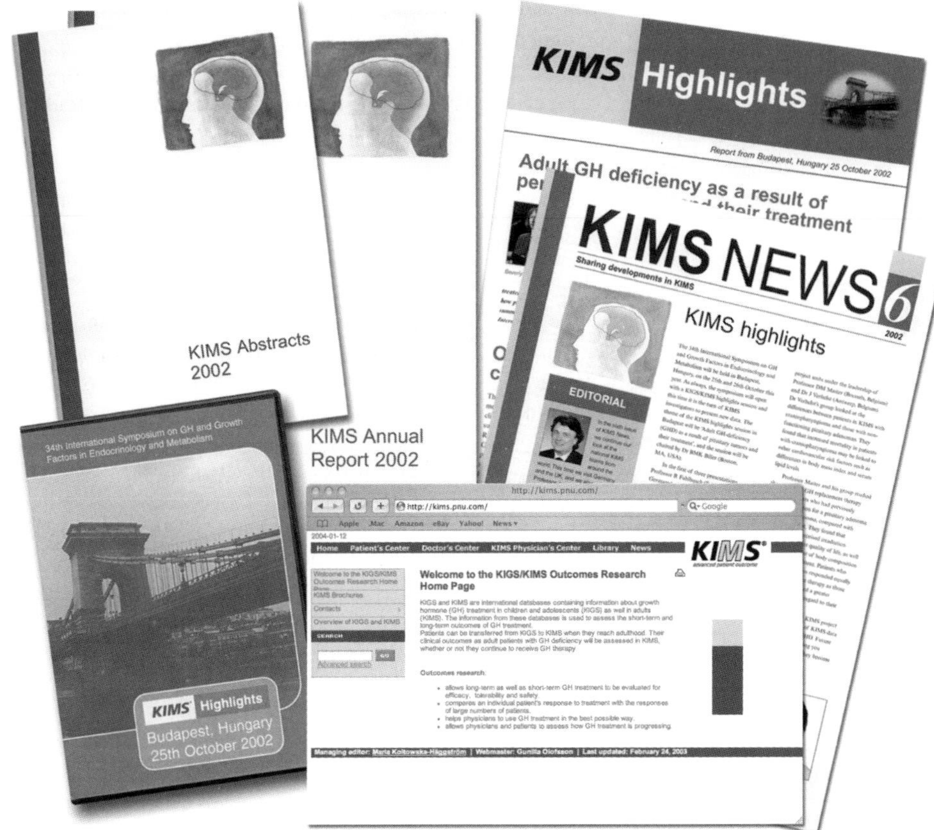

Figure 7. Selection of KIMS publications.

the investigation and analyses, and prepare publications.

KIMS is carefully managed at both the national and international levels. Physicians in each participating country may be elected or appointed to the KIMS National Boards, members of which are eligible for election to the KIMS International Board. The National Board governs all national activities, including meetings and publications based on the national KIMS data. National and international analyses of KIMS data are carried out regularly, and the KIMS International Board may also appoint KIMS physicians to Project Units to analyse data on specific topics or subgroups of patients. The overall structure of KIMS is thought to enable close international collaboration both among researchers interested in GH-related disorders, but also between researchers and the pharmaceutical industry.

In conclusion, it should be stated that whilst the randomized placebo-controlled clinical trial remains the gold standard, experience from KIMS has clearly demonstrated the value of outcomes research databases in documenting the real-life long-term consequences of specific therapeutic interventions, thus strengthening our evidence base. Therefore, KIMS is an important tool within evidence-based medicine, providing valuable information that enhances the management of patients with GHD and deepens our knowledge of this condition [43]. It is meaningful to highlight that the extensive data and long period of follow-up facilitated by pharmacoepidemiological surveys, mean that they provide outcome information that is not available from conventional clinical trials.

It only remains to thank all of the participants of KIMS from around the world whose enthusiasm, commitment and hard work have contributed to the success of this survey.

References

1. Ranke MB. The role of large databases in outcomes research. In: Bengtsson B-Å, Monson JP, editors. GH replacement in adults – the first 5 years of KIMS. Oxford: Oxford PharmaGenesis Ltd 2000:1–5

2. Feldt-Rasmussen U, Abs R, Bengtsson B-Å, Bennmarker H, Bramnert M, Hernberg-Ståhl E, Monson JP, Westberg B, Wilton P, Wüster C. Growth hormone deficiency and replacement in hypopituitary patients previously treated for acromegaly or Cushing's disease. Eur J Endocrinol 2002;146:67–74

3. Altman DG. What randomized trials and systematic reviews can offer decision makers. Horm Res 1999; 51 (Suppl 1):36–43

4. Black N. What observational studies can offer decision makers. Horm Res 1999;51 (Suppl 1):44–9

5. Abs R, Bengtsson B-Å, Hernberg-Ståhl E, Monson JP, Tauber JP, Wilton P, Wüster C. GH replacement in 1034 growth hormone deficient hypopituitary adults: demographic and clinical characteristics, dosing and safety. Clin Endocrinol (Oxf) 1999;50:703–13

6. Bengtsson B-Å, Abs R, Bennmarker H, Monson JP, Feldt-Rasmussen U, Hernberg-Ståhl E, Westberg B, Wilton P, Wüster C. The effects of treatment and the individual responsiveness to growth hormone (GH) replacement therapy in 665 GH-deficient adults. J Clin Endocrinol Metab 1999;54:3929–36

7. Brabant G, von zur Mühlen A, Wüster C, Ranke MB, Kratzsch J, Kiess W, Ketelslegers JM, Wilhelmsen L, Hulthén L, Saller B, Mattsson A, Wilde J, Schemer R, Kann P, on behalf of the German KIMS Board. Serum insulin-like growth factor I reference values for an automated chemiluminescence immunoassay system: results from a multicenter study. Horm Res 2003; 60:53–60

8. Hernberg-Ståhl E, Luger A, Abs R, Bengtsson B-Å, Feldt-Rasmussen U, Wilton P, Westberg B, Monson JP. Healthcare consumption decreases in parallel with improvements in quality of life during GH replacement in hypopituitary adults with GH deficiency. J Clin Endocrinol Metab 2001;86:5277–81

9. Wüster C, Abs R, Bengtsson B-Å, Bennmarker H, Feldt-Rasmussen U, Hernberg-Ståhl E, Monson JP, Westberg B, Wilton P. The influence of growth hormone deficiency, growth hormone replacement therapy, and other aspects of hypopituitarism on fracture rate and bone mineral density. J Bone Miner Res 2001;16:398–405

10. Lissett C, Jönsson P, Monson JP, Shalet SM. Determinants of IGF-I status in a large cohort of growth hormone-deficient (GHD) subjects: the role of timing of onset of GHD. Clin Endocrinol (Oxf) 2003;59:773–8

11. Monson JP, Bengtsson B-Å, Abs R, Feldt-Rasmussen U, Wüster C. Can growth hormone therapy cause diabetes? KIMS Strategic Committee. Lancet 2000;355:1728–9

12. Bengtsson B-Å, Koppeschaar HP, Abs R, Bennmarker H, Hernberg-Ståhl E, Westberg B, Wilton P, Monson JP, Feldt-Rasmussen U, Wüster C. Growth hormone replacement therapy is not associated with any increase in mortality. KIMS Study Group. J Clin Endocrinol Metab 1999;84:4291–2

13. Monson JP, Abs R, Bengtsson B-Å, Bennmarker H, Feldt-Rasmussen U, Hernberg-Ståhl E, Thorén M, Westberg B, Wilton P, Wüster C. Growth hormone deficiency and replacement in elderly hypopituitary adults. KIMS Study Group and the KIMS International Board. Pharmacia and Upjohn International Metabolic Database. Clin Endocrinol (Oxf) 2000;53:281–9

14. Dixon S, McEwan P, Currie CJ. Indirect estimation of the health utility of treatment in adults with growth hormone deficiency. J Outcomes Res 2003;7:1–12

15. Mukherjee A, Trainer PJ, Jönsson PJ, Monson JP, Shalet SM. Seeking the optimal target range for IGF-I during the treatment of adult GH disorders. J Clin Endocrinol Metab 2003;88:5865–70

16. Hernberg-Ståhl E, Wallström A. KIMS – rationale and organization. In: Bengtsson B-Å, Monson JP, editors. GH replacement in adults – the first 5 years of KIMS. Oxford: Oxford PharmaGenesis Ltd 2000:6–12

17. Monson JP. The KIMS database. The Endocrinologist Summer 2003;68:10

18. Rosén T, Bengtsson B-Å. Premature mortality due to cardiovascular disease in hypopituitarism. Lancet 1990;336:285–8

19. Bülow B, Hagmar L, Mikoczy Z, Nordström CH, Erfurth EM. Increased cerebrovascular mortality in patients with hypopituitarism. Clin Endocrinol (Oxf) 1997;46:75–81

20. Verhelst J, Abs R, Vandeweghe M, Mockel J, Legros JJ, Copinschi G, Mahler C, Velkeniers B, Vanhaelst L, Van Aelst A, De Rijdt D, Stevenaert A, Beckers A.

Two years of replacement therapy in adults with growth hormone deficiency. Clin Endocrinol (Oxf) 1997;47:485–94

21. Friedewald WT, Levy RI, Fredrickson DS. Estimation of the concentration of low-density lipoprotein cholesterol in plasma, without use of the preparative ultracentrifuge. Clin Chem 1972;18:499–502

22. Lopes-Virella MF, Stone P, Ellis S, Colwell JA. Cholesterol determination in high-density lipoproteins separated by three different methods. Clin Chem 1977;23:882–4

23. Fossati P, Prencipe L. Serum triglycerides determined colorimetrically with an enzyme that produces hydrogen peroxide. Clin Chem 1982;28:2077–80

24. Lie RF, Schmitz JM, Pierre KJ, Gochman N. Cholesterol oxidase-based determination, by continuous-flow analysis, of total and free cholesterol in serum. Clin Chem 1976;22:1627–30

25. Wallymahmed ME, Baker GA, Humphris G, Dewey M, MacFarlane IA. The development, reliability and validity of a disease specific quality of life model for adults with growth hormone deficiency. Clin Endocrinol (Oxf) 1996;44:403–11

26. Burman P, Deijen JB. Quality of life and cognitive function in patients with pituitary insufficiency. Psychother Psychosom 1998;67:154–67

27. McKenna SP, Doward LC, Alonso J, Kohlmann T, Niero M, Prieto L, Wirén L. The QoL-AGHDA: an instrument for the assessment of quality of life in adults with growth hormone deficiency. Qual Life Res 1999; 8:373–83

28. Holmes SJ, McKenna SP, Doward LC, Hunt SM, Shalet SM. Development of a questionnaire to assess the quality of life of adults with growth hormone deficiency. Endocrinol Metab 1995;2:63–9

29. Hakkaart-van Roijen L, Beckers A, Stevenaert A, Rutten FF. The burden of illness of hypopituitary adults with growth hormone deficiency. Pharmacoeconomics 1998;14:395–403

30. Ehrnborg C, Hakkaart-Van Roijen L, Jonsson B, Rutten FF, Bengtsson B-Å, Rosén T. Cost of illness in adult patients with hypopituitarism. Pharmacoeconomics 2000;17:621–8

31. Kendall-Taylor P. Baseline characteristics and effects of GH replacement therapy in adult GHD patients with craniopharyngioma compared to patients with pituitary adenomas. 21st Joint Meeting of the British Endocrine Societies 2002 Apr 8–11; Harrogate, UK. Oral communication

32. Abs R. A comparison of the clinical, endocrine and metabolic features of patients with adult-onset (AO) and childhood onset (CO) craniopharyngioma in the KIMS database. 10th Meeting of the European Neuroendocrine Assocation 2002 Sep 12–14; Munich, Germany. Oral communication

33. Keleştimur F. Baseline characteristics and the effects of GH replacement therapy in patients with Sheehan's syndrome as compared to non-functioning pituitary adenoma. The Endocrine Society's 85th Annual Meeting 2003 Jun 19–22; Philadelphia, USA. Poster

34. Casaneuva FF. Characteristics of GH deficiency (GHD) in adult patients who suffered traumatic brain injury (TBI), reflected in KIMS (Pharmacia International Metabolic Database). The Endocrine Society's 85th Annual Meeting 2003 Jun 19–22; Philadelphia, USA. Poster

35. Maiter DM, Abs R, Johansson G, Scanlon MF, Jönsson PJ, Kołtowska M, Wilton P. Influence of prior irradiation for pituitary adenoma or craniopharyngioma on the efficacy of growth hormone (GH) therapy in adult GH-deficient patients. The Endocrine Society's 84th Annual Meeting 2002 Jun 19–22; San Francisco, USA. Poster

36. Murray RD, Howell SJ, Lissett CA, Shalet SM. Pre-treatment IGF-I level is the major determinant of GH dosage in adult GH deficiency. Clin Endocrinol (Oxf) 2000;52:537–42

37. Rosén T, Johansson G, Mattsson A, Kołtowska M, Svensson J, Wirén L, Götherström G, Bengtsson B-Å. Growth hormone (GH) replacement therapy produces a sustained improvement in quality of life in hypopituitary adults with GH deficiency: Analysis of the KIMS database in the Swedish cohort. The Endocrine Society's 85th Annual Meeting 2003 Jun 19–22; Philadelphia, USA. Poster

38. Den Hartog M, van Kuijck MA, Mattsson A, Kołtowska-Häggström M, Koppeschaar H. Improvement in quality of life and healthcare utilization during growth hormone replacement therapy in hypopituitary adults: the Dutch KIMS experience. The Endocrine Society's 85th Annual Meeting 2003 Jun 19–22; Philadelphia, USA. Poster

39. Kann P, Buchfelder M, Mattsson A, Kołtowska-Häggström M, Metzeler H, Saller B. Healthcare consumption, QoL and patient-reported outcomes during GH replacement in hypopituitary adults: results from the German KIMS cohort. The Endocrine Society's 85th Annual Meeting 2003 Jun 19–22; Philadelphia, USA. Poster

40. Wilton P. Safety in growth hormone replacement therapy: a matter of varied responsiveness? Horm Res 2001;55 (Suppl 2):61–4

41. Monson JP, Abs R, Bengtsson B-Å, Feldt-Rasmussen U, Góth M, Kołtowska-Häggström M, Mattsson A, Wilton P. Safety and mortality during GH replacement therapy in 4457 adult GH-deficient patients – a KIMS database analysis. 192nd Society for Endocrinology Meeting 2001; London, UK. Poster

42. Bengtsson B-Å. The risk of diabetes mellitus in hypopituitary patients on growth hormone substitution. Growth Hormone Research Society 2002 Oct 5–9; Boston, USA. Oral communication

43. Ranke MB, Dowie J. KIGS and KIMS as tools for evidence-based medicine. Horm Res 1999;51 (Suppl 1):83–6

2 The physiology of the growth hormone/insulin-like growth factor axis

Aled Rees and Maurice Scanlon
Department of Medicine, University of Wales College of Medicine, Cardiff, UK

Summary

Growth hormone (GH) is produced principally in the pituitary gland as a 22 kDa polypeptide. It is secreted in a pulsatile fashion under the coordinate influences of several peptide hormones, including hypothalamic somatostatin, which is inhibitory, and stimulatory inputs from hypothalamic GH-releasing hormone and ghrelin, produced mainly in the stomach. This complex system of regulation is modified further by peripheral feedback mechanisms involving insulin-like growth factor I (IGF-I) and glucose among others, and through interaction with other hormone axes, including insulin, glucocorticoids, and thyroid and gonadal hormones. Under basal conditions, approximately 50% of GH in the circulation is bound to a high-affinity GH-binding protein, produced by proteolytic cleavage of the extracellular domain of the GH receptor (GHR). GH exerts its effects by binding to two extracellular GHR domains to induce activation of a variety of signal transduction cascades, including the Janus kinase 2 and signal transducer and activator of transcription 5 pathway, culminating in induction of gene transcription. The growth-promoting and metabolic actions of GH are mediated principally via IGF-I generation, though the relative importance of serum IGF-I, derived mainly from the liver, and locally produced IGF-I, has only recently become apparent. Approximately 80% of circulating IGF-I is bound to the 150 kDa IGF-binding protein (IGFBP) complex, consisting of IGFBP-3 and an acid-labile subunit, and this storage form of IGF-I is under GH control. GH has widespread actions on bone, lipid and carbohydrate metabolism, though its secretion and effects are modified by a number of physiological variables, such as gender, nutritional status, physical activity and age.

Introduction

The growth hormone (GH)/insulin-like growth factor (IGF) axis plays an important role in the regulation of postnatal growth and development and in the control of intermediary metabolism, energy balance and body composition. In this chapter we review the current understanding of the physiology of the GH/IGF axis, highlighting areas of particular clinical relevance.

The GH molecule

GH accounts for 10% of the pituitary hormonal content, and is stored and secreted by the somatotrophs located within the lateral aspects of the anterior pituitary. GH was originally characterized as a peptide hormone comprising a 191 amino acid, single-chain molecule with a molecular weight of 22 kDa [1]. Since then it has become apparent that the pituitary also produces a smaller GH variant with a molecular weight of 20 kDa, formed by alternative processing of the GH mRNA precursor. Besides these two most frequent isoforms, a large number of other isoforms are produced by the pituitary, including mass variants and charge variants, though the physiological role of these is unclear at present.

The *GH1* gene

The pituitary-expressed *GH1* gene is situated on the long arm of chromosome 17 within a cluster of five highly homologous genes: two chorionic somatomammotrophin genes (*CSH1* and *CSH2*), a second GH-related gene (*GH2*) and a chorionic somatomammotrophin pseudogene (*CSHP1*). We have recently shown that polymorphic and mutational variation in the promoter and coding regions of the human *GH1* gene is more frequent than had previously been recognized. A number of novel mutations in the *GH1* gene were identified by altering the selection criteria for *GH1* mutational screening in children with short stature [2] and variation in *GH1* promoter haplotype-influenced reporter gene expression *in vitro* [3]. An association was also demonstrated between the *in-vitro* expression value, corresponding to an individual's *GH1* promoter haplotype combination, and final adult height [3], suggesting that sequence variation in the *GH1* gene could influence GH levels *in vivo*. This relationship, if confirmed, could influence susceptibility to several diseases, such as cancer (acromegaly is associated with an increased risk of bowel cancer) and vascular disease (increased risk in GH deficiency [GHD] and excess), in addition to contributing to the physiological variation in human stature.

GH secretion

Although GH is secreted in discrete pulses every 3–4 hours, the vast majority of the daily GH output occurs during sleep, particularly slow-wave sleep (Stages III and IV).

Stress, physical activity and nutritional and metabolic pathways all have important influences on GH production, mediated via a complex network of signals converging at the hypothalamic and pituitary levels. These are reviewed in detail later in this chapter.

The GH receptor (GHR)

The GHR is a member of the cytokine receptor superfamily, with a wide tissue distribution and particularly high expression in the liver. It is a cell-surface-expressed transmembrane protein and the extracellular domain dimerizes upon GH binding [4]. In contrast to tyrosine kinase growth factor receptors, the GHR does not possess enzymatic activity in its cytoplasmic domain. Rather, following dimerization, it couples to non-receptor tyrosine kinases of the Janus family, principally Janus kinase 2 (JAK2). Activation of JAK2 leads to a cascade of events, including induction of signal transducers and activators of transcription (STAT) proteins, culminating in stimulation of target gene activation (Fig. 1). Of the STAT family of proteins, STAT5 is preferentially activated by GH. Furthermore, observations from the STAT5B knockout mouse, which is small and demonstrates loss of the normal GH-dependent sexual dimorphism of liver gene expression, suggest that STAT5B, rather than STAT5A, may be the isoform most relevant for GH signalling [5]. Other signal transduction cascades, such as the mitogen-activated protein kinase and phosphatidylinositol-3-kinase (PI3K) pathways are also activated by GH, with potentially important effects in regulation of cell growth, differentiation and apoptosis. Our own studies have recently identified a novel human *GH1* gene mutation (Ile179Met) exhibiting a reduced ability to activate the extracellular signal-regulated kinase pathway in a preadipocyte cell line despite normal activation of STAT5 [6]. The exact biological relevance of these additional pathways, however, is unclear at present.

GH-binding proteins (GHBPs)

In humans, two circulating GHBPs have been recognized thus far: a high-affinity form corresponding to the extracellular, ligand-binding domain of the hepatic GHR, and a low-affinity binding protein unrelated to the receptor. Most

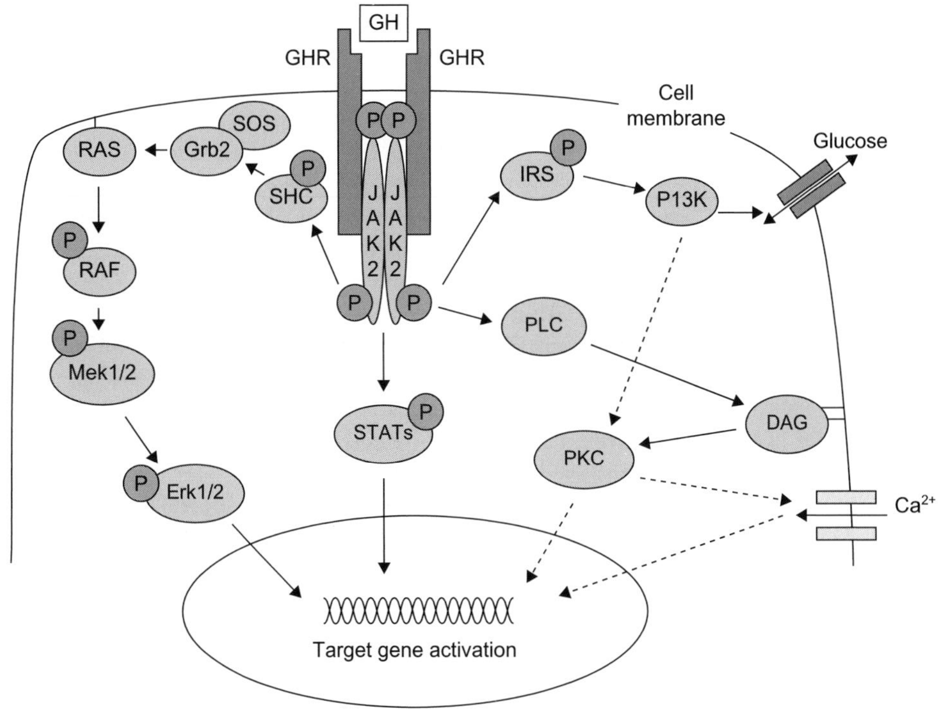

Figure 1. *Some of the pathways thought to be involved in GH signal transduction. Solid arrows indicate signal transduction cascades activated by GH. Dashed arrows relate to pathways used by other growth factors which may be involved in GH signalling.* Ca^{2+}*, calcium; DAG, diacylglycerol; Erk1/2, extracellular signal regulated kinase 1/2; Grb2, growth factor receptor-binding protein 2; IRS, insulin receptor substrate; JAK2, Janus kinase 2; Mek1/2, mitogen-activated/extracellular signal regulated kinase 1/2; P, phosphorylated tyrosine residues; PI3K, phosphatidylinositol-3-kinase; PKC, protein kinase C; PLC, phospholipase C; SOS, Son of Sevenless; STATs, signal transducers and activators of transcription.*

circulating GH is bound to the high-affinity form. In humans, the high-affinity GHBP is produced by proteolytic cleavage from the membrane-anchored GHR, in contrast to the alternative splicing of GHR mRNA in rodents. Tumour necrosis factor-α converting enzyme, a membrane-bound zinc-dependent metalloprotease, is involved in this [7], and proteolysis of the GHR can itself regulate GH signalling [8]. Under basal conditions, GHBP binds approximately half of the GH present in plasma (though GHBP is easily saturated at high GH concentrations) and acts to prolong its half-life, to dampen the oscillations in GH levels and to modify GH activity by competing for GH with the GHR.

Serum concentrations of GHBP approximate to tissue GHR expression, rising in parallel with GHR levels from low expression *in utero* to high levels in childhood and early adulthood, declining with advancing age. In fact, GHBP levels correlate closely with the concentration of GHRs across a wide spectrum of physiological, nutritional and disease states. The close relationship between GHBP levels and GHR status has led to the development of GHBP as a potential biochemical marker for GH insensitivity syndrome; however, up to 20% of patients with this condition may have normal or even high levels of serum GHBP [9], emphasizing the importance of detailed diagnostic testing of the entire GH/IGF-I axis, in addition to measurements of serum GHBP, in the assessment of GHR expression and GH functionality in individual patients.

Mode of action of GH

Generation of IGF-I

IGF-I and IGF-II share approximately 50% sequence homology with insulin, and the major source of both circulating IGFs is the liver. Hepatic IGF-I expression is responsive mainly to GH, and the levels of IGF-I in the circulation generally correlate well with GH secretion in postnatal life. Approximately 80% of circulating IGF-I is bound to the 150 kDa IGF-binding protein (IGFBP) complex, consisting of IGFBP-3 and an acid-labile subunit (ALS). However, the discovery that IGF-I is expressed in most tissues in the body has led to a debate as to the precise role of circulating versus locally produced IGF-I in mediating GH actions. Tissue IGF-I levels are often dependent on GH, as indicated by increased IGF-I mRNA expression in certain tissues following GH treatment [10], and, in many IGF-responsive tissues, local IGF-I production is partly regulated by GH [11]. In some tissues, however, IGF-I expression is independent of GH [12] and regulation of IGF-II is generally GH independent.

Data from a liver-specific IGF-I gene-deleted mouse model have helped clarify the relative contributions of circulating versus locally generated IGF-I to postnatal growth and development [13]. Although liver-specific deletion of IGF-I results in markedly reduced (> 80%) serum IGF-I concentrations, appendicular (though not axial) skeletal growth is unaffected in these animals, suggesting that locally generated IGF-I may be the major determinant of postnatal body growth. These and other data related to this mouse model are reviewed in detail in Chapter 3.

The IGFBPs

Serum IGFs are bound almost completely to a family of at least six IGFBPs, which are homologous and share a significant amount of their sequence. Hence, almost all serum IGFs form ternary complexes comprising one molecule each of IGF, IGFBP-3 (the predominant IGFBP in serum) or IGFBP-5 and ALS [14]. Lower molecular weight complexes of approximately 50 kDa, comprising several IGFBP species (IGFBP-1, -2, -4 and -6), are also present in plasma. These are incompletely saturated with IGFs, suggesting that very little free IGF-I or IGF-II is present in plasma, an assumption that has been challenged by studies using IGFBP-3 infusion in rats [15]. Unlike free IGFs and IGFs bound to the 50 kDa binary complexes, which can cross the vascular endothelium, formation of the ternary complexes restricts the IGFs to the vascular compartment and prolongs their half-lives to 12–15 hours [16], compared with the half-life of free binding proteins in plasma, estimated to be between 30 and 90 minutes, and the half-life of free IGF-I, estimated at less than 10 minutes. Formation of the ternary complexes also enables the IGFs to be stored at high concentrations, facilitating their endocrine actions yet minimizing local effects resulting from their insulin-like properties, such as hypoglycaemia.

GH is the predominant stimulus for ALS, IGF-I and IGFBP-3 formation. The importance of this regulation is clear from the almost complete absence of ALS in GHD [17], the temporal correlation between the appearance of ALS mRNA and functional hepatic GHRs [18] and the increase in plasma concentrations of IGFBP-3 and ALS after GH administration in hypophysectomized rats [19].

Physiological control of the GH/IGF-I axis

Effects of GHRH and somatostatin

GH is released in a pulsatile manner by the anterior pituitary gland and is tightly regulated by the coordinated actions of several peptide hormones and neurotransmitters. At the hypothalamic level, two principal peptides are secreted, at the median eminence, into the hypophyseal–portal circulation. GH-releasing hormone (GHRH), synthesized in the arcuate and ventromedial nuclei, stimulates both GH synthesis and secretion [20]. In contrast, somatostatin, synthesized in the periventricular and paraventricular nuclei, inhibits GH release without affecting GH synthesis [20]. Whereas GHRH is required for the initiation of GH pulses, pulse amplitude can be modified by somatostatin. Administration of a GHRH antagonist, for example, abolishes pulsatile GH release [21], whereas passive immunization with somatostatin antiserum eliminates the variability of GH response to GHRH in rats [22]. It is probable that GH pulses result from coincident peaks of hypothalamic GHRH release and troughs of somatostatin; however, direct synaptic interaction between somatostatinergic and GHRH neurones may also be important [23].

The role of neurotransmitters

Although it is clear from hypothalamic deafferentation studies that the major neural systems regulating the intermittent release of GHRH and somatostatin reside in the hypothalamus, neural inputs from extra-hypothalamic sites synapse on GHRH and somatostatinergic neurones in the mediobasal hypothalamus and are likely to play a role in the integrated control of GH release. Several neurotransmitters can also modify GH secretion, chiefly those of the adrenergic and cholinergic systems. Pharmacological agonism at both α_2-adrenergic receptors and muscarinic cholinergic receptors stimulates GH secretion [24], though the former may dominate, as co-administration of clonidine (an α_2-adrenergic agonist) and atropine (a muscarinic cholinergic antagonist) stimulates GH release, and yohimbine (an α_2-adrenergic antagonist) blocks the stimulatory effects on GH secretion of pyridostigmine (a cholinesterase inhibitor that enhances cholinergic tone) [25]. However, whether these pathways mediate their effects via stimulation of GHRH secretion, inhibition of somatostatin release, or both, is not entirely clear. For example, clonidine increases GHRH but not somatostatin concentration in sheep hypophyseal–portal blood [26]. In contrast, in humans, clonidine may decrease somatostatin secretion, as it potentiates the GH response to GHRH [25]. Cholinergic pathways are thought to suppress somatostatin release, as GHRH-stimulated GH release is augmented by cholinergic agonists and blocked by cholinergic antagonists in humans [27], and depletion of hypothalamic somatostatin content abolishes the effects of cholinergic agonists and antagonists on GH secretion in rats [28]. The importance of cholinergic mechanisms in regulating GH secretion in humans is reinforced by clinical studies demonstrating suppressed nocturnal, meal- and exercise-induced GH secretion in normal subjects and patients with type 1 diabetes treated with anticholinergics [29–31]. The potency of cholinergic blockade, using the antimuscarinic agent pirenzepine, for reducing GH, insulin and glucose production in normal subjects is illustrated in Figure 2.

Effects of ghrelin and GH secretagogues (GHSs)

Synthetic GHSs were initially developed based on the structure of metencephalin, a known GHS. GH-releasing peptide-6 was the first synthetic peptidic GHS able to induce GH release *in vivo*; however, several peptides have since been synthesized in addition to non-peptidic orally active molecules. The most representative of these is the spiroindoline MK-0677 [32], the development of which enabled the discovery and cloning of the GHS receptor, previously indicated by binding studies [32]. GHS receptors are expressed in high concentrations in the hypothalamus and pituitary gland but are also present in other central nervous system (CNS) sites and in peripheral tissues. Two types of human GHS receptor cDNAs, termed 1a and 1b, have been identified. The mRNA for the human GHS receptor type 1a results from a splicing event that removes 2152 nucleotides of intronic sequence, whereas the intron is not removed in the GHS receptor type 1b [33].

Ghrelin, a 28 amino acid peptide produced mainly by the stomach, is the natural ligand for the GHS receptor type 1a [34]. Apart from its well-recognized orexigenic properties and effects on regulation of energy homeostasis, ghrelin has a potent, dose-dependent action on GH release [35]. *In vivo*, ghrelin and other GHSs exhibit powerful synergistic effects with GHRH, suggesting that they act, at least in part, via different mechanisms. However, GHSs need GHRH activity to maximize their GH-releasing effect, as evidenced by

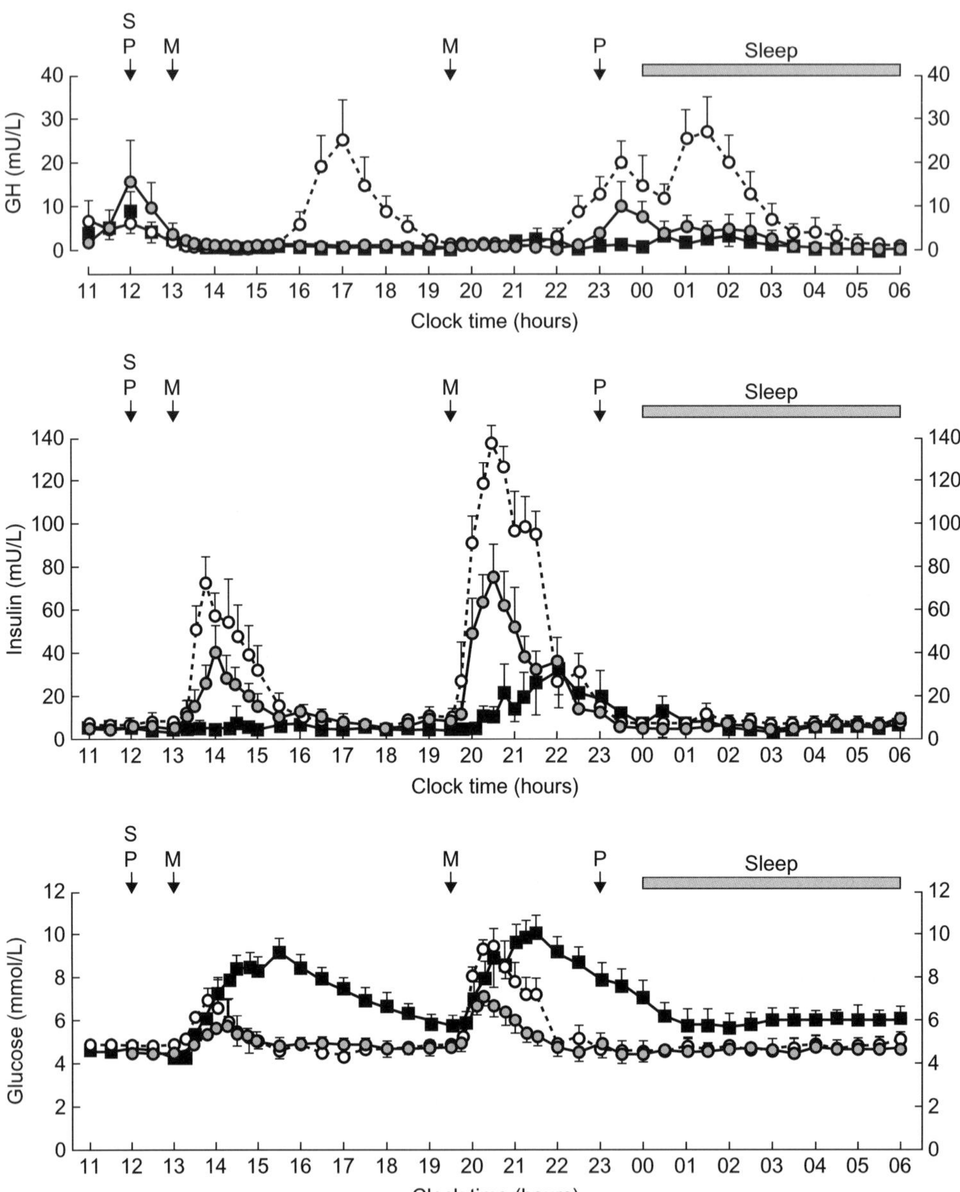

Figure 2. *Effect of pirenzepine (P; shaded circles) or placebo (P; open circles), or somatostatin (S; black squares) infusion on daily postprandial and fasting GH, insulin and glucose production in normal individuals. After fasting from midnight, subjects received on separate occasions pirenzepine 200 mg orally, or placebo, at 12.00 and 23.00 hours, or somatostatin infusion, 2 mg/minute from 12.00 to 06.00 hours. A standardized meal (M) was given at 13.00 and 19.30 hours. Glucose levels are elevated post-prandially in subjects receiving somatostatin, due to suppression of insulin secretion, in contrast to pirenzepine, where no such rises are observed due to the direct stimulatory effects of anticholinergics on pancreatic β-cells in addition to induction of somatostatin release. Results are expressed as the mean ± SEM in six normal subjects.*

potent inhibition, though not abolition, of the GH response to GHSs following both hypothalamic–pituitary disruption and administration of GHRH receptor antagonists [32]. Furthermore, patients with GHRH receptor deficiency are unable to increase GH secretion following GHS stimulation [36]. These studies suggest that the most important site of action of GHSs is the hypothalamus.

Ghrelin and synthetic GHSs can also act as functional somatostatin antagonists at both hypothalamic and pituitary levels. In humans, molecules that probably inhibit the release of somatostatin, such as arginine and acetylcholine receptor agonists, do not enhance the GH response to GHSs and ghrelin [37]. In contrast, the GH response to GHSs and ghrelin is partially refractory to compounds acting through induction of hypothalamic somatostatin secretion, such as β-adrenoceptor agonists, glucose and acetylcholine receptor antagonists [37], and even partially refractory to the inhibitory effects on GH release of substances acting directly on pituitary somatotrophs, such as somatostatin and free fatty acids (FFAs) [38, 39]. Furthermore, GHSs are also resistant to the negative feedback effects of GH and IGF-I.

Feedback regulation of GH secretion

GH itself has a direct feedback action on the secretory status of the somatotroph. For example, in normal human subjects pretreated with a single dose of human GH, subsequent acute GH responses to GHRH, administered prior to any rise in circulating IGF-I levels, were completely abolished, indicating an acute negative feedback action of GH on its own release [40]. This mechanism is likely to contribute significantly to the phenomenon of somatotroph desensitization, whereby GH responsiveness to GHRH falls with repeated administration of GHRH. An important observation in relation to the mechanism by which this phenomenon occurs is that this desensitization can be reversed by activation of cholinergic pathways [40, 41], and the mediator of this feedback may well be the hypothalamic somatostatinergic system, for the following reasons: drugs that prolong the action of acetylcholine, such as pyridostigmine, enhance the responsiveness of GH to GHRH, whereas drugs that block cholinergic muscarinic receptors, such as pirenzepine and atropine, abolish the GH response to most physiological stimuli [41]. These inhibitory effects of antimuscarinics are lost in animals pre-treated with neutralizing antibodies to somatostatin [28], supporting a critical role for the somatostatinergic system in mediating these actions.

In addition to direct feedback inhibition by GH itself, there are potent negative feedback effects of IGF-I on GH secretion at both pituitary and hypothalamic levels. In the early 1980s, rats given intracerebroventricular injections of plasma-derived IGF preparations exhibited a diminished GH pulse amplitude [42], though it was unclear from these observations whether IGF-I, IGF-II or both mediated these responses. In the hypothalamus, *in-vitro* studies have shown an acute concentration-dependent release of somatostatin by IGF-I, which probably contributes to the acute feedback control of the somatotroph [43]. In contrast, the effects of IGF-I at the pituitary level are more potent and sustained, and include inhibition of GH and pituitary transcription factor gene expression [44, 45]. IGF-I therefore regulates the basal tone of somatotroph responsiveness through direct pituitary mechanisms, as opposed to the more acute inhibition mediated by hypothalamic somatostatin.

Glucose is another important regulator of GH secretion, acting at the hypothalamic rather than the pituitary level. Acutely, glucose inhibits GH secretion in humans, with a rebound rise in GH levels some 3–4 hours later. In contrast, chronic elevation of glucose, as seen in patients with diabetes mellitus, often results in increased GH secretion, probably due to a combination of impaired sensitivity to glucose at the hypothalamic level and a reduction in negative feedback inhibition (low IGF-I levels). Glucose levels regulate somatostatinergic neurones (and possibly GHRH) through interaction with the well-established cholinergic regulation of these neurones. It is important to note, however, that blockade of cholinergic muscarinic receptors abolishes the GH response to all known secretagogues in humans, with the exception of stimulation by insulin-induced hypoglycaemia [41]. The actions of glucose therefore seem to override those of the cholinergic system on somatostatinergic neurones, which seems logical from a teleological perspective.

FFAs can regulate GH secretion, pharmacological reduction in FFAs increasing GH release and plasma FFA elevation reducing or blocking GH secretion *in vivo*. In fact, the tonic inhibitory influence of FFAs on GH secretion may be partly responsible for the reduction in GH secretion usually apparent in obese subjects.

Signals mediated by the nuclear receptor family, including glucocorticoids, thyroid hormones and gonadal hormones, are also important in the feedback regulation of the hypothalamic–somatotroph axis, and these interactions are reviewed in Chapter 4. A summary of the main pathways involved in the regulation of GH secretion is shown in Figure 3.

Effectors of the GH/IGF axis

Effects on lipids and lipolysis

The pulsatile pattern of GH secretion is amplified in fasting conditions, whereas meals inhibit GH release [46], suggesting that the main impact of GH is in the fasting and postabsorptive states. Studies have demonstrated a consistent dose-dependent action of GH on induction of lipolysis, with elevation of circulatory FFAs and glycerol and increased lipid oxidation rates [47]. These effects occur despite increased insulin levels, indicating that the lipogenic actions of insulin can easily be overcome by relatively low doses of GH. GH stimulates lipolysis by activation of hormone-sensitive lipase, with consequent increased lipid oxidation [48]. Lipid profiles show a characteristic pattern in patients with untreated GHD, comprising increased low-density lipoprotein (LDL)-cholesterol and triglycerides with normal or reduced high-density lipoprotein (HDL)-cholesterol. In addition, there is an accumulation, in particular, of atherogenic, small, dense LDL particles [49]. GH replacement in such patients appears to reduce total and LDL-cholesterol, tends to increase HDL-cholesterol and in general has no effect on triglyceride levels [49]. The mechanisms underpinning these changes are not fully understood; however, it is known that GH regulates cholesterol 7α-hydroxylase, and GHD may therefore lead to increased cholesterol accumulation in the liver and reduced LDL receptor expression [50]. Furthermore, GH increases hepatic LDL receptor expression and LDL-cholesterol clearance in humans [51] which may, at least in part, account for the observed reduction in plasma cholesterol following GH treatment.

Effects on bone

Clinical observations have long highlighted the importance of GH on bone metabolism (see Chapter 13), exemplified by the increased bone mass in patients with acromegaly compared with the delayed bone age in children with short stature due to GHD. GH is important for bone remodelling and the presence of GHRs in osteoblasts suggests a direct action of GH on osteoblast function. Furthermore, GHR numbers are modified by autocrine IGF (down-regulation) and IGFBP (up-regulation) activity in addition to synergistic interactions with oestrogens [52]. However, it remains unclear whether the principal effects of GH on osteoblast function are direct, or indirect via IGF-I formation. GH can also modulate bone resorption, as evidenced by studies in hypophysectomized rats treated with GH where numbers of osteoclasts in the tibial metaphysis were increased [53]. These direct actions may also be supplemented by indirect mechanisms of osteoclast activation via GH-induced production of osteoblast interleukin-6 [54]. In addition to effects on bone remodelling, GH can modify bone structure. For example, in aged rats, GH administration increases subperiosteal cortical bone formation with no major effect on cancellous bone mass [55]. Similarly, GH-transgenic mice show increased bone mineral content (BMC) compared with their wild-type littermates, but high and unphysiological serum levels of GH are generated in these animals [56].

Conclusions on bone formation drawn from studies in rodents can be difficult to apply to humans, as some effects may be due to bone growth and bone modelling consequent upon the relatively late closure of epiphyseal plates in rodent life. However, GH treatment in aged monkeys does increase bone formation [57]. Importantly, long-term GH therapy in adult humans with GHD consistently increases markers of bone turnover, BMC and, to a lesser extent, bone mineral density, but these promising improvements have not yet been reflected in a reduction in fracture risk.

Effects on carbohydrate metabolism

In the post-absorptive state, GH has a short-lived effect on reduction of plasma glucose and glucose production, and an increase in glucose clearance. Beyond this, however, sustained GH administration leads to glucose intolerance, secondary to increased hepatic glucose output from gluconeogenesis and glycogenolysis and to reduced insulin-mediated glucose uptake [58]. These alterations in carbohydrate handling are also reproduced in clinical studies of patients with GHD who have reduced insulin sensitivity compared with controls, though significant hyperinsulinaemia is not usually a feature and there is no evidence of an increased prevalence of diabetes mellitus. In these patients, short-term GH replacement causes a further deterioration in insulin sensitivity, which nevertheless usually returns to baseline with continued treatment for 3–12 months, partly due to the beneficial effects of GH on body composition [59]. The effects of GH on induction of lipolysis, with increased lipid oxidation and a rise in FFA concentrations, may reduce skeletal muscle glucose uptake and account for the reduction in insulin sensitivity [59]. The molecular mechanisms underlying the induction of insulin resistance by GH may also involve uncoupling of PI3K and its downstream signals, in addition to activation of suppressors of cytokine

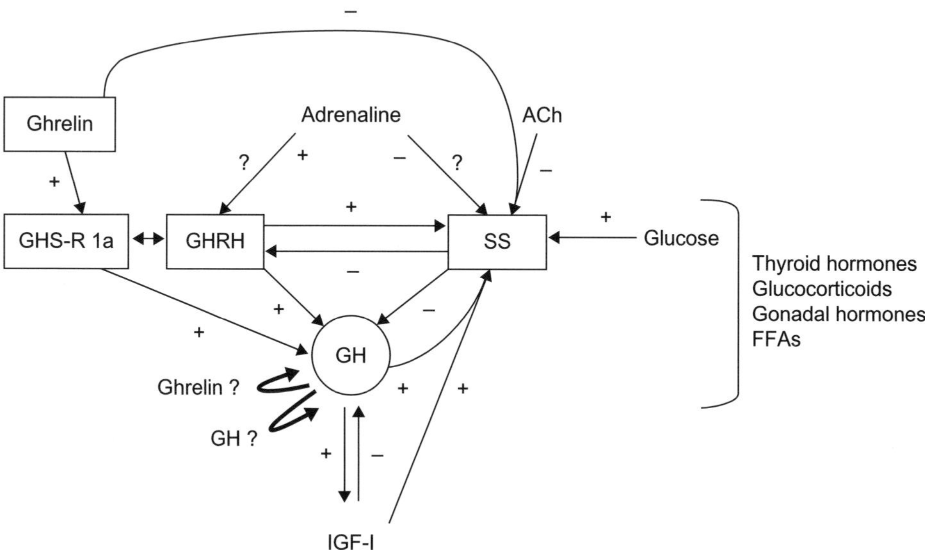

Figure 3. Overview of pathways involved in GH secretion. α_2-Adrenergic agonists may act via stimulation of GH-releasing hormone (GHRH), inhibition of somatostatin, or both. Ghrelin interacts with the GH secretagogue receptor type 1a (GHS-R 1a) and stimulates GH secretion via synergistic interactions with GHRH. It may also act as a functional somatostatin antagonist. The discovery of GH receptors, ghrelin and GHS-R 1a in pituitary somatotrophs suggests possible autocrine/paracrine effects on GH regulation within the pituitary. Thyroid hormones, glucocorticoids, gonadal hormones and free fatty acids (FFAs) probably act at both hypothalamic and pituitary levels. ACh, acetylcholine; SS, somatostatin.

signalling (SOCS) proteins, two of which (SOCS-1 and -6) have been found to inhibit insulin signalling *in vitro* and *in vivo* [60].

Physiological influences on the GH/IGF axis

Gender

Twenty-four-hour integrated GH concentrations are approximately 50% higher in young women than young men. In pre-menopausal women, GH production varies according to the phase of the menstrual cycle, approximately doubling in the late follicular compared with the early follicular and mid-luteal phases. This variation is likely to be related to changes in gonadal steroid production, as GH pulse amplitude is positively correlated with serum oestradiol and negatively correlated with serum progesterone levels [61]. These gender differences in GH production have clinical implications, as plasma GH levels after a glucose load are normally suppressed to a greater extent in young men than in young women in the early follicular phase of their menstrual cycle [62].

Nutrition

In humans, fasting results in enhanced GH production secondary to an increase in GH pulse frequency and amplitude [63], whereas refeeding rapidly suppresses fasting-enhanced GH secretion. The mechanisms responsible for these effects are likely to be multiple, including enhanced somatostatin release, reduced GH responses to GHRH consequent upon a rise in blood glucose, and increased ghrelin production during the fasting state.

Body composition can also influence GH production. Obese individuals have reduced GH concentrations, associated with decreased pulsatile GH secretion and a shorter GH half-life [64]. Furthermore, the peak GH response to GHRH is reduced in obese subjects, and this is often reversible with fasting or weight loss [65]; this raises the possibility that the elevated insulin levels associated with obesity may inhibit GH secretion, perhaps via regulation of IGF-I and/or IGFBP concentrations. Also, ghrelin levels are reduced in obese patients, but it is unclear whether this mediates any of the reduced GH secretion observed in visceral obesity. Patients with anorexia nervosa demonstrate an increased basal and GHRH-stimulated GH release and elevated ghrelin levels [66], reinforcing the importance of nutritional state on GH regulation. In fact, anorexia nervosa can be viewed as a state of functional GH resistance, as circulating IGF-I and IGFBP-3 levels are typically very low. Other central and peripherally generated peptides, such as leptin and neuropeptide Y, which have important roles in the regulation of food intake and energy balance, are also involved in the control of GH secretion, though the relative importance of these factors in GH regulation is not yet apparent.

Exercise

A stimulatory effect of physical exercise on GH secretion has long been recognized, though several studies have suggested that a threshold of exercise intensity may need to be crossed before any significant rise in GH concentration is observed. For example, in a study involving young eumenorrhoeic women, Weltman and colleagues [67] demonstrated a twofold rise in GH concentrations after a year of high-intensity aerobic training, but only in subjects who exercised consistently above the lactate threshold.

Age

Daily GH production rates increase threefold during puberty and are maximal during late puberty, when linear growth velocities are greatest. Thereafter, GH production falls progressively with advancing age, at a rate of approximately 14% per decade of adult life [64]. This age-related decline in GH secretion does not seem to be related to a reduction in GH storage, as appropriate stimuli can generate GH pulses in elderly subjects similar to those seen in their younger counterparts [68]. In addition, the frequency of GH pulses in the elderly is preserved, though the amplitude of the pulses is reduced in comparison with those observed in young adults, suggesting that GHRH activity may be diminished. In support of this hypothesis, GHRH administration in elderly individuals has been shown to increase spontaneous GH secretion and serum IGF-I to levels seen in young adults

[69]. Although GHRH activity may be reduced in the elderly, the age-related reduction in GH secretion may also be related to an increase in somatostatinergic tone, as the GH response to arginine, which inhibits the secretion of somatostatin from the hypothalamus, is not altered in healthy elderly individuals in comparison with young adults [68].

In parallel with the fall in GH secretion with advancing age, serum levels of IGF-I and IGFBP-3 also decline [70], though the concentration of the latter falls to a lesser degree than IGF-I and GH secretion [71]. However, studies have failed to demonstrate a correlation between GH secretion and IGF-I or IGFBP-3 in elderly individuals [68], suggesting that GH becomes less important in determining circulating IGF-I concentration with advancing age. Under these circumstances, other factors such as nutritional state, fragility and chronic disease may play a greater role in determining IGF-I and IGFBP-3 concentrations.

Conclusions

In summary, the regulation of GH secretion is complex, relying on the interaction of a wide range of central and peripheral feedback signals. These converge at the hypothalamic and pituitary levels to co-ordinate GH release in a pulsatile fashion. Our understanding of this regulatory system has been greatly advanced by the discovery of ghrelin as the natural ligand for the GHS receptor. Future studies will no doubt clarify the roles of other newly identified central and peripherally generated peptides in this intricate and important process.

References

1. Li CH, Dixon JS. Human pituitary growth hormone. 32. The primary structure of the hormone: revision. Arch Biochem Biophys 1971;146:233–6

2. Millar DS, Lewis MD, Horan M, Newsway V, Easter TE, Gregory JW, Fryklund L, Norin M, Crowne EC, Davies SJ, Edwards P, Kirk J, Waldron K, Smith PJ, Phillips JA 3rd, Scanlon MF, Krawczak M, Cooper DN, Procter AM. Novel mutations of the growth hormone 1 (*GH1*) gene disclosed by modulation of the clinical selection criteria for individuals with short stature. Hum Mutat 2003;21:424–40

3. Horan M, Millar DS, Hedderich J, Lewis G, Newsway V, Mo N, Fryklund L, Procter AM, Krawczak M, Cooper DN. Human growth hormone 1 (*GH1*) gene expression: complex haplotype-dependent influence of polymorphic variation in the proximal promoter and locus control region. Hum Mutat 2003;21:408–23

4. Frank SJ. Receptor dimerization in GH and erythropoietin action – it takes two to tango, but how? Endocrinology 2002;143:2–10

5. Udy GB, Towers RP, Snell RG, Wilkins RJ, Park SH, Ram PA, Waxman DJ, Davey HW. Requirement of STAT5b for sexual dimorphism of body growth rates and liver gene expression. Proc Natl Acad Sci USA 1997;94:7239–44

6. Lewis MD, Horan M, Millar DS, Newsway V, Easter TE, Fryklund L, Gregory JW, Norin M, del Valle C-J, Lopez-Siguero JP, Cañete R, Lopez-Canti LF, Diaz-Torrado N, Espino R, Ulied A, Scanlon MF, Procter AM, Cooper DN. A novel dysfunctional growth hormone variant (Ile179Met) exhibits a decreased ability to activate the extracellular signal-related kinase pathway. J Clin Endocrinol Metab 2004;89:1068–75

7. Zhang Y, Jiang J, Black RA, Baumann G, Frank SJ. Tumor necrosis factor-alpha converting enzyme (TACE) is a growth hormone binding protein (GHBP) sheddase: the metalloprotease TACE/ADAM-17 is critical for (PMA-induced) GH receptor proteolysis and GHBP generation. Endocrinology 2000;141: 4342–8

8. Wang X, He K, Gerhart M, Huang Y, Jiang J, Paxton RJ, Yang S, Lu C, Menon RK, Black RA, Baumann G, Frank SJ. Metalloprotease-mediated GH receptor proteolysis and GHBP shedding. Determination of extracellular domain stem region cleavage site. J Biol Chem 2002;277:50510–9

9. Woods KA, Dastot F, Preece MA, Clark AJ, Postel-Vinay MC, Chatelain PG, Ranke MB, Rosenfeld RG, Amselem S, Savage MO. Phenotype:genotype relationships in growth hormone insensitivity syndrome. J Clin Endocrinol Metab 1997;82:3529–35

10. Roberts CT Jr, Lasky SR, Lowe WL Jr, Seaman WT, LeRoith D. Molecular cloning of rat insulin-like growth factor I complementary deoxyribonucleic acids: differential messenger ribonucleic acid processing and regulation by growth hormone in extrahepatic tissues. Mol Endocrinol 1987;1:243–8

11. Jennische E, Isgaard J, Isaksson OGP. Local expression of insulin-like growth factors during tissue growth and regeneration. In: Schofield PN, editor. The insulin-like

growth factors: structure and biological functions. Oxford, New York, 1992:221–39

12. Murphy LJ, Murphy LC, Friesen HG. Estrogen induces insulin-like growth factor-I expression in the rat uterus. Mol Endocrinol 1987;1:445–50

13. Sjögren K, Liu JL, Blad K, Skrtic S, Vidal O, Wallenius V, LeRoith D, Tornell J, Isaksson OG, Jansson JO, Ohlsson C. Liver-derived insulin-like growth factor I (IGF-I) is the principal source of IGF-I in blood but is not required for postnatal body growth in mice. Proc Natl Acad Sci USA 1999;96:7088–92

14. Baxter RC. Insulin-like growth factor binding proteins in the human circulation: a review. Horm Res 1994; 42:140–4

15. Lewitt MS, Saunders H, Baxter RC. Bioavailability of insulin-like growth factors (IGFs) in rats determined by the molecular distribution of human IGF-binding protein-3. Endocrinology 1993;133:1797–802

16. Guler HP, Zapf J, Schmid C, Froesch ER. Insulin-like growth factors I and II in healthy man. Estimations of half-lives and production rates. Acta Endocrinol (Copenh) 1989;121:753–8

17. Aguiar-Oliveira MH, Gill MS, de A. Barretto ES, Alcantara MR, Miraki-Moud F, Menezes CA, Souza AH, Martinelli CE, Pereira FA, Salvatori R, Levine MA, Shalet SM, Camacho-Hubner C, Clayton PE. Effect of severe growth hormone (GH) deficiency due to a mutation in the GH-releasing hormone receptor on insulin-like growth factors (IGFs), IGF-binding proteins, and ternary complex formation throughout life. J Clin Endocrinol Metab 1999;84:4118–26

18. Tiong TS, Herington AC. Ontogeny of messenger RNA for the rat growth hormone receptor and serum binding protein. Mol Cell Endocrinol 1992;83:133–41

19. Zapf J, Hauri C, Waldvogel M, Futo E, Hasler H, Binz K, Guler HP, Schmid C, Froesch ER. Recombinant human insulin-like growth factor I induces its own specific carrier protein in hypophysectomized and diabetic rats. Proc Natl Acad Sci USA 1989;86:3813–7

20. Fukata J, Diamond DJ, Martin JB. Effects of rat growth hormone (rGH)-releasing factor and somatostatin on the release and synthesis of rGH in dispersed pituitary cells. Endocrinology 1985;117:457–67

21. Jaffe CA, Friberg RD, Barkan AL. Suppression of growth hormone (GH) secretion by a selective GH-releasing hormone (GHRH) antagonist. Direct evidence for involvement of endogenous GHRH in the generation of GH pulses. J Clin Invest 1993;92:695–701

22. Tannenbaum GS, Ling N. The interrelationship of growth hormone (GH)-releasing factor and somatostatin in generation of the ultradian rhythm of GH secretion. Endocrinology 1984;115:1952–7

23. Horvath S, Palkovits M. Synaptic interconnections among growth hormone-releasing hormone (GHRH)-containing neurons in the arcuate nucleus of the rat hypothalamus. Neuroendocrinology 1988;48:471–6

24. Müller EE. Neural control of somatotropic function. Physiol Rev 1987;67:962–1053

25. Devesa J, Diaz MJ, Tresguerres JA, Arce V, Lima L. Evidence that α_2-adrenergic pathways play a major role in growth hormone (GH) neuroregulation: α_2-adrenergic agonism counteracts the inhibitory effect of muscarinic cholinergic receptor blockade on the GH response to GH-releasing hormone, while α_2-adrenergic blockade diminishes the potentiating effect of increased cholinergic tone on such stimulation in normal men. J Clin Endocrinol Metab 1991;73:251–6

26. Magnan E, Cataldi M, Guillaume V, Mazzocchi L, Dutour A, Razafindraibe H, Sauze N, Renard M, Oliver C. Role of growth hormone (GH)-releasing hormone and somatostatin in the mediation of clonidine-induced GH release in sheep. Endocrinology 1994;134:562–7

27. Kelijman M, Frohman LA. The role of the cholinergic pathway in growth hormone feedback. J Clin Endocrinol Metab 1991;72:1081–7

28. Locatelli V, Torsello A, Redaelli M, Ghigo E, Massare F, Müller EE. Cholinergic agonist and antagonist drugs modulate the growth hormone response to growth hormone-releasing hormone in the rat: evidence for mediation by somatostatin. J Endocrinol 1986;111: 271–8

29. Atiea JA, Creagh F, Page M, Owens DR, Scanlon MF, Peters JR. Early morning hyperglycemia in insulin-dependent diabetes: acute and sustained effects of cholinergic blockade. J Clin Endocrinol Metab 1989; 69:390–5

30. Page MD, Bevan JS, Dieguez C, Peters JR, Scanlon MF. Cholinergic blockade with pirenzepine improves carbohydrate tolerance and abolishes the GH response to meals in normal subjects. Clin Endocrinol (Oxf) 1989;30:519–24

31. Ara J, Kang S, Creagh FM, Scanlon MF, Peters JR. Modulation of glucose and growth hormone responses to meals and exercise in type 1 diabetes by cholinergic muscarinic blockade. Diabet Med 1994;11:92–7

32. Smith RG, Van der Ploeg LH, Howard AD, Feighner SD, Cheng K, Hickey GJ, Wyvratt MJ Jr, Fisher MH, Nargund RP, Patchett AA. Peptidomimetic regulation of growth hormone secretion. Endocr Rev 1997; 18:621–45

33. Petersenn S, Rasch AC, Penshorn M, Beil FU, Schulte HM. Genomic structure and transcriptional regulation of the human growth hormone secretagogue receptor. Endocrinology 2001;142:2649–59

34. Kojima M, Hosoda H, Date Y, Nakazato M, Matsuo H, Kangawa K. Ghrelin is a growth-hormone-releasing acylated peptide from stomach. Nature 1999;402: 656–60

35. Takaya K, Ariyasu H, Kanamoto N, Iwakura H, Yoshimoto A, Harada M, Mori K, Komatsu Y, Usui T, Shimatsu A, Ogawa Y, Hosoda K, Akamizu T, Kojima M, Kangawa K, Nakao K. Ghrelin strongly stimulates growth hormone release in humans. J Clin Endocrinol Metab 2000;85:4908–11

36. Maheshwari HG, Rahim A, Shalet SM, Baumann G. Selective lack of growth hormone (GH) response to the GH-releasing peptide hexarelin in patients with GH-releasing hormone receptor deficiency. J Clin Endocrinol Metab 1999;84:956–9

37. Muccioli G, Tschop M, Papotti M, Deghenghi R, Heiman M, Ghigo E. Neuroendocrine and peripheral activities of ghrelin: implications in metabolism and obesity. Eur J Pharmacol 2002;440:235–54

38. Di Vito L, Broglio F, Benso A, Gottero C, Prodam F, Papotti M, Muccioli G, Dieguez C, Casanueva FF, Deghenghi R, Ghigo E, Arvat E. The GH-releasing effect of ghrelin, a natural GH secretagogue, is only blunted by the infusion of exogenous somatostatin in humans. Clin Endocrinol (Oxf) 2002;56:643–8

39. Broglio F, Benso A, Gottero C, Prodam F, Grottoli S, Tassone F, Maccario M, Casanueva FF, Dieguez C, Deghenghi R, Ghigo E, Arvat E. Effects of glucose, free fatty acids or arginine load on the GH-releasing activity of ghrelin in humans. Clin Endocrinol (Oxf) 2002;57:265–71

40. Ross RJ, Borges F, Grossman A, Smith R, Ngahfoong L, Rees LH, Savage MO, Besser GM. Growth hormone pretreatment in man blocks the response to growth hormone-releasing hormone; evidence for a direct effect of growth hormone. Clin Endocrinol (Oxf) 1987;26:117–23

41. Dieguez C, Page MD, Scanlon MF. Growth hormone neuroregulation and its alterations in disease states. Clin Endocrinol (Oxf) 1988;28:109–43

42. Tannenbaum GS, Guyda HJ, Posner BI. Insulin-like growth factors: a role in growth hormone negative feedback and body weight regulation via brain. Science 1983;220:77–9

43. Berelowitz M, Szabo M, Frohman LA, Firestone S, Chu L, Hintz RL. Somatomedin-C mediates growth hormone negative feedback by effects on both the hypothalamus and the pituitary. Science 1981;212:1279–81

44. Yamashita S, Melmed S. Insulin-like growth factor I regulation of growth hormone gene transcription in primary rat pituitary cells. J Clin Invest 1987;79: 449–52

45. Soto JL, Castrillo JL, Dominguez F, Dieguez C. Regulation of the pituitary-specific transcription factor GHF-I/Pit-1 messenger ribonucleic acid levels by growth hormone-secretagogues in rat anterior pituitary cells in monolayer culture. Endocrinology 1995;136:3863–70

46. Ho KY, Veldhuis JD, Johnson ML, Furlanetto R, Evans WS, Alberti KG, Thorner MO. Fasting enhances growth hormone secretion and amplifies the complex rhythms of growth hormone secretion in man. J Clin Invest 1988;81:968–75

47. Copeland KC, Nair KS. Acute growth hormone effects on amino acid and lipid metabolism. J Clin Endocrinol Metab 1994;78:1040–7

48. Dietz J, Schwartz J. Growth hormone alters lipolysis and hormone-sensitive lipase activity in 3T3-F442A adipocytes. Metabolism 1991;40:800–6

49. McCallum RW, Petrie JR, Dominiczak AF, Connell JM. Growth hormone deficiency and vascular risk. Clin Endocrinol (Oxf) 2002;57:11–24

50. Rudling M, Parini P, Angelin B. Growth hormone and bile acid synthesis. Key role for the activity of hepatic microsomal cholesterol 7alpha-hydroxylase in the rat. J Clin Invest 1997;99:2239–45

51. Angelin B, Rudling M. Growth hormone and hepatic lipoprotein metabolism. Curr Opin Lipidol 1994; 5:160–5

52. Slootweg MC, Swolin D, Netelenbos JC, Isaksson OG, Ohlsson C. Estrogen enhances growth hormone receptor expression and growth hormone action in rat osteosarcoma cells and human osteoblast-like cells. J Endocrinol 1997;155:159–64

53. Lewinson D, Shenzer P, Hochberg Z. Growth hormone involvement in the regulation of tartrate-resistant acid phosphatase-positive cells that are active in cartilage and bone resorption. Calcif Tissue Int 1993;52:216–21

54. Swolin D, Ohlsson C. Growth hormone increases interleukin-6 produced by human osteoblast-like cells. J Clin Endocrinol Metab 1996;81:4329–33

55. Andreassen TT, Jorgensen PH, Flyvbjerg A, Ørskov H, Oxlund H. Growth hormone stimulates bone formation and strength of cortical bone in aged rats. J Bone Miner Res 1995;10:1057–67

56. Sandstedt J, Törnell J, Norjavaara E, Isaksson OG, Ohlsson C. Elevated levels of growth hormone increase bone mineral content in normal young mice, but not in ovariectomized mice. Endocrinology 1996;137:3368–74

57. Sass DA, Jerome CP, Bowman AR, Bennett-Cain A, Ginn TA, LeRoith D, Epstein S. Short-term effects of growth hormone and insulin-like growth factor I on cancellous bone in rhesus macaque monkeys. J Clin Endocrinol Metab 1997;82:1202–9

58. Butler P, Kryshak E, Rizza R. Mechanism of growth hormone-induced postprandial carbohydrate intolerance in humans. Am J Physiol 1991;260:E513–20

59. Svensson J, Bengtsson B-Å. Growth hormone replacement therapy and insulin sensitivity. J Clin Endocrinol Metab 2003;88:1453–4

60. Mooney RA, Senn J, Cameron S, Inamdar N, Boivin LM, Shang Y, Furlanetto RW. Suppressors of cytokine signaling-1 and -6 associate with and inhibit the insulin receptor. A potential mechanism for cytokine-mediated insulin resistance. J Biol Chem 2001;276:25889–93

61. Faria AC, Bekenstein LW, Booth RA Jr, Vaccaro VA, Asplin CM, Veldhuis JD, Thorner MO, Evans WS. Pulsatile growth hormone release in normal women during the menstrual cycle. Clin Endocrinol (Oxf) 1992;36:591–6

62. Chapman IM, Hartman ML, Straume M, Johnson ML, Veldhuis JD, Thorner MO. Enhanced sensitivity growth hormone (GH) chemiluminescence assay reveals lower postglucose nadir GH concentrations in men than women. J Clin Endocrinol Metab 1994;78:1312–9

63. Hartman ML, Veldhuis JD, Johnson ML, Lee MM, Alberti KG, Samojlik E, Thorner MO. Augmented growth hormone (GH) secretory burst frequency and amplitude mediate enhanced GH secretion during a two-day fast in normal men. J Clin Endocrinol Metab 1992;74:757–65

64. Iranmanesh A, Lizarralde G, Veldhuis JD. Age and relative adiposity are specific negative determinants of the frequency and amplitude of growth hormone (GH) secretory bursts and the half-life of endogenous GH in healthy men. J Clin Endocrinol Metab 1991; 73:1081–8

65. Williams T, Berelowitz M, Joffe SN, Thorner MO, Rivier J, Vale W, Frohman LA. Impaired growth hormone responses to growth hormone-releasing factor in obesity. A pituitary defect reversed with weight reduction. N Engl J Med 1984;311:1403–7

66. Tolle V, Kadem M, Bluet-Pajot MT, Frere D, Foulon C, Bossu C, Dardennes R, Mounier C, Zizzari P, Lang F, Epelbaum J, Estour B. Balance in ghrelin and leptin plasma levels in anorexia nervosa patients and constitutionally thin women. J Clin Endocrinol Metab 2003;88:109–16

67. Weltman A, Weltman JY, Schurrer R, Evans WS, Veldhuis JD, Rogol AD. Endurance training amplifies the pulsatile release of growth hormone: effects of training intensity. J Appl Physiol 1992;72:2188–96

68. Toogood AA, Jones J, O'Neill PA, Thorner MO, Shalet SM. The diagnosis of severe growth hormone deficiency in elderly patients with hypothalamic–pituitary disease. Clin Endocrinol (Oxf) 1998;48:569–76

69. Corpas E, Harman SM, Pineyro MA, Roberson R, Blackman MR. Growth hormone (GH)-releasing hormone-(1-29) twice daily reverses the decreased GH and insulin-like growth factor-I levels in old men. J Clin Endocrinol Metab 1992;75:530–5

70. Janssen JA, Stolk RP, Pols HA, Grobbee DE, de Jong FH, Lamberts SW. Serum free IGF-I, total IGF-I, IGFBP-1 and IGFBP-3 levels in an elderly population: relation to age and sex steroid levels. Clin Endocrinol (Oxf) 1998;48:471–8

71. Donahue LR, Hunter SJ, Sherblom AP, Rosen C. Age-related changes in serum insulin-like growth factor-binding proteins in women. J Clin Endocrinol Metab 1990;71:575–9

3 Differential physiological effects of insulin-like growth factor I

Olle GP Isaksson, John-Olov Jansson, Claes Ohlsson and Klara Sjögren
Research Centre for Endocrinology and Metabolism (RCEM), Department of Internal Medicine, Sahlgrenska University Hospital, Gothenburg, Sweden

Summary

Insulin-like growth factor I (IGF-I), produced in multiple organs of the body, has important growth-promoting and metabolic functions. The production of IGF-I is particularly abundant in the liver, which is the main contributor to the circulatory pool of IGF-I in serum (endocrine IGF-I). It has been difficult to separate the functions of endocrine IGF-I from the effects of locally produced IGF-I in peripheral tissues (autocrine/paracrine IGF-I) and to determine the relative physiological role of endocrine IGF-I versus autocrine/paracrine IGF-I in different functions, such as skeletal growth and development, and lipid and carbohydrate metabolism. To address this issue, we developed a conditional gene-targeted mouse model, which allows liver-specific inducible deletion of the IGF-I gene. Serum levels of IGF-I decreased by approximately 80% in the liver-IGF-I-deficient mouse, confirming that the major part of serum IGF-I is derived from the liver. Surprisingly, appendicular skeletal growth was normal at 12 months of age, despite the profound decrease in circulating IGF-I levels, indicating that endocrine IGF-I is not required for a normal rate of appendicular skeletal growth. However, axial skeletal growth was clearly reduced in the liver-IGF-I-deficient mice. Furthermore, the amount of cortical bone was reduced due to decreased radial growth, but the amount of trabecular bone was unchanged, demonstrating differential effects of endocrine IGF-I on different morphological structures of the skeleton. The decreased level of circulating IGF-I was associated with increased serum levels of growth hormone (GH), indicating a role for endocrine IGF-I in the negative feedback regulation of GH secretion. Liver-IGF-I-deficient mice were found to be hyperinsulinaemic but normoglycaemic; a metabolic condition consistent with compensated insulin resistance. Interestingly, liver-IGF-I-deficient mice also exhibited a reduced age-dependent fat mass content compared with control mice. In conclusion, endocrine IGF-I is important for maintaining axial skeletal growth and periosteal growth of the long bones but is not required for a normal rate of appendicular skeletal growth. Furthermore, endocrine IGF-I is important for regulation of carbohydrate and lipid metabolism and for body composition.

Introduction

Growth hormone (GH) stimulates the growth and development of multiple organs and tissues, including liver, cartilage, bone, muscle and kidney, during the postnatal period. However, the mechanism(s) behind this stimulation are not fully understood and have been widely debated. In 1957, Daughaday and colleagues convincingly demonstrated that GH stimulates sulphate incorporation into cartilage indirectly via a factor found in serum. This factor was initially called sulphation factor and later renamed somatomedin [1]. According to the original somatomedin hypothesis, GH stimulates skeletal and organ growth by stimulating the liver production of somatomedin, which, in turn, stimulates muscular–skeletal growth in an endocrine manner [2]. Somatomedin was subsequently shown to be identical to insulin-like growth factor I (IGF-I) and insulin-like growth factor II (IGF-II) [2]. In the early 1980s the original somatomedin hypothesis was challenged by a study demonstrating that administration of GH locally to the rat tibial growth plate stimulates unilateral bone growth [3]. This initial observation has subsequently been confirmed and extended, and it is now well documented that GH stimulates the growth of many different organs directly [4]. It has also been demonstrated that GH, administered systemically or locally, stimulates the local production of IGF-I and, interestingly, that local administration of antibodies to IGF-I abolishes the stimulatory effect of GH on longitudinal bone growth [5], strongly suggesting that locally produced IGF-I has autocrine/paracrine functions. Until now it has been difficult to separate the endocrine effects of liver-derived IGF-I from the autocrine/paracrine effects of locally produced IGF-I. Moreover, the fact that both GH and IGF-I stimulate tissue growth makes an analysis of the relative importance of these two peptides, in terms of spatial and temporal patterns, very complex.

In the past 10 years, studies using genetically modified mice have greatly increased our knowledge of how GH and the IGFs stimulate body growth. In line with the original somatomedin hypothesis, GH treatment had no effect on the growth of mice carrying a null mutation in the *IGF-I* gene, indicating that IGF-I is essential as a mediator for the stimulatory effect of GH on postnatal growth [6]. Mice carrying a null mutation in the *GH receptor/GH receptor-binding protein* gene were normal in size at birth but at 3 weeks of age exhibited a decelerated growth rate that progressed with age compared with control animals. Thus, it is apparent that, postnatally, body growth becomes gradually GH dependent [7].

The components of the IGF system include IGF-I, IGF-II, type I and type II IGF receptors, IGF-binding proteins (IGFBPs) and IGFBP proteases. The actions of the IGFs are mediated primarily through the type I IGF receptor. At high concentrations, IGF-I also binds to the structurally related insulin receptor but with much lower affinity than insulin [8]. Mice carrying null mutations of the IGF-I receptor are severely growth retarded (45% of normal) and die at birth, confirming the importance of the IGF-I receptor in IGF signalling [9]. The IGF-II receptor binds IGF-II but has low or no affinity for IGF-I and does not bind insulin [8]. The IGF-II receptor in the IGF system has an important role as a scavenger receptor for IGF-II. Disruption of the IGF-II receptor in mice resulted in fetal and placental overgrowth, associated with a twofold increase in serum IGF-II levels [10].

These experimental and clinical studies clearly demonstrate that IGF-I plays a critical role in normal body growth; however, they do not clarify the role of liver-derived endocrine IGF-I versus IGF-I produced locally in peripheral tissues. To address this issue, and to study the importance of liver-derived IGF-I for growth and metabolism, we and other investigators developed a liver-IGF-I-deficient mouse model.

Liver-specific inducible IGF-I inactivation

The Cre/loxP system was used to achieve a tissue- and time-specific knockout mouse model that made possible the phenotypic analysis of organ and system function in mice during postnatal life [11]. By using this system, a transgenic mouse model with a liver-specific inducible inactivation of the *IGF-I* gene was established (Fig. 1). In brief, two different transgenic mouse lines were crossed. One line carried the *Cre* gene coupled to a liver-specific inducible promoter [12] and, in the other line, the normal *IGF-I* exon 4 was replaced with an *IGF-I* exon 4 flanked by two loxP sites [13]. Exon 4

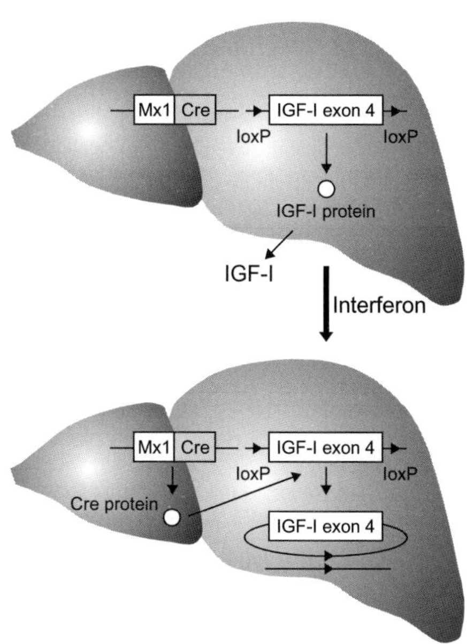

Figure 1. *Liver-specific inducible IGF-I inactivation. Mice homozygous for IGF-I exon 4 flanked with loxP sites and heterozygous for the Mx1–Cre construction were given interferon to induce Cre expression. Cre causes recombination of the loxP sites and subsequent excision of IGF-I exon 4 from genomic DNA. No functional IGF-I protein will be expressed in Cre expressing cells, whereas in other cells in which the Mx1 promoter is silent, IGF-I expression is normal. Cre-mediated excision in liver-IGF-I-deficient mice led to a decrease in IGF-I mRNA levels in the liver by 95%, whereas no significant effect was seen in other extra-hepatic tissues, including fat, muscle, bone, kidney, brain and heart.*

encodes several critical residues for ligand-receptor interaction of the IGF-I protein, and a lack of translation of exon 4 will result in a truncated IGF-I protein that has no functional capability [9].

The inducible promoter of the *Mx1* gene was used to drive the expression of *Cre* [14]. *Mx1* can be induced by interferon-α (IFN-α) and interferon-β (IFN-β) [9]. Interferon induction of the *Mx1–Cre* promoter has previously been shown to cause an almost 100% recombination of the *IGF-I* exon 4 in the liver and a partial recombination in the spleen, whereas the recombination in other peripheral tissues is very low or undetectable [14].

The end result of the two different crossings were mice that were all homozygous for the *IGF-I* allele in which exon 4 is flanked by loxP sites, and either heterozygous for or lacking the *Mx1–Cre* gene construct. The interferon activation of the *Mx1–Cre* construct was induced at the time of weaning (3–4 weeks after birth) by giving the animals human IFNα_2/α_1 for 4 days. An important advantage of this inducible gene targeting model is that the mice have normal gene function during embryogenesis and early neonatal life, allowing the study of loss of function of the IGF-I protein specifically at a determined time-point postnatally. This is important as it is well known that IGF-I has many important functions for growth and development during embryogenesis [9] that might distort the function of the IGF-I protein postnatally or induce compensatory mechanisms that might otherwise interfere with the physiological action of IGF-I.

Endocrine, autocrine and paracrine actions of IGF-I on skeletal growth – differential effects on appendicular and axial skeletal growth

We found that liver-inducible IGF-I-knockout mice had a complete deletion of exon 4 of the *IGF-I* gene in hepatocytes. Thus, IGF-I mRNA levels in liver-IGF-I gene targeted mice were decreased by more than 95% in the liver and by approximately 60% in the spleen, whereas no significant effect was seen in other extra-hepatic tissues including fat, muscle, bone, kidney, brain and heart [14, 15]. Serum IGF-I levels were decreased by approximately 80% in these animals, demonstrating that the liver is the major contributor to the circulating pool of IGF-I. This observation is in accordance with previous indirect calculations of the relative contribution of the liver to the circulating (endocrine) pool of IGF-I using isolated perfused rat liver [16]. Other investigators have recently demonstrated that the GH stimulation/drive of extra-hepatic tissues also contributes to the circulating pool of IGF-I. Thus, when liver-IGF-I-deficient mice were crossed with transgenic mice that produced a potent GH antagonist, a further significant reduction in serum IGF-I levels in the liver-IGF-I-deficient mice was observed, clearly demonstrating that IGF-I from extra-hepatic tissues – in response to GH – contributes to the circulatory pool of IGF-I [17].

Body growth (weight gain) and skeletal growth were normal in the liver-IGF-I-deficient mice during the first 2 months after loss of function of liver IGF-I, demonstrating that liver-derived IGF-I is not required for a normal rate of early postnatal growth, despite dramatically decreased serum IGF-I levels (Fig. 2) [14, 18]. To study the long-term effects of liver-specific IGF-I deletion on skeletal growth and body composition, we investigated mice lacking liver-produced IGF-I at 13 months of age. Interestingly, the adult axial skeletal growth was decreased by 24% in liver-IGF-I-deficient mice, with no major reduction of appendicular skeletal growth [15], demonstrating a differential effect of endocrine IGF-I on skeletal growth. Thus, endocrine IGF-I seems to be important in stimulating axial skeletal growth in mice during early adult life. If these results have any bearing on human physiology, they suggest that endocrine IGF-I might be of particular importance for 'sitting height' in children. It would be very interesting to study whether there is any statistical correlation between plasma levels of IGF-I and sitting height in prepubertal and pubertal children. Taken together, these data demonstrate that body and appendicular skeletal growth seem to be independent of endocrine IGF-I during early postnatal life. Endocrine IGF-I, however, is clearly of significant importance for axial skeletal growth during adult life in mice.

IGFBP-2 and IGFBP-3 in serum were decreased in mice with liver-specific inactivation of the *IGF-I* gene [14, 18]. It could be argued that the decrease in serum IGF-I is not within the fraction of free and dissociable IGF-I due to altered binding kinetics to IGFBPs, explaining the fact that skeletal growth occurred at a normal rate, in spite of the marked decrease in serum IGF-I levels. Such an interpretation is supported by a study that showed that there was no difference in serum levels of free IGF-I between liver-IGF-I-deficient mice and

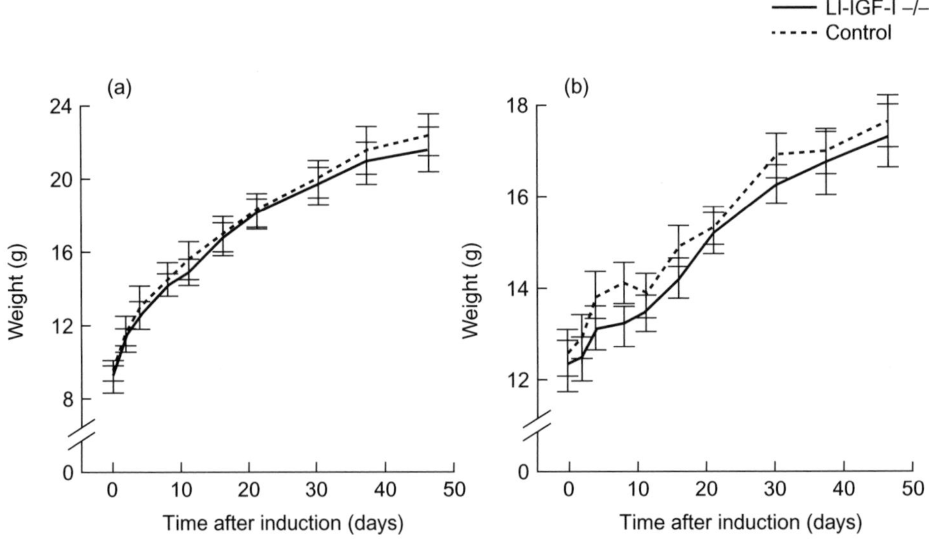

Figure 2. Body growth in liver-inducible IGF-I –/– (LI-IGF-I –/–) mice. Mice were given interferon at 3 weeks of age to induce Cre expression. The weights of (a) male and (b) female mice at various times after induction are indicated. Number of observations (n) = 4–5. Reproduced from [14] with permission. Copyright 1999, National Academy of Sciences USA.

controls [19]. However, we think it unlikely that the method used to estimate dissociable IGF-I gives a true value of *in vivo* biologically active IGF-I [20]. Furthermore, marked alterations in several physiological functions in the liver-IGF-I-deficient mice, including increased GH secretion, increased insulin resistance, decreased fat mass, increased leptin levels, decreased periosteal bone growth and reduced axial skeletal growth, indicate that the levels of *in vivo* biologically active IGF-I are altered in liver-IGF-I-deficient mice [14, 15, 18, 21, 22].

The relative importance of local versus systemic effects of IGF-I on body growth has been addressed indirectly in a few studies from other laboratories. Suppressor of cytokine signalling-2 (SOCS-2) is part of a family of proteins that is up-regulated by GH and decreases GH action by inhibiting the stimulatory effect of GH on the Janus kinase–signal tranducer and activator of transcription signal transduction pathway [23]. Metcalf *et al.* [24] demonstrated that loss of suppressor function of the SOCS-2 protein in mice resulted in gigantism that was associated with a clear up-regulation of IGF-I in peripheral tissues but unchanged serum levels of IGF-I. This study strongly supports the notion that the local concentration of IGF-I in peripheral tissues, rather than endocrine IGF-I, determines the magnitude of local tissue growth.

Musaro *et al.* [25] demonstrated that locally produced IGF-I has the capacity to preserve muscle architecture and regenerative capacity in the skeletal muscle of ageing mice. These investigators used an IGF-I transgenic model that expresses an isoform of IGF-I that normally dominates in muscle tissue, making it possible to study the isolated effect of a local increase in IGF-I concentration without a concomitant increase of IGF-I in the circulation. In other IGF-I transgenic models, the increases in muscle mass and strength have been accompanied by a release of IGF-I into the circulation, making it difficult to differentiate between local and systemic effects of IGF-I [26–29]. Furthermore, inactivation of the *acid labile subunit* gene in mice resulted in only a modest growth-retardation, despite significant reductions in the concentrations of serum IGF-I (62%) and IGFBP-3 (88%), again suggesting that normal skeletal growth is not particularly dependent upon the level of IGF-I in the circulation [30]. On the other hand, the growth phenotype of GH receptor null mice was almost completely reversed by IGF-I treatment [31], suggesting that systemically administered IGF-I has the capacity to compensate for a lack of autocrine/paracrine IGF-I. However, these data suggest that under normal physiological conditions autocrine/paracrine IGF-I, and not endocrine IGF-I, is the main determinant (regulator) of muscular–skeletal growth.

Differential effect of IGF-I on growth and development of trabecular and cortical bone

GH and IGF-I are important for normal adult bone growth and development. GH deficiency (GHD) results in a decreased bone mass in both humans and experimental animals [4]. Long-term GH replacement therapy in patients with GHD increases bone mass and accumulation of IGF-I in cortical and trabecular bone [32, 33]. The effects of GHD and GH replacement on bone are discussed in Chapter 13.

Although it is clear that IGF-I affects adult bone mass and structure, it is (again) difficult to separate the systemic from the local effects of IGF-I. In an effort to clarify this relationship, we measured cortical and trabecular bone parameters in IGF-I-deficient mice at different ages. Interestingly, there was a clear reduction in the amount of cortical bone in liver-IGF-I-deficient mice, suggesting that endocrine IGF-I is an important determinant of cortical bone mass. The decreased cortical bone mineral content in these mice was mainly due to a reduced periosteal circumference, associated with decreased cortical thickness [15]. Several studies have shown that GH treatment of normal, as well as ovariectomized rats, results in an increase in cortical bone formation at the periosteal surface [34–36]. Results from liver-IGF-I-deficient mice suggest that at least some of the stimulatory effect of GH on cortical radial bone growth is dependent on endocrine IGF-I. In contrast, the trabecular bone mineral density was unchanged in the liver-IGF-I-deficient mice [15]. In summary, it appears that endocrine IGF-I exerts a significant effect on cortical periosteal bone growth, while endocrine IGF-I is not required for the maintenance of trabecular bone in adult mice.

Endocrine IGF-I and insulin resistance

Mice with loss of function of liver-produced IGF-I had elevated basal insulin levels, as well as elevated glucose-induced insulin levels, but normal glucose levels. Thus, it appears that these animals had an adequately compensated insulin resistance (Fig. 3) [19, 22]. A similar phenotype is seen in transgenic mice that over-express IGFBP-1, which results in partial IGF-I deficiency [37]. In contrast, mice over-expressing IGF-I have reduced basal insulin levels [38]. Thus, there seems to be an inverse relationship between serum levels of IGF-I and insulin in all these different transgenic mouse models.

It is well known from earlier clinical studies that infusion of IGF-I decreases glucose levels in the blood, and treatment with IGF-I has been suggested as a potential therapy for diabetes as it reduces insulin resistance [39, 40]. Interestingly, two of the insulin sensitive tissues – the liver and white adipose tissue – express no or very low levels of IGF-I receptors. As a result, stimulatory effects of IGF-I on glucose metabolism in the whole body are probably caused by effects on glucose uptake in skeletal muscle. Interestingly, Yakar and co-workers [19] found that insulin-induced auto-phosphorylation of the insulin receptor, as well as tyrosine phosphorylation of the insulin receptor substrate 1, were absent in muscle but normal in liver and white adipose tissue of liver-IGF-I-deficient mice, indicating muscle-specific insulin resistance in these animals. Interestingly, in a recent epidemiological study in humans, high circulating levels of IGF-I were associated with a reduced risk of developing impaired glucose tolerance and type 2 diabetes [41]. These studies indicate an important and beneficial role of endocrine IGF-I in normal glucose homeostasis, and perhaps in delaying the development of type 2 diabetes.

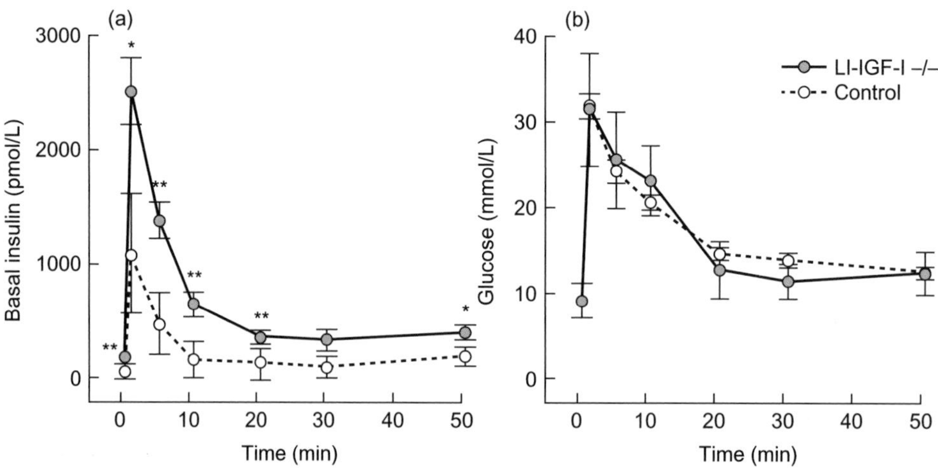

Figure 3. *Intravenous glucose tolerance test. (a) Plasma insulin and (b) glucose were measured immediately before and 1, 5, 10, 20, 30 and 50 minutes after intravenous injection of glucose (1 g/kg) in 4-month-old anaesthetized female mice. Values are expressed as means ± SEM. *$p < 0.05$ **$p < 0.01$, liver-inducible IGF-I –/– (LI-IGF-I –/–) versus control, Student's t-test, n = 4–7. Similar results were obtained for male mice. Reproduced from [22] with permission. Copyright 2001, The American Diabetes Assocation.*

The compensatory increase in GH levels in the liver-IGF-I-deficient animals, rather than the decreased serum IGF-I levels, may be the cause of the increased insulin levels. It is well known that very high endogenous GH levels, as seen in GH transgenic mice or acromegalic patients, result in insulin resistance [38, 42]. In order to find out whether the hyperinsulinaemia in liver-IGF-I-deficient mice is caused by the low endocrine levels of IGF-I or by the compensatory increased GH levels, mice were treated with a GH receptor antagonist. This treatment resulted in a partial improvement of insulin sensitivity, but not to the same level as in control animals, indicating that liver-derived IGF-I regulates glucose homeostasis both directly via decreased serum levels of IGF-I and indirectly via increased GH levels [17].

Role of endocrine IGF-I in lipid metabolism and body composition

Liver-IGF-I-deficient mice had a decreased body fat content at 13 months of age (Fig. 4) [22]. The mechanism(s) behind this alteration in body composition are not fully understood. One possibility is that the decreased fat mass may be secondary to elevated GH levels in liver-IGF-I-deficient mice, as GH is known to promote lipolysis directly in adipose tissue by enhancing the reactivity of hormone-sensitive triglyceride lipase to lipolytic hormones [43].

(a)

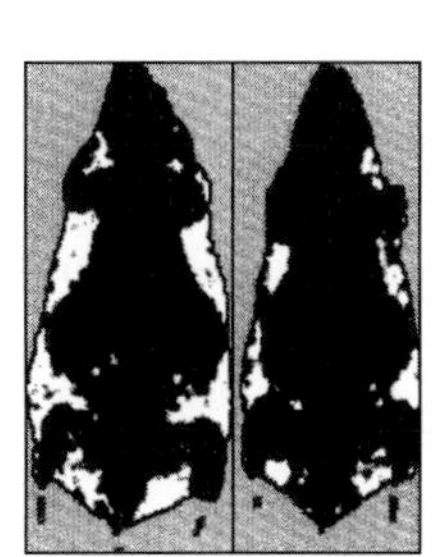

(b)

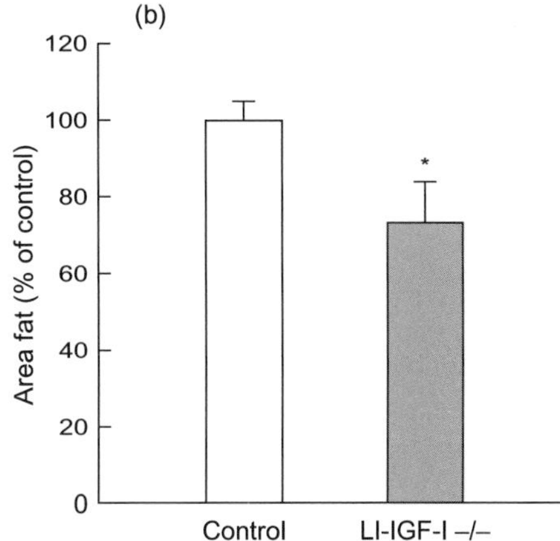

*Figure 4. Total body fat, as measured using dual-energy X-ray absorptiometry (DXA), in 13-month-old pooled male and female liver-inducible IGF-I –/– (LI-IGF-I –/–) and control mice. (a) DXA analysis of fat content in representative LI-IGF-I –/– and control mice. Areas with more than 50% fat are white, and areas with lean mass and bone are black. (b) Fat area. Values are expressed as a percentage of control and given as means ± SEM. *$p < 0.05$, LI-IGF-I –/– versus control, Student's t-test, $n = 11$. Reproduced from [22] with permission. Copyright 2001, The American Diabetes Association.*

Several experimental studies have indicated a role for IGF-I in preadipocyte proliferation and differentiation. IGFBP-1 transgenic mice, like liver-IGF-I-deficient mice, have a lean phenotype. IGFBPs limit the bioavailability of IGF-I, and IGFBP-1 transgenic mice have a phenotype consistent with partial inhibition of IGF-I action in all tissues. Interestingly, IGFBP-1 transgenic mice exhibited impaired preadipocyte proliferation and differentiation [44]. Mice with partial IGF-I receptor deficiency in all tissues had a decreased fat mass, with fewer but larger adipocytes, indicating decreased preadipocyte proliferation and differentiation into mature adipocytes [45]. In comparison, liver-IGF-I-deficient mice have a decreased fat mass, but the loss of IGF-I function is limited to the liver, with normal IGF-I expression in peripheral tissues, including adipose tissue [14]. Further studies are required to investigate whether adipocyte formation is impaired in liver-IGF-I-deficient mice.

Leptin is produced in adipose tissue and is known to reduce fat mass by decreasing food intake [46]. Interestingly, leptin levels were clearly increased in liver-IGF-I-deficient mice [22]. One of the most important regulators of leptin is insulin [47]. Thus, the increased leptin levels in liver-IGF-I-deficient mice might be secondary to the elevated insulin levels. Food intake was normal in liver-IGF-I-deficient mice when measured over a 2-week period, although a slightly reduced food intake cannot be excluded (unpublished observations). Further studies are required for the determination of the exact mechanism(s) behind the decreased fat mass in liver-IGF-I-deficient mice.

In conclusion, endocrine IGF-I is important for maintaining axial skeletal growth and periosteal growth of the long bones postnatally, but it is not required for a normal rate of longitudinal bone growth. Furthermore, endocrine IGF-I has an important role in determining insulin sensitivity and is also involved in the regulation of lipid metabolism and body composition.

References

1. Daughaday WH, Hall K, Raben MS, Salmon WD Jr, van den Brande JL, van Wyk JJ. Somatomedin: proposed designation for sulphation factor. Nature 1972;235:107
2. Daughaday WH. Growth hormone and somatomedins. In: Daughaday WH, editor. Endocrine control of growth. New York: Elsevier 1981:1–24
3. Isaksson OG, Jansson JO, Gause IA. Growth hormone stimulates longitudinal bone growth directly. Science 1982;216:1237–9
4. Ohlsson C, Bengtsson B-Å, Isaksson OG, Andreassen TT, Slootweg MC. Growth hormone and bone. Endocr Rev 1998;19:55–79
5. Isaksson OG, Lindahl A, Nilsson A, Isgaard J. Mechanism of the stimulatory effect of growth hormone on longitudinal bone growth. Endocr Rev 1987; 8:426–38
6. Liu JL, LeRoith D. Insulin-like growth factor I is essential for postnatal growth in response to growth hormone. Endocrinology 1999;140:5178–84
7. Zhou Y, Xu BC, Maheshwari HG, He L, Reed M, Lozykowski M, Okada S, Cataldo L, Coschigamo K, Wagner TE, Baumann G, Kopchick JJ. A mammalian model for Laron syndrome produced by targeted disruption of the mouse growth hormone receptor/binding protein gene (the Laron mouse). Proc Natl Acad Sci USA 1997;94:13215–20
8. Jones JI, Clemmons DR. Insulin-like growth factors and their binding proteins: biological actions. Endocr Rev 1995;16:3–34
9. Liu JP, Baker J, Perkins AS, Robertson EJ, Efstratiadis A. Mice carrying null mutations of the genes encoding insulin-like growth factor I (Igf-I) and type 1 IGF receptor (Igf1r). Cell 1993;75:59–72
10. Lau MM, Stewart CE, Liu Z, Bhatt H, Rotwein P, Stewart CL. Loss of the imprinted IGF2/cation-independent mannose 6-phosphate receptor results in fetal overgrowth and perinatal lethality. Genes Dev 1994;8:2953–63
11. Gu H, Marth JD, Orban PC, Mossmann H, Rajewsky K. Deletion of a DNA polymerase beta gene segment in T cells using cell type-specific gene targeting. Science 1994;265:103–6
12. Kuhn R, Schwenk F, Aguet M, Rajewsky K. Inducible gene targeting in mice. Science 1995;269:1427–9
13. Liu JL, Grinberg A, Westphal H, Sauer B, Accili D, Karas M, LeRoith D. Insulin-like growth factor-I affects perinatal lethality and postnatal development in a gene dosage-dependent manner: manipulation using the Cre/loxP system in transgenic mice. Mol Endocrinol 1998;12:1452–62
14. Sjögren K, Liu JL, Blad K, Skrtic S, Vidal O, Wallenius V, LeRoith D, Törnell J, Isaksson OG, Jansson JO, Ohlsson C. Liver-derived insulin-like growth factor I (IGF-I) is the principal source of IGF-I in blood but is not required for postnatal body growth in mice. Proc Natl Acad Sci USA 1999;96:7088–92
15. Sjögren K, Sheng M, Moverare S, Liu JL, Wallenius K, Tornell J, Isaksson O, Jansson JO, Mohan S, Ohlsson C. Effects of liver-derived insulin-like growth factor I on bone metabolism in mice. J Bone Miner Res 2002;17:1977–87
16. Froesch ER, Schmid C, Schwander J, Zapf J. Actions of insulin-like growth factors. Annu Rev Physiol 1985;47:443–67
17. Yakar S, Setser J, Kopchick JJ, LeRoith D. Growth hormone antagonists inhibit extrahepatic IGF-I secretion into the circulation and increase peripheral insulin sensitivity. The Endocrine Society's 84th Annual Meeting 2002 Jun 19–22; San Francisco, USA
18. Yakar S, Liu JL, Stannard B, Butler A, Accili D, Sauer B, LeRoith D. Normal growth and development in the absence of hepatic insulin-like growth factor I. Proc Natl Acad Sci USA 1999;96:7324–9
19. Yakar S, Liu JL, Fernandez AM, Wu Y, Schally AV, Frystyk J, Chernausek SD, Mejia W, LeRoith D. Liver-specific Igf-1 gene deletion leads to muscle insulin insensitivity. Diabetes 2001;50:1110–8

20. Bang P, Ahlsen M, Berg U, Carlsson-Skwirut C. Free insulin-like growth factor I: are we hunting a ghost? Horm Res 2001;55 (Suppl 2):84–93

21. Wallenius K, Sjögren K, Peng XD, Park S, Wallenius V, Liu JL, Umaerus M, Wennbo H, Isaksson O, Frohman L, Kineman R, Ohlsson C, Jansson JO. Liver-derived IGF-I regulates GH secretion at the pituitary level in mice. Endocrinology 2001;142:4762–70

22. Sjögren K, Wallenius K, Liu JL, Bohlooly YM, Pacini G, Svensson L, Törnell J, Isaksson OG, Ahren B, Jansson JO, Ohlsson C. Liver-derived IGF-I is of importance for normal carbohydrate and lipid metabolism. Diabetes 2001;50:1539–45

23. Starr R, Willson TA, Viney EM, Murray LJ, Rayner JR, Jenkins BJ, Gonda TJ, Alexander WS, Metcalf D, Nicola NA, Hilton DJ. A family of cytokine-inducible inhibitors of signalling. Nature 1997;387:917–21

24. Metcalf D, Greenhalgh CJ, Viney E, Willson TA, Starr R, Nicola NA, Hilton DJ, Alexander WS. Gigantism in mice lacking suppressor of cytokine signalling-2. Nature 2000;405:1069–73

25. Musaro A, McCullagh K, Paul A, Houghton L, Dobrowolny G, Molinaro M, Barton ER, Sweeney HL, Rosenthal N. Localized Igf-1 transgene expression sustains hypertrophy and regeneration in senescent skeletal muscle. Nat Genet 2001;27:195–200

26. Mathews LS, Hammer RE, Behringer RR, D'Ercole AJ, Bell GI, Brinster RL, Palmiter RD. Growth enhancement of transgenic mice expressing human insulin-like growth factor I. Endocrinology 1988;123:2827–33

27. Coleman ME, DeMayo F, Yin KC, Lee HM, Geske R, Montgomery C, Schwartz RJ. Myogenic vector expression of insulin-like growth factor I stimulates muscle cell differentiation and myofiber hypertrophy in transgenic mice. J Biol Chem 1995;270:12109–16

28. Delaughter MC, Taffet GE, Fiorotto ML, Entman ML, Schwartz RJ. Local insulin-like growth factor I expression induces physiologic, then pathologic, cardiac hypertrophy in transgenic mice. Faseb J 1999;13:1923–9

29. Reiss K, Cheng W, Ferber A, Kajstura J, Li P, Li B, Olivetti G, Homcy CJ, Baserga R, Anversa P. Overexpression of insulin-like growth factor-1 in the heart is coupled with myocyte proliferation in transgenic mice. Proc Natl Acad Sci USA 1996;93: 8630–5

30. Ueki I, Ooi GT, Tremblay ML, Hurst KR, Bach LA, Boisclair YR. Inactivation of the acid labile subunit gene in mice results in mild retardation of postnatal growth despite profound disruptions in the circulating insulin-like growth factor system. Proc Natl Acad Sci USA 2000;97:6868–73

31. Sims NA, Clement-Lacroix P, Da Ponte F, Bouali Y, Binart N, Moriggl R, Goffin V, Coschigano K, Gaillard-Kelly M, Kopchick J, Baron R, Kelly PA. Bone homeostasis in growth hormone receptor-null mice is restored by IGF-I but independent of Stat5. J Clin Invest 2000;106:1095–103

32. Ueland T, Bollerslev J, Flyvbjerg A, Hansen TB, Vahl N, Mosekilde L. Effects of 12 months of GH treatment on cortical and trabecular bone content of IGFs and OPG in adults with acquired GH deficiency: a double-blind, randomized, placebo-controlled study. J Clin Endocrinol Metab 2002;87:2760–3

33. Johannsson G, Rosén T, Bosæus I, Sjöstrom L, Bengtsson B-Å. Two years of growth hormone (GH) treatment increases bone mineral content and density in hypopituitary patients with adult-onset GH deficiency. J Clin Endocrinol Metab 1996;81:2865–73

34. Oxlund H, Andersen NB, Ortoft G, Ørskov H, Andreassen TT. Growth hormone and mild exercise in combination markedly enhance cortical bone formation and strength in old rats. Endocrinology 1998; 139:1899–904

35. Andreassen TT, Jorgensen PH, Flyvbjerg A, Ørskov H, Oxlund H. Growth hormone stimulates bone formation and strength of cortical bone in aged rats. J Bone Miner Res 1995;10:1057–67

36. Andreassen TT, Melsen F, Oxlund H. The influence of growth hormone on cancellous and cortical bone of the vertebral body in aged rats. J Bone Miner Res 1996;11:1094–102

37. Crossey PA, Jones JS, Miell JP. Dysregulation of the insulin/IGF binding protein-1 axis in transgenic mice is associated with hyperinsulinemia and glucose intolerance. Diabetes 2000;49:457–65

38. Quaife CJ, Mathews LS, Pinkert CA, Hammer RE, Brinster RL, Palmiter RD. Histopathology associated with elevated levels of growth hormone and insulin-like growth factor I in transgenic mice. Endocrinology 1989;124:40–8

39. Moses AC, Young SC, Morrow LA, O'Brien M, Clemmons DR. Recombinant human insulin-like growth factor I increases insulin sensitivity and improves glycemic control in type II diabetes. Diabetes 1996;45:91–100

40. Clemmons DR, Moses AC, McKay MJ, Sommer A, Rosen DM, Ruckle J. The combination of insulin-like growth factor I and insulin-like growth factor-binding protein-3 reduces insulin requirements in insulin-dependent type 1 diabetes: evidence for in vivo biological activity. J Clin Endocrinol Metab 2000; 85:1518–24

41. Sandhu MS, Heald AH, Gibson JM, Cruickshank JK, Dunger DB, Wareham NJ. Circulating concentrations of insulin-like growth factor-I and development of glucose intolerance: a prospective observational study. Lancet 2002;359:1740–5

42. Møller N, Jørgensen JO, Møller J, Ørskov L, Ovesen P, Schmitz O, Christiansen JS, Ørskov H. Metabolic effects of growth hormone in humans. Metabolism 1995; 44:33–6

43. Dietz J, Schwartz J. Growth hormone alters lipolysis and hormone-sensitive lipase activity in 3T3-F442A adipocytes. Metabolism 1991;40:800–6

44. Rajkumar K, Modric T, Murphy LJ. Impaired adipogenesis in insulin-like growth factor binding protein-1 transgenic mice. J Endocrinol 1999; 162:457–65

45. Holzenberger M, Hamard G, Zaoui R, Leneuve P, Ducos B, Beccavin C, Perin L, Le Bouc Y. Experimental IGF-I receptor deficiency generates a sexually dimorphic pattern of organ-specific growth deficits in mice, affecting fat tissue in particular. Endocrinology 2001;142:4469–78

46. Friedman JM, Halaas JL. Leptin and the regulation of body weight in mammals. Nature 1998;395:763–70

47. Saladin R, De Vos P, Guerre-Millo M, Leturque A, Girard J, Staels B, Auwerx J. Transient increase in obese gene expression after food intake or insulin administration. Nature 1995;377:527–9

4 Interaction of the growth hormone/ insulin-like growth factor axis with other hormone axes

Gerhard Baumann

Center for Endocrinology, Metabolism and Molecular Medicine, Northwestern University Feinberg School of Medicine and Veterans Administration, Chicago Health Care System, Chicago, Illinois, USA

Summary

The growth hormone (GH)/insulin-like growth factor I (IGF-I) axis is the major anabolic hormone system responsible for linear growth; it has numerous and complex interactions with other hormone systems. The structure and function of IGF-I resemble those of insulin, for example, and the respective receptors for these hormones are also related. The anabolic activities of the GH/IGF-I and insulin hormone systems together ensure tissue growth and maintain normal body composition. Glucocorticoids are potent suppressors of GH secretion and inhibit GH and/or IGF-I action through multiple mechanisms, including down-regulation of GH receptor expression. Conversely, GH/IGF-I inhibits type 1 11β-hydroxysteroid dehydrogenase (11β-HSD1). GH treatment normalizes the imbalance in cortisone–cortisol interconversion characteristic of GH deficiency, which results from enhanced 11β-HSD1 activity. Oestrogens enhance GH secretion; this is largely due to the induction of GH resistance via inhibition of the GH receptor signalling cascade. Aromatizable, but not non-aromatizable, androgens enhance GH secretion, mainly due to the effects of oestrogens derived from them. Otherwise, there appears to be little direct interaction between androgens and GH/IGF-I, although the two hormone systems have similar anabolic actions. Thyroid hormone and GH and/or IGF-I act synergistically to potentiate their effects at the epiphyseal growth plate in linear growth. Most associations between the GH/IGF-I axis and the leptin system are indirect and relate to their similar respective roles in adipose tissue, body composition and energy metabolism. The GH/IGF-I axis is thus of universal importance in many tissues and interconnects with many other hormonal systems through a diverse variety of mechanisms.

Introduction

The growth hormone (GH)/insulin-like growth factor I (IGF-I) axis represents the major anabolic hormone system responsible for linear growth as well as accretion and maintenance of lean body mass. The GH/IGF axis interacts with several other hormonal axes in multiple ways, including effects on hormone production, secretion, transport and action. This chapter reviews the principal known interactions between the GH/IGF axis and other hormones, with particular emphasis on their biology in humans.

Insulin

The interplay of the GH/IGF axis on the one hand, and insulin and its metabolic spectrum on the other, is complex and bi-directional. IGF-I, a proinsulin-like peptide, has many features that resemble insulin, both in structure and function. The insulin receptor and the IGF-I receptor (type I IGF receptor) are also structurally and functionally related. IGF-I and insulin have the highest affinity for their cognate receptors, respectively, but they also bind with lower affinity to the related, non-cognate receptor, resulting in some cross-talk between insulin receptors and IGF receptors, and their signalling pathways. Furthermore, insulin/IGF-I hybrid receptors exist, though their precise physiological role in insulin and IGF signalling remains to be delineated. GH/IGF and insulin, the two hormone systems principally responsible for anabolism, together assure tissue accretion, fuel homeostasis and normal body composition (Fig. 1).

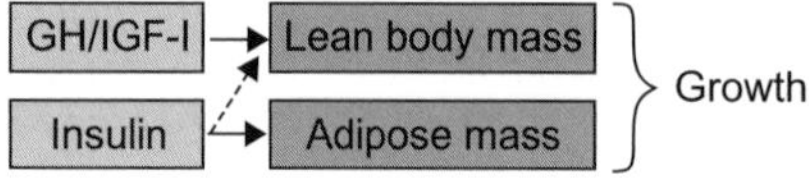

Figure 1. *The principal anabolic hormone systems. The GH/IGF axis is primarily responsible for lean tissue accretion. Insulin has a major role in adipose tissue accretion, but is also important for the growth of other tissues, both directly and by facilitating GH/IGF-I action.*

Insulin effects on GH secretion

Insulin, through its effect on blood glucose, and perhaps also through other central nervous system (CNS) effects, is an important factor in the regulation of GH release and secretion. This property is exploited pharmacologically in the insulin tolerance test, a classic stimulus for GH release from the pituitary gland. This action is mediated by hypoglycaemia, and no direct effect of insulin is implicated. The physiological fluctuations of GH secretion associated with fasting and eating are probably also mediated by changing metabolic fuel levels, which are, in turn, linked to blood insulin levels. The changes in overall GH secretion rate associated with nutritional status (in humans GH secretion is enhanced in malnutrition and reduced in over-nutrition), while principally governed by IGF-I feedback on GH secretion, are also partly linked to prevailing insulin levels. Other hormones, such as leptin and ghrelin, and metabolic fuels may also play a role. A possible direct effect of insulin on GH production is difficult to differentiate from these indirect associations, but cannot be excluded.

Insulin effects on GH and IGF action (Fig. 2)

Insulin has a permissive effect on GH action through its effect on GH receptor up-regulation in the liver [1]. In uncontrolled (insulinopenic) diabetes, a GH-resistant state prevails, which in its most extreme form can lead to growth failure (Mauriac syndrome). Hepatic GH receptors in rats, as well as serum GH-binding protein (GHBP) levels in humans, are decreased in insulin deficiency, be it from pancreatic β-cell failure or other causes, such as malnutrition [2–4]. Post-receptor mechanisms of impaired GH signalling, such as increased expression of suppressor of cytokine signalling (SOCS) proteins, also contribute to this type of GH resistance [5, 6]. Conversely, over-nutrition and hyperinsulinaemia

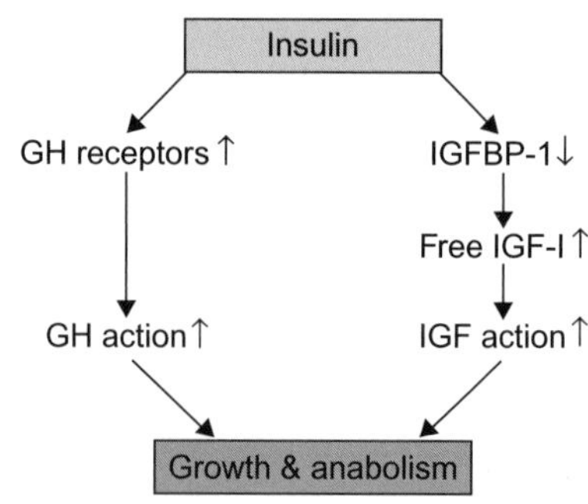

Figure 2. *The influence of insulin on GH/IGF action. Insulin enhances GH action by up-regulating GH receptors, particularly in the liver. This leads to enhanced GH action and increased IGF-I production. In addition, insulin enhances IGF-I action by down-regulating IGF-binding protein-1 (IGFBP-1), the major circulating inhibitor of IGF action. Circulating free IGF-I concentrations are thereby increased and IGF action is augmented.*

result in a state of GH hypersensitivity and elevated GHBP levels [4, 7] (see [8] for review).

Insulin also has an important effect on IGF blood transport and IGF action through its regulation of IGF-binding protein-1 (IGFBP-1). *IGFBP-1* gene expression is negatively regulated by insulin [9], and IGFBP-1 levels in blood vary widely and inversely with insulin levels [10]. IGFBP-1 acts primarily as a circulating inhibitor of IGF action, thereby acutely regulating the anabolic and mitogenic activities of IGF-I as a function of the nutritional/metabolic state. This mechanism contributes to the adaptive response of fuel allocation towards either storage or energy production, depending on the abundance of available fuel.

GH effects on insulin secretion (Fig. 3)

GH has insulotropic activity, promoting pancreatic β-cell proliferation and insulin production. This includes both indirect (hyperglycaemia-mediated) and direct effects. Evidence for the latter is provided *in vitro*, where GH stimulates β-cell proliferation and insulin production [11]. *In vivo*, this insulotropic effect is further enhanced by the anti-insulin effect of GH (see below), which results in elevated levels of blood glucose (and probably other fuels) that are stimulatory to the β-cell. Increased blood insulin levels then act to bring the level of blood glucose back to normal. The relative contributions of these direct and indirect insulotropic effects of GH *in vivo* are difficult to separate.

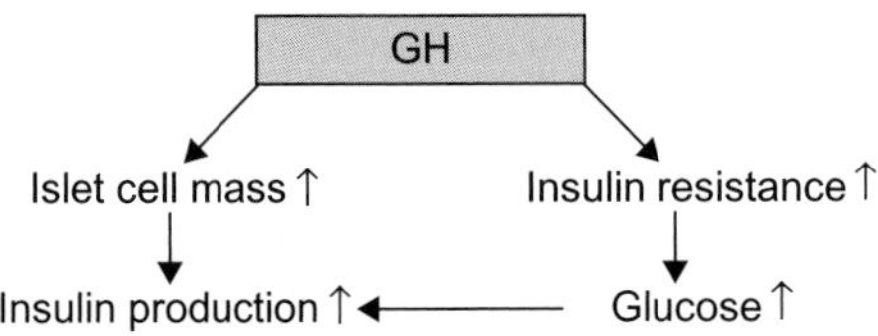

Figure 3. *The effect of GH on pancreatic islet mass and function. GH directly stimulates β-cell mass and insulin output. This effect is indirectly abetted by GH-induced peripheral insulin resistance, which raises blood glucose and thereby stimulates insulin secretion. The result of both actions is a higher circulating insulin level, which returns glucose levels to baseline and contributes to tissue anabolism.*

GH effects on insulin action

GH has potent anti-insulin activity, in part through its lipolytic action/free fatty acid liberation. GH also has acute 'insulin-like activity', which is short-lived and probably attributable to cross-talk between insulin and GH signalling pathways, specifically insulin receptor substrate molecules, which participate in signalling cascades, not only for insulin, but also for GH [12]. *In vivo*, this insulin-like activity is only demonstrable in a state of preceding GH deficiency (GHD); it probably has only minor physiological importance. In contrast, the anti-insulin property of GH is very prominent and prevails over the long term. The clinical manifestations of this property of GH are the enhanced insulin sensitivity in hypopituitarism and the insulin resistance in acromegaly. In GHD, endogenous insulin levels are low; they rise to normal levels after the institution of GH replacement therapy. Acromegaly is associated with elevated insulin levels, frequently carbohydrate intolerance, and sometimes frank diabetes mellitus. Because of its insulin-antagonistic property, GH is known as a 'diabetogenic hormone', and glucose tolerance should be carefully monitored in patients on GH therapy. It should be mentioned in this context that there are also reasons for insulin resistance in GHD, such as visceral obesity. In this case, insulin sensitivity may improve with GH therapy because of the reversal of obesity – an outcome opposite to the expected direct action of GH. Thus, the net *in-vivo* effect of GH status on insulin action represents a composite of several direct and indirect influences.

IGF-I effects on insulin action

At high concentrations, IGF-I can activate the insulin receptor, but this occurs only at supraphysiological levels. Furthermore, IGF-I, presumably acting through its own receptor, can partially supplant insulin action and has been used with some success as a surrogate for insulin in patients with defects in the insulin receptor or its function [13]. In insulin receptor knockout mice, IGF-I was shown to activate IGF-I receptor-mediated phosphatidylinositol 3-kinase and glucose transport [14]. IGF-I given as a therapeutic agent improves metabolic control in type 1 and type 2 diabetes – an effect partially, but not fully, explained by suppression of elevated GH levels [15]. The precise mechanism(s) by which IGF-I improves metabolic control are complex and still incompletely understood.

Thyroid hormones

Thyroid hormone effects on GH secretion and IGF-I production

In the rat, *GH* gene expression is under strong positive control by tri-iodothyronine (T_3) due to a critical thyroid response element in the promoter region of the *GH* gene [16]. This T_3 dependence is less marked in humans, where hypothyroidism results in only moderately impaired GH secretion [17]. Decreased GH secretion, while not the sole factor, probably contributes to the growth retardation caused by hypothyroidism. Hypothyroidism also impairs IGF-I generation in response to GH [18].

Hyperthyroidism has been shown to increase GH production in humans, but serum GH levels are generally lower than normal, presumably because of accelerated GH clearance [19, 20].

Thyroid hormone effects on GH and IGF action

Thyroid hormone plays an important role in linear growth through its effects on growth and maturation of epiphyseal cartilage. In the absence of thyroid hormone, growth cartilage is poorly responsive to GH and/or IGF-I, and IGF-I production in response to GH is impaired [21]. This results in a maturation arrest and delayed ossification manifesting itself clinically as 'stippled' epiphyses. GH and thyroid hormone appear to potentiate each other's effects at the growth plate; the combined action of both is therefore critically important for normal linear growth.

GH/IGF-I effects on thyroid hormone secretion

IGF-I is mitogenic for many tissues, including the thyroid; it is probably a locally active cytokine important for optimizing thyroid growth and function [22]. IGF-I has also been implicated in the formation of thyroid nodules and multi-nodular goitre, especially in acromegaly [23].

GH/IGF-I effects on thyroid hormone metabolism/activity (Fig. 4)

GH increases peripheral conversion of thyroxine (T_4) to T_3 by stimulating 5'-deiodinase activity [24, 25]. This effect is only partially mediated by IGF-I [26]. As a result, there is a rise in circulating T_3, a decline in reverse T_3, a rise in the T_3/T_4 ratio, and in most studies a decline in T_4 or free T_4 when GH is given to normal or GH-deficient subjects [27]. This phenomenon has implications for treating hypopituitarism in patients with combined hormone deficiencies. When thyrotrophin-deficient patients treated with T_4 start GH replacement therapy, the effect of GH on thyroid hormone interconversion should be taken into account, with careful adjustment of the T_4 dose as needed.

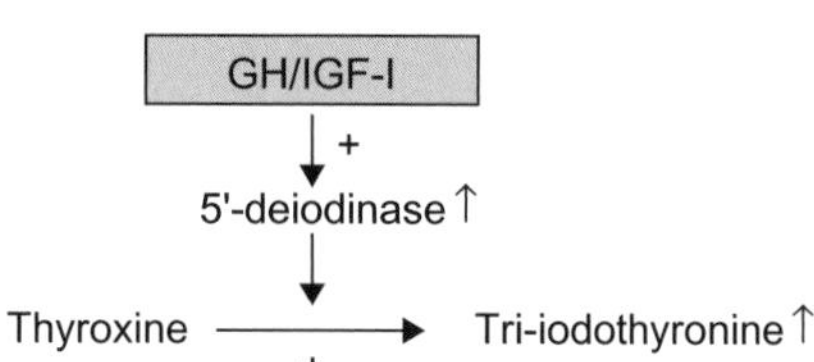

Figure 4. *The effect of GH and IGF-I on peripheral conversion of thyroxine (T_4) to tri-iodothyronine (T_3). GH/IGF stimulates 5'-deiodinase activity, which results in enhanced T_3 production from its T_4 precursor in peripheral tissues. Homeostatic mechanisms then lead to a lower T_4 level and maintain the organism in a euthyroid state.*

IGF-I effects on thyroid hormone action

As mentioned above, there is a synergistic relationship between IGF-I and thyroid hormone at the epiphyseal growth plate. Similar cooperative effects between IGF-I and thyroid hormones may exist in other tissues and organs, but there is relatively little information on this possibility.

Corticosteroids

Corticosteroid effects on GH secretion and IGF-I production (Fig. 5)

GH production at the pituitary level is stimulated by corticosteroids [28, 29], and a glucocorticoid response element is present in the *GH* gene [30]. However, *in vivo*, corticosteroids inhibit GH secretion through a hypothalamic mechanism involving increased somatostatin tone [31] and possibly other pathways. The net effect of the hypothalamic and pituitary actions of glucocorticoids is potent inhibition of GH secretion. Indeed, corticosteroid treatment is an important and prevalent cause of growth retardation, which, in part, is due to suppressed GH secretion. Glucocorticoids are also strong catabolic agents for lean body mass (especially bone and muscle); attenuated GH production plays a contributory role in this phenomenon.

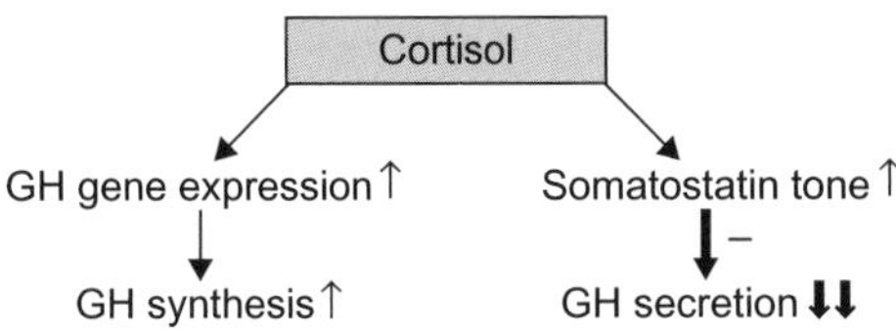

Figure 5. *The dual effects of glucocorticoids on GH production. At the pituitary level, glucocorticoids enhance GH gene expression. At the hypothalamic level, glucocorticoids strongly inhibit GH secretion. The latter is thought to be mediated by increasing somatostatin tone. The net in-vivo effect of these dual and opposing actions is a strong inhibition of GH secretion.*

Corticosteroid effects on GH and IGF action

Glucocorticoids inhibit GH and/or IGF action through multiple mechanisms. GH receptor expression is under negative regulation by glucocorticoids [32]. A circulating IGF-I inhibitor associated with steroid treatment has been demonstrated [33]. Inhibitory effects at the epiphyseal growth plate include suppressed IGF-I and IGFBP production, attenuated chondrocyte proliferation, impaired proteoglycan formation, accelerated chondrocyte apoptosis, and diminished vascular endothelial growth factor expression (see [34, 35] for review). Glucocorticoids have a profound catabolic effect on skeletal muscle. The resulting steroid myopathy can be partially overcome by GH [36], thereby implying that glucocorticoids induce partial resistance to GH and/or IGF-I. Mechanisms implicated include up-regulation of glutamine synthetase by steroids (and inhibition thereof by GH/IGF-I), as well as interference with IGF-I signalling pathways by corticosteroids (reviewed in [37]).

GH/IGF-I effects on corticosteroid secretion

No major direct effect of GH and IGF-I on corticosteroid secretion has been identified. However, secondary adjustments in the hypothalamic–pituitary–adrenal axis may occur in response to alterations in cortisol metabolism induced by GH/IGF-I (see below).

GH/IGF-I effects on corticosteroid metabolism/activity (Fig. 6)

One of the enzymes involved in cortisol metabolism, type 1 11β-hydroxysteroid dehydrogenase (11β-HSD1), is under inhibitory control by IGF-I and hence GH. This enzyme catalyses interconversion between cortisol and its inactive metabolite, cortisone, in a bidirectional manner, with the 'activating' direction of cortisone to cortisol conversion predominating. It is expressed in liver, adipose tissue (visceral fat more than subcutaneous fat), bone, gonadal tissue and the CNS. In GHD, 11β-HSD1-mediated cortisone to cortisol conversion is enhanced, a fact that has been implicated in the disproportionate visceral fat accumulation seen in that condition (see [38] for review). Indeed, over-expression of 11β-HSD1 in a mouse model leads to a Cushing's- or metabolic syndrome-like phenotype, including visceral obesity, glucose intolerance and hyperlipidaemia [39]. GH treatment restores normal cortisol

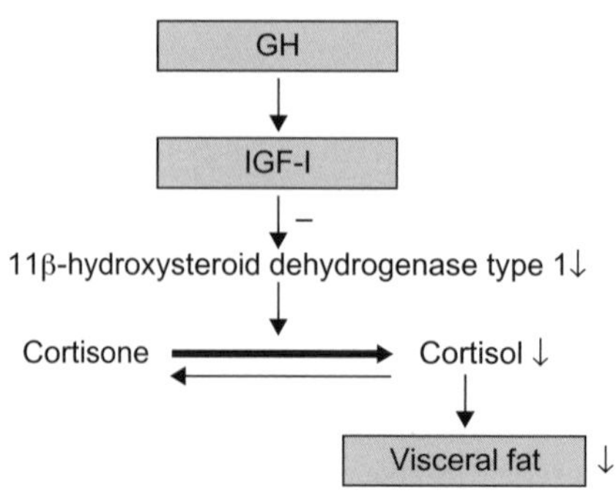

Figure 6. *The effect of GH/IGF-I on cortisol-dependent visceral fat mass. Visceral fat accumulation is in part a function of local conversion of inactive cortisone to active cortisol, a process mediated by type 1 11β-hydroxysteroid dehydrogenase (11β-HSD1). IGF-I inhibits 11β-HSD1 activity, thereby shifting the cortisone–cortisol equilibrium towards the inactive metabolite cortisone. In GHD, the situation is reversed, with excessive local cortisol production and enhanced visceral fat accumulation.*

metabolism, with concomitant loss of body fat, especially in the truncal area. Thus, the remarkably consistent effect of GH in promoting adipose tissue loss *in vivo* may result from a combination of its lipolytic effect and its regulation of 11β-HSD1 activity in favour of cortisol inactivation.

The effect of GH on cortisol metabolism has therapeutic implications in hypopituitary patients on corticosteroids, where institution of GH therapy may necessitate an increase in dose and/or switching from cortisone acetate to hydrocortisone [40].

GH/IGF-I effects on corticosteroid action

GH treatment can counteract the catabolic action of corticosteroids on muscle and bone [36, 41], an effect that is, at least in part, mediated by IGF-I [42, 43]. However, the potential clinical use of GH as a therapeutic agent in preventing steroid-induced catabolism has not found wide application and is still to be tested in clinical trials.

Oestrogens

Oestrogen effects on GH secretion and IGF-I production

Oestrogens enhance GH secretion, in large part indirectly by inducing GH resistance (see below) and consequent diminished negative feedback by IGF-I on GH production. One manifestation of this oestrogen effect is the sexual dimorphism of GH secretion. Women of reproductive age have higher serum GH levels, their secretion pattern is characterized by higher trough levels and a more ‘disordered’ pulsatile profile [44, 45], and their GH production rate is about twice that observed in men. Sexual dimorphism of GH secretion is even more pronounced in some other species, such as the rat. Oestrogens promote enhanced GH secretion during puberty, which results in the pubertal growth spurt [46]. This applies to both sexes as, in males, oestrogens derived from aromatized testosterone are primarily responsible for stimulating GH secretion [46].

Oestrogen effects on GH transport

Oestrogens, especially when given by the oral route, increase the circulating concentration of GHBPs, the soluble ectodomains of GH receptors [47]. Women have slightly higher GHBP levels than men and, in some species (e.g. rodents), females have markedly higher GHBP levels than males [48]. By influencing GHBP levels, oestrogens modulate GH blood transport, GH metabolism and GH action (see [48] for review).

Oestrogen effects on GH action (Fig. 7)

Oestrogens inhibit GH actions, including IGF-I generation, an effect that has been known for a long time and has been proposed as a medical treatment for acromegaly [49, 50]. The mechanism for this inhibition has recently been identified at the level of GH receptor signalling. Specifically, oestrogens induce SOCS-2, which, in turn, inhibits Janus kinase 2 phosphorylation, the first and a critical step in the GH receptor signalling cascade [51]. The result is not only diminished GH action, but also the aforementioned compensatory increase in GH secretion.

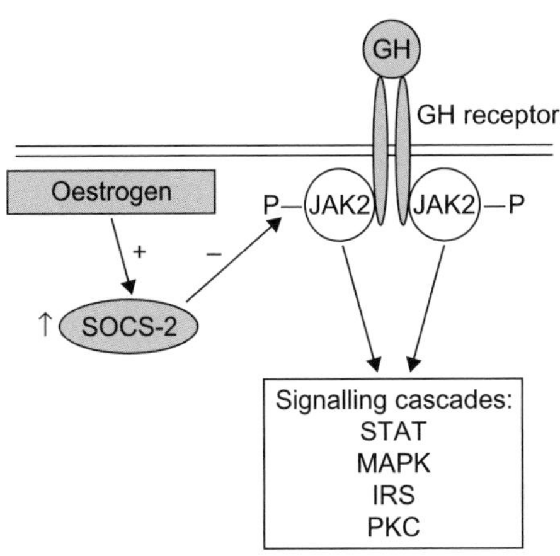

Figure 7. *The inhibitory effect of oestrogens on GH action. The liganded GH receptor dimer associated with phospho-Janus kinase 2 (JAK2) is shown. Recruitment of JAK2 to the GH receptor and the subsequent phosphorylation of JAK2 (and the GH receptor) is the first step in GH signal transduction; it serves as the trigger for downstream phosphorylation cascades, such as the activation of signal transducer and activator of transcription (STAT), mitogen-activated protein kinase (MAPK), insulin receptor substrate (IRS) and protein kinase C (PKC) pathways. Oestrogens induce suppressor of cytokine signalling 2 (SOCS-2), an inhibitor of JAK2 phosphorylation, thereby decreasing JAK2 enzymatic (kinase) activity, with corresponding dampening of all downstream signalling events.*

Oestrogens also limit the most obvious aspect of GH/IGF-I action, linear growth, by promoting epiphyseal closure during puberty. This involves no direct interaction with the GH/IGF system, but nevertheless impacts on an important endpoint of GH/IGF-I action.

GH/IGF-I effects on oestrogen secretion and action

IGF-I is important for the proper development and function of many tissues, including the ovary. Various effects of IGF-I on ovarian function are demonstrable in experimental settings. However, *in vivo*, in humans, no major abnormalities in oestrogen secretion have been attributed to derangements in GH or IGF-I physiology. Similarly, oestrogen action does not appear to be directly influenced by GH or IGF-I. For the effect of GH on pubertal timing, see below.

Androgens

Androgen effects on GH secretion and IGF-I production

The increased androgen production during adrenarche and puberty leads to enhanced GH secretion; however, as mentioned above, the stimulatory effects of aromatizable androgens (e.g. testosterone) on GH secretion are largely due to oestrogens derived from them. Non-aromatizable androgens, such as dihydrotestosterone, do not enhance GH secretion. Despite this, a possible direct role of androgens in the elaboration of the appropriate mixture of bioactive GH forms during puberty has been postulated and needs further evaluation [52].

Androgen effects on GH action

Androgens have potent anabolic actions that parallel those of GH and IGF-I. They appear to be independent of the GH/IGF axis, but the combination of androgen and GH results in a significant increase in muscle mass, as is seen most dramatically in male puberty. Body builders also strongly believe that a combination of anabolic/androgenic steroids and GH results in muscle growth. With respect to bone elongation, androgens (oxandrolone) have been used to accelerate growth in patients with Turner syndrome. This appears to be an effect independent of GH or IGF-I; the effect parallels and perhaps adds to that of GH. Thus, the available evidence suggests that, with respect to hormone action, there is little direct interaction between androgens and GH/IGF-I. Rather, the anabolic effects of the two hormone classes resemble each other in certain target tissues.

GH/IGF-I effects on androgen secretion

Adrenal androgen production is partially under GH/IGF control. Patients with GHD have subnormal adrenal androgen levels, which can be normalized with GH therapy in at least some patients [53, 54]. Conversely, patients with acromegaly show evidence of increased adrenal androgen production [55] and increased sebum production. The mechanism for this effect of GH/IGF-I is probably complex; it may include direct stimulation of the adrenal gland, as well as indirect effects mediated through activation of the hypothalamic–pituitary–adrenal axis [54]. The GH/IGF-I effect on adrenal androgens is relatively minor, and its physiological or clinical significance is uncertain. No consistent effect of GH/IGF-I on gonadal androgen production has been identified. For the effect of androgens on pubertal timing, see below.

Gonadotrophins

Early studies have suggested that GH, acting as a co-gonadotrophin, may amplify gonadotrophin action in women undergoing ovulation-induction protocols [56] or in hypogonadal men treated to induce spermatogenesis [57]. However, the efficacy of GH as a co-gonadotrophin has not been consistently observed; and GH use for this purpose has been largely abandoned.

GH effects on pubertal timing

The awakening of enhanced and pulsatile gonadotrophin secretion is the hallmark of puberty. It is still largely unknown what triggers the onset of puberty, but body size and fat mass appear to be important determinants. GHD, regardless of aetiology, markedly delays the onset of puberty in both sexes. This striking effect is probably mediated through retardation of the attainment of a critical body mass, rather than through a direct GH effect on gonadotrophin secretion. Among other factors, a rise in leptin, as an index of adipose tissue mass, has been shown to be associated with pubertal onset in some studies. This probably reflects achievement of a threshold body/adipose mass rather than a direct effect of leptin.

Leptin

Numerous associations between the GH/IGF system and the leptin system have been reported. However, most of the interconnections between the two systems relate to their respective roles in the regulation of adipose tissue mass, body composition, and fuel metabolism; they are thus primarily indirect associations rather than causal links. However, a few intriguing observations are not explained by these indirect connections. For example, GH given as an injection acutely stimulates serum leptin levels [58]. Patients with an inactivating mutation in the leptin receptor show growth retardation and GHD [59], yet patients with genetic deficiency of leptin itself appear to have normal GH function [60]. These observations suggest that additional studies of the interconnections between the leptin and the GH/IGF systems are warranted.

Conclusions

The GH/IGF axis, by virtue of its universal importance for most tissues, interacts with most other hormone systems in one way or another. Major interactions occur with insulin (the other major anabolic hormone system), with glucocorticoids (the principal catabolic hormone system), as well as with sex steroids and thyroid hormones. The interactions are complex and diverse; they involve direct influences on hormone secretion, metabolism, actions and more indirect modulations mediated by feedback loops and signals derived from secondary events promoted by hormone action. Detailed knowledge of these interconnections is important for optimal treatment of patients with hypopituitarism and GHD, as well as those with acromegaly.

Acknowledgement

Supported in part by a Merit Review grant from the Department of Veterans Affairs.

References

1. Baxter RC, Turtle JR. Regulation of hepatic growth hormone receptors by insulin. Biochem Biophys Res Commun 1978;84:350–7

2. Postel-Vinay MC, Cohen-Tanugi E, Charrier J. Growth hormone receptors in rat liver membranes: effects of fasting and refeeding, and correlation with plasma somatomedin activity. Mol Cell Endocrinol 1982; 28:657–69

3. Mercado M, Molitch ME, Baumann G. Low plasma growth hormone binding protein in IDDM. Diabetes 1992;41:605–9

4. Hochberg Z, Hertz P, Colin V, Ish-Shalom S, Yeshurun D, Youdim MB, Amit T. The distal axis of growth hormone (GH) in nutritional disorders: GH-binding protein, insulin-like growth factor-I (IGF-I), and IGF-I receptors in obesity and anorexia nervosa. Metabolism 1992;41:106–12

5. Maes M, Underwood LE, Ketelslegers JM. Low serum somatomedin-C in insulin-dependent diabetes: evidence for a postreceptor mechanism. Endocrinology 1986; 118:377–82

6. Beauloye V, Ketelslegers JM, Moreau B, Thissen JP. Dexamethasone inhibits both growth hormone (GH)-induction of insulin-like growth factor-I (IGF-I) mRNA and GH receptor (GHR) mRNA levels in rat primary cultured hepatocytes. Growth Horm IGF Res 1999; 9:205–11

7. Forbes GB. Nutrition and growth. J Pediatr 1977;91:40–2

8. Baumann G, Mercado M. Growth hormone-binding proteins in plasma. Nutrition 1993;9:546–53

9. Cichy SB, Uddin S, Danilkovich A, Guo S, Klippel A, Unterman TG. Protein kinase B/Akt mediates effects of insulin on hepatic insulin-like growth factor-binding protein-1 gene expression through a conserved insulin response sequence. J Biol Chem 1998;273:6482–7

10. Holly JM, Biddlecombe RA, Dunger DB, Edge JA, Amiel SA, Howell R, Chard T, Rees LH, Wass JA. Circadian variation of GH-independent IGF-binding protein in diabetes mellitus and its relationship to insulin. A new role for insulin? Clin Endocrinol (Oxf) 1988;29:667–75

11. Nielsen JH, Linde S, Welinder BS, Billestrup N, Madsen OD. Growth hormone is a growth factor for the differentiated pancreatic beta-cell. Mol Endocrinol 1989;3:165–73

12. Souza SC, Frick GP, Yip R, Lobo RB, Tai LR, Goodman HM. Growth hormone stimulates tyrosine phosphorylation of insulin receptor substrate-1. J Biol Chem 1994;269:30085–8

13. Kuzuya H, Matsuura N, Sakamoto M, Makino H, Sakamoto Y, Kadowaki T, Suzuki Y, Kobayashi M, Akazawa Y, Nomura M. Trial of insulin-like growth factor I therapy for patients with extreme insulin resistance syndromes. Diabetes 1993;42:696–705

14. Di Cola G, Cool MH, Accili D. Hypoglycemic effect of insulin-like growth factor-1 in mice lacking insulin receptors. J Clin Invest 1997;99:2538–44

15. O'Connell T, Clemmons DR. IGF-I/IGF-binding protein-3 combination improves insulin resistance by GH-dependent and independent mechanisms. J Clin Endocrinol Metab 2002;87:4356–60

16. Flug F, Copp RP, Casanova J, Horowitz ZD, Janocko L, Plotnick M, Samuels HH. *cis*-acting elements of the rat growth hormone gene which mediate basal and regulated expression by thyroid hormone. J Biol Chem 1987;262:6373–82

17. Chernausek SD, Turner R. Attenuation of spontaneous, nocturnal growth hormone secretion in children with hypothyroidism and its correlation with plasma insulin-like growth factor I concentrations. J Pediatr 1989; 114:968–72

18. Wolf M, Ingbar SH, Moses AC. Thyroid hormone and growth hormone interact to regulate insulin-like growth factor-I messenger ribonucleic acid and circulating levels in the rat. Endocrinology 1989;125:2905–14

19. Iranmanesh A, Lizarralde G, Johnson ML, Veldhuis JD. Nature of altered growth hormone secretion in hyperthyroidism. J Clin Endocrinol Metab 1991; 72:108–15

20. Sasaki N, Tsuyusaki T, Nakamura H, Sanayama K, Niimi H, Nakajima H. Sleep-related growth hormone release in thyrotoxic patients before and during propylthiouracil therapy. Endocrinol Jpn 1985;32: 39–44

21. Thorngren KG, Hansson LI. Effect of thyroxine and growth hormone on longitudinal bone growth in the hypophysectomized rat. Acta Endocrinol (Copenh) 1973;74:24–40

22. Bachrach LK, Eggo MC, Hintz RL, Burrow GN. Insulin-like growth factors in sheep thyroid cells: action, receptors and production. Biochem Biophys Res Commun 1988;154:861–7

23. Dumont JE, Lamy F, Roger P, Maenhaut C. Physiological and pathological regulation of thyroid cell proliferation and differentiation by thyrotropin and other factors. Physiol Rev 1992;72:667–97

24. Gotzsche LS, Flyvbjerg A, Marshall S, Jorgensen KD, Weeke J. The influence of growth hormone and thyroxine on iodothyronine deiodinase activity in the liver, kidney and brown adipose tissue in hypophysectomized rats. Acta Endocrinol (Copenh) 1991;125:219–26

25. MacLatchy DL, Eales JG. Growth hormone stimulates hepatic thyroxine 5'-monodeiodinase activity and 3,5,3'-triiodothyronine levels in rainbow trout (*Salmo gairdneri*). Gen Comp Endocrinol 1990;78:164–72

26. Hussain MA, Schmitz O, Jørgensen JO, Christiansen JS, Weeke J, Schmid C, Froesch ER. Insulin-like growth factor I alters peripheral thyroid hormone metabolism in humans: comparison with growth hormone. Eur J Endocrinol 1996;134:563–7

27. Møller J, Jørgensen JO, Møller N, Christiansen JS, Weeke J. Effects of growth hormone administration on fuel oxidation and thyroid function in normal man. Metabolism 1992;41:728–31

28. Kohler PO, Bridson WE, Rayford PL. Cortisol stimulation of growth hormone production by monkey adenohypophysis in tissue culture. Biochem Biophys Res Commun 1968;33:834–40

29. Baumann G, MacCart JG. Growth hormone production by human pituitary glands in organ culture: evidence for predominant secretion of the single-chain 22,000 molecular weight form (isohormone B). J Clin Endocrinol Metab 1982;55:611–8

30. Moore DD, Marks AR, Buckley DI, Kapler G, Payvar F, Goodman HM. The first intron of the human growth hormone gene contains a binding site for glucocorticoid receptor. Proc Natl Acad Sci USA 1985;82:699–702

31. Wehrenberg WB, Janowski BA, Piering AW, Culler F, Jones KL. Glucocorticoids: potent inhibitors and stimulators of growth hormone secretion. Endocrinology 1990;126:3200–3

32. Gabrielsson BG, Carmignac DF, Flavell DM, Robinson IC. Steroid regulation of growth hormone (GH) receptor and GH-binding protein messenger ribonucleic acids in the rat. Endocrinology 1995;136:209–17

33. Unterman TG, Phillips LS. Glucocorticoid effects on somatomedins and somatomedin inhibitors. J Clin Endocrinol Metab 1985;61:618–26

34. Hochberg Z. Mechanisms of steroid impairment of growth. Horm Res 2002;58 (Suppl 1):33–8

35. Robson H, Siebler T, Shalet SM, Williams GR. Interactions between GH, IGF-I, glucocorticoids, and thyroid hormones during skeletal growth. Pediatr Res 2002;52:137–47

36. Horber FF, Haymond MW. Human growth hormone prevents the protein catabolic side effects of prednisone in humans. J Clin Invest 1990;86:265–72

37. Kanda F, Okuda S, Matsushita T, Takatani K, Kimura KI, Chihara K. Steroid myopathy: pathogenesis and effects of growth hormone and insulin-like growth factor-I administration. Horm Res 2001;56 (Suppl 1):24–8

38. Stewart JK, Clifton DK, Koerker DJ, Rogol AD, Jaffe T, Goodner CJ. Pulsatile release of growth hormone and prolactin from the primate pituitary *in vitro*. Endocrinology 1985;116:1–5

39. Masuzaki H, Paterson J, Shinyama H, Morton NM, Mullins JJ, Seckl JR, Flier JS. A transgenic model of visceral obesity and the metabolic syndrome. Science 2001;294:2166–70

40. Gelding SV, Taylor NF, Wood PJ, Noonan K, Weaver JU, Wood DF, Monson JP. The effect of growth hormone replacement therapy on cortisol-cortisone interconversion in hypopituitary adults: evidence for growth hormone modulation of extrarenal 11 beta-hydroxysteroid dehydrogenase activity. Clin Endocrinol (Oxf) 1998;48:153–62

41. Ortoft G, Andreassen TT, Oxlund H. Growth hormone increases cortical and cancellous bone mass in young growing rats with glucocorticoid-induced osteopenia. J Bone Miner Res 1999;14:710–21

42. Mauras N, Beaufrere B. Recombinant human insulin-like growth factor-I enhances whole body protein anabolism and significantly diminishes the protein catabolic effects of prednisone in humans without a diabetogenic effect. J Clin Endocrinol Metab 1995; 80:869–74

43. Kanda F, Takatani K, Okuda S, Matsushita T, Chihara K. Preventive effects of insulinlike growth factor-I on steroid-induced muscle atrophy. Muscle Nerve 1999; 22:213–7

44. Ho KY, Evans WS, Blizzard RM, Veldhuis JD, Merriam GR, Samojlik E, Furlanetto R, Rogol AD, Kaiser DL, Thorner MO. Effects of sex and age on the 24-hour profile of growth hormone secretion in man: importance of endogenous estradiol concentrations. J Clin Endocrinol Metab 1987;64:51–8

45. Winer LM, Shaw MA, Baumann G. Basal plasma growth hormone levels in man: new evidence for rhythmicity of growth hormone secretion. J Clin Endocrinol Metab 1990;70:1678–86

46. Mauras N. Growth hormone and sex steroids. Interactions in puberty. Endocrinol Metab Clin North Am 2001;30:529–44

47. Weissberger AJ, Ho KK, Lazarus L. Contrasting effects of oral and transdermal routes of estrogen replacement therapy on 24-hour growth hormone (GH) secretion, insulin-like growth factor I, and GH-binding protein in postmenopausal women. J Clin Endocrinol Metab 1991;72:374–81

48. Baumann G. Growth hormone binding protein 2001. J Pediatr Endocrinol Metab 2001;14:355–75

49. McCullagh EP, Beck JC, Schaffenburg CA. Control of diabetes and other features of acromegaly following treatment with estrogens. Diabetes 1955;4:13–23

50. Clemmons DR, Underwood LE, Ridgway EC, Kliman B, Kjellberg RN, Van Wyk JJ. Estradiol treatment of acromegaly. Reduction of immunoreactive somatomedin-C and improvement in metabolic status. Am J Med 1980;69:571–5

51. Leung KC, Doyle N, Ballesteros M, Sjögren K, Watts CK, Low TH, Leong GM, Ross RJ, Ho KK. Estrogen inhibits GH signaling by suppressing GH-induced JAK2 phosphorylation, an effect mediated by SOCS-2. Proc Natl Acad Sci USA 2003;100:1016–21

52. Cemeroglu AP, Barkan AL, Kletter GB, Beitins IZ, Foster CM. Changes in serum immunoreactive and bioactive growth hormone concentrations in boys with advancing puberty and in response to a 20-hour estradiol infusion. J Clin Endocrinol Metab 1997;82:2166–71

53. Rudd BT, Rayner PH, Bassett RM, Williams JW. Serum dehydroepiandrosterone (DHA) and sulphate (DHAS) after acute growth hormone therapy. Acta Paediatr Scand 1980;69:287–92

54. Isidori AM, Kaltsas GA, Perry L, Burrin JM, Besser GM, Monson JP. The effect of growth hormone replacement therapy on adrenal androgen secretion in adult onset hypopituitarism. Clin Endocrinol (Oxf) 2003;58:601–11

55. Lim NY, Dingman JF. Androgenic adrenal hyperfunction in acromegaly. N Engl J Med 1964;271:1189–94

56. Homburg R, West C, Torresani T, Jacobs HS. Cotreatment with human growth hormone and gonadotropins for induction of ovulation: a controlled clinical trial. Fertil Steril 1990;53:254–60

57. Shoham Z, Conway GS, Ostergaard H, Lahlou N, Bouchard P, Jacobs HS. Cotreatment with growth hormone for induction of spermatogenesis in patients with hypogonadotropic hypogonadism. Fertil Steril 1992;57:1044–51

58. Lissett CA, Clayton PE, Shalet SM. The acute leptin response to GH. J Clin Endocrinol Metab 2001; 86:4412–5

59. Clement K, Vaisse C, Lahlou N, Cabrol S, Pelloux V, Cassuto D, Gourmelen M, Dina C, Chambaz J, Lacorte JM, Basdevant A, Bougneres P, Lebouc Y, Froguel P, Guy-Grand B. A mutation in the human leptin receptor gene causes obesity and pituitary dysfunction. Nature 1998;392:398–401

60. Montague CT, Farooqi IS, Whitehead JP, Soos MA, Rau H, Wareham NJ, Sewter CP, Digby JE, Mohammed SN, Hurst JA, Cheetham CH, Earley AR, Barnett AH, Prins JB, O'Rahilly S. Congenital leptin deficiency is associated with severe early-onset obesity in humans. Nature 1997;387:903–8

5 Overview of growth hormone deficiency in adults

Annice Mukherjee and Stephen M Shalet
Department of Endocrinology, Christie Hospital, Wilmslow Road, Withington, Manchester, UK

Summary

The study of human growth hormone (GH) and its physiological effects was pioneered in the middle of the 20th Century. During the 1960s and '70s GH was used primarily for the treatment of childhood growth disorders and, in general, use was restricted by the limited supply of cadaveric GH. As early as 1962, however, Raben [1] reported improved vigour, well-being, and ambition in a 35-year-old hypopituitary patient treated with extracted pituitary GH, suggesting that GH might continue to play a significant role in adults. The introduction of recombinant human GH [2], which became widely available in the middle of the 1980s, provided an opportunity for more detailed study of the effects of GH in adults. The first double-blind, randomized, placebo-controlled trials investigating the effects of GH in adults were completed in 1989 and initiated a new era in the study of GH and its physiological effects. By the mid-1990s a plethora of data provided a basis for the existence of an adult GH deficiency syndrome, which was noted to include a wide variety of biological features. These consisted of adverse metabolic changes, abnormal body composition, an adverse cardiovascular risk profile, reduced bone mineral density and impairment in quality of life [3]. Many endocrine units began to advocate the widespread use of GH replacement therapy in GH-deficient adults because of its beneficial effects on these parameters. The identification of appropriate dosing schedules remained unresolved at this stage, as a dichotomy in the dose requirements between adults and children had become even more evident than predicted. In addition, the heterogeneity of response of patients to GH replacement therapy meant that some patients displayed dramatic changes in biological endpoints, whereas others exhibited no noticeable benefits. This was partly explained by the fact that the degree of improvement in many of the endpoints studied was proportional to the deviation from normality at the outset.

In the late 1990s and into the new millennium, more detailed studies have been undertaken, addressing many of the issues arising from the earlier studies. These recent studies have examined the effects of GH on bone mass accrual, the identification of optimal dosing schedules for GH replacement during the transition from adolescence to adulthood and the identification of a safety-derived target range for insulin-like growth factor I, to aid dose titration during GH replacement in adulthood. Since the initial trials of GH replacement in adults, vigilance over safety has been an overriding concern. To date, no definite association has been identified between GH and either de novo tumours or recurrence of treated, pre-existing tumours.

Early observations on the metabolic effects of growth hormone

The isolation and purification of cadaveric pituitary-derived growth hormone (GH) occurred in the late 1950s [4]. Soon afterwards, GH was demonstrated to be potently effective both as an anabolic agent and a growth stimulator in humans [5]. A further breakthrough in the study of the effects of GH in adults came with the development of an immunoassay for human GH [6], which identified significant amounts of the hormone in healthy adults, thereby supporting the idea of a meaningful biological role. Multiple studies investigating the effects of GH in healthy and hypopituitary adults followed, which revealed pronounced metabolic effects in both [7]. However, the limited supply of cadaveric GH during the subsequent two decades necessitated that its use was primarily restricted to hypopituitary children with severe growth retardation.

Renaissance of GH studies in adults

The introduction of recombinant human GH [2], which became widely available in the mid-1980s, provided an opportunity for further study of the effects of GH in adults. With a background of information on the potential metabolic effects of GH in adults, but no documentation of the actual physiological importance of these effects [8], a number of investigators set out to examine the *in-vivo* effect of GH in hypopituitary adults with GH deficiency (GHD). The first two randomized controlled trials were published in 1989 [9, 10]. These initial studies illustrated a number of biological effects of GH and were followed by an unprecedented interest in GHD. Moreover, it became evident that GH-deficient adults have impairment in both physical and psychological health, compared with age-matched healthy adults. Subsequently, evidence for 'adult GHD syndrome' became established [11]. Adults with GHD were found to have abnormalities of body composition, bone mineral density (BMD), muscle strength, exercise performance, cardiovascular function and risk factors, energy, protein, carbohydrate and lipid metabolism, skin, immune system and psychological well-being [3]. Furthermore, beneficial effects of GH replacement on many aspects of homeostasis in adults were demonstrated [3].

Diagnostic tests

As GHD in adulthood became increasingly recognized and GH replacement possible, greater focus was placed on the criteria used for diagnosis. The diagnostic criteria used in childhood could not simply be extrapolated to the adult population. Partial GHD in childhood may have an impact on statural growth, whereas partial GHD in adulthood remains of unproven significance and, to date, studies in GH-deficient adults have been predominantly limited to those with severe GHD. Consensus guidelines for the diagnosis of GHD in adults have been established [12], and the criteria differ from those used in childhood [13].

The emergence of GH dose titration regimens

Many early studies of GH replacement in adults stimulated as many questions as answers. The doses of GH used in these early studies were derived largely from the paediatric doses used to achieve statural growth in childhood, with GH replacement regimens based on weight. It rapidly became apparent that GH dose requirements in adults were even lower than had been anticipated, and significantly less than those used in childhood. The sodium retention and increased total body water, observed in patients with acromegaly [14] and in the early studies of GH replacement for statural growth in childhood [15], gave early indications that GH may play a role in body fluid homeostasis. Indeed in the early studies of GH replacement in adults, the most common side-effects were symptoms associated with fluid retention, reflecting over-replacement. Thus a gradual refinement of the GH dose followed, and more widespread use of dose titration of GH, based on insulin-like growth factor I (IGF-I) monitoring, has been advocated [16, 17]. In GH-deficient adults such regimens are better tolerated than the weight-based regimens adapted from paediatric practice. This approach is also aimed at satisfying long-term safety concerns, as many adult patients treated with weight-based regimens in the early studies displayed supraphysiological IGF-I values [18].

Long-term GH replacement studies – continued benefits

The long-term efficacy of GH replacement with the lower dose regimens has been demonstrated in single-centre studies [19–26] and large multinational databases [18, 27, 28]. By virtue of their size, the latter are likely to detect rare adverse events, evaluate beneficial changes in various endpoints and permit analysis of mortality rates. KIMS – Pfizer International Metabolic Database – is currently the largest database, with information on over 8000 patients from a total of 27 countries. Long-term follow-up of patients in KIMS has confirmed that beneficial effects are maintained for at least 2 years after the initiation of therapy in both men and women. An increase within the normal range for fasting glucose and glycated haemoglobin has been observed in short-term studies of GH replacement. These changes are maintained during longer term follow-up, but do not tend to rise further above baseline in subjects with pre-existing impaired glucose tolerance [28].

Unresolved issues

GH dose changes

Evidence for considerable individual variation in response to GH replacement arose from a number of studies, performed in the early 1990s, using weight-based regimens. In some cases the patients studied exhibited supraphysiological IGF-I values, which raised the question of whether the observed beneficial effects of GH were the result of physiological replacement or were pharmacological effects. However, because the strength of the argument for GH replacement was felt to be strong after the original weight-based studies, GH was licensed in many countries and GH replacement became routine practice simultaneously with the emergence of dose titration regimens. Since the initiation of dose titration of GH, resulting in more predictable physiological replacement of GH as guided by IGF-I monitoring, ongoing audit of practice has continued. The ethics of further randomized, placebo-controlled studies to investigate the effects of physiological replacement doses of GH remain controversial because they would deny, for at least a period of time, a proportion of patients a therapy from which benefits have purportedly already been substantiated. On the other hand, in many countries GH replacement is not universally prescribed for adults with severe GHD, a decision partly based on health economics, but also on a reluctance on the part of some endocrinologists to accept that the beneficial effects have been irrefutably established; under these circumstances the moral imperative to perform further controlled therapeutic studies in selected subsets of GH-deficient patients is a strong one.

Patient selection

As the number of studies of GH replacement in GH-deficient adults increased, a dichotomy became evident, based on the realization that in the untreated state, some patients reported a severe impairment in quality of life (QoL) and some a normal QoL [29]. Historically, generic self-rating QoL questionnaires have been used but, with the establishment of an association between GHD in adulthood and QoL impairment, disease-generated QoL assessment questionnaires have been validated and are now widely used [30]. The mechanism underlying QoL impairment in GH-deficient adults has not been fully explained but is likely to be multifactorial in origin because of the widespread physiological actions of GH. An inevitable controversy ensued as GH-deficient patients reporting no QoL impairment in the untreated state were unlikely to exhibit improvement in this endpoint in response to GH replacement; therefore, some studies investigating effects of GH replacement in unselected cohorts of patients with GHD documented no significant improvement in QoL [31]. However, studies investigating cohorts of GH-deficient patients selected because of severe impairment in QoL have demonstrated significant improvements in QoL after GH replacement [16, 17]. Furthermore, the degree of improvement in many biological endpoints affected by GH are proportional to the degree of deviation from normality at baseline [15].

Mortality risk

There is an increased mortality risk in hypopituitary adults in whom all pituitary hormones other than GH are fully replaced [32–34]. The increased standardized mortality rate in hypopituitary adults with untreated GHD is in the region of 1.8, compared with the general population. Furthermore, GH replacement has beneficial effects on markers of adverse cardiovascular risk in GH-deficient adults [3]. However, the increased mortality risk in GH-deficient adults could, in part, relate to under- or over-replacement of other pituitary hormones rather than the GHD itself; additional confounding variables include the use of pituitary radiotherapy. Longitudinal data, demonstrating an improvement in mortality in GH-replaced hypopituitary adults, are required to resolve this issue.

Divergence of opinion

Many countries have now approved the use of GH replacement for hypopituitary adults with GHD, akin to any other hormone replacement therapy. However, some countries do not advocate GH replacement in GH-deficient adults. In the UK, the indication for GH replacement is based primarily on severe QoL impairment. Moreover, although guidelines exist [12], there is no current international conformity of approach.

Recent advances

A number of unusual associations with GHD have recently been identified including parathyroid disease [35] and traumatic brain injury [36]. GH replacement may, in future, be considered in patients suffering from these disease states. To date, however, no data are available relating to GH treatment for such patients. More established causes of GHD in adulthood include radiation-induced hypothalamic–pituitary damage in adult survivors of childhood cancer. Other non-GH-deficient states have also been targets for GH therapy with varying results.

Effects of GH replacement therapy in unusual cohorts

Adult survivors of childhood cancer

A specific group of patients at risk of GHD include the long-term survivors of childhood cancers who have received treatment with cranial irradiation either for primary brain tumours, nasopharyngeal carcinoma or acute lymphoblastic leukaemia, or total body irradiation in preparation for bone marrow transplantation. These individuals are at risk of developing deficiency in one or more pituitary hormones [37–40]. GH is the most vulnerable of the pituitary hormones to radiation-induced damage, with doses as low as 18 gray shown to result in GH insufficiency many years later [41]. Long-term survival in this cohort is improving. Only one study has investigated the effect of GH replacement in this group of patients [42], and has demonstrated significant improvements in QoL at up to 12 months following commencement of GH replacement (Fig. 1). Minor improvements in body composition, lipid profile and BMD were also observed.

Effects of GHD on BMD

Influences of GH on accretion of peak bone mass (PBM)

The timing of acquisition of PBM in young adults with GHD is not known, but may be more protracted than in normal individuals. Many studies, including those measuring markers of bone turnover and bone remodelling, have suggested a major role for GH in the accrual of PBM and bone preservation in children and young adults [43, 44].

Differences between adults with childhood-onset GHD (CO-GHD) and adult-onset GHD (AO-GHD)

Children with GHD exhibit relative osteopenia before the start of exogenous GH replacement [45], but the significance and implications of this are unknown. Adults with CO-GHD are also osteopenic [46–49]. Until recently, there has been

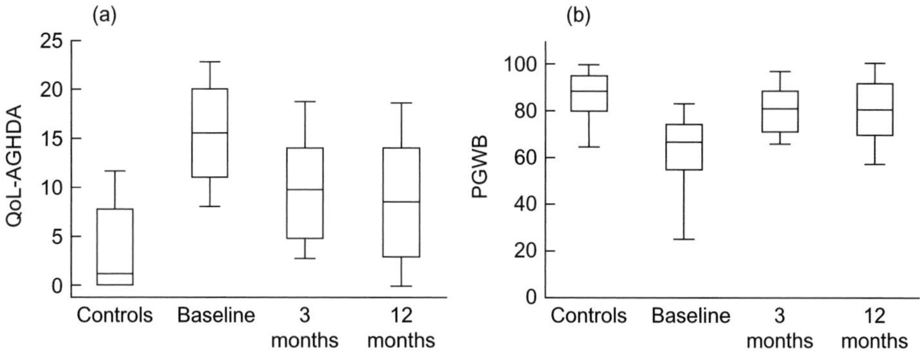

Figure 1. *Box and whisker plots representing quality of life as assessed by (a) the Quality of Life Assessment of GHD in Adults (QoL-AGHDA) (range 0–25; high values represent greater morbidity) and (b) the Psychological General Well-being (PGWB) index (range, 0–110; low values represent greater morbidity) in GH-deficient survivors of childhood cancer during 12 months of GH treatment and in healthy control subjects. The lower boundary of the box indicates the 25th percentile, the line within the box marks the median, and the upper boundary of the box indicates the 75th percentile. Error bars above and below the box indicate the 90th and 10th percentiles respectively. Adapted from [42] with permission. Copyright 2002, The Endocrine Society.*

no consensus as to whether AO-GHD is associated with osteopenia [50–55].

Recently, the effect of GHD on BMD has been shown to be closely correlated with age [56]. Relative osteopenia was confirmed in younger patients below the age of 30 years, regardless of whether they had CO- or AO-GHD. However, patients over 60 years of age demonstrated normal BMD at all sites compared with the control population (Table 1). These data are in agreement with previous work by Toogood *et al.* [53], demonstrating normal BMD in adults with GHD over the age of 60 years. The influence of age on BMD may, to a large extent, explain variations in BMD in adults with GHD in previous studies; in other words, the degree of abnormality in BMD at baseline may have been determined by the mean age of the cohort studied. Whilst acknowledging the impact of GHD on the skeleton, the evidence of a wide variation in BMD around the mean for all ages indicates other, significant, confounding variables. Nonetheless, it has become clear that GHD has a significant effect on the skeletal health of young adults, regardless of the age of onset or aetiology of their GHD, but GH status appears to play a much less important role in patients diagnosed with AO-GHD beyond the age of 30 years. This finding is strongly supportive of a major role for GH in the accrual of PBM.

Table 1. *Percentage of bone mineral density Z-scores of < –2 at four skeletal sites, related to age, in 200 severely GH-deficient adults [56].*

	Age (years)			
	< 30	**30–45**	**45–60**	**> 60**
Lumbar spine	23%	11%	11%	6%
Femoral neck	29%	12%	7%	0%
Ultra–distal radius	22%	14%	3%	7%
Distal radius	42%	13%	4%	0%

In a recent large study involving 92 adults with CO-GHD and 35 GH-naive adults with AO-GHD of comparable age [57], a significant maturational deficit of bone mineral content (BMC) in the CO-GHD group was demonstrated, despite GH replacement during childhood. In this study, a large proportion of patients with CO-GHD had not reached their full growth potential. In addition, the height deficit of these patients was highly negatively correlated with BMC, suggesting that bone density may be detrimentally affected in those who fail to reach target height. Furthermore, if somatic development during childhood GH replacement therapy had been adequate, it would be expected that body composition and BMD would be comparable in patients with AO- and CO-GHD, which was not the case, confirming previous reports in non age-matched patients [48, 58]. This study by Attanasio *et al.* [57] has demonstrated that failure to reach target height has detrimental consequences in terms of skeletal health. However, whether this maturational deficit has irrevocable consequences for bone mass potential in these subjects remains undetermined.

GHD in the transition from adolescence to adulthood

Historically, the typical approach to the adolescent GH-deficient patient has been to discontinue GH replacement at completion of linear growth. Since the onset of adult GH replacement for psychological and metabolic indications, many adults with CO-GHD have undergone re-testing of GH reserve. In some cases, these adults have been offered GH replacement. However, the skeletal impact of discontinuing GH replacement at completion of linear growth has only recently been considered in detail [59, 60].

A recent multicentre study has assessed the optimal GH replacement dose in young adults with CO-GHD [60]. In this study, 128 patients were randomized to receive either adult-dose GH replacement, paediatric-dose GH or no treatment. After 1 year, markers of bone turnover were considerably reduced in the untreated group and significantly increased in the treatment groups. At 2 years, total BMC was significantly greater in the treatment groups, with no significant dose effect, suggesting that adult dose regimens are satisfactory for ongoing accrual of bone mass after completion of linear growth. This study strongly supports the hypothesis that a reduction in bone turnover, associated with discontinuation of GH therapy at the completion of linear growth, will ultimately result in reduced BMD as the bone remodelling cycle progresses in the absence of GH. Furthermore, the study by Lissett *et al.* [61] also provides new data regarding GH dose requirements for optimal bone mass accretion after epiphyseal closure.

Optimal target range for IGF-I during the treatment of adult GH disorders

A large overlap exists between values for IGF-I in normal subjects and patients with AO-GHD matched for age (Tables 2 and 3), even in those with the most severe GHD identified by provocative tests of GH secretion [61] or number of additional pituitary hormone deficits [13, 62]. IGF-I is not, therefore, considered as a reliable marker for the diagnosis of GHD, although its usefulness has been shown to vary with the age of the patient and the time of onset of GHD [63–68]. The situation is different for monitoring treatment of GH disorders in adulthood, the literature to date suggesting that IGF-I is a better marker than IGF-binding protein-3 or acid-labile subunit [69]. During GH replacement therapy in adults with GHD, IGF-I monitoring is widely used to aid dose titration, in order to minimize the risk of over-treatment. However, targeting IGF-I levels broadly to within the normal age-related reference range during treatment of GH disorders in adults does not preclude the presence of a functional GH-deficient state. To date, no data are available that quantify the risk of under-treatment of such patients. Thus, sub-optimal replacement therapy may be associated with unresolved morbidity and an increased risk of mortality from a continuing state of relative GHD. A recent study utilizing baseline IGF-I data from the KIMS database has identified a range of IGF-I values, which are higher than those found in untreated GHD, with high sensitivity [62]. These data may be of use during GH dose titration for GH-deficient patients

Table 2. IGF-I and IGF-I SD scores (SDS) in women with adult-onset GHD, demonstrating the percentage overlap of IGF-I values with the normal age-related range. Reproduced from [62] with permission. Copyright 2003, The Endocrine Society.

Age range (years)	Number per group	Median IGF-I (µg/L) n = 376	Median IGF-I SDS n = 376	Patients with IGF-I within the age-related normal range (%)
21–30	24	99.5 (37.5–124.0)	–2.91 (–6.16 to –2.59)	8.3
31–40	74	78.0 (53.0–122.0)	–2.76 (–3.50 to –1.76)	31.1
41–50	123	77.0 (52.5–105.5)	–2.22 (–3.10 to –1.39)	41.5
51–60	93	69.0 (34.8–96.3)	–1.97 (–3.25 to –1.10)	49.5
61–70	51	56.0 (38.0–87.0)	–1.92 (–3.14 to –1.03)	52.9
71–80	11	57.0 (39.3–77.8)	–1.78 (–2.42 to –1.17)	54.5

Table 3. IGF-I and IGF-I SD scores (SDS) in men with adult-onset GHD, demonstrating the percentage overlap of IGF-I values with the normal age-related range. Reproduced from [62] with permission. Copyright 2003, The Endocrine Society.

Age range (years)	Number per group	Median IGF-I (µg/L) n = 434	Median IGF-I SDS n = 434	Patients with IGF-I within the age-related normal range (%)
21–30	30	125.5 (94.0–178.0)	–2.56 (–3.49 to –1.912)	26.7
31–40	62	125.0 (79.0–173.0)	–1.63 (–2.55 to –0.597)	62.9
41–50	102	103.5 (61.0–158.0)	–1.37 (–2.72 to –0.319)	61.8
51–60	149	90.0 (65.0–130.5)	–1.36 (–2.13 to –0.436)	73.1
61–70	75	73.0 (46.0–106.8)	–1.51 (–2.50 to –0.187)	60.0
71–80	16	60.0 (44.0–64.5)	–1.65 (–2.11 to –1.247)	75.0

who do not respond clinically to a conventional therapeutic trial of GH replacement, especially if the IGF-I level has remained below the 95th percentile for functional GHD.

Long-term safety

Extensive long-term follow-up data, relating to GH replacement from single centres and large multinational databases, have found no increase in the overall occurrence of *de novo* neoplasia or the rate of re-growth of primary pituitary tumours [24, 27, 28]. An apparent increase in intracranial neoplasia detected from KIMS data may reflect an inherent bias in comparing a surveillance population with general population data [28].

Conclusions

Over the past 10 years a vast amount of information has been accrued relating to GH replacement therapy in hypopituitary adults. The need for careful patient selection and optimization of dosing regimens with dose titration against IGF-I levels, and the emergence of evidence for specific benefits in certain sub-groups of patients, are factors that have become evident with time. However, these factors were not taken into account in earlier studies. In particular, the benefits of using an individually titrated GH regimen in patients selected on the basis of significant morbidity at baseline, have not been studied in the setting of randomized, placebo-controlled studies. Although a strong basis for GH replacement in adulthood has been established, considerable further study will be required to determine the magnitude of the effect of physiological GH replacement on biological endpoints in hypopituitary adults and to aid understanding of the mechanisms by which these effects are achieved.

References

1. Raben MS. Clinical use of human growth hormone. N Engl J Med 1962;266:82–6
2. Olson KC, Fenno J, Lin N, Harkins RN, Snider C, Kohr WH, Ross MJ, Fodge D, Prender G, Stebbing N. Purified human growth hormone from E. coli is biologically active. Nature 1981;293:408–11
3. Carroll PV, Christ ER, Bengtsson B-Å, Carlsson L, Christiansen JS, Clemmons D, Hintz R, Ho K, Laron Z, Sizonenko P, Sönksen PH, Tanaka T, Thorne M. Growth hormone deficiency in adulthood and the effects of growth hormone replacement: a review. Growth Hormone Research Society Scientific Committee. J Clin Endocrinol Metab 1998;83:382–95
4. Li CH, Papkoff H. Preparation and properties of growth hormone from human and monkey pituitary glands. Science 1956;124:1293–4
5. Raben MS. Human growth hormone. Recent Prog Horm Res 1959;15:71–114
6. Glick SM, Roth J, Yallow RS, Berson SA. Immunoassay of human growth hormone in plasma. Nature 1963; 199:784–7
7. Press M. Growth hormone and metabolism. Diabetes Metab Rev 1988;4:391–414
8. Thorner MO, Vance ML. Growth hormone, 1988. J Clin Invest 1988;82:745–7
9. Salomon F, Cuneo RC, Hesp R, Sönksen PH. The effects of treatment with recombinant human growth hormone on body composition and metabolism in adults with growth hormone deficiency. N Engl J Med 1989; 321:1797–803
10. Jørgensen JO, Pedersen SA, Thuesen L, Jørgensen J, Ingemann-Hansen T, Skakkebæk NE, Christiansen JS. Beneficial effects of growth hormone treatment in GH-deficient adults. Lancet 1989;1:1221–5
11. Cuneo RC, Salomon F, McGauley GA, Sönksen PH. The growth hormone deficiency syndrome in adults. Clin Endocrinol (Oxf) 1992;37:387–97
12. Hartman ML. The Growth Hormone Research Society consensus guidelines for the diagnosis and treatment of adult GH deficiency. Growth Horm IGF Res 1998; 8 (Suppl A):25–9
13. Shalet SM, Toogood A, Rahim A, Brennan BM. The diagnosis of growth hormone deficiency in children and adults. Endocr Rev 1998;19:203–23
14. Bengtsson B-Å, Brummer RJ, Edén S, Bosæus I. Body composition in acromegaly. Clin Endocrinol (Oxf) 1989;30:121–30
15. Parra A, Argote RM, Garcia G, Cervantes C, Alatorre S, Perez-Pasten E. Body composition in hypopituitary dwarfs before and during human growth hormone therapy. Metabolism 1979;28:851–7
16. Murray RD, Skillicorn CJ, Howell SJ, Lissett CA, Rahim A, Shalet SM. Dose titration and patient selection increases the efficacy of GH replacement in severely GH deficient adults. Clin Endocrinol (Oxf) 1999; 50:749–57
17. Drake WM, Coyte D, Camacho-Hubner C, Jivanji NM, Kaltsas G, Wood DF, Trainer PJ, Grossman AB, Besser GM, Monson JP. Optimizing growth hormone replacement therapy by dose titration in hypopituitary adults. J Clin Endocrinol Metab 1998;83:3913–9
18. Abs R, Bengtsson B-Å, Hernberg-Ståhl E, Monson JP, Tauber JP, Wilton P, Wüster C. GH replacement in 1034 growth hormone deficient hypopituitary adults: demographic and clinical characteristics, dosing and safety. Clin Endocrinol (Oxf) 1999;50:703–13
19. Wallymahmed ME, Foy P, Shaw D, Hutcheon R, Edwards RH, MacFarlane IA. Quality of life, body composition and muscle strength in adult growth hormone deficiency: the influence of growth hormone replacement therapy for up to 3 years. Clin Endocrinol (Oxf) 1997;47:439–46
20. Chrisoulidou A, Beshyah SA, Rutherford O, Spinks TJ, Mayet J, Kyd P, Anyaoku V, Haida A, Ariff B, Murphy M, Thomas E, Robinson S, Foale R, Johnston DG. Effects of 7 years of growth hormone replacement therapy in hypopituitary adults. J Clin Endocrinol Metab 2000;85:3762–9
21. Rosenfalck AM, Maghsoudi S, Fisker S, Jørgensen JO, Christiansen JS, Hilsted J, Vølund AA, Madsbad S. The effect of 30 months of low-dose replacement therapy with recombinant human growth hormone (rhGH) on insulin and C-peptide kinetics, insulin secretion, insulin sensitivity, glucose effectiveness, and body composition

in GH-deficient adults. J Clin Endocrinol Metab 2000;85:4173–81

22. Clanget C, Seck T, Hinke V, Wüster C, Ziegler R, Pfeilschifter J. Effects of 6 years of growth hormone (GH) treatment on bone mineral density in GH-deficient adults. Clin Endocrinol (Oxf) 2001;55:93–9

23. Drake WM, Rodriguez-Arnao J, Weaver JU, James IT, Coyte D, Spector TD, Besser GM, Monson JP. The influence of gender on the short and long-term effects of growth hormone replacement on bone metabolism and bone mineral density in hypopituitary adults: a 5-year study. Clin Endocrinol (Oxf) 2001;54:525–32

24. Götherström G, Svensson J, Koranyi J, Alpsten M, Bosæus I, Bengtsson B, Johannsson G. A prospective study of 5 years of GH replacement therapy in GH-deficient adults: sustained effects on body composition, bone mass, and metabolic indices. J Clin Endocrinol Metab 2001;86:4657–65

25. van der Sluis IM, Boot AM, Hop WC, De Rijke YB, Krenning EP, de Muinck Keizer-Schrama SM. Long-term effects of growth hormone therapy on bone mineral density, body composition, and serum lipid levels in growth hormone deficient children: a 6-year follow-up study. Horm Res 2002;58:207–14

26. Gilchrist FJ, Murray RD, Shalet SM. The effect of long-term untreated growth hormone deficiency (GHD) and 9 years of GH replacement on the quality of life (QoL) of GH-deficient adults. Clin Endocrinol (Oxf) 2002;57:363–70

27. Attanasio AF, Bates PC, Ho KK, Webb SM, Ross RJ, Strasburger CJ, Bouillon R, Crowe B, Selander K, Valle D, Lamberts SW. Human growth hormone replacement in adult hypopituitary patients: long-term effects on body composition and lipid status – 3-year results from the HypoCCS Database. J Clin Endocrinol Metab 2002;87:1600–6

28. Monson JP. Long-term experience with GH replacement therapy: efficacy and safety. Eur J Endocrinol 2003;148 (Suppl 2):S9–14

29. Holmes SJ, Shalet SM. Factors influencing the desire for long-term growth hormone replacement in adults. Clin Endocrinol (Oxf) 1995;43:151–7

30. Holmes SJ, McKenna SP, Doward LC, Shalet SM. Development of a questionnaire to assess the quality of life of adults with growth hormone deficiency. Endocrinol Metab 1995;2:63–9

31. Baum HB, Katznelson L, Sherman JC, Biller BM, Hayden DL, Schoenfeld DA, Cannistraro KE, Klibanski A. Effects of physiological growth hormone (GH) therapy on cognition and quality of life in patients with adult-onset GH deficiency. J Clin Endocrinol Metab 1998;83:3184–9

32. Rosén T, Bengtsson B-Å. Premature mortality due to cardiovascular disease in hypopituitarism. Lancet 1990;336:285–8

33. Bates AS, Van't Hoff W, Jones PJ, Clayton RN. The effect of hypopituitarism on life expectancy. J Clin Endocrinol Metab 1996;81:1169–72

34. Tomlinson JW, Holden N, Hills RK, Wheatley K, Clayton RN, Bates AS, Sheppard MC, Stewart PM. Association between premature mortality and hypopituitarism. West Midlands Prospective Hypopituitary Study Group. Lancet 2001;357:425–31

35. Gasperi M, Cecconi E, Grasso L, Bartalena L, Centoni R, Aimaretti G, Broglio F, Miccoli P, Marcocci C, Ghigo E, Martino E. GH secretion is impaired in patients with primary hyperparathyroidism. J Clin Endocrinol Metab 2002;87:1961–4

36. Lieberman SA, Oberoi AL, Gilkison CR, Masel BE, Urban RJ. Prevalence of neuroendocrine dysfunction in patients recovering from traumatic brain injury. J Clin Endocrinol Metab 2001;86:2752–6

37. Shalet SM, Beardwell CG, Morris-Jones PH, Pearson D. Pituitary function after treatment of intracranial tumours in children. Lancet 1975;2:104–7

38. Shalet SM, Beardwell CG, Pearson D, Jones PH. The effect of varying doses of cerebral irradiation on growth hormone production in childhood. Clin Endocrinol (Oxf) 1976;5:287–90

39. Shalet SM, Beardwell CG, Jones PH, Pearson D. Growth hormone deficiency after treatment of acute leukaemia in children. Arch Dis Child 1976;51:489–93

40. Shalet SM, Clayton PE, Price DA. Growth and pituitary function in children treated for brain tumours or acute lymphoblastic leukaemia. Horm Res 1988;30:53–61

41. Brennan BM, Rahim A, Mackie EM, Eden OB, Shalet SM. Growth hormone status in adults treated for acute lymphoblastic leukaemia in childhood. Clin Endocrinol (Oxf) 1998;48:777–83

42. Murray RD, Darzy KH, Gleeson HK, Shalet SM. GH-deficient survivors of childhood cancer: GH replacement during adult life. J Clin Endocrinol Metab 2002;87:129–35

43. Saggese G, Baroncelli GI, Bertelloni S, Barsanti S. The effect of long-term growth hormone (GH) treatment on bone mineral density in children with GH deficiency. Role of GH in the attainment of peak bone mass. J Clin Endocrinol Metab 1996;81:3077–83

44. Attie KM. The importance of growth hormone replacement therapy for bone mass in young adults with growth hormone deficiency. J Pediatr Endocrinol Metab 2000;13 (Suppl 2):1011–21

45. Shore RM, Chesney RW, Mazess RB, Rose PG, Bargman GJ. Bone mineral status in growth hormone deficiency. J Pediatr 1980;96:393–6

46. Kaufman JM, Taelman P, Vermeulen A, Vandeweghe M. Bone mineral status in growth hormone-deficient males with isolated and multiple pituitary deficiencies of childhood onset. J Clin Endocrinol Metab 1992; 74:118–23

47. O'Halloran DJ, Tsatsoulis A, Whitehouse RW, Holmes SJ, Adams JE, Shalet SM. Increased bone density after recombinant human growth hormone (GH) therapy in adults with isolated GH deficiency. J Clin Endocrinol Metab 1993;76:1344–8

48. de Boer H, Blok GJ, van Lingen A, Teule GJ, Lips P, van der Veen EA. Consequences of childhood-onset growth hormone deficiency for adult bone mass. J Bone Miner Res 1994;9:1319–26

49. Sartorio A, Ortolani S, Conti A, Cherubini R, Galbiati E, Faglia G. Effects of recombinant growth hormone (GH) treatment on bone mineral density and body composition in adults with childhood onset growth hormone deficiency. J Endocrinol Invest 1996;19:524–9

50. Holmes SJ, Economou G, Whitehouse RW, Adams JE, Shalet SM. Reduced bone mineral density in patients with adult onset growth hormone deficiency. J Clin Endocrinol Metab 1994;78:669–74

51. Rosén T, Hansson T, Granhed H, Szucs J, Bengtsson B-Å. Reduced bone mineral content in adult patients with growth hormone deficiency. Acta Endocrinol (Copenh) 1993;129:201–6

52. Johansson AG, Burman P, Westermark K, Ljunghall S. The bone mineral density in acquired growth hormone deficiency correlates with circulating levels of insulin-like growth factor I. J Intern Med 1992;232:447–52

53. Toogood AA, Adams JE, O'Neill PA, Shalet SM. Elderly patients with adult-onset growth hormone deficiency are not osteopenic. J Clin Endocrinol Metab 1997; 82:1462–6

54. Janssen YJ, Hamdy NA, Frolich M, Roelfsema F. Skeletal effects of two years of treatment with low physiological doses of recombinant human growth hormone (GH) in patients with adult-onset GH deficiency. J Clin Endocrinol Metab 1998;83:2143–8

55. Fernholm R, Bramnert M, Hagg E, Hilding A, Baylink DJ, Mohan S, Thorén M. Growth hormone replacement therapy improves body composition and increases bone metabolism in elderly patients with pituitary disease. J Clin Endocrinol Metab 2000;85:4104–12

56. Murray R, Columb B, Adams J, Shalet S. The osteopenia of adult GH deficiency is age-dependent. 20th Joint Meeting of the British Endocrine Societies, 2001:107

57. Attanasio AF, Howell S, Bates PC, Frewer P, Chipman J, Blum WF, Shalet SM. Body composition, IGF-I and IGFBP-3 concentrations as outcome measures in severely GH-deficient (GHD) patients after childhood GH treatment: a comparison with adult onset GHD patients. J Clin Endocrinol Metab 2002;87: 3368–72

58. Attanasio AF, Lamberts SW, Matranga AM, Birkett MA, Bates PC, Valk NK, Hilsted J, Bengtsson B-Å, Strasburger CJ. Adult growth hormone (GH)-deficient patients demonstrate heterogeneity between childhood onset and adult onset before and during human GH treatment. Adult Growth Hormone Deficiency Study Group. J Clin Endocrinol Metab 1997;82:82–8

59. Drake WM, Carroll PV, Maher KT, Metcalfe KA, Camacho-Hubner C, Shaw NJ, Dunger DB, Cheetham TD, Savage MO, Monson JP. The effect of cessation of growth hormone (GH) therapy on bone mineral accretion in GH-deficient adolescents at the completion of linear growth. J Clin Endocrinol Metab 2003; 88:1658–63

60. Shalet SM, Shavrikowa E, Cromer M, Child CJ, Keller E, Zapletalova J, Moshang T, Blum WF, Chipman JJ, Quigley CA, Attanasio AF. Effect of growth hormone (GH) treatment on bone in post-pubertal GH deficient (GHD) patients: a 2-year randomized, controlled, dose-ranging study. J Clin Endocrinol Metab 2003;88:4124–9

61. Lissett CA, Murray RD, Shalet SM. Timing of onset of growth hormone deficiency is a major influence on insulin-like growth factor I status in adult life. Clin Endocrinol (Oxf) 2002;57:35–40

62. Mukherjee A, Monson JP, Jonsson PJ, Trainer PJ, Shalet SM. Seeking the optimal target range for insulin-like growth factor 1 during the treatment of adult growth hormone disorders. J Clin Endocrinol Metab 2003;88: 5865–70.

63. Juul A, Holm K, Kastrup KW, Pedersen SA, Michaelsen KF, Scheike T, Rasmussen S, Müller J, Skakkebæk NE. Free insulin-like growth factor I serum levels in 1430 healthy children and adults, and its diagnostic value in patients suspected of growth hormone deficiency. J Clin Endocrinol Metab 1997;82:2497–502

64. Weinzimer SA, Homan SA, Ferry RJ, Moshang T. Serum IGF-I and IGFBP-3 concentrations do not accurately predict growth hormone deficiency in children with brain tumours. Clin Endocrinol (Oxf) 1999;51:339–45

65. Bussieres L, Souberbielle JC, Pinto G, Adan L, Noel M, Brauner R. The use of insulin-like growth factor 1 reference values for the diagnosis of growth hormone deficiency in prepubertal children. Clin Endocrinol (Oxf) 2000;52:735–9

66. Marzullo P, Di Somma C, Pratt KL, Khosravi J, Diamandis A, Lombardi G, Colao A, Rosenfeld RG. Usefulness of different biochemical markers of the insulin-like growth factor (IGF) family in diagnosing growth hormone excess and deficiency in adults. J Clin Endocrinol Metab 2001;86:3001–8

67. Clemmons DR. Commercial assays available for insulin-like growth factor I and their use in diagnosing growth hormone deficiency. Horm Res 2001;55 (Suppl 2):73–9

68. Lange M, Svendsen OL, Skakkebæk NE, Müller J, Juul A, Schmiegelow M, Feldt-Rasmussen U. An audit of the insulin-tolerance test in 255 patients with pituitary disease. Eur J Endocrinol 2002;147:41–7

69. Monson JP. Biochemical markers of individual response to growth hormone replacement in adults. Horm Res 2001;55 (Suppl 2):49–54

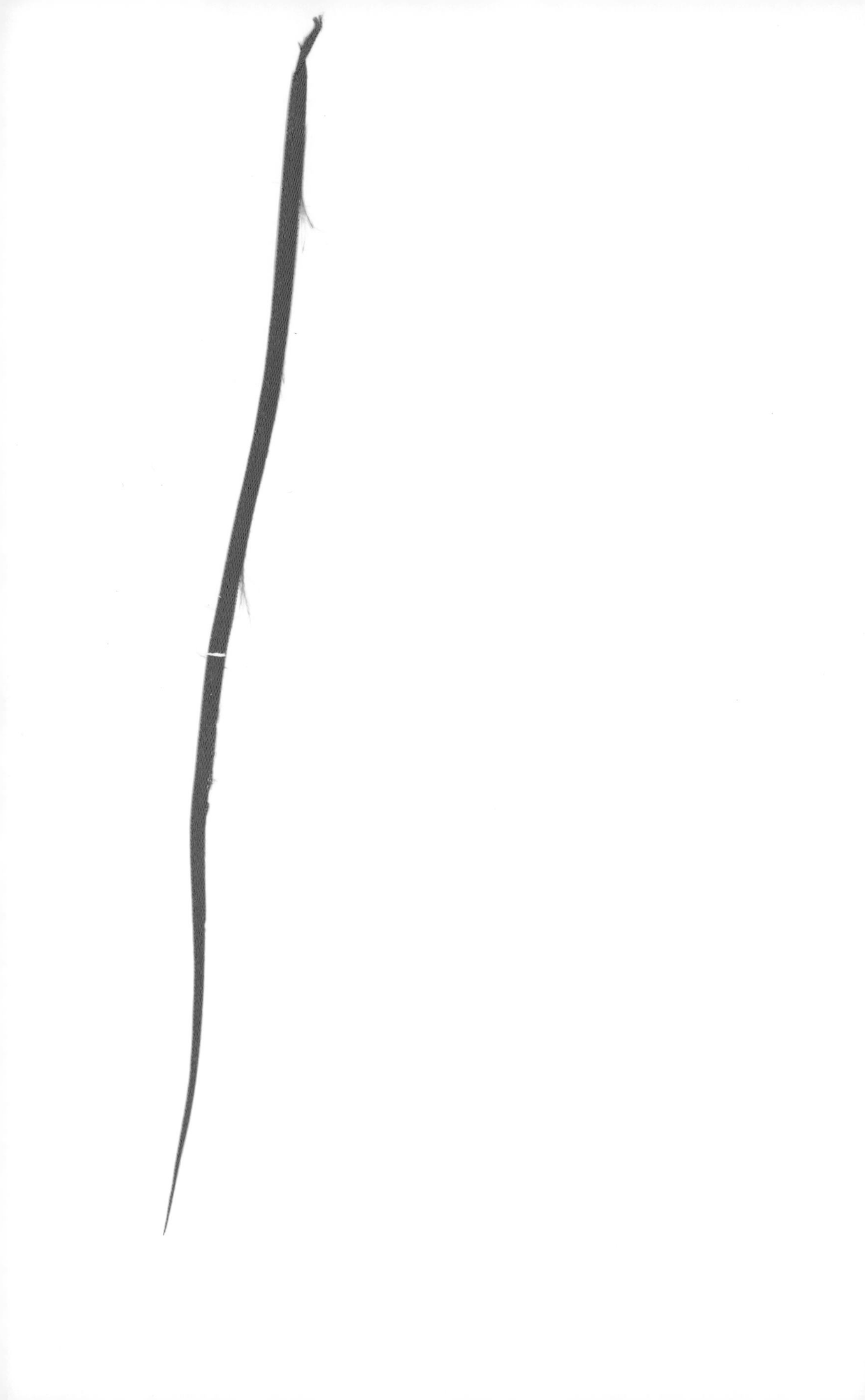

Cardiovascular risk and mortality in patients with growth hormone deficiency

Andrew A Toogood

Division of Medical Sciences, Department of Medicine, Queen Elizabeth Hospital, University of Birmingham, Edgbaston, Birmingham, UK

Summary

Hypopituitarism is a heterogeneous condition that represents a broad range of endocrine disorders caused by a variety of different insults to the hypothalamic–pituitary axis. Patients with hypopituitarism suffer an almost twofold increase in mortality compared with the normal population. In particular, mortality from cardiovascular and cerebrovascular causes, and respiratory disease, is increased; however, the factors that impact on mortality in these patients often remain obscure. Age at diagnosis, gender, treatment with radiotherapy, an underlying diagnosis of craniopharyngioma, and changes in body composition associated with growth hormone (GH) deficiency have all been linked to an increase in mortality in adults with hypopituitarism. In addition, it is possible that treatment for hypopituitarism may itself contribute to this increased risk. Studies of GH replacement therapy in hypopituitary patients have shown that GH has a positive impact on cardiovascular risk factors. Changes in body composition, serum lipid profile, inflammatory markers and structural markers of cardiovascular risk have all been shown to improve during a relatively short period of treatment with GH. However, it will take many years of follow-up to determine whether GH treatment prolongs life in hypopitutary patients.

Introduction

Since the first reports of growth hormone (GH) replacement therapy in adults with hypopituitarism were published in 1989 [1, 2] its use for this indication has been increasingly accepted by endocrinologists around the world. Over the past 15 years, clinical practice has evolved and differences now exist between countries, particularly with regard to the policies adopted for initiating GH replacement therapy in GH-deficient patients. In the UK, for example, the decision to treat is based primarily upon assessment of quality of life, with only those who have the most severe impairment being offered a trial of GH replacement therapy. This practice was recently formalized in the guidelines published in the UK by the National Institute for Clinical Excellence. In other countries, such as Sweden, it is normal practice to offer GH replacement therapy to all GH-deficient patients on the grounds that it has other benefits, particularly on the cardiovascular risk profile. This chapter reviews the evidence that mortality is increased in patients with GH deficiency (GHD), and discusses the potential contribution of GHD to this increase in mortality and the benefits that GH replacement therapy may offer.

Mortality in patients with hypopituitarism

There are now five studies in the literature regarding mortality in hypopituitary patients [3–7], four of which demonstrate a significant increase in all-cause mortality in patients with hypothalamic–pituitary disease. In their seminal study, Rosén and Bengtsson [3] reviewed the notes of 333 patients treated for pituitary disease in their institution between 1956 and 1987. During this period there were 104 deaths in the patient population, almost twice as many as expected in the normal population (standardized mortality ratio [SMR], 1.81). Cardiovascular disease accounted for 60 of the observed deaths, significantly more than the 30.4 that would have been predicted (SMR, 1.98) (Fig. 1). These observations were independent of gender and underlying pituitary pathology.

Bülow *et al.* [4] reported mortality rates amongst 344 patients receiving conventional hormone replacement for hypopituitarism following neurosurgery for pituitary tumours, presenting between 1946 and 1988 to their department in Lund, Sweden. The SMR from all causes was 2.17 in this cohort. There was an increase in cardiovascular deaths (SMR, 1.75) but the greatest increase was in deaths from cerebrovascular disease (SMR, 3.39).

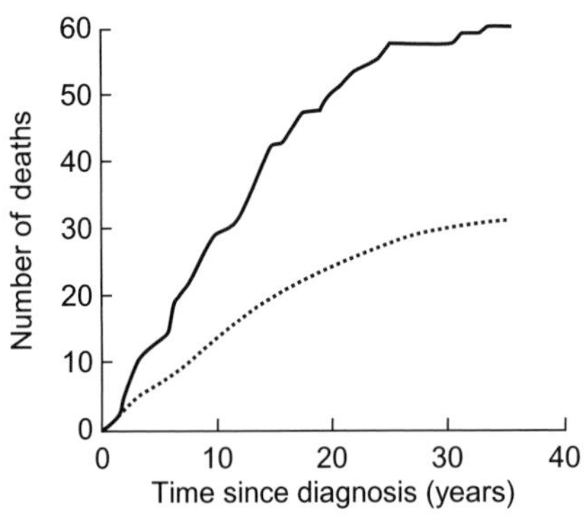

Figure 1. *Death rates from cardiovascular disease in patients with hypopituitarism (solid line) and in the normal population matched for age and sex distribution (dotted line). Adapted from [3] with permission from Elsevier.*

In the first of three studies from the West Midlands in the UK, Bates *et al.* [5] reviewed the case notes of 172 patients treated for pituitary disease between 1967 and 1993. In this study, all-cause mortality was significantly increased (SMR, 1.73), but the number of deaths from cardiovascular disease was similar to that in the normal population. The authors found that age and gonadal hormone status were important factors in determining the outcome of their patients. Survival was improved in those patients who had gonadotrophin deficiency, an observation that was confirmed in the second study from the West Midlands [6]. On this occasion, Bates *et al.* [6] reviewed the notes of 335 patients undergoing pituitary surgery between 1970 and 1992. In this cohort there was a small increase in mortality that did not reach statistical significance.

In the third study from the West Midlands, which is the largest study of mortality in hypopituitary patients to date, Tomlinson *et al.* [7] studied 1014 patients prospectively between 1992 and 2000. During this 8-year period there were 181 deaths, compared with the expected 96.7 (SMR, 1.87). Patients in this cohort were at an increased risk of death from cardiovascular disease (SMR, 1.82), cerebrovascular disease (SMR, 2.44) and respiratory disease (SMR, 2.66).

Overall the data from these studies demonstrate that patients with hypopituitarism suffer an almost twofold increase in mortality compared with the normal population.

Factors that contribute to mortality in patients with hypopituitarism

Hypopituitarism is a heterogeneous condition that represents a broad spectrum of endocrine disorders caused by a variety of different insults to the hypothalamic–pituitary axis, and can occur in people of all ages. The therapeutic interventions used to treat the underlying disorder vary from patient to patient and there can be considerable differences in hormone replacement strategies. Many of these factors can impact upon the cardiovascular risk profile.

Diagnosis and treatment of the disorder underlying hypopituitarism

The commonest cause of hypopituitarism occurring in adult life is a non-functioning pituitary adenoma and its treatment. Other causes include craniopharyngioma, functioning pituitary adenomas, parasellar lesions, hypophysitis, pituitary infarction or haemorrhage and radiotherapy [7, 8]. Perhaps the most notable diagnosis in terms of its impact on mortality is craniopharyngioma. The SMR amongst patients treated for craniopharyngioma is markedly increased. In two cohorts from Sweden and the UK, the SMR was 5.5 (confidence interval [CI], 3.68–8.22) [9] and 8.68 (CI, 5.46–13.8) [7], respectively. There was a marked increase in mortality caused by cerebrovascular disease (SMR, 19.4) and respiratory disease (SMR, 22.1). Craniopharyngioma can be difficult to manage and often occurs in young patients. The latter may explain why the SMR is significantly higher in this patient group than in patients with pituitary adenomas; either because only a small number of deaths are required to cause a high SMR in a young cohort, or because the duration of panhypopituitarism is greater. Patients with craniopharyngioma are more likely to undergo surgery via the transcranial route than other patients with pituitary tumours, but it is not known whether this directly impacts upon cerebrovascular mortality.

Cerebrovascular disease

The impact of radiotherapy on mortality from cerebrovascular disease in patients treated for a pituitary adenoma is unclear at the present time. Tomlinson *et al.* [7] reported that the SMR was significantly greater in patients who had received pituitary irradiation and that the risk of death from cerebrovascular disease was increased in this cohort (SMR for cerebrovascular disease, 4.36 [CI, 2.48–7.68] versus 1.64 [CI, 0.91–2.96]). However, multivariate analysis did not demonstrate a relationship between radiotherapy and increased mortality, indicating that the contribution of other factors was greater in determining outcome in this cohort. Brada *et al.* [10] reported a similar increase in risk of cerebrovascular death in patients with pituitary adenomas (relative risk [RR], 4.11 [CI, 2.84–5.75]). This increased risk was primarily attributable to patients who had undergone debulking surgery (RR, 5.19 [CI, 3.5–7.42]) and was not present in those who had undergone pituitary biopsy or who had not had surgery (RR, 1.33 [CI, 0.27–3.88]). However, the risk of cerebrovascular death did not increase with time from irradiation, suggesting that the size of the lesion, which may relate to the duration of undiagnosed hypopituitarism, may have been important. Erfurth *et al.* [11] compared a cohort of 31 patients operated and irradiated for pituitary tumours who had died of cerebrovascular disease, with 62 controls who had been managed in a similar way for their pituitary disease but had no history of cerebrovascular events. The two groups were similar in terms of radiation dose and distribution, but the patients who died had reported a longer duration of symptoms of hypopituitarism than the controls. It appears that radiotherapy is a surrogate for more severe pituitary disease, larger tumours, possibly more aggressive tumours and a longer duration of untreated hypopituitarism. More work is required, including long-term prospective studies, to define the relative contribution of radiotherapy and hypopituitarism to the increase in cerebrovascular disease in patients with hypopituitarism.

Gender

Two of the four studies that demonstrated increased mortality reported that women were at a significantly greater risk than men; the SMRs in men compared with women were reported as 1.91 versus 2.93 [4] and 1.57 versus 2.29 [7]. This trend was also present in a third study, but did not reach statistical significance [5]. Bülow *et al.* [12] studied the detailed cardiovascular risk profile of a small group of women with hypopituitarism and found an increased incidence of cardiovascular disease, an adverse lipid profile and abnormal indices of cardiac function, compared with normal controls. The Framingham Heart Study equation [13] was used by others to calculate the cardiovascular risk of patients with pituitary disease; the serum lipid profiles were found to be the primary factor contributing to risk. Relative risk was increased in women, but not in men [14], which suggests that the lipid abnormalities may have a greater clinical impact in women than men.

Age at diagnosis

The age at which the diagnosis of hypopituitarism is made has a major impact on mortality rate. Tomlinson *et al.* [7] demonstrated that patients diagnosed before the age of 20 had an SMR of 12.36 (CI, 5.47–27.95), whereas those diagnosed between the ages of 20 and 40, and 40 and 60 years had SMRs of 3.17 (CI, 1.73–5.82) and 2.40 (CI, 1.77–3.26), respectively. The marked increase in SMR in patients diagnosed before 20 years of age may reflect the higher incidence of craniopharyngioma in this age group. The SMR of patients aged over 60 when hypopituitarism was diagnosed was not increased significantly.

Cardiovascular risk factors

GHD consists of a cluster of symptoms and clinical abnormalities that are not specific for the condition, many of which impact upon cardiovascular risk. Patients with untreated GHD have an abnormal body composition [15]. Studies utilizing a range of methods to determine body composition consistently demonstrate an increased fat mass compared with controls of similar age, sex and body mass index. Abdominal computed tomography (CT) has demonstrated that intra-abdominal or visceral fat mass is increased [16]. The importance of this is clear when it is considered that central obesity in the normal population is associated with hyperlipidaemia, increased insulin resistance [17, 18] and increased cardiovascular morbidity and mortality [19].

Serum lipid profiles are abnormal in GH-deficient adults; total cholesterol, low-density lipoprotein (LDL)-cholesterol and triglyceride levels are increased [8, 14, 20]. The situation regarding high-density lipoprotein (HDL)-cholesterol is less clear. In some studies, serum HDL-cholesterol has been reported to be unchanged [21] while others have shown that HDL-cholesterol levels are lower in patients with untreated GHD [22]. More recently, Abdu *et al.* [14] studied detailed lipid profiles in men and women with hypopituitarism and found that HDL-cholesterol levels were similar to those in control subjects in men, but were significantly reduced in women. Similar findings have been reported from patients in KIMS – Pfizer International Metabolic Database. Patients with untreated GHD also have impaired insulin sensitivity, which has been attributed to the presence of central adiposity [23].

The development of thrombus plays an important role in the evolution of cardiovascular events and diseases associated with increased cardiovascular risk, such as diabetes mellitus and obesity. A similar prothrombotic state has been described in patients with hypopituitarism in whom plasma fibrinogen and plasminogen activator inhibitor-1 activity were increased [24]. This finding is not consistent with other studies, however, which have reported levels of fibrinogen, tissue plasminogen activator, and other factors involved in thrombogenesis or thrombolysis that were not significantly different between patients and controls [25, 26].

Inflammation is now understood to play a critical role in the development of atheroma [27]. Serum markers of inflammation such as interleukin-6 (IL-6) and C-reactive protein (CRP) are elevated in patients with atherosclerotic disease, and have been shown to be predictive of cardiovascular events. In patients with hypopituitarism receiving conventional replacement therapy, but not GH, both IL-6 and CRP levels in the serum are significantly elevated compared with controls [28, 29].

Patients with untreated GHD have multiple abnormalities that promote the development of atherosclerotic disease. Ultrasound-Doppler techniques can be used to determine the severity of atherosclerotic change present in a vessel. Aortic compliance provides a measure of the stiffness of the aorta, which is decreased in the presence of atherosclerotic disease, and carotid intima–media thickness (IMT) provides a direct measure of risk of myocardial infarction and stroke [30]. In adults with hypopituitarism and GHD, aortic compliance was decreased [31] and carotid IMT was increased [32–34] compared with matched controls. Carotid IMT correlated with circulating risk factors, such as IL-6, confirming that the adverse cardiovascular risk profile observed in these patients impacts upon the development of atherosclerosis and the subsequent risk of events such as myocardial infarction or stroke [29].

GHD versus hypopituitarism?

In their seminal paper, Rosén and Bengtsson [3] suggested that the lack of GH replacement in their cohort might have contributed to the increased cardiovascular mortality in patients with hypopituitarism. They also recognized that pituitary hormone replacement therapy was far from perfect, and that such therapy could also impact upon cardiovascular risk factors. Similar observations were made in other studies, while some studies argue strongly in favour of hypopituitarism as the primary cause of increased mortality in these patients.

Glucocorticoid replacement therapy may contribute to the increased cardiovascular morbidity and mortality observed in hypopituitarism. Untreated Cushing's syndrome has a poor outcome, leading to central obesity, insulin resistance, hypertension, hyperlipidaemia and a marked increase in cardiovascular morbidity. Some have suggested that GHD has a similar phenotype to that of Cushing's disease [35]. A large proportion of patients with hypopituitarism receives glucocorticoid replacement therapy that, until recently, was probably excessive; typically patients would receive 30 mg of hydrocortisone per day, administered in divided doses. It is now recognized that the initial cortisol generation studies overestimated daily cortisol production by almost twofold, and the majority of patients now receive 15–20 mg/day. The state of relative hypercortisolaemia is further aggravated by the metabolism of cortisol, under the control of two isoforms of the enzyme 11β-hydroxysteroid dehydrogenase (11β-HSD), which is affected by the patient's GH status. Bioactive cortisol is inactivated by type 2 11β-HSD, which is found in the kidney, colon, salivary glands and skin, where it protects the mineralocorticoid receptor from exposure to cortisol. In contrast, type 1 11β-HSD, present in liver and adipose tissue, amongst others, has the net effect of converting cortisone to cortisol, and can therefore influence tissue exposure to cortisol. GH modulates the activity of type 1 11β-HSD, thus reducing the generation of cortisol within tissues expressing the enzyme [36, 37]. In patients with GHD who may already be exposed to excessive levels of cortisol through inappropriate steroid replacement regimens, the exposure of some tissues is further increased by the conversion of the inactive cortisone to cortisol. In adipose tissue this increases the differentiation of pre-adipocytes to adipocytes and promotes fat accumulation, and in the liver can impact upon insulin sensitivity [38].

The adequacy of thyroid hormone replacement in patients with hypopituitarism is difficult to judge, because the normal negative feedback mechanisms are disrupted and serum thyrotrophin (TSH) levels cannot be used as a marker to determine the correct dose of thyroxine (T_4). Instead, one has to rely upon estimates of the serum T_4 level. In the normal population, a suppressed TSH level is associated with an increased risk of atrial fibrillation [39], placing the individual at increased risk of embolic events, such as stroke. Furthermore, in a population study based in Birmingham (UK), deaths from cardiovascular disease were significantly increased in subjects who had a suppressed TSH level but a normal free T_4 concentration [40]. Thus, mild over-treatment with T_4 in patients with hypopituitarism may contribute to the increased cardiovascular mortality observed.

To date, gonadotrophin deficiency is the only anterior pituitary hormone deficit that has been shown to impact significantly on mortality in hypopituitarism. In two of three studies from the UK, hypopituitary patients with a diagnosis of gonadotrophin deficiency seemed to have an advantage in terms of survival [5, 6]. The third, more recent report [7], was large enough to be able to study this in more detail and found that the mortality rate was improved in patients receiving sex-steroid replacement (Fig. 2). Mortality was significantly higher in patients with untreated gonadotrophin deficiency compared with patients who were receiving sex-steroid replacement and those with an intact pituitary–gonadal axis; mortality in the latter two groups was similar. Further analysis of the data has shown that the reduced risk of mortality was largely seen in men treated with testosterone (SMR, 1.22 versus 3.03 in untreated patients) rather than women receiving hormone replacement therapy (HRT) (SMR, 2.61 versus 2.93 in untreated patients) (J Tomlinson, personal communication). The previous observation that gonadotrophin deficiency was associated with a better outcome can now be clarified: treated gonadotrophin deficiency improves outcome, particularly in men.

For many years the use of sex-steroid replacement in normal, post-menopausal women was advocated for the amelioration of menopausal symptoms and the prevention of cardiovascular disease. This practice has been thrown into doubt

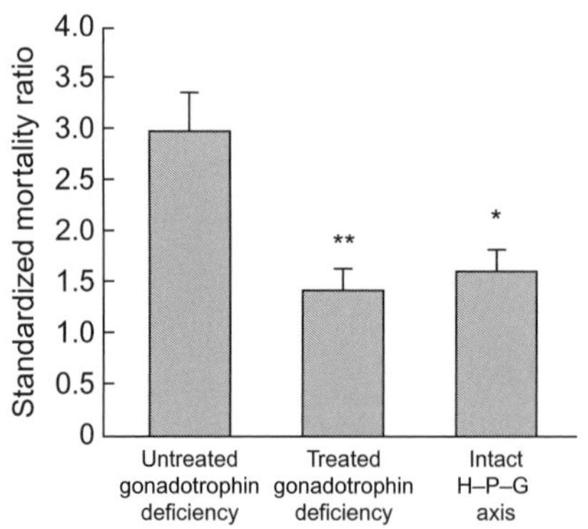

Figure 2. *Mortality in patients with untreated gonadotrophin deficiency (n = 218) compared with that in patients with treated gonadotrophin deficiency receiving sex-steroid replacement therapy (n = 449) or with an intact hypothalamic–pituitary–gonadal (H–P–G) axis (n = 253). *p < 0.0005; **p = 0.0001 compared with patients with untreated gonadotrophin deficiency. Adapted from [7] with permission from Elsevier.*

by two recent, large, randomized, placebo-controlled studies that have reported increased cerebrovascular and cardiovascular events and an increased risk of developing breast cancer after prolonged HRT [41, 42]. These findings raise particular concern in the hypopituitary population, some of whom take HRT for several decades. The data available in hypopituitary women, however, suggest that sex-steroid replacement therapy does not increase mortality. Furthermore, studies of mortality in hypopituitarism do not demonstrate an increased risk of death from malignancy compared with the normal population; in fact, one study reported a 50% reduction in deaths from this cause [3]. More detailed studies of sex-steroid replacement strategies and their long-term effect on cardiovascular risk factors and outcome in women with hypopituitarism are required to ensure that current practice is not placing patients at risk.

It is clear that deficits of anterior pituitary hormones other than GH can impact upon cardiovascular risk factors. One might expect, therefore, that mortality would increase as the severity of hypopituitarism increases; however, this is not the case. Tomlinson *et al.* [7] demonstrated that mortality remained similar when their cohort was divided into groups defined by the number of hormone deficiencies present. The authors suggested that this observation weakened the case for the contribution of GHD to mortality in hypopituitary patients. Using the observation that the severity of GHD increases as the number of anterior pituitary hormone deficiencies increases [43], they argued that as the mortality rate was not affected by the severity of hypopituitarism, GHD could not be a contributing factor; however, the patients in this study all had at least one anterior pituitary hormone deficiency. The implication of this is that approximately 93% had severe GHD (calculated from the observations of Toogood *et al.* [43]). The remaining patients almost certainly did not have normal GH secretory dynamics. Thus, severe GHD is the one consistent feature across this heterogeneous group, suggesting that GHD makes an important contribution to the increased mortality observed in these patients. Further studies are required to determine at what level of GH impairment or hypopituitarism the cardiovascular risk profile starts to deteriorate.

Impact of GH replacement therapy on cardiovascular risk

There is an increasing body of evidence that suggests that GH replacement therapy could impact upon the increased mortality observed in patients with hypopituitarism. Changes in body composition, serum lipid profile, inflammatory markers and structural markers of cardiovascular risk have all been shown to improve during a relatively short period of treatment with GH.

The effects of GH on body composition are well known; lean body mass is increased and there is a reduction in fat mass (see Chapter 11). Although obesity *per se* is associated with increased morbidity and mortality, fat distribution is also an important determinant of cardiovascular risk. Central adiposity has a more detrimental effect upon metabolic parameters than peripheral fat deposition. Central adiposity is reduced in GH-deficient patients receiving GH replacement therapy. This has been demonstrated using simple measurements of waist/hip ratio [44], but some studies have shown a reduction in intra-abdominal adipose mass using CT [16]. The waist/hip ratio provides a simple marker of cardiovascular risk; the higher the ratio, the greater the risk of developing cardiovascular disease [19]. A reduction in the waist/hip ratio caused by GH-mediated changes in body composition would have a beneficial impact upon cardiovascular risk in patients with hypopituitarism and should contribute to an improvement in outcome.

GH also impacts upon the abnormal serum lipid profile seen in patients with GHD (Fig. 3) (see Chapter 12). Studies have consistently shown that total serum cholesterol, LDL-cholesterol and triglyceride levels fall significantly after 6 months of GH replacement [20, 21, 45, 46]. The effects of GH on HDL-cholesterol levels are less clear; some studies have reported no effect [20, 46] while others have shown a small but significant increase in HDL-cholesterol concentration [45, 47]; however, the ratio of LDL- to HDL-cholesterol improves significantly in the majority of studies reported. Data from KIMS suggested that GH improves HDL-cholesterol levels in women, but not in men [44]. The magnitude of change in serum cholesterol concentration observed in patients receiving GH replacement is comparable with that achieved in the West of Scotland Coronary Prevention Study [48]. This was a primary prevention study in men aged 45–64 years treated with pravastatin or placebo for 5 years, which demonstrated a 31% reduction in myocardial infarction and a 32% relative reduction in risk of death as a result of myocardial infarction.

Other markers of cardiovascular risk implicated in atherogenesis are also affected by GH (see Chapter 15). Serum concentrations of IL-6 and CRP, markers of inflammation implicated in the evolution of atherosclerotic disease, fall during GH replacement therapy in hypopituitary adults [49]. In addition, fibrinogen levels are decreased, reducing the propensity for thrombus formation [21, 50].

These beneficial effects of GH replacement suggest that GH replacement therapy may have a significant impact on the increased cardiovascular mortality observed in adults with hypopituitarism; however, other determinants of cardiovascular risk are either unaffected or deteriorate during GH treatment. Insulin sensitivity is reduced in patients with GHD and has been shown to either deteriorate further [51] or remain unchanged [52, 53] during GH treatment. The doses of GH used in early studies were higher than those recommended now, which may have impacted upon insulin sensitivity; however, when the GH dose was titrated against serum insulin-like growth factor I levels, insulin sensitivity did not improve after 6 months of treatment [54]. Serum lipoprotein (a) is an independent risk factor for cardiovascular disease that has been reported to remain unchanged [55, 56], to rise [57] or to fall during GH replacement therapy, although this may represent problems with methodology [58].

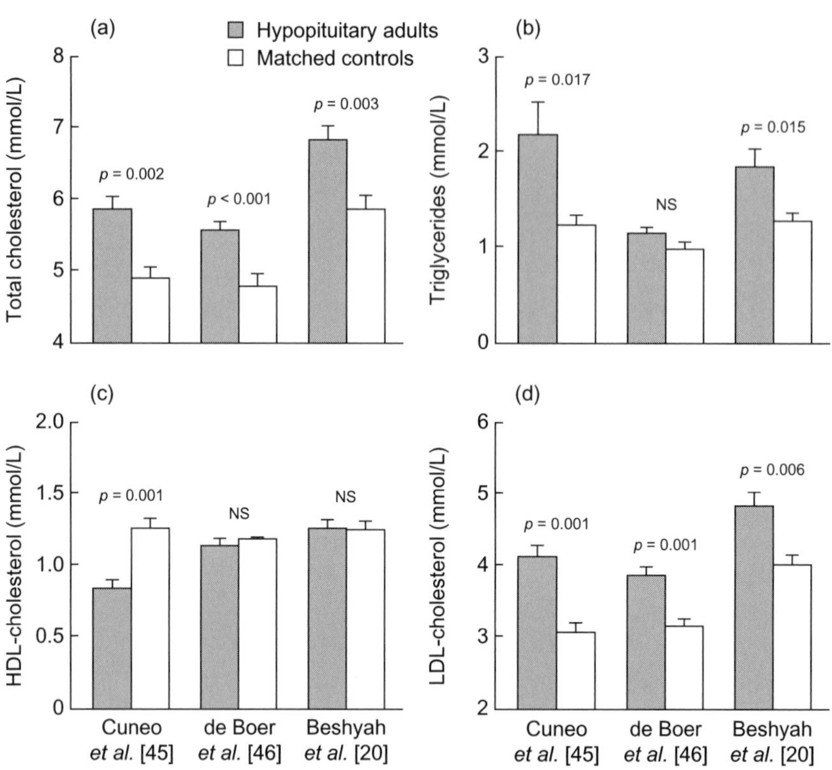

Figure 3. *Serum lipid levels in hypopituitary adults and matched controls. Data are derived from three studies [20, 45, 46]. HDL, high-density lipoprotein; LDL, low-density lipoprotein. Adapted from [60] with permission from Blackwell Publishing.*

GH replacement therapy has a beneficial effect upon many serological markers of cardiovascular risk. In order to advocate a possible improvement in cardiovascular outcome it is important to demonstrate a functional benefit of GH on the cardiovascular system. Measurement of carotid IMT provides a measure of risk for both myocardial infarction and cerebrovascular accident [30]. After only 6 months of GH replacement therapy the carotid IMT in hypopituitary patients was reduced to a level similar to that observed in controls, a change that was sustained after 18 months of therapy (Fig. 4) [32]. In addition, measures of vascular function improved. After 6 months of GH replacement therapy, flow-mediated dilatation, a marker of endothelial function, and aortic compliance, had improved significantly [59]. Echocardiographic studies have found that GH improves left ventricular mass and cardiac function. The improvement in cardiac function is particularly apparent during exercise [21]. The effects of GHD and GH replacement therapy on cardiovascular function are reviewed in Chapter 14.

The improvement in functional parameters suggests that GH has a beneficial effect upon cardiovascular risk. It is not yet known, however, whether this benefit will translate into a better prognosis for patients with hypothalamic–pituitary disease. Long-term studies are required to answer this question. Based on the SMR from the most recent study from Birmingham, power calculations suggest that a controlled study to determine whether GH replacement therapy improves the SMR of patients with hypopituitarism would require 2000 patients, randomized to receive either treatment or no treatment, observed for a period

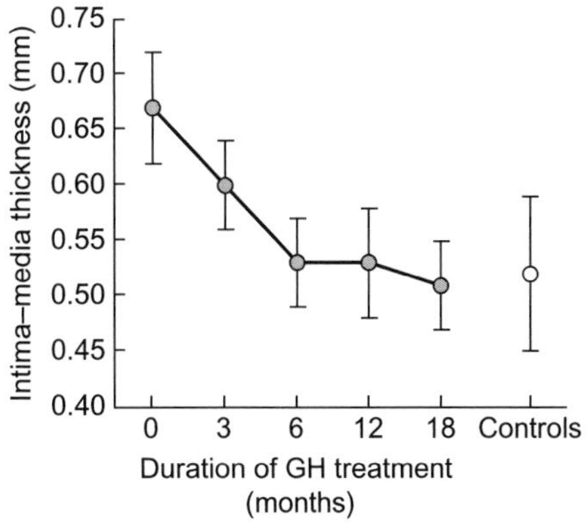

Figure 4. *Change in carotid intima–media thickness (mean ± SD) in 11 patients receiving GH replacement therapy over 18 months and in 12 controls. Adapted from [32] with permission. Copyright 1999, The Endocrine Society.*

of 5 years. Such a study is prohibitively expensive (drug costs alone would approach $20 million) and is unlikely to be embarked upon. Instead, we must rely upon long-term surveillance databases, such as KIMS, that follow a large number of patients over many years, to provide the answer.

Conclusions

Patients with hypothalamic–pituitary disease who have received conventional treatment, and appropriate endocrine replacement therapy, have a twofold increase in mortality compared with the general population. The risk is increased significantly in patients with an underlying diagnosis of craniopharyngioma and in those diagnosed before the age of 60. It is important that patients receive optimal endocrine replacement, with particular attention given to sex-steroid substitution. There are now considerable data demonstrating that factors that impact on cardiovascular function and cardiovascular risk are adversely affected in patients with treated hypopituitarism not receiving GH replacement therapy, implying a role for GH. There are, however, many unanswered questions. We do not know whether all patients with hypopituitarism suffer adverse cardiovascular effects. How do other endocrine abnormalities impact upon risk, and would manipulation of 'conventional' endocrine agents improve outcome?

Finally, what is the role of GH? Will GH replacement therapy reduce mortality in patients with hypopituitarism? GH replacement therapy improves many of the adverse effects of GHD and the cardiovascular risk profile in these patients. These improvements should support the use of GH in all patients who have GHD; however, it is not yet known whether GH replacement therapy reduces mortality. It will take many years of individual patient follow-up to determine whether GH prolongs life in hypopituitary patients. Whatever the outcome, it will have important implications for the future management of patients with hypopituitarism.

References

1. Jørgensen JO, Pedersen SA, Thuesen L, Jorgensen J, Ingemann-Hansen T, Skakkebæk NE, Christiansen JS. Beneficial effects of growth hormone treatment in GH-deficient adults. Lancet 1989;1:1221–5

2. Salomon F, Cuneo RC, Hesp R, Sönksen PH. The effects of treatment with recombinant human growth hormone on body composition and metabolism in adults with growth hormone deficiency. N Engl J Med 1989; 321:1797–803

3. Rosén T, Bengtsson B-Å. Premature mortality due to cardiovascular disease in hypopituitarism. Lancet 1990; 336:285–8

4. Bülow B, Hagmar L, Mikoczy Z, Nordström CH, Erfurth EM. Increased cerebrovascular mortality in patients with hypopituitarism. Clin Endocrinol (Oxf) 1997;46:75–81

5. Bates AS, Van't Hoff W, Jones PJ, Clayton RN. The effect of hypopituitarism on life expectancy. J Clin Endocrinol Metab 1996;81:1169–72

6. Bates AS, Bullivant B, Sheppard MC, Stewart PM. Life expectancy following surgery for pituitary tumours. Clin Endocrinol (Oxf) 1999;50:315–9

7. Tomlinson JW, Holden N, Hills RK, Wheatley K, Clayton RN, Bates AS, Sheppard MC, Stewart PM. Association between premature mortality and hypopituitarism. West Midlands Prospective Hypopituitary Study Group. Lancet 2001;357:425–31

8. Abs R, Bengtsson B-Å, Hernberg-Ståhl E, Monson JP, Tauber JP, Wilton P, Wüster C. GH replacement in 1034 growth hormone deficient hypopituitary adults: demographic and clinical characteristics, dosing and safety. Clin Endocrinol (Oxf) 1999;50:703–13

9. Bülow B, Attewell R, Hagmar L, Malmstrom P, Nordström CH, Erfurth EM. Postoperative prognosis in craniopharyngioma with respect to cardiovascular mortality, survival, and tumor recurrence. J Clin Endocrinol Metab 1998;83:3897–904

10. Brada M, Ashley S, Ford D, Traish D, Burchell L, Rajan B. Cerebrovascular mortality in patients with pituitary adenoma. Clin Endocrinol (Oxf) 2002; 57:713–7

11. Erfurth EM, Bülow B, Svahn-Tapper G, Norrving B, Odh K, Mikoczy Z, Bjork J, Hagmar L. Risk factors for cerebrovascular deaths in patients operated and irradiated for pituitary tumors. J Clin Endocrinol Metab 2002;87:4892–9

12. Bülow B, Hagmar L, Eskilsson J, Erfurth EM. Hypopituitary females have a high incidence of cardiovascular morbidity and an increased prevalence of cardiovascular risk factors. J Clin Endocrinol Metab 2000;85:574–84

13. Anderson M, Hansen TB, Stoving RK, Bertelsen J, Hangaard J, Hyltoft Petersen P, Hagen C. The pyridostigmine-growth hormone releasing hormone test in adults. The reference interval and a comparison with the insulin tolerance test. Endocrinol Metab 1996; 3:197–206

14. Abdu TA, Neary R, Elhadd TA, Akber M, Clayton RN. Coronary risk in growth hormone deficient hypopituitary adults: increased predicted risk is due largely to lipid profile abnormalities. Clin Endocrinol (Oxf) 2001;55:209–16

15. Beshyah SA, Freemantle C, Thomas E, Rutherford O, Page B, Murphy M, Johnston DG. Abnormal body composition and reduced bone mass in growth hormone deficient hypopituitary adults. Clin Endocrinol (Oxf) 1995;42:179–89

16. Lonn L, Kvist H, Grangard U, Bengtsson B-Å, Sjöström L. CT-determined body composition changes with recombinant human growth hormone treatment to adults with growth hormone deficiency. Basic Life Sci 1993;60:229–31

17. Kissebah AH, Vydelingum N, Murray R, Evans DJ, Hartz AJ, Kalkhoff RK, Adams PW. Relation of body fat distribution to metabolic complications of obesity. J Clin Endocrinol Metab 1982;54:254–60

18. Haffner SM, Stern MP, Hazuda HP, Rosenthal M, Knapp JA, Malina RM. Role of obesity and fat distribution in non-insulin-dependent diabetes mellitus in Mexican Americans and non-Hispanic whites. Diabetes Care 1986;9:153–61

19. Lapidus L, Bengtsson C, Larsson B, Pennert K, Rybo E, Sjöström L. Distribution of adipose tissue and risk of cardiovascular disease and death: a 12 year follow up of participants in the population study of women in Gothenburg, Sweden. Br Med J (Clin Res Ed) 1984; 289:1257–61

20. Beshyah SA, Henderson A, Niththyanathan R, Sharp P, Richmond W, Johnston DG. Metabolic abnormalities in growth hormone deficient adults: carbohydrate tolerance and lipid metabolism. Endocrinol Metab 1994;1:173–80

21. Colao A, di Somma C, Cuocolo A, Spinelli L, Tedesco N, Pivonello R, Bonaduce D, Salvatore M, Lombardi G. Improved cardiovascular risk factors and cardiac performance after 12 months of growth hormone (GH) replacement in young adult patients with GH deficiency. J Clin Endocrinol Metab 2001;86:1874–81

22. al-Shoumer KA, Cox KH, Hughes CL, Richmond W, Johnston DG. Fasting and postprandial lipid abnormalities in hypopituitary women receiving conventional replacement therapy. J Clin Endocrinol Metab 1997;82:2653–9

23. Hew FL, Koschmann M, Christopher M, Rantzau C, Vaag A, Ward G, Beck-Nielsen H, Alford F. Insulin resistance in growth hormone-deficient adults: defects in glucose utilization and glycogen synthase activity. J Clin Endocrinol Metab 1996;81:555–64

24. Johansson JO, Landin K, Tengborn L, Rosén T, Bengtsson B-Å. High fibrinogen and plasminogen activator inhibitor activity in growth hormone-deficient adults. Arterioscler Thromb 1994;14:434–7

25. Beshyah SA, Markussis V, Harbourne T, Nicolaides AN, Johnston DG. Haemostatic mechanisms are normal despite increased vascular mortality in hypopituitary adults. Horm Metab Res 1993;25:449–50

26. Jørgensen JO, Pedersen SA, Ingerslev J, Møller J, Skakkebæk NE, Christiansen JS. Growth hormone (GH) therapy in GH-deficient patients, the plasma factor VIII-von Willebrand factor complex, and capillary fragility. A double-blind, placebo-controlled crossover study. Scand J Clin Lab Invest 1990;50:417–20

27. Ross R. Atherosclerosis – an inflammatory disease. N Engl J Med 1999;340:115–26

28. Klibanski A. Growth hormone and cardiovascular risk markers. Growth Horm IGF Res 2003;13 (Suppl A): S109–15

29. Leonsson M, Hulthe J, Johannsson G, Wiklund O, Wikstrand J, Bengtsson B-Å, Oscarsson J. Increased interleukin-6 levels in pituitary-deficient patients are independently related to their carotid intima–media thickness. Clin Endocrinol (Oxf) 2003;59:242–50

30. O'Leary DH, Polak JF, Kronmal RA, Manolio TA, Burke GL, Wolfson SK Jr. Carotid-artery intima and media thickness as a risk factor for myocardial infarction and stroke in older adults. Cardiovascular Health Study Collaborative Research Group. N Engl J Med 1999;340:14–22

31. Lehmann ED, Hopkins KD, Weissberger AJ, Gosling RG, Sönksen PH. Aortic distensibility in growth hormone deficient adults. Lancet 1993;341:309

32. Pfeifer M, Verhovec R, Zizek B, Prezelj J, Poredos P, Clayton RN. Growth hormone (GH) treatment reverses early atherosclerotic changes in GH-deficient adults. J Clin Endocrinol Metab 1999;84:453–7

33. Leonsson M, Hulthe J, Oscarsson J, Johannsson G, Wendelhag I, Wikstrand J, Bengtsson B-Å. Intima–media thickness in cardiovascularly asymptomatic hypopituitary adults with growth hormone deficiency: relation to body mass index, gender, and other cardiovascular risk factors. Clin Endocrinol (Oxf) 2002;57:751–9

34. Markussis V, Beshyah SA, Fisher C, Sharp P, Nicolaides AN, Johnston DG. Detection of premature atherosclerosis by high-resolution ultrasonography in symptom-free hypopituitary adults. Lancet 1992;340: 1188–92

35. Stewart PM, Sheppard MC. Mortality and hypopituitarism. Growth Horm IGF Res 1999;9 (Suppl A):15–19

36. Gelding SV, Taylor NF, Wood PJ, Noonan K, Weaver JU, Wood DF, Monson JP. The effect of growth hormone replacement therapy on cortisol-cortisone interconversion in hypopituitary adults: evidence for growth hormone modulation of extrarenal 11 beta-hydroxysteroid dehydrogenase activity. Clin Endocrinol (Oxf) 1998;48:153–62

37. Moore JS, Monson JP, Kaltsas G, Putignano P, Wood PJ, Sheppard MC, Besser GM, Taylor NF, Stewart PM. Modulation of 11 beta-hydroxysteroid dehydrogenase isozymes by growth hormone and insulin-like growth factor: in vivo and in vitro studies. J Clin Endocrinol Metab 1999;84:4172–7

38. Stewart PM, Tomlinson JW. Cortisol, 11 beta-hydroxysteroid dehydrogenase type 1 and central obesity. Trends Endocrinol Metab 2002;13:94–6

39. Sawin CT, Geller A, Wolf PA, Belanger AJ, Baker E, Bacharach P, Wilson PW, Benjamin EJ, D'Agostino RB. Low serum thyrotropin concentrations as a risk factor for atrial fibrillation in older persons. N Engl J Med 1994;331:1249–52

40. Parle JV, Maisonneuve P, Sheppard MC, Boyle P, Franklyn JA. Prediction of all-cause and cardiovascular mortality in elderly people from one low serum thyrotropin result: a 10-year cohort study. Lancet 2001;358:861–5

41. Rossouw JE, Anderson GL, Prentice RL, LaCroix AZ, Kooperberg C, Stefanick ML, Jackson RD, Beresford SA, Howard BV, Johnson KC, Kotchen JM, Ockene J. Risks and benefits of estrogen plus progestin in healthy postmenopausal women: principal results from the Women's Health Initiative randomized controlled trial. JAMA 2002;288:321–33

42. Beral V. Breast cancer and hormone-replacement therapy in the Million Women Study. Lancet 2003; 362:419–27

43. Toogood AA, Beardwell CG, Shalet SM. The severity of growth hormone deficiency in adults with pituitary disease is related to the degree of hypopituitarism. Clin Endocrinol (Oxf) 1994;41:511–6

44. Bengtsson B-Å, Abs R, Bennmarker H, Monson JP, Feldt-Rasmussen U, Hernberg-Ståhl E, Westberg B, Wilton P, Wüster C. The effects of treatment and the individual responsiveness to growth hormone (GH) replacement therapy in 665 GH-deficient adults. KIMS Study Group and the KIMS International Board. J Clin Endocrinol Metab 1999;84:3929–35

45. Cuneo RC, Salomon F, Watts GF, Hesp R, Sönksen PH. Growth hormone treatment improves serum lipids and lipoproteins in adults with growth hormone deficiency. Metabolism 1993;42:1519–23

46. de Boer H, Blok GJ, Voerman HJ, Phillips M, Schouten JA. Serum lipid levels in growth hormone-deficient men. Metabolism 1994;43:199–203

47. Colao A. Are patients with acromegaly at high risk for dysrhythmias? Clin Endocrinol (Oxf) 2001;55:305–6

48. West of Scotland Coronary Prevention Study: identification of high-risk groups and comparison with other cardiovascular intervention trials. Lancet 1996; 348:1339–42

49. Sesmilo G, Biller BM, Llevadot J, Hayden D, Hanson G, Rifai N, Klibanski A. Effects of growth hormone administration on inflammatory and other cardiovascular risk markers in men with growth hormone deficiency. A randomized, controlled clinical trial. Ann Intern Med 2000;133:111–22

50. Smith JC, Lane HA, Lewis J, Dann S, Goodfellow J, Collins P, Evans LM, Scanlon MF, Davies JS. Endothelial function and coagulant factors in growth hormone-treated hypopituitary adults receiving desmopressin. J Clin Endocrinol Metab 2003;88:2152–6

51. Christopher M, Hew FL, Oakley M, Rantzau C, Alford F. Defects of insulin action and skeletal muscle glucose metabolism in growth hormone-deficient adults persist after 24 months of recombinant human growth hormone therapy. J Clin Endocrinol Metab 1998; 83:1668–81

52. O'Neal DN, Kalfas A, Dunning PL, Christopher MJ, Sawyer SD, Ward GM, Alford FP. The effect of

3 months of recombinant human growth hormone (GH) therapy on insulin and glucose-mediated glucose disposal and insulin secretion in GH-deficient adults: a minimal model analysis. J Clin Endocrinol Metab 1994;79:975–83

53. Fowelin J, Attvall S, Lager I, Bengtsson B-Å. Effects of treatment with recombinant human growth hormone on insulin sensitivity and glucose metabolism in adults with growth hormone deficiency. Metabolism 1993;42:1443–7

54. McConnell EM, Atkinson AB, Ennis C, Hadden DR, McCance DR, Sheridan B, Bell PM. The effects on insulin action in adult hypopituitarism of recombinant human GH therapy individually titrated for six months. J Clin Endocrinol Metab 2001;86:5342–7

55. Russell-Jones DL, Watts GF, Weissberger A, Naoumova R, Myers J, Thompson GR, Sönksen PH. The effect of growth hormone replacement on serum lipids, lipoproteins, apolipoproteins and cholesterol precursors in adult growth hormone deficient patients. Clin Endocrinol (Oxf) 1994;41:345–50

56. Leese GP, Wallymahmed M, Wieringa G, VanHeyningen C, MacFarlane IA. Apo E phenotype and changes in serum lipids in adult patients during growth hormone replacement. Eur J Endocrinol 1999;140:174–9

57. Edén S, Wiklund O, Oscarsson J, Rosén T, Bengtsson B-Å. Growth hormone treatment of growth hormone-deficient adults results in a marked increase in Lp(a) and HDL cholesterol concentrations. Arterioscler Thromb 1993;13:296–301

58. Wieringa G, Toogood AA, Ryder WD, Anderson JM, Mackness M, Shalet SM. Changes in lipoprotein(a) levels measured by six kit methods during growth hormone treatment of growth hormone-deficient adults. Growth Horm IGF Res 2000;10:14–19

59. Smith JC, Evans LM, Wilkinson I, Goodfellow J, Cockcroft JR, Scanlon MF, Davies JS. Effects of GH replacement on endothelial function and large-artery stiffness in GH-deficient adults: a randomized, double-blind, placebo-controlled study. Clin Endocrinol (Oxf) 2002;56:493–501

60. Beshyah SA, Johnston DG. Cardiovascular disease and risk factors in adults with hypopituitarism. Clin Endocrinol (Oxf) 1999;50:1–15

7 Aetiology and demography of adult growth hormone deficiency

Miklós I Góth[1], Erika Hubina[1] and Márta Korbonits[2]

[1]*Division of Endocrinology, National Medical Centre, Budapest, Hungary;* [2]*Department of Endocrinology, St Bartholomew's Hospital, London, UK*

Summary

Growth hormone deficiency (GHD) in adult life has serious implications for health and life expectancy. Variation between centres and countries in the diagnosis of patients with GHD, and the fact that patients with childhood-onset GHD (CO-GHD) are not automatically reassessed in adulthood, makes it difficult to establish the incidence of GHD in the adult population. Based on the estimated incidence of pituitary tumours, the incidence of adult-onset GHD in the USA and Europe is ten cases per million people. When adult patients with CO-GHD are considered the prevalence of GHD can be estimated as 200 per million. The most common causes of GHD are previous hypothalamic–pituitary diseases, such as a pituitary tumour and/or its treatment, cranial irradiation, head trauma/vascular injury and infiltrative disease. In line with other reports, analysis of data from KIMS – Pfizer International Metabolic Database – shows that 47% of cases of GHD are the result of pituitary tumours, 11% the result of craniopharyngiomas and 3.5% the result of other tumours affecting the pituitary or hypothalamus; 17% are from idiopathic and 1.6% from congenital causes and approximately 4% of cases are caused by trauma, infiltrative diseases or inflammatory diseases. The majority of adults with GHD have additional pituitary hormone deficiencies, the number of additional deficiencies being highest in patients with craniopharyngiomas. Growth hormone replacement therapy has been shown to have beneficial effects in adults with GHD. It is therefore important that every patient with a history of hypothalamic–pituitary disease, cranial irradiation, head trauma or CO-GHD is investigated for GHD in adulthood.

Introduction

Growth hormone deficiency (GHD) can develop as the result of a variety of conditions, and may begin during childhood or adulthood. Although GHD may occur in isolation, it is often observed in the context of multiple pituitary hormone deficiencies, where growth hormone (GH) is typically the first hormone to become clearly deficient. Among the most frequent causes of GHD in adults are previous hypothalamic–pituitary disease, such as a pituitary tumour and/or its treatment, cranial irradiation, head trauma/vascular injury and infiltrative disease [1]; however, in some cases the cause of GHD is unknown.

The most common cause of hypopituitarism is a pituitary tumour [2], which may progressively damage the pituitary/hypothalamus as a result of tumour growth, with compression of the hypothalamus, pituitary stalk or portal vessels. A further major cause of hypopituitarism, including GHD, is the treatment of these pituitary tumours. Surgery is the treatment of choice for the majority of pituitary tumours; however, surgery itself may cause hypopituitarism. Radiotherapy may also result in hypopituitarism, although the onset is typically delayed. Other cranial tumours, especially craniopharyngiomas, may also lead to GHD. Traumatic brain injury or subarachnoid haemorrhage that affects the hypothalamus or pituitary are also known to cause immediate or delayed hypopituitarism. Other causes include autoimmune hypophysitis and post-partum atrophy (Sheehan's syndrome).

Recent studies have shown that hypopituitarism may also be caused by alterations in the genes associated with the hypothalamic–pituitary axis (see Chapter 8); for example, deletions of the pituitary GH gene (*GH-1*) have been associated with familial isolated GHD [3], and mutations of the pituitary transcription factor gene, *POU1F1* (*Pit-1* in the old nomenclature), have been associated with combined GH, thyroid-stimulating hormone and prolactin deficiencies [4].

The importance of GHD in adult life is becoming increasingly apparent. GHD is associated with serious effects on health and quality of life [5] and life expectancy may be reduced in patients who develop chronic diseases associated with GHD [1, 6–9]. For example, the mortality rate is approximately 1.4–1.9 times higher in patients with hypopituitarism due to the increased occurrence of arteriosclerosis and vascular disease [6, 9–11].

This chapter examines the aetiology of GHD during adulthood with special reference to data from KIMS – Pfizer International Metabolic Database.

Incidence and prevalence of GHD in adults

The incidence and prevalence of GHD in adults in a given population is difficult to establish with certainty as it depends on numerous factors, such as the diagnostic techniques used, selection criteria and indications for surgical intervention. These factors may vary considerably in different countries, as well as between individual centres. Moreover, children with GHD were previously not automatically re-assessed for GHD when they reach final height [12, 13]. Although approximately one-third of children with GHD who are re-tested after the cessation of GH replacement therapy show a normal GH response, a large proportion continue to show an inadequate GH response [14–19].

Although there are only a few epidemiological studies specifically regarding GHD in adulthood [20, 21], data on patients with pituitary tumours [22, 23] may help in estimating the annual incidence of new cases of GHD and the prevalence of GHD within the population as a whole. The incidence rate of adult-onset GHD (AO-GHD), based on the estimated incidence of pituitary tumours, is suggested to be ten per million annually in the USA and Europe [1, 24]. The prevalence of GHD in adults is estimated by the Society for Endocrinology to be approximately 200 per million of the adult population, with AO-GHD accounting for approximately half of these cases [24]. According to Monson and Besser [11], about 100–200 per million of the UK population are thought to be GH deficient; however, a higher prevalence has been recorded in northern Spain. The prevalence of hypopituitarism in north-western Spain is 455 per million and the average annual incidence rate is 42.1 cases per million. In this population, the cause of hypopituitarism was most often a pituitary tumour, and about 50% of patients had three to five pituitary hormone deficiencies. GHD tended to be more frequent in patients with tumour-induced hypopituitarism than in those with non-tumour related hypopituitarism [21]. In France, the prevalence of GHD was estimated to be 46 per million of the population, based on an analysis of the population of Bouches du Rhône. Considering only the adult population, the annual incidence is approximately 12 per million [20].

Incidence and prevalence of pituitary adenoma

Pituitary adenomas and their treatment are the most common cause of GHD in adulthood [2]. In a study by Littley *et al.* [25], for example, it was shown that about 50% of patients with pituitary tumours evaluated before surgery already had GHD; after surgery, however, about 80% showed evidence of GHD. In addition, GHD developed after 5 years in all patients who had received post-operative radiotherapy.

The frequency of pituitary adenoma in the general population varies widely, ranging from between 3.4 and 23.2% of primary brain tumours [23]. The most frequent type of pituitary adenoma is prolactinoma (19–50%), followed by non-functioning adenoma (23–30%), GH-secreting adenoma (13–21%), adrenocorticotrophin (ACTH)-secreting adenoma (4–16%), thyrotrophin (TSH)-secreting adenoma and gonadotrophin-secreting adenoma (0.2–1.4%) [23, 26–29]. The incidence of pituitary adenomas in clinical studies peaks in the third to fifth decades of life. Generally, hormone-secreting adenomas are characteristic of younger patients, whereas non-functioning adenomas tend to occur in older patients. Micro-prolactinomas are more common in women, whereas the prevalence of macroprolactinomas is almost the same in men and women. ACTH-secreting adenomas are more frequent in women, with 3–15:1 female to male ratios having been reported. No gender differences have been observed in patients with acromegaly or non-functioning pituitary adenomas. ACTH- and prolactin-secreting tumours are the most common pituitary tumours in children, whereas non-functioning pituitary adenomas and TSH-secreting adenomas are extremely rare. Primary empty sella is a relatively frequent finding in the general population, and in a recent study was found to be associated with GHD in 15 out of 43 cases [30].

A higher incidence of pituitary tumours is suggested by analyses of autopsy material from the general population, with tumours found in 3–27% of unselected autopsies, dependent on the level of examination in the different studies. The age distribution is also wider in autopsy studies, ranging from 2–98 years, with the highest incidence starting in the fifth decade [23].

Demography and aetiology of GHD

The KIMS Scientific Committee has developed a classification list for the aetiology of GHD (see Appendix D) [31]. Data were analysed from the 7396 adult patients (mean age, 44 ± 15 years) in KIMS who have received GH replacement therapy. The number of males was 3763 (51%) and females 3633 (49%). The onset of GHD occurred during childhood in 23.1%. Of those patients in the KIMS database, 29% (2171) had received GH treatment before enrolling in the database (either in childhood or adulthood) [32]. The mean age at diagnosis of pituitary disease was 34 years and the mean age at diagnosis of GHD was 40 years. Patients were enrolled in KIMS at an average of 4 years after the diagnosis of GHD.

A variety of other co-morbidities are reported in patients with GHD in KIMS. The most frequent of these is hypertension, which is reported in 15% of

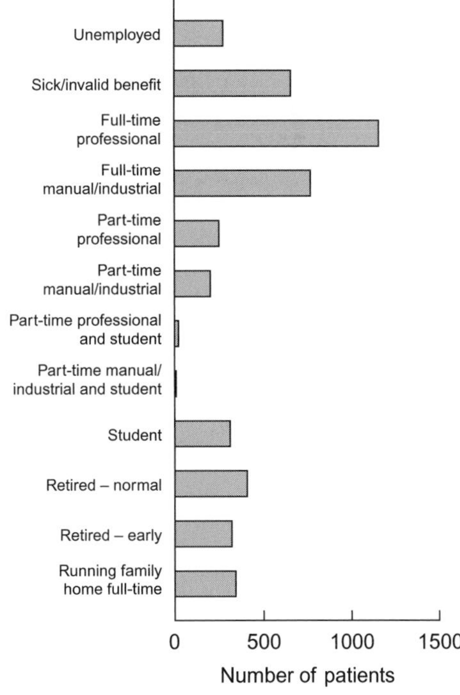

Figure 1. *Employment of patients with GHD in the KIMS database.*

Table 1. *Aetiology of GHD during adulthood in patients in KIMS.*

	Male	Female	Total	Percentage of total KIMS population (n = 7396)
Pituitary adenoma	1893	1595	3488	47.2
Non-functioning	1174	742	1916	25.9
Prolactin-secreting	373	335	708	9.6
Adrenocorticotrophin-secreting	130	343	473	6.4
GH-secreting	64	73	137	1.9
Gonadotrophin-secreting	34	7	41	0.6
Thyrotrophin-secreting	8	3	11	0.1
Co-secreting	2	2	4	0.1
Other[1]	108	90	198	2.7
Craniopharyngioma	453	393	846	11.4
Other pituitary/hypothalamic tumours	102	157	259	3.5
Cranial tumour distant from the pituitary	116	141	257	3.5
Germ cell tumour	71	41	112	1.5
Treatment of tumour outside the cranium	20	30	50	0.7
Other acquired GHD[2]	377	600	977	13.2
Traumatic brain injury	77	55	132	1.8
Idiopathic GHD	663	624	1287	17.4
Congenital GHD	67	53	120	1.6

[1]Not specified in database. [2]Including perinatal head trauma, traumatic brain injury, central nervous system infection, hydrocephalus, granulomatous diseases, Langerhans cell histiocytosis, infarction, Sheehan's syndrome, aneurysm, sickle cell anaemia, other vascular and lymphocytic hypophysitis.

patients, followed by arthrosis, which is reported in 7% of patients. Others include neoplasm (6%), diabetes mellitus (5%), coronary disease (4%), stroke (2%) and claudication (1%). In addition, it has previously been reported that GH-deficient patients with a childhood onset of disease are less likely to be married than subjects of the same age in the general population [33–35]. In a Canadian study [33], only 15 of the 116 adults studied were married. Of the patients in KIMS, 30% are unmarried. Several studies have also found higher rates of unemployment or underemployment among patients with GHD compared with the general population [33, 36]. The employment status of the GH-deficient patients in KIMS shows that a relatively high number of patients are unemployed or receiving sick/invalid benefit (Fig. 1).

The aetiology of GHD recorded in KIMS corresponds to other reports (Table 1). The most frequent cause of GHD during adulthood, seen in 47.2% of patients in KIMS, was a pituitary tumour. Of this group, more than half of the pituitary tumours (54.9%) were non-functioning adenomas. In 11.4% of cases GHD was caused by craniopharyngiomas, and in 3.5% by other tumours affecting the hypothalamus or pituitary. Interestingly, the aetiology of GHD was unknown (idiopathic) in 17.4% of cases, while in only 1.6% was the aetiology congenital. GHD was the result

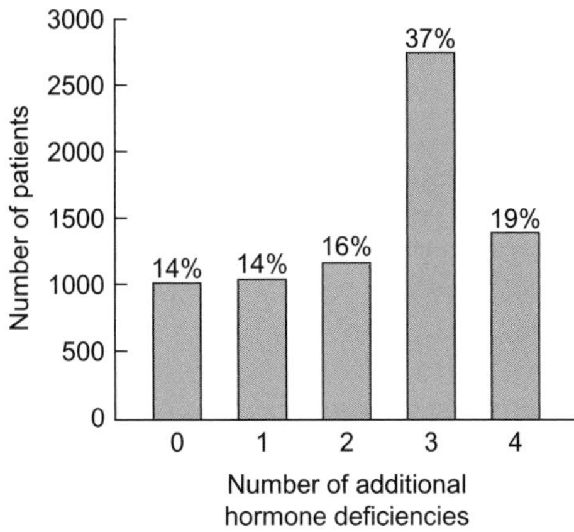

Figure 2. *Number of additional pituitary hormone deficiencies in patients with GHD in the KIMS database.*

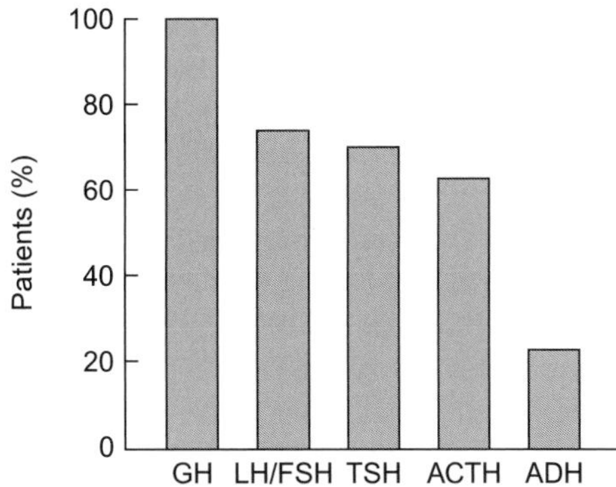

Figure 3. *Pituitary hormone deficiencies in patients in the KIMS database. ACTH, adrenocorticotrophin; ADH, antidiuretic hormone; LH/FSH, luteinizing hormone/follicle-stimulating hormone; TSH, thyrotrophin.*

of head trauma in 2.2% of cases, while 3.2% of cases were patients who had Sheehan's syndrome.

The data in KIMS show that the majority of adult GH-deficient patients have multiple pituitary hormone deficiencies, with only 14% having isolated GHD (Figs 2 and 3). The most frequently reported additional hormone deficiency was luteinizing hormone (LH)/follicle-stimulating hormone (FSH) deficiency, followed by TSH and ACTH deficiencies. The incidence of antidiuretic hormone (ADH) deficiency was substantially lower, being reported in approximately 22% of patients. It has been shown previously that the greater the number of pituitary hormone deficits, the more severe is the GHD [37]. The proportion of patients diagnosed with severe GHD (peak GH < 2.5 μg/L) was 41%, 67%, 83%, 96%, and 99% for patients with zero, one, two, three and four additional pituitary hormone deficiencies, respectively [38, 39]. Several studies have suggested that approximately 80% of patients with one or two, and nearly 100% of patients with three or four, other pituitary hormone deficits have GHD [37]. According to a Spanish survey of 69 patients with hypopituitarism, 87% of the patients had LH/FSH deficiency, 64% had TSH deficiency, 62% had ACTH deficiency, 61% had GHD, 20% had ADH deficiency and 17% had prolactin deficiency [21]. Twenty-one per cent of the patients with hypopituitarism had only one hormone deficit, and 15%, 23%, 19%, 15% and 7% of patients had two, three, four, five and six pituitary hormone deficiencies, respectively [21].

In the KIMS cohort, patients with tumours associated with the pituitary/hypothalamus are generally more likely to have additional hormone deficiencies. In particular, patients with craniopharyngioma have, on average, a significantly higher number of additional pituitary hormone deficiencies compared with all other aetiologies ($p < 0.001$) (Fig. 4). Of those studied, the aetiology least likely to be associated with additional pituitary hormone deficiencies is treatment of a tumour outside the cranium. For all aetiologies, excluding cranial tumours distant from the pituitary, the most frequently reported additional hormone deficiency was of LH/FSH (Fig. 5).

Conclusion

GHD may develop in adult life as a result of a variety of conditions, most commonly pituitary tumour, and has serious implications for health and life expectancy. Nevertheless, adult GHD is probably under-diagnosed, and it is proposed that

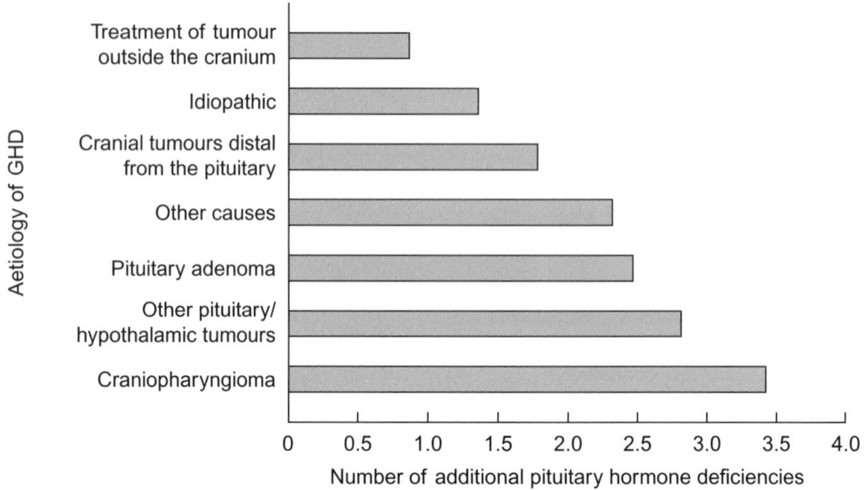

Figure 4. *Mean number of other pituitary hormone deficiencies in different aetiologies of GHD. Treatment for malignancy outside the cranium, n = 50; idiopathic, n = 1287; cranial tumours distal from the pituitary/hypothalamic area, n = 257; other causes, n = 977; pituitary adenoma, n = 3488; other pituitary/hypothalamic tumours, n = 259; craniopharyngioma, n = 846. All aetiologies differ significantly (p ≤ 0.01).*

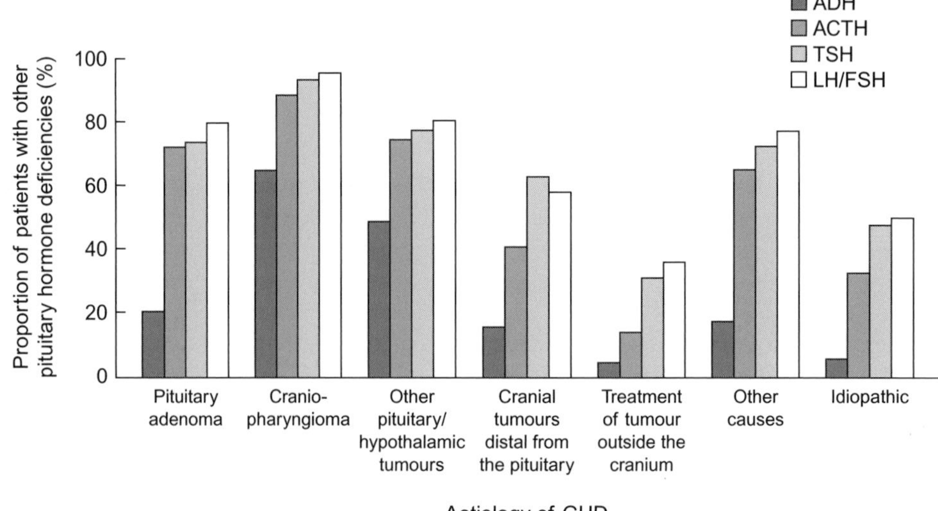

Figure 5. *Pituitary hormone deficiencies other than GHD expressed as a percentage of the different aetiologies. Pituitary adenoma, n = 3488; craniopharyngioma, n = 846; other pituitary/hypothalamic tumours, n = 259; cranial tumours distal from the pituitary/hypothalamic area, n = 257; treatment for malignancy outside the cranium, n = 50; other causes, n = 977; idiopathic, n = 1287. ACTH, adrenocorticotrophin; ADH, antidiuretic hormone; LH/FSH, luteinizing hormone/follicle-stimulating hormone; TSH, thyrotrophin.*

all patients with a history of hypothalamic–pituitary disease, cranial irradiation, head trauma or childhood-onset GHD should be investigated for GHD in adulthood.

References

1. Monson JP, Cook DM. Growth hormone deficiency in adults: a pocket guide to clinical management. Pennsylvania: ApotheCom Associates LLC, Yardley 2003

2. Vance ML. Hypopituitarism. N Eng J Med 1994; 330:1651–62

3. Phillips JA 3rd, Hjelle BL, Seeburg PH, Zachmann M. Molecular basis for familial isolated growth hormone deficiency. Proc Natl Acad Sci USA 1981;78:6372–5

4. Parks JS, Brown MR, Hurley DL, Phelps CJ, Wajnrajch MP. Heritable disorders of pituitary development. J Clin Endocrinol Metab 1999;84:4362–70

5. de Boer H, Blok GJ, van der Veen EA. Clinical aspects of growth hormone deficiency in adults. Endocr Rev 1995;16:63–86

6. Rosén T, Bengtsson B-Å. Premature mortality due to cardiovascular disease in hypopituitarism. Lancet 1990;336:285–8

7. Bates AS, Van't Hoff W, Jones PJ, Clayton RN. The effect of hypopituitarism on life expectancy. J Clin Endocrinol Metab 1996;81:1169–72

8. Ho KKZ. Growth hormone deficiency in adults. In: DeGroot LJ, Jameson JL, editors. Endocrinology. 4th Edition. Philadelphia: WB Saunders 2001:520–7

9. McCallum RW, Petrie JR, Dominiczak AF, Connell JM. Growth hormone deficiency and vascular risk. Clin Endocrinol (Oxf) 2002;57:11–24

10. Bülow B, Hagmar L, Mikoczy Z, Nordström CH, Erfurth EM. Increased cerebrovascular mortality in patients with hypopituitarism. Clin Endocrinol (Oxf) 1997;46:75–81

11. Monson JP, Besser GM. Premature mortality and hypopituitarism. Lancet 2001;357:1972–3

12. Nicolson A, Toogood AA, Rahim A, Shalet SM. The prevalence of severe growth hormone deficiency in adults who received growth hormone replacement in childhood. Clin Endocrinol (Oxf) 1996;44:311–6

13. Monson JP, Chatelain P. How should we transfer patients from paediatric to adult clinics? In: Monson JP, editor. Challenges in growth hormone therapy. Oxford: Blackwell Science 1999:222–31

14. Cacciari E, Tassoni P, Cicognani A, Pirazzoli P, Salardi S, Balsamo A, Cassio A, Zucchini S, Colli C, Tassinari D. Value and limits of pharmacological and physiological tests to diagnose growth hormone (GH) deficiency and predict therapy response: first and second retesting during replacement therapy of patients defined as GH deficient. J Clin Endocrinol Metab 1994;79:1663–9

15. Cacciari E, Tassoni P, Parisi G, Pirazzoli P, Zucchini S, Mandini M, Cicognani A, Balsamo A. Pitfalls in diagnosing impaired growth hormone (GH) secretion: retesting after replacement therapy of 63 patients defined as GH deficient. J Clin Endocrinol Metab 1992;74:1284–9

16. Wacharasindhu S, Cotterill AM, Camacho-Hubner C, Besser GM, Savage MO. Normal growth hormone secretion in growth hormone insufficient children retested after completion of linear growth. Clin Endocrinol (Oxf) 1996;45:553–6

17. Tauber M, Moulin P, Pienkowski C, Jouret B, Rochiccioli P. Growth hormone (GH) retesting and auxological data in 131 GH-deficient patients after completion of treatment. J Clin Endocrinol Metab 1997;82:352–6

18. Toogood AA, Shalet SM. Diagnosis of severe growth hormone (GH) deficiency in young adults who received GH replacement therapy during childhood. Acta Paediatr Suppl 1997;423:117–20

19. Attanasio AF, Howell S, Bates PC, Blum WF, Frewer P, Quigley C, Shalet SM. Confirmation of severe GH deficiency after final height in patients diagnosed as GH deficient during childhood. Clin Endocrinol (Oxf) 2002;56:503–7

20. Sassolas G, Chazot FB, Jaquet P, Bachelot I, Chanson P, Rudelli CC, Tauber JP, Allannic H, Bringer J, Roudaut N, Rohmer V, Roger P, Latapie JL, Reville P, Leutenegger M. GH deficiency in adults: an epidemiological approach. Eur J Endocrinol 1999; 141:595–600

21. Regal M, Paramo C, Sierra SM, Garcia-Mayor RV. Prevalence and incidence of hypopituitarism in an adult Caucasian population in northwestern Spain. Clin Endocrinol (Oxf) 2001;55:735–40

22. Ambrosi B, Faglia G. Epidemiology of pituitary tumours. In: Faglia G, Beck-Peccoz P, Ambrosi B, Travaglini P, Spada A, editors. Pituitary adenomas: new trends in basic and clinical research. Amsterdam: Excerpta Medica 1991:159–61

23. Yamada S. Epidemiology of pituitary tumours. In: Thapar K, Kovacs K, Scheithauer BW, Lloyd RV, editors. Diagnosis and management of pituitary tumours. Totowa: Humana Press Inc 2001:57–68

24. Bryant J, Loveman E, Chase D, Mihaylova B, Cave C, Gerard K, Milne R. Clinical effectiveness and cost-effectiveness of growth hormone in adults in relation to impact on quality of life: a systematic review and economic evaluation. Health Technol Assess 2002; 6:1–106

25. Littley MD, Shalet SM, Beardwell CG, Ahmed SR, Applegate G, Sutton ML. Hypopituitarism following external radiotherapy for pituitary tumours in adults. Q J Med 1989;70:145–60

26. Lloyd RV, Jin L, Tsumanuma I, Vidal S, Kovacs K, Horvath E, Scheithauer BW, Couce ME, Burguera B. Leptin and leptin receptor in anterior pituitary function. Pituitary 2001;4:33–47

27. Mindermann T, Wilson CB. Age-related and gender-related occurrence of pituitary adenomas. Clin Endocrinol (Oxf) 1994;41:359–64

28. Kovacs K, Horvath E, Vidal S. Classification of pituitary adenomas. J Neurooncol 2001;54:121–7

29. Terada T, Kovacs K, Stefaneanu L, Horvath E. Incidence, pathology, and recurrence of pituitary adenomas: study of 647 unselected surgical cases. Endocr Pathol 1995;6:301–10

30. Cannavo S, Curto L, Venturino M, Squadrito S, Almoto B, Narbone MC, Rao R, Trimarchi F. Abnormalities of hypothalamic–pituitary–thyroid axis in patients with primary empty sella. J Endocrinol Invest 2002;25:236–9

31. Ranke MB. The KIGS aetiology classification system. In: Ranke MB, Wilton P, Editors. Growth hormone therapy in KIGS – 10 years' experience. Heidelberg: Leipzig: Barth 1999

32. KIMS Annual Report. London: OCC Europe Ltd 2002

33. Dean HJ, McTaggart TL, Fish DG, Friesen HG. The educational, vocational, and marital status of growth hormone-deficient adults treated with growth hormone during childhood. Am J Dis Child 1985;139:1105–10

34. Takano K, Tanaka T, Saito T. Psychosocial adjustment in a large cohort of adults with growth hormone deficiency treated with growth hormone in childhood: summary of a questionnaire survey. Committee for the Study Group of Adult GH Deficiency. Acta Paediatr Suppl 1994;399:16–19

35. Rikken B, van Busschbach J, le Cessie S, Manten W, Spermon T, Grobbee R, Wit JM. Impaired social status of growth hormone deficient adults as compared to controls with short or normal stature. Dutch Growth Hormone Working Group. Clin Endocrinol (Oxf) 1995;43:205–11

36. Mitchell CM, Joyce S, Johanson AJ, Libber S, Plotnick L, Migeon CJ, Blizzard RM. A retrospective evaluation of psychosocial impact of long-term growth hormone therapy. Clin Pediatr (Phila) 1986;25:17–23

37. Toogood AA, Beardwell CG, Shalet SM. The severity of growth hormone deficiency in adults with pituitary disease is related to the degree of hypopituitarism. Clin Endocrinol (Oxf) 1994;41:511–6

38. Hartman ML, Crowe BJ, Biller BM, Ho KK, Clemmons DR, Chipman JJ. Which patients do not require a GH stimulation test for the diagnosis of adult GH deficiency? J Clin Endocrinol Metab 2002;87:477–85

39. Abs R. Update on the diagnosis of GH deficiency in adults. Eur J Endocrinol 2003;148 (Suppl 2):S3–8

8 Genetic causes of growth hormone deficiency

Thierry Brue[1,3], Rachel Reynaud[2,3], Albert Beckers[5], Patrick Petrossians[5], Alexandre Saveanu[1,3], Anne Barlier[3,4] and Alain Enjalbert[3,4]

[1]Department of Endocrinology and [2]Department of Pediatrics, Centre Hospitalier Universitaire Timone; [3]Laboratory Interactions Cellulaires Neuroendocriniennes, CNRS UMR 6544, Institut Fédératif Jean Roche, Faculté de Médecine, Université de la Méditerranée; [4]Laboratory of Biochemistry and Molecular Biology, Hôpital de la Conception, Marseille, France; [5]Department of Endocrinology, Centre Hospitalier Universitaire Sart Tilman, Liège, Belgium

Summary

Over the past 15 years, molecular biology has identified several genetic alterations that are responsible for pituitary hormone deficits. Several types of isolated or combined hypopituitarism have been shown to involve mutations in different pituitary transcription factors that regulate hormone gene expression, cell differentiation and cell proliferation during anterior pituitary organogenesis. This chapter provides an overview of the genes and mutations that are currently implicated in pituitary hormone deficits, such as the GH-releasing hormone receptor gene and the pituitary transcription factor gene POU1F1. Undoubtedly, further studies will help to identify other genes and mutations that are involved in pituitary disease and development. This will allow accurate identification of patients who have a genetic mutation that causes GH deficiency (GHD), particularly delayed-onset GHD, thus enabling the early initiation of treatment.

Introduction

Albeit modulated by environmental factors such as nutrition, somatic diseases or psychological factors, growth is a genetically determined process. Over the past 15 years, molecular biology techniques have identified several genetic alterations that are responsible for growth hormone deficiency (GHD) [1]. Alterations in several of the numerous genes that play a role in growth regulation in man have been shown to result in the abnormal secretion or action of growth hormone (GH). These genes include the pituitary *GH* gene, the *GH-releasing hormone receptor (GHRHR)* gene, or pituitary transcription factor genes, such as *POU1F1* (*Pit-1* in the old nomenclature), *PROP1*, *Lhx3* and *Hesx1* [2].[1] Other molecular abnormalities affecting GH action without causing GHD – and hence not discussed in this overview – may also be responsible for short stature, such as GH receptor gene defects associated with Laron-syndrome [3] or insulin-like growth factor I (IGF-I) gene alterations (Fig. 1).

---

[1]**Abbreviations:** HESX1, Homeobox gene expression in embryonic stem cells; Lhx3, LIM homeobox transcription factor 3; Pit-1, Pituitary transcription factor 1; Pitx2, Pituitary homeobox 2; POU1F1, “Pit-1,Oct,Unc” transcription factor 1; PROP1, Prophet of Pit-1

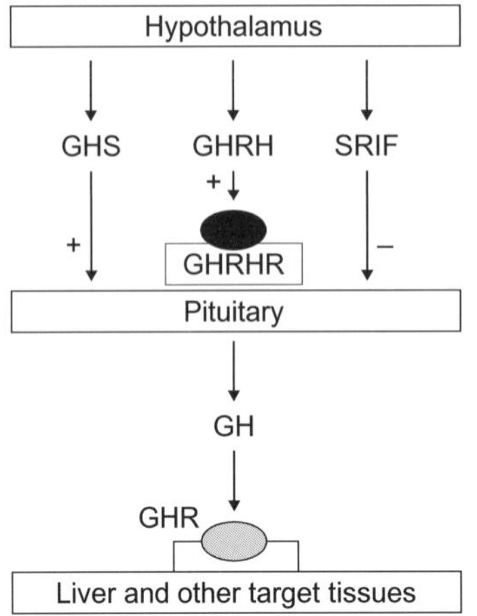

Figure 1. *Molecular defects resulting in abnormal GH secretion and action: involvement of different genes of the somatotrophic axis. The somatotrophic axis involves several interdependent genes. The corresponding proteins include ligands, such as GH and IGF-I; transcription factors, such as POU1F1, Prop1, Lhx3, Lhx4, Hesx1 and Pitx2; stimulatory and inhibitory hypothalamic hormones, such as GH-releasing hormone (GHRH) and somatostatin, and hormone receptors, such as the GHRH receptor (GHRHR) and the GH receptor (GHR). GHS, GH secretagogue; SRIF, somatostatin-release inhibiting factor.*

The mature anterior pituitary is composed of five neuroendocrine cell types, each defined by the hormone produced. The development of this gland is similar in all vertebrates, but has been best studied in the mouse. Anterior pituitary ontogenesis is dependent upon a cascade of signalling molecules and developmental genes that function as transcription factors. A number of homeobox genes and signalling molecules are implicated in the various stages of pituitary gland development. Although the general transcription factors are widely expressed in various tissues, many of these proteins are restricted to the pituitary or to one of its sublineages. Many of these cell-restricted transcription factors first play a role in the control of morphogenesis, lineage differentiation, and/or proliferation, and are then recruited to regulate cell-specific gene expression.

Defects in the hypothalamic–pituitary–GH axis result in GHD and are often associated with other pituitary hormone deficiencies. GHD induces IGF-I deficiency, which results in severe growth retardation and also in more minor morphological changes, including a doll-like face, a marked nasal bridge, frontal bossing and increased abdominal adiposity. Birth length is typically normal, but postnatal growth is retarded, especially after 6 months of age. A family history of GHD is suggestive of a genetic cause in between 5% and 30% of cases [4]. Sporadic cases, however, may also be due to a genetic cause. Two types of GHD may be distinguished: isolated GHD (IGHD) and multiple pituitary hormone deficiency (MPHD), in which GHD is associated with deficits of at least one other pituitary hormone. The latter condition has been associated in the past decade with genetic alterations of several pituitary transcription factors. GHD may also be part of syndromic alterations of embryonic development due to a number of monogenic or chromosomal defects.

IGHD

There are several ways of classifying IGHD, based either on a combination of phenotypic traits and a suspected mode of inheritance, or on the genotypic abnormality, if identified. Four main categories of IGHD have been proposed [5, 6].

- Type I IGHD Subtype IA is characterized by a severe phenotype. Despite a normal birth length, growth velocity is very low after 6 months of age and is associated with neonatal hypoglycaemia. GH concentrations are undetectable, both at baseline and during stimulation tests. Subtype IA is transmitted in an autosomal recessive manner.
- Type I IGHD Subtype IB IGHD has a less severe phenotype, with very low basal but detectable stimulated GH levels. Subtype IB is transmitted in an autosomal recessive manner.
- Type II IGHD has clinical and biological features similar to that of subtype IB, but the disease is transmitted as an autosomal dominant trait.
- Type III IGHD, inherited as an X-linked recessive disease, is associated with hypogammaglobulinaemia in male subjects. Alterations of the *XLA* gene (located at Xq21.3–q22), which encodes the btk tyrosine kinase, and/or contiguous loci appear to be involved in the pathogenesis of this rare disorder [7].

IGHD is mainly caused by mutations in the *GH* gene or in the *GHRHR* gene.

GH-1

The human pituitary *GH* gene (*GH-1*) is located on the long arm of chromosome 17 (17q23), close to *CSHP-1* (chorionic somatomammotrophin pseudogene 1), *CSH-1* (chorionic somatomammotrophin gene 1), *GH-2* and *CSH-2* (chorionic somatomammotrophin gene 2). These highly homologous genes (which share 92–98% of their sequence) form a cluster spanning 66.5 kilobases (kb). *GH-1* contains five exons and four introns. It is expressed in anterior pituitary somatotrophs and encodes a 22 kDa, 191 amino-acid protein.

Several homozygous *GH-1* gene mutations have been associated with a phenotype of subtype IA severe IGHD. They usually consist of bi-allelic deletions (such as a 6.7 kb deletion found in up to 70% of affected patients with this type of IGHD), stop mutations or intronic mutations that predict the production of truncated GH proteins [5]. Mono-allelic mutations affecting intron 3 of the *GH-1* gene have also been implicated in type II IGHD. These are intronic substitutions or deletions that result in a lack of transcription of exon 3 of *GH-1* into mature mRNA, leading to an abnormal 17.5 kDa GH isoform lacking amino acids 32–71 [6].

GHRH

The *GHRH* gene, which was initially cloned from ectopic GHRH-secreting tumours, is located on the long arm of chromosome 20 (20q11.2). It spans approximately 10 kb and contains five exons. It encodes a 107–108 amino-acid peptide, secondarily cleaved into the 44 amino-acid mature GHRH. No such mutation has been described in man.

GHRHR

The *GHRHR* gene is located on the short arm of chromosome 7 (7p14) and contains more than ten exons. A homozygous mutation of this gene has been shown to be responsible for the 'little mouse' phenotype, a dwarf mouse model for recessively transmitted IGHD with pituitary hypoplasia. Bi-allelic anomalies of this gene have been found in patients with familial subtype IB IGHD and hypoplastic pituitaries [8].

MPHD

MPHD is due mainly to anomalies of pituitary transcription factors. A combination of cell-specific and hormone-regulated transcription factors cooperate to integrate the developmental and endocrine signals necessary for the homeostatic production of pituitary hormones. Despite interspecies phenotypic variability, animal models have given a valuable insight into human pituitary disease. For example, Snell or Jackson mice, known to have GH, prolactin and thyrotrophin (TSH) deficiencies associated with a hypoplastic pituitary, have allowed the identification of alterations of the *POU1F1* transcription factor gene [9]. The human phenotype associated with mutations in this gene is similar to that of mouse mutants [10, 11]. Mutations of the *Prop1* transcription factor [12] and *GHRHR* genes were first described in other spontaneous animal models: Ames and little mice, respectively. Several murine knockout models induced phenotypical conditions similar to human diseases, implying homologous human genes, such as *HESX1* [13], *LHX3* [14] and *LHX4* [15] transcription factors. Currently, *HESX1, PITX2, LHX3, LHX4, PROP1* and *POU1F1* transcription factors have been shown to be involved in disorders of human pituitary development [2].

POU1F1 (Pit-1)

In humans, at least 15 distinct recessive or dominant autosomal mutations of the *POU1F1* gene have been shown to be responsible for GH, prolactin and TSH deficiencies [10, 11, 16–33]. Interestingly, the inheritance pattern and phenotype in affected patients are variable. Phenotypical presentation is characterized by severe somatotroph and lactotroph deficiencies, with variable thyrotroph deficiency. The pituitary can be hypoplastic or normal, without stalk interruption syndrome. The majority of the mutations are located in the POU-specific and POU-homeodomain regions, which are both necessary for high-affinity DNA binding on the GH and prolactin genes. Two mutations were described in the *N*-terminal transactivation domain. Several *POU1F1* mutations have been analysed *in vitro* in co-transfection experiments, which has revealed different molecular mechanisms responsible for the MPHD phenotype. Some of the mutant proteins act as dominant inhibitors of transcription, such as R271W; some have defective DNA-binding, such as R143Q, E174G, W193R, 747delA and the Snell mouse W261C mutation, and some display alterations of protein–protein interactions, such as A158P, P239S and the recessive F135C mutation that we have recently described and analysed in terms of molecular structure and function [19].

PROP1 (Fig. 2)

In man, at least 12 distinct recessive mutations of the *PROP1* gene have been documented in a total of 50 unrelated families with MPHD [34–46]. In contrast to patients with *POU1F1* defects, all of these patients presented with hypogonadotrophic hypogonadism, and some of them also with adrenocorticotrophin (ACTH) deficiency; however, only moderately altered fertility and preserved corticotroph function are reported in the Ames mouse, the animal model for the *PROP1* gene defect. Moreover, the pituitary was hypoplastic, normal or hyperplastic with subsequent involution. The possibility that the pituitary may have a tumour-like appearance must be emphasized, as it may lead to an incorrect diagnosis (Fig. 2). We have identified several mutations of the *PROP1* gene, including three new mutations, in ten unrelated families with MPHD. That study showed the predominance of *PROP1* defects in MPHD, a marked phenotypic variability with delayed appearance of the different deficiencies and an underestimated frequency of ACTH deficiency [35].

LHX3

Recessive mutations of *LHX3* were described in four patients from two unrelated and consanguineous families [47]. Two of these patients presented with the same phenotype: GH, prolactin, TSH and gonadotrophin deficiencies associated with a rigid cervical spine leading to limited head rotation. The pituitary was found to be either hypoplastic or dramatically enlarged, as has been described in patients with *PROP1* gene mutations [46]. In one patient, a homozygous mutation predicted a change from a tyrosine to a cysteine in the LIM2 domain involved in the zinc finger structure of this transcription factor. In

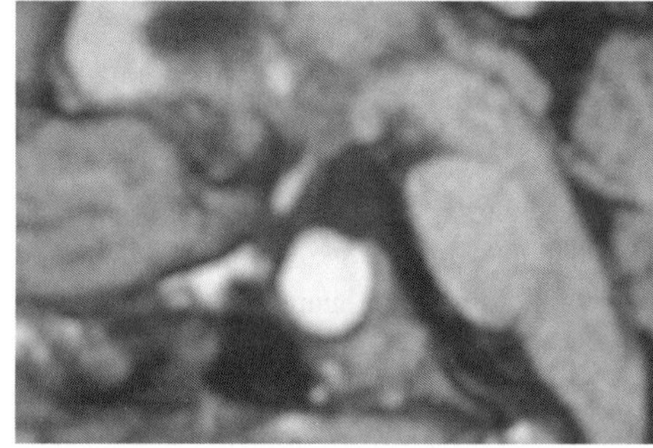

Figure 2. *Sagittal magnetic resonance imaging section (T1 weighted) in a patient harbouring the 301–302delGA PROP1 2-base-pair deletion showing an enlarged, hyperintense pituitary gland. Courtesy of Dr C Adamsbaum, Paris.*

another family, a 23 base-pair deletion was responsible for a severely truncated protein lacking the homeodomain.

LHX4

The *LHX4* gene was recently cloned in man. A dominant intronic mutation of *LHX4* was found in a familial case presenting with a complex disease phenotype. It was characterized by GH, TSH and ACTH deficiencies associated with a hypoplastic pituitary, stalk interruption syndrome and extrapituitary abnormalities, pointed cerebellar tonsils and a poorly developed sella turcica [15]. Should additional extrapituitary anomalies be described in other patients or families, this gene defect may also legitimately fall into the category of syndromic GHD.

Syndromic GHD

Septo-optic dysplasia

Hesx1, also known as *Rpx*, is a 'paired'-like homeodomain pituitary transcription factor that plays a role in early anterior pituitary development [13]. The human *HESX1* gene, spanning 1.7 kb, is located on the short arm of chromosome 3 (3p21.2), contains four exons and encodes a 185 amino-acid protein. Gene inactivation experiments generate, in homozygous and a minority of heterozygote mice, a phenotype reminiscent of septo-optic dysplasia, including anophthalmia, severe microphthalmia, an abnormal corpus callosum and septum pellucidum, and a hypoplastic anterior pituitary with an absent pituitary stalk [13]. In recent years, *HESX1* has been implicated in septo-optic dysplasia in humans. This rare condition, often referred to as de Morsier syndrome, is characterized by the classic triad of optic nerve hypoplasia, midline neuroradiological abnormalities, such as agenesis of the corpus callosum or absence of the septum pellucidum, and pituitary hypoplasia with variable hypopituitarism. Endocrine defects vary from IGHD to panhypopituitarism. Delayed or precocious puberty, diabetes insipidus and abnormal hypothalamic neuroanatomy or function may be observed [13, 48]. A recessive mutation of the *HESX1* gene has been described in two familial cases of septo-optic dysplasia [13], and some six pedigrees [48]. It should be emphasized, however, that this syndrome is usually sporadic, and that *HESX1* defects are only observed in a minority (less than 5%) of cases, suggesting involvement of other genes.

Rieger syndrome

Pitx2, also known as *Ptx2* or *Rieg*, is a 'bicoid' homeodomain transcription factor that is expressed from the early stages of pituitary development through to adult age [49]. Its gene, localized on chromosome 4 (4q25–q26), spans 18 kb, contains four exons and three introns and encodes a 271 amino-acid protein. At least six different mutations in *PITX2* have been found in patients with Rieger syndrome, most of them affecting the homeodomain [49].

Rieger syndrome is an autosomal dominant disease with variable manifestations including anomalies of the anterior chamber of the eye (coloboma and an increased risk of glaucoma), dental hypoplasia, a protuberant umbilicus, mental retardation and variable degrees of pituitary alteration.

Other syndromes

Various types of malformation syndromes may be found in association with GHD, such as holoprosencephaly, EEC syndrome (ectrodactyly–ectodermal dysplasia–clefting), Fanconi's anaemia or Bloom's syndrome [2]. A rare X-linked recessive form of hypopituitarism, which may range from IGHD to panhypopituitarism, has recently been reported to be due to a gene duplication at Xq26–q27. Affected males may also suffer from varying degrees of mental retardation [50].

Conclusions

The molecular bases of pituitary defects are just beginning to be elucidated in humans. Several types of isolated or combined hypopituitarism have recently been shown to involve different pituitary transcription factors that regulate hormone gene expression, cell differentiation and proliferation during anterior pituitary organogenesis. Anterior pituitary development is indeed dependent upon the normal cascade of a number of transcription factors and signalling molecules. Mutations of these lead to different phenotypes. The identification of the genes underlying these heterogeneous conditions has so far relied on the analysis of mouse mutations, resulting in analogous disease phenotypes. Identification of other pituitary genes and mutations will contribute to a better understanding of both human disease and pituitary development. In large cohorts of patients, such as the GH-deficient population included in KIMS – Pfizer International Metabolic Database – genetic causes of GHD may be increasingly identified in patients with so-called idiopathic GHD. Identification of a given molecular defect can be of direct benefit to the patient, allowing early diagnosis and treatment of associated hormone deficiencies, particularly in cases with a delayed onset. Therefore, where appropriate, consideration should be given to sending DNA samples to research teams working in this field.

References

1. Pfäffle R, Blankenstein O, Wuller S, Heimann K, Heimann G. Idiopathic growth hormone deficiency: a vanishing diagnosis? Horm Res 2000;53 (Suppl 3):1–8
2. Dattani MT, Robinson IC. The molecular basis for developmental disorders of the pituitary gland in man. Clin Genet 2000;57:337–46
3. Woods KA, Clark AJ, Amselem S, Savage MO. Relationship between phenotype and genotype in growth hormone insensitivity syndrome. Acta Paediatr Suppl 1999;88:158–62
4. Procter AM, Phillips JA, 3rd, Cooper DN. The molecular genetics of growth hormone deficiency. Hum Genet 1998;103:255–72
5. Phillips JA 3rd, Cogan JD. Genetic basis of endocrine disease. 6. Molecular basis of familial human growth hormone deficiency. J Clin Endocrinol Metab 1994; 78:11–16
6. Massa GG, Binder G, Oostdijk W, Ranke MB, Wit JM. De novo mutations of the growth hormone gene: an important cause of congenital isolated growth hormone deficiency? Eur J Pediatr 1998;157:272–5
7. Duriez B, Duquesnoy P, Dastot F, Bougneres P, Amselem S, Goossens M. An exon-skipping mutation in the btk gene of a patient with X-linked agammaglobulinemia and isolated growth hormone deficiency. FEBS Lett 1994;346:165–70
8. Wajnrajch MP, Gertner JM, Harbison MD, Chua SC Jr, Leibel RL. Nonsense mutation in the human growth hormone-releasing hormone receptor causes growth failure analogous to the little (lit) mouse. Nat Genet 1996;12:88–90
9. Li S, Crenshaw EB 3rd, Rawson EJ, Simmons DM, Swanson LW, Rosenfeld MG. Dwarf locus mutants lacking three pituitary cell types result from mutations in the POU-domain gene *pit-1*. Nature 1990;347:528–33
10. Radovick S, Nations M, Du Y, Berg LA, Weintraub BD, Wondisford FE. A mutation in the POU-homeodomain of Pit-1 responsible for combined pituitary hormone deficiency. Science 1992;257:1115–18
11. Pfäffle RW, DiMattia GE, Parks JS, Brown MR, Wit JM, Jansen M, Van der Nat H, Van den Brande JL, Rosenfeld MG, Ingraham HA. Mutation of the POU-specific domain of Pit-1 and hypopituitarism without pituitary hypoplasia. Science 1992;257:1118–21
12. Sornson MW, Wu W, Dasen JS, Flynn SE, Norman DJ, O'Connell SM, Gukovsky I, Carriere C, Ryan AK, Miller AP, Zuo L, Gleiberman AS, Andersen B, Beamer WG, Rosenfeld MG. Pituitary lineage determination by the Prophet of Pit-1 homeodomain factor defective in Ames dwarfism. Nature 1996;384:327–33
13. Dattani MT, Martinez-Barbera JP, Thomas PQ, Brickman JM, Gupta R, Martensson IL, Toresson H, Fox M, Wales JK, Hindmarsh PC, Krauss S, Beddington RS, Robinson IC. Mutations in the homeobox gene HESX1/Hesx1 associated with septo-optic dysplasia in human and mouse. Nat Genet 1998;19:125–33
14. Sheng HZ, Zhadanov AB, Mosinger B Jr, Fujii T, Bertuzzi S, Grinberg A, Lee EJ, Huang SP, Mahon KA, Westphal H. Specification of pituitary cell lineages by the LIM homeobox gene Lhx3. Science 1996; 272:1004–7
15. Machinis K, Pantel J, Netchine I, Leger J, Camand OJ, Sobrier ML, Dastot-Le Moal F, Duquesnoy P, Abitbol M, Czernichow P, Amselem S. Syndromic short stature in patients with a germline mutation in the LIM homeobox LHX4. Am J Hum Genet 2001;69:961–8
16. Fofanova OV, Takamura N, Kinoshita E, Yoshimoto M, Tsuji Y, Peterkova VA, Evgrafov OV, Dedov, II, Goncharov NP, Yamashita S. Rarity of PIT1 involvement in children from Russia with combined pituitary hormone deficiency. Am J Med Genet 1998;77:360–5
17. Hendriks-Stegeman BI, Augustijn KD, Bakker B, Holthuizen P, van der Vliet PC, Jansen M. Combined pituitary hormone deficiency caused by compound heterozygosity for two novel mutations in the POU

domain of the Pit1/POU1F1 gene. J Clin Endocrinol Metab 2001;86:1545–50

18. Brown MR, Parks JS, Adess ME, Rich BH, Rosenthal IM, Voss TC, VanderHeyden TC, Hurley DL. Central hypothyroidism reveals compound heterozygous mutations in the Pit-1 gene. Horm Res 1998;49:98–102

19. Vallette-Kasic S, Pellegrini-Bouiller I, Sampieri F, Gunz G, Diaz A, Radovick S, Enjalbert A, Brue T. Combined pituitary hormone deficiency due to the F135C human Pit-1 (pituitary-specific factor 1) gene mutation: functional and structural correlates. Mol Endocrinol 2001;15:411–20

20. Blankenstein O, Muhlenberg R, Kim C, Wuller S, Pfäffle R, Heimann G. A new C-terminal located mutation (V272ter) in the PIT-1 gene manifesting with severe congenital hypothyroidism. Possible functionality of the PIT-1 C-terminus. Horm Res 2001;56:81–6

21. Gat-Yablonski G, Lazar L, Pertzelan A, Phillip M. A novel mutation in PIT-1: phenotypic variability in familial combined pituitary hormone deficiencies. J Pediatr Endocrinol Metab 2002;15:325–30

22. Hashimoto Y, Cisternino M, Cohen LE. A novel nonsense mutation in the Pit-1 gene: evidence for a gene dosage effect. J Clin Endocrinol Metab 2003;88:1241–7

23. Cohen LE, Wondisford FE, Salvatoni A, Maghnie M, Brucker-Davis F, Weintraub BD, Radovick S. A "hot spot" in the Pit-1 gene responsible for combined pituitary hormone deficiency: clinical and molecular correlates. J Clin Endocrinol Metab 1995;80: 679–84

24. Cohen LE, Zanger K, Brue T, Wondisford FE, Radovick S. Defective retinoic acid regulation of the Pit-1 gene enhancer: a novel mechanism of combined pituitary hormone deficiency. Mol Endocrinol 1999;13:476–84

25. de Zegher F, Pernasetti F, Vanhole C, Devlieger H, Van den Berghe G, Martial JA. The prenatal role of thyroid hormone evidenced by fetomaternal Pit-1 deficiency. J Clin Endocrinol Metab 1995;80:3127–30

26. Irie Y, Tatsumi K, Ogawa M, Kamijo T, Preeyasombat C, Suprasongsin C, Amino N. A novel E250X mutation of the PIT1 gene in a patient with combined pituitary hormone deficiency. Endocr J 1995;42:351–4

27. Irie Y, Tatsumi K, Kusuda S, Kawawaki H, Boyages SC, Nose O, Ichiba Y, Katsumata N, Amino N. Screening for PIT1 abnormality by PCR direct sequencing method. Thyroid 1995;5:207–11

28. Ohta K, Nobukuni Y, Mitsubuchi H, Fujimoto S, Matsuo N, Inagaki H, Endo F, Matsuda I. Mutations in the Pit-1 gene in children with combined pituitary hormone deficiency. Biochem Biophys Res Commun 1992;189:851–5

29. Okamoto N, Wada Y, Ida S, Koga R, Ozono K, Chiyo H, Hayashi A, Tatsumi K. Monoallelic expression of normal mRNA in the PIT1 mutation heterozygotes with normal phenotype and biallelic expression in the abnormal phenotype. Hum Mol Genet 1994;3:1565–8

30. Pellegrini-Bouiller I, Bélicar P, Barlier A, Gunz G, Charvet JP, Jaquet P, Brue T, Vialettes B, Enjalbert A. A new mutation of the gene encoding the transcription factor Pit-1 is responsible for combined pituitary hormone deficiency. J Clin Endocrinol Metab 1996; 81:2790–6

31. Pernasetti F, Milner RD, al Ashwal AA, de Zegher F, Chavez VM, Muller M, Martial JA. Pro239Ser: a novel recessive mutation of the Pit-1 gene in seven Middle Eastern children with growth hormone, prolactin, and thyrotropin deficiency. J Clin Endocrinol Metab 1998; 83:2079–83

32. Tatsumi K, Miyai K, Notomi T, Kaibe K, Amino N, Mizuno Y, Kohno H. Cretinism with combined hormone deficiency caused by a mutation in the PIT1 gene. Nat Genet 1992;1:56–8

33. Tatsumi K, Amino N. PIT1 abnormality. Growth Horm IGF Res 1999;9 (Suppl B):18–22

34. Deladoey J, Fluck C, Buyukgebiz A, Kuhlmann BV, Eble A, Hindmarsh PC, Wu W, Mullis PE. "Hot spot" in the PROP1 gene responsible for combined pituitary hormone deficiency. J Clin Endocrinol Metab 1999; 84:1645–50

35. Vallette-Kasic S, Barlier A, Teinturier C, Diaz A, Manavela M, Berthezene F, Bouchard P, Chaussain JL, Brauner R, Pellegrini-Bouiller I, Jaquet P, Enjalbert A, Brue T. PROP1 gene screening in patients with multiple pituitary hormone deficiency reveals two sites of hypermutability and a high incidence of corticotroph deficiency. J Clin Endocrinol Metab 2001;86: 4529–35

36. Duquesnoy P, Roy A, Dastot F, Ghali I, Teinturier C, Netchine I, Cacheux V, Hafez M, Salah N, Chaussain JL, Goossens M, Bougneres P, Amselem S. Human Prop-1: cloning, mapping, genomic structure. Mutations in familial combined pituitary hormone deficiency. FEBS Lett 1998;437:216–20

37. Wu W, Cogan JD, Pfäffle RW, Dasen JS, Frisch H, O'Connell SM, Flynn SE, Brown MR, Mullis PE, Parks JS, Phillips JA 3rd, Rosenfeld MG. Mutations in PROP1 cause familial combined pituitary hormone deficiency. Nat Genet 1998;18:147–9

38. Cogan JD, Wu W, Phillips JA, 3rd, Arnhold IJ, Agapito A, Fofanova OV, Osorio MG, Bircan I, Moreno A, Mendonca BB. The PROP1 2-base pair deletion is a common cause of combined pituitary hormone deficiency. J Clin Endocrinol Metab 1998;83:3346–9

39. Fofanova O, Takamura N, Kinoshita E, Vorontsov A, Vladimirova V, Dedov I, Peterkova V, Yamashita S. MR imaging of the pituitary gland in children and young adults with congenital combined pituitary hormone deficiency associated with PROP1 mutations. Am J Roentgenol 2000;174:555–9

40. Mendonca BB, Osorio MG, Latronico AC, Estefan V, Lo LS, Arnhold IJ. Longitudinal hormonal and pituitary imaging changes in two females with combined pituitary hormone deficiency due to deletion of A301,G302 in the PROP1 gene. J Clin Endocrinol Metab 1999;84:942–5

41. Pernasetti F, Toledo SP, Vasilyev VV, Hayashida CY, Cogan JD, Ferrari C, Lourenco DM, Mellon PL. Impaired adrenocorticotropin–adrenal axis in combined pituitary hormone deficiency caused by a two-base pair deletion (301-302delAG) in the prophet of Pit-1 gene. J Clin Endocrinol Metab 2000;85:390–7

42. Agarwal G, Bhatia V, Cook S, Thomas PQ. Adrenocorticotropin deficiency in combined pituitary hormone deficiency patients homozygous for a novel PROP1 deletion. J Clin Endocrinol Metab 2000;85:4556–61

43. Fluck C, Deladoey J, Rutishauser K, Eble A, Marti U, Wu W, Mullis PE. Phenotypic variability in familial combined pituitary hormone deficiency caused by a PROP1 gene mutation resulting in the substitution of Arg->Cys at codon 120 (R120C). J Clin Endocrinol Metab 1998;83:3727–34

44. Osorio MG, Kopp P, Marui S, Latronico AC, Mendonca BB, Arnhold IJ. Combined pituitary hormone deficiency caused by a novel mutation of a highly conserved residue (F88S) in the homeodomain of PROP-1. J Clin Endocrinol Metab 2000;85:2779–85

45. Takamura N, Fofanova OV, Kinoshita E, Yamashita S. Gene analysis of PROP1 in dwarfism with combined pituitary hormone deficiency. Growth Horm IGF Res 1999;9 (Suppl B):12–17

46. Teinturier C, Vallette S, Adamsbaum C, Bendaoud M, Brue T, Bougneres PF. Pseudotumor of the pituitary due to PROP-1 deletion. J Pediatr Endocrinol Metab 2002;15:95–101

47. Netchine I, Sobrier ML, Krude H, Schnabel D, Maghnie M, Marcos E, Duriez B, Cacheux V, Moers A, Goossens M, Gruters A, Amselem S. Mutations in LHX3 result in a new syndrome revealed by combined pituitary hormone deficiency. Nat Genet 2000;25:182–6

48. Thomas PQ, Dattani MT, Brickman JM, McNay D, Warne G, Zacharin M, Cameron F, Hurst J, Woods K, Dunger D, Stanhope R, Forrest S, Robinson IC, Beddington RS. Heterozygous HESX1 mutations associated with isolated congenital pituitary hypoplasia and septo-optic dysplasia. Hum Mol Genet 2001; 10:39–45

49. Semina EV, Reiter R, Leysens NJ, Alward WL, Small KW, Datson NA, Siegel-Bartelt J, Bierke-Nelson D, Bitoun P, Zabel BU, Carey JC, Murray JC. Cloning and characterization of a novel bicoid-related homeobox transcription factor gene, RIEG, involved in Rieger syndrome. Nat Genet 1996;14:392–9

50. Solomon NM, Nouri S, Warne GL, Lagerstrom-Fermer M, Forrest SM, Thomas PQ. Increased gene dosage at Xq26-q27 is associated with X-linked hypopituitarism. Genomics 2002;79:553–9

9 Biochemical diagnosis of growth hormone deficiency in adults

Felipe F Casanueva[1], Manuel Pombo[2], Alfonso Leal[4], Vera Popovic[5] and Carlos Dieguez[3]

[1]Department of Medicine, Endocrine Section, [2]Department of Paediatrics and [3]Department of Physiology, School of Medicine and Complejo Hospitalario Universitario de Santiago, University of Santiago de Compostela, Santiago de Compostela, Spain; [4]Division of Endocrinology, Hospital Virgen del Rocio, Seville, Spain; [5]Institute of Endocrinology, University Clinical Centre, Belgrade, Serbia and Montenegro

Summary

Although growth hormone deficiency (GHD) in adults is now recognized as a distinct clinical syndrome associated with increased morbidity and mortality, its diagnosis is often problematic. This is due to the fact that none of the many signs and symptoms exhibited by adults with GHD are pathognomonic of the disease, making biochemical diagnosis essential. This is usually carried out by assessing growth hormone (GH) secretory capacity after stimulation by a variety of agents. A widely used method for assessing GH secretion is the insulin tolerance test (ITT), which has been considered, until now, the 'gold standard'. In common with other tests, however, the ITT has certain disadvantages. This has led to the development of the GH-releasing hormone (GHRH)–arginine test and, more recently, the GHRH–GH-releasing peptide-6 (GHRP-6) test, which have been shown to be useful in discriminating between GH-sufficient and GH-deficient adults. An alternative approach has been the consideration of additional pituitary hormone deficiencies plus low IGF-I levels as a probabilistic diagnostic procedure. This chapter critically assesses the ITT, GHRH–arginine and GHRH–GHRP-6 tests, and outlines the features required for the ideal biochemical test for diagnosis of GHD in adults. In addition, the probabilistic approach to diagnosis will be assessed.

Introduction

In the late 1980s, Salomon *et al.* [1] and Jørgensen *et al.* [2] demonstrated unambiguously that growth hormone deficiency (GHD) in adults is a disease. Following this, many epidemiological studies and placebo-controlled trials have demonstrated that GHD is associated with increased morbidity and mortality, and that growth hormone (GH) replacement therapy is beneficial [3–7].

In children, GHD is associated with clear auxological signs – reduced growth velocity and short stature. In GH-deficient adults, however, the signs and symptoms of the disease are less clear and none is pathognomonic. In addition, many of the signs and symptoms are common in other situations, for example in normal ageing. This has generated an ongoing search for clear-cut biochemical criteria for diagnosing GHD in adults, and the development and validation of a variety of different stimulation tests to assess GH reserve [8].

For pituitary hormones other than GH and adrenocorticotrophin (ACTH), diagnosis of excessive or defective secretion is commonly established by analysing the levels of that hormone in a basal state relative to the hormone levels of the target gland or peripheral tissue. The logical test for GHD would therefore be the measurement of serum levels of GH in relation to insulin-like growth factor I (IGF-I), which is the major peripheral hormone of the somatotroph axis. However, GH is secreted in a pulsatile manner, which renders assessment of random serum GH concentrations essentially worthless for diagnosis of GHD [9, 10]. Likewise, regular sampling of GH throughout the day, or the measurement of integrated 24-hour urinary GH concentrations, have been shown to be of little value [11–13]. Confounding the interpretation of peripheral GH measurements is the normal decline in GH levels that occurs with ageing or with increased adiposity [14]. As adults with suspected GHD are usually over 40 years of age (mean age of adults with GHD in KIMS – Pfizer International Metabolic Database – is 44–45 years) and have a body mass index (BMI) generally higher than that of the general population, GH values need to be adjusted for age and BMI [15]. IGF-I levels are also subject to an age-related decline [14, 16]; moreover, most studies have demonstrated that about one-third of patients with GHD, diagnosed by GH stimulation tests, have IGF-I levels in the normal gender- and age-adjusted range [15–18]. This problem is compounded by the incomplete availability of normative IGF-I data, and analytical difficulties that make comparison between different laboratories difficult [16]. Furthermore, measurement of static values of GH, IGF-I or IGF-binding proteins are considered unsuitable for reliable diagnosis, as values from patients with adult-onset GHD and healthy individuals clearly overlap [13].

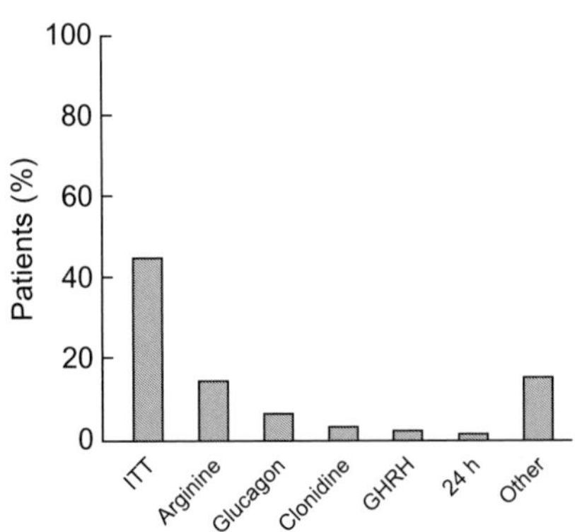

Figure 1. *Proportion of patients in the KIMS pharmacoepidemiological database diagnosed by different GH-stimulation tests. The column labelled 'Other' includes less frequently used tests such as, L-dopa, GH-releasing hormone (GHRH)–arginine, IGF-I values etc. ITT, insulin tolerance test.*

Diagnostic methods

Based on the above, and in accordance with the consensus published by the Growth Hormone Research Society, it is commonly assumed that, within an appropriate clinical context, diagnosis of GHD must be biochemically established by a provocative test of GH secretory reserve [18]. In the past decades, various stimuli, alone or in combination, have been proposed for use in GH-stimulation tests, including insulin (the insulin tolerance test [ITT]), GH-releasing hormone (GHRH), glucagon, arginine, GH secretagogues, free fatty acid depression, clonidine, L-dopa, pyridostigmine, physical exercise and increased temperature [19–27]. Some of these stimuli have been widely used in the clinical setting, as reflected in KIMS. Figure 1 shows the provocative tests of GH reserve used by clinicians from 28 countries worldwide, in 8500 GH-deficient patients currently in KIMS. Some of these tests, such as the L-dopa test, were more popular in the past than now, and some, such as exercise or pyridostigmine plus GHRH, still await stringent validation. Recent reports indicate that some previous tests used in adults, for example GHRH and clonidine [26–28], are of little or no diagnostic value. Arginine and glucagon alone may be useful, but are less discriminatory than the ITT [21, 28].

Today, the three most extensively studied and validated tests are insulin-induced hypoglycaemia (the ITT), the combined administration of GHRH and arginine (GHRH–arginine) and the combined administration of GHRH and the GH secretagogue, GH-releasing peptide-6 (GHRH–GHRP-6). These tests are considered in detail in this chapter. As the likelihood of GHD increases with increasing numbers of pituitary hormone deficiencies, it has been suggested that a probabilistic diagnosis of GHD in adulthood can be made on the basis of low IGF-I levels plus this clinical information [29]. This approach will also be evaluated.

The ITT

Diagnosis of impaired GH release has generally depended on the demonstration that a significant rise in peripheral GH levels does not occur after one or more GH-provoking stimuli [30]. The most widely used GH-stimulation test is the ITT, in which GH secretion is provoked by marked insulin-induced hypoglycaemia (Fig. 2). Until now it has been considered the 'gold standard' and the test of choice for evaluating adults with suspected GHD [31]. Using the ITT, Hoffman *et al.* [13] found that there was clear separation between normal individuals (GH peak above 5 µg/L) (µg/L is equal to ng/ml) and patients with multiple pituitary hormone deficiencies and clinical signs and symptoms of GHD, who had a GH peak less than 3 µg/L (Fig. 3). Although this finding was not replicated by other groups [32], an ITT-mediated GH peak equal to or less than 3 µg/L is widely considered to be the cut off for biochemical diagnosis of GHD in adults. However, as the Growth Hormone Research Society stated [18], the cut-off values above were defined before 1995 using polyclonal antibody-based competitive radioimmunoassays. Today all assay manufacturers use immunoradiometric two-site monoclonal antibody-based assays, which provide values roughly 50% of those measured by classic radioimmunoassays. Therefore, no current international diagnostic cut-off value exists for the ITT, and each research group needs to establish its own reference values.

A disadvantage of the ITT is that normative control values are based mostly on young and lean subjects, and there is little experience of its use in individuals over 60 years of age. The normative

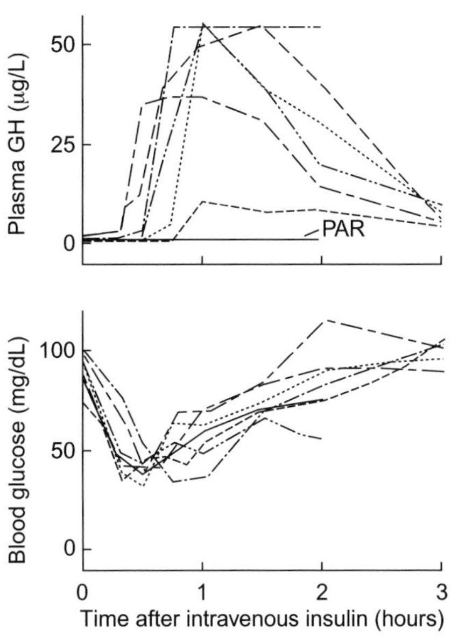

Figure 2. *Plasma levels of GH and blood glucose after intravenous administration of insulin. PAR, hypophysectomized patient. This work, published in 1963, is probably the first dynamic test of GH secretion assessed by radioimmunoassay. Reproduced from [19] with permission.*

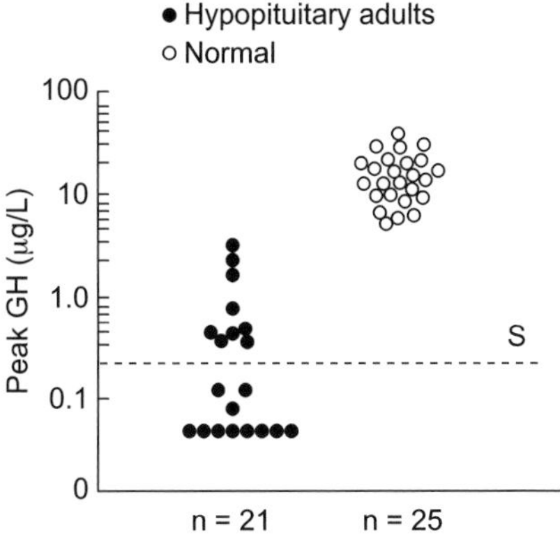

Figure 3. *The insulin tolerance test discriminates well between normal individuals and those with multiple pituitary hormone deficiencies and clinical signs and symptoms of GHD. S, assay sensitivity (0.2 µg/L). Adapted from [13] with permission from Elsevier.*

values are therefore not very representative of those individuals likely to be suspected of having GHD. Additionally, it has a low degree of reproducibility [32–36]. Although most provocative tests of GH reserve perform poorly in terms of individual reproducibility, the ITT in particular shows a high number of false positives (15%) with an intra-individual coefficient of variation of 41% for men and 104% for women [35–37]. However, it should be noted that these values are based on measurements in small numbers of individuals. Furthermore, the ITT must be performed by experienced personnel under careful medical supervision, and is contraindicated in some common clinical conditions, such as in patients with uncontrolled seizure disorders or a history of ischaemic heart disease. Having said that, a detailed audit of the ITT, conducted in a large cohort of patients, concluded that the test was a safe procedure when performed in an experienced endocrine unit under adequate supervision [33].

Despite the drawbacks mentioned above, the ITT is the most commonly used stimulation test, possibly because it was the first test to be used in the history of clinical endocrinology [19] and is capable of exploring the prolactin and ACTH reserve concomitantly with GH. Currently, the use of the ITT in the USA, as reflected in the Hypopituitary Control and Complications Study, is just 11% of the total tests employed [29]. In European practice, as reflected in KIMS, the use of the ITT has progressively declined from 53% in 1994 to 28% in 2002. Although its use is declining due to the introduction of other tests (see below), it is likely that the ITT will continue as an important tool for assessing pituitary function.

The GHRH–arginine test

The GHRH–arginine test has been validated by Ghigo *et al.* [27]. In normal individuals, GHRH alone produces random GH responses, whereas prior administration of pyridostigmine, an indirect cholinergic agonist, which presumably inhibits endogenous somatostatin release, transforms GHRH into a potent and reproducible GH stimulus [20]. Arginine probably acts by a similar mechanism to inhibit endogenous somatostatin tone, allowing GHRH to determine somatotroph reserve with very little variability. In this way, administration of an arginine infusion followed by GHRH yields a reliable and potent GH peak [37, 38].

GHRH–arginine is one of the most potent and reproducible GH stimuli for evaluating the releasable pituitary GH pool. It has the advantage that, in contrast to the ITT, it is not affected by age [39]; however, it is affected by adiposity [40], although this is not as marked as for the ITT. The cut-off value for severe GHD in this test is 9 μg/L, which was established with modern two-site immunoradiometric assays. The GHRH–arginine test has been shown to be at least as sensitive as the ITT in diagnosing GHD in adults, but with less side-effects and better specificity, presenting a low degree of false positives (less than 6.6%) (Fig. 4) [39]. As with the ITT, the GHRH–arginine test can be used to explore the whole hypothalamus–pituitary–somatotroph unit, and hypothalamic damage, such as that seen in patients who have received cranial irradiation for leukaemia or brain tumours, can be detected after an appropriate time interval [41]. This test has the advantage that both GHRH and arginine are widely available for use and that it is practically devoid of contraindications.

The GHRH–GHRP-6 test

In the past few years, the combined administration of GHRH plus GHRP-6 has been investigated by different groups as a GH-stimulation test [42–45]. GHRP-6 is an artificial hexapeptide [46] that activates a hypothalamic and pituitary receptor, the natural ligand of which is ghrelin. Combined administration of GHRP-6 and GHRH is one of the most potent GH releasers known to date [47], with excellent reproducibility, absence of side-effects and no known contraindications [48].

The GHRH–GHRP-6 test has been extensively validated in normal subjects. Unlike the ITT, the GHRH–GHRP-6-induced GH peak is not affected by metabolic variables, such as a previous meal [49], and is not affected by gender or gonadal

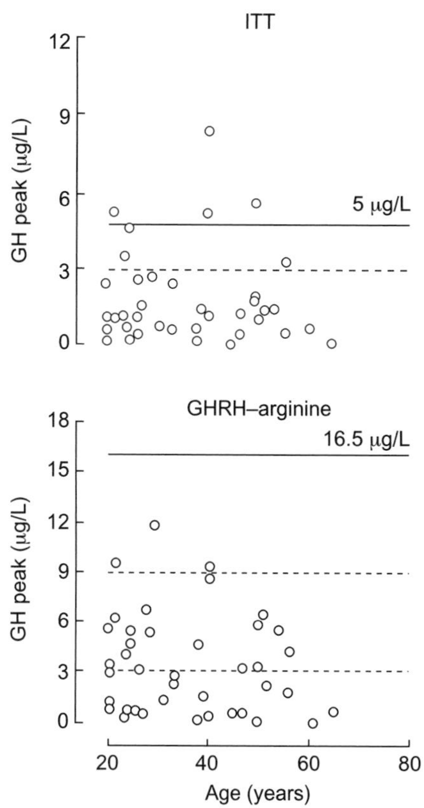

Figure 4. *Peak GH response to an insulin tolerance test (ITT) compared with the peak GH response to GH-releasing hormone–arginine (GHRH–arginine) in the same adult patients with GHD (n = 40). The limits for normality are 5 µg/L and 16.5 µg/L, and the limits for GHD are 3 µg/L and 9 µg/L for the ITT and GHRH–arginine test, respectively. Adapted from [39] with permission. Copyright 1998, The Endocrine Society.*

status [50], thyroid status [51], diabetes mellitus [52], previous treatment with GH, or time of day when the test is performed [49]. The combined GHRH–GHRP-6 test also assesses the whole hypothalamus–pituitary–somatotroph unit [53]. The fact that this test is not affected by age [54] and scarcely affected by adiposity (only when the BMI is over 35) [55] makes it very useful for the type of patient with suspected GHD.

The GHRH–GHRP-6 test has been shown to be highly effective in discriminating between normal and GH-deficient patients [48]. Recently, we have shown that the elicited GH peak is independent of the baseline GH level, confirming that the test is robust and potent, and that a 30-minute sample provides similar diagnostic information to the peak sample [56]. This can reduce the average provocative test from a 150-minute six-sample test to a 30-minute single-sample one, reducing time and cost and increasing convenience.

The GHRH–GHRP-6 test was the first to be validated by the receiver operating characteristic (ROC) curve analysis method [57, 58], which assessed its ability to discriminate between normal and impaired cases, and which indicated its suitability as a GH-stimulation test [48]. In the ROC curve analysis the value of 15 µg/L provided the best pairing of sensitivity and specificity using modern immunoradiometric assays, and was selected as the cut-off for this test. In the clinical setting, a test that is not 100% accurate with regard to sensitivity is unacceptable for clinicians and patients, and a test that is not 100% accurate with regard to specificity is questionable for health administrators. Therefore, it was suggested for operational purposes to use the GHRH–GHRP-6 test with a cut-off point for normality of greater than or equal to 20 µg/L, and a cut-off point of 10 µg/L or less for diagnosing GHD. This provides 100% sensitivity and 100% specificity (Fig. 5). The diagnosis of GHD in individuals with a GHRH–GHRP-6-induced peak between 11 and 19 µg/L should be considered uncertain, and the final diagnosis based either on a second stimulation test [59], or according to Bayes' theorem [60]. Briefly, Bayes' theorem states that if you perform any test in a population suspected of harbouring a given disease, the obtained values are more meaningful than if you perform it in a healthy population. Translated to this example, an uncertain value in a subject suspected on clinical grounds of having GHD can be considered a positive test. This two-step method of analysis with a 'grey zone' is a new approach to diagnosis, and a way of circumventing the inherent imprecision of any test or biochemical parameter that lacks clear biological signs on which to base the appropriate cut-offs for diagnosis. In clinical practice, if there is a clear limit above which GH secretion can be

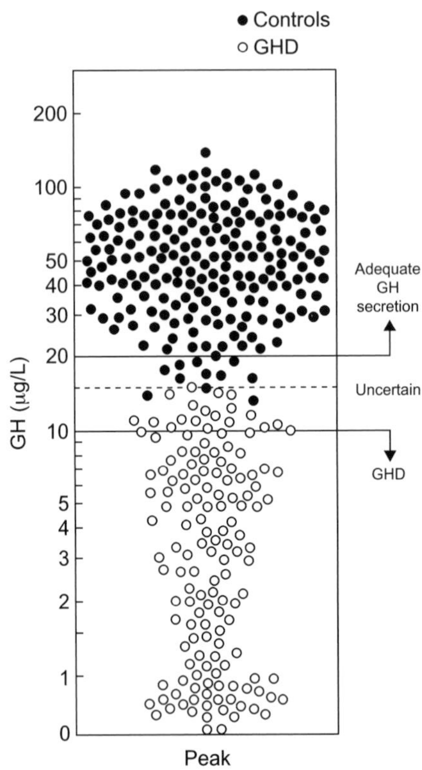

Figure 5. *Individual GH peaks obtained in 203 control individuals and 146 GH-deficient patients after administration of GH-releasing hormone–GH-releasing peptide-6. The cut-off point for the test is 15 μg/L. For operational purposes, values over 20 μg/L are considered normal and lower than 10 μg/L GH deficient. In patients with uncertain values (11–19 μg/L) diagnosis should be confirmed using clinical criteria, such as additional pituitary hormone deficiencies, or a second test.*

considered normal, and a similarly robust limit for GHD, then most individuals can be confidently assigned to the correct diagnostic group. No false positives have been detected with this test, which has a coefficient of variation lower than 25% [61]. The drawback of the GHRH–GHRP-6 test is that it only provides information about organic lesions, and is probably not useful for functional alterations, such as those commonly seen in children with GHD. In addition, this test is more expensive than the ITT because GHRP-6 is not widely available.

Importance of using appropriate cut-off values

It should be remembered that all biochemical methods of diagnosis are dependent not only on the stimulation test used but also on the subsequent GH assay method [62]. For example, the normally accepted cut-off for the ITT was based on data generated before 1995 using the classic polyclonal antibody-based competitive radioimmunoassay. Current assays, however, are immunoradiometric and based on a two-site methodology with monoclonal antibodies. These assays read approximately 50% lower as they are selective for the 22 kDa GH molecule [63]. Similarly, the classic radioimmunoassays used an International Reference Preparation (IRP), the pituitary-derived World Health Organization (WHO) IRP 80/505 (1 mg GH = 2.6 U), while modern assays have changed to recombinant human GH, WHO IRP 88/624 (1 mg GH = 3.0 U) [18, 63]. This emphasizes the need for selecting the appropriate cut-off point for different tests and assays and why GH values published before 1995 may need to be adapted considerably to current methodology until new international criteria can be adopted for the diagnosis of GHD. Currently there is no good IGF-I reference preparation.

The search for the perfect GH-stimulation test

The GHRH–arginine and GHRH–GHRP-6 tests, although having certain advantages over the ITT and other classic tests, need to be more extensively validated by different research groups. In the validation of a test, stringent criteria for selection of the cohort and thorough statistical analysis must be applied, but are lacking for most tests. One of the most common errors is to validate the test in GH-deficient patients who have been diagnosed by the same test that is under scrutiny. To prevent circular validation, the diagnosis of such patients needs to be carried out using clinical information and a different GH-stimulation test. Similarly, reproducibility must be evaluated in normal control subjects and never in patients. GH-deficient patients, by definition, have less GH reserve and provide more homogeneous responses. The conditions for validation are detailed in Table 1.

Table 1. Validation of a GH-stimulation test.

- The test needs to be potent and reproducible
- Reproducibility must be assessed in normal subjects
- The influence of gender, age and adiposity on the test should be validated in control subjects
- The effectiveness of the test needs to be assessed in controls and patients and evaluated by receiver operating characteristic (ROC) curve analysis
- The cut-off point for the test should be established by ROC curve analysis and not by SD calculations
- The cut-off point is the value which in ROC analysis provides the best pairing of sensitivity and specificity

The ideal, or 'gold standard', test needs to provide a good pairing of sensitivity and specificity indices in the diagnostic cut-off point used, and to be able to separate controls from patients. The diagnostic capability and the absence of false positives are of foremost importance. In addition, the test should be able to assess the whole hypothalamus–stalk–pituitary–somatotroph unit and, for use in adults, should not be unduly affected by age and adiposity (Table 2).

Probabilistic diagnosis of GHD

Ten years ago, Toogood *et al.* [64] assessed pituitary hormone deficiencies in a group of patients with pituitary disease who had a GH response lower than 20 mU/L (approximately 9.2 µg/L according to the assay used) in an ITT. These patients were divided into those with isolated GHD (GHD_0), or GHD plus one (GHD_1), two (GHD_2) or three (GHD_3) additional hormone deficiencies (gonadotrophins, ACTH and thyrotrophin in any combination). They found that the degree of GHD varied according to the degree of hypopituitarism (Fig. 6); the greater the number of pituitary hormone deficits, the more severe the GHD. In fact, 91% of patients with GHD_2 and GHD_3 had a GH peak lower than 2.3 µg/L. These results have been replicated by other groups [11, 17, 65]. Based on these findings, Hartman and co-workers [29] performed a similar analysis on the database of the Hypopituitary Control and Complications Study, using a peak GH level of 2.5 µg/L as the cut-off point for GHD after any type of GH-stimulation test. When they analysed patients according to the number of additional pituitary hormone deficits (including antidiuretic hormone deficiency, to give four possible additional deficiencies [GHD_4]), they found that the percentage of patients with GHD in each group was: GHD_0, 41%; GHD_1, 67%; GHD_2, 83%; GHD_3, 96% and GHD_4, 99%. On the other hand, an IGF-I value of –3 SD also predicted GHD in 96% of cases. As three or four additional pituitary hormone deficits and an IGF-I level lower than –3 SD had a positive predictive value of 95%, the authors proposed that GHD in these patients can be diagnosed without using a GH-stimulation test [29]. This procedure has a sensitivity of 95–99% and a low specificity of

Table 2. Criteria for an ideal GH-stimulation test.

- Safe, no side-effects
- Reproducible
- Able to assess the whole axis, that is hypothalamus, stalk and pituitary
- Not affected by adiposity
- Not affected by age
- Not affected by gonadal factors (gender, menstrual cycle, puberty, menopause, hypogonadism)
- Not affected by thyroid or glucocorticoid status
- Not affected by metabolic variables
- Provide similar results with different assays
- Convenient, no need for medical supervision
- Economical

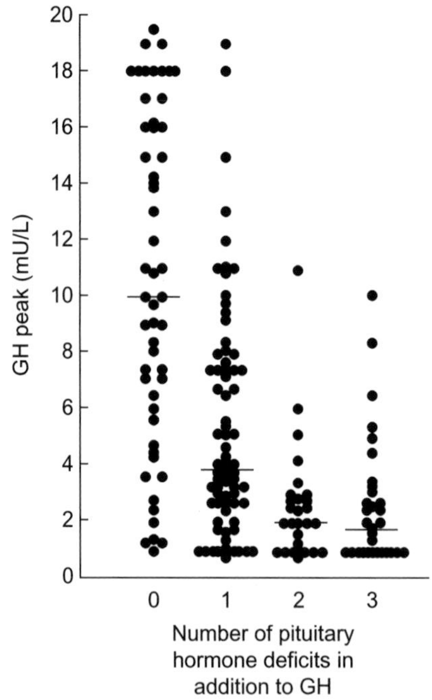

Figure 6. *Peak GH concentrations in standard GH-stimulation tests according to the number of additional pituitary hormone deficiencies. The horizontal lines represent median values. Reproduced from [64] with permission from Blackwell Publishing.*

16–33%, and has the advantage of eliminating dynamic testing of GH secretion, although identification of some additional deficits, such as ACTH, also requires a fully validated dynamic test.

As the 5% error rate based on IGF-I levels together with evidence of multiple pituitary hormone deficiency is identical to the error inherent in most dynamic tests of GH reserve, probabilistic diagnosis may be useful in some cases of suspected GHD, and in the absence of a reliable provocative test of GH secretion.

Conclusions

Although the probabilistic approach will help in the clinical diagnosis of patients with suspected GHD, biochemical tests remain mandatory [66]. Both patients and health administrators require precise biochemical diagnosis before initiation of expensive, long-term and inconvenient treatment. In addition, a biochemically based discipline, such as endocrinology, should not accept the fact that GH is the only hormone deficiency that does not have stringent biochemical cut-off points for its diagnosis. Only through further research will the biochemical diagnosis of GHD be refined.

Acknowledgements

The technical collaboration of Ms Mary Lage is gratefully acknowledged. The results presented were supported by research grants from the Fondo de Investigación Sanitaria and the Instituto de Salud Carlos III, Ministerio de Sanidad y Consumo, Red de Grupos RGTO (G03/028), Red de Centros RCMN (C03/08), Secretaría Xeral de Investigación e Desenvolvemento (PGIDIT02BTF91801PR), Xunta de Galicia, and the Ministerio Español de Ciencia y Tecnología.

References

1. Salomon F, Cuneo RC, Hesp R, Sönksen PH. The effects of treatment with recombinant human growth hormone on body composition and metabolism in adults with growth hormone deficiency. N Engl J Med 1989; 321:1797–803

2. Jørgensen JO, Pedersen SA, Thuesen L, Jørgensen J, Ingemann-Hansen T, Skakkebæk NE, Christiansen JS. Beneficial effects of growth hormone treatment in GH-deficient adults. Lancet 1989;1:1221–5

3. Cuneo RC, Salomon F, Wiles CM, Hesp R, Sönksen PH. Growth hormone treatment in growth hormone-deficient adults. II. Effects on exercise performance. J Appl Physiol 1991;70:695–700

4. Verhelst J, Abs R. Long-term growth hormone replacement therapy in hypopituitary adults. Drugs 2002;62:2399–412

5. Rosén T, Bengtsson B-Å. Premature mortality due to cardiovascular disease in hypopituitarism. Lancet 1990;336:285–8

6. Amato G, Carella C, Fazio S, La Montagna G, Cittadini A, Sabatini D, Marciano-Mone C, Sacca L, Bellastella A. Body composition, bone metabolism, and heart structure and function in growth hormone (GH)-deficient adults before and after GH replacement

therapy at low doses. J Clin Endocrinol Metab 1993; 77:1671–6

7. de Boer H, Blok GJ, Van der Veen EA. Clinical aspects of growth hormone deficiency in adults. Endocr Rev 1995;16:63–86

8. Jørgensen JO, Christiansen JS. Testing for growth hormone deficiency in adults – how to respond? Clin Endocrinol (Oxf) 2003;58:18–19

9. Rosenfeld RG. Is growth hormone deficiency a viable diagnosis? J Clin Endocrinol Metab 1997;82:349–51

10. Casanueva FF. Diagnosis of growth hormone deficiency in adulthood. Eur J Endocrinol 1996;135:168–70

11. Weissberger AJ, Verikiou K, Sönksen PH. Diagnosis of growth hormone deficiency in adults. Lancet 1994; 344:483

12. Shalet SM, Toogood A, Rahim A, Brennan BM. The diagnosis of growth hormone deficiency in children and adults. Endocr Rev 1998;19:203–23

13. Hoffman DM, Nguyen TV, O'Sullivan AJ, Baxter RC, Ho KK. Diagnosis of growth hormone deficiency in adults. Lancet 1994;344:482–3

14. Rudman D, Kutner MH, Rogers CM, Lubin MF, Fleming GA, Bain RP. Impaired growth hormone secretion in the adult population: relation to age and adiposity. J Clin Invest 1981;67:1361–9

15. Molitch ME. Diagnosis of GH deficiency in adults – how good do the criteria need to be? J Clin Endocrinol Metab 2002;87:473–6

16. Clemmons DR. Commercial assays available for insulin-like growth factor I and their use in diagnosing growth hormone deficiency. Horm Res 2001; 55 (Suppl 2):73–9

17. Bates AS, Evans AJ, Jones P, Clayton RN. Assessment of GH status in adults with GH deficiency using serum growth hormone, serum insulin-like growth factor-I and urinary growth hormone excretion. Clin Endocrinol (Oxf) 1995;42:425–30

18. Consensus guidelines for the diagnosis and treatment of adults with growth hormone (GH) deficiency: summary statement of the Growth Hormone Research Society Workshop on Adult Growth Hormone Deficiency. J Clin Endocrinol Metab 1998;83:379–81

19. Roth J, Glick SM, Yalow RS, Berson SA. Hypoglycemia: a potent stimulus to secretion of growth hormone. Science 1963;140:987–8

20. Andersen M, Hansen TB, Stoving RK, Bertelsen J, Hangaard J, Petersen PH, Hagen C. The pyridostigmine-growth hormone releasing hormone test in adults. The reference interval and a comparison with the insulin tolerance test. Endocrinol Metab 1996;3:197–206

21. Baum HB, Biller BM, Katznelson L, Oppenheim DS, Clemmons DR, Cannistraro KB, Schoenfeld DA, Best SA, Klibanski A. Assessment of growth hormone (GH) secretion in men with adult-onset GH deficiency compared with that in normal men – a clinical research center study. J Clin Endocrinol Metab 1996;81:84–92

22. Reiter EO, Martha PM, Jr. Pharmacological testing of growth hormone secretion. Horm Res 1990;33:121–7

23. de Boer H, Blok GJ, Popp-Snijders C, van der Veen EA. Diagnosis of growth hormone deficiency in adults. Lancet 1994;343:1645–6

24. Fisker S, Jørgensen JO, Ørskov H, Christiansen JS. L-arginine and insulin-tolerance tests in the diagnosis of adult growth hormone deficiency: influence of confounding factors. Clin Endocrinol (Oxf) 1998;48:109–15

25. Cordido F, Dieguez C, Casanueva FF. Effect of central cholinergic neurotransmission enhancement by pyridostigmine on the growth hormone secretion elicited by clonidine, arginine, or hypoglycemia in normal and obese subjects. J Clin Endocrinol Metab 1990; 70:1361–70

26. Vierhapper H, Nowotny P, Czech T, Bieglmayer C, Raber W, Waldhausl W. How (not) to diagnose growth hormone deficiency in adults: stimulated serum concentrations of growth hormone in healthy subjects and in patients with pituitary macroadenomas. Metabolism 1997;46:680–3

27. Ghigo E, Aimaretti G, Gianotti L, Bellone J, Arvat E, Camanni F. New approach to the diagnosis of growth hormone deficiency in adults. Eur J Endocrinol 1996;134:352–6

28. Rahim A, Toogood AA, Shalet SM. The assessment of growth hormone status in normal young adult males using a variety of provocative agents. Clin Endocrinol (Oxf) 1996;45:557–62

29. Hartman ML, Crowe BJ, Biller BM, Ho KK, Clemmons DR, Chipman JJ. Which patients do not require a GH stimulation test for the diagnosis of adult GH deficiency? J Clin Endocrinol Metab 2002; 87:477–85

30. Daughaday WH. Growth hormone assay in acromegaly, gigantism, dwarfism and hypopituitarism. Postgrad Med 1969;46:84–91

31. Lange M, Svendsen OL, Skakkebæk NE, Müller J, Juul A, Schmiegelow M, Feldt-Rasmussen U. An audit of the insulin-tolerance test in 255 patients with pituitary disease. Eur J Endocrinol 2002;147:41–7

32. Hoeck HC, Vestergaard P, Jakobsen PE, Laurberg P. Test of growth hormone secretion in adults: poor reproducibility of the insulin tolerance test. Eur J Endocrinol 1995;133:305–12

33. Jones SL, Trainer PJ, Perry L, Wass JA, Bessser GM, Grossman A. An audit of the insulin tolerance test in adult subjects in an acute investigation unit over one year. Clin Endocrinol (Oxf) 1994;41:123–8

34. Greenwood FC, Landon J, Stamp TC. The plasma sugar, free fatty acid, cortisol, and growth hormone response to insulin. I. In control subjects. J Clin Invest 1966; 45:429–36

35. Vestergaard P, Hoeck HC, Jakobsen PE, Laurberg P. Reproducibility of growth hormone and cortisol responses to the insulin tolerance test and the short ACTH test in normal adults. Horm Metab Res 1997; 29:106–10

36. Hoeck HC, Jakobsen PE, Vestergaard P, Falhof J, Laurberg P. Differences in reproducibility and peak growth hormone responses to repeated testing with various stimulators in healthy adults. Growth Horm IGF Res 1999;9:18–24

37. Ghigo E, Goffi S, Nicolosi M, Arvat E, Valente F, Mazza E, Ghigo MC, Camanni F. Growth hormone (GH) responsiveness to combined administration of arginine and GH-releasing hormone does not vary with age in man. J Clin Endocrinol Metab 1990;71:1481–5

38. Valetto MR, Bellone J, Baffoni C, Savio P, Aimaretti G, Gianotti L, Arvat E, Camanni F, Ghigo E. Reproducibility of the growth hormone response to stimulation with growth hormone-releasing hormone plus arginine during lifespan. Eur J Endocrinol 1996;135:568–72

39. Aimaretti G, Corneli G, Razzore P, Bellone S, Baffoni C, Arvat E, Camanni F, Ghigo E. Comparison between insulin-induced hypoglycemia and growth hormone (GH)-releasing hormone + arginine as provocative tests for the diagnosis of GH deficiency in adults. J Clin Endocrinol Metab 1998;83:1615–8

40. Popovic V, Pekic S, Doknic M, Micic D, Damjanovic S, Aimaretti G, Corneli G, Ghigo E, Dieguez C, Casanueva FF. The effectiveness of arginine + GHRH test compared with GHRH + GHRP-6 test in diagnosing growth hormone deficiency in adults. Clin Endocrinol (Oxf) 2003;59:251–7

41. Darzy KH, Aimaretti G, Wieringa G, Gattamaneni HR, Ghigo E, Shalet SM. The usefulness of the combined growth hormone (GH)-releasing hormone and arginine stimulation test in the diagnosis of radiation-induced GH deficiency is dependent on the post-irradiation time interval. J Clin Endocrinol Metab 2003;88:95–102

42. Casanueva FF, Dieguez C. Growth hormone secretagogues: physiological role and clinical utility. Trends Endocrinol Metab 1999;10:30–8

43. Mahajan T, Lightman SL. A simple test for growth hormone deficiency in adults. J Clin Endocrinol Metab 2000;85:1473–6

44. Giustina A, Bussi AR, Deghenghi R, Imbimbo B, Licini M, Poiesi C, Wehrenberg WB. Comparison of the effects of growth hormone-releasing hormone and hexarelin, a novel growth hormone-releasing peptide-6 analog, on growth hormone secretion in humans with or without glucocorticoid excess. J Endocrinol 1995; 146:227–32

45. Petersenn S, Jung R, Beil FU. Diagnosis of growth hormone deficiency in adults by testing with GHRP-6 alone or in combination with GHRH: comparison with the insulin tolerance test. Eur J Endocrinol 2002; 146:667–72

46. Bowers CY, Sartor AO, Reynolds GA, Badger TM. On the actions of the growth hormone-releasing hexapeptide, GHRP. Endocrinology 1991;128:2027–35

47. Bowers CY, Reynolds GA, Durham D, Barrera CM, Pezzoli SS, Thorner MO. Growth hormone (GH)-releasing peptide stimulates GH release in normal men and acts synergistically with GH-releasing hormone. J Clin Endocrinol Metab 1990;70:975–82

48. Popovic V, Leal A, Micic D, Koppeschaar HP, Torres E, Paramo C, Obradovic S, Dieguez C, Casanueva FF. GH-releasing hormone and GH-releasing peptide-6 for diagnostic testing in GH-deficient adults. Lancet 2000; 356:1137–42

49. Popovic V, Pekic S, Simic M, Damjanovic S, Micic D, Dieguez C, Casanueva FF. Physical activity or food intake prior to testing did not affect the reproducibility of GH secretion elicited by GH releasing hormone plus GH-releasing hexapeptide in normal adult subjects. Clin Endocrinol (Oxf) 2002;56:89–94

50. Peñalva A, Pombo M, Carballo A, Barreiro J, Casanueva FF, Dieguez C. Influence of sex, age and adrenergic pathways on the growth hormone response to GHRP-6. Clin Endocrinol (Oxf) 1993;38:87–91

51. Ramos-Dias JC, Pimentel-Filho F, Reis AF, Lengyel AM. Different growth hormone (GH) response to GH-releasing peptide and GH-releasing hormone in hyperthyroidism. J Clin Endocrinol Metab 1996; 81:1343–6

52. Micic D, Macut D, Popovic V, Kendereski A, Sumarac-Dumanovic M, Zoric S, Dieguez C, Casanueva FF. Growth hormone (GH) response to GH-releasing peptide-6 and GH-releasing hormone in normal-weight and overweight patients with non-insulin-dependent diabetes mellitus. Metabolism 1999;48:525–30

53. Popovic V, Damjanovic S, Micic D, Djurovic M, Dieguez C, Casanueva FF. Blocked growth hormone-releasing peptide (GHRP-6)-induced GH secretion and absence of the synergic action of GHRP-6 plus GH-releasing hormone in patients with hypothalamo-pituitary disconnection: evidence that GHRP-6 main

action is exerted at the hypothalamic level. J Clin Endocrinol Metab 1995;80:942–7

54. Micic D, Popovic V, Doknic M, Macut D, Dieguez C, Casanueva FF. Preserved growth hormone (GH) secretion in aged and very old subjects after testing with the combined stimulus GH-releasing hormone plus GH-releasing hexapeptide-6. J Clin Endocrinol Metab 1998;83:2569–72

55. Ozata M, Dieguez C, Casanueva FF. The inhibition of growth hormone secretion presented in obesity is not mediated by the high leptin levels: a study in human leptin deficiency patients. J Clin Endocrinol Metab 2003;88:312–6

56. Leal A, Lage M, Popovic V, Torres E, Koppeschaar HP, Paramo C, Micic D, Garcia-Mayor RV, Dieguez C, Casanueva FF. A single growth hormone (GH) determination is sufficient for the diagnosis of GH-deficiency in adult patients using the growth hormone releasing hormone plus growth hormone releasing peptide-6 test. Clin Endocrinol (Oxf) 2002;57:377–84

57. Hanley JA, McNeil BJ. The meaning and use of the area under a receiver operating characteristic (ROC) curve. Radiology 1982;143:29–36

58. DeLong ER, DeLong DM, Clarke-Pearson DL. Comparing the areas under two or more correlated receiver operating characteristic curves: a nonparametric approach. Biometrics 1988;44:837–45

59. Lissett CA, Thompson EG, Rahim A, Brennan BM, Shalet SM. How many tests are required to diagnose growth hormone (GH) deficiency in adults? Clin Endocrinol (Oxf) 1999;51:551–7

60. Spicer CC. Test reduction: II – Bayes's theorem and the evaluation of tests. Br Med J 1980;281:592–4

61. Popovic V, Pekic S, Micic D, Damjanovic S, Marikovic J, Simic M, Dieguez C, Casanueva FF. Evaluation on the reproducibility of the GHRH plus GHRP-6 test of growth hormone reserve in adults. Clin Endocrinol (Oxf) 2004;60:185–91

62. Andersson AM, Ørskov H, Ranke MB, Shalet S, Skakkebæk NE. Interpretation of growth hormone provocative tests: comparison of cut-off values in four European laboratories. Eur J Endocrinol 1995; 132:340–3

63. Jansson C, Boguszewski C, Rosberg S, Carlsson L, Albertsson-Wikland K. Growth hormone (GH) assays: influence of standard preparations, GH isoforms, assay characteristics, and GH-binding protein. Clin Chem 1997;43:950–6

64. Toogood AA, Beardwell CG, Shalet SM. The severity of growth hormone deficiency in adults with pituitary disease is related to the degree of hypopituitarism. Clin Endocrinol (Oxf) 1994;41:511–6

65. Sassolas G, Chazot FB, Jaquet P, Bachelot I, Chanson P, Rudelli CC, Tauber JP, Allannic H, Bringer J, Roudaut N, Rohmer V, Roger P, Latapie JL, Reville P, Leutenegger M. GH deficiency in adults: an epidemiological approach. Eur J Endocrinol 1999; 141:595–600

66. Giustina A, Veldhuis JD. Pathophysiology of the neuroregulation of growth hormone secretion in experimental animals and the human. Endocr Rev 1998;19:717–97

10 Dosing and individual responsiveness to growth hormone replacement therapy

Rolf-Christian Gaillard and Vittorio Giusti

Division of Endocrinology, Diabetology and Metabolism, Department of Medicine, University Hospital, Lausanne, Switzerland

Summary

Although growth hormone (GH) replacement in GH-deficient adults is now approved in many countries, there are still some outstanding questions concerning the optimization and individualization of treatment. There is no biological or clinical marker with which to assess the efficacy of GH replacement in adulthood that is equivalent to the linear growth observed in those treated during childhood. In the absence of a specific marker, it is proposed that a combination of clinical responses and serum IGF-I levels should be used to monitor the dose, in order to maximize the clinical benefits, whilst minimizing side-effects. Early studies of GH replacement in adults were based on paediatric experience, and used GH doses that were clearly excessive, resulting in a high frequency of side-effects. We now know that there is great variability in individual responsiveness to GH, with dosing regimens based on body weight and surface area alone proving unsuitable for adult patients. For example, by not taking into consideration age and adiposity, such regimens wrongly suggest high doses for elderly and obese patients. Doses of GH clearly, therefore, need to be individually tailored, taking into account all of the factors that influence GH responsiveness.

Introduction

Growth hormone (GH) is classically linked with linear growth during childhood, but we now know that it continues to exert numerous important actions throughout life. Thus, GH deficiency (GHD) in adulthood causes a distinct clinical syndrome characterized by a constellation of signs and symptoms, including abnormal body composition, osteopenia, reduced physical performance, poor muscle strength, impaired quality of life (QoL), alterations in lipid metabolism, cardiac dysfunction, decreased fibrinolysis and premature atherosclerosis [1–3]. The most visible feature of GHD in adults is the disturbance of body composition, characterized by increased fat mass and decreased lean body mass. Fat accumulates preferentially in the visceral compartment, a distribution that has clearly been shown to be associated with an increased risk of cardiovascular disease, diabetes and hypertension [4–6]. Patients with GHD have increased activity of the enzyme 11β-hydroxysteroid dehydrogenase, which converts inactive cortisone to active cortisol. Thus, the central obesity of GH-deficient patients may reflect hypercortisolism [7].

All of these metabolic changes increase the risk of cardiovascular disease and bone fracture and may lead to greater overall mortality [8–13]. It seems obvious, therefore, that this syndrome warrants treatment, just as deficiencies in cortisol, thyroid hormone and sex hormones are routinely replaced.

Although the ultimate clinical efficacy of GH replacement on morbidity and mortality is not known, numerous clinical trials have clearly shown that substitutive treatment reverses many features of this clinical syndrome, improving the metabolic profile of patients and enhancing QoL [14–16]. Furthermore, the beneficial effects of GH replacement have also been shown to decrease the direct and indirect costs of GHD. Indeed, GH replacement is associated with a significant reduction in sick leave, physicians' visits and hospital admissions [17], leading to a diminished consumption of healthcare resources.

As a result of the favourable effects of GH, the use of GH replacement in adult GHD has now been approved in many countries; however, there are still some issues that remain to be fully addressed. Foremost amongst these is the individualization of treatment and its monitoring. A clear consensus is still required on how to optimize GH dosing and how to predict individual responsiveness, in order to accurately manage the needs of the patient. Another area of some concern remains the long-term safety of GH. Even if currently available data are reassuring, it seems prudent to avoid the use of GH doses that produce supraphysiological serum levels of insulin-like growth factor I (IGF-I), as epidemiological data suggest that an individual's risk of developing prostate or breast carcinoma may be influenced by serum IGF-I levels [18, 19]. However, some caution should be used in the interpretation of these studies, as they were performed in normal adults with a well-functioning GH/IGF-I axis, and it may not be appropriate to extrapolate these findings to adult hypopituitary patients receiving GH replacement therapy. Nevertheless, these findings justify the question of whether over-treatment with GH is acceptable in the management of GHD in adults. This chapter reviews the dosing of GH replacement in GH-deficient adults, as well as the various causes of differences in individual responsiveness to GH replacement therapy.

Endogenous GH secretion versus GH replacement therapy

When considering methods to calculate the optimal GH replacement dose, it is important to remember that exact physiological replacement, mimicking the normal patterns of GH secretion and action, may not be possible. In healthy individuals, GH is secreted in a pulsatile manner. This creates a very different pattern than that obtained with a single daily subcutaneous injection of GH (Fig. 1). In addition, endogenous GH secretion and action vary according to gender, age, nutritional status and adiposity [21–23]. In

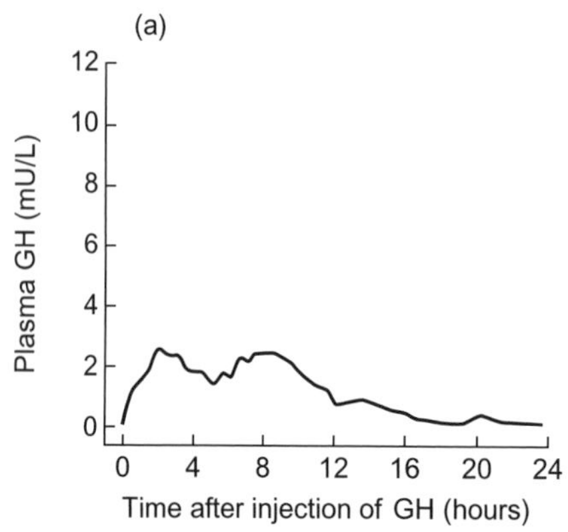

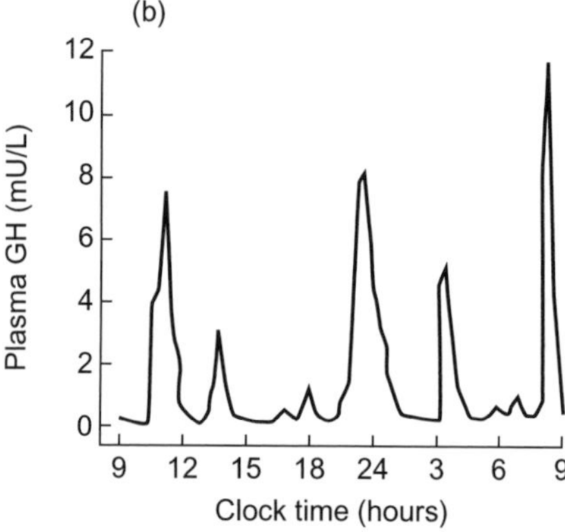

Figure 1. *Plasma time curve for GH (a) after one subcutaneous injection of 1.2 IU GH given to an adult with GHD compared with (b) the physiological pattern of endogenous GH secretion in a healthy man. Courtesy of Dr Y Janssen, personal communication. Adapted from [20] with permission.*

a recent study, Hansen and colleagues [24] have demonstrated that body composition and circulating levels of insulin, IGF-binding protein-1 (IGFBP-1) and GH-binding protein (GHBP) affect the pharmacokinetics of GH in healthy adults independently of age. The amount of abdominal fat has been shown to determine GHBP levels in healthy non-obese adults [25]. As GH binds to GHBPs, this has implications for the selection of the GH dose and for monitoring, because the bioactivity of the same dose of GH given to two individuals of the same age, sex and gonadal status will depend, at least partially, on their degree of abdominal obesity. It is therefore clear that doses of GH chosen for replacement therapy must be individualized to take into consideration all of the various factors influencing GH responsiveness.

Does the mode of administration of GH influence its effects?

The mode of administration seems to affect not only the pharmacokinetics of GH but also its effects. The bioavailability of intravenously injected GH is greater than an equivalent subcutaneous injection, suggesting a possible local degradation of GH when injected subcutaneously [26]. In addition, subcutaneous absorption is influenced by several parameters, such as subcutaneous blood flow and the depth and site of injection [27–29]. Because absorption is faster from an abdominal site than from the thigh, the peak concentration of GH is obtained more rapidly after abdominal injection. However, injections in both areas have a similar effect on serum IGF-I levels.

In the rat, linear growth and IGF-I generation are more sensitive to pulsatile GH administration than to continuous delivery, whereas GHBP and hepatic GH receptor levels are regulated through continuous GH exposure [30, 31]. By contrast, in man, short-term comparisons of continuous versus intermittent delivery of GH have revealed only minor differences in metabolic parameters [32], both modes of administration being equally effective in increasing serum IGF-I and IGFBP levels [32, 33]. However, longer treatment, comparing continuous and pulsatile GH administration, has shown that only continuous treatment increases levels of GHBPs [34].

It remains uncertain whether close imitation of the physiological pulsatile pattern of GH secretion is important for the effect of GH treatment in humans. Indeed, constant GH exposure might, in theory, down-regulate the GH receptor. A recent study [35], comparing the long-term effects of continuous subcutaneous infusion with daily subcutaneous injection, clearly demonstrates that both modes of GH administration are comparable with respect to the IGF/IGFBP axis, GHBPs, bone metabolism, body composition, insulin sensitivity and lipoproteins. Therefore, data from this study challenge the assumption that the effects of GH depend strongly on a pulsatile pattern of exposure.

IGF-I as a biochemical marker of GH action

GH has some direct effects on peripheral tissues, but most of its actions are mediated through IGF-I. In contrast to GH, IGF-I levels remain more or less stable throughout the day because it circulates bound principally to IGFBP-3. However, the use of circulating IGF-I measurement as a marker of GH action is probably too simplistic, because the IGF-I response to GH can be affected by many variables modulating both hepatic and local tissue IGF-I production. Most circulating IGF-I is produced in the liver, but it is also synthesized in non-hepatic tissues where it acts in an autocrine/paracrine fashion [36]. Sex steroids are also important modulators of IGF-I generation in response to a given GH stimulus. Testosterone administration increases circulating IGF-I levels in men, while oral oestrogen treatment lowers circulating IGF-I in post-menopausal women [37]. In addition, oestrogens have different effects on GH secretion and action depending on the route of administration. The oral route attenuates IGF-I production despite an increase in mean GH levels, whereas the transdermal route does not influence GH secretion but causes a slight increase in circulating IGF-I [38, 39].

GH dosing strategies

During childhood, the efficacy of GH replacement can be judged according to linear growth. Unfortunately, no such marker is available during adult life, making the assessment of optimal GH replacement difficult. Optimizing GH therapy in adults means finding the dose that maximizes the potential clinical benefit, whilst minimizing the risks that may result from excessive GH exposure. Dosing strategies for the adolescent GH-deficient patient are discussed in Chapter 20.

The initial trials of GH treatment in adults with GHD all employed doses of GH based on body weight or body surface area [40, 41]. This strategy was adopted essentially from paediatric practice, and unfortunately the existence of individual responsiveness to GH was ignored. It was also thought that clinical monitoring, using markers such as body composition, by analogy with linear growth used in paediatric practice, would be sufficient. We now know that such dosing strategies are too simplistic and that the dose of GH given on the basis of these regimens is clearly excessive for adults [42, 43]. Indeed, such dosing regimens do not take into consideration that the tolerance of adult patients for GH is much lower than that of children. Therefore most of these early trials reported a rather high frequency of side-effects, mainly related to fluid retention. Physiological GH secretion is inversely correlated with age and adiposity [44]. Consequently, older patients and patients with a high body mass index are more prone to side-effects if GH is given according to body weight. By not taking age and adiposity into consideration, GH dosing regimens based on body weight and surface area have therefore wrongly delivered excessive doses to elderly and/or obese patients. Furthermore, using such dosing regimens, most GH-deficient women have received a lower dose of GH compared with men, despite the fact that fertile healthy women physiologically secrete more GH than young men [23]. As factors such as age, gender and adiposity influence an individual's responsiveness to GH, they should always be taken into consideration when determining the appropriate GH dose for a patient. In current trials using an individualized GH-dosing schedule, women receive more GH per kg body weight than men, and older patients receive less than younger patients [45].

Numerous recent clinical studies have demonstrated that optimal GH doses for replacement therapy are significantly lower than the weight-based doses used in the past; for example, for adult patients with childhood-onset GHD (CO-GHD), the appropriate dose of GH would appear to be in the range of 0.37–0.57 mg/m^2/day (1.1–1.7 IU/m^2/day) while, for patients with adult-onset GHD (AO-GHD), a smaller dose of 0.2–0.47 mg/m^2/day (0.6–1.4 IU/m^2/day) seems to be appropriate, confirming that patients with AO-GHD often require less GH replacement [46–48]. Low doses of GH have recently been shown to produce additional beneficial effects on insulin resistance and β-cell function as well as on bone [46, 48].

In a short term study, Yuen *et al.* [49] showed that a low 'physiological' GH dose of 0.0017 mg/kg/day, which represents a close approximation to daily physiological GH production rates in adults, produced important beneficial effects on β-cell function, without compromising insulin sensitivity or modifying fasting glucose and insulin levels. These observations support previous findings that GH and IGF-I are of physiological importance for the regulation and proliferation of β-cells [50]. In contrast to the beneficial effects of the low dose, a higher GH dose of 0.025 mg/kg/day induced insulin resistance. These findings confirm the importance of starting treatment with low GH doses. The low dose used in this study could represent the optimum starting dose, as it appears to provide the additional benefit of enhancing β-cell function without compromising insulin sensitivity. In addition, the deterioration of insulin sensitivity associated with the highest dose further confirms the importance of avoiding over-treatment.

A low dose of GH (0.004 mg/kg/day) seems optimal for restoring bone mass in AO-GHD [51], as it avoids the initial decline in bone mineral density (BMD) usually observed when GH treatment is introduced. GH is indeed a stimulator of both bone resorption and bone formation [52], and it increases bone remodelling, leading, particularly when high doses are used, to an initial decrease in BMD [53]. The demonstration that low doses of GH do not produce this decrease in BMD confirms previous observations that a low dose of IGF-I stimulates bone formation more markedly than bone resorption [54], and that low doses of GH may generate a more marked anabolic action on bone than higher doses [55].

The above data are consistent with the recommendations of the Growth Hormone Research Society that GH replacement therapy should start with a low dose (0.15–0.30 mg/day; 0.45–0.90 IU/day) administered as daily subcutaneous injections in the evening. The dosage should be increased gradually on the basis of clinical and biochemical responses, no more frequently than at monthly intervals. The increasing steps should be between 0.1–0.2 mg/day (0.3–0.6 IU/day). The maintenance dose seldom exceeds 1.0 mg/day (3 IU/day). Clinical status and serum IGF-I levels should be monitored and the dose titrated so that IGF-I levels are kept within the normal range (not exceeding +2 SD scores). In the initial stages, IGF-I should be measured as frequently as necessary (every 1 or 2 months). Once a stable dose has been reached, IGF-I should be monitored every 6–12 months [43].

Biochemical markers for monitoring GH replacement therapy

IGF-I is the tissue effector of many of the actions of GH. Almost all circulating IGF-I is bound to one of several IGFBPs, the most abundant of which is IGFBP-3. Together with the acid-labile subunit (ALS), IGF-I and IGFBP-3 form a ternary complex. All three proteins are GH dependent and may theoretically be considered as potential markers of GH efficacy. However, although IGF-I is considered useful for dose monitoring, measurements of serum IGFBP-3 and ALS are too variable for routine clinical use [56].

Serum IGF-I is a sensitive marker of GH treatment and may reflect over-treatment better than measurement of clinical effects, such as body composition. Unfortunately, there is diurnal variation in serum IGF-I concentrations following subcutaneous administration of GH in the evening, such that IGF-I levels peak in the morning and nadir at night [57]. Therefore, in patients receiving a subcutaneous injection of GH in the evening, serum IGF-I concentrations in the morning could be approximately 15% higher than the predicted mean values for healthy adults. This may therefore falsely suggest high over-replacement, as judged by supranormal IGF-I levels. Furthermore, IGF-I may not always be clinically useful for assessing GH status, as a substantial number of patients with verified GHD have normal serum IGF-I levels [58]. IGF-I has been shown to be a good marker in adults with CO-GHD, the percentage of patients with a value below the 5th percentile of the normal range for IGF-I being more than 95%. The sensitivity of this marker is much lower in patients with AO-GHD, as less than 65% of patients have such low values. The score is even worse for IGFBP-3, as less than 30% of patients have IGFBP-3 values below the 5th percentile. IGF-I seems, therefore, to be the most sensitive serum marker of GH status and, despite some limitations, is probably the best available marker of GH replacement in adults. However, with regard to the occurrence of side-effects, IGF-I levels are not always an optimal marker. Indeed, it has been observed that normalization of serum levels of IGF-I does not exclude the possibility that the GH dose is too high in an individual patient [46]. This could be due to the fact that side-effects seem to be more associated with the increment, rather than the absolute values, of serum IGF-I. It is therefore possible that the higher frequency of side-effects in patients receiving larger GH doses according to their body weight could be due to a more marked increment in IGF-I. Thus, to avoid side-effects, the starting dose of GH should always be low, as proposed by the consensus guidelines of the Growth Hormone Research Society.

Tolerability as a marker for monitoring GH replacement therapy

Almost all side-effects of GH replacement therapy are due to excess dosing. They are clearly dose dependent, and a reduction of the dose usually resolves the problems. Furthermore, side-effects are typically observed at the beginning of treatment and/or when increasing the dose too quickly. The most common side-effects are linked to water retention due to the antinatriuretic actions of GH. Oedema is observed in about 40% of treated patients, arthralgia in 20%, myalgia in 16%, paraesthesia in 8% and carpal tunnel syndrome in 2% [59]. In the early trials when weight-based dosing regimens were used, side-effects, as previously discussed, were more common in elderly and obese patients [60]. The use of smaller individualized doses of GH (taking age, gender and obesity into account) has significantly reduced the occurrence of side-effects.

It was suggested that GH doses should be adapted according to tolerability. This strategy, however, was quickly shown to be inadequate. Indeed even when GH doses were decreased because of adverse symptoms, serum IGF-I levels remained elevated in up to one-third of patients [46], suggesting that the absence of adverse symptoms due to GH excess was too crude a method with which to judge GH over-replacement (Fig. 2).

Clinical responses as markers of GH efficacy

As GH replacement reverses many clinical symptoms of GHD, such as impaired QoL, abnormal body composition and osteopenia, it was suggested that improvements of these symptoms could be used as markers of GH efficacy during substitution therapy.

QoL

Reduced QoL and well-being, including low energy levels, social isolation and increased emotional stress, are well recognized features of the GHD syndrome in adults [61] (see Chapter 19). It was therefore thought that improvement of these symptoms could be used to judge the efficacy of GH replacement. However, although many studies have documented significant improvements in well-being during GH treatment [61, 62], some controversies remain [63]. The reasons for such discrepancies are not clear. It has been suggested that, in some studies, compliance with GH therapy was suboptimal, or that patients who participated in the early GH trials were often the most severely affected in terms of psychological distress [64]. However, it has recently been shown that clinical

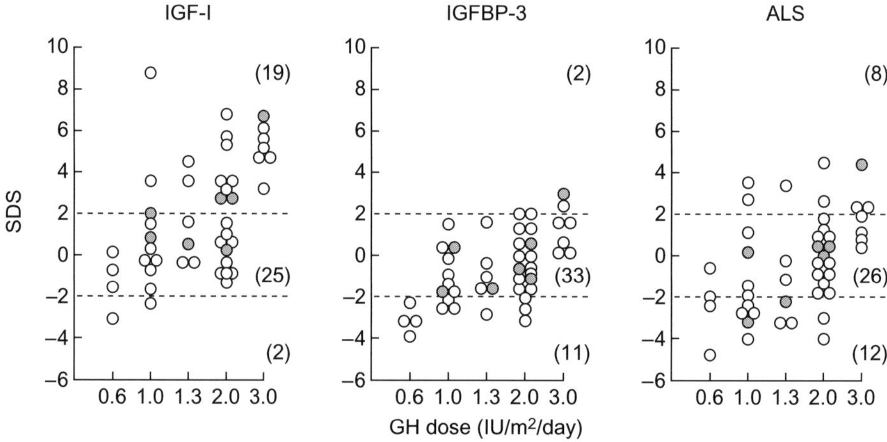

__Figure 2.__ Levels of IGF-I, IGF-binding protein-3 (IGFBP-3) and acid-labile subunit (ALS) obtained in GH-deficient patients randomized to receive one of three starting doses of GH with subsequent adjustment according to clinical symptoms of GH excess. Filled symbols indicate patients with symptoms of GH excess and open symbols patients with no symptoms of GH excess. The number of patients with levels within and outside the normal range are shown in parentheses. Reproduced from [46] with permission. Copyright 1996, The Endocrine Society.

benefits, in terms of well-being, do not adequately reflect the efficacy of GH therapy. In one report [65], the effect of two different GH doses (0.012 and 0.024 mg/kg/day) on well-being were studied. The improvement in well-being was similar in both groups, but 45% of the patients in the higher dose group had an elevated serum IGF-I compared with 24% in the lower dose group. This indicates that the extra GH administered did not produce greater clinical benefits in terms of well-being, but induced biochemical over-treatment in about twice as many patients. In the same study, among the patients who decided to discontinue GH therapy after the end of the study period due to a lack of improvement in well-being, 30% had a supra-normal serum IGF-I level. Thus, if the GH dose in these non-responders had been increased because of a poor clinical response, it may have further increased the IGF-I levels into the pathological range of acromegalic patients. More recently, the use of the Quality of Life Assessment of GHD in Adults (QoL-AGHDA), a scoring system for psychosocial morbidity that is specific to GHD [66], has shown improvements even in patients treated with a GH dose that was too low to cause a significant increase in serum IGF-I [56]. These results suggest that improvements in QoL and well-being may, at least in part, be mediated directly by GH rather that through the production of IGF-I [56].

Body composition

GH-deficient patients have abnormal body composition, with an increased fat mass (mostly abdominal or visceral), decreased lean body mass and decreased total body water compared with age-matched healthy controls. Many studies have shown that GH replacement therapy produces beneficial effects on all these parameters. However, the use of body composition parameters as markers of GH treatment efficacy does not seem to be totally reliable. Indeed a recent study [45], in which a low starting dose of GH was followed by individual dose adjustments according to serum IGF-I levels and changes in body composition, has shown that in some patients dose increments on the basis of persistently abnormal body composition resulted in elevated circulating IGF-I levels. This suggests that using normalization of body composition as a marker of GH efficacy may not be appropriate, as increasing the GH dose in an attempt to normalize body composition may result in over-treatment as judged by circulating IGF-I levels.

Bone density

GH-deficient patients are osteopenic compared with age-matched healthy controls [67] and have an increased rate of bone fractures [68]. The severity of bone loss is proportional to the biochemical severity of GHD [69]. GH replacement has a biphasic effect on bone metabolism and BMD. In the short term, GH replacement is associated with a reduction in bone density [70], whereas prolonged treatment significantly increases bone density [71]. However, many studies have shown that the individual responses of markers of bone metabolism are highly variable and that measurement of such parameters have little use outside the clinical trial [40] and cannot be used to monitor replacement therapy.

In conclusion, it appears that clinical monitoring is important during GH replacement therapy. Because of the high degree of variability in the individual response to GH, however, the failure to observe improvements in a single clinical parameter should not automatically lead to dose increments. Circulating IGF-I levels should always be measured before increasing the dose of GH.

Using markers of clinical response and tolerability (that is, occurrence of side-effects) to monitor GH dose titration unfortunately does not exclude over-treatment. All measurements of efficacy have limitations and are probably only crude markers of GH status. Thus, it is suggested that to improve safety during long-term GH replacement therapy a combination of markers should be used, including, for example, clinical responses, tolerability and measurement of IGF-I.

GH replacement in GH-deficient women during pregnancy

In humans, two related genes with tissue-specific expression are responsible for the production of distinct isoforms of GH – the *GH-N* gene in the anterior pituitary and the *GH-V* gene in the placenta [72, 73]. During pregnancy, the pulsatile release of pituitary GH is progressively suppressed and replaced by continuous secretion of placental GH [74]. Interestingly, placental GH has similar metabolic and somatogenic effects as pituitary GH, but lower lactogenic activity [75]. Placental GH plays a definite role in fetal growth and development [76]. The maternal GH/IGF-I axis may not be essential for the development of a normal pregnancy, as normal pregnancies have been reported in GH-deficient women [77]. However, some clinical studies have found a correlation between low maternal GH and IGF-I levels and intrauterine growth retardation [76], suggesting that maternal GHD might be potentially deleterious for placental development and fetal growth.

GH replacement therapy is currently not licensed for use during pregnancy because of a lack of safety data, and the label recommendation is therefore to discontinue GH replacement in hypopituitary women when they become pregnant. According to the Growth Hormone Research Society Consensus Guidelines, GH replacement is not contraindicated during early pregnancy, but GH treatment should be discontinued in the second trimester, as GH is produced by the placenta [43].

Discontinuation of GH replacement in hypopituitary pregnant women may lead to severe psychological symptoms [78] during the first trimester of pregnancy. To prevent such problems, it is suggested that the same pregestational dose of GH is maintained during the first trimester, followed by a gradual decrease of the dose during the second trimester and discontinuation of treatment at the beginning of the third trimester, when sufficient placental production of GH is achieved [78].

Factors influencing individual responsiveness to GH replacement therapy

As already mentioned, the individual response of GH-deficient adults to GH is variable [40]. The variability in the individual GH response is related to factors, such as age, adiposity, gender, sex steroid status and age at onset of GHD.

Age

Age-related changes in GH secretion have been documented in both men and women [79, 80]. GH secretion increases at the onset of sexual maturation and reaches its highest levels during puberty. After puberty, the GH secretion rate declines by approximately 14% per decade. This decline with age is related to a progressive decrease of secretion and action of GH-releasing hormone and an increase in somatostatin tone [81, 82]. Ageing also induces an increase in metabolic clearance and the distribution volume of GH, with a consequent reduction of the responsiveness to GH administration [83]. Finally, each passing decade shortens GH half-life by 6% [84]. These age-related changes in GH are paralleled by a decline in IGF-I in both men and women, with a 30–50% decrease observed between the third and seventh decade [85]. Elderly GH-deficient patients are sensitive to GH and need low daily doses to normalize their serum IGF-I levels [86]. However, in terms of anabolic effects and muscle performance, elderly patients are less responsive than younger patients [87]. Adult GHD should not be viewed as a single clinical entity, as there are marked differences in baseline data between AO- and CO-GHD [88]. Patients with AO-GHD are often regarded as being more sensitive to GH and more prone to side-effects than patients with CO-GHD.

Adiposity

Adiposity may also influence the responsiveness to GH. There is a positive correlation between body mass index and the GH dose necessary to obtain the same clinical results. This correlation could be due to the increased levels of GHBP, increased clearance of GH and/or hepatic resistance to GH action observed in obesity.

Sexual dimorphism of the response to GH

Numerous studies have demonstrated that the sensitivity of GH-deficient adults to GH is gender dependent [56, 89, 90]. Thus, because of the antagonistic effect of oestrogen on GH actions, women require more GH than men to obtain equivalent clinical and biochemical responses. The reasons for this discrepancy are not fully understood, but an attenuation of GH action by oestrogen certainly plays an important role. Indeed, to reach the same IGF-I concentration as men, women without oral oestrogen therapy need an 18% higher GH dose, whereas an increase of more than 125% is necessary in women receiving oral oestrogen therapy [91] (Fig. 3). This gender difference is largely due to interactions between sex steroids and the GH/IGF-I axis [92]. Oestrogens have a direct effect on the liver, leading to attenuated serum IGF-I generation, inhibited lipid oxidation, increased fat mass and decreased lean body mass [93]. If oestrogen replacement blunts the IGF-I response to GH in women, androgen substitution increases the responsivity in men, causing a risk of undertreatment in women and overtreatment in men [90]. The IGF-I lowering effect of oestrogen could be partly due to an increased production of GHBP which attenuates GH-stimulated IGF-I generation by the liver. Very recently, Leung *et al.* [94] proposed a cellular mechanism for the inhibitory effects of oestrogens on GH actions. Using hepatoma and breast cancer cells, they provide strong evidence that oestradiol may inhibit some GH signalling events by suppressing GH-induced Janus kinase phosphorylation, an effect mediated by suppressor of cytokine signalling-2. The route of administration seems to be a major determinant in the effect of oestrogen. Transdermal oestrogen does not seem to modulate hepatic IGF-I production to the same extent as oral oestrogen, although a similar effect can be observed when the number of oestrogen patches is increased [38]. In a recent study [91], it has been demonstrated that women on oral oestrogen required twice as much GH to maintain serum IGF-I levels in the upper part of the normal range as women taking transdermal oestrogen. Indeed, as depicted in Figure 4, one patient in this study [91] was switched from oral to transdermal oestrogen administration after several weeks. Within 2 weeks of the changed route of administration, the patient complained of adverse effects due to GH excess (muscle and joint aching) and had an elevated IGF-I level. After reduction of the GH dose to half of that previously used when on oral oestrogen, symptoms of GH excess were relieved and IGF-I was normalized (Fig. 4). Thus, if oestrogen is replaced transdermally in women,

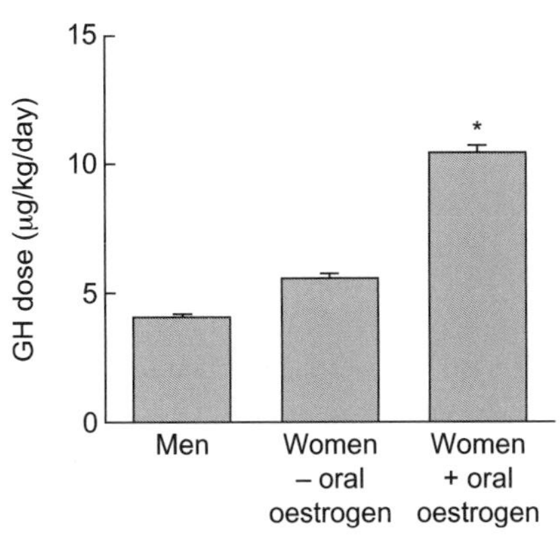

Figure 3. *Final GH dose by weight (μg/kg/day) in men, women not receiving oral oestrogen and women receiving oral oestrogen to obtain similar IGF-I response.*
**Statistical difference from the other groups (by ANOVA). Adapted from [91] with permission. Copyright 1999, The Endocrine Society.*

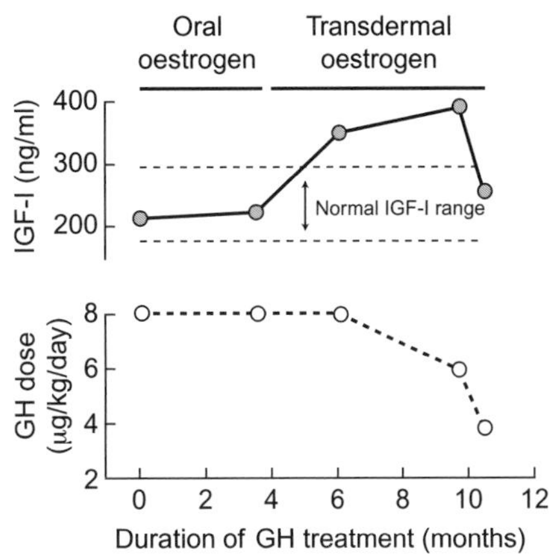

Figure 4. *Time course of GH dose (μg/kg/day) and IGF-I (ng/ml) in a patient who was switched from oral to transdermal oestrogen during her course of treatment. Adapted from [91] with permission. Copyright 1999, The Endocrine Society.*

GH requirements are much less than when receiving oral oestrogen therapy. The effect of oral oestrogen on liver IGF-I production is probably due to the higher concentrations of oestrogen as it passes through the liver after oral administration. This observation has implications in terms of the cost of GH. Indeed, the cost can be significantly reduced if women needing both GH replacement and exogeneous oestrogen therapy receive oestrogen transdermally rather than orally.

Conclusions

To realize optimal GH replacement therapy in GH-deficient adults is more complex that was first thought. There is no biological or clinical marker in adulthood that is equivalent to linear growth in childhood with which to assess the efficacy of GH replacement. In the absence of such a marker, it is proposed to use a combination of clinical responses and measurement of serum IGF-I in order to avoid over-treatment. Side-effects are a poor guide to excess GH exposure.

As a result of great individual variability in GH responsiveness, dosing strategies based on weight and body surface should not be used in adults. Instead, the dose of GH needs to be individually tailored for each patient, considering that responsiveness to GH is influenced by age, adiposity, gender and sex steroids.

References

1. Cuneo RC, Salomon F, McGauley GA, Sönksen PH. The growth hormone deficiency syndrome in adults. Clin Endocrinol (Oxf) 1992;37:387–97
2. Vance ML, Mauras N. Growth hormone therapy in adults and children. N Engl J Med 1999;341:1206–16
3. Cummings DE, Merriam GR. Growth hormone therapy in adults. Annu Rev Med 2003;54:513–33
4. Kannel WB, Cupples LA, Ramaswami R, Stokes J, Kreger BE, Higgins M. Regional obesity and risk of cardiovascular disease; the Framingham Study. J Clin Epidemiol 1991;44:183–90
5. Lapidus L, Bengtsson C, Larsson B, Pennert K, Rybo E, Sjöström L. Distribution of adipose tissue and risk of cardiovascular disease and death: a 12-year follow up of participants in the population study of women in Gothenburg, Sweden. Br Med J 1984;289:1257–61
6. Montague CT, O'Rahilly S. The perils of portliness: causes and consequences of visceral adiposity. Diabetes 2000;49:883–8
7. Stewart PM, Toogood AA, Tomlinson JW. Growth hormone, insulin-like growth factor-I and the cortisol-cortisone shuttle. Horm Res 2001;56 (Suppl 1):1–6
8. Abs R, Bengtsson B-Å, Hernberg-Ståhl E, Monson JP, Tauber JP, Wilton P, Wüster C. GH replacement in 1034 growth hormone deficient hypopituitary adults: demographic and clinical characteristics, dosing and safety. Clin Endocrinol (Oxf) 1999;50:703–13
9. Rosén T, Bengtsson B-Å. Premature mortality due to cardiovascular disease in hypopituitarism. Lancet 1990;336:285–8
10. Bates AS, Van't Hoff W, Jones PJ, Clayton RN. The effect of hypopituitarism on life expectancy. J Clin Endocrinol Metab 1996;81:1169–72
11. Bülow B, Hagmar L, Mikoczy Z, Nordström CH, Erfurth EM. Increased cerebrovascular mortality in patients with hypopituitarism. Clin Endocrinol (Oxf) 1997;46:75–81
12. Tomlinson JW, Holden N, Hills RK, Wheatley K, Clayton RN, Bates AS, Sheppard MC, Stewart PM. Association between premature mortality and hypopituitarism. West Midlands Prospective Hypopituitary Study Group. Lancet 2001;357:425–31
13. Wüster C, Abs R, Bengtsson B-Å, Bennmarker H, Feldt-Rasmussen U, Hernberg-Ståhl E, Monson JP, Westberg B, Wilton P. The influence of growth hormone deficiency, growth hormone replacement therapy, and other aspects of hypopituitarism on fracture rate and bone mineral density. J Bone Miner Res 2001;16:398–405
14. Monson JP. Long-term experience with GH replacement therapy: efficacy and safety. Eur J Endocrinol 2003;148 (Suppl 2):S9–14
15. Attanasio AF, Bates PC, Ho KK, Webb SM, Ross RJ, Strasburger CJ, Bouillon R, Crowe B, Selander K, Valle D, Lamberts SW. Human growth hormone replacement in adult hypopituitary patients: long-term effects on body composition and lipid status – 3-year results from the HypoCCS Database. J Clin Endocrinol Metab 2002;87:1600–6
16. Florakis D, Hung V, Kaltsas G, Coyte D, Jenkins PJ, Chew SL, Grossman AB, Besser GM, Monson JP. Sustained reduction in circulating cholesterol in adult hypopituitary patients given low dose titrated growth hormone replacement therapy: a two year study. Clin Endocrinol (Oxf) 2000;53:453–9

17. Hernberg-Ståhl E, Luger A, Abs R, Bengtsson B-Å, Feldt-Rasmussen U, Wilton P, Westberg B, Monson JP. Healthcare consumption decreases in parallel with improvements in quality of life during GH replacement in hypopituitary adults with GH deficiency. J Clin Endocrinol Metab 2001;86:5277–81

18. Wolk A, Mantzoros CS, Andersson SO, Bergstrom R, Signorello LB, Lagiou P, Adami HO, Trichopoulos D. Insulin-like growth factor 1 and prostate cancer risk: a population-based, case-control study. J Natl Cancer Inst 1998;90:911–5

19. Hankinson SE, Willett WC, Colditz GA, Hunter DJ, Michaud DS, Deroo B, Rosner B, Speizer FE, Pollak M. Circulating concentrations of insulin-like growth factor-I and risk of breast cancer. Lancet 1998; 351:1393–6

20. Drake WM, Johannsson G. Individual susceptibility to growth hormone. In: Bengtsson B-Å, Monson JP, editors. GH replacement in adults: the first 5 years of KIMS: Oxford PharmaGenesis Ltd 2000:165–81

21. Iranmanesh A, Lizarralde G, Veldhuis JD. Age and relative adiposity are specific negative determinants of the frequency and amplitude of growth hormone (GH) secretory bursts and the half-life of endogenous GH in healthy men. J Clin Endocrinol Metab 1991;73:1081–8

22. Rosenbaum M, Gertner JM. Metabolic clearance rates of synthetic human growth hormone in children, adult women, and adult men. J Clin Endocrinol Metab 1989;69:820–4

23. Ho KY, Evans WS, Blizzard RM, Veldhuis JD, Merriam GR, Samojlik E, Furlanetto R, Rogol AD, Kaiser DL, Thorner MO. Effects of sex and age on the 24-hour profile of growth hormone secretion in man: importance of endogenous estradiol concentrations. J Clin Endocrinol Metab 1987;64:51–8

24. Hansen TK, Jørgensen JO, Christiansen JS. Body composition and circulating levels of insulin, insulin-like growth factor-binding protein-1 and growth hormone (GH)-binding protein affect the pharmacokinetics of GH in adults independently of age. J Clin Endocrinol Metab 2002;87:2185–93

25. Fisker S, Vahl N, Jørgensen JO, Christiansen JS, Ørskov H. Abdominal fat determines growth hormone-binding protein levels in healthy nonobese adults. J Clin Endocrinol Metab 1997;82:123–8

26. Jørgensen JO. Human growth hormone replacement therapy: pharmacological and clinical aspects. Endocr Rev 1991;12:189–207

27. Laursen T, Jørgensen JO, Christiansen JS. Pharmacokinetics and metabolic effects of growth hormone injected subcutaneously in growth hormone deficient patients: thigh versus abdomen. Clin Endocrinol (Oxf) 1994;40:373–8

28. Blok GJ, van der Veen EA, Susgaard S, Larsen F. Influence of concentration and injection volume on the bioavailability of subcutaneous growth hormone: comparison of administration by ordinary syringe and by injection pen. Pharmacol Toxicol 1991;68:355–9

29. Laursen T, Jørgensen JO, Christiansen JS. Metabolic effects of growth hormone administered subcutaneously once or twice daily to growth hormone deficient adults. Clin Endocrinol (Oxf) 1994;41:337–43

30. Gevers EF, Wit JM, Robinson IC. Growth, growth hormone (GH)-binding protein, and GH receptors are differentially regulated by peak and trough components of the GH secretory pattern in the rat. Endocrinology 1996;137:1013–18

31. Maiter D, Underwood LE, Maes M, Davenport ML, Ketelslegers JM. Different effects of intermittent and continuous growth hormone (GH) administration on serum somatomedin-C/insulin-like growth factor I and liver GH receptors in hypophysectomized rats. Endocrinology 1988;123:1053–9

32. Laursen T, Jørgensen JO, Jakobsen G, Hansen BL, Christiansen JS. Continuous infusion versus daily injections of growth hormone (GH) for 4 weeks in GH-deficient patients. J Clin Endocrinol Metab 1995; 80:2410–8

33. Johansson JO, Oscarsson J, Bjarnason R, Bengtsson B-Å. Two weeks of daily injections and continuous infusion of recombinant human growth hormone (GH) in GH-deficient adults: I. Effects on insulin-like growth factor-I (IGF-I), GH and IGF binding proteins, and glucose homeostasis. Metabolism 1996;45:362–9

34. Tauber M, De Bouet Du Portal H, Sallerin-Caute B, Rochiccioli P, Bastide R. Differential regulation of serum growth hormone (GH)-binding protein during continuous infusion versus daily injection of recombinant human GH in GH-deficient children. J Clin Endocrinol Metab 1993;76:1135–9

35. Laursen T, Gravholt CH, Heickendorff L, Drustrup J, Kappelgaard AM, Jørgensen JO, Christiansen JS. Long-term effects of continuous subcutaneous infusion versus daily subcutaneous injections of growth hormone (GH) on the insulin-like growth factor system, insulin sensitivity, body composition, and bone and lipoprotein metabolism in GH-deficient adults. J Clin Endocrinol Metab 2001;86:1222–8

36. D'Ercole AJ, Stiles AD, Underwood LE. Tissue concentrations of somatomedin C: further evidence for multiple sites of synthesis and paracrine or autocrine mechanisms of action. Proc Natl Acad Sci USA 1984;81:935–9

37. Goodman-Gruen D, Barrett-Connor E. Effect of replacement estrogen on insulin-like growth factor-I in

postmenopausal women: the Rancho Bernardo Study. J Clin Endocrinol Metab 1996;81:4268–71

38. Weissberger AJ, Ho KK, Lazarus L. Contrasting effects of oral and transdermal routes of estrogen replacement therapy on 24-hour growth hormone (GH) secretion, insulin-like growth factor I, and GH-binding protein in postmenopausal women. J Clin Endocrinol Metab 1991;72:374–81

39. Friend KE, Hartman ML, Pezzoli SS, Clasey JL, Thorner MO. Both oral and transdermal estrogen increase growth hormone release in postmenopausal women – a clinical research center study. J Clin Endocrinol Metab 1996;81:2250–6

40. Drake WM, Howell SJ, Monson JP, Shalet SM. Optimizing GH therapy in adults and children. Endocr Rev 2001;22:425–50

41. Salomon F, Cuneo RC, Hesp R, Sönksen PH. The effects of treatment with recombinant human growth hormone on body composition and metabolism in adults with growth hormone deficiency. N Engl J Med 1989; 321:1797–803

42. Carroll PV, Christ ER, Bengtsson B-Å, Carlsson L, Christiansen JS, Clemmons D, Hintz R, Ho K, Laron Z, Sizonenko P, Sönksen PH, Tanaka T, Thorne M. Growth hormone deficiency in adulthood and the effects of growth hormone replacement: a review. Growth Hormone Research Society Scientific Committee. J Clin Endocrinol Metab 1998;83:382–95

43. Consensus guidelines for the diagnosis and treatment of adults with growth hormone deficiency: summary statement of the Growth Hormone Research Society Workshop on Adult Growth Hormone Deficiency. J Clin Endocrinol Metab 1998;83:379–81

44. Rudman D, Kutner MH, Rogers CM, Lubin MF, Fleming GA, Bain RP. Impaired growth hormone secretion in the adult population: relation to age and adiposity. J Clin Invest 1981;67:1361–9

45. Johannsson G, Rosén T, Bengtsson B-Å. Individualized dose titration of growth hormone (GH) during GH replacement in hypopituitary adults. Clin Endocrinol (Oxf) 1997;47:571–81

46. de Boer H, Blok GJ, Popp-Snijders C, Stuurman L, Baxter RC, van der Veen E. Monitoring of growth hormone replacement therapy in adults, based on measurement of serum markers. J Clin Endocrinol Metab 1996;81:1371–7

47. Janssen YJ, Frölich M, Roelfsema F. A low starting dose of genotropin in growth hormone-deficient adults. J Clin Endocrinol Metab 1997;82:129–35

48. de Boer H, Blok GJ, Voerman B, de Vries P, Popp-Snijders C, van der Veen E. The optimal growth hormone replacement dose in adults, derived from bioimpedance analysis. J Clin Endocrinol Metab 1995; 80:2069–76

49. Yuen K, Cook D, Ong K, Chatelain P, Fryklund L, Gluckman P, Ranke MB, Rosenfeld R, Dunger D. The metabolic effects of short-term administration of physiological versus high doses of GH therapy in GH deficient adults. Clin Endocrinol (Oxf) 2002;57:333–41

50. Nielsen JH, Galsgaard ED, Moldrup A, Friedrichsen BN, Billestrup N, Hansen JA, Lee YC, Carlsson C. Regulation of beta-cell mass by hormones and growth factors. Diabetes 2001;50 (Suppl 1):S25–9

51. Abrahamsen B, Hangaard J, Horn HC, Hansen TB, Gregersen G, Hansen-Nord M, Vahl N, Junker P, Andersen M, Hagen C. Evaluation of the optimum dose of growth hormone (GH) for restoring bone mass in adult-onset GH deficiency: results from two 12-month randomized studies. Clin Endocrinol (Oxf) 2002; 57:273–81

52. Bravenboer N, Holzmann P, de Boer H, Roos JC, van der Veen EA, Lips P. The effect of growth hormone (GH) on histomorphometric indices of bone structure and bone turnover in GH-deficient men. J Clin Endocrinol Metab 1997;82:1818–22

53. Holmes SJ, Whitehouse RW, Swindell R, Economou G, Adams JE, Shalet SM. Effect of growth hormone replacement on bone mass in adults with adult onset growth hormone deficiency. Clin Endocrinol (Oxf) 1995;42:627–33

54. Ghiron LJ, Thompson JL, Holloway L, Hintz RL, Butterfield GE, Hoffman AR, Marcus R. Effects of recombinant insulin-like growth factor-I and growth hormone on bone turnover in elderly women. J Bone Miner Res 1995;10:1844–52

55. Amato G, Izzo G, La Montagna G, Bellastella A. Low dose recombinant human growth hormone normalizes bone metabolism and cortical bone density and improves trabecular bone density in growth hormone deficient adults without causing adverse effects. Clin Endocrinol (Oxf) 1996;45:27–32

56. Drake WM, Coyte D, Camacho-Hubner C, Jivanji NM, Kaltsas G, Wood DF, Trainer PJ, Grossman AB, Besser GM, Monson JP. Optimizing growth hormone replacement therapy by dose titration in hypopituitary adults. J Clin Endocrinol Metab 1998;83:3913–9

57. Oscarsson J, Johannsson G, Johansson JO, Lundberg PA, Lindstedt G, Bengtsson B-Å. Diurnal variation in serum insulin-like growth factor (IGF)-I and IGF binding protein-3 concentrations during daily sub-cutaneous injections of recombinant human growth hormone in GH-deficient adults. Clin Endocrinol (Oxf) 1997;46:63–8

58. Hoffman DM, O'Sullivan AJ, Baxter RC, Ho KK. Diagnosis of growth-hormone deficiency in adults. Lancet 1994;343:1064–8

59. Mardh G, Lundin K, Borg G, Jönsson B, Lindeberg A. Growth hormone replacement therapy in adult hypopituitary patients with growth hormone deficiency: combined data from 12 European placebo-controlled clinical trials. Endocrinol Metab 1994;1 (Suppl A):43–9

60. Amato G, Carella C, Fazio S, La Montagna G, Cittadini A, Sabatini D, Marciano-Mone C, Saccà L, Bellastella A. Body composition, bone metabolism, and heart structure and function in growth hormone (GH)-deficient adults before and after GH replacement therapy at low doses. J Clin Endocrinol Metab 1993;77:1671–6

61. Burman P, Broman JE, Hetta J, Wiklund I, Erfurth EM, Hagg E, Karlsson FA. Quality of life in adults with growth hormone (GH) deficiency: response to treatment with recombinant human GH in a placebo-controlled 21-month trial. J Clin Endocrinol Metab 1995; 80:3585–90

62. McGauley GA, Cuneo RC, Salomon F, Sönksen PH. Psychological well-being before and after growth hormone treatment in adults with growth hormone deficiency. Horm Res 1990;33 (Suppl 4):52–4

63. Baum HB, Katznelson L, Sherman JC, Biller BM, Hayden DL, Schoenfeld DA, Cannistraro KE, Klibanski A. Effects of physiological growth hormone (GH) therapy on cognition and quality of life in patients with adult-onset GH deficiency. J Clin Endocrinol Metab 1998;83:3184–9

64. Holmes SJ, Shalet SM. Characteristics of adults who wish to enter a trial of growth hormone replacement. Clin Endocrinol (Oxf) 1995;42:613–8

65. Carroll PV, Littlewood R, Weissberger AJ, Bogalho P, McGauley G, Sönksen PH, Russell-Jones DL. The effects of two doses of replacement growth hormone on the biochemical, body composition and psychological profiles of growth hormone-deficient adults. Eur J Endocrinol 1997;137:146–53

66. McKenna SP, Doward LC, Alonso J, Kohlmann T, Niero M, Prieto L, Wirén L. The QoL-AGHDA: an instrument for the assessment of quality of life in adults with growth hormone deficiency. Qual Life Res 1999; 8:373–83

67. Holmes SJ, Economou G, Whitehouse RW, Adams JE, Shalet SM. Reduced bone mineral density in patients with adult onset growth hormone deficiency. J Clin Endocrinol Metab 1994;78:669–74

68. Rosén T, Wilhelmsen L, Landin-Wilhelmsen K, Lappas G, Bengtsson B-Å. Increased fracture frequency in adult patients with hypopituitarism and GH deficiency. Eur J Endocrinol 1997;137:240–5

69. Colao A, Di Somma C, Pivonello R, Loche S, Aimaretti G, Cerbone G, Faggiano A, Corneli G, Ghigo E, Lombardi G. Bone loss is correlated to the severity of growth hormone deficiency in adult patients with hypopituitarism. J Clin Endocrinol Metab 1999; 84:1919–24

70. Vandeweghe M, Taelman P, Kaufman JM. Short and long-term effects of growth hormone treatment on bone turnover and bone mineral content in adult growth hormone-deficient males. Clin Endocrinol (Oxf) 1993; 39:409–15

71. Baum HB, Biller BM, Finkelstein JS, Cannistraro KB, Oppenhein DS, Schoenfeld DA, Michel TH, Wittink H, Klibanski A. Effects of physiologic growth hormone therapy on bone density and body composition in patients with adult-onset growth hormone deficiency. A randomized, placebo-controlled trial. Ann Intern Med 1996;125:883–90

72. Boguszewski CL, Svensson PA, Jansson T, Clark R, Carlsson LM, Carlsson B. Cloning of two novel growth hormone transcripts expressed in human placenta. J Clin Endocrinol Metab 1998;83:2878–85

73. Barsh GS, Seeburg PH, Gelinas RE. The human growth hormone gene family: structure and evolution of the chromosomal locus. Nucleic Acids Res 1983; 11:3939–58

74. Eriksson L, Frankenne F, Eden S, Hennen G, Von Schoultz B. Growth hormone 24-h serum profiles during pregnancy – lack of pulsatility for the secretion of the placental variant. Br J Obstet Gynaecol 1989; 96:949–53

75. Igout A, Frankenne F, L'Hermite-Baleriaux M, Martin A, Hennen G. Somatogenic and lactogenic activity of the recombinant 22 kDa isoform of human placental growth hormone. Growth Regul 1995;5:60–5

76. McIntyre HD, Serek R, Crane DI, Veveris-Lowe T, Parry A, Johnson S, Leung KC, Ho KK, Bougoussa M, Hennen G, Igout A, Chan FY, Cowley D, Cotterill A, Barnard R. Placental growth hormone (GH), GH-binding protein, and insulin-like growth factor axis in normal, growth-retarded, and diabetic pregnancies: correlations with fetal growth. J Clin Endocrinol Metab 2000;85:1143–50

77. Verhaeghe J, Bougoussa M, Van Herck E, de Zegher F, Hennen G, Igout A. Placental growth hormone and IGF-I in a pregnant woman with Pit-1 deficiency. Clin Endocrinol (Oxf) 2000;53:645–7

78. Wirén L, Boguszewski CL, Johannsson G. Growth hormone (GH) replacement therapy in GH-deficient women during pregnancy. Clin Endocrinol (Oxf) 2002; 57:235–9

79. Florini JR, Prinz PN, Vitiello MV, Hintz RL. Somatomedin-C levels in healthy young and old men: relationship to peak and 24-hour integrated levels of growth hormone. J Gerontol 1985;40:2–7

80. Clemmons DR, Van Wyk JJ. Factors controlling blood concentration of somatomedin C. Clin Endocrinol Metab 1984;13:113–43

81. Iovino M, Monteleone P, Steardo L. Repetitive growth hormone-releasing hormone administration restores the attenuated growth hormone (GH) response to GH-releasing hormone testing in normal aging. J Clin Endocrinol Metab 1989;69:910–3

82. Müller EE, Cocchi D, Ghigo E, Arvat E, Locatelli V, Camanni F. Growth hormone response to GHRH during lifespan. J Pediatr Endocrinol 1993;6:5–13

83. Vahl N, Møller N, Lauritzen T, Christiansen JS, Jørgensen JO. Metabolic effects and pharmacokinetics of a growth hormone pulse in healthy adults: relation to age, sex, and body composition. J Clin Endocrinol Metab 1997;82:3612–8

84. Zadik Z, Chalew SA, McCarter RJ Jr, Meistas M, Kowarski AA. The influence of age on the 24-hour integrated concentration of growth hormone in normal individuals. J Clin Endocrinol Metab 1985;60:513–6

85. Corpas E, Harman SM, Pineyro MA, Roberson R, Blackman MR. Growth hormone (GH)-releasing hormone-(1-29) twice daily reverses the decreased GH and insulin-like growth factor-I levels in old men. J Clin Endocrinol Metab 1992;75:530–5

86. Toogood AA, Shalet SM. Growth hormone replacement therapy in the elderly with hypothalamic–pituitary disease: a dose-finding study. J Clin Endocrinol Metab 1999;84:131–6

87. Johannsson G, Grimby G, Sunnerhagen KS, Bengtsson B-Å. Two years of growth hormone (GH) treatment increase isometric and isokinetic muscle strength in GH-deficient adults. J Clin Endocrinol Metab 1997;82:2877–84

88. Attanasio AF, Lamberts SW, Matranga AM, Birkett MA, Bates PC, Valk NK, Hilsted J, Bengtsson B-Å, Strasburger CJ. Adult growth hormone (GH)-deficient patients demonstrate heterogeneity between childhood onset and adult onset before and during human GH treatment. Adult Growth Hormone Deficiency Study Group. J Clin Endocrinol Metab 1997;82:82–8

89. Johansson AG, Engstrom BE, Ljunghall S, Karlsson FA, Burman P. Gender differences in the effects of long term growth hormone (GH) treatment on bone in adults with GH deficiency. J Clin Endocrinol Metab 1999; 84:2002–7

90. Span JP, Pieters GF, Sweep CG, Hermus AR, Smals AG. Gender difference in insulin-like growth factor I response to growth hormone (GH) treatment in GH-deficient adults: role of sex hormone replacement. J Clin Endocrinol Metab 2000;85:1121–5

91. Cook DM, Ludlam WH, Cook MB. Route of estrogen administration helps to determine growth hormone (GH) replacement dose in GH-deficient adults. J Clin Endocrinol Metab 1999;84:3956–60

92. Lieberman SA, Mitchell AM, Marcus R, Hintz RL, Hoffman AR. The insulin-like growth factor I generation test: resistance to growth hormone with aging and estrogen replacement therapy. Horm Metab Res 1994;26:229–33

93. O'Sullivan AJ, Crampton L, Freund J, Ho KK. The route of estrogen replacement therapy confers divergent effects on substrate oxidation and body composition in postmenopausal women. J Clin Invest 1998; 102:1035–40

94. Leung KC, Doyle N, Ballesteros M, Sjögren K, Watts CK, Low TH, Leong GM, Ross RJ, Ho KK. Estrogen inhibits GH signaling by suppressing GH-induced JAK2 phosphorylation, an effect mediated by SOCS-2. Proc Natl Acad Sci USA 2003;100:1016–21

11 Body composition – methods and effects of growth hormone

Henriette Mersebach, Åse K Rasmussen and Ulla Feldt-Rasmussen
Department of Endocrinology, Copenhagen University Hospital, Copenhagen, Denmark

Summary

In 1942, Behnke [1] demonstrated that American football players had excess weight but not excess fat mass. Thereafter, the development and application of methods for assessment of body composition in vivo rapidly increased. Today, there are several techniques available for the measurement of body composition that serve as important tools for monitoring the response to growth hormone (GH) therapy in patients with GH deficiency (GHD). At present, the most accurate in-vivo methods of measuring body composition are multislice magnetic resonance imaging and axial computed tomography (CT). The limited capacity and costs of the procedures, and the exposure to radiation during CT measurement, however, leave dual-energy X-ray absorptiometry as the preferred method.

GH is a potent anabolic and lipolytic hormone with a variety of metabolic functions, including an antinatriuretic action. Each of these properties has an impact on body composition. One of the most important effects of GHD is on body composition. Using a variety of techniques, adults with GHD have consistently been shown to have subnormal tissue hydration, reduced lean body mass (LBM) and increased fat mass (FM). Long-term GH treatment produces a sustained favourable redistribution of the body compartments, increasing LBM and tissue hydration and concomitantly reducing FM, with a particular reduction in central obesity. The greater responsiveness of insulin-like growth factor I to GH treatment in men with GHD compared with women with GHD is accompanied by more pronounced changes in body composition in the former, at least in the short term. Individual dose titration of GH, with regard to both sex and age, is required for the most favourable response.

Methods used for assessment of body composition

Measurement of body composition is important in the management and treatment surveillance of adult growth hormone deficiency (GHD). The classic method of investigating body composition *in vivo* is by densitometry. In 1942, Behnke [1] used hydrodensitometry to show that American football players had excess weight but not excess fat mass (FM). Since then the development and application of methods to measure body fat have increased rapidly. Today, although there are several techniques available for assessment of body composition *in vivo*, none has been established as the 'gold standard'. The simple field methods are cheap, quick and easy to use, and they rely on formulae based on more accurate methods. The advanced techniques are more expensive, more complex and less available than simple field methods. Other methodological differences concern the body compartments measured, the use of invasive or non-invasive procedures and exposure to radiation (Table 1). Despite procedural diversity, the findings using different methods are remarkably similar.

Simple methods

Body mass index

Body mass index (BMI) is calculated as body weight in kilograms divided by the square of height in metres and is therefore the cheapest way of assessing body composition. According to the World Health Organization (WHO)-endorsed international classification, BMI may be used to describe the type and severity of obesity. The normal range of BMI is 18.5–25 kg/m^2, while a BMI below 18.5 kg/m^2 indicates that the individual is underweight. If BMI exceeds 25 or 30 kg/m^2, an individual is considered to be overweight or obese, respectively. The BMI estimate does not distinguish between FM and lean body mass (LBM) and covers huge variations in adiposity. BMI correlates reasonably well, however, with FM and relative FM, defined as total body fat expressed as a percentage of body weight. When using age- and sex-specific prediction equations, the relative FM can be predicted with an error of 3–5% ($R^2 = 0.6–0.8$) in most patients [2, 3].

Bioelectrical impedance (BI)

In BI measurement, a small alternating current (50 kHz) is applied to the body. Different tissues have differences in electrical conductivity, and it is assumed that lean tissue, which contains large amounts of water and electrolytes, is a good electrical conductor and fat, which is anhydrous, is a poor conductor [4]. The technical error is less than 2%. However, this method relies on a statistical relationship between the measured variables and a method of reference. It is clear that the validity is less compared with laboratory techniques, not least because more assumptions are made on top of those already made for the method of reference. The prediction of fat-free mass (FFM) can be improved by adding other independent variables into the model; for example sex, age and weight. Nevertheless, FM is computed based on the prediction of FFM. One source of error is the distribution of body water between intra- and extracellular spaces. The use of this method for assessment of body composition in patients with GHD has been questioned by de Boer *et al.* [5], who reported a higher conductivity in these patients compared with controls, due to subnormal tissue hydration in the former. BI measurement may, however, be clinically valuable in monitoring rapid changes in tissue hydration during initial growth hormone (GH) therapy [6]. Body shape also affects BI measurements. In subjects with relatively long legs, BI generally overestimates body fat. Furthermore, impedance depends on body and skin temperature, body posture during measurement, skin humidity, timing of food consumption and the amount of exercise taken prior to measurement. The advantages of this method include the fact that it is non-invasive, portable, cheap and rapid.

Body circumferences

Body circumferences can be used to predict the amount of body fat. It has been shown that waist circumference alone or the ratio of waist circumference to hip circumference (WHR) correlates well with intra-abdominal fat as measured by computed tomography (CT) or magnetic resonance imaging (MRI). The WHO suggests cut-off points for abdominal obesity at a WHR above 0.85 for women and 1.00 for men.

Skinfold thickness

The sum of skinfold thicknesses at four to seven different sites (e.g. biceps, triceps, subscapular, suprailiac) provides an approximation of the FM [7]. Skinfolds are measured with a skinfold calliper, or by ultrasound. A constant relationship between subcutaneous fat and total FM is assumed. The sum of skinfolds is used to reduce the error in measurement and to correct for possible differences in subcutaneous fat distribution between individuals of the same age and sex. The technical error is 3–5% depending on age, sex and level of body fatness. However, most skinfold callipers may not widen beyond 4 cm. The thickness of a skinfold is also influenced by the content of water and connective tissues. As with BI, this method relies on a statistical relationship

Table 1. *Available methods for assessment of body composition.*

Method	Compartments	Irradiation	Technical error	Advantages	Disadvantages
Body mass index	–	No	3–5%	Timesaving, cheap, portable	Indirect method No distinction between FM and LBM
Bioelectrical impedance	FM, FFM	No	< 2%	Timesaving, cheap, non-invasive, portable	Indirect method; population (race) specific; depends on body shape, tissue hydration, body and skin temperature, skin humidity, posture, time of food consumption and prior exercise
Waist circumference	–	No	–	Timesaving, portable	Indirect method
Skinfold thickness	–	No	3–5%	Cheap, portable	Indirect method
Densitometry	FM, FFM	No	1%	Accuracy, timesaving	Indirect method; assumes constant density of FM (not applicable in obese and elderly); co-operation from patients required; patients required to wear swimsuits
DXA	FM, LBM, BMC	Low	1–3%	Measurement of regional body composition Repeated measurements	No distinction between water and lean mass; tissue depth affects measurements
Total body potassium	FM, fat free extracellular solids, body cell mass, ECW	No	–	Reliable method for measurement of total ^{40}K	Costs; access to facilities is limited; requires exact calibration; assumes constant potassium in FFM
Computed tomography	FM, muscle mass, water, bone, tissue specific	High	< 1%	Tissue-specific 3D imaging Measurement of total body composition and fat distribution	Irradiation; costs; time-consuming
Magnetic resonance imaging	FM, muscle mass, water, bone, tissue specific	No	< 1%	Tissue-specific 3D imaging Measurement of total body composition and fat distribution Repeated measurements	Costs; lack of access to facilities; time-consuming

BMC, bone mineral content; 3D, three-dimensional; DXA, dual-energy X-ray absorptiometry; ECW, extracellular water; FFM, fat-free mass; FM, fat mass; ^{40}K, radioactive potassium; LBM, lean body mass.

between the measured variables and a reference method. Trained and experienced observers are required for reliable measurements. The calculation of relative FM is very simple. In the adult population the prediction equation of Durnin and Womersley [8] is most often used.

Advanced methods

Densitometry

Densitometry is a classic method, which assumes that the body consists of two compartments, FM and FFM, the sum providing the total body weight [9]. Density is weight divided by volume, and the specific and constant density for FM is 0.9 kg/L, whereas FFM has a density of 1.1 kg/L. The methods that are now used to determine body volume are water displacement, underwater weighing and air displacement. Correction for air trapped in the lungs and gut must be made. The technical error is small and hardly exceeds 1%. However, in elderly individuals the density of FFM is likely to be lower than 1.1 kg/L, as there is less bone mineral and more water in the FFM. In obese individuals the density of the FFM may also be lower due to a higher water content than in normal individuals. In both circumstances, body fat is overestimated, when using the normal formula for calculation. Other concerns are the necessity for the subject to co-operate (maximal exhaling during immersion in water) and the need to wear a swimsuit.

Dual-energy X-ray absorptiometry (DXA)

DXA is a non-invasive method for estimating body composition. Measurements are performed as whole-body scans. Based on the different attenuation coefficients of minerals and soft tissue on the one hand, and of FM and LBM soft tissue on the other, body composition in terms of total FM, total LBM and total bone mineral content can be calculated [10]. The sum of these compartments provides the total body weight. This method also has the advantage that regional body composition (e.g. of the legs, arms, trunk and abdomen) can be determined. Exposure to radiation is minimal, even over repeated measurements. The technical error for relative FM varies from 1 to 3%, being lowest for whole-body scans and highest for the extremities. The DXA method has been criticized because it does not distinguish lean mass from water. This should be taken into consideration when evaluating LBM in relation to GH treatment, which may induce fluid retention [11]. Tissue depth also has an impact on the total attenuation of the body, so the accuracy may differ between obese and lean individuals.

Total body potassium

This method uses the four-compartment model comprising body cell mass, FM, extracellular water and fat-free extracellular solids. Body potassium is distributed entirely in the FFM compartment. Body composition is estimated from measurement of total body potassium (calculated by measuring the amount of ^{40}K), total body water and body weight and subsequent calculation, using the algorithms described by Bruce *et al.* [12]. The accuracy depends on a constant level of potassium in the FFM (FFM = total body potassium divided by 69.1 mmol/kg). Due to low intracellular potassium in GH-deficient patients, LBM may be underestimated by measurement of total ^{40}K. The equipment for measuring total ^{40}K is expensive, and access to the facilities necessary for measurements is limited. These factors restrict the use of this method for assessment of body composition.

Imaging techniques

At present, the most accurate *in-vivo* methods of measuring body composition are multislice MRI and axial CT. The use of CT or MRI provides three-dimensional information on body composition. CT and MRI can be used to assess total body composition (multiple scans), but are normally used only to obtain data on body fat distribution, by employing single scans at the L4/L5 level. Exposure to radiation rules out the use of CT scans for repetitive measurements. MRI does not require the use of radiation, and therefore may be preferred to CT scanning. A recent study by Snel *et al.* [13] using MRI to assess visceral and subcutaneous abdominal adipose tissue and subcutaneous hip adipose tissue in patients with GHD has confirmed previous findings [14], with a higher FM in the GH-deficient state and a decline in FM following GH replacement therapy. The cost of the measurements and restricted access to instruments are limiting factors in the utility of these techniques.

Body composition in GHD – baseline characteristics

One of the most important effects of GHD is on body composition. Using a variety of techniques, adult patients with GHD have consistently been shown to have subnormal tissue hydration, reduced LBM and increased FM [14, 15]. Body weight is usually increased compared with control subjects, and the presence of multiple pituitary hormone deficiencies appears to favour increased body weight and development of obesity [16, 17]. This was confirmed in a large number of patients; data obtained from 1552 patients enrolled in KIMS – Pfizer International Metabolic Database – demonstrated that 445 patients (29%) were obese, with a BMI above 30 kg/m^2 prior to commencement of GH replacement therapy. In the same cohort, BMI was significantly higher (all $p < 0.001$) in patients with multiple hormone deficiencies (four additional pituitary hormone deficiencies) compared with those in other groups (Fig. 1). BMI was also found to increase with increasing age (Fig. 2) and was significantly higher in patients who had received radiotherapy compared with those who had not (Fig. 3).

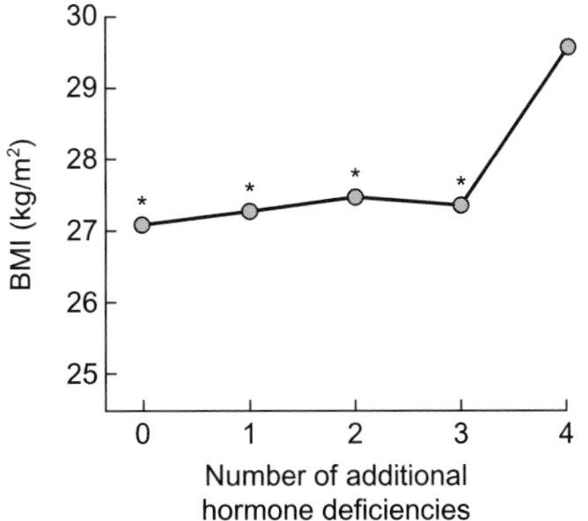

*Figure 1. Relationship between mean body mass index (BMI) and number of additional pituitary hormone deficiencies in adults with GHD. Data are presented as means. Patients with four additional hormone deficiencies had a higher BMI compared with patients with one, two, three or no additional hormone deficiencies, *p < 0.001.*

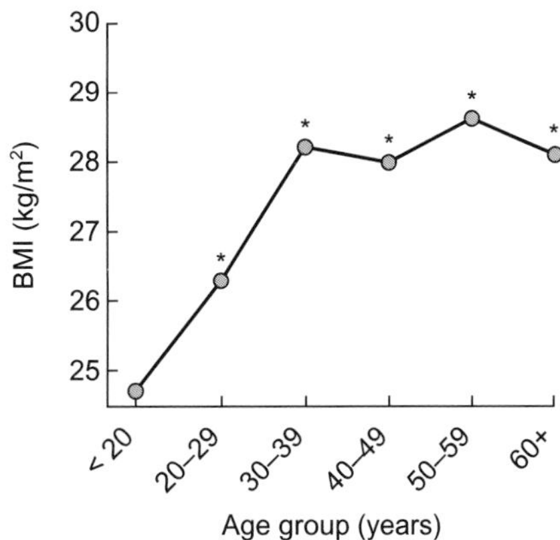

*Figure 2. Relationship between mean body mass index (BMI) and age. Data are presented as means. Patients younger than 20 years of age had a lower BMI compared with patients in older age groups, *p < 0.001.*

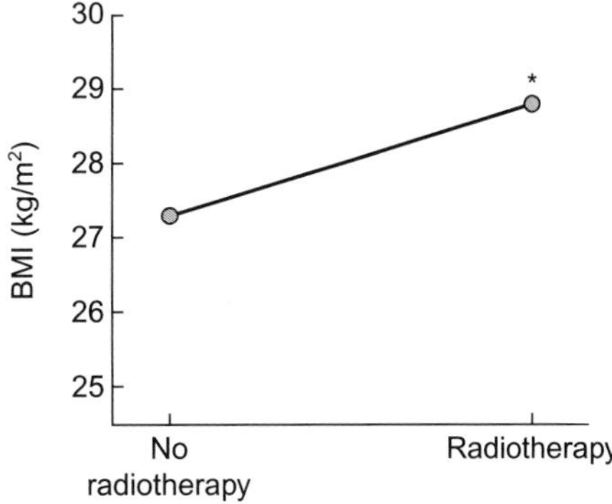

*Figure 3. Relationship between mean body mass index (BMI) and previous radiotherapy. Data are presented as means. Patients who had received radiotherapy had a higher BMI compared with patients who had not received radiotherapy, *p < 0.001.*

FM

Salomon *et al.* [14] were the first to demonstrate that FM was higher by a mean of 7% in patients with GHD compared with predicted values based on age, gender and height. The excess fat accumulates in a central (abdominal) pattern, mostly in visceral tissue. The reduced lipolytic tone in patients with GHD accounts for the majority of the excess adiposity. The average size and lipid content of subcutaneous adipocytes in GH-deficient patients is greater than that in normal subjects.

LBM

Reduced LBM is an important feature of GHD. Initial studies reported a mean reduction in LBM of 7–8% (measured by whole-body ^{40}K counting), corresponding to approximately 4 kg of lean tissue [14].

Total body weight

Patients with GHD are characteristically overweight. Rosenfalck *et al.* [18] have presented baseline data of patients with GHD with a relative body weight of 116.8 ± 20.1% (mean ± SD) of ideal body weight. Weight was increased compared with ideal weight primarily because of an FM that was 1.5 SD scores (SDS) above age- and sex-matched mean values [18]. In a study of more than 100 adults with GHD, body weight was increased by 7.5 kg in men and 3.6 kg in women compared with that of healthy individuals [19]. The difference in men was explained by an average increase of 6.6 kg in FM and 1.6 kg in body cell mass, and a simultaneous reduction of 0.7 kg in extracellular water. An increase in FM of 6.0 kg and a concurrent decrease of 2.4 kg in extracellular water accounted for the change seen in women.

Effect of GH treatment on body composition

GH is a potent anabolic and lipolytic hormone with a variety of metabolic functions, including an anti-natriuretic action. Each of these properties has an impact on body composition. The effects of GH on fuel metabolism include amplified lipolytic activity [20] and protein synthesis [21] and indirect inhibition of proteolysis via insulin-like growth factor I (IGF-I) [22]. GH-enhanced lipolytic activity in adipose tissue, in conjunction with reduced triglyceride accumulation via inhibition of lipoprotein lipase activity, appear to be the major mechanisms by which GH diminishes total FM [23]. The effects of GH on preadipocyte and adipocyte function, however, are complex, and are mediated via the GH receptor. Hypophysectomy decreases GH receptor gene expression in adipose tissue in the rat and GH replacement restores expression of the receptor gene [24]. The acute lipolytic response to GH administration is an increase in serum free fatty acids – probably via an amplified catecholaminergic tone.

Short-term effects

Several short-term studies have confirmed that initiation of GH replacement therapy in adults with GHD improves body composition [25]. GH has consistently been shown to induce an increase in LBM and a concomitant reduction in FM, with a particular reduction in central obesity. In all reported studies the increase in LBM varied from 2.0 to 5.5 kg after 6 months of GH replacement [16, 25, 26]. In these studies the changes in LBM were associated with reductions in FM of approximately 4–6 kg. Anthropometric measurements indicated that the most important change occurs in the abdominal region, corresponding to reduced visceral FM [13, 25]. Additionally, GH therapy increased the muscle to fat ratio of the thigh [27]. The total cross-sectional area, as well as volume of thigh muscle, were also increased following GH treatment both in patients with childhood-onset GHD and adult-onset GHD [15, 28]. Finally, GH replacement results in an increase in total body water, particularly extracellular water, within 3–5 days [29].

Long-term effects

The long-term effects of GH treatment on body composition comprise a sustained favourable redistribution of the body compartments [18, 30, 31]. KIMS data on the long-term effects are shown in Table 2. Data from 331 patients enrolled in KIMS have revealed a significant reduction compared with baseline in total FM, measured by DXA, following 12 and 24 months of GH replacement therapy. GH replacement therapy was also accompanied by a significant increase in LBM, from baseline to 12 and 24 months. Data on waist circumference and WHR obtained from 1421 KIMS patients consistently showed significant improvement at 12 and 24 months compared with baseline values. Consistent with these findings, 10 years of GH replacement therapy in adults with GHD induced significant increases in LBM and thigh muscle area and a significant reduction in FM [31]. Götherström *et al.* [30] examined patients with GHD during 5 years of follow-up, and showed a sustained increase in LBM, whereas body fat was reduced by 1.2–2.7 kg as measured by DXA, or using a four- or five-compartment model. The changes in FM and LBM were generally observed after 1 year of treatment [30]. Three years of GH therapy normalized muscle mass and the muscle to fat ratio from initial subnormal levels. The normalization, however, reflected the fact that the muscle to fat ratio decreased with age in the control group [32].

Despite an improved body composition in patients following GH replacement therapy, both Rosenfalck *et al.* [18] and Götherström *et al.* [30] have demonstrated a minor reduction in body weight after the first year of therapy, followed by regain of weight to levels above baseline after 2–5 years. Data obtained from KIMS have shown unaltered BMI during 24 months of treatment, despite the changes in distribution of mass, because the BMI estimate does not distinguish between FM and LBM.

Gender difference in GH-induced changes in body composition

The greater responsiveness of IGF-I to GH treatment in men compared with women with GHD is accompanied by more pronounced changes in body composition in the former, at least in the short term. Johansson *et al.* [33] found a greater loss of FM in men than in women with GHD, when treated with GH. Treatment with GH for 6 and 12 months caused significantly greater increments in FFM in GH-deficient men than in GH-deficient women [26]. Data obtained from 665 adults with GHD enrolled in KIMS revealed a greater decrease in WHR, but not in FM, in men than in women following 1 year of GH treatment [34]. Finally, Span *et al.* [35] reported a significant increase in body weight and FFM during GH replacement. The increases were more pronounced in men than in women, reflecting the higher responsiveness of IGF-I in men. The FM decline was also more pronounced in men than in women at 6 months, but the gender difference in FM levelled off and was subsequently insignificant.

Effect of GH on body composition in the elderly

Normal ageing is associated with a decreased amplitude of GH pulses and reduced serum levels of IGF-I. Increasing age is also coupled with a redistribution of body fat to the visceral compartment. The cause–effect relationship between age, body composition and GH, however, is not fully understood. Nevertheless, Toogood *et al.* [36] have demonstrated reduced spontaneous GH secretion and a reduced GH response to arginine in elderly patients with pituitary disease when compared with healthy age-matched subjects, and current data verify that elderly

Table 2. *Anthropometry and body composition, measured by dual-energy X-ray absorptiometry, before and after 12 and 24 months of GH replacement therapy in patients with GHD enrolled in KIMS. Values are means ± SEM. *p < 0.05 compared with baseline values.*

	Baseline	12 months	24 months
Body mass index (kg/m^2)	27.8 ± 5.8 (n = 1552)	27.6 ± 5.8 (n = 558)	27.6 ± 5.2 (n = 308)
Waist circumference (cm)	93.9 ± 14.9 (n = 1421)	91.1 ± 13.8* (n =556)	92.2 ± 13.5* (n = 317)
Waist/hip ratio	0.92 ± 0.11 (n = 1419)	0.89 ± 0.09* (n = 555)	0.90 ± 0.08* (n = 317)
Fat mass (kg)	26.8 ± 11.3 (n = 331)	24.6 ± 10.6* (n = 103)	24.5 ± 10.7* (n = 78)
Lean body mass (kg)	46.5 ± 12.8 (n = 331)	49.6 ± 12.0* (n = 103)	51.6 ± 12.6* (n = 78)

patients with GHD respond to GH replacement therapy similarly to their young and middle-aged counterparts, with improvements in body composition, bone metabolism and quality of life [37–39]. Data from 265 GH-deficient patients aged over 65 years commencing GH replacement at the time of entry into KIMS were analysed. At baseline, waist circumference and WHR were slightly higher in the elderly patients compared with 2469 younger patients (Fig. 4). Despite more pronounced clinical abnormalities at baseline in the elderly population, the improvements in body composition as determined by waist and hip measurements and LBM measured by BI, were of the same order of magnitude in response to GH replacement in elderly and younger patients with GHD (Fig. 4).

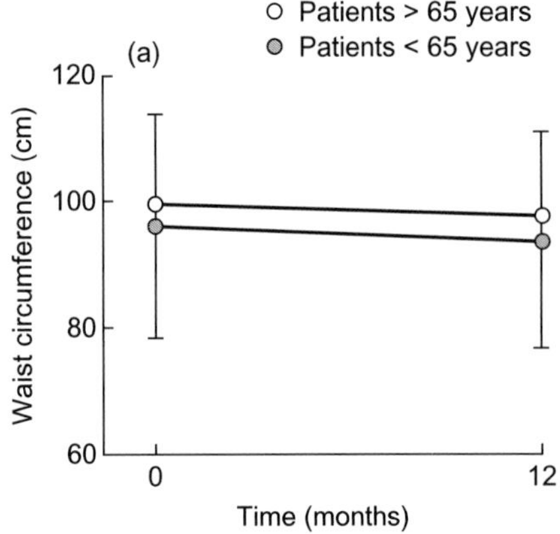

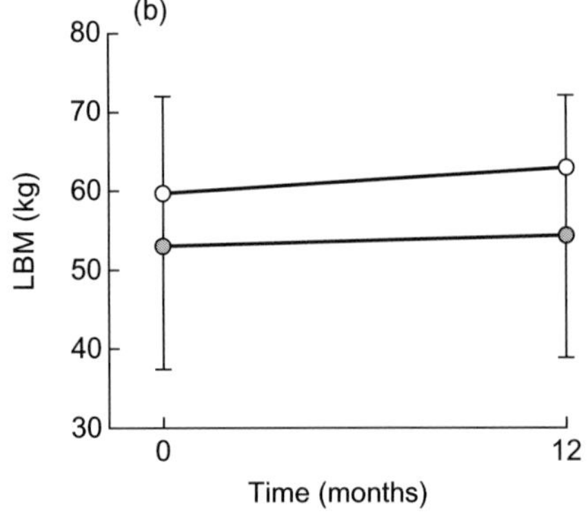

Figure 4. *Effect of 12 months of GH therapy on (a) waist circumference and (b) lean body mass (LBM), as measured by bioelectrical impedance, in patients aged over 65 years and under 65 years. Data are presented as medians and the 10th to 90th percentiles.*

Conclusions

In general, the most accurate methods of measuring body composition *in vivo* are multislice MRI and axial CT; however, the limited capacity, costs and, in CT, exposure to radiation, leave DXA as the method of choice.

Using a variety of techniques, adults with GHD have consistently been shown to have subnormal tissue hydration, reduced LBM and increased FM. For baseline characteristics the most appropriate methods for evaluation of body composition in adults with GHD are WHR and DXA. For follow-up of individual patients, waist circumference is the most sensitive method, if combined with DXA, which can also provide an estimate of abdominal fat.

GH replacement therapy normalizes body composition and fluid homeostasis, including reduction of adipose tissue and concomitant increases in LBM and tissue hydration. Improvements in body composition following GH replacement therapy should be seen not only as a cosmetic goal, but as a normalization of metabolism. Individual dose titration of GH, with regards to both gender and age, is required to achieve the most favourable response.

References

1. Behnke AR Jr, Feen BG, Welham WC. The specific gravity of healthy men. Body weight divided by volume as an index of obesity. 1942. Obes Res 1995;3:295–300
2. Deurenberg P, Weststrate JA, Seidell JC. Body mass index as a measure of body fatness: age- and sex-specific prediction formulas. Br J Nutr 1991;65:105–14
3. Gallagher D, Visser M, Sepulveda D, Pierson RN, Harris T, Heymsfield SB. How useful is body mass index for comparison of body fatness across age, sex, and ethnic groups? Am J Epidemiol 1996;143:228–39
4. Heymsfield SB, Nunez C, Pietrobelli A. Bioimpedance analysis: what are the next steps? Nutr Clin Practice 1997;12:201–3

5. de Boer H, Blok GJ, Voerman HJ, De Vries PM, van der Veen EA. Body composition in adult growth hormone-deficient men, assessed by anthropometry and bio-impedance analysis. J Clin Endocrinol Metab 1992; 75:833–7

6. de Boer H, Blok GJ, Voerman B, de Vries P, Popp-Snijders C, van der Veen E. The optimal growth hormone replacement dose in adults, derived from bioimpedance analysis. J Clin Endocrinol Metab 1995; 80:2069–76

7. Cameron N, Human growth. Vol. 2. London: Tindall 1978

8. Durnin JV, Womersley J. Body fat assessed from total body density and its estimation from skinfold thickness: measurements on 481 men and women aged from 16 to 72 years. Br J Nutr 1974;32:77–97

9. Siri WE. Body composition from fluid spaces and density: analysis of methods. 1961. Nutrition 1993; 9:480–91

10. Pietrobelli A, Formica C, Wang Z, Heymsfield SB. Dual-energy X-ray absorptiometry body composition model: review of physical concepts. Am J Physiol 1996;271:E941–51

11. Ho KY, Kelly JJ. Role of growth hormone in fluid homeostasis. Horm Res 1991;36 (Suppl 1):44–8

12. Bruce A, Andersson M, Arvidsson B, Isaksson B. Body composition. Prediction of normal body potassium, body water and body fat in adults on the basis of body height, body weight and age. Scand J Clin Lab Invest 1980;40:461–73

13. Snel YE, Doerga ME, Brummer RM, Zelissen PM, Koppeschaar HP. Magnetic resonance imaging-assessed adipose tissue and serum lipid and insulin concentrations in growth hormone-deficient adults. Effect of growth hormone replacement. Arterioscler Thromb Vasc Biol 1995;15:1543–8

14. Salomon F, Cuneo RC, Hesp R, Sönksen PH. The effects of treatment with recombinant human growth hormone on body composition and metabolism in adults with growth hormone deficiency. N Engl J Med 1989; 321:1797–803

15. Cuneo RC, Salomon F, Wiles CM, Hesp R, Sönksen PH. Growth hormone treatment in growth hormone-deficient adults. I. Effects on muscle mass and strength. J Appl Physiol 1991;70:688–94

16. Jørgensen JO, Pedersen SA, Thuesen L, Jørgensen J, Ingemann-Hansen T, Skakkebæk NE, Christiansen JS. Beneficial effects of growth hormone treatment in GH-deficient adults. Lancet 1989;1:1221–5

17. Libber SM, Plotnick LP, Johanson AJ, Blizzard RM, Kwiterovich PO, Migeon CJ. Long-term follow-up of hypopituitary patients treated with human growth hormone. Medicine (Baltimore) 1990;69:46–55

18. Rosenfalck AM, Maghsoudi S, Fisker S, Jørgensen JO, Christiansen JS, Hilsted J, Vølund AA, Madsbad S. The effect of 30 months of low-dose replacement therapy with recombinant human growth hormone (rhGH) on insulin and C-peptide kinetics, insulin secretion, insulin sensitivity, glucose effectiveness, and body composition in GH-deficient adults. J Clin Endocrinol Metab 2000;85:4173–81

19. Rosén T, Bosæus I, Tolli J, Lindstedt G, Bengtsson B-Å. Increased body fat mass and decreased extracellular fluid volume in adults with growth hormone deficiency. Clin Endocrinol (Oxf) 1993;38:63–71

20. Raben MS, Hollenberg CH. Effect of growth hormone on plasma fatty acids. J Clin Invest 1959;38:484–8

21. Russell-Jones DL, Weissberger AJ, Bowes SB, Kelly JM, Thomason M, Umpleby AM, Jones RH, Sönksen PH. Protein metabolism in growth hormone deficiency, and effects of growth hormone replacement therapy. Acta Endocrinol (Copenh) 1993;128 (Suppl 2):44–7

22. Umpleby AM, Russell-Jones DL. The hormonal control of protein metabolism. Baillieres Clin Endocrinol Metab 1996;10:551–70

23. Richelsen B. Action of growth hormone in adipose tissue. Horm Res 1997;48 (Suppl 5):105–10

24. Frick GP, Leonard JL, Goodman HM. Effect of hypophysectomy on growth hormone receptor gene expression in rat tissues. Endocrinology 1990; 126:3076–82

25. Bengtsson B-Å, Edén S, Lonn L, Kvist H, Stokland A, Lindstedt G, Bosæus I, Tolli J, Sjöstrom L, Isaksson OG. Treatment of adults with growth hormone (GH) deficiency with recombinant human GH. J Clin Endocrinol Metab 1993;76:309–17

26. Cuneo RC, Judd S, Wallace JD, Perry-Keene D, Burger H, Lim-Tio S, Strauss B, Stockigt J, Topliss D, Alford F, Hew L, Bode H, Conway A, Handelsman D, Dunn S, Boyages S, Cheung NW, Hurley D. The Australian Multicenter Trial of Growth Hormone (GH) Treatment in GH-Deficient Adults. J Clin Endocrinol Metab 1998;83:107–16

27. Jørgensen JO, Pedersen SA, Thuesen L, Jørgensen J, Møller J, Müller J, Skakkebæk NE, Christiansen JS. Long-term growth hormone treatment in growth hormone deficient adults. Acta Endocrinol (Copenh) 1991;125:449–53

28. Whitehead HM, Boreham C, McIlrath EM, Sheridan B, Kennedy L, Atkinson AB, Hadden DR. Growth hormone treatment of adults with growth hormone deficiency: results of a 13-month placebo controlled cross-over study. Clin Endocrinol (Oxf) 1992;36:45–52

29. Hoffman DM, Crampton L, Sernia C, Nguyen TV, Ho KK. Short-term growth hormone (GH) treatment of GH-deficient adults increases body sodium and extracellular water, but not blood pressure. J Clin Endocrinol Metab 1996;81:1123–8

30. Götherström G, Svensson J, Koranyi J, Alpsten M, Bosæus I, Bengtsson B-Å, Johannsson G. A prospective study of 5 years of GH replacement therapy in GH-deficient adults: sustained effects on body composition, bone mass, and metabolic indices. J Clin Endocrinol Metab 2001;86:4657–65

31. Gibney J, Wallace JD, Spinks T, Schnorr L, Ranicar A, Cuneo RC, Lockhart S, Burnand KG, Salomon F, Sönksen PH, Russell-Jones D. The effects of 10 years of recombinant human growth hormone (GH) in adult GH-deficient patients. J Clin Endocrinol Metab 1999; 84:2596–602

32. Jørgensen JO, Thuesen L, Müller J, Ovesen P, Skakkebæk NE, Christiansen JS. Three years of growth hormone treatment in growth hormone-deficient adults: near normalization of body composition and physical performance. Eur J Endocrinol 1994;130:224–8

33. Johansson AG, Engstrom BE, Ljunghall S, Karlsson FA, Burman P. Gender differences in the effects of long-term growth hormone (GH) treatment on bone in adults with GH deficiency. J Clin Endocrinol Metab 1999;84:2002–7

34. Bengtsson B-Å, Abs R, Bennmarker H, Monson JP, Feldt-Rasmussen U, Hernberg-Ståhl E, Westberg B, Wilton P, Wüster C. The effects of treatment and the individual responsiveness to growth hormone (GH) replacement therapy in 665 GH-deficient adults. KIMS Study Group and the KIMS International Board. J Clin Endocrinol Metab 1999;84:3929–35

35. Span JP, Pieters GF, Sweep FG, Hermus AR, Smals AG. Gender differences in rhGH-induced changes in body composition in GH-deficient adults. J Clin Endocrinol Metab 2001;86:4161–5

36. Toogood AA, O'Neill PA, Shalet SM. Beyond the somatopause: growth hormone deficiency in adults over the age of 60 years. J Clin Endocrinol Metab 1996;81:460–5

37. Fernholm R, Bramnert M, Hagg E, Hilding A, Baylink DJ, Mohan S, Thorén M. Growth hormone replacement therapy improves body composition and increases bone metabolism in elderly patients with pituitary disease. J Clin Endocrinol Metab 2000; 85:4104–12

38. Monson JP, Jönsson P. Aspects of growth hormone (GH) replacement in elderly patients with GH deficiency: data from KIMS. Horm Res 2003;60:112–20

39. Monson JP, Abs R, Bengtsson B-Å, Bennmarker H, Feldt-Rasmussen U, Hernberg-Ståhl E, Thorén M, Westberg B, Wilton P, Wüster C. Growth hormone deficiency and replacement in elderly hypopituitary adults. KIMS Study Group and the KIMS International Board. Pharmacia and Upjohn International Metabolic Database. Clin Endocrinol (Oxf) 2000;53:281–9

12 The lipid profile in adult hypopituitary patients with growth hormone deficiency

Pascale Abrams and Roger Abs
Department of Endocrinology and Antwerp Metabolic Research Unit (AMRU), University of Antwerp, Antwerp, Belgium

Summary

It is now a well accepted phenomenon that adult hypopituitary patients have an increased mortality if not supplemented for growth hormone deficiency (GHD). The adverse lipid profile of GHD is probably one of the main causes of the increased prevalence of cardiovascular risk factors. GHD is associated with a dual abnormality in lipid metabolism: a defect in the low-density lipoprotein (LDL) pathway and in the triglyceride-rich lipoprotein pathway. This results in an increase in serum concentrations of total cholesterol and LDL-cholesterol on one hand, and an increase in triglycerides and decrease in high-density lipoprotein (HDL)-cholesterol on the other. The combination of these factors confers an increased risk for cardiovascular disease. Growth hormone (GH) replacement therapy induces a dichotomous response upon both pathways. GH will stimulate the induction of LDL receptors and consequently decrease the LDL serum concentration. However, the disturbance in triglycerides and HDLs is not rectified by GH replacement, probably because of an increase in hepatic very low-density lipoprotein secretion. The information retrieved from KIMS – Pfizer International Metabolic Database – is in line with the data reported in the literature. The findings in a large number of severely GH-deficient patients confirm the adverse cholesterol profile and undoubtedly show the impact of age and gender. The pronounced favourable effect of GH therapy is documented for each age group and gender.

Introduction

Studies have shown that hypopituitarism acquired during adulthood is associated with an increased mortality and prevalence of cardiovascular risk factors when patients receive only conventional replacement therapy [1–4]. The increase in cardiovascular risk factors has been established by comparing hypopituitary patients with the normal population [2, 5] and with age-, gender- and weight-matched normal controls [6–8]. It is thus highly probable that growth hormone deficiency (GHD) plays an important role in the increased occurrence of vascular disease in hypopituitarism. Acting in concert, the different metabolic disturbances associated with GHD are probably responsible for the strikingly unfavourable cardiovascular risk profile of GH-deficient adults [9]. Although the mechanisms of vascular deterioration induced by GHD are multiple, the adverse lipid changes in GH-deficient patients are likely to play a major role, as anticipated by the potent actions of growth hormone (GH) on lipid metabolism [10].

This chapter gives a brief summary of the relationship between lipid metabolism and the effects of GH and reviews the abnormalities in lipid metabolism in adult patients with GHD. The effects of GH replacement are assessed from data available in the literature and KIMS – Pfizer International Metabolic Database – is used to give an overview of the lipid profile in a large population of adult GH-deficient patients.

Lipid metabolism

Triglycerides are used for production and storage of energy, while cholesterol is a component of the cell membrane structure and a precursor of bile acid and steroids. Both dietary and *de novo* synthesized cholesterol are transported through the circulation in lipoprotein particles. The protein component of a lipoprotein is called an apolipoprotein. The various lipoproteins are distinguished by the proportions of their components. Large lipoproteins, like chylomicrons and very low-density lipoproteins (VLDLs), have cores that are rich in triglycerides. Smaller and denser lipoproteins, such as high-density lipoproteins (HDLs) and low-density lipoproteins (LDLs), have cores that mostly contain cholesterol esters. HDL helps to remove cholesterol from the blood and prevents cholesterol from building up. LDLs are the principal serum carriers of cholesterol, delivering cholesterol from the liver to peripheral tissues, primarily the adrenal glands and the adipose tissue. LDLs also return cholesterol to the liver.

The cellular uptake of cholesterol from LDLs occurs following the interaction of LDLs with the LDL receptor, also called the apolipoprotein B-100/apolipoprotein E (apoB-100/apoE) receptor. While the extracellular domain of the receptor accounts for the apoB-100/apoE binding, the intracellular domain is responsible for the clustering of LDL receptors into regions of the plasma membrane termed coated pits. Ligand binding by the liver receptors clears the lipoproteins from the circulation, but ligand binding to cells in the blood vessel wall can result in foam cell formation, which initiates atherosclerosis. Once LDL binds to the receptor, the complex is rapidly internalized. The portion of the endosomal membrane harbouring the receptor is then recycled to the plasma membrane and the LDL-containing endosomes fuse with lysosomes. Acid hydrolases of the lysosomes degrade the apolipoproteins and release free fatty acids (FFAs) and cholesterol. The free cholesterol is either incorporated into plasma membranes or esterified by acyl-coenzyme A:cholesterol acyltransferase (ACAT) and stored within the cell. The level of intracellular cholesterol is regulated through cholesterol-induced suppression of LDL receptor synthesis and cholesterol-induced inhibition of cholesterol synthesis. The increased level of intracellular cholesterol that results from LDL uptake has the additional effect of activating ACAT, thereby allowing the storage of excess cholesterol within cells. However, the effect of cholesterol-induced suppression of LDL receptor synthesis is a decrease in the rate at which LDLs are removed from the serum. This can lead to excess circulating levels of cholesterol and cholesteryl esters when the dietary intake of fat and cholesterol exceeds the needs of the body. The excess cholesterol tends to be deposited in the skin, tendons and, more seriously, within the arteries, leading to atherosclerosis.

Regulation of lipid metabolism by GH

GH status in healthy adults is known to be an independent determinant of total cholesterol, LDL-cholesterol and triglycerides [11]. GH has physiological effects on both VLDL and cholesterol metabolism, which explains the lipid disturbances observed in patients with GHD.

Effect of GH on VLDL metabolism

GH has important effects on intrahepatic substrate availability, as it stimulates VLDL apoB liver secretion by a relative increase in intrahepatic lipid concentration. GH has a lipolytic effect, especially on visceral fat, leading to a decrease in re-esterification of non-esterified FFAs in the peripheral tissues. FFAs appear in the portal circulation and are directly cleared by the liver through a GH-dependent mechanism [12]. An increased hepatic esterification leads to an increase in intrahepatic triglycerides and cholesterol esters. This, in turn, stimulates VLDL apoB secretion.

On the other hand, GH also stimulates VLDL apoB catabolism. An increased hydrolysation of triglyceride through lipoprotein lipase (LPL) will lead to the formation of triglyceride-depleted LDL particles. However, evidence concerning the effect of GH on LPL, which is necessary for the clearance of VLDL apoB, is contradictory. GH increases total postheparin LPL activity in rats [13], but in humans GH appears to reduce total plasma postheparin LPL [14] and adipose tissue LPL activity [15]. VLDL particles can be cleared through two pathways: a non-LDL pathway and an LDL pathway [16]. GH stimulates direct hepatic removal through different receptors, such as the LDL receptor, LDL receptor-related protein, and/or the VLDL receptor. GH also directly affects the expression of hepatic LDL receptors and key enzymes [17]. The up-regulation of LDL receptors increases the conversion of VLDL to LDL, resulting in an enhanced clearance of apoB-containing lipoprotein particles.

In adults with GHD, VLDL secretion is enhanced and LDL receptor activity is decreased, resulting in elevated levels of serum triglycerides and LDL-cholesterol, and abnormal postprandial lipoprotein clearance, despite normal LPL activity [18, 19]. GH replacement in GH-deficient patients will thus enhance the uptake of VLDL particles by LDL receptor-related protein and/or the VLDL receptor, and will deplete the particles of cholesterol.

In conclusion, although GH therapy stimulates VLDL apoB secretion by increasing intrahepatic lipid availability, Christ *et al.* [20] suggest that GH replacement therapy improves the lipid profile by increasing the removal of VLDL particles as a result of up-regulating LDL receptors and modifying the VLDL composition. However, as VLDL synthesis remains elevated, serum triglyceride levels may not normalize.

Effect of GH on cholesterol metabolism

GH stimulates the expression and activity of key enzymes involved in cholesterol synthesis and bile acid metabolism. Cholesterol 7α-hydroxylase controls the conversion of cholesterol to bile acids. In GHD, reduced activity of this enzyme results in intrahepatic cholesterol accumulation. This, in turn, will down-regulate LDL-receptor numbers and increase 3-hydroxy-3-methylglutaryl coenzyme A-reductase activity, which will subsequently increase cholesterol synthesis [21].

Cholesteryl transfer protein (CETP) transfers triglycerides from triglyceride-rich lipoprotein particles to HDL, in exchange for cholesteryl esters from HDL. HDL then transports cholesterol from the peripheral tissues toward the liver for excretion into the bile. As plasma CETP activity is lower in GH-deficient patients, the decrease in HDL cholesteryl ester concentration may lead to a decreased serum HDL concentration.

Effect of GH on lipoprotein (a)

Lipoprotein (a) has been proposed to be an independent risk factor for cardiovascular disease. Several studies have revealed increases in lipoprotein (a) after initiation of GH replacement in GH-deficient patients [22–24], although this observation has not been uniform [19, 25]. Wieringa *et al.* [26] showed that the change in lipoprotein (a) concentration during GH therapy is assay dependent.

The lipid profile in GH-deficient adults

The relationship between GHD and an adverse lipid profile was observed for the first time in GH-deficient dwarfs, one-third of whom showed abnormal lipid and lipoprotein concentrations [27]. Since then, lipid and lipoprotein abnormalities have been well documented by several authors in numerous patients with hypopituitarism.

In a retrospective study, Wüster *et al.* [2] found that 77% of 122 adult GH-deficient patients, adequately treated with conventional replacement therapy but not with GH, had dyslipidaemia, which was complicated in 14% by a history of vascular events. These figures were higher than the incidence shown in the PROCAM (Prospective Cardiovascular Münster) study [28].

Baseline data reported in a double-blind placebo-controlled trial with GH in 24 GH-deficient patients clearly showed significantly higher serum concentrations of total cholesterol, LDL-cholesterol, apoB and triglycerides, and lower concentrations of HDL-cholesterol [6]. Rosén *et al.* [5] compared 104 GH-deficient patients with the MONICA (Monitoring trends and determinants in cardiovascular disease) study control population and found a significant increase in serum triglycerides, no difference in total cholesterol, but a significant decrease in HDL-cholesterol.

de Boer *et al.* [7] evaluated the lipid profile in 64 young adults with GHD who were compared with an age- and gender-matched control group. Total cholesterol, LDL-cholesterol and apoB levels were significantly higher in GH-deficient patients, while HDL-cholesterol and triglycerides were normal. An inverse association between insulin-like growth factor I (IGF-I) and LDL indicated that the abnormality in lipid metabolism could be related to the severity of GHD.

Vahl *et al.* [29] compared serum lipid and lipoprotein levels in 27 adults with GHD with those of healthy matched controls. Total cholesterol, LDL-cholesterol and triglycerides were significantly higher in patients compared with healthy controls, with no difference in HDL-cholesterol or apoA levels.

Sanmarti *et al.* [30] conducted a retrospective study of the health status of 926 hypopituitary patients with adult-onset GHD who were not treated with GH, including 1-year follow-up data, which were available in 356 patients. Clinical evaluations and laboratory tests showed a higher incidence of cardiovascular risk factors. Total cholesterol, LDL-cholesterol, and triglyceride levels were significantly higher, and HDL-cholesterol levels significantly lower, compared with those of a reference population.

Abdu *et al.* [31] compared the serum lipid and lipoprotein levels of 50 hypopituitary adults with GHD on conventional hormone replacement with those of 45 healthy matched controls. Compared with controls, serum triglyceride levels were significantly increased in male and female patients, total cholesterol and LDL-cholesterol were significantly increased in male patients, HDL-cholesterol was significantly reduced in female patients, the ratio of total- to HDL-cholesterol was significantly increased in both male and female patients, and apoA1 levels were significantly reduced in female patients. Risk-factor modelling showed an increased coronary risk associated with hypopituitarism, particularly among females, due largely to the abnormal lipid profile, which appeared to be related to GHD either directly, or indirectly through central adiposity.

Kearney *et al.* [32] compared the VLDL composition and apoB kinetics in 16 hypopituitary patients and 16 controls. They suggested that the triglyceride enrichment of VLDL may be an important mechanism underlying VLDL overproduction in GHD and may contribute to the vascular mortality of hypopituitarism.

Recent evidence indicates that markers of increased cardiovascular risk are already present in GH-deficient children and adolescents. Gleeson *et al.* [33] examined lipid levels in eight children and adolescents, and seven adults from the same Brazilian community with untreated severe, congenital GHD caused by a mutation in the *GH-releasing hormone receptor* gene and compared the results with those of 29 controls from the same extended kindred and with an age- and gender-matched USA reference population. More GH-deficient children had plasma levels of total- and LDL-cholesterol above the 95th percentile for the reference population compared with controls, and the median total cholesterol and LDL levels were higher in the GH-deficient adults than in controls. These results show that the lipid profile is abnormal in children as well as adults with isolated GHD, although there appeared to be no significant worsening of the lipid abnormality with duration of GHD or attainment of adulthood. Another study has shown that LDL levels were also increased in 12 untreated GH-deficient adolescents when compared with healthy controls, whereas cholesterol, HDL-cholesterol, and triglyceride concentrations were similar to controls [34]. Similar results were found in a study comparing 15 GH-deficient adolescents receiving GH replacement therapy with matched controls [35]. After GH discontinuation, a further deterioration of the lipid profile occurred, as evidenced by increased total/HDL-cholesterol, LDL-cholesterol and triglycerides.

As indicated by the previous study by Colao *et al.* [35], discontinuation of GH replacement has an adverse effect on the lipid profile, which is a strong argument in favour of GH therapy as an appropriate option in adults with GHD. This finding has also been demonstrated in other studies. Kohno *et al.* [36] showed that 6 months after stopping GH therapy a significant increase in total cholesterol was observed in 18 young male adults, while HDL-cholesterol remained unchanged. Johannsson *et al.* [37] demonstrated an accumulation of important cardiovascular risk factors in 21 adolescents with childhood-onset GHD 2 years after discontinuation of GH replacement. Apart from the increase in abdominal fat mass, an increase in total cholesterol, LDL-cholesterol and apoB, and a decrease in HDL-cholesterol, were found.

In conclusion, although not all studies have been consistent in their findings, a picture has emerged of two distinct abnormalities in lipid metabolism characteristic of GHD; namely, LDL and triglyceride pathway defects.

Effect of GH replacement on the lipid profile in GH-deficient adults

Clinical trials of GH therapy in adults with GHD indicate that treatment of such patients may reduce cardiovascular risk, at least by the effect of GH on lipid metabolism [6, 20, 22, 29, 37–56]. The results of these trials are summarized in Table 1.

Although there have been a number of negative results, the majority of studies demonstrate a significant reduction in total and LDL-cholesterol during GH replacement therapy, associated with an improvement of LDL receptor function resulting in an increased uptake of LDL-cholesterol. In contrast to the changes found in LDL-cholesterol metabolism, the abnormalities observed in the metabolism of triglyceride-rich lipoproteins appear not to be corrected by GH replacement. Indeed, triglyceride level, LDL particle size, and HDL level remained unaffected by GH replacement. This may be explained by the relative hyperinsulinaemia induced by GH and the availability of FFA, resulting in an increased hepatic VLDL secretion [57]. Hypertriglyceridaemia ensues, despite the GH-induced reduction in visceral adiposity.

KIMS: total cholesterol concentration in GH-deficient adults

The KIMS project allows determination of serum cholesterol concentrations in every adult GH-deficient patient included in the database. The measurement of this parameter in a single laboratory permits the follow-up of an important factor related to the increased mortality associated with GHD. Patients enrolled in the KIMS database were included in the analysis reported here if they satisfied the criteria of severe GHD.

Cholesterol profile at baseline

There were 2589 patients (mean age, 44.2 ± 14.6 years; mean body mass index [BMI], 28.2 ± 5.7 kg/m^2; mean IGF-I SD score [SDS], –2.4 ± 2.0) included in the study. Females numbered 1263 (48.8%; mean age, 43.6 ± 14.2 years; mean BMI, 28.3 ± 6.4 kg/m^2; mean IGF-I SDS, –2.8 ± 2.0), of which 769 were pre-menopausal (29.7%; mean age, 39.5 ± 12.5 years; mean BMI, 27.5 ± 5.9 kg/m^2; mean IGF-I SDS, –2.9 ± 2.1) and 494 were post-menopausal (19.1%; mean age, 50.1 ± 14.4 years; mean BMI, 29.5 ± 6.9 kg/m^2; mean IGF-I SDS, –2.5 ± 1.9). Males numbered 1326 (51.2%; mean age, 44.8 ± 15.0 years; mean BMI, 28.1 ± 5.0 kg/m^2; mean IGF-I SDS, –2.1 ± 2.0).

Table 1. *Results of clinical trials of GH in adults with GHD.*

Study	Design	Effect of GH replacement on lipid levels
Salomon *et al.* [38]	Double-blind, placebo-controlled, GH for 6 months, in 24 GH-deficient adults	Cholesterol decreased significantly; no difference in triglycerides
Cuneo *et al.* [6]	Double-blind, placebo-controlled, GH for 6 months, in 24 GH-deficient adults	Total cholesterol, LDL, LDL/HDL ratio and apoB decreased significantly; no change in HDL or apoA1
Snel *et al.* [39]	Open study, GH for 6 months, in 12 GH-deficient adults	Total cholesterol decreased significantly; HDL increased significantly
Beshyah *et al.* [40]	Double-blind, placebo-controlled, GH for 6 months, open for 12 months, in 40 GH-deficient adults	No significant changes at 6 months for total cholesterol, LDL, HDL, apoA1, apoB and triglycerides; at 18 months a downward trend in total cholesterol and LDL, and a significant increase in HDL
Weaver *et al.* [22]	Double-blind, placebo-controlled, GH for 6 months, in 22 hypopituitary adults	Total cholesterol and apoB decreased significantly
Nolte *et al.* [41]	Double-blind, placebo-controlled, GH for 12 months, in 17 GH-deficient adults (placebo group crossed over to GH after 12 months)	Total cholesterol, LDL, total cholesterol/LDL ratio, LDL/HDL ratio and triglycerides decreased significantly
Lucidi *et al.* [42]	Double blind, placebo-controlled, two GH doses for 1 week, in 6 GH-deficient adults	GH, 3.3 μg/kg/day but not 2.0 μg/kg/day or placebo, normalized lipid metabolism as determined by rate of lipolysis after [1,1,2,3,3-D5]glycerol
al-Shoumer *et al.* [43]	Open study, GH for 4 years, in 13 GH-deficient adults	Total cholesterol and LDL decreased significantly at 1 and 4 years; triglycerides, HDL, apoA1 and apoB did not change significantly
Vahl *et al.* [29]	Double-blind, placebo-controlled, GH for 12 months, in 27 GH-deficient adults	Total cholesterol decreased significantly, but remained significantly elevated; LDL decreased non-significantly; HDL and triglycerides were unchanged
Cuneo *et al.* [44]	Double-blind, placebo-controlled, GH for 6 months, in 166 GH-deficient adults (placebo group crossed over to GH after 6 months)	Total cholesterol and LDL decreased significantly
Christ *et al.* [20]	Double-blind, placebo-controlled, GH for 3 months, in 14 GH-deficient adults	Total cholesterol, LDL and VLDL cholesterol/VLDL apoB ratio decreased significantly
O'Neal *et al.* [45]	Open study, GH for 24 months, in 22 GH-deficient adults	Total cholesterol and LDL decreased significantly; triglycerides, HDL, apoA, apoB and LDL size did not change significantly
Bengtsson *et al.* [47]	Open study, GH for 12 months, in 665 GH-deficient adults (KIMS database)	Total cholesterol decreased significantly in men; HDL increased in women

Table 1. *Results of clinical trials of GH in adults with GHD (continued).*

Study	Design	Effect of GH replacement on lipid levels
Leonsson *et al.* [46]	Open, cross-over study, GH for 17 days followed by no treatment for 17 days in 6 GH-deficient adults on a high cholesterol/saturated fat diet	Total cholesterol, LDL, apoB and apoA1 increased on diet and GH therapy and tended to increase on diet without GH therapy; no change in triglycerides, VLDL, HDL and apoE
Johannsson *et al.* [37]	Open study of discontinuation of GH for 2 years in 40 GH-deficient adolescents, 21 of whom had severe GHD	Total cholesterol, LDL and apoB increased more in severe GH-deficient subjects; HDL decreased in patients with severe GHD and increased in GH-deficient patients with sufficient endogenous GH secretion
Kamarudin *et al.* [48]	Open study, GH for 6 and 24 months, in 10 GH-deficient adults	Total cholesterol decreased
Chrisoulidou *et al.* [49]	Open study, GH for 7 years or for 6–18 months versus no GH, in 33 GH-deficient adults	No significant difference in lipid levels
Amato *et al.* [50]	Open study, GH daily or 3 times weekly for 12 months, in 34 GH-deficient adults	Total cholesterol, LDL and triglycerides decreased significantly; HDL increased significantly after 6 months with no further change at 12 months
Florakis *et al.* [51]	Open study, GH for 6–24 months, in 90 GH-deficient adults	Total cholesterol and LDL decreased significantly at 6 months and the decrease was maintained during the study; HDL increased modestly at 18 months; no significant change in triglycerides
Sesmilo *et al.* [52]	Single-blind, placebo-controlled, GH for 18 months, in 40 GH-deficient adult men	Total cholesterol, LDL and total cholesterol/HDL ratio decreased significantly in first 3 months, but the decrease was not maintained
Koranyi *et al.* [53]	Open study, GH for 5 years, in 21 adults with adult-onset GHD and 21 adults with childhood-onset GHD	Lipid profile more disturbed and decrease in total cholesterol more marked in subjects with adult-onset GHD
Götherström *et al.* [54]	Open study, GH for 5 years, in 118 GH-deficient adults	Total cholesterol and LDL decreased; HDL increased after 1 year; triglycerides decreased after 5 years
Colao *et al.* [55]	Open study, GH for 12 months, in 20 GH-deficient adults	Total cholesterol, LDL and triglyceride decreased significantly; HDL increased significantly
Colao *et al.* [56]	Open study, GH for 12 months, in 15 GH-deficient adults versus no GH in 15 GH-deficient adults	Total cholesterol and LDL decreased significantly; HDL increased significantly; GH deprivation for 12 months induced further impairment of lipid profile

apo, apolipoprotein; HDL, high-density lipoprotein; LDL, low-density lipoprotein; VLDL, very low-density lipoprotein.

Table 2. Total cholesterol concentration at baseline in 2589 adult GH-deficient patients in KIMS. Mean values are adjusted to the 40–49 year group and a 50/50 gender distribution ± SD. $^{*}p < 0.001$ *and* $^{**}p < 0.0001$ *versus males*

Total cholesterol	mean ± SD (mmol/L)	95% CI (mmol/L)	mean ± SD (mg/dL)
Target	< 5.20	–	< 200
All	6.06 ± 1.28	5.96–6.16	233 ± 49
Males	5.95 ± 1.27	5.84–6.06	229 ± 49
Pre-menopausal females	6.14 ± 1.25*	6.02–6.26	236 ± 48
Post-menopausal females	6.22 ± 1.30**	6.07–6.37	239 ± 50

Baseline concentrations of total cholesterol for the whole cohort of GH-deficient patients were markedly higher than the currently accepted target range (Table 2). Baseline mean values of total cholesterol were above the target value in all age groups, except for the under 20-year-old age group (Fig. 1). The total cholesterol concentration increased progressively with age and reached a plateau from the age of 40–49 years onwards (Fig. 1). Compared with the 40–49 year age group, values were significantly lower in the under 20, 20–29 and 30–39 year age groups. The total cholesterol concentration was highest in post-menopausal women and lowest in men. Compared with men, the values were significantly higher in both pre-menopausal and post-menopausal women.

Of the 15 different variables examined besides age and gender, nine did not significantly influence the baseline cholesterol concentration (country, onset of GHD, duration of GHD, severity of hypopituitarism, severity of GHD, aetiology, previous GH replacement, radiotherapy, and use of

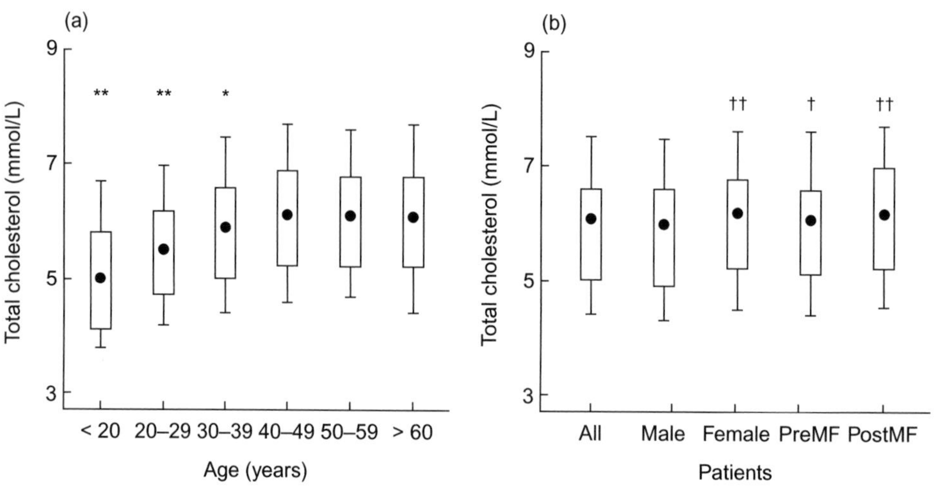

Figure 1. Total cholesterol concentration at baseline according to (a) age group ($^{*}p < 0.05$, $^{**}p < 0.0001$ *versus 40–49 year age group), and (b) gender (*$^{\dagger}p < 0.001$, $^{\dagger\dagger}p < 0.0001$ *versus males). 10th, 25th, 75th and 90th percentiles and mean values adjusted to a 50/50 gender distribution and the 40–49 year group. preMF, pre-menopausal; postMF, post-menopausal.*

Table 3. Total cholesterol concentration at baseline and after 1 year and 2 years of GH replacement therapy in 1206 adult patients with GHD in KIMS. $^{*}p < 0.01$, $^{**}p < 0.001$ *versus 1 year;* $^{\dagger}p < 0.0001$ *versus baseline.*

Total cholesterol	Baseline (mean ± SD) (mmol/L)	1 year (mean ± SD) (mmol/L)	2 years (mean ± SD) (mmol/L)
All	5.92 ± 1.21	5.54 ± 1.14†	5.45 ± 1.05**†
Males	5.79 ± 1.21	5.37 ± 1.09†	5.30 ± 1.08*†
Pre-menopausal females	5.98 ± 1.17	5.68 ± 1.16†	5.63 ± 1.07†
Post-menopausal females	6.19 ± 1.24	5.85 ± 1.27†	5.63 ± 1.20**†

lipid-lowering drugs). Six variables were found to have an effect: BMI (the BMI < 20 kg/m^2 group have a slightly lower total cholesterol compared with the BMI > 20 kg/m^2 groups), waist/hip ratio (total cholesterol is lower in the < 0.85 ratio group compared with each other ratio group), waist (total cholesterol is significantly higher in males with a waist circumference of 92–102 cm), smoking (total cholesterol is significantly higher in smokers), epilepsy (total cholesterol is significantly higher in patients receiving anti-epileptic drugs), diabetes mellitus (total cholesterol concentration is significantly lower in patients with diabetes mellitus).

Effect of GH replacement on total cholesterol (Table 3)

Mean total cholesterol concentration was measured at the 1- and 2-year time-points for the 1206 patients in whom longitudinal data were available. The characteristics were similar to the group consisting of 2589 patients.

A significant reduction in total cholesterol was observed at both the 1- and 2-year intervals. The mean decrease in total cholesterol was 0.38 ± 0.03 mmol/L after 12 months and 0.47 ± 0.03 mmol/L after 24 months. The change in cholesterol was also significant between year 1 and year 2: –0.09 ± 0.04. The decrease in total cholesterol after 1 year was significant for each gender group, and a further significant decrease was observed during the second year of treatment. A significant decrease in total cholesterol was found in each age group, except for the under 20-year-old age group. Moreover, a further decrease was observed between 1 and 2 years of treatment, which was significant in the age groups 50–59 and over 60.

The change in total cholesterol concentration during GH replacement therapy was essentially unaffected by any of the other baseline variables examined. In all subgroups, total cholesterol concentration was reduced after both 1 and 2 years. In most subgroups, the reductions after 1 and 2 years were statistically significant. The only subgroups for which this was not the case were the patients aged less than 20 years, with a BMI less than 20 kg/m^2, or with a baseline IGF-I SDS between 0 and 2.

Conclusion

From published studies and the information retrieved from the KIMS database, it is obvious that GHD in adults is associated with an unfavourable lipid profile. The lipid disturbances are twofold and involve an increase in both serum LDL and triglyceride concentrations. Recent studies have indicated that the lipid abnormalities are already present in adolescents with GHD. GH replacement therapy is accompanied by a favourable effect on LDL levels, independent of age and gender, while there are no apparent changes in triglyceride levels. Discontinuation of GH replacement results in a deterioration of the lipid profile. Moreover, data from KIMS show that long-term continuation of therapy is associated with a sustained improvement of the lipid parameters.

References

1. Rosén T, Bengtsson B-Å. Premature mortality due to cardiovascular disease in hypopituitarism. Lancet 1990; 336:285–8

2. Wüster C, Slenczka E, Ziegler R. Increased prevalence of osteoporosis and arteriosclerosis in conventionally substituted anterior pituitary insufficiency: need for additional growth hormone substitution? [German] Klin Wochenschr 1991;69:769–73

3. Bates AS, Van't Hoff W, Jones PJ, Clayton RN. The effect of hypopituitarism on life expectancy. J Clin Endocrinol Metab 1996;81:1169–72

4. Erfurth EM, Bülow B, Hagmar LE. Is vascular mortality increased in hypopituitarism? Pituitary 2000;3:77–81

5. Rosén T, Edén S, Larson G, Wilhelmsen L, Bengtsson B-Å. Cardiovascular risk factors in adult patients with growth hormone deficiency. Acta Endocrinol (Copenh) 1993;129:195–200

6. Cuneo RC, Salomon F, Watts GF, Hesp R, Sönksen PH. Growth hormone treatment improves serum lipids and lipoproteins in adults with growth hormone deficiency. Metabolism 1993;42:1519–23

7. de Boer H, Blok GJ, Voerman HJ, Phillips M, Schouten JA. Serum lipid levels in growth hormone-deficient men. Metabolism 1994;43:199–203

8. Beshyah SA, Henderson A, Niththyananthan R, Sharp P, Richmond W, Johnston DG. Metabolic abnormalities in growth hormone deficient adults II, carbohydrate tolerance and lipid metabolism. Endocrinol Metab 1994;1:173–80

9. Hew FL, O'Neal D, Kamarudin N, Alford FP, Best JD. Growth hormone deficiency and cardiovascular risk. Baillieres Clin Endocrinol Metab 1998;12:199–216

10. Davidson MB. Effect of growth hormone on carbohydrate and lipid metabolism. Endocr Rev 1987; 8:115–31

11. Vahl N, Klausen I, Christiansen JS, Jørgensen JO. Growth hormone (GH) status is an independent determinant of serum levels of cholesterol and triglycerides in healthy adults. Clin Endocrinol (Oxf) 1999;51:309–16

12. Angelin B, Rudling M. Growth hormone and hepatic lipoprotein metabolism. Curr Opin Lipidol 1994; 5:160–5

13. Vikman-Adolfsson K, Oscarsson J, Nilsson-Ehle P, Edén S. Growth hormone but not gonadal steroids influence lipoprotein lipase and hepatic lipase activity in hypophysectomized rats. J Endocrinol 1994; 140:203–9

14. Asayama K, Amemiya S, Kusano S, Kato K. Growth-hormone-induced changes in postheparin plasma lipoprotein lipase and hepatic triglyceride lipase activities. Metabolism 1984;33:129–31

15. Ottosson M, Vikman-Adolfsson K, Enerback S, Elander A, Bjorntorp P, Edén S. Growth hormone inhibits lipoprotein lipase activity in human adipose tissue. J Clin Endocrinol Metab 1995;80:936–41

16. Packard CJ, Shepherd J. Lipoprotein heterogeneity and apolipoprotein B metabolism. Arterioscler Thromb Vasc Biol 1997;17:3542–56

17. Rudling M, Norstedt G, Olivecrona H, Reihner E, Gustafsson JA, Angelin B. Importance of growth hormone for the induction of hepatic low density lipoprotein receptors. Proc Natl Acad Sci USA 1992;89:6983–7

18. Angelin B, Rudling M, Olivecrona H, Ericsson S. Effects of growth hormone on low-density lipoprotein metabolism. Acta Paediatr Suppl 1992;383:67–8

19. Russell-Jones DL, Watts GF, Weissberger A, Naoumova RP, Myers J, Thompson GR, Sönksen PH. The effects of growth hormone replacement of serum lipids, lipoproteins, apolipoproteins and cholesterol precursors in adult growth hormone deficient patients. Clin Endocrinol (Oxf) 1994;41:345–50

20. Christ ER, Cummings MH, Albany E, Umpleby AM, Lumb PJ, Wierzbicki AS, Naoumova RP, Boroujerdi MA, Sönksen PH, Russell-Jones DL. Effects of growth hormone (GH) replacement therapy on very low density lipoprotein apolipoprotein B100 kinetics in patients with adult GH deficiency: a stable isotope study. J Clin Endocrinol Metab 1999;84:307–16

21. Rudling M, Parini P, Angelin B. Growth hormone and bile acid synthesis. Key role for the activity of hepatic microsomal cholesterol 7alpha-hydroxylase in the rat. J Clin Invest 1997;99:2239–45

22. Weaver JU, Monson JP, Noonan K, John WG, Edwards A, Evans KA, Cunningham J. The effect of low dose recombinant human growth hormone replacement on regional fat distribution, insulin sensitivity, and cardiovascular risk factors in hypopituitary adults. J Clin Endocrinol Metab 1995;80:153–9

23. O'Halloran DJ, Wieringa G, Tsatsoulis A, Shalet SM. Increased serum lipoprotein(a) concentrations after growth hormone (GH) treatment in patients with isolated GH deficiency. Ann Clin Biochem 1996; 33:330–4

24. Burman P, Johansson AG, Siegbahn A, Vessby B, Karlsson FA. Growth hormone (GH)-deficient men are more responsive to GH replacement therapy than women. J Clin Endocrinol Metab 1997;82:3514–5

25. Garry P, Collins P, Devlin JG. An open 36-month study of lipid changes with growth hormone in adults: lipid changes following replacement of growth hormone in adult acquired growth hormone deficiency. Eur J Endocrinol 1996;134:61–6

26. Wieringa G, Toogood AA, Ryder WD, Anderson JM, Mackness M, Shalet SM. Changes in lipoprotein(a) levels measured by six kit methods during growth hormone treatment of growth hormone-deficient adults. Growth Horm IGF Res 2000;10:14–19

27. Merimee TJ. A follow-up study of vascular disease in growth-hormone-deficient dwarfs with diabetes. N Engl J Med 1978;298:1217–22

28. Assmann G, Schulte H. The Prospective Cardiovascular Münster (PROCAM) study: prevalence of hyperlipidemia in persons with hypertension and/or diabetes mellitus and the relationship to coronary heart disease. Am Heart J 1988;116:1713–24

29. Vahl N, Jørgensen JO, Hansen TB, Klausen IB, Jurik AG, Hagen C, Christiansen JS. The favourable effects of growth hormone (GH) substitution on hypercholesterolaemia in GH-deficient adults are not associated with concomitant reductions in adiposity. A 12 month placebo-controlled study. Int J Obes Relat Metab Disord 1998;22:529–36

30. Sanmarti A, Lucas A, Hawkins F, Webb SM, Ulied A. Observational study in adult hypopituitary patients with untreated growth hormone deficiency (ODA study). Socio-economic impact and health status. Collaborative ODA (Observational GH Deficiency in Adults) Group. Eur J Endocrinol 1999;141:481–9

31. Abdu TA, Neary R, Elhadd TA, Akber M, Clayton RN. Coronary risk in growth hormone deficient hypopituitary adults: increased predicted risk is due largely to lipid profile abnormalities. Clin Endocrinol (Oxf) 2001;55:209–16

32. Kearney T, Navas de Gallegos C, Chrisoulidou A, Gray R, Bannister P, Venkatesan S, Johnston DG. Hypopituitarism is associated with triglyceride enrichment of very low-density lipoprotein. J Clin Endocrinol Metab 2001;86:3900–6

33. Gleeson HK, Souza AH, Gill MS, Wieringa GE, Barretto ES, Barretto-Filho JA, Shalet SM, Aguiar-Oliveira MH, Clayton PE. Lipid profiles in untreated severe congenital isolated growth hormone deficiency through the lifespan. Clin Endocrinol (Oxf) 2002; 57:89–95

34. Lanes R, Gunczler P, Lopez E, Esaa S, Villaroel O, Revel-Chion R. Cardiac mass and function, carotid artery intima-media thickness, and lipoprotein levels in growth hormone-deficient adolescents. J Clin Endocrinol Metab 2001;86:1061–5

35. Colao A, Di Somma C, Salerno M, Spinelli L, Orio F, Lombardi G. The cardiovascular risk of GH-deficient adolescents. J Clin Endocrinol Metab 2002;87:3650–5

36. Kohno H, Ueyama N, Honda S. Unfavourable impact of growth hormone (GH) discontinuation on body composition and cholesterol profiles after the completion of height growth in GH-deficient young adults. Diabetes Obes Metab 1999;1:293–6

37. Johannsson G, Albertsson-Wikland K, Bengtsson B-Å. Discontinuation of growth hormone (GH) treatment: metabolic effects in GH-deficient and GH-sufficient adolescent patients compared with control subjects. Swedish Study Group for Growth Hormone Treatment in Children. J Clin Endocrinol Metab 1999;84:4516–24

38. Salomon F, Cuneo RC, Hesp R, Sönksen PH. The effects of treatment with recombinant human growth hormone on body composition and metabolism in adults with growth hormone deficiency. N Engl J Med 1989; 321:1797–803

39. Snel YE, Doerga ME, Brummer RM, Zelissen PM, Koppeschaar HP. Magnetic resonance imaging-assessed adipose tissue and serum lipid and insulin concentrations in growth hormone-deficient adults. Effect of growth hormone replacement. Arterioscler Thromb Vasc Biol 1995;15:1543–8

40. Beshyah SA, Henderson A, Niththyananthan R, Skinner E, Anyaoku V, Richmond W, Sharp P, Johnston DG. The effects of short and long-term growth hormone replacement therapy in hypopituitary adults on lipid metabolism and carbohydrate tolerance. J Clin Endocrinol Metab 1995;80:356–63

41. Nolte W, Radisch C, Armstrong VW, Hufner M, von zur Muhlen A. The effect of recombinant human GH replacement therapy on lipoprotein(a) and other lipid parameters in adults with acquired GH deficiency: results of a double-blind and placebo-controlled trial. Eur J Endocrinol 1997;137:459–66

42. Lucidi P, Lauteri M, Laureti S, Celleno R, Santoni S, Volpi E, Angeletti G, Santeusanio F, De Feo P. A dose-response study of growth hormone (GH) replacement on whole body protein and lipid kinetics in GH-deficient adults. J Clin Endocrinol Metab 1998;83:353–7

43. al-Shoumer KA, Gray R, Anyaoku V, Hughes C, Beshyah S, Richmond W, Johnston DG. Effects of four years' treatment with biosynthetic human growth hormone (GH) on glucose homeostasis, insulin secretion and lipid metabolism in GH-deficient adults. Clin Endocrinol (Oxf) 1998;48:795–802

44. Cuneo RC, Judd S, Wallace JD, Perry-Keene D, Burger H, Lim-Tio S, Strauss B, Stockigt J, Topliss D, Alford F, Hew L, Bode H, Conway A, Handelsman D, Dunn S, Boyages S, Cheung NW, Hurley D. The

Australian multicenter trial of growth hormone (GH) treatment in GH-deficient adults. J Clin Endocrinol Metab 1998;83:107–16

45. O'Neal DN, Hew FL, Best JD, Alford F. The effect of 24 months recombinant human growth hormone (rh-GH) on LDL cholesterol, triglyceride-rich lipoproteins and apo [a] in hypopituitary adults previously treated with conventional replacement therapy. Growth Horm IGF Res 1999;9:165–73

46. Leonsson M, Oscarsson J, Bosæus I, Lundgren BK, Johannsson G, Wiklund O, Bengtsson B-Å. Growth hormone (GH) therapy in GH-deficient adults influences the response to a dietary load of cholesterol and saturated fat in terms of cholesterol synthesis, but not serum low density lipoprotein cholesterol levels. J Clin Endocrinol Metab 1999;84:1296–303

47. Bengtsson B-Å, Abs R, Bennmarker H, Monson JP, Feldt-Rasmussen U, Hernberg-Ståhl E, Westberg B, Wilton P, Wüster C. The effects of treatment and the individual responsiveness to growth hormone (GH) replacement therapy in 665 GH-deficient adults. KIMS Study Group and the KIMS International Board. J Clin Endocrinol Metab 1999;84:3929–35

48. Kamarudin N, Hew FL, Christopher M, Alford J, Rantzau C, Ward G, Alford F. Insulin secretion in growth hormone-deficient adults: effects of 24 months' therapy and five days' acute withdrawal of recombinant human growth hormone. Metabolism 1999;48:1387–96

49. Chrisoulidou A, Beshyah SA, Rutherford O, Spinks TJ, Mayet J, Kyd P, Anyaoku V, Haida A, Ariff B, Murphy M, Thomas E, Robinson S, Foale R, Johnston DG. Effects of 7 years of growth hormone replacement therapy in hypopituitary adults. J Clin Endocrinol Metab 2000;85:3762–9

50. Amato G, Mazziotti G, Di Somma C, Lalli E, De Felice G, Conte M, Rotondi M, Pietrosante M, Lombardi G, Bellastella A, Carella C, Colao A. Recombinant growth hormone (GH) therapy in GH-deficient adults: a long-term controlled study on daily versus thrice weekly injections. J Clin Endocrinol Metab 2000;85:3720–5

51. Florakis D, Hung V, Kaltsas G, Coyte D, Jenkins PJ, Chew SL, Grossman AB, Besser GM, Monson JP. Sustained reduction in circulating cholesterol in adult hypopituitary patients given low dose titrated growth hormone replacement therapy: a two-year study. Clin Endocrinol (Oxf) 2000;53:453–9

52. Sesmilo G, Biller BM, Llevadot J, Hayden D, Hanson G, Rifai N, Klibanski A. Effects of growth hormone administration on inflammatory and other cardiovascular risk markers in men with growth hormone deficiency. A randomized, controlled clinical trial. Ann Intern Med 2000;133:111–22

53. Koranyi J, Svensson J, Götherström G, Sunnerhagen KS, Bengtsson B, Johannsson G. Baseline characteristics and the effects of five years of GH replacement therapy in adults with GH deficiency of childhood or adulthood onset: a comparative, prospective study. J Clin Endocrinol Metab 2001;86:4693–9

54. Götherström G, Svensson J, Koranyi J, Alpsten M, Bosæus I, Bengtsson B-Å, Johannsson G. A prospective study of 5 years of GH replacement therapy in GH-deficient adults: sustained effects on body composition, bone mass, and metabolic indices. J Clin Endocrinol Metab 2001;86:4657–65

55. Colao A, di Somma C, Cuocolo A, Spinelli L, Tedesco N, Pivonello R, Bonaduce D, Salvatore M, Lombardi G. Improved cardiovascular risk factors and cardiac performance after 12 months of growth hormone (GH) replacement in young adult patients with GH deficiency. J Clin Endocrinol Metab 2001;86:1874–81

56. Colao A, di Somma C, Pivonello R, Cuocolo A, Spinelli L, Bonaduce D, Salvatore M, Lombardi G. The cardiovascular risk of adult GH deficiency (GHD) improved after GH replacement and worsened in untreated GHD: a 12-month prospective study. J Clin Endocrinol Metab 2002;87:1088–93

57. Christopher M, Hew FL, Oakley M, Rantzau C, Alford F. Defects of insulin action and skeletal muscle glucose metabolism in growth hormone-deficient adults persist after 24 months of recombinant human growth hormone therapy. J Clin Endocrinol Metab 1998;83:1668–81

13 Effects of growth hormone (GH) deficiency and GH replacement therapy on bone

Peter H Kann

Centre for Internal Medicine, Division of Endocrinology and Diabetology, Philipps University Medical School, Marburg, Germany

Summary

Longitudinal bone growth ceases after final height is reached. Bone mineral density (BMD), however, continues to increase until peak bone mass (PBM) is achieved, probably within the third decade of life. Even after PBM is achieved, remodelling of bone continues throughout life, and is important for maintaining the health and strength of the skeleton and for mineral homeostasis. As bone growth and metabolism are stimulated by the growth hormone (GH)/insulin-like growth factor I axis, GH deficiency (GHD) of childhood onset reduces PBM and adult BMD. Adult-onset GHD, by reducing bone turnover, also leads to a lower BMD. Both childhood-onset and adult-onset GHD result in an increased fracture risk in later life. Although long-term data on the effect of GH replacement therapy on the incidence of fractures are not yet available, the increased BMD seen after GH replacement therapy in both children and adults indicates that GH replacement should reduce the risk of fractures in hypopituitary patients.

Introduction

Growth hormone (GH) is important not only for stimulating longitudinal bone growth in children, but also for the accumulation of bone mineral density (BMD) in adolescence and the attainment of a normal peak bone mass (PBM) in young adults [1]. PBM is achieved after the cessation of linear growth [2], and adults with childhood-onset GH deficiency (CO-GHD) have a reduced BMD [1, 3]. This osteopenia is irrespective of whether patients have isolated GHD or multiple pituitary hormone deficiencies, indicating that at least some of the reduction in BMD is due to GHD [4, 5]. BMD has also been shown to be reduced in patients with adult-onset GHD (AO-GHD) [6], and a reduced BMD in adults is associated with an increased risk of fractures [7].

This chapter examines the basic physiology and structure of bone, particularly in relation to the effects of GH and GHD, and describes the techniques used for assessing bone growth and metabolism. Evidence for the beneficial effect of GH replacement therapy on bone is also reviewed.

Bone structure and physiology

Bone tissue consists of living cells and a mineralized extracellular matrix. The matrix is composed of organic material, mainly type I collagen, and inorganic material, mainly calcium phosphate in a crystalline form – hydroxyapatite. There are two main morphological types of bone, called cortical (compact) and cancellous (trabecular or spongy) (Fig. 1). Cortical bone

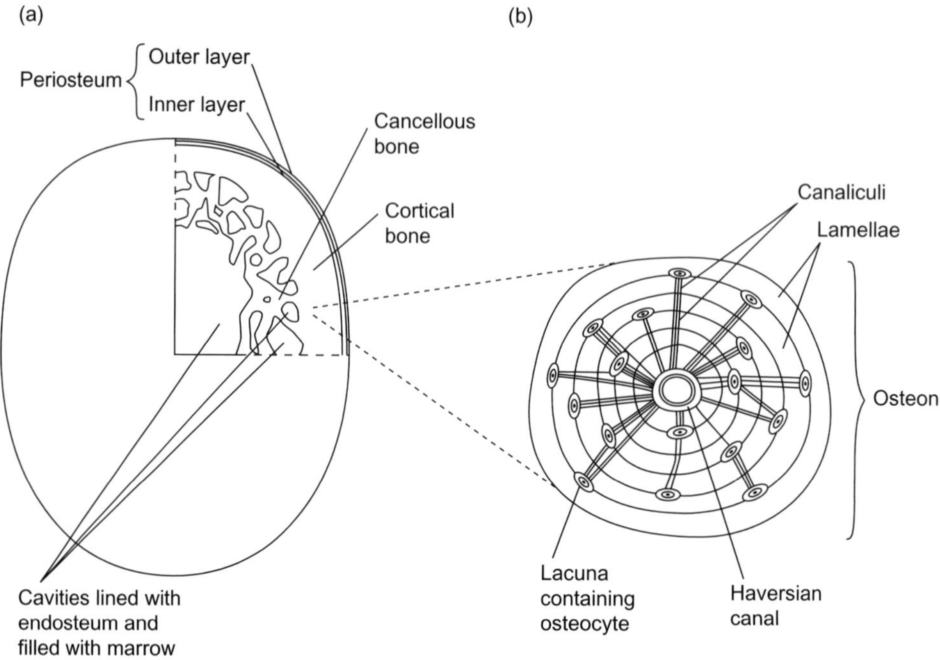

Figure 1. *Schematic structure of bone, showing a cross-section through (a) a long bone and (b) an osteon.*

consists of densely packed cylindrical units called osteons or Haversian systems, each of which is constructed of layers of matrix (lamellae) surrounding a central canal (Haversian canal). Spaces within the lamellae contain osteocytes, which are mature osteoblasts that have become surrounded by bone matrix. The osteocytes are connected to each other and to the Haversian canal by strands of protoplasms called canaliculi. Cortical bone generally forms the outer layer of bones and has a supportive and protective function. Cancellous bone occurs inside the cortical layer. It also consists of lamellae, but these are not organized into cylindrical osteons. The open structure of cancellous bone helps to reduce bone mass whilst, at the same time, conferring strength on the rigid cortical layer. Cancellous bone also performs much of the calcium regulatory function of the skeleton.

The two main types of cells concerned with bone metabolism are osteoblasts and osteoclasts. Osteoblasts, derived from mesenchymal stem cells, produce bone matrix and regulate bone mineralization. Osteoclasts, derived from bone marrow cells of the monocyte–macrophage lineage, resorb bone material. Both these cell types are necessary for bone growth and remodelling. Bone growth increases the length of the long bones (endochondral growth) and the diameter of the long bones and all the dimensions of other bones (appositional growth). Although this bone growth ceases when an individual reaches adulthood, bone remodelling occurs throughout life. Remodelling consists of the resorption of old bone by osteoclasts and the subsequent deposition of new bone by osteoblasts. The purpose of this process is thought to be to adapt the skeleton to mechanical stress, to repair damage, to prevent the accumulation of old and brittle bone and to regulate levels of calcium in the body.

GH regulates bone metabolism by stimulating osteoblasts and osteoclasts [8–10], leading to both bone formation and resorption [11, 12]. This occurs directly through binding to GH receptors on the cell surface, and indirectly through stimulation of hepatic production of insulin-like growth factor I (IGF-I). There is also evidence that some of the 'direct' effects of GH are mediated in an autocrine or paracrine manner by locally produced IGF-I [13, 14]. In addition, GH appears to be involved in the coupling of osteoclast and osteoblast activity, which is mediated by cytokines [9, 15].

Methods for studying bone metabolism

Numerous non-invasive methods have been developed for studying bone metabolism and structure in clinical practice. These involve measuring biochemical markers of bone formation and resorption, and various imaging techniques.

Biochemical markers

Peptides and proteins secreted by osteoclasts or osteoblasts, and components of the bone matrix released into the circulation during bone resorption or formation, can be used as markers of bone metabolism (Table 1). As levels of biochemical markers of bone formation and resorption are age dependent, measurements should be compared with established reference ranges for clinical interpretation [17]. Biochemical markers of bone metabolism are particularly useful for monitoring treatment, as they indicate short-term changes in the remodelling process. Typically, biochemical markers change within a few weeks of the initiation of treatment, whereas changes in BMD may be observed only after several months [18]. Assays for bone markers are widely available and have been used in studies of GHD and GH replacement therapy [11, 19–22].

Imaging

Imaging techniques for assessing bone size, bone mineral content (BMC, in grams) and BMD include radiography, single-energy or dual-energy photon absorptiometry, single-energy or dual-energy X-ray absorptiometry (DXA), computed tomography (CT) and neutron activation. DXA is the most appropriate technique in most clinical situations. It is accurate, fast, cost-effective and involves low doses of radiation. It also allows the analysis of whole-body composition.

Bone size can be measured directly from the produced images, and BMC can be calculated using computer software. BMD is then calculated from these two variables. The ability to estimate BMD is important as it relates directly to bone strength and the risk of fractures [23].

Because DXA images are two-dimensional, BMD is usually expressed in terms of mass per area of bone (areal BMD [BMC/cm^2]). Areal BMD, however, is strongly dependent on bone size. Bone mineral mass increases with the cube of bone length, whereas cross-sectional area increases with the square of bone length. Areal BMD will therefore increase as bone grows, making interpretation of measurements difficult, especially during childhood and adolescence. A more accurate way of assessing bone density is to use volumetric measures of BMD (expressed as mass of mineral per volume of bone [BMC/cm^3]) (Fig. 2). The volume of bone can be measured using quantitative CT, although this is relatively expensive and involves high doses of radiation. Alternatively, bone volume can be calculated assuming that the section of bone examined conforms to a regular geometric shape, such as a cube or cylinder [24–26].

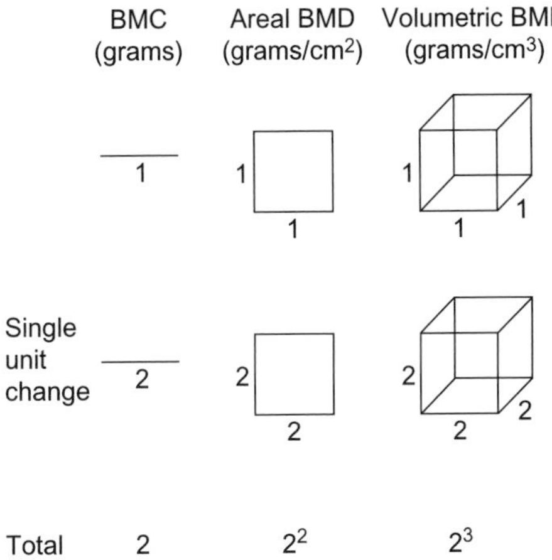

***Figure 2.** Differences between measurements of bone mineral content (BMC), areal bone mineral density (BMD) and volumetric BMD.*

Table 1. Biochemical markers of bone resorption and formation. Adapted from [16] with permission. Copyright 1996, Elsevier.

	Assayed in	Comments
Bone resorption markers		
Tartrate-resistant acid phosphatase (TRAP)	Plasma	Enzyme secreted by osteoclasts; precise function unknown.
Calcium	Urine	Released when bone matrix is broken down.
Hydroxyproline	Urine	Amino acid found mainly in collagen; released when bone matrix is broken down.
Hydroxylysine glycosides	Urine	Hydroxylysine is an amino acid unique to collagen and related proteins, in which it is present in two glycosylated forms; released when bone matrix is broken down.
Pyridinoline and deoxypyridinoline	Urine	Molecules that form cross-links between collagen molecules; released when bone matrix is broken down.
Carboxy-terminal and amino-terminal cross-linked telopeptides of type I collagen (ICTP and INTP, respectively)	Serum (ICTP) Urine (INTP)	Peptide fragments from the ends of type I collagen molecules (where cross-links form); released when bone matrix is broken down.
Bone formation markers		
Alkaline phosphatase	Serum	Enzyme secreted by osteoblasts; precise function in bone obscure, but known to play a key role in mineralization; a bone-specific isozyme exists and can be assayed.
Osteocalcin (bone gla-protein)	Serum	Small protein synthesized by osteoblasts. Most is incorporated into bone matrix, but a fraction is released into the circulation. Its precise function is unknown.
Carboxy-terminal and amino-terminal propeptides of type I procollagen	Serum	Peptide fragments cleaved from type I procollagen during its conversion to type I collagen.

Effects of hypopituitarism and GHD

Hypopituitarism is associated with an increased risk of osteoporosis not only due to GHD, but also to a lack of sex-steroid hormones, if they are not adequately replaced.

Adults with GHD have reduced rates of bone turnover [27–29] and a subnormal BMD [4–6, 11, 30–32]. This is clinically important, as a decreased BMD is associated with an increased risk of fractures [7, 33, 34].

The possible role of disturbances of the somatotrophic axis in the pathogenesis of idiopathic osteoporosis has also been discussed [35], as has the possible role of GH therapy in idiopathic [36, 37] and glucocorticoid-induced [38] osteoporosis. Conflicting data from studies in these areas mean that it is currently difficult to draw firm conclusions on the involvement of the somatotrophic axis or the potential benefits of GH treatment. Recently, however, 2 years of GH treatment was shown to increase BMD in men with idiopathic osteoporosis [39].

Is GH replacement therapy beneficial?

Several studies in hypopituitary patients have shown that GH replacement therapy stimulates bone turnover [11, 19, 28, 40–44]. These effects *in vivo* are consistent with data from studies *in vitro* that have demonstrated a stimulatory effect of GH on the differentiation, proliferation and activity of osteoblasts and osteoclasts [8–10, 13, 14].

Randomized placebo-controlled trials have demonstrated that BMD is increased by long-term GH replacement therapy in hypopituitary patients [11, 43–51]. In several studies, however, the long-term gain in BMD has been shown to occur after an initial decrease in BMD during the first year of treatment [11, 19, 52]. This is explained by the biphasic effect of GH on bone. Initially, resorption of matrix material is stimulated by osteoclasts. This is followed by new bone formation, leading – in the long term – to a new steady state of bone turnover with anabolism dominating [11, 12, 19] (Fig. 3).

Based on current knowledge, it is assumed that the bone produced as a result of GH replacement has normal physiological composition with regard to its quality and microarchitecture [11]. It is therefore reasonable to expect that the normalization of BMD due to GH administration may counter the increased risk of fractures in hypopituitary patients. However, no randomized controlled trials have yet been completed to support this assumption.

Importance of PBM

The decreased BMD in adults with CO-GHD is thought to be due to a failure to achieve a PBM (see Chapter 20). Most bone mass is acquired during late adolescence or early adulthood. The PBM achieved during this time, and the subsequent age-related decline in BMD, determines an individual's risk of fractures in later life [53].

GH replacement therapy in children results in an increase in BMD to normal levels, but only after several years of treatment [1, 54]. Hence, Saggese and colleagues [1] have suggested that GH treatment should be continued until the attainment of PBM, irrespective of the height achieved. In a recent 2-year randomized controlled trial of GH replacement in young adults who had terminated GH therapy at final height, the reintroduction of GH therapy induced significant progression towards the expected PBM [55].

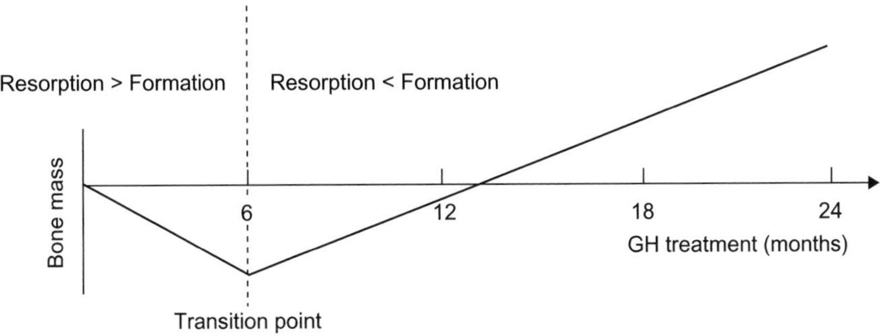

Figure 3. *The biphasic model of GH action in bone remodelling. The transition point is the time when bone formation is stimulated more than bone resorption. After this point, bone mass increases. Reproduced from [12] with permission. Copyright 1998, The Endocrine Society.*

Evidence from KIMS

BMD

Data on BMD are collected in KIMS – Pfizer International Metabolic Database. As KIMS is an international pharmacoepidemiological survey, and not a controlled, prospective trial, data on BMD are available from only a subset of patients – those treated in centres where there is a special interest and which have the necessary technical equipment. However, because KIMS contains data from patients treated outside the constraints of a trial environment, but within the normal clinical context, it provides a valuable contribution to evidence-based medicine.

As the measuring sites and techniques used for assessing BMD in KIMS are not standardized, the BMD data shown in Figure 4 are pooled from measurements taken using a variety of imaging techniques, and are given as changes compared with baseline values.

Taking into account the methodological and statistical problems of pooling measurements performed under non-standard and technically different conditions, the data documented in KIMS are consistent with those from randomized controlled studies performed to investigate the influence of GH substitution on BMD, referred to above. In KIMS, significant increases were seen in the skeletal load-bearing sites of the femoral neck and lumbar spine at 2 years and at 1–4 years of GH treatment, respectively (Fig. 4).

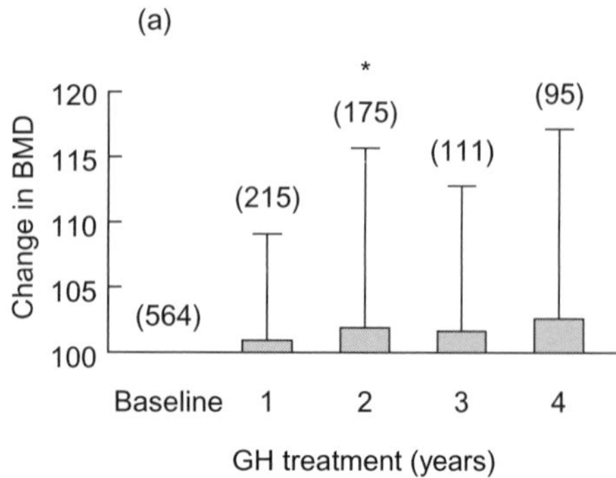

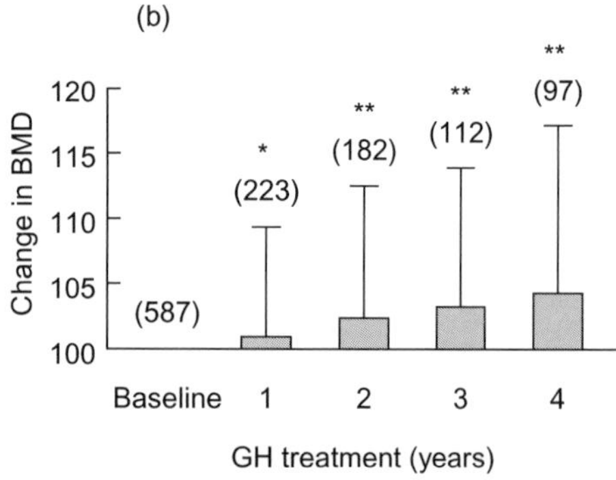

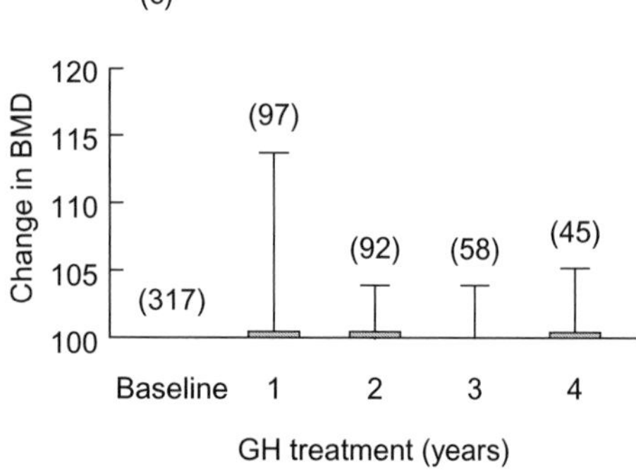

Figure 4. *Changes in bone mineral density (BMD) in (a) the femoral neck, (b) the lumbar spine and (c) the whole body in adult patients with GHD in KIMS after 1–4 years of GH replacement therapy. Values are mean changes (± SD) from baseline for the numbers of patients in parentheses; paired t-test *$p < 0.05$, **$p < 0.001$ compared with baseline.*

Fracture rates

Fracture rates in patients in KIMS have been analysed by comparing them to the expected prevalence calculated from a comparable age group in the European Vertebral Osteoporosis Study [7]. The fracture rate was higher in both men (29% compared with 6%; $p < 0.05$) and women (34% compared with 18%; $p = 0.06$) in KIMS compared with the control population (Fig. 5). In a post-hoc analysis, there was evidence for a similar increase in the fracture risk in patients with isolated GHD and those with multiple pituitary hormone deficiencies. In addition, patients with AO-GHD had a higher fracture risk than GH-deficient adults with CO-GHD. Data from KIMS thus support a close link between GHD-induced osteopenia and an increased fracture risk.

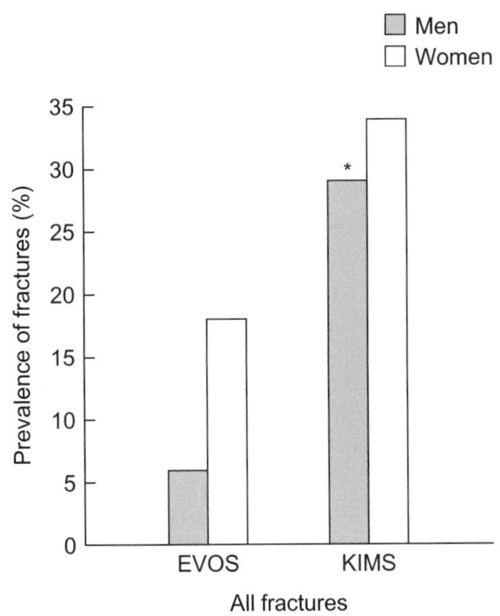

Figure 5. *Prevalence of all fractures in patients over 60 years of age in KIMS compared with the fracture rate in age- and sex-matched individuals in the European Vertebral Osteoporosis Study (EVOS); *p < 0.05 compared with patients in EVOS. Adapted from [7] with permission from the American Society for Bone and Mineral Research.*

Conclusions

Data from KIMS and from controlled clinical trials clearly implicate GHD in the osteopenia and increased fracture risk seen in hypopituitary patients. Although the long-term effects of GH replacement therapy on the risk of fractures are not yet known, the increases in bone turnover and BMD associated with such therapy indicate that the fracture risk is likely to be reduced. Future analyses of data from long-term surveillance studies, such as KIMS, will be important in determining the exact clinical benefits of GH replacement on skeletal tissue.

References

1. Saggese G, Baroncelli GI, Bertelloni S, Barsanti S. The effect of long-term growth hormone (GH) treatment on bone mineral density in children with GH deficiency. Role of GH in the attainment of peak bone mass. J Clin Endocrinol Metab 1996;81:3077–83

2. Carrascosa A, Gussinyé M, Yeste D, del Rio L, Audi L, Enrubia M, Vargas D. Skeletal mineralization during infancy, childhood and adolescence in the normal population and in populations with nutritional and hormonal disorders. Dual X-ray absorptiometry (DEXA) evaluation. In: Schönau E. Paediatric osteology. New developments in diagnostics and therapy. Amsterdam: Elsevier 1996:93–102

3. Cuneo RC, Judd S, Wallace JD, Perry-Keene D, Burger H, Lim-Tio S, Strauss B, Stockigt J, Topliss D, Alford F, Hew L, Bode H, Conway A, Handelsman D, Dunn S, Boyages S, Cheung NW, Hurley D. The Australian Multicenter Trial of Growth Hormone (GH) Treatment in GH-Deficient Adults. J Clin Endocrinol Metab 1998;83:107–16

4. Kaufman JM, Taelman P, Vermeulen A, Vandeweghe M. Bone mineral status in growth hormone-deficient males with isolated and multiple pituitary deficiencies of childhood onset. J Clin Endocrinol Metab 1992;74:118–23

5. de Boer H, Blok GJ, van Lingen A, Teule GJ, Lips P, van der Veen EA. Consequences of childhood-onset growth hormone deficiency for adult bone mass. J Bone Miner Res 1994;9:1319–26

6. Holmes SJ, Economou G, Whitehouse RW, Adams JE, Shalet SM. Reduced bone mineral density in patients with adult onset growth hormone deficiency. J Clin Endocrinol Metab 1994;78:669–74

7. Wüster C, Abs R, Bengtsson B-Å, Bennmarker H, Feldt-Rasmussen U, Hernberg-Ståhl E, Monson JP, Westberg B, Wilton P. The influence of growth hormone deficiency, growth hormone replacement therapy, and other aspects of hypopituitarism on fracture rate and bone mineral density. J Bone Miner Res 2001; 16:398–405

8. Maor G, Hochberg Z, von der Mark K, Heinegard D, Silbermann M. Human growth hormone enhances chondrogenesis and osteogenesis in a tissue culture system of chondroprogenitor cells. Endocrinology 1989;125:1239–45

9. Nishiyama K, Sugimoto T, Kaji H, Kanatani M, Kobayashi T, Chihara K. Stimulatory effect of growth hormone on bone resorption and osteoclast differentiation. Endocrinology 1996;137:35–41

10. Slootweg MC, van Buul-Offers SC, Herrmann-Erlee MP, van der Meer JM, Duursma SA. Growth hormone is mitogenic for fetal mouse osteoblasts but not for undifferentiated bone cells. J Endocrinol 1988; 116:R11–13

11. Kann P, Piepkorn B, Schehler B, Andreas J, Lotz J, Prellwitz W, Beyer J. Effect of long-term treatment with GH on bone metabolism, bone mineral density and bone elasticity in GH-deficient adults. Clin Endocrinol (Oxf) 1998;48:561–8

12. Ohlsson C, Bengtsson B-Å, Isaksson OG, Andreassen TT, Slootweg MC. Growth hormone and bone. Endocr Rev 1998;19:55–79

13. Stracke H, Schulz A, Moeller D, Rossol S, Schatz H. Effect of growth hormone on osteoblasts and demonstration of somatomedin-C/IGF I in bone organ culture. Acta Endocrinol (Copenh) 1984;107:16–24

14. Ernst M, Froesch ER. Growth hormone dependent stimulation of osteoblast-like cells in serum-free cultures via local synthesis of insulin-like growth factor I. Biochem Biophys Res Commun 1988;151:142–7

15. Swolin D, Ohlsson C. Growth hormone increases interleukin-6 produced by human osteoblast-like cells. J Clin Endocrinol Metab 1996;81:4329–33

16. Seibel MJ, Pols APP. Clinical applications of biochemical markers of bone metabolism. In: Bilezikian JP, Raisz LG, Rodan GA, editors. Principles of bone biology. San Diego: Academic Press 1996:1293–312

17. van der Sluis IM, Hop WC, van Leeuwen JP, Pols HA, de Muinck Keizer-Schrama SM. A cross-sectional study on biochemical parameters of bone turnover and vitamin D metabolites in healthy dutch children and young adults. Horm Res 2002;57:170–9

18. Cowell CT, Wüster C. The effects of growth hormone deficiency and growth hormone replacement therapy on bone. A meeting report. Horm Res 2000;54 (Suppl 1):68–74

19. Vandeweghe M, Taelman P, Kaufman JM. Short and long-term effects of growth hormone treatment on bone turnover and bone mineral content in adult growth hormone-deficient males. Clin Endocrinol (Oxf) 1993; 39:409–15

20. Saggese G, Baroncelli GI. Bone mineral density and biochemical parameters of bone turnover in children with growth hormone deficiency. Horm Res 1996;45 (Suppl 1):67–8

21. Rodriguez-Arnao J, James I, Jabbar A, Trainer PJ, Perrett D, Besser GM, Ross RJ. Serum collagen crosslinks as markers of bone turn-over during GH replacement therapy in growth hormone deficient adults. Clin Endocrinol (Oxf) 1998;48:455–62

22. Nilsson AG. Effects of growth hormone replacement therapy on bone markers and bone mineral density in growth hormone-deficient adults. Horm Res 2000;54 (Suppl 1):52–7

23. World Health Organization. Assessment of fracture risk and its application to screening for post-menopausal osteoporosis. WHO Technical Report Series, Geneva 1994

24. Carter DR, Bouxsein ML, Marcus R. New approaches for interpreting projected bone densitometry data. J Bone Miner Res 1992;7:137–45

25. Jergas M, Breitenseher M, Gluer CC, Yu W, Genant HK. Estimates of volumetric bone density from projectional measurements improve the discriminatory capability of dual X-ray absorptiometry. J Bone Miner Res 1995; 10:1101–10

26. Lu PW, Cowell CT, Lloyd-Jones SA, Briody JN, Howman-Giles R. Volumetric bone mineral density in normal subjects, aged 5–27 years. J Clin Endocrinol Metab 1996;81:1586–90

27. Amato G, Carella C, Fazio S, La Montagna G, Cittadini A, Sabatini D, Marciano-Mone C, Saccà L, Bellastella A. Body composition, bone metabolism, and heart structure and function in growth hormone (GH)-deficient adults before and after GH replacement therapy at low doses. J Clin Endocrinol Metab 1993;77:1671–6

28. Amato G, Izzo G, La Montagna G, Bellastella A. Low dose recombinant human growth hormone normalizes bone metabolism and cortical bone density and improves trabecular bone density in growth hormone deficient adults without causing adverse effects. Clin Endocrinol (Oxf) 1996;45:27–32

29. Sartorio A, Conti A, Monzani M. New markers of bone and collagen turnover in children and adults with growth hormone deficiency. Postgrad Med J 1993;69:846–50

30. Bing-You RG, Denis MC, Rosén CJ. Low bone mineral density in adults with previous hypothalamic-pituitary tumors: correlations with serum growth hormone responses to GH-releasing hormone, insulin-like growth factor I, and IGF binding protein 3. Calcif Tissue Int 1993;52:183–7

31. Elgindy N, Grunditz R, Thorén M, Degerblad M, Sjöberg HE, Ringertz H. Long-term follow-up of metacarpal cortical thickness and bone mineral density in panhypopituitarism. Radiol Diag 1991;32:326–30

32. Rosén T, Hansson T, Granhed H, Szucs J, Bengtsson B-Å. Reduced bone mineral content in adult patients with growth hormone deficiency. Acta Endocrinol (Copenh) 1993;129:201–6

33. Rosén T, Wilhelmsen L, Landin-Wilhelmsen K, Lappas G, Lindstedt G, Wilske J, Bengtsson B-Å. Increased fracture rate in adults with growth hormone deficiency. Endocrinol Metab 1996;3:121

34. Wüster C, Slenczka E, Ziegler R. Increased prevalence of osteoporosis and arteriosclerosis in conventionally substituted anterior pituitary insufficiency: need for additional growth hormone substitution? [German] Klin Wochenschr 1991;69:769–73

35. Dennison EM, Hindmarsh PC, Kellingray S, Fall CH, Cooper C. Growth hormone predicts bone density in elderly women. Bone 2003;32:434–40

36. Li G, Zeng M. Relation of serum growth hormone and estradiol levels and osteoporosis in postmenopausal women. [Chinese] Zhonghua Yi Xue Za Zhi 1990;70:16–19

37. Rubin CD. Southwestern internal medicine conference: growth hormone – aging and osteoporosis. Am J Med Sci 1993;305:120–9

38. Franco P, Marelli O, Lattuada D, Locatelli V, Cocchi D, Muller EE. Influence of growth hormone on the immunosuppressive effect of prednisolone in mice. Acta Endocrinol (Copenh) 1990;123:339–44

39. Gillberg P, Mallmin H, Petren-Mallmin M, Ljunghall S, Nilsson AG. Two years of treatment with recombinant human growth hormone increases bone mineral density in men with idiopathic osteoporosis. J Clin Endocrinol Metab 2002;87:4900–6

40. Ahmad AM, Thomas J, Clewes A, Hopkins MT, Guzder R, Ibrahim H, Durham BH, Vora JP, Fraser WD. Effects of growth hormone replacement on parathyroid hormone sensitivity and bone mineral metabolism. J Clin Endocrinol Metab 2003;88:2860–8

41. Balducci R, Toscano V, Pasquino AM, Mangiantini A, Municchi G, Armenise P, Terracina S, Prossomariti G, Boscherini B. Bone turnover and bone mineral density in young adult patients with panhypopituitarism before and after long-term growth hormone therapy. Eur J Endocrinol 1995;132:42–6

42. Beshyah SA, Kyd P, Thomas E, Fairney A, Johnston DG. The effects of prolonged growth hormone replacement on bone metabolism and bone mineral density in hypopituitary adults. Clin Endocrinol (Oxf) 1995;42:249–54

43. Degerblad M, Bengtsson B-Å, Bramnert M, Johnell O, Manhem P, Rosén T, Thorén M. Reduced bone mineral density in adults with growth hormone (GH) deficiency: increased bone turnover during 12 months of GH substitution therapy. Eur J Endocrinol 1995;133:180–8

44. Hansen TB, Brixen K, Vahl N, Jørgensen JO, Christiansen JS, Mosekilde L, Hagen C. Effects of 12 months of growth hormone (GH) treatment on calciotropic hormones, calcium homeostasis, and bone metabolism in adults with acquired GH deficiency: a double blind, randomized, placebo-controlled study. J Clin Endocrinol Metab 1996;81:3352–9

45. Abrahamsen B, Hangaard J, Horn HC, Hansen TB, Gregersen G, Hansen-Nord M, Vahl N, Junker P, Andersen M, Hagen C. Evaluation of the optimum dose of growth hormone (GH) for restoring bone mass in adult-onset GH deficiency: results from two 12-month randomized studies. Clin Endocrinol (Oxf) 2002; 57:273–81

46. Baum HB, Biller BM, Finkelstein JS, Cannistraro KB, Oppenhein DS, Schoenfeld DA, Michel TH, Wittink H, Klibanski A. Effects of physiologic growth hormone therapy on bone density and body composition in patients with adult-onset growth hormone deficiency. A randomized, placebo-controlled trial. Ann Intern Med 1996;125:883–90

47. Bex M, Abs R, Maiter D, Beckers A, Lamberigts G, Bouillon R. The effects of growth hormone replacement therapy on bone metabolism in adult-onset growth hormone deficiency: a 2-year open randomized controlled multicenter trial. J Bone Miner Res 2002; 17:1081–94

48. Finkenstedt G, Gasser RW, Hofle G, Watfah C, Fridrich L. Effects of growth hormone (GH) replacement on bone metabolism and mineral density in adult onset of GH deficiency: results of a double-blind placebo-controlled study with open follow-up. Eur J Endocrinol 1997;136:282–9

49. Gomez JM, Gomez N, Fiter J, Soler J. Effects of long-term treatment with GH in the bone mineral density of adults with hypopituitarism and GH deficiency and after discontinuation of GH replacement. Horm Metab Res 2000;32:66–70

50. Holmes SJ, Whitehouse RW, Swindell R, Economou G, Adams JE, Shalet SM. Effect of growth hormone replacement on bone mass in adults with adult onset growth hormone deficiency. Clin Endocrinol (Oxf) 1995;42:627–33

51. Sneppen SB, Hoeck HC, Kollerup G, Sorensen OH, Laurberg P, Feldt-Rasmussen U. Bone mineral content and bone metabolism during physiological GH treatment in GH-deficient adults – an 18-month randomised, placebo-controlled, double blinded trial. Eur J Endocrinol 2002;146:187–95

52. Johannsson G, Rosén T, Bosæus I, Sjöström L, Bengtsson B-Å. Two years of growth hormone (GH) treatment increases bone mineral content and density in hypopituitary patients with adult-onset GH deficiency. J Clin Endocrinol Metab 1996;81:2865–73

53. Drake WM, Howell SJ, Monson JP, Shalet SM. Optimizing GH therapy in adults and children. Endocr Rev 2001;22:425–50

54. Greig F, Greenfield E, Prasad V, AvRushkin TW, Bastian W, Yasumura S, Castells S. Increase in bone density and plasma osteocalcin during growth hormone therapy in growth hormone deficient children. J Pediatr Endocrinol Metab 1997;10:11–17

55. Shalet SM, Shavrikova E, Cromer M, Child CJ, Keller E, Zapletalova J, Moshang T, Blum WF, Chipman JJ, Quigley CA, Attanasio AF. Effect of growth hormone (GH) treatment on bone in post-pubertal GH-deficient patients: a 2-year randomized, controlled, dose-ranging study. J Clin Endocrinol Metab 2003;88:4124–9

14 Growth hormone (GH) deficiency and GH replacement therapy: effects on cardiovascular function

Hugo L Fideleff and Hugo R Boquete
Endocrinology Unit, Department of Medicine, Hospital T. Alvarez, Buenos Aires, Argentina

Summary

In recent years, the important role of the growth hormone (GH)/insulin-like growth factor I (IGF-I) axis in cardiac structure and function and endothelial function has become apparent. Despite the well-known effects of GH on the heart and on various cardiovascular risk factors, the effects of GH deficiency (GHD) in adulthood are still unclear. A frequent, but inconsistent, finding is diastolic dysfunction, which has been reported in up to 65% of patients with GHD. Systolic function is typically within the normal range, although marked impairment has been reported in some studies. Analysis of data from KIMS – Pfizer International Metabolic Database – shows evidence of a restrictive pattern of diastolic function in a number of patients with childhood-onset adult GHD and a prolonged pattern of diastolic function in some patients with adult-onset GHD. Systolic dysfunction was observed in some patients, and cardiac mass was decreased in a considerable number of patients in both adult- and childhood-onset groups. There is still no consensus as to the medium- and long-term effects of GH replacement therapy on these cardiovascular abnormalities, largely as a result of the use of high doses of GH in early studies. Recent studies, however, using lower doses, suggest that there may be an improvement in diastolic function. Physical performance capacity, which is often impaired in adults with GHD, has also been found to improve following GH replacement therapy. Future long-term studies will enable us to examine in more detail the role of GH and the effects of GH replacement therapy on cardiac function in adults with GHD.

Introduction

The effects of growth hormone (GH) on somatic growth, body composition and metabolism are well known. However, only in recent years has the role of the GH/insulin-like growth factor I (IGF-I) axis on cardiovascular structure and function become evident. Cardiomegaly and impaired cardiac function had been reported in acromegalic patients many years ago, although it was only in the late 1980s that the impact of GH deficiency (GHD) on cardiac structure and performance started to be recognized in adults [1]. Increased classic and non-classic cardiovascular risk factors and increased morbidity and mortality were observed in this group of patients [2–4] (see Chapter 6). Cardiac abnormalities are associated with impaired endothelial and vascular function, which, in conjunction with changes in the metabolic profile, enhance the risk of atherogenesis and would partly account for the above-mentioned increased cardiovascular mortality [4, 5].

Even though some of these abnormalities may be reversed by GH replacement, the sustained benefits of GH therapy in the long term remain controversial.

In this chapter, we will critically analyse some aspects related to GH therapy and the heart, with particular reference to patients enrolled in KIMS – Pfizer International Metabolic Database – and discuss the advances in our understanding of the physiology and pathophysiology of GHD and the effect of GH replacement therapy.

Physiological aspects

It has been demonstrated that GH receptors are expressed in the myocardium and that, by interacting with circulating GH, they stimulate the biosynthesis of IGF-I [6, 7]. Locally produced IGF-I acts in an autocrine or paracrine manner by binding to its specific high-affinity sarcolemmatic receptor. This may activate multiple signal transduction pathways, increasing protein synthesis with accumulation of myofibrils and an increase in myocyte cell mass and volume [7]. Few data are currently available on the physiological role of IGF-binding proteins in heart growth and development and it is not clear whether these binding proteins are synthesized in cardiac tissue [6].

The importance of the GH/IGF-I axis in the regulation of myocardial growth *in vivo* has been investigated in several animal models. In some of them, cardiac hypertrophy induced by GH/IGF-I activation translated into significant enhancement of systolic and diastolic left ventricular (LV) function and was not accompanied by an increase in collagen content [7]. These findings contribute to the understanding of the complex mechanisms involved in the development of cardiac hypertrophy, suggesting that both GH and IGF-I play an important role in the sequence of events that control cardiac growth [6]. In humans, the role of the GH/IGF-I axis in the cardiovascular system has been extensively evaluated in pathological models such as acromegaly, GHD in children and adults, anorexia nervosa, heart failure and certain genetic syndromes associated with dilated cardiomyopathy [6, 8–12]. On the other hand, the administration of recombinant IGF-I to healthy subjects increased cardiac performance, without any correlation with metabolic changes [13]. As IGF-I has been shown to have a vasodilatory effect, it has been hypothesized that its cardiac action might be partly related to vascular mechanisms [14]. The relationship between such effects and catecholamine release remains controversial [15]. In recent years, the anti-apoptotic properties of IGF-I in cultured rat cardiomyocytes have become a new area of research [16].

GHD and cardiac function

Multiple epidemiological studies showing increased mortality in hypopituitary patients suggested that GHD was responsible for the increased mortality [2, 3, 17]. Other factors should also be considered, however, such as the aetiology of the process resulting in hypopituitarism, the primary therapy administered, other hormonal deficiencies and the adequate or inadequate replacement therapy for those hormonal deficiencies. Despite the well-known effects of GH on the heart and various cardiovascular risk factors, findings concerning cardiac structure and function in adult GHD, as well as the results of short-, medium- and long-term therapy, remain controversial. Some studies reported a decrease in the thickness of the LV posterior wall and of the interventricular septum, and a decrease in LV internal diameter, together with an average decrease in cardiac size of 36% in adults with childhood-onset GHD (CO-GHD) [18]. In contrast, other studies on patients with CO-GHD and adult-onset GHD (AO-GHD) have shown no morphological or functional differences between patients and controls [19, 20]. On the other hand, Colao *et al.* [10] reported a decrease in cardiac mass in young patients, both with CO- and AO-GHD; however, such findings have not been confirmed in patients over 60 years of age. In 77 adults with GHD, we observed a decrease in cardiac mass index (CMI; the relationship between calculated LV mass and body surface area) compared with that in adults without GHD. In over 50% of the patients, and in up to 85% of females with CO-GHD, a CMI of less than 90 g/m^2 was observed (reference range for normal population: 110 ± 20 g/m^2) [21].

The underlying pathophysiology of cardiac abnormalities in adults with GHD is still not fully understood. The mechanisms involved may be related to functional impairments secondary to the reduced growth of the cardiac muscle, to the absence of the direct effect of GH on myocardial cells and/or to indirect effects: cardiac pre-load and after-load (Fig. 1). In addition, abnormalities in heart rate, an indirect marker of cardiac autonomic tone, have been described [22].

A frequent – though not consistent – finding is the presence of diastolic dysfunction in GH-deficient adults, reported in up to 65% of cases, depending on the study [5, 23]. The use of isotopic angiography techniques may allow early detection of impaired LV filling. Diastolic function is usually evaluated by Doppler echocardiography. Mitral Doppler flow is recorded between the mid-portion and tip of the mitral valve leaflets. Two waves are identified: the E-wave (passive early flow from the left atrium to the left ventricle) and the A-wave (active flow produced by auricular contraction). The normal A/E wave ratio ranges from 0.82 to 1.04. A pattern is considered to be restrictive when this ratio is below 0.40, and prolonged when the ratio is above 1.05. With regard to diastolic function, we have observed a tendency towards restrictive patterns in adults with CO-GHD and a larger number of cases with a prolonged pattern in AO-GHD [24]. The frequent observation of a restrictive pattern in adults with CO-GHD (considered physiological during childhood) may be related to a failure of proper maturation of diastolic function due to GHD [9, 24]. As the prolonged diastolic pattern is frequently observed during ageing, a relatively early impairment of diastolic function is likely in our patients. On the other hand, we found no correlation between the extent of diastolic dysfunction and the duration of GHD or the severity of the disease (expressed in terms of the decrease in IGF-I levels) [24].

With regard to systolic function, many papers report a decrease in the different parameters evaluated (shortening fraction, ejection fraction, systolic volume and cardiac index) when comparing GH-deficient adults with healthy controls [5, 10, 25]; however, reported values are within the normal range in most cases. Not all adults with GHD can therefore be assumed to have ventricular failure. Some authors have found a more marked impairment of systolic function in adults with CO-GHD, both at rest and during exercise [11]. Such impairment has been associated with a decrease in cardiac wall thickness, which in extreme cases may lead to dilated cardiomyopathy, ultimately resulting in cardiac failure [9, 25]. Colao *et al.* [23] reported impairment of ventricular performance only in young patients, and characterized this finding as a hypokinetic syndrome caused either by a direct

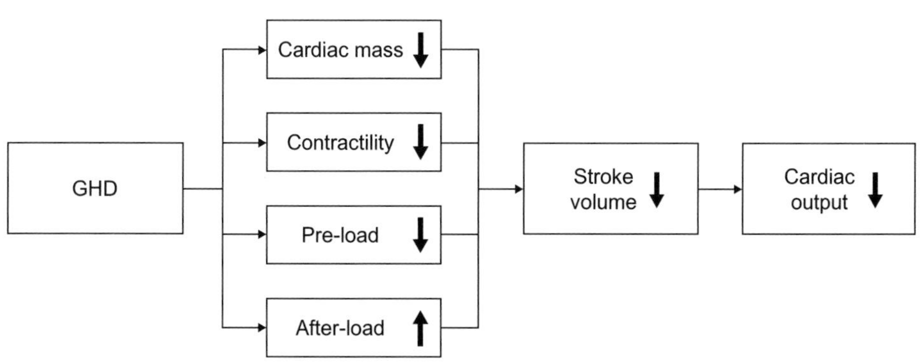

Figure 1. *Adult GHD and heart abnormalities: possible mechanisms involved.*

cardiac effect or by altered haemodynamic parameters secondary to GHD. On the other hand, many authors have reported systolic function to be normal in AO-GHD [19, 20]. Nevertheless, Ezzat *et al.* [26] have recently stated that there is evidence that many men and women with GHD have systolic dysfunction as evidenced by a decrease in ejection fraction. Interestingly, these authors consider as normal an ejection fraction over 60%, while for most investigators the cut-off value is 50%. As cardiac parameters vary according to age, results should be compared with age-matched reference ranges. In our experience, we found only a small number of male patients with a minimal decrease in ejection fraction, both in CO-GHD and AO-GHD. Multicentre studies have reported hypertension in 26% of GH-deficient adults [27], which is similar to the prevalence of hypertension in the general population. Hypertension in some of these patients could be attributed to impaired vascular reactivity related to the generation and/or metabolism of nitric oxide (NO) in the vascular wall [4, 28]. In our experience, a variable percentage of both men and women with GHD show a mild increase in systolic blood pressure; however, elevated diastolic blood pressure is seen in some men.

GH replacement therapy and the heart

There is still no consensus as to the medium- and long-term effects of GH replacement on cardiovascular abnormalities. Discrepancies in the results obtained from different studies may be attributed to protocol-related differences in the selection of patients and the therapy administered. Not all studies performed in large series of patients on GH therapy differentiate between CO- and AO-GHD, males and females and young and elderly subjects. Interestingly, Ezzat *et al.* [26] did not find any differences in echocardiographic changes between men and women after 6 months of therapy. On the other hand, there is marked heterogeneity in the doses of GH used, with a clear tendency in recent years towards the use of lower doses [29]. For this reason, there are considerable variations in the IGF-I levels attained and in the impact on myocardial cell receptors. This might explain why some early studies using high GH doses found cardiac hypertrophy. Moreover, no comparison can be made between results obtained from short-, medium- and long-term therapy. Finally, the variability in responses may also be attributed to the heterogeneity of individual characteristics.

Short-term studies have reported results ranging from the absence of changes to a clear increase in cardiac mass [10, 20]. Colao *et al.* [30] reported that, after 12 months of GH replacement therapy, IGF-I levels normalized and LV mass index, LV ejection fraction (LVEF) at peak exercise, peak-filling rate, and exercise duration and capacity significantly increased. Systolic function at rest and during exercise was further impaired in patients left untreated for the same period. In 10-year studies, however, other authors observed few changes in cardiac size from baseline [31, 32]. Moreover, some of these studies showed variable results over time, including a reversal of the initial beneficial effects [31]. It should be noted, however, that the doses of GH employed were supraphysiological during the first years of therapy and were subsequently reduced; hence the variation in IGF-I levels. Ter Maaten *et al.* [31] reported an increase in stroke volume during the first year of GH therapy, attributed to fluid retention and increased pre-load; however, a direct inotropic effect of GH should not be ruled out, as the increase in the cardiac index was sustained in the long term.

In our studies, we observed a significant improvement in diastolic function in patients with CO-GHD treated for 12–24 months, as demonstrated by an increase in the A/E wave ratio, and no significant changes – but a tendency towards an increase – in CMI. However, no progression was observed in these changes after 4 years of therapy [33]. Recently, in a 6-year longitudinal follow-up of a subset of adults with CO-GHD and AO-GHD receiving GH replacement therapy, whose IGF-I levels were maintained between 0 and 2 SD scores (SDSs), we observed a significant heterogeneity in the cardiac response. Even though we found no significant differences in the group as a whole, either in CMI or in diastolic and systolic functions, there was an improvement in diastolic function in 50% of adults with CO-GHD and in 86% of those with AO-GHD on GH therapy (Fig. 2). It should be emphasized that CMI was improved most in those patients with a more severe impairment and lower pre-treatment values (CMI < 60 g/m^2) [21].

In a recent meta-analysis, Maison and Chanson [34] carried out a systematic review of the echocardiographic findings from controlled trials comparing GH treatment with placebo, and open studies in adults with GHD, giving data for before and after GH treatment. These data suggest that GH treatment is associated with positive cardiac effects: a significant increase in LV mass, interventricular septum thickness, LV posterior wall thickness, LV end-diastolic diameter and stroke volume. The authors suggest a dose–effect relationship; however, the dose range employed in the different studies analysed varied from 0.03 to 0.50 IU/kg/week, making it difficult to confirm this relationship. Moreover, in the majority of reports, IGF-I values were given in absolute terms, without reference to gender- and age-adjusted ranges, which would enable calculation of the SDS. In a recent publication we have discussed the importance of expressing IGF-I values in terms of SDS to allow comparison between results obtained from different laboratories [35].

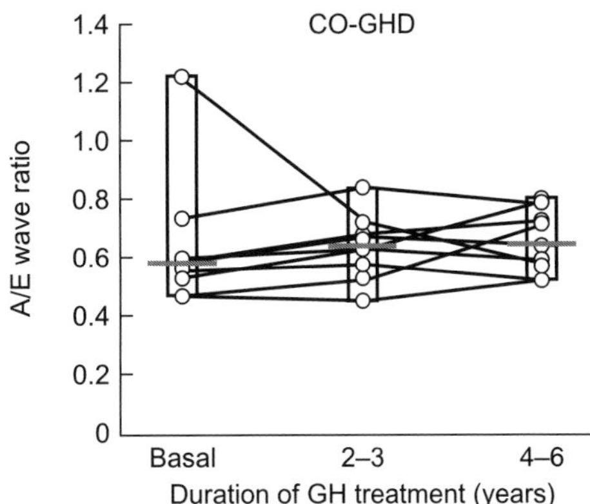

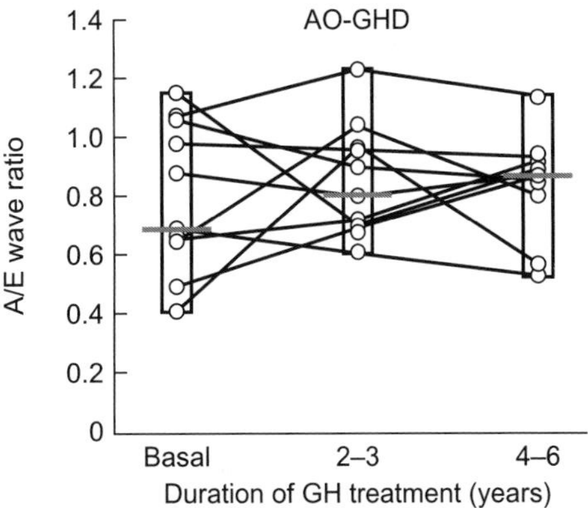

Figure 2. *Effects of medium- and long-term GH replacement therapy on the A/E wave ratio in adults with childhood-onset GHD (CO-GHD; upper) and adult-onset GHD (AO-GHD; lower). Medians are shown as horizontal lines.*

GHD, endothelial function and vascular structure

Premature atherosclerosis has been described in hypopituitary patients, demonstrated by an increase in the intima–media thickness (IMT) of the carotid arteries [36]. Increased risk factors for vascular disease have been well established in this group of patients, including lipid abnormalities, increased visceral adiposity, glucose intolerance and insulin resistance, hypertension, coagulation disorders and fibrinolysis with an increased thrombogenic risk [37, 38].

Endothelial dysfunction is an early and potentially reversible event in the pathogenesis of atherosclerosis [39]. It should be noted that the vascular endothelium plays a vital and complex role in homeostasis and the regulation of vascular tone [38]. Endothelial dysfunction is associated with decreased NO production. NO has been shown to inhibit platelet aggregation and leukocyte adhesion to the vascular endothelium [40]. Endothelial permeability and some endothelial cell functions are linked to the activity of endothelial NO synthase. This enzyme is capable of producing the superoxide anion, with deleterious vascular effects, in situations of oxidative stress [40]. Other injurious factors have also been observed, such as tumour necrosis factor-α and interleukin-1, which induce the expression of adhesion glycoproteins, including E-selectin and intracellular adhesion molecule-1 (ICAM-1) by endothelial cells. Such molecules facilitate macrophage and leukocyte adhesion and their migration to the subendothelial space, thus favouring the atherogenic process and the increase in IMT. The activated endothelium is also known to express other markers of endothelial dysfunction, such as von Willebrand factor and thrombomodulin [38]. For a review of the role of GH in coagulation and inflammation see Chapter 15.

IGF-I receptors have been characterized in the vascular endothelium, and the haemodynamic effects of IGF-I are mediated by NO [28]. The negative correlation of ICAM-1 and some biochemical markers of endothelial dysfunction with IGF-I, suggests that the GH/IGF-I axis is involved in the expression of cell adhesion molecules by the endothelium [38]. IGF-I deficiency might therefore be an early event in the pathogenesis of atherosclerosis in GH-deficient adults. These patients have been reported to show reduced urinary excretion of NO metabolites, which is normalized on GH replacement therapy [41]. These findings, together with the evidence for a direct stimulatory effect of IGF-I on NO production in endothelial cell cultures, would support the role of the GH/IGF-I axis in endothelial dysfunction [28]. In conclusion, there is sufficient evidence of increased vascular risk in adults with GHD; however, it is difficult to differentiate between the specific role of GHD and that of other pituitary deficiencies. It has been well established that the improvement observed after GH therapy is mediated by an increase in NO availability, changes in different lipid fractions, changes in vascular wall composition and decreased inflammatory mediators [38]. These changes indicate that GH therapy may partially or completely reverse some of the processes associated with atherogenesis, and warrant further research.

GHD and physical work capacity

From the early description of the adult GHD syndrome, alterations in body composition, with reduced lean body mass (LBM) and a concomitant reduction in muscle mass and physical performance, have been recognized [5, 42]. Some authors have shown reduced isometric quadriceps force, which may be explained by the reduction in cross-sectional muscle area [42]. Koranyi *et al.* [43] reported that the knee extensor muscle, knee flexor muscle and handgrip strength were more impaired in adults with CO-GHD than in those with AO-GHD. Additionally, the reduced physical work capacity observed in adults with GHD might also be partly related to decreased cardiac performance during exercise [5]. Several studies have reported alterations in the LVEF at peak exercise in young, middle-aged and elderly patients [10]. On the other hand, GH-deficient adults have also shown a reduction in maximum oxygen uptake and submaximal aerobic performance, which could account for their perception of increased fatigue and reduced physical performance [44]. Muscle biopsies in adults with GHD revealed significant changes in some isoforms of the myosin heavy chain. These changes did not correlate with circulating IGF-I levels or with changes in body composition after 6 months of GH replacement therapy [5]. The effect of GH on muscle tissue appears to be mediated by stimulation of protein synthesis, rather than by inhibition of proteolysis. This effect might be due to a direct action of GH or to the *in-situ* production of IGF-I, although the contribution of circulating IGF-I cannot be ruled out [45]. It is not known whether the increase in insulin or lipid intermediates contributes to the anabolic action of GH in muscle [45].

It has been reported that after GH replacement therapy, maximum oxygen uptake increases significantly, reaching values approaching those predicted for age, sex and height [44]. Such an increase has been associated with improvements in exercise capacity [42]. The increase in LBM and muscle strength while on GH therapy might vary according to sex and the time of onset of the deficiency. A more marked increase in LBM has been reported in males after 6 months of GH therapy [26] and a more marked response in muscle strength has been reported in adults with CO-GHD after 5 years of replacement

Table 1. *Basal cardiac parameters and physical work capacity variables in adult patients with untreated GHD in KIMS. Values are expressed as medians and 10th and 90th centiles of the population evaluated; n corresponds to the number of observations of each variable.*

	CO-GHD		AO-GHD	
Cardiac parameter	**Men**	**Women**	**Men**	**Women**
Left atrium diameter systole (mm)	31 (26–35) n = 31	30 (24–35) n = 21	36 (29–44) n = 74	33 (23–41) n = 67
LV diameter diastole (mm)	45 (38–52) n = 37	42.5 (40.0–48.0) n = 22	49 (41–56) n = 76	46 (38–54) n = 68
LV diameter systole (mm)	28 (23–37) n = 37	28.5 (23.0–35.0) n = 22	31 (24–37) n = 71	28 (23–36) n = 66
Septum width diastole (mm)	8 (6–11) n = 36	7 (6–11) n = 22	10 (7–13) n = 78	9 (7–13) n = 65
Posterior wall thickness diastole (mm)	8 (6–10) n = 36	7 (5–10) n = 21	9.1 (7.0–12.0) n = 77	9 (7–12) n = 62
A/E wave ratio	0.64 (0.43–0.85) n = 25	0.60 (0.43–0.96) n = 19	0.93 (0.62–1.39) n = 51	0.79 (0.49–1.23) n = 50
Deceleration time (ms)	179 (120–439) n = 18	160 (110–210) n = 15	182.5 (110.0–294.0) n = 44	185 (110–263) n = 46
Fractional shortening (%)	36.0 (24.1–45.2) n = 37	33.3 (26.8–46.0) n = 22	37.7 (30.0–45.7) n = 71	38.1 (22.2–46.0) n = 64
Ejection fraction (%)	52.0 (36.4–64.3) n = 18	49.2 (37.8–66.0) n = 10	56.9 (37.2–69.1) n = 43	51.8 (44.6–71.3) n = 37
Cardiac mass index (g/m^2)	81.2 (48.3–111.0) n = 36	66.8 (53.3–110.3) n = 21	90.0 (61.1–144.8) n = 74	82.1 (60.8–127.9) n = 60
Heart rate (beats/minute)	72 (60–82) n = 489	72 (60–85) n = 392	72 (60–84) n = 1539	72 (60–84) n = 1609
Systolic blood pressure (mmHg)	120 (100–138) n = 527	112.5 (100.0–132.0) n = 412	130 (110–150) n = 1637	125 (106–150) n = 1712
Diastolic blood pressure (mmHg)	75 (60–86) n = 527	70 (60–85) n = 412	80 (70–95) n = 1636	80 (66–90) n = 1708
Maximum workload (watts)	200 (125–250) n = 25	100 (75–200) n = 15	150 (75–245) n = 48	100 (75–175) n = 52
Maximum load heart rate (beats/minute)	155.5 (130.0–185.0) n = 26	163 (145–188) n = 16	150 (110–170) n = 49	145 (116–176) n = 53
Maximum load systolic blood pressure (mmHg)	150 (130–200) n = 26	145 (120–185) n = 16	183.5 (140.0–209.0) n = 48	160 (130–210) n = 53

AO-GHD, adult-onset GHD; CO-GHD, childhood-onset GHD; LV, left ventricular.

Table 2. Diastolic and systolic functions and cardiac mass index (CMI) in adults with GHD enrolled in KIMS and treated with GH. Values are shown for adult patients with childhood-onset GHD (CO-GHD) after 1 year of GH treatment and for patients with adult-onset GHD (AO-GHD) after 5 years of GH treatment (longitudinal data), and expressed as medians and 10th and 90th centiles of the population evaluated; n corresponds to the number of observations of each variable.

	Adults with CO-GHD (1 year of GH therapy)	Adults with AO-GHD (5 years of GH therapy)
Delta A/E wave ratio	0.00 (–0.16 to 0.43) n = 8	–0.02 (–0.55 to 0.60) n = 8
Delta deceleration time (ms)	30.5 (–25.0 to 280.0) n = 6	–16.5 (–224.0 to 102.0) n = 10
Delta fractional shortening (%)	–4.15 (–13.50 to 0.03) n = 13	2.12 (–11.48 to 12.91) n = 10
Delta ejection fraction (%)	0.22 (–3.80 to 15.06) n = 7	4.43 (–25.74 to 15.18) n = 9
Delta CMI (g/m^2)	4.15 (–10.51 to 23.45) n = 10	14.95 (–1.53 to 22.44) n = 7

therapy [43]. Some studies have shown a significant increase in both exercise capacity and duration during GH replacement [5, 42]. We have observed an increase in physical work capacity in almost half of our patients during long-term treatment with GH [21]. Increased physical performance has been associated with an improvement in LVEF at peak exercise, both in adults with CO-GHD and in those with AO-GHD, but values remained lower than in controls [10]. Finally, an increase in oxygen transport capacity due to a stimulatory effect of IGF-I on erythropoiesis may also contribute to increased physical capacity [46].

Experience from KIMS

Electrocardiography, ergometry, echocardiography and/or mitral Doppler were performed in 310 men and 292 women. The results of the different variables obtained in untreated GH-deficient adults are shown in Table 1. In this cohort, there were considerable numbers of men and women with CO-GHD who had a tendency towards a restrictive pattern of diastolic function, and some patients with AO-GHD with a prolonged pattern. With regard to systolic function, low ejection fraction values were observed in a large number of patients in all groups, particularly in those with CO-GHD. In some cases, such values were consistent with systolic dysfunction. The CMI was decreased (< 90 g/m^2) in a considerable number of patients in all groups, but mainly in women with CO-GHD.

Longitudinal data in GH-treated adults with GHD are available for two different time periods: 1 year for CO-GHD and 5 years for AO-GHD (Table 2). It is worth noting that, after 1 year of therapy, the increase observed in LV diameter in systole was greater in adults with CO-GHD than in those with AO-GHD. No significant differences were found in physical work capacity. After 5 years of therapy, there was no evidence of cardiac hypertrophy or significant changes in heart rate or diastolic or systolic blood pressure.

Conclusions

In hypopituitary patients, the association of GHD with increased mortality suggests that this hormone deficiency increases the likelihood of various cardiovascular risk factors. Additionally, evidence of a direct action of GH on the heart has been reported both in healthy subjects and in adults with GHD. Despite the large number of basic and clinical research studies, impairment of cardiac structure and function in GH-deficient patients remains a source of contention. Controversy also persists about some of the findings obtained with long-term GH replacement therapy and as to whether the different subsets of patients (AO-GHD and CO-GHD, females and males, young and elderly) would benefit in a similar manner.

In the future, basic research on the complex intracellular pathways of GH and IGF-I, as well as longitudinal clinical trials and a comparison with adequate control groups, will make it possible to draw conclusions about the exact role of GH, not only in adults with GHD but also in different pathologies affecting the cardiovascular system.

References

1. Cuneo RC, Wilmshurst P, Lowy C, McGauley G, Sönksen PH. Cardiac failure responding to growth hormone. Lancet 1989;1:838–9
2. Rosén T, Bengtsson B-Å. Premature mortality due to cardiovascular disease in hypopituitarism. Lancet 1990;336:285–8
3. Tomlinson JW, Holden N, Hills RK, Wheatley K, Clayton RN, Bates AS, Sheppard MC, Stewart PM. Association between premature mortality and hypopituitarism. West Midlands Prospective Hypopituitary Study Group. Lancet 2001;357:425–31
4. McCallum RW, Petrie JR, Dominiczak AF, Connell JM. Growth hormone deficiency and vascular risk. Clin Endocrinol (Oxf) 2002;57:11–24
5. Simpson H, Savine R, Sönksen P, Bengtsson B-Å, Carlsson L, Christiansen JS, Clemmons D, Cohen P, Hintz R, Ho K, Mullis P, Robinson I, Strasburger C, Tanaka T, Thorner M. Growth hormone replacement therapy for adults: into the new millennium. Growth Horm IGF Res 2002;12:1–33
6. Isgaard J. GH effects on cardiac function. In: Bengtsson B-Å. Growth hormone. Massachusetts: Kluwer Academic Publishers 1999:253–60
7. Fazio S, Palmieri EA, Biondi B, Cittadini A, Saccà L. The role of the GH–IGF-I axis in the regulation of myocardial growth: from experimental models to human evidence. Eur J Endocrinol 2000;142:211–6
8. Saccà L, Cittadini A, Fazio S. Growth hormone and the heart. Endocr Rev 1994;15:555–73
9. Bengtsson B-Å, Christiansen JS, Cuneo RC, Saccà L. Cardiovascular effects of GH. J Endocrinol 1997; 152:1–3
10. Colao A, Marzullo P, Di Somma C, Lombardi G. Growth hormone and the heart. Clin Endocrinol (Oxf) 2001;54:137–54
11. Drake WM, Howell SJ, Monson JP, Shalet SM. Optimizing GH therapy in adults and children. Endocr Rev 2001;22:425–50
12. Kaplinsky E, Perandones C, Galiana MG, Fideleff H, Favaloro RR, Carlos V, Perrone SV. Borjeson-Forssman-Lehmann syndrome and dilated cardiomyopathy: a previously unreported association. Can J Cardiol 2001;17:80–3
13. Donath MY, Jenni R, Brunner HP, Anrig M, Kohli S, Glatz Y, Froesch ER. Cardiovascular and metabolic effects of insulin-like growth factor I at rest and during exercise in humans. J Clin Endocrinol Metab 1996; 81:4089–94
14. Copeland KC, Nair KS. Recombinant human insulin-like growth factor-I increases forearm blood flow. J Clin Endocrinol Metab 1994;79:230–2
15. Bisi G, Podio V, Valetto MR, Broglio F, Bertuccio G, Del Rio G, Boghen MF, Berti F, Müller EE, Ghigo E. Radionuclide angiocardiographic evaluation of the cardiovascular effects of recombinant human IGF-I in normal adults. Eur J Endocrinol 1999;140:322–7
16. Wang L, Ma W, Markovich R, Chen JW, Wang PH. Regulation of cardiomyocyte apoptotic signaling by insulin-like growth factor I. Circ Res 1998;83:516–22
17. Bülow B, Hagmar L, Mikoczy Z, Nordström CH, Erfurth EM. Increased cerebrovascular mortality in patients with hypopituitarism. Clin Endocrinol (Oxf) 1997;46:75–81
18. Merola B, Cittadini A, Colao A, Longobardi S, Fazio S, Sabatini D, Saccà L, Lombardi G. Cardiac structural and functional abnormalities in adult patients with growth hormone deficiency. J Clin Endocrinol Metab 1993; 77:1658–61
19. Beshyah SA, Shahi M, Skinner E, Sharp P, Foale R, Johnston DG. Cardiovascular effects of growth hormone replacement therapy in hypopituitary adults. Eur J Endocrinol 1994;130:451–8
20. Valcavi R, Gaddi O, Zini M, Iavicoli M, Mellino U, Portioli I. Cardiac performance and mass in adults with hypopituitarism: effects of one year of growth hormone treatment. J Clin Endocrinol Metab 1995;80:659–66
21. Boquete H, Fideleff HR, Giaccio A, Sobrado P, Barmat R, Stalldecker G. Heterogeneity of cardiac response in adults with GH deficiency during medium- and long-term replacement therapy. Proceedings of the 35th International symposium: GH and growth factors in endocrinology and metabolism, Prague 2003;Abstract 30
22. Leong KS, Mann P, Wallymahmed M, MacFarlane IA, Wilding JP. Abnormal heart rate variability in adults with growth hormone deficiency. J Clin Endocrinol Metab 2000;85:628–33
23. Colao A, Cuocolo A, Di Somma C, Cerbone G, Morte AM, Pivonello R, Nicolai E, Salvatore M, Lombardi G.

Does the age of onset of growth hormone deficiency affect cardiac performance? A radionuclide angiography study. Clin Endocrinol (Oxf) 2000;52:447–55

24. Boquete H, Fideleff H, Stalldecker G, Barmat R, Sobrado P, Caravelli A, Giaccio A, Claus Hernberg H, Chervin A, Levalle O, Miras M, Sinay I. Childhood- and adult-onset growth hormone deficiency: differences in cardiac function patterns in adults. Growth Horm IGF Res 2000;10:148

25. Cittadini A, Longobardi L, Fazio S, Saccà L. Growth hormone and cardiac function. In: Juul A, Jørgensen JOL, editors. Growth hormone in adults. Cambridge: Cambridge University Press 1996:251–64

26. Ezzat S, Fear S, Gaillard RC, Gayle C, Landy H, Marcovitz S, Mattioni T, Nussey S, Rees A, Svanberg E. Gender-specific responses of lean body composition and non-gender-specific cardiac function improvement after GH replacement in GH-deficient adults. J Clin Endocrinol Metab 2002;87:2725–33

27. Luger A. Baseline characteristics of patients enrolled in KIMS. In: Bengtsson B-Å, Monson JP, editors. GH replacement in adults. Oxford: Oxford PharmaGenesis 2000:105–11

28. Christ ER, Chowienczyk PJ, Sönksen PH, Russel-Jones DL. Growth hormone replacement therapy in adults with growth hormone deficiency improves vascular reactivity. Clin Endocrinol (Oxf) 1999;51:21–5

29. Sneppen SB, Steensgaard-Hansen F, Feldt-Rasmussen U. Cardiac effects of low-dose growth hormone replacement therapy in growth hormone-deficient adults. An 18-month randomised, placebo-controlled, double-blind study. Horm Res 2002;58:21–9

30. Colao A, di Somma C, Pivonello R, Cuocolo A, Spinelli L, Bonaduce D, Salvatore M, Lombardi G. The cardiovascular risk of adult GH deficiency (GHD) improved after GH replacement and worsened in untreated GHD: a 12-month prospective study. J Clin Endocrinol Metab 2002;87:1088–93

31. Ter Maaten JC, De Boer H, Kamp O, Stuurman L, van der Veen EA. Long-term effects of growth hormone (GH) replacement in men with childhood-onset GH deficiency. J Clin Endocrinol Metab 1999;84:2373–80

32. Gibney J, Wallace JD, Spinks T, Schnorr L, Ranicar A, Cuneo RC, Lockhart S, Burnand KG, Salomon F, Sönksen PH, Russell-Jones D. The effects of 10 years of recombinant human growth hormone (GH) in adult GH-deficient patients. J Clin Endocrinol Metab 1999; 84:2596–602

33. Boquete HR, Fideleff HL, Giaccio A, Barmat R, Stalldecker G, Sobrado P, Claus Hernberg H, Chervin A, Levalle O, Miras M, Sinay I. Intratreatment changes in heart structure and function in adults with childhood onset GH deficiency. Proceedings of the XIV meeting of the Latin American Paediatric Endocrinology Society, Ushuaia, Argentina 2000;P43

34. Maison P, Chanson P. Cardiac effects of growth hormone in adults with growth hormone deficiency: a meta-analysis. Circulation 2003;108:2648–52

35. Boquete HR, Sobrado PG, Fideleff HL, Sequera AM, Giaccio AV, Suarez MG, Ruibal GF, Miras M. Evaluation of diagnostic accuracy of insulin-like growth factor (IGF)-I and IGF-binding protein-3 in growth hormone-deficient children and adults using ROC plot analysis. J Clin Endocrinol Metab 2003;88:4702–8

36. Pfeifer M, Verhovec R, Žižek B, Preželj J, Poredoš P, Clayton RN. Growth hormone (GH) treatment reverses early atherosclerotic changes in GH-deficient adults. J Clin Endocrinol Metab 1999;84:453–7

37. Abs R, Bengtsson B-Å, Hernberg-Ståhl E, Monson JP, Tauber JP, Wilton P, Wüster C. GH replacement in 1034 growth hormone deficient hypopituitary adults: demographic and clinical characteristics, dosing and safety. Clin Endocrinol (Oxf) 1999;50:703–13

38. Elhadd TA, Abdu TA, Oxtoby J, Kennedy G, McLaren M, Neary R, Belch JJ, Clayton RN. Biochemical and biophysical markers of endothelial dysfunction in adults with hypopituitarism and severe GH deficiency. J Clin Endocrinol Metab 2001;86:4223–32

39. Evans LM, Davies JS, Goodfellow J, Rees JA, Scanlon MF. Endothelial dysfunction in hypopituitary adults with growth hormone deficiency. Clin Endocrinol (Oxf) 1999;50:457–64

40. Evans LM, Davies JS, Anderson RA, Ellis GR, Jackson SK, Lewis MJ, Frenneaux MP, Rees A, Scanlon MF. The effect of GH replacement therapy on endothelial function and oxidative stress in adult growth hormone deficiency. Eur J Endocrinol 2000;142:254–62

41. Boger RH, Skamira C, Bode-Boger SM, Brabant G, von zur Muhlen A, Frölich JC. Nitric oxide may mediate the hemodynamic effects of recombinant growth hormone in patients with acquired growth hormone deficiency. A double-blind, placebo-controlled study. J Clin Invest 1996;98:2706–13

42. Carroll PV, Christ ER, Bengtsson B-Å, Carlsson L, Christiansen JS, Clemmons D, Hintz R, Ho K, Laron Z, Sizonenko P, Sönksen PH, Tanaka T, Thorne M. Growth hormone deficiency in adulthood and the effects of growth hormone replacement: a review. Growth Hormone Research Society Scientific Committee. J Clin Endocrinol Metab 1998;83:382–95

43. Koranyi J, Svensson J, Götherström G, Sunnerhagen KS, Bengtsson B, Johannsson G. Baseline characteristics and the effects of five years of GH replacement therapy in adults with GH deficiency of childhood or adult-

hood onset: a comparative, prospective study. J Clin Endocrinol Metab 2001;86:4693–9

44. Woodhouse LJ, Asa SL, Thomas SG, Ezzat S. Measures of submaximal aerobic performance evaluate and predict functional response to growth hormone (GH) treatment in GH-deficient adults. J Clin Endocrinol Metab 1999;84:4570–7

45. Jørgensen JO, Dall R, Vahl N, Nørrelund H, Christiansen JS. Effects of growth hormone on muscle mass and function. In: Bengtsson B-Å, editor. Growth hormone. Massachusetts: Kluwer Academic Publishers 1999:227–36

46. Christ ER, Cummings MH, Westwood NB, Sawyer BM, Pearson TC, Sönksen PH, Russell-Jones DL. The importance of growth hormone in the regulation of erythropoiesis, red cell mass, and plasma volume in adults with growth hormone deficiency. J Clin Endocrinol Metab 1997;82:2985–90

15 Growth hormone, coagulation and inflammation

Michaela Riedl[1], Harald Kotzmann[1] and Anton Luger[1,2]

[1]Department of Medicine III, Clinical Division of Endocrinology and Metabolism, [2]University of Vienna and Ludwig Boltzmann Institute for Experimental Endocrinology, Vienna, Austria

Summary

Patients with growth hormone deficiency (GHD) are at increased risk of cardiovascular mortality. Besides obesity, hypertension, insulin resistance, elevated plasma lipid concentrations and endothelial dysfunction, abnormalities in the coagulation and fibrinolytic systems also appear to contribute to this excess mortality. Among other derangements, plasma concentrations of fibrinogen, tissue-type plasminogen activator, plasminogen activator inhibitor type 1, von Willebrand factor and soluble adhesion molecules are elevated in patients with GHD, and decrease with growth hormone (GH) replacement therapy. This is also true for several pro-inflammatory cytokines, which in turn increase plasma concentrations of soluble adhesion molecules and inhibit GH action. As data on cardiovascular mortality in GH-deficient patients receiving GH replacement therapy are not yet available, it remains to be established whether this therapy will normalize the reduced life expectancy of these patients. GH also has stimulatory effects on cells and mediators of the inflammatory/immune response and, conversely, pro-inflammatory cytokines affect GH secretion and action. In addition, GH is produced by lymphoid tissues. The exact mechanisms of the communication between the GH/insulin-like growth factor I axis and the immune system are not yet understood.

GH and coagulation

Deviations of growth hormone (GH) serum concentrations from the normal range have a negative impact on survival: GH deficiency (GHD), as well as GH excess, has been reported to be associated with increased mortality [1–4]. This excess mortality is mainly due to cardiovascular events (see Chapter 6). Besides hypertension and insulin resistance, which are present in both pathological situations, central obesity and elevated plasma lipid concentrations may contribute to the increased mortality in GHD [5, 6]. In addition to these changes, left ventricular hypertrophy is an almost universal finding in acromegalic patients [5]. While efforts to normalize both elevated and decreased GH concentrations have shown beneficial effects on the adverse cardiovascular risk profile and parameters of cardiac function [5, 7–9], it remains to be demonstrated that these therapeutic interventions will ultimately reduce the increased mortality in both diseases. For a review of GH and cardiovascular function see Chapter 14.

Other pathophysiological mechanisms by which GHD may cause increased cardiovascular mortality include alterations of the coagulation and fibrinolytic systems (Fig. 1). Indeed, increased plasma concentrations of fibrinogen, tissue-type plasminogen activator (t-PA) and plasminogen activator inhibitor type 1 (PAI-1) in GHD have

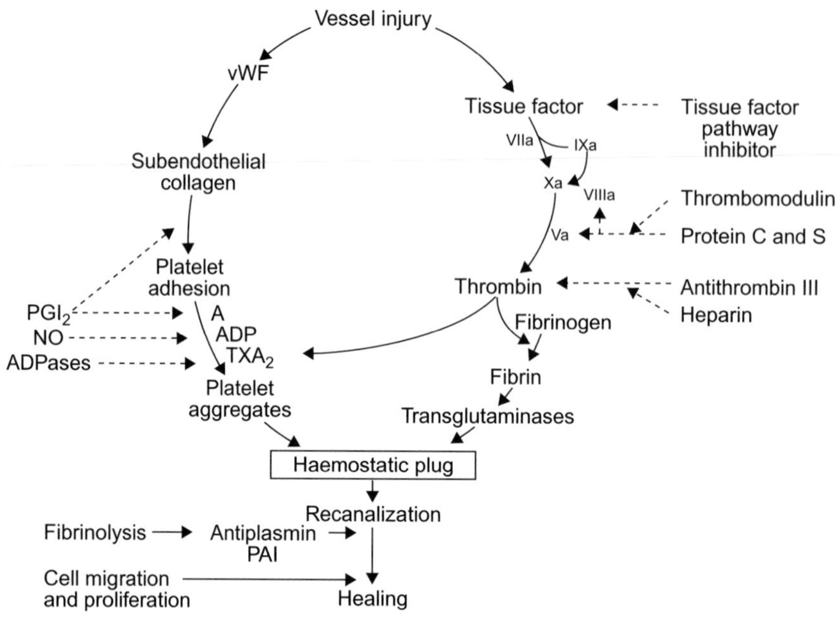

Figure 1. *Overview of haemostasis. A, adrenaline; ADP, adenosine diphosphate; ADPases, adenosine diphosphatases; NO, nitric oxide; PAI, plasminogen activation inhibitor;* PGI_2*, prostacyclin;* TXA_2*, thromboxane* a_2*; vWF, von Willebrand factor. Adapted from [47] with permission from Lippincott, Williams & Wilkins.*

been described in several studies [6, 10–12]. Interestingly, some of these alterations have also been observed in acromegaly [5, 11, 13]. t-PA and PAIs are produced by the endothelium and modulate fibrinolysis. In addition, factor VIII and von Willebrand factor (vWF) have been reported to be elevated in GHD [14]. vWF, also produced by the endothelium, stabilizes factor VIII and induces platelet recruitment and aggregation. All of these factors have been shown to be independent risk factors for cardiovascular disease [15–18]. Furthermore, it has been demonstrated that long-term GH treatment decreases plasma concentrations of PAI-1, PAI antigen and t-PA antigen [12, 19]. Although it cannot be excluded that these observations are secondary to changes in body composition and plasma lipids, they represent favourable sequelae of such therapy. In rats, however, hypophysectomy has been shown to be associated with decreased levels of vitamin K-dependent coagulation factors, particularly of factor VII, which binds to the tissue factor and initiates the blood coagulation cascade, but also factor VIII. Substitution of GH, but not cortisol or thyroxine, reversed these alterations [20].

Serum concentrations of the soluble adhesion molecules E-selectin, P-selectin and intercellular adhesion molecule-1 (ICAM-1) have also been found to be elevated in GH-deficient patients and to normalize after 1 year of GH replacement therapy [12, 14]. E-selectin and ICAM-1 are produced by endothelial cells, whereas P-selectin is synthesized by activated platelets. They are involved in the process of platelet adhesion to the endothelium, and have been shown to be associated with atherosclerosis. It is noteworthy that production of adhesion molecules is increased by pro-inflammatory cytokines, such as tumour necrosis factor-α (TNF-α) and interleukin-6 (IL-6), which are also elevated in GHD [21, 22], and suppressed by GH *in vitro* and *in vivo* [23, 24]. Therefore, it has been speculated that GH may inhibit the inflammatory response related to the onset of atherosclerosis [6]. This hypothesis is further supported by the decrease of acute-phase reactants, such as C-reactive protein, in a randomized, controlled clinical trial in GH-deficient patients receiving GH replacement therapy [24]. In addition, plasma concentrations of homocysteine are elevated in patients with GHD, and decrease with GH replacement therapy [25]. Homocysteine is also considered as an independent cardiovascular risk factor [26].

Endothelial dysfunction is an early marker of cardiovascular disease and can be detected before the onset of atherosclerosis [27]. As mentioned above, the endothelium is metabolically highly active, has important antithrombotic and fibrinolytic functions and modulates vascular tone. Nitric oxide is a central paracrine mediator of these processes. In patients with GHD, flow-mediated endothelium-derived dilatation (FMD) of the brachial artery was compromised following ischaemia induced by inflation of a blood pressure tourniquet to supra-systolic pressure [28]. FMD represents an established functional test of the capacity of medium-sized arteries to increase blood flow following ischaemia. Furthermore, premature atherosclerosis was detected [14, 28, 29]. Again, GH replacement therapy reversed these early morphological and functional changes in the major arteries of GH-deficient patients [28]. These findings are further supported by the demonstration of improved endothelium-dependent vascular relaxation *ex vivo* when hypophysectomized rats received GH [30].

Although no definitive conclusions on the long-term effects of GH replacement therapy in adults can be drawn at this point, as data on the endpoint of cardiovascular mortality are not yet available, strong evidence has accumulated that such therapy improves many of the cardiovascular risk factors, as well as morphological and functional changes of blood vessels, in GH-deficient patients.

GH and inflammation

Numerous reports document a close interaction between the endocrine and immune systems (for review see [31]). Figure 2 shows the activation of innate immune mechanisms. There is also convincing evidence for bidirectional communication between the GH/insulin-like growth factor I (IGF-I) axis and the immune system. GH has been shown to be produced locally by lymphoid tissues, and lymphocytes express GH receptors [32, 33] (B-lymphocytes and monocytes in a higher proportion than T-lymphocytes). Also in bone marrow, GH receptors are expressed to various extents on all haematopoietic lineages, including B-lymphocytes, T-lymphocytes, macrophages and granulocyte precursors [33]. Furthermore, it has been demonstrated that both GH and IGF-I are able to enhance lymphopoiesis and immune function *in vitro* and *in vivo* [34].

In contrast to these findings, it is well known that children with GHD do not exhibit severe immune deficiency, and do not show extreme susceptibility to infections. Nevertheless, several lines of evidence suggest that GH affects inflammatory and immune processes in man. Long-term GH replacement therapy induces a significant increase in myeloid and also erythroid progenitor cells, while peripheral white and red blood cells are only marginally affected [35]. Furthermore, GH-deficient adults have an impaired basal and (interferon-α and IL-2) stimulated natural killer (NK) cell activity, as well as changes in lymphocyte subsets [36]. Interestingly, 18 months of GH replacement therapy did not normalize any of these parameters. In contrast, short-term and long-term supraphysiological doses of GH increased the phagocytic activity of polymorphonuclear leukocytes in patients with chronic renal failure [37, 38]. This finding may be of particular interest, as this population is known to be GH resistant, and infections are major contributors to morbidity and mortality [39]. In addition, chronically elevated GH concentrations in patients with acromegaly have been shown to significantly enhance phagocytic activity and T-cell activity, while many other parameters, such as serum concentrations of immunoglobulins, lymphocyte subsets and NK activity, were not affected [40].

An acute effect of GH has also been demonstrated in children undergoing an IGF-I generation test, where significant increases in the serum

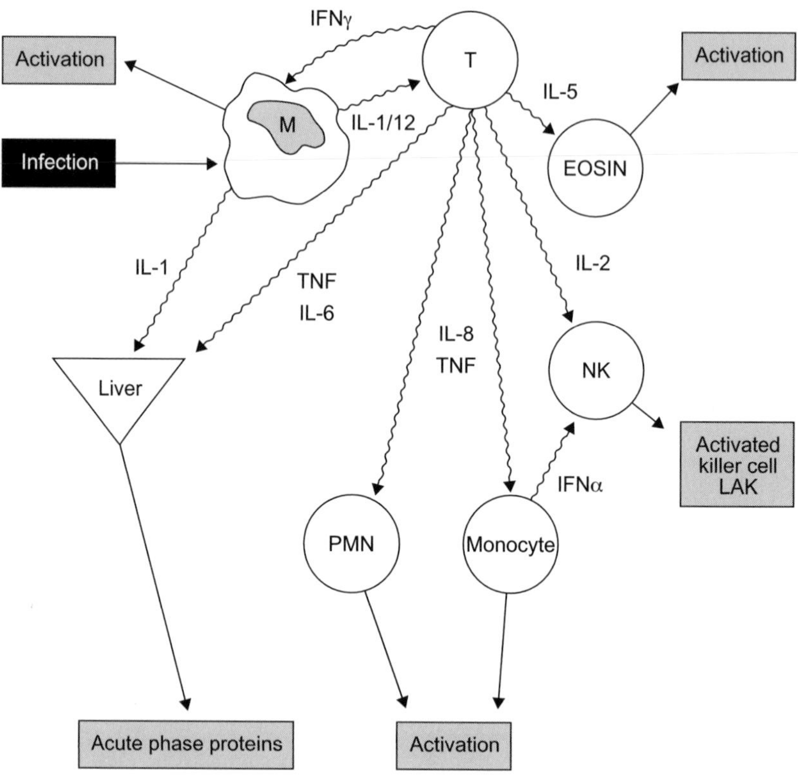

Figure 2. *Activation of innate immune mechanisms. EOSIN, eosinophil; IFN, interferon; IL, interleukin; LAK, lymphokine-activated killer; M, macrophage; NK, natural killer cell; PMN, polymorphonuclear neutrophil; T, T-lymphocyte; TNF, tumour necrosis factor. Adapted from [48] with permission from Blackwell Publishing.*

concentrations of several pro-inflammatory cytokines (IL-1, IL-2, IL-12, TNF-α and interferon-γ) have been described [41]. In contrast, enhanced IL-6 and TNF-α plasma concentrations and monocyte production have been observed in patients with GHD, which decreased after 3 months of GH therapy [23, 24, 42]. As a further indication of a bidirectional cross-talk between the endocrine and immune systems, elevated cytokine concentrations have been shown to impair GH action [43]. IL-6, IL-1β and TNF-α inhibit the GH/signal transducer and activator of transcription 5 signalling pathway, leading to down-regulation of GH-responsive genes during an acute-phase response [43]. The interaction between GH and cytokines appears to be complex; thus acute and chronic effects of GHD and GH excess may differ.

In a recent report, serum mannan binding lectin (MBL) concentrations have been determined in GH-deficient patients before and during GH or IGF-I therapy, as well as in acromegalic patients before and during therapy with octreotide or pegvisomant [44]. MBL is an innate plasma protein that binds to specific receptors on the surface of microbes and subsequently activates the complement cascade through serine proteases. The role of MBL in immune defence is underlined by the increased susceptibility of subjects with low serum MBL concentrations to recurrent infections [45]. GH, but not IGF-I, replacement therapy increased the basally decreased serum MBL concentrations in GH-deficient patients, whereas the somatostatin analogue octreotide and the GH-antagonist pegvisomant, decreased the initially elevated MBL levels in acromegalic patients.

Together these findings clearly indicate a relationship between GH and peripheral blood mononuclear cell phenotype and function, although the mechanisms are not yet entirely understood. Autocrine and paracrine regulatory pathways may play an important role [46].

References

1. Rosén T, Bengtsson B-Å. Premature mortality due to cardiovascular disease in hypopituitarism. Lancet 1990;336:285–8
2. Bülow B, Hagmar L, Mikoczy Z, Nordström CH, Erfurth EM. Increased cerebrovascular mortality in patients with hypopituitarism. Clin Endocrinol (Oxf) 1997;46:75–81
3. Tomlinson JW, Holden N, Hills RK, Wheatley K, Clayton RN, Bates AS, Sheppard MC, Stewart PM. Association between premature mortality and hypopituitarism. West Midlands Prospective Hypopituitary Study Group. Lancet 2001;357:425–31
4. Orme SM, McNally RJ, Cartwright RA, Belchetz PE. Mortality and cancer incidence in acromegaly: a retrospective cohort study. United Kingdom Acromegaly Study Group. J Clin Endocrinol Metab 1998;83:2730–4
5. Colao A, Marzullo P, Di Somma C, Lombardi G. Growth hormone and the heart. Clin Endocrinol (Oxf) 2001;54:137–54
6. McCallum RW, Petrie JR, Dominiczak AF, Connell JM. Growth hormone deficiency and vascular risk. Clin Endocrinol (Oxf) 2002;57:11–24
7. Jørgensen JO, Pedersen SA, Thuesen L, Jørgensen J, Ingemann-Hansen T, Skakkebæk NE, Christiansen JS. Beneficial effects of growth hormone treatment in GH-deficient adults. Lancet 1989;1:1221–5
8. Gibney J, Wallace JD, Spinks T, Schnorr L, Ranicar A, Cuneo RC, Lockhart S, Burnand KG, Salomon F, Sönksen PH, Russell-Jones D. The effects of 10 years of recombinant human growth hormone (GH) in adult GH-deficient patients. J Clin Endocrinol Metab 1999; 84:2596–602
9. Colao A, di Somma C, Pivonello R, Cuocolo A, Spinelli L, Bonaduce D, Salvatore M, Lombardi G. The cardiovascular risk of adult GH deficiency (GHD) improved after GH replacement and worsened in untreated GHD: a 12-month prospective study. J Clin Endocrinol Metab 2002;87:1088–93
10. Johansson JO, Landin K, Tengborn L, Rosén T, Bengtsson B-Å. High fibrinogen and plasminogen activator inhibitor activity in growth hormone-deficient adults. Arterioscler Thromb 1994;14:434–7
11. Sartorio A, Cattaneo M, Bucciarelli P, Bottasso B, Porretti S, Epaminonda P, Faglia G, Arosio M. Alterations of haemostatic and fibrinolytic markers in adult patients with growth hormone deficiency and with acromegaly. Exp Clin Endocrinol Diabetes 2000; 108:486–92
12. Kvasnicka J, Marek J, Kvasnicka T, Weiss V, Markova M, Stepan J, Umlaufova A. Increase of adhesion molecules, fibrinogen, type-1 plasminogen activator inhibitor and orosomucoid in growth hormone (GH) deficient adults and their modulation by recombinant human GH replacement. Clin Endocrinol (Oxf) 2000;52:543–8
13. Wildbrett J, Hanefeld M, Fucker K, Pinzer T, Bergmann S, Siegert G, Breidert M. Anomalies of lipoprotein pattern and fibrinolysis in acromegalic patients: relation to growth hormone levels and insulin-like growth factor I. Exp Clin Endocrinol Diabetes 1997;105:331–5
14. Elhadd TA, Abdu TA, Oxtoby J, Kennedy G, McLaren M, Neary R, Belch JJ, Clayton RN. Biochemical and biophysical markers of endothelial dysfunction in adults with hypopituitarism and severe GH deficiency. J Clin Endocrinol Metab 2001;86:4223–32
15. Wilhelmsen L, Svardsudd K, Korsan-Bengtsen K, Larsson B, Welin L, Tibblin G. Fibrinogen as a risk factor for stroke and myocardial infarction. N Engl J Med 1984;311:501–5
16. Juhan-Vague I, Alessi MC. PAI-1, obesity, insulin resistance and risk of cardiovascular events. Thromb Haemost 1997;78:656–60
17. Folsom AR, Aleksic N, Park E, Salomaa V, Juneja H, Wu KK. Prospective study of fibrinolytic factors and incident coronary heart disease: the Atherosclerosis Risk in Communities (ARIC) Study. Arterioscler Thromb Vasc Biol 2001;21:611–7
18. Jager A, van Hinsbergh VW, Kostense PJ, Emeis JJ, Yudkin JS, Nijpels G, Dekker JM, Heine RJ, Bouter LM, Stehouwer CD. von Willebrand factor, C-reactive protein, and 5-year mortality in diabetic and non-diabetic subjects: the Hoorn Study. Arterioscler Thromb Vasc Biol 1999;19:3071–8
19. Johansson JO, Landin K, Johannsson G, Tengborn L, Bengtsson B-Å. Long-term treatment with growth hormone decreases plasminogen activator inhibitor-1 and tissue plasminogen activator in growth hormone-deficient adults. Thromb Haemost 1996;76: 422–8
20. Savendahl LS, Grankvist K, Engstrom KG. Growth hormone deficiency impairs blood clotting and reduces factor VII coagulant activity in rat. Thromb Haemost 1995;73:626–9

21. Bülow B, Ahrén B, Erfurth EM. Increased leptin and tumour necrosis factor-alpha per unit fat mass in hypopituitary women without growth hormone treatment. Eur J Endocrinol 2001;145:737–42

22. Twickler TB, Dallinga-Thie GM, Visseren FL, de Vries WR, Erkelens DW, Koppeschaar HP. Induction of postprandial inflammatory response in adult onset growth hormone deficiency is related to plasma remnant-like particle-cholesterol concentration. J Clin Endocrinol Metab 2003;88:1228–33

23. Galdiero M, Donnarumma G, Cipollaro de l'Ero G, Marcatili A, Scarfogliero P, Sommese L. Effect of growth hormone, prolactin and insulin on the release of IL-1 alpha, IFN-gamma and IL-4 by staphylococcal enterotoxin A-stimulated splenocytes. Eur Cytokine Netw 1995;6:187–94

24. Sesmilo G, Biller BM, Llevadot J, Hayden D, Hanson G, Rifai N, Klibanski A. Effects of growth hormone administration on inflammatory and other cardiovascular risk markers in men with growth hormone deficiency. A randomized, controlled clinical trial. Ann Intern Med 2000;133:111–22

25. Sesmilo G, Biller BM, Llevadot J, Hayden D, Hanson G, Rifai N, Klibanski A. Effects of growth hormone (GH) administration on homocyst(e)ine levels in men with GH deficiency: a randomized controlled trial. J Clin Endocrinol Metab 2001;86:1518–24

26. Wald NJ, Watt HC, Law MR, Weir DG, McPartlin J, Scott JM. Homocysteine and ischemic heart disease: results of a prospective study with implications regarding prevention. Arch Intern Med 1998;158:862–7

27. Abdu TA, Elhadd T, Pfeifer M, Clayton RN. Endothelial dysfunction in endocrine disease. Trends Endocrinol Metab 2001;12:257–65

28. Pfeifer M, Verhovec R, Zizek B, Prezelj J, Poredos P, Clayton RN. Growth hormone (GH) treatment reverses early atherosclerotic changes in GH-deficient adults. J Clin Endocrinol Metab 1999;84:453–7

29. Markussis V, Beshyah SA, Fisher C, Sharp P, Nicolaides AN, Johnston DG. Detection of premature atherosclerosis by high-resolution ultrasonography in symptom-free hypopituitary adults. Lancet 1992; 340:1188–92

30. Rossoni G, Locatelli V, De Gennaro Colonna V, Torsello A, Schweiger F, Boghen M, Nilsson M, Bernareggi M, Müller EE, Berti F. Growth hormone and hexarelin prevent endothelial vasodilator dysfunction in aortic rings of the hypophysectomized rat. J Cardiovasc Pharmacol 1999;34:454–60

31. Dardenne M, Savino W. Interdependence of the endocrine and immune systems. Adv Neuroimmunol 1996;6:297–307

32. Hattori N, Ikekubo K, Ishihara T, Moridera K, Hino M, Kurahachi H. Spontaneous growth hormone (GH) secretion by unstimulated human lymphocytes and the effects of GH-releasing hormone and somatostatin. J Clin Endocrinol Metab 1994;79:1678–80

33. Dardenne M, Mello-Coelho V, Gagnerault MC, Postel-Vinay MC. Growth hormone receptors and immuno-competent cells. Ann N Y Acad Sci 1998;840:510–7

34. Clark R. The somatogenic hormones and insulin-like growth factor-1: stimulators of lymphopoiesis and immune function. Endocr Rev 1997;18:157–79

35. Kotzmann H, Riedl M, Clodi M, Barnas U, Kaider A, Hocker P, Luger A. The influence of growth hormone substitution therapy on erythroid and myeloid progenitor cells and on peripheral blood cells in adult patients with growth hormone deficiency. Eur J Clin Invest 1996; 26:1175–81

36. Sneppen SB, Mersebach H, Ullum H, Feldt-Rasmussen U. Immune function during GH treatment in GH-deficient adults: an 18-month randomized, placebo-controlled, double-blinded trial. Clin Endocrinol (Oxf) 2002;57:787–92

37. Kotzmann H, Yilmaz N, Lercher P, Riedl M, Schmidt A, Schuster E, Kreuzer S, Geyer G, Frisch H, Horl WH, Mayer G, Luger A. Differential effects of growth hormone therapy in malnourished hemodialysis patients. Kidney Int 2001;60:1578–85

38. Kotzmann H, Schmidt A, Lercher P, Schuster E, Geyer G, Frisch H, Horl WH, Mayer G, Luger A. One-year growth hormone therapy improves granulocyte function without major effects on nutritional and anthropometric parameters in malnourished hemo-dialysis patients. Nephron Clin Pract 2003;93:C75–82

39. Port FK. Morbidity and mortality in dialysis patients. Kidney Int 1994;46:1728–37

40. Kotzmann H, Koller M, Czernin S, Clodi M, Svoboda T, Riedl M, Boltz-Nitulescu G, Zielinski CC, Luger A. Effect of elevated growth hormone concentrations on the phenotype and functions of human lymphocytes and natural killer cells. Neuroendocrinology 1994; 60:618–25

41. Bozzola M, De Benedetti F, De Amici M, Jouret B, Travaglino P, Pagani S, Conte F, Tauber M. Stimulating effect of growth hormone on cytokine release in children. Eur J Endocrinol 2003;149:397–401

42. Serri O, St-Jacques P, Sartippour M, Renier G. Alterations of monocyte function in patients with growth hormone (GH) deficiency: effect of substitutive GH therapy. J Clin Endocrinol Metab 1999;84:58–63

43. Bergad PL, Schwarzenberg SJ, Humbert JT, Morrison M, Amarasinghe S, Towle HC, Berry SA. Inhibition of

growth hormone action in models of inflammation. Am J Physiol Cell Physiol 2000;279:C1906–17

44. Hansen TK, Thiel S, Dall R, Rosenfalck AM, Trainer P, Flyvbjerg A, Jørgensen JO, Christiansen JS. GH strongly affects serum concentrations of mannan-binding lectin: evidence for a new IGF-I independent immunomodulatory effect of GH. J Clin Endocrinol Metab 2001;86:5383–8

45. Super M, Thiel S, Lu J, Levinsky RJ, Turner MW. Association of low levels of mannan-binding protein with a common defect of opsonisation. Lancet 1989;2:1236–9

46. Haeffner A, Thieblemont N, Deas O, Marelli O, Charpentier B, Senik A, Wright SD, Haeffner-Cavaillon N, Hirsch F. Inhibitory effect of growth hormone on TNF-α secretion and nuclear factor-β translocation in lipopolysaccharide-stimulated human monocytes. J Immunol 1997;158:1310–4

47. Colman RW, Hirsh J, Marder VJ, Clowes AW, George JN. Hemostasis and thrombosis: basic principles and clinical practice. 4th edition. Philadelphia: Lippincott, Williams and Wilkins 2001

48. Roitt IM, Delves PJ. Roitt's essential immunology. 10th edition. Malden: Blackwell Science 2001

16 Growth hormone and renal function

James Gibney[1], Hans Herlitz[2] and Gudmundur Johannsson[3]

[1]Department of Endocrinology, St Vincent's University Hospital, Dublin, Ireland; [2]Department of Nephrology and [3]Department of Endocrinology, Sahlgrenska University Hospital, Gothenburg, Sweden

Summary

Renal size and function are influenced by the somatotrophic axis. In patients with acromegaly, renal size and haemodynamic function are increased and in adults with growth hormone deficiency (GHD), renal haemodynamic function is reduced. Through renal tubular effects, short-term growth hormone (GH) administration induces sodium and water retention, resulting in an increase in extracellular water (ECW) that is sustained following long-term GH treatment. Increased ECW can also be demonstrated in patients with acromegaly. The mechanisms underlying these effects are not known, but possibly include direct effects mediated through GH and/or insulin-like growth factor I (IGF-I) receptors and indirect effects mediated through the renin–angiotensin–aldosterone system and natriuretic peptides. Pressure or escape natriuresis, which characterizes other sodium-retaining (antinatriuretic) agents, such as mineralocorticoids, does not occur with GH. Long-term treatment with GH in children and adults does not appear to influence renal function, although this has not explicitly been studied. In contrast, GH treatment in children with chronic renal failure and those who have had a kidney transplant has been carefully monitored and appears to be safe. GH may play a role in the development and progression of diabetic nephropathy. A small number of trials of IGF-I treatment in patients with acute renal failure and patients with diabetes mellitus have been reported. Here we review the clinical literature concerning the impact of GH and IGF-I on renal function, with particular attention to GHD and GH replacement in adults.

Renal tubular function

The salt- and water-retaining (antinatriuretic) effects of growth hormone (GH) have been known for decades. These effects explain the reduction in extracellular water (ECW) content that is found in adults with severe GH deficiency (GHD) and the marked increase in extracellular fluid volume that is found in patients with acromegaly [1, 2]. The mechanism behind these effects remains unknown, but several direct and indirect actions are possible.

The observations that receptors for GH and insulin-like growth factor I (IGF-I) are expressed in renal tubules [3] and that GH stimulates sodium–potassium adenosine triphosphatase activity in the kidney [4] provide a mechanistic explanation by which GH could exert direct antinatriuretic effects. Further evidence for a direct effect of GH/IGF-I on the renal tubule comes from the finding that the antinatriuretic effect of GH also occurs in patients with adrenal insufficiency [5], although this does not rule out the possibility that additional indirect effects are mediated through the renin–angiotensin–aldosterone system (RAAS) [6] and/or through natriuretic peptides.

Some [6, 7] but not all studies [8] have concluded that the antinatriuretic effect of GH occurs indirectly through an interaction with the RAAS. Other studies have reported that short-term administration of GH and IGF-I respectively suppress plasma atrial natriuretic peptide (ANP) and impair the ANP response to a saline load, which may contribute to sodium retention [9, 10], but these findings are also inconsistent [8, 11].

Despite the volume expansion induced by GH administration, blood pressure is either unchanged [12–15] or reduced [16, 17]. This observation can be explained by decreased peripheral resistance during GH replacement therapy [16], which may, at least in part, be explained by increased endothelial nitric oxide (NO) formation [15].

Decreased urinary sodium excretion in the presence of unchanged lithium clearance indicates that increased renal tubular sodium reabsorption in response to GH treatment takes place mainly in the distal nephron. Enhanced tubular sodium reabsorption and increased ECW in response to GH treatment does not offset pressure natriuresis, which would be anticipated to eliminate the 'sodium load' [18]. With unchanged or even decreased blood pressure, together with decreased or unchanged plasma concentrations of natriuretic peptides, pressure or escape natriuresis does not occur, resulting in increased ECW both during short- and long-term GH replacement and in acromegaly. An inverse relationship has also been found between the decrease in diastolic blood pressure and the increase in ECW during 12 months of GH treatment, which favours blood pressure reduction [19] as a potential mechanism in preventing the pressure natriuresis reported with other antinatriuretic agents. Moreover, the escape from the antinatriuretic effect of mineralocorticoids is coincident with an increased concentration of plasma ANP, suggesting that natriuretic peptides also play a role in this phenomenon [20]. The trend for reduced plasma ANP and brain natriuretic peptide concentrations seen after GH treatment [9, 10, 19] may be important in preventing sodium and water escape during GH replacement.

Several factors may contribute to the increase in renal tubular sodium reabsorption that occurs in response to administration of GH. Two trials using GH replacement doses closer to physiological production rates, indicate that RAAS stimulation may be important, although the mechanism does not seem to be stimulation of the adrenal cortex, as plasma aldosterone levels did not change in response to GH treatment [8, 19]. The primary effect may be increased plasma renin activity (PRA), a consistent finding in response to GH administration [6, 8, 11, 21, 22]. Elevated PRA will increase serum angiotensin II levels, which directly increase the sodium reabsorption in renal tubules.

Renin release is increased by renal sympathetic activity and circulating catecholamines. A relationship between an increase in 24-hour urinary noradrenaline excretion and an increase in PRA has been found in response to short-term GH treatment, suggesting that GH treatment increases renal sympathetic activity, which may, in turn, increase PRA. Although urinary noradrenaline excretion is not a specific measure of renal sympathetic nervous function, the increase in urinary nitrate excretion seen following short-term GH treatment may indicate an acute selective increase in renal sympathetic activity, as sympathetic outflow to other vascular beds remains unaffected by short-term GH treatment [23]. All of these indirect effects disappear during long-term GH replacement, suggesting that the more prolonged effects of GH/IGF-I are mediated through direct actions on the distal nephron and not through interaction with renal sympathetic activity and the RAAS. This is supported by unchanged or even reduced activity of the RAAS in patients with acromegaly [24, 25].

From the available data it can be summarized that the sodium- and water-retaining effects of GH mainly take place in the distal nephron by a direct action of GH/IGF-I, as other plausible indirect mechanisms are only modestly or transiently affected. Of importance for the sustained increase in ECW in response to GH is the parallel action on blood pressure and plasma natriuretic peptides, which prevents pressure-induced natriuresis.

Renal haemodynamic function

There is circumstantial evidence linking GH to increased renal plasma flow (RPF) and glomerular filtration rate (GFR). In patients with acromegaly, the kidneys are enlarged and renal haemodynamic function is increased. These observations were preceded by the findings of White and colleagues [26, 27], who described reduced clearance rates of inulin, diodrast, creatinine and urea, indicating reduction in RPF and GFR, after hypophysectomy in the dog. They also demonstrated the absence of compensatory hypertrophy of the remaining kidney after unilateral nephrectomy in hypophysectomized dogs, indicating both a functional and a structural influence of the pituitary gland on the kidney. Talbott *et al.* [28] subsequently showed that GFR and RPF were reduced in humans with hypopituitarism.

The first studies of renal function in patients with acromegaly were carried out in the 1950s. Luft and Sjögren [29], measuring clearance rates of inulin and diodrast, demonstrated that mean GFR was 26% greater in patients with acromegaly compared with normal subjects, while simultaneously RPF was slightly decreased. Measuring clearance rates of inulin and para-aminohippurate (PAH), Ikkos *et al.* [30] demonstrated greater GFR (27%) and RPF (29%) in patients with acromegaly compared with normal subjects, with the filtration fraction being similar in the two groups. The authors also noted an increase in extracellular volume (ECV) that seemed to parallel the increase in renal haemodynamic function. This was later confirmed by Falkheden and Sjögren [31], who also found the filtration fraction to be normal in their study of 12 patients with acromegaly. The latter authors noted that the relationship between changes in renal function and ECV was not necessarily a causal one. Falkheden [32] also investigated 12 patients who had undergone a hypophysectomy. In these patients, GFR and RPF were significantly reduced without a concomitant change in ECV. Gershberg *et al.* [33] compared the results of renal haemodynamic studies with the autopsy findings in one patient with acromegaly. GFR measured close to the time of death was markedly enhanced, and during post-mortem examination the kidneys were enlarged, weighing 655 and 550 g, respectively, and histological examination revealed markedly enlarged glomeruli.

In the 1960s and 1970s, interest focussed on the effect of treatment of acromegaly on renal function. Falkheden and Wickbom [34] studied renal function in patients with acromegaly or breast carcinoma before and after hypophysectomy. They measured inulin and PAH clearance and estimated kidney size and weight by means of radiological techniques. The estimated kidney size and weight, GFR and RPF all decreased after hypophysectomy, but there was no correlation between renal structural and functional changes in their patients. Furthermore, a decrease in renal function could be demonstrated before a reduction in renal mass.

Effect of GH on renal haemodynamic function

Both GFR and RPF are elevated in the presence of high circulating levels of GH and are reduced in hypopituitarism. Hoogenberg *et al.* [35] demonstrated that treatment with octreotide, which reduced serum levels of GH by 63%, also reduced creatinine clearance. In a similar study, Dullaart *et al.* [36] determined GFR and RPF by means of ^{125}I-iothalamate and ^{131}I-hippuran, respectively, in seven patients with acromegaly before and following 3 months of octreotide treatment. Octreotide reduced plasma GH concentration by 65% and decreased GFR and RPF to normal values. In line with these studies, Manelli *et al.* [37] demonstrated that exercise-induced microalbuminuria in patients with active acromegaly was reversed by treatment with a long-acting somatostatin analogue.

Corvilain *et al.* [38] were the first to show that administration of GH-containing pituitary extracts increased GFR in normal subjects. Since then, several studies have shown that administration of GH to healthy subjects and to patients with glomerulonephritis, diabetes and hypopituitarism, significantly increased GFR [39–42]. In contrast to previous studies, Johannsson *et al.* [19] showed that renal haemodynamic function did not change in response to GH treatment. Several factors could explain this difference. Previous trials used pharmacological doses for a short period of time, whereas in this study a more physiological replacement dose was used, resulting in smaller effects on IGF-I than in previous studies. In addition, sodium and protein intake were controlled during the measurement period. Notably, in the study of Johannsson *et al.*, a marked effect on renal tubular sodium reabsorption occurred despite a lack of effect on renal haemodynamic function.

Effect of IGF-I on renal haemodynamic function

The renal effects of recombinant GH are apparent 3–4 days after the initiation of treatment and disappear approximately 2 days after treatment is stopped. These findings suggest that the ability of GH to increase GFR is not a direct effect, but occurs through another mediator, such as IGF-I.

Several studies have been performed to test the hypothesis that IGF-I increases glomerular dynamics and mediates the effect of GH to increase GFR. Acute intravenous infusion of recombinant human IGF-I in normal anaesthetized rats rapidly elevates RPF and GFR and reduces renal vascular resistance [43]. The increase in GFR is dose dependent and can be as large as 35%.

While there is substantial evidence that IGF-I increases GFR when administered in pharmacological doses *in vivo*, plasma IGF-I has also been correlated with GFR in a number of physiological and pathophysiological conditions. Both IGF-I and GFR are increased in patients with acromegaly and during intake of a high protein diet, and reduced in patients with GHD, in patients with panhypopituitarism, in acromegalic or diabetic patients during treatment with somatostatin analogues and during low protein intake.

Mechanism of the IGF-I-induced increase in renal haemodynamics

Micropuncture studies have revealed that IGF-I induces a decrease in arteriolar and renal vascular resistance, resulting in an increase in nephron plasma flow and single nephron GFR. The increase in nephron ultrafiltration exceeds the increase in plasma flow, probably due to a twofold increase in the glomerular ultrafiltration coefficient, LpA or Kf [44]. Relaxation of the glomerular mesangium caused by IGF-I could lead to an expansion of the capillary surface area.

Circumstantial evidence suggests that IGF-I-induced renal arteriolar vasodilatation is mediated by an increased NO production and requires the presence of an intact renal cyclooxygenase system. The acute increase in GFR by IGF-I may be mediated by vasodilatory prostaglandins, as concomitant administration of a cyclooxygenase inhibitor blocks the IGF-I-induced increase in GFR and renal blood flow [43]. This concept is supported by the finding that co-administration of indomethacin completely blocks the increase in GFR induced by GH, despite a similar increase in serum IGF-I levels [45].

Experimental evidence for a role of NO in the acute renal haemodynamic response to IGF-I comes from the finding that co-administration of an NO-synthase inhibitor completely abolishes IGF-I-induced vasodilatation [46, 47]. Böger *et al.* [15] showed that systemic NO formation was diminished in adults with GHD, and that treatment with GH normalized urinary nitrate and cyclic GMP excretion.

GH and IGF-I influence renal haemodynamic function in acromegaly, severe GHD and hypopituitarism. Short-term interventions with both hormones increase GFR and RPF through mechanisms mediated by NO and cyclooxygenase. The somatotrophic axis may therefore be important in the regulation of renal haemodynamic function in normal physiology and in pathological states, such as diabetes mellitus.

Administration of GH and IGF-I in patients with renal impairment

Insights into the effects of GH and IGF-I in the context of reduced functional renal mass can be derived from a number of diverse clinical settings in which recombinant human GH and IGF-I have been administered to patients with renal impairment. GH has been used extensively to increase linear growth in children with chronic renal failure (CRF), and has also been investigated for its anabolic properties in adults with CRF. A small number of clinical trials have investigated the potential of IGF-I to improve renal function in adults with acute renal failure (ARF) and those with CRF. Finally, changes in renal function have been meticulously studied in patients with type 1 diabetes mellitus, who have been treated with IGF-I in an attempt to improve metabolic control.

Although changes in renal function under all of these conditions provide useful information, assessment of the effects of GH or IGF-I on renal function in patients with renal impairment is complicated by a number of factors. Firstly, assessment of changes in renal function in response to treatment is possible when there is some preservation of renal function or following renal transplantation, but is not possible in the setting of end-stage renal failure (ESRF). Secondly, CRF is characterized by an inexorable decline in renal function and, therefore, assessment of the effects of GH on renal function can only be made in the context of an appropriate control population. Thirdly, changes in renal function during interventional studies in CRF are frequently assessed using formulae based on serum creatinine, with or without the inclusion of height as an additional variable. As these formulae do not take into account GH-induced increases in muscle mass, this effect will inevitably be associated with an increase in creatinine and an apparent decrease in renal function.

GH treatment in children and adolescents with CRF

Children with renal insufficiency suffer from growth retardation, which begins when the GFR falls to 50% of normal, and becomes an increasing problem once the GFR falls below 25%. It is likely that abnormalities of the GH/IGF-I axis play an important role in this problem, which is not improved by intensive conventional treatment or dialysis [48]. Demonstration that the administration of supraphysiological doses of GH to uraemic rats improved rates of linear growth [49] provided proof of concept that GH might be useful in human subjects. This led to extensive studies, initially in children and adolescents with CRF, and later in children following renal transplantation. The results of these studies, with specific reference to their effects on renal function are reviewed below.

Early studies of GH in patients with CRF were conducted cautiously in view of theoretical concerns that GH might impair renal function. While supraphysiological doses of GH had been shown to increase growth in 5/6 nephrectomized rats [49], there was also evidence that GH may have a causative role in the development of glomerulosclerosis in mice [50], and it had been hypothesized that hyperfiltration could lead to a similar effect in human subjects. Initial uncontrolled studies, with small numbers of participants, uniformly demonstrated improvement in linear growth compared with the period prior to the commencement of GH. These studies provided reassurance that GH did not cause any further decline in renal function, although they relied on calculated values of GFR. One exception was a small study by Andersson *et al.* [51] in which calculated GFR appeared to deteriorate in two of three children with cystinosis who were treated with GH.

The first placebo-controlled study of GH treatment in children with CRF demonstrated that administration of GH (4 IU/m^2/day) resulted in increased height velocity in 16 children who were managed conservatively [52]. Reassuringly, no change in calculated GFR was observed in the children taking part in this study. A larger study in which 125 children were randomized to treatment with GH (0.05 mg/kg/day) or placebo for 2 years confirmed the ability of GH to increase height velocity [53]. A non-significant increase in creatinine was observed in the GH-treated group, but no change in calculated creatinine clearance was observed.

Evidence that GH treatment might actually improve renal function in CRF came from a later double-blind study in which 23 children with CRF were randomized to receive a higher or a lower dose of GH for 2.5 years [54]. Increased efficacy was observed with 4 compared with 2 IU/m^2/day, but, unexpectedly, all four children who had a baseline GFR of more than 15 ml/min/1.73 m^2 and were managed conservatively exhibited an initial improvement in calculated GFR following GH replacement. This finding may be relevant in the context of the ability of GH to increase GFR in subjects with a normal renal function, and suggests that this effect may also occur in patients with less severe renal impairment.

That the short-term improvements in height velocity resulted in improved adult height has been demonstrated in patients treated with GH for a mean of 5.3 years compared with patients who had not received GH treatment [55]. GH treatment normalized final height, while there was a decline in height SD score in children who did not receive GH. GFR was comparable at baseline in the treated and untreated patients, and decreased to a similar extent in both groups, both when managed conservatively and following transplantation.

In summary, therefore, there is no evidence from controlled studies that GH exerts any effect on renal function in the setting of renal failure, and there is some evidence that it may be beneficial when renal impairment is less severe. However, few studies using gold-standard techniques have been carried out in this setting.

Clinical trials of GH in children following renal transplantation

Soon after the successful use of GH in children with CRF, studies were carried out to determine whether GH would also increase growth rates in children following successful renal transplantation; however, in addition to concerns about the potentially deleterious effect of GH on renal (graft) function, there were also concerns that exogenous GH might increase the incidence of graft rejection by antagonizing the immunosuppressive effect of glucocorticoid treatment. At least partly because of these potential side-effects, changes in renal function during GH treatment have been more meticulously described in renal transplant recipients compared with patients with CRF. While early, uncontrolled, studies of GH treatment in renal transplant recipients provided preliminary evidence that GH was efficacious in increasing growth rates, some of these studies also raised concerns that GH might have a deleterious effect on graft function. However, studies that used more rigorous methods to estimate GFR provided more reassuring data.

The first controlled study of GH treatment in transplant recipients was reported by Hokken-Koelega *et al.* [56], who treated 18 adolescent patients for 2 years following renal transplantation. GFR and effective RPF were tested in a subset of 14 patients with ^{125}I-thalamate and ^{131}I-hippuran, respectively, at the start of the study and after 2 and 12 months of GH treatment, and GFR was calculated in all patients throughout the study. In the patients in whom formal testing of GFR was carried out, no significant decline was observed over the first year of the study. Calculated GFR decreased by more than 25% in seven of the 18 patients over 2 years, but this change did not differ from a group of non-GH-treated control subjects (GFR decreased in 29 of 90). Subsequently, in a double-blind placebo-controlled crossover study using ^{125}I-thalamate and ^{131}I-hippuran clearances, the same investigators demonstrated that administration of GH, 4 IU/m^2/day, to 11 prepubertal children for 6 months did not influence GFR or RPF [56].

By combining two large databases (the North American Pediatric Renal Transplant Cooperative Study, with data on 2390 renal transplant recipients, and the National Cooperative Growth Study, with data on a large number of children treated with GH for a variety of indications),

Mentser *et al.* [57] identified 59 transplant recipients who had been treated with GH for between 1 and 3 years. There was no difference in either acute rejection episodes or change in calculated creatinine clearance rates between patients who had received GH and the overall group of transplant recipients. Finally, to further investigate safety issues, Fine *et al.* [58] randomized 68 allograft recipients to a GH treatment or control group. No rejection episodes occurred in the first year in the treatment group compared with three in the control group.

Taken together, therefore, the overwhelming body of evidence suggests that GH does not exert deleterious effects on renal function or increase acute rejection episodes in renal transplant recipients. This has been borne out, both by small studies using gold-standard techniques, and by larger observational and controlled studies.

Use of IGF-I in the treatment of ARF and CRF

In contrast to GH, which is used in patients with CRF for its growth-promoting and anabolic effects, IGF-I has been used in adults with ARF and CRF in an attempt to improve renal function. In initial studies, high doses of IGF-I increased renal function for several days but caused serious side-effects. O'Shea *et al.* [59] administered IGF-I for 4 days to patients with moderate CRF and observed a progressive increase in inulin and PAH clearance, reflecting improved renal function. The same group administered IGF-I for 4 days to patients with ESRF and reported increased clearance of inulin and PAH, and the percent tubular reabsorption of filtered phosphate, and decreased plasma creatinine, urea and phosphate [60]. However, in a subset of patients, inulin and PAH clearance no longer differed from baseline values following 20 days of administration of IGF-I. It was hypothesized that reduced circulating levels of total IGF-I and reduced IGF-binding protein-3 might have contributed to this unsustained effect. Vijayan *et al.* [61] demonstrated that in patients with ESRF, treatment with a lower intermittent dose of IGF-I was well tolerated and resulted in a sustained improvement in renal function. While these data were promising, studies of IGF-I have now been limited by unavailability of the drug.

As well as these studies in CRF, two randomized placebo-controlled trials have been carried out in patients with ARF. Franklin *et al.* [62] examined the effects of IGF-I on recovery of renal function in 58 patients who underwent vascular surgery of the renal artery or aorta, and observed that renal function declined in fewer patients who received IGF-I (22%) compared with those who received placebo (33%). Hirschberg *et al.* [63] administered IGF-I for a mean duration of 14 days to 72 intensive-care patients with confirmed ARF from a variety of different causes. No changes were seen in GFR, creatinine clearance, daily urine volume, serum urea nitrogen, creatinine, albumin or transferrin. The mortality rate was not altered by IGF-I. Overall, therefore, despite promising data from animal models, no data are available to suggest that IGF-I has a therapeutic role in ARF in humans.

GH and IGF-I in patients with diabetes mellitus

Poorly controlled type 1 diabetes mellitus is associated with increased GH secretion, which is thought to arise partly through the negative feedback of low serum concentrations of IGF-I, reflecting reduced biosynthesis by the liver. Increased GH secretion may contribute to insulin resistance and the development of complications. To try to overcome this defect, IGF-I has been used as a therapeutic agent in both type 1 and type 2 diabetes mellitus. Acerini *et al.* [64] administered two doses of IGF-I (20 and 40 μg/kg/day) to patients with type 1 diabetes mellitus for 24 weeks, and measured urinary albumin/creatinine ratio, and GFR using inulin clearance and chromium edetate clearance, at baseline and the end of the study. No significant changes were observed in any of these variables, although it is notable that no patient had established nephropathy on entry to the study. Thus, while data are limited, long-term treatment with IGF-I does not appear to alter renal function in patients with diabetes without established nephropathy.

Conclusions

Renal function is influenced by the somatotrophic axis. In severe GHD, renal tubular sodium and water retention is probably reduced, and renal haemodynamic function, measured as RPF and GFR, is attenuated. These changes are normalized by GH replacement therapy. The opposite effects are seen in patients with acromegaly, and return to normal following correction of GH excess. In diabetes mellitus it has been suggested that GH/IGF-I may play a role in glomerular hyperfiltration. The observation that glomerulonephritis is not a frequent finding in acromegaly, despite greatly increased GFR and a high prevalence of hypertension and glucose intolerance, suggests that GH/IGF-I does not play a causative role in this condition. Safety concerns surrounding the administration of GH to patients with reduced renal function have been meticulously addressed in children with CRF and particularly in those who have received a renal transplant. Current data suggest that GH does not exert any deleterious effect on renal function in this setting. Based on current information therefore, it appears that GH treatment is safe in patients with reduced renal function, although it must be recognized that experience is limited in adults receiving GH replacement therapy.

References

1. Bengtsson B-Å, Brummer RJ, Edén S, Bosæus I. Body composition in acromegaly. Clin Endocrinol (Oxf) 1989;30:121–30
2. Rosén T, Bosæus I, Tölli J, Lindstedt G, Bengtsson B-Å. Increased body fat mass and decreased extracellular fluid volume in adults with growth hormone deficiency. Clin Endocrinol (Oxf) 1993;38:63–71
3. Chin E, Zhou J, Bondy CA. Renal growth hormone receptor gene expression: relationship to renal insulin-like growth factor system. Endocrinology 1992;131:3061–6
4. Shimomura Y, Lee M, Oku J, Bray GA, Glick Z. Sodium potassium dependent ATPase in hypophysectomized rats: response to growth hormone, triiodothyronine, and cortisone. Metabolism 1982;31:213–6
5. Biglieri EG, Watlington CO, Forsham PH. Sodium retention with human growth hormone and its subfractions. J Clin Endocrinol Metab 1961;21:361–70
6. Ho KY, Weissberger AJ. The antinatriuretic action of biosynthetic human growth hormone in man involves activation of the renin–angiotensin system. Metabolism 1990;39:133–7
7. Honeyman TW, Goodman HM, Fray JC. The effects of growth hormone on blood pressure and renin secretion in hypophysectomized rats. Endocrinology 1983; 112:1613–7
8. Hoffman DM, Crampton L, Sernia C, Nguyen TV, Ho KK. Short-term growth hormone (GH) treatment of GH-deficient adults increases body sodium and extracellular water, but not blood pressure. J Clin Endocrinol Metab 1996;81:1123–8
9. Møller J, Jørgensen JO, Møller N, Hansen KW, Pedersen EB, Christiansen JS. Expansion of extracellular volume and suppression of atrial natriuretic peptide after growth hormone administration in normal man. J Clin Endocrinol Metab 1991;72:768–72
10. Møller J, Jørgensen JO, Marqversen J, Frandsen E, Christiansen JS. Insulin-like growth factor I administration induces fluid and sodium retention in healthy adults: possible involvement of renin and atrial natriuretic factor. Clin Endocrinol (Oxf) 2000;52:181–6
11. Møller J, Frandsen E, Fisker S, Jørgensen JO, Christiansen JS. Decreased plasma and extracellular volume in growth hormone deficient adults and the acute and prolonged effects of GH administration: a controlled experimental study. Clin Endocrinol (Oxf) 1996;44:533–9
12. Amato G, Carella C, Fazio S, La Montagna G, Cittadini A, Sabatini D, Marciano-Mone C, Saccà L, Bellastella A. Body composition, bone metabolism, and heart structure and function in growth hormone (GH)-deficient adults before and after GH replacement therapy at low doses. J Clin Endocrinol Metab 1993;77:1671–6
13. Cittadini A, Cuocolo A, Merola B, Fazio S, Sabatini D, Nicolai E, Colao A, Longobardi S, Lombardi G, Saccà L. Impaired cardiac performance in GH-deficient adults and its improvement after GH replacement. Am J Physiol 1994;267:E219–25
14. Valcavi R, Gaddi O, Zini M, Iavicoli M, Mellino U, Portioli I. Cardiac performance and mass in adults with hypopituitarism: effects of one year of growth hormone treatment. J Clin Endocrinol Metab 1995;80:659–66
15. Böger RH, Skamira C, Bode-Böger SM, Brabant G, von zur Mühlen A, Frölich JC. Nitric oxide may mediate the hemodynamic effects of recombinant growth hormone in patients with acquired growth hormone deficiency. A double-blind, placebo-controlled study. J Clin Invest 1996;98:2706–13
16. Caidahl K, Edén S, Bengtsson B-Å. Cardiovascular and renal effects of growth hormone. Clin Endocrinol (Oxf) 1994;40:393–400

17. Johannsson G, Rosén T, Lindstedt G, Bosæus I, Bengtsson B-Å. Effects of 2 years of growth hormone treatment on body composition and cardiovascular risk factors in adults with growth hormone deficiency. Endocrinol Metab 1996;3 (Suppl A):3–12

18. Guyton AC, Coleman TG. Quantitative analysis of the pathophysiology of hypertension. Circ Res 1969; 24:1–19

19. Johannsson G, Sverrisdottir YB, Ellegard L, Lundberg PA, Herlitz H. GH increases extracellular volume by stimulating sodium reabsorption in the distal nephron and preventing pressure natriuresis. J Clin Endocrinol Metab 2002;87:1743–9

20. Yokota N, Bruneau BG, Kuroski de Bold ML, de Bold AJ. Atrial natriuretic factor significantly contributes to the mineralocorticoid escape phenomenon. Evidence for a guanylate cyclase-mediated pathway. J Clin Invest 1994;94:1938–46

21. Møller J, Møller N, Frandsen E, Wolthers T, Jørgensen JO, Christiansen JS. Blockade of the renin–angiotensin–aldosterone system prevents growth hormone-induced fluid retention in humans. Am J Physiol 1997;272:E803–8

22. Cuneo RC, Salomon F, Wilmshurst P, Byrne C, Wiles CM, Hesp R, Sönksen PH. Cardiovascular effects of growth hormone treatment in growth-hormone-deficient adults: stimulation of the renin–aldosterone system. Clin Sci (Lond) 1991;81:587–92

23. Sverrisdottir YB, Elam M, Caidahl K, Soderling AS, Herlitz H, Johannsson G. The effect of growth hormone (GH) replacement therapy on sympathetic nerve hyperactivity in hypopituitary adults: a double-blind, placebo-controlled, crossover, short-term trial followed by long-term open GH replacement in hypopituitary adults. J Hypertens 2003;21:1905–14

24. Karlberg BE, Ottosson AM. Acromegaly and hypertension: role of the renin–angiotensin–aldosterone system. Acta Endocrinol (Copenh) 1982;100:581–7

25. Cain JP, Williams GH, Dluhy RG. Plasma renin activity and aldosterone secretion in patients with acromegaly. J Clin Endocrinol Metab 1972;34:73–81

26. White HL, Heinbecker P, Rolf D. Effects of hypophysectomy on some renal functions. Proc Soc Exp Biol Med 1941;461:44–7

27. White HL, Heinbecker P. Observations on creatinine and urea clearances, on responses to water ingestion and on concentrating power of the kidneys in normal, diabetes insipidus and hypophysectomized dog. Am J Physiol 1938;123:566–76

28. Talbott JH, Pecora LH, Melville RS, Consolazio WV. Renal function in patients with Addison's disease and in patients with adrenal insufficiency secondary to pituitary panhypofunction. J Clin Invest 1942; 21:107–19

29. Luft R, Sjögren B. The significance of adenohypophysis, adrenal cortex and thyroid in renal function in man. Acta Endocrinol (Copenh) 1950;4:352–62

30. Ikkos D, Ljunggren H, Luft R. Glomerular filtration rate and renal plasma flow in acromegaly. Acta Endocrinol (Copenh) 1956;21:226–36

31. Falkheden T, Sjögren B. Extracellular fluid volume and renal function in pituitary insufficiency and acromegaly. Acta Endocrinol (Copenh) 1964;46:80–8

32. Falkheden T. Renal function following hypophysectomy in man. Acta Endocrinol (Copenh) 1963;42:571–90

33. Gershberg H, Heinemann HO, Stumpf HH. Renal function studies and autopsy report in a patient with gigantism and acromegaly. J Clin Endocrinol Metab 1957;17:377–85

34. Falkheden T, Wickbom I. Renal function and kidney size following hypophysectomy in man. Acta Endocrinol (Copenh) 1965;48:348–54

35. Hoogenberg K, Sluiter WJ, Dullaart RP. Effect of growth hormone and insulin-like growth factor I on urinary albumin excretion: studies in acromegaly and growth hormone deficiency. Acta Endocrinol (Copenh) 1993; 129:151–7

36. Dullaart RP, Meijer S, Marbach P, Sluiter WJ. Effect of a somatostatin analogue, octreotide, on renal haemodynamics and albuminuria in acromegalic patients. Eur J Clin Invest 1992;22:494–502

37. Manelli F, Bossoni S, Burattin A, Doga M, Solerte SB, Romanelli G, Giustina A. Exercise-induced microalbuminuria in patients with active acromegaly: acute effects of slow-release lanreotide, a long-acting somatostatin analog. Metabolism 2000;49:634–9

38. Corvilain J, Abramow M, Bergans A. Some effects of human growth hormone on renal hemodynamics and on tubular phosphate transport in man. J Clin Invest 1962;41:1230–5

39. Haffner D, Zacharewicz S, Mehls O, Heinrich U, Ritz E. The acute effect of growth hormone on GFR is obliterated in chronic renal failure. Clin Nephrol 1989;32:266–9

40. Gershberg H. Metabolic and renotropic effects of human growth hormone in disease. J Clin Endocrinol Metab 1960;20:1107–19

41. Christiansen JS, Gammelgaard J, Frandsen M, Ørskov H, Parving HH. Kidney function and size in type 1 (insulin-dependent) diabetic patients before and during growth hormone administration for one week. Diabetologia 1982;22:333–7

42. Hirschberg RR, Kopple JD. Increase in renal plasma flow and glomerular filtration rate during growth hormone treatment may be mediated by insulin-like growth factor I. Am J Nephrol 1988;8:249–54

43. Hirschberg R, Kopple JD. Evidence that insulin-like growth factor I increases renal plasma flow and glomerular filtration rate in fasted rats. J Clin Invest 1989;83:326–30

44. Hirschberg R, Kopple JD, Blantz RC, Tucker BJ. Effects of recombinant human insulin-like growth factor I on glomerular dynamics in the rat. J Clin Invest 1991;87:1200–6

45. Tönshoff B, Nowack R, Kurilenko S, Blum WF, Seyberth HW, Mehls O, Ritz E. Growth hormone-induced glomerular hyperfiltration is dependent on vasodilating prostanoids. Am J Kidney Dis 1993; 21:145–51

46. Tönshoff B, Kaskel FJ, Moore LC. Effects of insulin-like growth factor I on the renal juxtamedullary microvasculature. Am J Physiol 1998;274:F120–8

47. Haylor J, Singh I, el Nahas AM. Nitric oxide synthesis inhibitor prevents vasodilation by insulin-like growth factor I. Kidney Int 1991;39:333–5

48. Rees L, Rigden SP, Ward GM. Chronic renal failure and growth. Arch Dis Child 1989;64:573–7

49. Mehls O, Ritz E, Hunziker EB, Eggli P, Heinrich U, Zapf J. Improvement of growth and food utilization by human recombinant growth hormone in uremia. Kidney Int 1988;33:45–52

50. Doi T, Striker LJ, Quaife C, Conti FG, Palmiter R, Behringer R, Brinster R, Striker GE. Progressive glomerulosclerosis develops in transgenic mice chronically expressing growth hormone and growth hormone releasing factor but not in those expressing insulin like growth factor-1. Am J Pathol 1988;131: 398–403

51. Andersson HC, Markello T, Schneider JA, Gahl WA. Effect of growth hormone treatment on serum creatinine concentration in patients with cystinosis and chronic renal disease. J Pediatr 1992;120:716–20

52. Hokken-Koelega AC, Stijnen T, de Muinck Keizer-Schrama SM, Wit JM, Wolff ED, de Jong MC, Donckerwolcke RA, Abbad NC, Bot A, Blum WF. Placebo-controlled, double-blind, cross-over trial of growth hormone treatment in prepubertal children with chronic renal failure. Lancet 1991;338:585–90

53. Fine RN, Kohaut EC, Brown D, Perlman AJ. Growth after recombinant human growth hormone treatment in children with chronic renal failure: report of a multicenter randomized double-blind placebo-controlled study. Genentech Cooperative Study Group. J Pediatr 1994;124:374–82

54. Hokken-Koelega AC, Stijnen T, De Jong MC, Donckerwolcke RA, de Muinck Keizer-Schrama SM, Blum WF, Drop SL. Double blind trial comparing the effects of two doses of growth hormone in prepubertal patients with chronic renal insufficiency. J Clin Endocrinol Metab 1994;79:1185–90

55. Haffner D, Schaefer F, Nissel R, Wühl E, Tönshoff B, Mehls O. Effect of growth hormone treatment on the adult height of children with chronic renal failure. German Study Group for Growth Hormone Treatment in Chronic Renal Failure. N Engl J Med 2000;343:923–30

56. Hokken-Koelega AC, Stijnen T, de Jong RC, Donckerwolcke RA, Groothoff JW, Wolff ED, Blum WF, de Muinck Keizer-Schrama SM, Drop SL. A placebo-controlled, double-blind trial of growth hormone treatment in prepubertal children after renal transplant. Kidney Int Suppl 1996;53:S128–34

57. Mentser M, Breen TJ, Sullivan EK, Fine RN. Growth-hormone treatment of renal transplant recipients: the National Cooperative Growth Study experience – a report of the National Cooperative Growth Study and the North American Pediatric Renal Transplant Cooperative Study. J Pediatr 1997;131:S20–4

58. Fine RN, Stablein D, Cohen AH, Tejani A, Kohaut E. Recombinant human growth hormone post-renal transplantation in children: a randomized controlled study of the NAPRTCS. Kidney Int 2002;62:688–96

59. O'Shea MH, Miller SB, Hammerman MR. Effects of IGF-I on renal function in patients with chronic renal failure. Am J Physiol 1993;264:F917–22

60. Miller SB, Moulton M, O'Shea M, Hammerman MR. Effects of IGF-I on renal function in end-stage chronic renal failure. Kidney Int 1994;46:201–7

61. Vijayan A, Franklin SC, Behrend T, Hammerman MR, Miller SB. Insulin-like growth factor I improves renal function in patients with end-stage chronic renal failure. Am J Physiol 1999;276:R929–34

62. Franklin SC, Moulton M, Sicard GA, Hammerman MR, Miller SB. Insulin-like growth factor I preserves renal function postoperatively. Am J Physiol 1997; 272:F257–9

63. Hirschberg R, Kopple J, Lipsett P, Benjamin E, Minei J, Albertson T, Munger M, Metzler M, Zaloga G, Murray M, Lowry S, Conger J, McKeown W, O'Shea M, Baughman R, Wood K, Haupt M, Kaiser R, Simms H, Warnock D, Summer W, Hintz R, Myers B, Haenftling K, Capra W. Multicenter clinical trial of recombinant human insulin-like growth factor I in patients with acute renal failure. Kidney Int 1999; 55:2423–32

64. Acerini CL, Patton CM, Savage MO, Kernell A, Westphal O, Dunger DB. Randomised placebo-controlled trial of human recombinant insulin-like growth factor I plus intensive insulin therapy in adolescents with insulin-dependent diabetes mellitus. Lancet 1997;350:1199–204

17 Role of growth hormone and insulin-like growth factor I in cognitive function

Hans PF Koppeschaar[1], P Sytze van Dam[1], Andre Aleman[2] and Edward HF de Haan[2]

[1]Department of Endocrinology, University Medical Centre, Utrecht, and [2]Department of Psychonomics, Utrecht University, Utrecht, The Netherlands

Summary

A number of recent studies show that growth hormone (GH) and GH receptors, and insulin-like growth factor I (IGF-I) and IGF-I receptors, are located in several areas of the brain. The distribution of receptors suggests that GH and IGF-I contribute to the function of the hippocampus, a brain structure important for cognitive functions, such as learning and memory. It is feasible that GH and IGF-I play a role in the early development of these areas of the brain and subsequently have an effect on cognitive function. Evidence for cognitive deficits in GH-deficient individuals has been found in various studies, some of which have shown that these deficits can be reversed by GH replacement therapy.

Introduction

In recent years it has been speculated that cognitive performance may be affected by growth hormone (GH) and insulin-like growth factor I (IGF-I). This is supported by the presence of GH and IGF-I in the cerebrospinal fluid and of binding sites for GH and IGF-I in the brain [1–3]. In particular, the presence of a high number of binding sites for GH in the hippocampus, a brain structure of major importance in the process of learning and memory, is suggestive of a specific effect of the GH/IGF-I axis on cognition. Indeed, impaired cognitive function has been observed in adults with either childhood-onset (CO-) or adult-onset (AO-) GH deficiency (GHD) [4, 5], and a few studies have demonstrated improvement in cognitive deficits in adults with GHD given GH replacement therapy [6, 7].

The detrimental impact of insufficient GH and IGF-I concentrations on cognitive function is not limited to GH-deficient individuals. As the activity of the somatotrophic hormone axis declines with advancing age, it has been suggested that a condition of relative hyposomatotrophism may be a factor in the impaired cognitive function associated with ageing [8, 9] and in neurodegenerative diseases such as Alzheimer's disease [10, 11]. Therefore, in an ageing population, the interaction of the somatotrophic axis with the brain has become a major target for basic and clinical research. After a short review concerning the role of GH and IGF-I in the brain, especially in the hippocampal area, this chapter will focus on cognitive functions in GH-deficient adults and on the effects of GH replacement therapy.

GH and IGF-I in the central nervous system (CNS)

It has been demonstrated that both GH and IGF-I can cross the blood–brain barrier, but local synthesis of IGF-I and, to a lesser degree, GH also occurs in most areas of the brain [12, 13]. In GH-deficient patients, concentrations of GH and IGF-I in the cerebrospinal fluid are increased by subcutaneous administration of GH [1].

In humans, GH receptors are found throughout the brain but are mainly concentrated in the choroid plexus, pituitary, hippocampus, putamen and hypothalamus [14]. The most abundant specific binding of ^{125}I-labelled GH to membranes in the human brain is found in the choroid plexus and the pituitary. In the choroid plexus, GH receptors presumably serve as a system to transport GH across the blood–brain barrier. The high number of GH receptors in the hippocampus (approximately two- to fourfold higher than in most other areas of the brain) suggests that GH plays a relatively important role in hippocampal functions; however, the localization of binding sites for GH in the hippocampus has not been specified. Both animal and human studies make it clear that the number of GH receptors declines with age throughout the brain (Fig. 1) [14–17]. In humans, a significant negative correlation has been observed between advancing age (over 60 years) and the density of cerebral binding sites for GH, particularly in the pituitary, hypothalamus, hippocampus and putamen [16, 17]. One study found an age-related reduction in the expression of GH receptor mRNA in different regions of the brain, especially in the areas that affect mood, cognition, memory and learning [16]. Hence, it can be speculated that alterations in the status of the GH receptor in the hippocampus or in other brain areas may contribute to age-related cognitive decline.

Similar to binding sites for GH, IGF-I receptors are relatively concentrated in the hippocampus and the parahippocampal areas, but they are also present in the amygdala, cerebellum and cortex in humans [3]. In one study in rats, hippocampal IGF-I receptors were shown to be concentrated in the dentate gyrus and the CA3 region, but no changes in IGF-I binding sites occurred with age or in a specific subgroup of memory-impaired elderly rats [18]. In humans, no alterations in the density of cortical IGF-I receptors could be shown in connection with ageing or Alzheimer's disease [19].

A large variety of biological effects of IGF-I on different brain structures has been demonstrated. In general, IGF-I can stimulate the viability and function of different neuronal cell types, such as cortical, cerebellar and hypothalamic neurones, and contributes to neuronal DNA synthesis, as well as myelination. In addition, IGF-I modifies synaptic transmission and increases neuronal excitability and synaptic recruiting [10, 20]. Furthermore, it has been demonstrated that IGF-I can protect hippocampal neurones against β-amyloid-induced toxicity – increased deposition of this peptide in the CNS has been associated with the development of Alzheimer's disease [21]. Thus, IGF-I is believed to have both neurotrophic and neuroprotective effects. The wide distribution of binding sites for IGF-I in the brain, with a high density in the hippocampus, may reflect the physiological effects of IGF-I on the CNS, as well as the vulnerability of specific brain areas to GH and IGF-I deficiency. Age-related decreased IGF-I levels are associated with altered synaptic plasticity, cell loss and/or impairment, a reduced reparative capacity and neurogenesis, altered glucose metabolism and impaired angiogenesis [16, 17]. Thus, the ability of IGF-I to keep nerve cells alive and functional is compromised in old age.

Effects of age-related decreased IGF-I and GH levels on cognitive function

Activity of the somatotrophic axis decreases with age, and some studies have focussed on the relationship between hyposomatotrophism and age-related changes in cognitive function. In a study of 104 healthy elderly men, Papadakis *et al.* [22] found a significant association between IGF-I levels and a measure of mental processing speed, but not with another timed test of executive cognitive function. The relationship

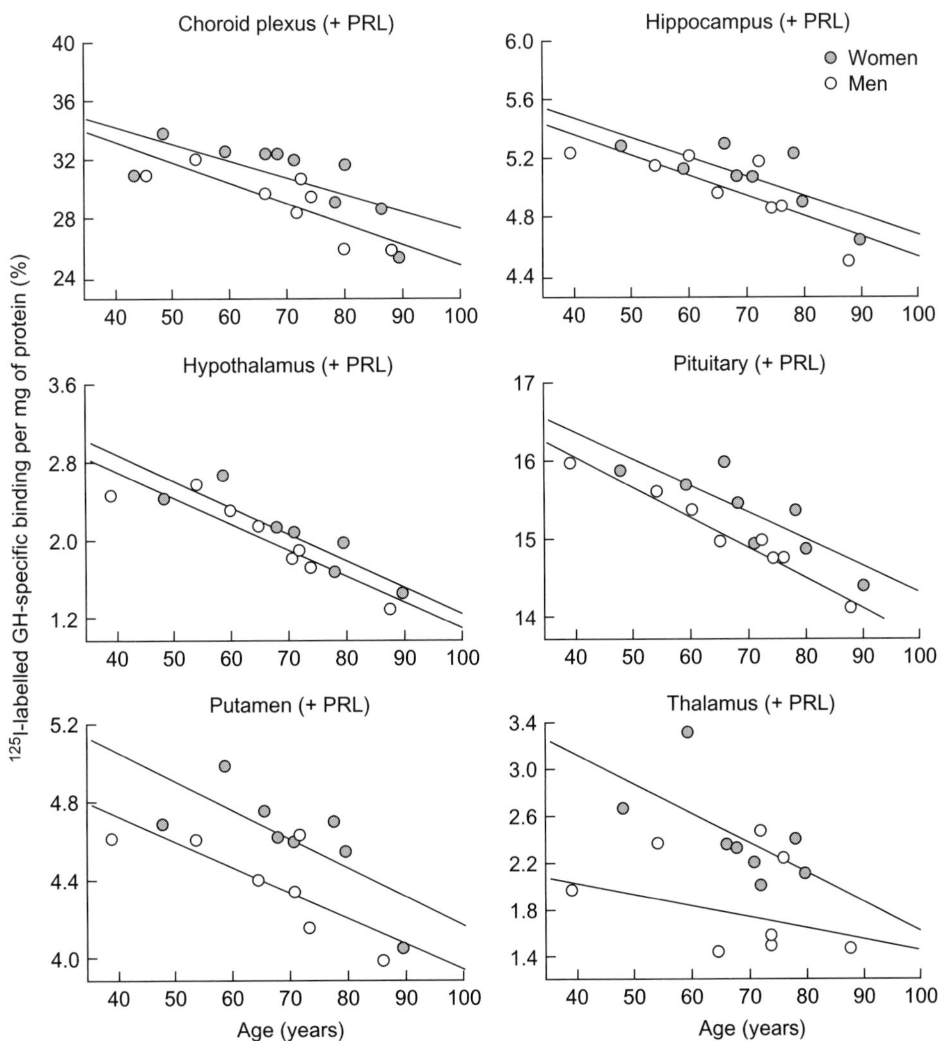

Figure 1. *Binding sites for* ^{125}*I-labelled GH in different regions of the brain of women and men, as a function of age. In all regions except the thalamus, the decrease in receptor binding with age was significant. Lactogenic binding sites were blocked by the addition of an excess of unlabelled human prolactin (PRL). Reproduced from [17] with permission. Copyright 1993, Elsevier Science.*

between hormone levels and cognitive function in a sample of 56 men (age range, 20–84 years) was studied by Morley *et al.* [23], who observed significant correlations between the IGF-I to GH ratio and cognitive performance, including measures of visual and verbal memory. Rollero *et al.* [8] reported a positive correlation between IGF-I levels and cognitive function, as measured by the Mini-Mental State Examination in 22 elderly individuals with varying degrees of mild cognitive impairment.

In a study of 25 healthy elderly men, Aleman *et al.* [9] observed an association between plasma IGF-I levels and age-sensitive cognitive function, particularly cognitive speed and motor performance (Table 1). Vitiello *et al.* [24] evaluated the correlation between IGF-I levels and the results of

Table 1. Relationship of age-independent and age-sensitive cognitive test scores to circulating IGF-I levels in healthy elderly adults (n = 25). Adapted from [9] with permission. Copyright 1999, The Endocrine Society.

	Function measured	*r* value	*p* value
Age-independent functions			
Information	General knowledge	−0.16	0.47
Vocabulary	Verbal ability	0.11	0.60
Brus reading	Reading ability and speed	0.31	0.14
Judgement of line orientation	Basic visuo-spatial perception	−0.07	0.74
Age-sensitive functions			
Digit–symbol substitution	Cognitive and perceptual-motor processing speed	0.52	0.009
Block design	Visuo-spatial perceptual organization and construction	0.03	0.90
Concept shifting task	Planning of movement and cognitive speed	−0.55	0.005
15-word test	Verbal long-term memory	−0.22	0.29

age-sensitive performance tests that involve problem-solving abilities. Their findings were consistent with those of the study of Aleman *et al.* [9], further supporting the hypothesis that IGF-I concentration may be related to the age-related decline in cognitive function. Recently, Vitiello *et al.* [25] reported a study of 89 carefully screened, community-recruited, healthy elderly men and women (age range, 60–85 years) who were randomized to either placebo or synthetic GH-releasing hormone (GHRH[1–29]-NH_2 [sermorelin acetate]) treatment. Five months of treatment increased IGF-I and GH levels by 30 and 50%, respectively, in the GHRH group, while no change was observed in the placebo-treated group. Cognitive functions improved significantly in the GHRH-treated group, particularly those cognitive functions that involve perceptual-motor speed [25]. Aleman *et al.* [26] reported a dissociation between IGF-I levels and maximal pituitary GH secretion (assessed by the combined administration of GHRH and GH-releasing peptide-6) as correlates of cognitive function. A higher GH response was associated with poorer cognitive performance, whereas higher levels of IGF-I were associated with better performance, particularly on tests of perceptual-motor and mental processing speed. Hence, IGF-I and GH levels appear to correlate independently with cognitive function.

Papadakis *et al.* [27] observed only marginally positive effects of GH treatment in one of three tests of cognitive function in healthy elderly men, with executive function improving in patients receiving GH and deteriorating in the placebo group. As cognitive processing speed and motor performance are predominantly controlled by the frontal cerebral cortex rather than other brain areas, these observations suggest that reduced concentrations of IGF-I rather than GH are more directly implicated in cognitive dysfunction in the elderly. In addition to the possibility that GH and/or IGF-I interact directly with the brain, it has been shown in ageing rats that decreased cerebral microvasculature is associated with attenuated levels of GH and IGF-I [28]. Hence, hyposomatotrophism and reduced vascular supply in the brain could contribute to the cognitive changes observed in the elderly. Further studies should focus on the cause of this association between ageing, hyposomatotrophism and vascular changes in the brain, should investigate the specific roles of GH and IGF-I and should characterize the cognitive changes in the elderly in relation to changes in the activity of the somatotrophic axis.

Practical definitions

Short-term memory

Short-term memory (also known as working memory) is the ability to hold on to and work with small amounts of information for a matter of seconds. This enables us to, for example, remember speech so that we can interpret the flow of a conversation, or remember a short sequence of numbers, such as a telephone number.

Long-term memory

Long-term memory is the ability to store information for longer time intervals, ranging from minutes to years.

Recognition memory

Recognition memory is the ability to judge that you have previously been exposed to something when you are presented with it.

Iconic memory

Iconic memory is a type of visual memory and describes the ability to recall information about visual stimuli following a very brief presentation.

Perceptual-motor memory

Perceptual-motor memory (also known as perceptual-motor skill memory) is used to describe situations in which sensory input is integrated with muscular response to obtain a goal. This type of memory is often assessed by examining the acquisition of a 'skill', or the performance of an already learned 'skill', in terms of speed and/or errors. Measurement of speed can be broken down into the time taken for the motor component (Perceptual-motor speed) and the time taken for the cognitive component (cognitive/mental processing speed).

Executive functions

Executive functions are higher-order functions that enable performance to be optimized in situations requiring the operation of a number of cognitive processes. Examples of executive functions include selective attention, planning, response inhibition, concept shifting and the manipulation of information in problem-solving tasks.

Selective attention

Selective attention is the ability to focus selectively on certain stimuli and ignore others that are present at the same time.

Concept shifting

Having acquired a concept about a particular situation, concept shifting is the ability to discard this concept and acquire a new concept based on a different aspect of the same situation. Tasks may require subjects to alternate between two concepts, for example requiring them to switch between selecting numbers and letters from an array of stimuli. A motor component may also be involved in some tasks.

Mini-Mental State Examination (MMSE)

The MMSE is a brief, quantitative measure of cognitive status in adults. It assesses orientation, attention, immediate and short-term recall, language and the ability to follow simple verbal and written commands, and provides a total score that places the individual on a scale of cognitive function. The MMSE is used to screen for cognitive impairment.

Event-related potentials

Event-related potentials can be recorded at the scalp. They are electrical potentials generated in the brain as a result of the synchronized activation of populations of neurones, and can be temporally linked to external events or stimuli. Event-related potentials can be divided into components that occur at different latencies with respect to the event; one such component is N2b.

Cognitive function: effects of GHD and GH therapy

Cognitive dysfunction has been demonstrated in adults with CO-GHD and AO-GHD.

CO-GHD

The most comprehensive study of cognitive function in individuals with CO-GHD was carried out by Deijen *et al.* [5], who evaluated 48 men with this condition. Impaired memory performance (short-term, long-term and iconic memory), as well as lower intelligence scores were demonstrated in men with either isolated GHD or multiple pituitary hormone deficits, including GHD. In contrast, perceptual-motor performance and emotional well-being were impaired only in men with multiple pituitary hormone deficits, including GHD, but not in patients with isolated GHD. Therefore, the authors suggested that cognitive defects, but not alterations in mood and general well-being, are associated with the GH-deficient state [5].

In a second study of the same group of men with CO-GHD [7], short- and long-term memory were found to improve after 26 weeks of treatment with GH in comparison with placebo, and supraphysiological doses of GH were found to accelerate the memory improvement. After 2 years of GH treatment in this open-label study, iconic memory was also significantly improved, and no differences in cognitive performance were observed between the GH-treated patients and normal controls. Assessment of perceptual-motor skill and psychological well-being did not reveal major treatment effects, except for a lower anxiety score after 2 years of treatment. These data suggest a selective effect of GH (and/or IGF-I) on memory performance, with no influence on emotional well-being.

In a small series of uncontrolled observations, Sartorio *et al.* [4, 29] found normal intellectual profiles in adults with CO-GHD, and symbol–number association (digit–symbol substitution) was the only cognitive task involving non-verbal intelligence that improved after GH treatment. There were contradictory results from two earlier studies focussing on cognitive function in patients with isolated GHD or multiple pituitary hormone deficits, including GHD. Almqvist *et al.* [30] demonstrated improved recognition memory in five individuals with multiple pituitary hormone deficits, including CO-GHD, who were treated with GH for 4 weeks in an open-label study. In contrast, a placebo-controlled crossover study performed by Degerblad *et al.* [31] found no beneficial effects of GH substitution on cognitive function in six individuals with either multiple pituitary hormone deficits, including GHD, or isolated GHD. Considering the small numbers of patients and, in the study by Almqvist *et al.*, the absence of a placebo-treated control group, the data from these studies are difficult to interpret.

Using electrophysiological measurement of event-related brain potentials, we recently demonstrated that adults with CO-GHD have attentional deficits in association with reduced N2b depolarization [32]. Alterations in N2b are associated with functional deficits in the cingulate cortex, and are also observed in the ageing population. In addition, we could demonstrate small cognitive deficits, which were identified as attenuated performance on a delayed verbal memory test and a test evaluating processing speed and planning behaviour (executive functioning). Furthermore, plasma IGF-I levels in these patients were correlated with *N*-acetylaspartate/choline levels in the brain, which suggests an inverse association between circulating IGF-I levels and neuronal damage [33].

AO-GHD

AO-GHD has been associated with other forms of cognitive dysfunction, in particular attenuated concentration ability [6]. In an extensive placebo-controlled intervention study, Baum *et al.* [34] evaluated cognitive function in 40 patients with AO-GHD, either isolated or combined with other pituitary deficits.

At baseline, they observed reduced verbal learning and visual memory scores in comparison with normal controls, but normal performance on a variety of other cognitive tasks, suggesting a mild deficit in the ability to learn and remember new information as a consequence of AO-GHD. They reported that, after 18 months of GH replacement therapy, there were no changes in cognitive performance in the GH-treated group compared with a placebo-treated GH-deficient control group [34]. The different effect of GH on cognitive performance, in comparison with the study by Deijen *et al.* [7], may be due to the difference in age at the time of onset of GHD. Other variations between the two studies, such as effects of radiotherapy, the aetiology of pituitary disease or the relatively high number of patients with combined pituitary hormone deficits in the study by Baum *et al.* [34], should also be considered as possible explanations for the observed differences.

Impact of GH on CNS metabolism

Johansson *et al.* [1] and Burman *et al.* [35] have demonstrated that GH substitution in GH-deficient patients increases the concentrations of dopamine metabolites and β-endorphin in the cerebrospinal fluid, suggesting that GH substitution in these patients affects dopamine and endorphin metabolism.

Limited data and difficult interpretation

Overall, the data on cognitive function in GHD are limited and controversial, making the interpretation of the effects of GH substitution therapy on cognition speculative. To gain further insight into the importance of cognitive deficits in GHD, studies are needed that can unravel the impact of CO- versus AO-GHD, as well as isolated GHD versus GHD combined with other pituitary hormone deficits. Another complication, making it difficult to interpret studies of patients with multiple pituitary hormone deficits, is the possibility of inadequate substitution of the deficient hormones. In summary, the available data are too limited to answer adequately the question of whether the impairment of cognitive function in patients with GHD is a direct consequence of the GH-deficient state. As there are no data on the effects of IGF-I treatment on cognition in GH-deficient individuals, it is still unclear whether the reported cognitive deficits are related specifically to GHD or to insufficient IGF-I levels.

Conclusions and future perspectives

The attenuated cognitive performance observed in GH-deficient states may be caused by defective binding of GH and/or IGF-I to their respective binding sites, leading to reduced secretion of neurotransmitters. Moreover, the age-related decrease in activity of the somatotrophic axis may affect cognitive function in a way that differs from the effect seen in syndromes of GHD. Recently published reviews have focussed extensively on the interaction between the somatotrophic axis and the brain, in particular in relation to cognitive performance [36, 37]. The specific brain areas involved and the contribution of changes in the secretion of either GH or IGF-I are still unclear. Differences in the distribution of binding sites for GH and IGF-I in the brain suggest that each of these proteins may play a specific role. The elucidation of these questions is an important issue for research on the role of the somatotrophic axis in cognitive function.

References

1. Johansson JO, Larson G, Andersson M, Elmgren A, Hynsjo L, Lindahl A, Lundberg PA, Isaksson OG, Lindstedt S, Bengtsson B-Å. Treatment of growth hormone-deficient adults with recombinant human growth hormone increases the concentration of growth hormone in the cerebrospinal fluid and affects neurotransmitters. Neuroendocrinology 1995;61:57–66

2. Nyberg F, Burman P. Growth hormone and its receptors in the central nervous system – location and functional significance. Horm Res 1996;45:18–22

3. Adem A, Jossan SS, d'Argy R, Gillberg PG, Nordberg A, Winblad B, Sara V. Insulin-like growth factor 1 (IGF-1) receptors in the human brain: quantitative autoradiographic localization. Brain Res 1989;503:299–303

4. Sartorio A, Conti A, Molinari E, Riva G, Morabito F, Faglia G. Growth, growth hormone and cognitive functions. Horm Res 1996;45:23–9

5. Deijen JB, de Boer H, Blok GJ, van der Veen EA. Cognitive impairments and mood disturbances in growth hormone deficient men. Psychoneuroendocrinology 1996;21:313–22

6. Burman P, Broman JE, Hetta J, Wiklund I, Erfurth EM, Hagg E, Karlsson FA. Quality of life in adults with growth hormone (GH) deficiency: response to treatment with recombinant human GH in a placebo-controlled 21-month trial. J Clin Endocrinol Metab 1995;80:3585–90

7. Deijen JB, de Boer H, van der Veen EA. Cognitive changes during growth hormone replacement in adult men. Psychoneuroendocrinology 1998;23:45–55

8. Rollero A, Murialdo G, Fonzi S, Garrone S, Gianelli MV, Gazzerro E, Barreca A, Polleri A.

Relationship between cognitive function, growth hormone and insulin-like growth factor I plasma levels in aged subjects. Neuropsychobiology 1998;38:73–9

9. Aleman A, Verhaar HJ, de Haan EH, de Vries WR, Samson MM, Drent ML, van der Veen EA, Koppeschaar HP. Insulin-like growth factor-I and cognitive function in healthy older men. J Clin Endocrinol Metab 1999; 84:471–5

10. Connor B, Dragunow M. The role of neuronal growth factors in neurodegenerative disorders of the human brain. Brain Res Rev 1998;27:1–39

11. Connor B, Beilharz EJ, Williams C, Synek B, Gluckman PD, Faull RL, Dragunow M. Insulin-like growth factor-I (IGF-I) immunoreactivity in the Alzheimer's disease temporal cortex and hippocampus. Mol Brain Res 1997;49:283–90

12. Han VK. Is the central nervous system a target for growth hormone and insulin-like growth factors? Acta Paediatr Suppl 1995;411:3–8

13. Johansson JO, Bengtsson B-Å. Central nervous effects of growth hormone. Endocrinol Metab 1997; 4 (Suppl B):103–107

14. Lai ZN, Emtner M, Roos P, Nyberg F. Characterization of putative growth hormone receptors in human choroid plexus. Brain Res 1991;546:222–6

15. Zhai Q, Lai Z, Roos P, Nyberg F. Characterization of growth hormone binding sites in rat brain. Acta Paediatr Suppl 1994;406:92–5

16. Nyberg F. Aging effects on growth hormone receptor binding in the brain. Exp Gerontol 1997;32:521–8

17. Lai Z, Roos P, Zhai O, Olsson Y, Fholenhag K, Larsson C, Nyberg F. Age-related reduction of human growth hormone-binding sites in the human brain. Brain Res 1993;621:260–6

18. Doré S, Kar S, Rowe W, Quirion R. Distribution and levels of [^{125}I]IGF-I, [^{125}I]IGF-II and [^{125}I]insulin receptor binding sites in the hippocampus of aged memory-unimpaired and -impaired rats. Neuroscience 1997;80:1033–40

19. De Keyser J, Wilczak N, Goossens A. Insulin-like growth factor-I receptor densities in human frontal cortex and white matter during aging, in Alzheimer's disease, and in Huntington's disease. Neurosci Lett 1994;172:93–6

20. Baskin DG, Wilcox BJ, Figlewicz DP, Dorsa DM. Insulin and insulin-like growth factors in the CNS. Trends Neurosci 1988;11:107–11

21. Dore S, Kar S, Quirion R. Insulin-like growth factor I protects and rescues hippocampal neurons against beta-amyloid- and human amylin-induced toxicity. Proc Natl Acad Sci USA 1997;94:4772–7

22. Papadakis MA, Grady D, Tierney MJ, Black D, Wells L, Grunfeld C. Insulin-like growth factor 1 and functional status in healthy older men. J Am Geriatr Soc 1995; 43:1350–5

23. Morley JE, Kaiser F, Raum WJ, Perry HM 3rd, Flood JF, Jensen J, Silver AJ, Roberts E. Potentially predictive and manipulable blood serum correlates of aging in the healthy human male: progressive decreases in bioavailable testosterone, dehydroepiandrosterone sulfate, and the ratio of insulin-like growth factor I to growth hormone. Proc Natl Acad Sci USA 1997; 94:7537–42

24. Vitiello MV, Merriam GR, Moe KE, Drolet G, Barsness S, Kletke M, Schwartz RS. IGF-I correlates with cognitive function in healthy older men and estrogenized women. Gerontologist 1999;39:6

25. Vitiello MV, Baker LD, Mazzoni G. Growth hormone releasing hormone treatment improves cognitive function in healthy older men and women. Gerontologist 2003;43:S1–4

26. Aleman A, de Vries WR, de Haan EH, Verhaar HJ, Samson MM, Koppeschaar HP. Age-sensitive cognitive function, growth hormone and insulin-like growth factor 1 plasma levels in healthy older men. Neuropsychobiology 2000;41:73–8

27. Papadakis MA, Grady D, Black D, Tierney MJ, Gooding GA, Schambelan M, Grunfeld C. Growth hormone replacement in healthy older men improves body composition but not functional ability. Ann Intern Med 1996;124:708–16

28. Sonntag WE, Lynch CD, Cooney PT, Hutchins PM. Decreases in cerebral microvasculature with age are associated with the decline in growth hormone and insulin-like growth factor 1. Endocrinology 1997; 138:3515–20

29. Sartorio A, Molinari E, Riva G, Conti A, Morabito F, Faglia G. Growth hormone treatment in adults with childhood onset growth hormone deficiency: effects on psychological capabilities. Horm Res 1995;44:6–11

30. Almqvist O, Thorén M, Sääf M, Eriksson O. Effects of growth hormone substitution on mental performance in adults with growth hormone deficiency: a pilot study. Psychoneuroendocrinology 1986;11:347–52

31. Degerblad M, Almqvist O, Grunditz R, Hall K, Kaijser L, Knutsson E, Ringertz H, Thorén M. Physical and psychological capabilities during substitution therapy with recombinant growth hormone in adults with growth hormone deficiency. Acta Endocrinol (Copenh) 1990;123:185–93

32. Lijffijt M, Van Dam PS, Kenemans JL, Koppeschaar HPF, de Vries WR, Drent ML, Wittenberg A. Somatotropic-axis deficiency affects brain substrated of selective attention in childhood-onset growth

hormone-deficient patients. Neurosci Lett 2003; 353:123–6

33. van Dam PS, Lijffijt M, de Vries WR, de Winter CF, Drent ML, Van der Grond J, Verbaten MN, Kenemans JL, Aleman A, de Haan EHF, Koppeschaar HPF. Cognitive function, selective attention, event-related potentials and 1H magnetic resonance spectroscopy in childhood-onset growth hormone deficiency. Growth hormone and growth factors in endocrinology and metabolism symposium abstracts 2002;32

34. Baum HB, Katznelson L, Sherman JC, Biller BM, Hayden DL, Schoenfeld DA, Cannistraro KE, Klibanski A. Effects of physiological growth hormone (GH) therapy on cognition and quality of life in patients with adult-onset GH deficiency. J Clin Endocrinol Metab 1998;83:3184–9

35. Burman P, Hetta J, Wide L, Mansson JE, Ekman R, Karlsson FA. Growth hormone treatment affects brain neurotransmitters and thyroxine. Clin Endocrinol (Oxf) 1996;44:319–24

36. Schneider HJ, Pagotto U, Stalla GK. Central effects of the somatotropic system. Eur J Endocrinol 2003; 147:377–92

37. van Dam PS, Aleman A. IGF-I, cognition and brain ageing. Eur J Pharmacol 2004 in press

18 Methodological issues in the assessment of quality of life

Paul Kind

Outcomes Research Group, Centre for Health Economics, University of York, York, UK

Summary

Measurement of health outcomes, which is essential in evaluating and comparing treatment effects, requires a reliable and consistent method of describing health status. For some conditions, a single parameter may suffice, but for many conditions, including growth hormone deficiency (GHD), there are no such unambiguous markers of health status or outcome. In recent years, quality of life has emerged as an important indicator of health outcome, particularly with the shift of medical attention towards the alleviation of chronic conditions. In its broadest sense, quality of life is a multidimensional construct that embraces the human condition as a whole, and so includes a potentially large number of parameters. Health-related quality of life (HrQoL) is more narrowly defined and provides a more focussed description of quality of life that is relevant in the context of health and healthcare. There is clear evidence that the adverse changes associated with GHD impact on the quality of life of affected patients, and measurement of HrQoL is central to the diagnosis of GHD in adults and to the monitoring of treatment effects.

Introduction

Measuring health outcomes is fundamental to the delivery of any treatment. For individual patients we must know whether treatment produces any effects and, if so, whether these effects are positive or negative. The health status of a patient must therefore be compared at two points in time. Subtraction of one observation from the second generates an index of change. To have the greatest practical value such an index needs to go beyond the qualitative better/same/worse and must be capable of reflecting the magnitude of change as well as its direction. It is not enough to know that a patient responds positively to treatment – we need to know by how much he or she benefits. Such information is relevant to clinicians in improving their accumulated knowledge about the impact of treatment, as well as helping to distinguish the relative benefits of one treatment over another. The latter use is not restricted to clinicians but has potential in the wider evaluation of new treatment options. Health authorities and other regulatory agencies want to know the size of the additional benefit of one treatment compared with another. The measurement of that benefit relies heavily upon our capacity to measure health outcomes. For some conditions it is possible to select a single marker that unambiguously represents health status. In managing the overweight patient, for example, body weight may be selected as the relevant index of health status. Observations before and after the introduction of a diet/exercise programme allows quantification of any weight loss. However, for many conditions, and perhaps the majority, there are no such unambiguous indicators of health status or outcome.

The diagnosis of growth hormone deficiency (GHD) in adults is determined by the analysis of biochemical markers and the patient's presenting history [1]. However, the impact of GHD on patients extends far beyond the mere fact of diagnosis, being associated with cardiovascular risk factors and changes in body composition, including reduced lean body mass and impaired bone mineral density. Additional symptoms, such as memory loss, attenuated levels of concentration, tiredness, irritability and higher levels of perceived health problems, are also reported. GHD also impacts on specific areas of function, capacity and performance. More broadly, however, GHD affects quality of life itself (see Chapter 19).

The established tests of growth hormone (GH) status, which tend to be the basis for diagnostic and treatment decision, focus on the biochemical parameters of the condition. Investigation of the impact of GHD on quality of life, however, is less well developed and is the focus of this chapter.

Basic concepts

In its broadest interpretation, quality of life is a multidimensional construct that embraces the full spectrum of human experience, going well beyond the physical, mental and social dimensions identified in the World Health Organization definition of health.[1] The boundaries of the construct that we term quality of life are somewhat ill-defined, being largely dictated by the context in which the term is used. For example, if the quality of life of citizens in rural and urban settings is compared, then different dimensions are selected to those that would be incorporated in, for example, the measurement of quality of life in a clinical study. The former might take account of the environment, transport, housing, social and recreational amenities and level of crime amongst other things. To these external factors might be added person-centred indicators of freedom, happiness, well-being, fulfilment and satisfaction. In such a study the catalogue of measurable elements of quality of life is potentially large. In the specific setting of a clinical study, the quality of life construct covers an altogether narrower and more specific set of dimensions, such as pain, mood or physical function, and excludes those dimensions that lie outside the healthcare system's capacity to influence. Housing or the perception of crime may impact on an individual's quality of life, but there is little by way of healthcare interventions that can be done to remedy the negative impact of these factors. It is for this reason that the term health-related quality of life (HrQoL) is often used, being a more accurate description of quality of life when applied in the context of health and healthcare. HrQoL is concerned with those aspects of life beyond survival that are influenced by the provision or withholding of healthcare.

The terms quality of life, HrQoL and health status are often used synonymously; however, this is both inaccurate and misleading. HrQoL and health status are related elements that contribute to the wider quality of life construct. It may be expedient to treat HrQoL as a subjective indicator of health status, but neither HrQoL nor health status should be regarded as more than an imperfect proxy for overall quality of life. As there is no agreed standard definition there is consequentially enormous variability in the measurement of quality of life. This laxity has been rightly criticized [2], it being equally important to be as accurate and precise in this area of scientific enquiry as it is in clinical practice or research. However, whilst definition may be desirable and useful, it can also be problematic. Consider, for example the following statements, sampled from the literature:

Quality of life is a uniquely personal perception, denoting the way that individual patients feel about their health status and/or nonmedical aspects of their lives [2].

[1]Health is a state of complete physical, mental and social well-being and not merely the absence of disease or infirmity. World Health Organization (1948) Constitution as adopted by the International Health Conference, New York, 19–22 June, 1946; signed on 22 July 1946 by the representatives of 61 States (Official Records of the World Health Organization, no. 2, p. 100) and entered into force on 7 April 1948.

Quality of life as an outcome could be explored more clearly if (it) was replaced with a more easily handled notion such as that of "subjective health status" [3].

Quality of life in clinical medicine represents the functional effect of an illness and its consequent therapy upon a patient as perceived by the patient [4].

If one accepts the assertion that quality of life can be measured only by the individual patient, then there is no legitimate scope for quality of life assessment made by third parties. Such a position challenges the status of clinician-based assessments or those of others concerned with patient care. Additionally, it denies the measurement of quality of life in patients for whom intellectual functioning or communication are problematic. Clearly, such a restrictive view is unhelpful. So too is an exclusive focus on functional status. Quality of life measurement goes beyond the assessment of function and captures the subjective experience of functional loss or impairment. Despite the obvious lack of an agreed definition, there is a high degree of consensus that any measure of HrQoL should include aspects of physical, psychological, social and general health [5].

Wilson and Cleary [6] proposed a useful model in which elements of health status are represented along a continuum of increasing complexity. At one end, representing the fundamental determinants of health status are, they suggest, molecular and genetic factors. At the opposite end is quality of life, with a mediating role assigned to symptoms, functional status and general health perceptions. Such a conceptual model is, of course, useful in providing a general schematic that identifies the relationship between the various components of quality of life. Turning such a model into a practical measurement instrument, however, presents a challenge.

Measurement

Measurement in the laboratory or in clinical practice implies the application of a standard process with reproducible results, albeit with known margins of error. Our experience of measurement is largely related to its use with the concrete, tangible or physical and, consequentially, with the use of standard units. We are comfortable with, for example, the measurement of height or weight, as the units are universally recognized and accepted. By contrast, the measurement of subjective phenomena, such as quality of life, is regarded as less robust, more liable to error and not easily interpreted. It is worth noting, however, that the measurement of blood pressure, for which there is an effective 'gold standard', is prone to significant variability in its execution, often lacks precision, is subject to observer bias and requires different procedures according to the patient's body mass and handedness. Set against this benchmark, the measurement of quality of life is, to say the least, its technical equal.

The basis of all forms of measurement is a capacity to describe. If we wish to count objects we must be able to distinguish two elementary categories (same or different). A nominal classification of this type is qualitative in nature but provides the gateway to all higher level measurement. Descriptive classification may appear a trivial form of measurement but may nevertheless have great utility. A binary classification of health status (alive or dead) allows us to count outcomes for hospital in-patients and hence compute mortality rates. The International Classification of Diseases provides a mechanism for assigning patients to one or more diagnostic category. Where such a descriptive classification allows us not only to distinguish between different categories, but to place categories in some sort of hierarchical order, then our measurement is of a more sophisticated form. In such an ordinal classification we are not only able to identify whether objects belong to the same category, but are able to establish whether one category dominates another. The ubiquitous 'none/mild/moderate/severe' classification used, for example, to categorize symptom severity, contains just such information. Different patients categorized as 'moderate' are regarded as having a broadly similar level of symptom severity. Despite its qualitative status, such an ordinal system may have powerful applications. For example, in the measurement of health outcomes, such a classification can be used to indicate the direction of change. A patient with pre- and post-treatment assessments of 'severe' and 'moderate', respectively, demonstrates, by inference, a positive change in symptoms. Quantitative measurement, which generates data with true cardinal properties, becomes possible when we are able to specify the units of measure. By assigning the numbers 1 to 4 to the symptom classification, we confer a form of value or weighting to the basic descriptive system. This measurement process assigns 4 to the category 'severe' and 2 to the category 'mild'. Such interval scales can be used to quantify the distance between points along the scale. Ratio scales, having both a defined unit of measure and a non-arbitrary zero, dominate this hierarchy of measurement types.

Nominal and ordinal scales generate non-cardinal information. Despite this essentially non-metric form of measurement, data based on such scales are widely misreported. The median or mode are the appropriate measures of central tendency, and non-parametric statistical tests should be used with such data. Of equal concern is the interpretation of numeric labels as 'values'. If the 'none/mild/moderate/severe' classification were re-coded as the numbers 1 to 4, this does not change the status of the original classification. It simply gives the classification the *appearance* of having cardinal properties. The real danger lies in the subtle imposition of value. The category 'severe', having a coded value of 4, carries twice the weight of the category 'mild' that is coded as 2. The relative value of categories in such circumstances is imposed by the instrument designer and by the researcher who uses the instrument. This is unacceptable practice in the world of scientific investigation in general and particularly so in the measurement of HrQoL, in which value plays such a pivotal role.

In the measurement of quality of life, we have to deal with the twin components of description and valuation that underpin all forms of measurement. First, we require a descriptive system that gives physical expression to the concept itself. A system of this sort would, as a minimum, list the dimensions that were identified as relevant in the measurement of quality of life. This descriptive system might be used to construct vignettes or health states that characterize different levels of quality of life. The real potential of quality of life measurement can be realized once this descriptive system is linked to a valuation system that enables a numeric score to be assigned to different quality of life states. We can then define measurement as the assignment of numbers to objects according to a rule [7]. Figure 1 provides a graphical representation of this process.

Using such a schematic, several health states may be identified: a, b, c and d. We know something about their relative 'severity', in that c is closer to full health than a or b. State d is worse than dead. Other things being equal, moving a patient from b to c would represent an improvement in their health status. Moving from b to a represents a deterioration in health status. It should be noted that the inferences we are able to draw from such a descriptive system are constrained because the system is ordinal in nature. We can identify the direction of change but not its magnitude. To quantify the magnitude of change, we need to have an indication of the value associated with health states a to d. State b is closer to state c than it is to state a, hence $c^* - b^* < b^* - a^*$. State d being worse than dead has a negative value, as dead in this measurement system has a value of zero.

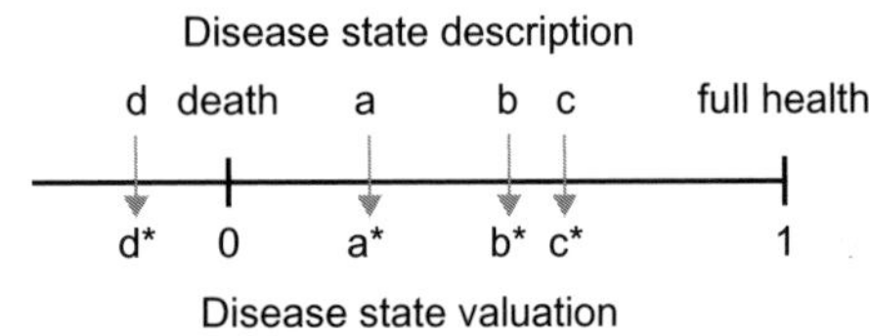

Figure 1. *Schematic representation of the process of measuring health-related quality of life by description and valuation of different health states. The letters a, b, c and d describe four different health states, which, using a linked valuation system, are assigned the numeric scores of a*, b*, c* and d*, respectively.*

Despite this negative value, it is still possible to derive positive health gain from treatment if it results in moving a patient to any state to the right (i.e. moving towards full health).

Although different measures of quality of life take different forms, they are all the product of description and valuation. The points of difference, when they occur, are in the content of the descriptive system and the form of the valuation system, and often arise as a result of differences in beliefs about whose perspective counts or should count.

Form of quality of life measures

Quality of life measures generally take one of two forms. Information about discrete dimensions may be presented as a series of concurrent scores that, for example, report separately on physical and social functioning. Such a profile maintains the individual components and provides the user with some insight into the impact a condition has on specific dimensions of quality of life. In its basic form a profile is incapable of providing an overall assessment of quality of life, as its separate dimension scores cannot be aggregated to generate a total sum. Figure 2 presents hypothetical pre- and post-treatment scenarios based on a hypothetical measure of HrQoL in GHD. The measure used defines HrQoL in terms of four dimensions (energy/tiredness, mood, social isolation and physical strength) and, for this example, a high rating on a given dimension indicates more problems.

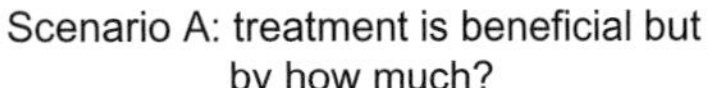

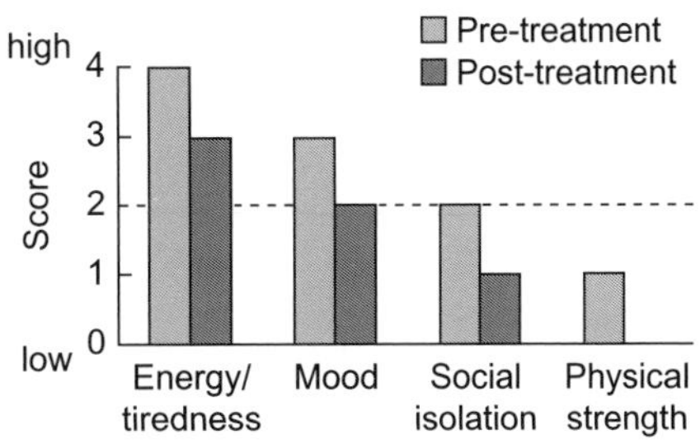

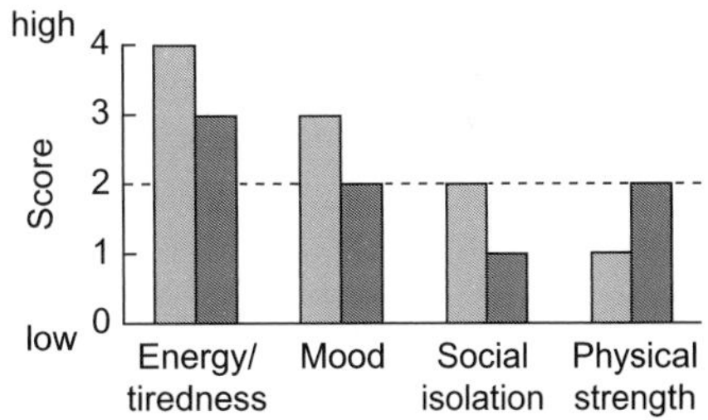

Figure 2. *Two scenarios of pre- and post-treatment health-related quality of life (HrQoL) profiles based on hypothetical measures of HrQoL dimensions in patients with GHD. For the four HrQoL dimensions – energy/tiredness, mood, social isolation and physical strength – a higher score indicates more problems.*

In scenario A, each of the dimensions has a post-treatment rating that is lower than its corresponding pre-treatment observation; hence, it is reasonable to conclude that there has been an improvement in the patient's HrQoL. Although the direction of change is known, its magnitude remains uncertain. In scenario B, the pre- and post-treatment profiles indicate improvement in three dimensions, but deterioration in physical strength. These profiles tell us simply that there has been a change in HrQoL, but we are not even in a position to assess whether that change is positive or negative. How do we balance the improvement on three dimensions against the worsened situation on the fourth? This is the fundamental weakness of all profile measures. In general, we know nothing about the relative value of the dimensions – about how gains/losses of physical functioning might be traded against compensating changes in mood or social functioning, for example. Without a formal investigation of such relative values, it is both dangerous and simplistic to attempt to reduce profile sub-scores to a single aggregate total.

Were the relative value of each dimension (and level within each dimension) known, then such profile data could be made into a single aggregate score, representing overall HrQoL. In possession of such an algorithm, we could easily compute the value of a profile and, from that information, derive a quantitative measure of change. Such an index format, in which HrQoL is represented by a single number, is essential for certain types of application but may be criticized as forcing users to accept a simplistic model of HrQoL that denies its multidimensional character. Critics would argue that it is not meaningful to compute summary scores across diverse dimensions that are both conceptually and practically separate. Index measurement, however, is a practical requirement in many settings, which makes such theoretical niceties irrelevant.

Perspective of quality of life measures

Amongst the different possible approaches to constructing quality of life measures, the so-called individualistic approach is based on the concept that quality of life is 'what the individual says it is' [8]. Proponents of this approach argue that the legitimate source of all information relating to quality of life is the individual person or patient him- or herself. The practical limitations of this approach, however, are so manifestly obvious as to rule it out in designing tools for use in clinical studies. We might ask a patient with newly diagnosed GHD to take part in a semi-structured interview in which they are encouraged to describe the impact of the condition on their quality of life. Without being offered prompts or suggestions of any sort it is highly likely that they will describe problems encountered with, for example, a lack of energy or inability to participate fully in social activity. The patient might then be invited to rank or otherwise value these problems. Over time, the patient may accommodate to some aspects of their condition, so that a repeat interview conducted some time later might reveal a different set of problems. What had originally been regarded as being relatively minor might now assume greater importance, and problems that had been successfully resolved might not be raised in the repeat interview. The practical limitation of this approach becomes clearer if we seek to aggregate data across patients. Problem areas identified by one patient may not be mentioned by others. Furthermore, the value attached by different patients to the same problem obstructs the aggregation process. This does not mean that the views of individual patients do not count – merely that their views represent one perspective among many possible.

A case can be made for adopting other approaches. For example, as patients' views are likely to change during the course of their condition and treatment, it might be considered better to rely on the assessments of professional health carers, whose training enables them to take a more informed and detached approach than the patient. However, their knowledge of prognosis and responses to treatment may influence their assessment of current HrQoL. If it is known that fatigue or mood state is improved by treatment, then the rating of HrQoL may be lowered – treatable HrQoL effects may be trivialized. In a wider social setting, as decisions about treatment ultimately affect us all, it could be argued that the views of the general public are relevant (as tax payers and potential future patients). As no single reference group dominates, it is sensible to accept that different perspectives will yield different HrQoL data and that different interpretations may follow as a consequence.

Application of HrQoL assessments

HrQoL assessments are made, or should be made, for a specific purpose and, in selecting an instrument, we need to take account of that intended application. If an instrument is to be used to inform clinical judgements then it needs to capture information that is relevant to clinicians and patients. Given the broad spectrum of the effects of GHD on HrQoL, it is reasonable to suppose that a generic instrument will have potential as a suitable measure of outcome. Even a profile measure can be useful as a descriptive vehicle. At the level of individual clinical decision making, the issues exemplified in Figure 2 could be resolved through discussion with the patient. Where HrQoL is an outcome variable in a clinical study, it will be advantageous to present data in both profile and index formats. The former provides information about separate dimensions and the latter provides a summary measure of outcome.

For use in economic evaluation, quality of life measurements must fulfil additional requirements. Economic analysis is concerned with the balance between inputs and outputs, the resources consumed or used and the consequential change in a patient's health status, and the balance between the costs and benefits of healthcare. At its simplest we might wish to know the cost per patient treated for GHD. Of more interest, when comparing the costs and benefits of alternative therapies, we are concerned with differences in costs and differences in benefits. In these circumstances, quality of life measurement has particular use in generalizing the results of economic evaluation by standardizing the measurement of health benefits. Healthcare interventions may influence the quantity of life and/or the quality of life. The quality-adjusted life year (QALY) is a unit of measure that combines both these elements and is the arithmetic product of quality and quantity. One QALY represents 1 year of life with full HrQoL. If we could plot the HrQoL of treated patients with GHD over time, it might produce curve A in Figure 3. The y-axis represents HrQoL measured using a single index instrument calibrated so that 'full health' has a value of 1 and 'dead' has a value of 0. HrQoL levels with a negative value are technically possible. The x-axis represents time, in this case measured in years.

If curve B resulted from GH-deficient patients not receiving treatment, then the marginal benefit, measured in QALYs, over the time t_0 to t_1 is given by the shaded area between the two curves. For this type of analysis to be sustained, we require two particular properties in the instrument used to measure quality of life. First, the instrument has to have a single index format. This means that profile measures, such as the Short Form-36 or the Nottingham Health Profile (NHP), cannot be used for this type of economic analysis, as they generate multiple scores. Secondly, quality of life must be measured on a scale that assigns a value of 1 to full

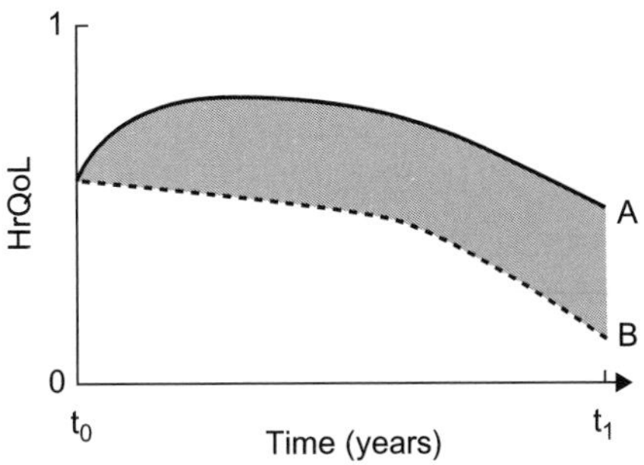

Figure 3. *Graphical representation of the difference between HrQoL in treated (A) and untreated (B) patients with GHD over time, assuming HrQoL was measured using a single index format ranging from 0 (dead) to 1 (full health).*

health and a value of zero to dead. This latter property is peculiar only to the calculation of QALYs. Representation of treatment pathways in this form also has potential value for clinicians and patients who might want to assess the consequences of current interventions on future levels of HrQoL. Information based on longitudinal studies of patient cohorts would be an invaluable source of information for these purposes.

Quality of life in GHD

The measurement of quality of life or, more appropriately, the measurement of HrQoL, is clearly as exacting in its methodology as is any other form of scientific measurement. In GHD, HrQoL measurement has been dominated by the NHP and, more recently, by the Quality of Life Assessment of GHD in Adults (QoL-AGHDA; see Appendix B) [9]. The NHP is a generic instrument based on 'yes/no' responses to 38 questions covering six dimensions – mobility, pain, energy, sleep, emotional reactions and social isolation. Items were selected from 2200 statements made by 768 individuals in open-ended interviews [10]. The instrument's designers took the view that perceived health status could only be represented as a profile, and that an index form lacked justification or meaning. As a consequence of that choice, the

NHP cannot be used as a summary measure of HrQoL, as the relative importance of each dimension is unknown. Dimensions within the NHP are made up of groups of items. The following two questions are taken from the group of five that constitutes the sleep dimension: "I need tablets to help me sleep" and "I wake up feeling tired". Answering yes to either of these questions leaves us knowing only that the respondent has some problem(s). We may personally feel that requiring tablets to aid sleep indicates a more serious problem than feeling tired on waking. However, that assessment depends upon our opinion – there is no external evidence to support (or challenge) that view. The responses in their 'raw' form provide us with descriptive clues that have limited quantitative value. One might consider counting the number of positive responses to the items within the sleep dimension, as this will generate a number with true cardinal properties. Taking this approach we might find, for example, three questions with positive answers out of the total of five. Whilst it is the case that this represents 60% of the maximum number of items in this dimension, it would be dangerous to represent that percentage as an index of value.

Why, then, is the abuse of such data so potentially hazardous? The use of item counts as exemplified in the NHP sleep dimension imposes a set of assumptions that good scientific practice demands should be tested. Counting positive responses implies that all items have the same importance. Taking tablets to aid sleep has the same (negative) weight as feeling tired when waking. This equality may or may not be true for the individual patient, for all patients with GHD, or for the general population as a whole. Although assigning equal weight to each item or statement may appear a simple expedient, it carries a significant risk of distorting patient responses by imposing external arbitrary values that have no foundation in empirical evidence. This limitation was recognized by the NHP's developers who devised a weighting system for groups of items within dimensions [11]. It is worth noting that these weights were based upon the views of healthy members of the general public – a perfectly acceptable, indeed desirable, reference source in the construction of a generic measure. As the importance of health as judged by individuals with different experiences of ill-health differs accordingly [12], a safe interpretation of NHP dimension scores in GHD is that they represent HrQoL as reported by patients, but as valued by healthy people.

The emergence of QoL-AGHDA [13] as a second-generation measure appears to have been driven by the need for a condition-specific instrument that was more closely allied to the concerns of GH-deficient patients themselves. Its descriptive content was derived in interviews with patients, thus ensuring that items are more likely to be relevant in assessing outcomes in GHD. This can represent a significant advantage over more broadly based generic measures. However, QoL-AGHDA retains the same 'yes/no' response system that is used in the NHP, yielding a total 'score' based on the number of positive items, and carrying with it the assumption of equal weight for all items. Efforts to redress this limitation have centred on the use of Rasch analysis [14, 15], an approach that is essentially probabilistic in character and is, in that sense, 'value' free. Weights produced through Rasch analysis tell us nothing about the relative importance of items as judged by patients or any other reference group. They are essentially the product of a statistical model. For QoL-AGHDA responses to be converted into an index that captures patient preferences, additional information is required that not only establishes the fact that a given item represents a problem for the patient, but in addition indicates the degree to which that problem impacts on their quality of life.

Conclusions

The measurement of quality of life involves a complex set of well-defined methodological issues for which there is a range of practical solutions. Far from being an optional variable of interest with limited value, HrQoL is central to the measurement of outcomes and, as a consequence, forms an integral part of treatment and management – especially in GHD. In making decisions about individual patients, we need data that adequately reflect their views. In the wider context of priority setting, where there is competition for healthcare resources, we must be able to establish the case for treatment of GHD using a different metric – one calibrated in terms of the preferences of the wider population. In these circumstances, a generic instrument can be a useful adjunct to our arsenal of outcome measures.

In GHD, where quality of life issues predominate, the choice of HrQoL measure will ultimately be driven by the data requirements of the intended application – and these will vary. A single index format that incorporates social preferences of the general population is essential for certain types of economic analysis. A profile format based on patient preferences may suffice for some clinical uses. In either event, it is the responsibility of the user to confront the questions – whose descriptions and whose values form the basis of the HrQoL measurement? Despite its technical problems, quality of life measurement represents a major advance in demonstrating the outcomes of treatment in conditions such as GHD. It is no longer acceptable, if indeed it ever was, to represent outcomes exclusively in terms of biological markers selected by clinicians as their favoured index. Quality of life measurement has transformed the mechanism for capturing outcome data in a way that is transparent to patients and healthcare professionals alike.

References

1. Consensus guidelines for the diagnosis and treatment of adults with growth hormone deficiency: summary statement of the Growth Hormone Research Society Workshop on Adult Growth Hormone Deficiency. J Clin Endocrinol Metab 1998;83:379–81

2. Gill TM, Feinstein AR. A critical appraisal of the quality of quality-of-life measurements. JAMA 1994; 272:619–26

3. Leplege A, Hunt S. The problem of quality of life in medicine. JAMA 1997;278:47–50

4. Schipper H, Clinch JJ, Olweny CLM. Quality of life studies: definitions and conceptual issues. In: Spilker B, editor. Quality of life and pharmacoeconomics in clinical trials. 2nd edition. Philadelphia: Lippincott-Raven 1996:11–23

5. Cramer JA, Spilker B. Quality of life and pharmaco-economics: an introduction. Philadelphia: Lippincott-Raven 1998

6. Wilson IB, Cleary PD. Linking clinical variables with health-related quality of life. A conceptual model of patient outcomes. JAMA 1995;273:59–65

7. Stevens SS. On the theory of scales of measurement. Science 1946;103:677–80

8. Joyce CR, Hickey A, McGee HM, O'Boyle CA. A theory-based method for the evaluation of individual quality of life: the SEIQoL. Qual Life Res 2003;12:275–80

9. Kołtowska-Häggström M, Kind P. Evaluating outcomes in adult growth hormone deficiency: the status of quality of life measurement in clinical studies. ENDO 2003. The Endocrine Society 85th Annual Meeting 2003 Jun 19–22; Philadelphia, USA. Poster P2–320

10. McEwen J, McKenna SP. Nottingham Health Profile. In: Spilker B, editor. Quality of life and pharmacoeconomics in clinical trials. 2nd edition. Philadelphia: Lippincott-Raven 1996:281–6

11. McKenna SP, Hunt SM, McEwen J. Weighting the seriousness of perceived health problems using Thurstone's method of paired comparisons. Int J Epidemiol 1981;10:93–7

12. Kind P, Dolan P. The effect of past and present illness experience on the valuations of health states. Med Care 1995;33:AS255–63

13. McKenna SP, Doward LC, Alonso J, Kohlmann T, Niero M, Prieto L, Wirén L. The QoL-AGHDA: an instrument for the assessment of quality of life in adults with growth hormone deficiency. Qual Life Res 1999;8:373–83

14. Prieto L, Roset M, Badia X. Rasch measurement in the assessment of growth hormone deficiency in adult patients. J Appl Meas 2001;2:48–64

15. Wirén L, Whalley D, McKenna S, Wilhelmsen L. Application of a disease-specific, quality-of-life measure (QoL-AGHDA) in growth hormone-deficient adults and a random population sample in Sweden: validation of the measure by rasch analysis. Clin Endocrinol (Oxf) 2000;52:143–52

19 Effects of growth hormone (GH) deficiency and GH replacement on quality of life

Václav Hána

3rd Department of Internal Medicine, Faculty of Medicine, Charles University, Prague, Czech Republic

Summary

Long-term growth hormone (GH) replacement in GH-deficient adults has been demonstrated to have a significant beneficial effect on quality of life (QoL) – one of the aims of treatment for any chronic condition. The duration of treatment is important, as demonstrated by the variable results reported in short-term studies. However, in most studies lasting for more than 6 months, it is clear that QoL is improved. In the longest studies, conducted for up to 10 years, improvements have been demonstrated in energy levels, vitality, emotional well-being and overall QoL. Importantly, positive effects of GH replacement have also been reported by patients' partners in a long-term placebo-controlled trial. Discontinuation of GH replacement consistently results in a deterioration of QoL. The mechanisms behind the psychological benefits of GH are poorly understood, but could work through direct effects on receptors in the brain and/or GH-induced changes in metabolism and interaction with other hormones, such as thyroxine.

Introduction

The term quality of life (QoL) refers to psychological and social well-being as assessed from the patient's perspective. In the past two decades, medicine in developed countries has concentrated on improving the QoL of patients with chronic diseases. Reducing handicap and integrating the patient back into society with a normal life have become two of the main aims of modern medicine.

The impact of growth hormone (GH) on QoL was first recorded by Raben [1] in 1962, who treated a 35-year-old woman with hypopituitarism who, after 2 months, reported increased vigour, ambition and sense of well-being. This observation stimulated the assessment of psychological status and perceived QoL in GH-deficient adults, both in untreated patients and those treated with recombinant GH, which was introduced into clinical practice in 1985. An unexpected and very high level of psychological morbidity was revealed to be associated with GH deficiency (GHD). Assessment of QoL is now assuming increasing importance, with GH treatment in adults in some countries, such as the UK, being conditional upon the demonstration of an impairment in QoL without treatment [2].

This chapter reviews the evidence that adult GHD is a serious clinical condition in terms of its effects on QoL, and summarizes the known benefits of GH replacement therapy.

QoL in GH-deficient adults

A reduced QoL in untreated GH-deficient adults was confirmed in studies comparing patients with normal controls. Detailed assessment of psychological well-being showed that adults with GHD perceived themselves as having much greater physical and psychological health problems. Over one-third of the patients scored in the range consistent with psychiatric disturbance requiring therapy [3–7]. Using a self-rating questionnaire – the Nottingham Health Profile (NHP) – Rosén *et al.* [6] proved a decreased psychological well-being in terms of energy, social isolation and emotional reaction (psycho-logically labile), and a disturbed sex life in GH-deficient adults compared with matched controls. Wallymahmed *et al.* [7] found that GH-deficient patients were psychosocially disadvantaged in terms of depression, self-esteem, mental fatigue and life fulfilment compared with matched controls. The lack of energy, and emotional problems, in patients with adult-onset GHD (AO-GHD) were the two most pronounced findings in the study by Burman *et al.* [3]. The most prominent problems reported by patients in these studies were lack of energy, emotional lability, low mood and social isolation.

Children with GHD have been found to be psychologically immature and to have problems in socializing [8]. Long-term follow-up studies of adults previously treated with GH in childhood have shown that these patients were approximately three times more likely to be single and unemployed, and more likely not to have a driving licence [9]. Similarly, in a mixed group of patients with isolated GHD (IGHD) and idiopathic multiple pituitary hormone deficiency (MPHD), Björk*et al.* [10] found that the GH-deficient group experienced a poorer QoL in terms of greater social isolation, decreased amounts of physical mobility, poorer sleep and a perceived poorer level of general health. There was no difference between patients with IGHD and those with MPHD. When patients with AO- and childhood-onset GHD (CO-GHD) were compared, a more severe impairment in QoL (psychosocial distress) was observed in patients with AO-GHD [11, 12].

QoL in elderly GH-deficient patients was evaluated by Li Voon Chong *et al.* [13]. When elderly GH-deficient patients (over 65 years of age) were compared with matched healthy controls using various questionnaires (NHP, Short Form-36 Health Survey, Hospital Anxiety and Depression Scale, Self-Esteem Scale, Mental Fatigue Questionnaire, Life Fulfilment Scale, Disease Impact Scale), significantly worse scores for personal life fulfilment, mental fatigue, general health and mental health were reported by the GH-deficient patients. However, after 2 years of follow-up without GH treatment, only depression was significantly worse in the GH-deficient patients compared with the controls [13].

In some series of patients no negative effects of GHD have been reported [14, 15]. This is not surprising, considering the relatively low numbers of patients investigated in each study, the variety of instruments used and the heterogeneity of the patient groups studied. For instance, both gender and the duration of GHD influence the perception of QoL. Women tend to report more problems than men and patients with GHD of recent onset tend to feel better than those with long-standing disease [3].

Assessment of QoL

The first assessments of QoL were carried out using generic instruments, such as the NHP, the Psychological General Well-Being (PGWB) schedule (see Appendix A) and the Hopkins Symptom Checklist. These generic questionnaires were designed for use in a wide range of health states and therefore have the advantage of allowing comparison of patients with different conditions; however, they have a number of weaknesses when assessing specific patient populations. In particular, general questionnaires may not capture some of the disease-specific aspects of health-related QoL (HrQoL), for example in GHD. The questions asked may not focus on issues that are relevant for patients with GHD, and they may not even cover areas in which there are major concerns. Furthermore, they may measure other areas that are irrelevant for patients with this condition.

A disease-specific questionnaire was therefore developed that would take account of even the relatively minor – but often underestimated – manifestations of GHD in adults. This questionnaire – the Quality of Life Assessment of GHD in Adults (QoL-AGHDA, see Appendix B) [16] – confirmed that there was an impaired QoL in GH-deficient patients in comparison with a reference population [17, 18]. Deterioration of HrQoL in GH-deficient patients was marked, with patients achieving scores almost double those of the general population (mean score, 9.4 versus 5.5; a higher score indicates poorer perceived health) [17]. QoL-AGHDA questionnaires became a standard part of the evaluation of adults with GHD in the largest database of such patients – KIMS – Pfizer International Metabolic Database. Analyses of data from this large cohort have confirmed the poor QoL in GH-deficient patients. QoL-AGHDA scores from 275 naive patients entering KIMS were 7.1 ± 6.1 (mean ± SD) in men and 10.2 ± 6.3 in women, and were considerably higher (indicating a worse QoL) than those reported for normal adults in the MONICA (Monitoring trends and determinants in cardiovascular disease) study (2.7–3.3 for men and 4.0–4.6 for women). Mean scores in CO-GHD and AO-GHD were similar [19]. Analysis of 665 patients from the KIMS database provided similar results, with a mean baseline QoL-AGHDA score of 7.4 for men and 9.8 for women, and no significant difference between CO- and AO-GHD [20].

QoL in GHD in comparison with other conditions

A few studies have addressed the question of whether the poor QoL in GH-deficient patients is simply the result of a general chronic condition or whether it is disease specific. Using a battery of tests Wallymahmed *et al.* [21] found a significantly poorer QoL in GH-deficient patients when compared with patients with diabetes mellitus. The GH-deficient group reported significantly more depression and mental fatigue, lower self-esteem and less life-fulfilment than either the group with diabetes or the controls. Within the GH-deficient group there were no differences in QoL scores between patients with pituitary, hypothalamic or other brain tumours and no significant differences according to surgical treatment modality or radiotherapy (although the patients who had undergone transcranial surgery tended to have the greatest impairment) [21]. In a study of psychiatric morbidity in GH-deficient adults in comparison with diabetic patients, an increased prevalence of anxiety and depression was found in those with GHD [22]. Other data showing marked psychopathology in GH-deficient patients – 42% were evaluated as sufficiently depressed to need psychiatric referral and 31% sufficiently depressed to be considered a suicide risk – have also been reported (personal communication cited in [23]).

Page *et al.* [24] compared QoL in adult patients with GHD after treatment for non-functioning pituitary tumours with those who had undergone mastoid surgery. Overall, no significant difference was found. However, a subgroup of patients who had received radiotherapy reported significantly more depression and emotional lability than those in the mastoid group.

Effect of GH replacement on QoL

Both placebo-controlled and other studies have documented statistically significant improvements in well-being in GH-deficient adults receiving GH replacement, although the results have not been uniform. Whereas most studies have shown a definite benefit [5, 20, 25–27], other improvements were limited to some of the questionnaires used or to their subsections [28, 29], or to some subgroups of GH-deficient patients [11]. In addition, some studies have failed to demonstrate any significant improvement in QoL [30], or have shown improvements in some aspects and deterioration in others [31]. In a placebo-controlled study by Cuneo *et al.* [31], for example, modest improvements in QoL were reported following GH treatment in terms of energy, emotional reaction and overall score on part I of the NHP, while there was a decrease in physical mobility during the first 3 months of treatment.

The reasons for such discrepancies are not entirely clear. One explanation may be that there is minimal impairment of QoL in unselected GH-deficient cohorts at baseline, such that demonstrating an improvement is difficult. In fact, in the study by Cuneo and colleagues [31], one- to two-thirds of patients reported little or no impairment in QoL at baseline. Most clinicians are aware that some GH-deficient patients do not complain as much as others, who report a very poor QoL before GH treatment and appear to benefit enormously from GH replacement. Studies on selected cohorts of patients with the most impaired QoL demonstrated the highest degree of improvement, as assessed using the PGWB and QoL-AGHDA. The overall QoL-AGHDA score improved from 15.3 ± 6.0 to 9.8 ± 6.5 after 8 months of GH replacement. Baseline PGWB and QoL-AGHDA scores were the most important variables for predicting the level of improvement in both scores during GH therapy [12, 32]. These results were consistent with those described previously by Holmes and Shalet [33], who looked at the factors that determined a patient's desire to continue long-term GH replacement as an adult. Those adults who wished to continue on GH replacement tended to have more severe GHD, to experience more distress in terms of energy and vitality at entry into the study and to experience an improvement in energy after 6 months of treatment with GH [33]. Another factor influencing the QoL outcome of GH replacement could be that supraphysiological doses of GH were used in the initial trials. An increased incidence of side-effects may have masked some of the beneficial effects of GH replacement in these early studies.

Analysis of the effect of GH replacement in a cohort of 665 GH-deficient patients in the KIMS database has demonstrated a significant improvement in QoL, as assessed using the QoL-AGHDA questionnaire. The median decrease was 3 points at 6 months ($p < 0.0001$) and 4 points at 12 months [20]. A significant relationship between improvement in the QoL-AGHDA score and the maintenance dose of GH was observed in this study – patients receiving the highest doses of GH demonstrated the greatest improvement in QoL. In contrast to this observation, another study comparing two doses of GH did not report a better effect on QoL in patients receiving a higher dose, although a significant self-perceived improvement in well-being was clearly documented in the NHP and PGWB [25].

The latest analysis of data on QoL in patients enrolled in the KIMS database confirmed the positive effect of GH treatment on QoL. There was an improvement compared with baseline in all of the QoL measures assessed – QoL-AGHDA, PGWB and NHP – in naive (had never received GH prior to entry into KIMS) and semi-naive (had not received GH during the 6 months prior to entry into KIMS) patients treated with GH for 24 months (Figs 1–3) [34]. For details of the latest data on GH and QoL in elderly patients with GHD see Chapter 21.

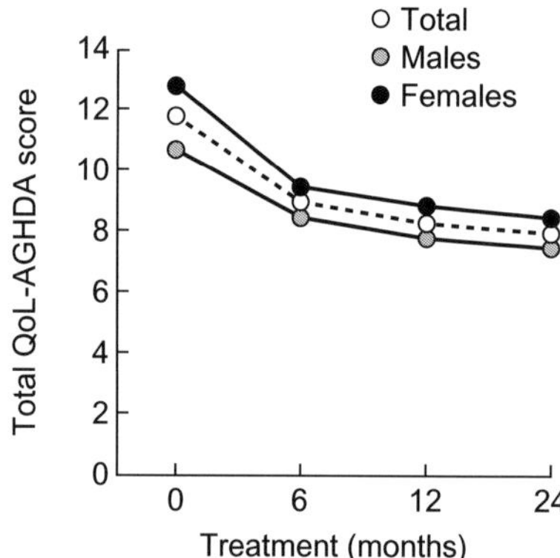

Figure 1. *Quality of Life Assessment of GHD in Adults (QoL-AGHDA) scores of KIMS patients over 24 months of treatment with GH. After 24 months of treatment with GH there was a significant improvement ($p < 0.0001$) in the QoL-AGHDA score compared with baseline (1055 patients evaluated at 24 months compared with 3268 patients at baseline). The mean improvement in score was significantly greater in women than in men ($p < 0.02$) (1609 males and 1659 females at baseline compared with 525 males and 530 females at 24 months).*

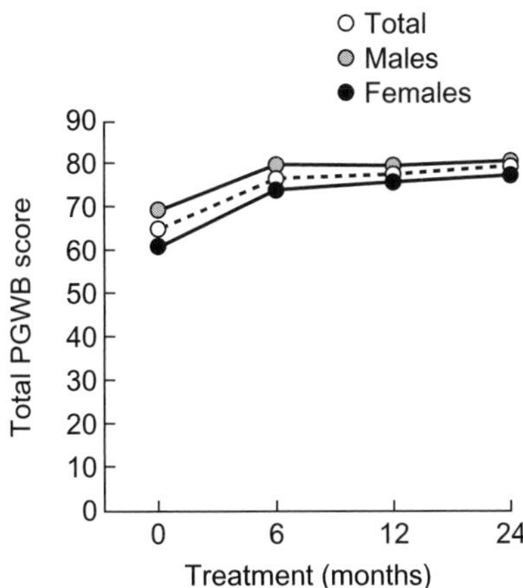

***Figure 2.** Psychological General Well-Being (PGWB) schedule scores of KIMS patients over 24 months of treatment with GH. After 24 months of treatment with GH there was a significant improvement ($p < 0.0001$) in the PGWB score compared with baseline (690 patients evaluated at 24 months compared with 1357 patients at baseline). The mean improvement in score was significantly greater in women than in men ($p < 0.001$) (659 males and 698 females at baseline compared with 334 males and 356 females at 24 months).*

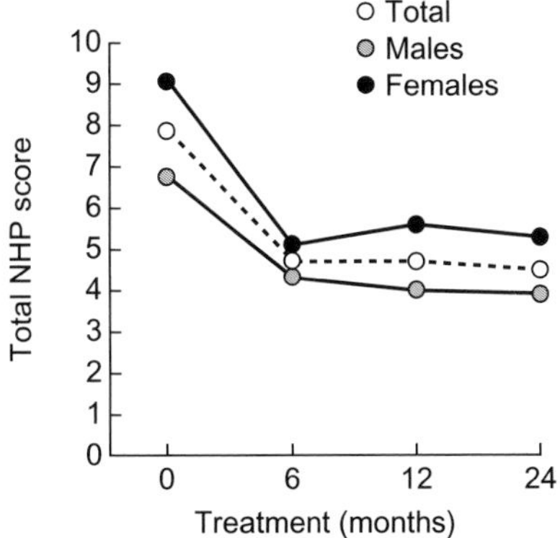

***Figure 3.** Nottingham Health Profile (NHP) scores of KIMS patients over 24 months of treatment with GH. After 24 months of treatment with GH there was a significant reduction ($p < 0.0001$) in the NHP score compared with baseline (584 patients evaluated at 24 months compared with 1575 patients at baseline). There were no gender differences in response to treatment (847 males and 728 females at baseline compared with 334 males and 250 females at 24 months).*

Duration of treatment appears to be an important factor in the effect of GH on QoL. In the prospective long-term study by Wirén *et al.* [27] 71 GH-deficient adults were treated with GH for 20–50 months. NHP part I mean overall score (concerning problems with emotional reaction, sleep, energy, pain, physical mobility and social life) significantly improved during the first 6 months and remained at the new level thereafter. Scores in all areas of the NHP part II (covering patient problems in paid employment, house work, social life, family life, sex life, hobbies and holidays) improved significantly between baseline and 20–50 months, as did the total score and five (anxiety, depression, well-being, self-control and vitality) of six area scores on the PGWB index. The total PGWB score and three area scores (depression, self-control and vitality) improved significantly between 6 or 12 months and 20–50 months. In the retrospective stage, 92.7% of the patients reported that they had experienced positive effects of GH therapy. In 30.3% of patients, however, such effects did not become apparent until GH had been administered for more than 6 months. This study suggests that once started, GH therapy should be continued for at least 6 months before any judgement is made regarding its efficacy in improving QoL. Wallymahmed *et al.* [29] found that, compared with baseline levels, energy increased at 6 and 12 months in a group of GH-deficient adults on GH therapy. In patients continuing on GH, energy levels continued to improve after 2 years, but then fell after 3 years. A similar pattern was observed for emotional reactions. Only improvements in self-esteem, which were apparent after 6 months, were maintained throughout the 3 years of the study. The authors speculated that the initial improvements in subjective well-being might have led to greater expectations and a desire for further improvement, which may not occur beyond 2 years of GH replacement.

The long-term effects of GH replacement on QoL have been addressed in studies lasting for up to 10 years [28, 35]. Gilchrist *et al.* [28] observed improvements in the energy and vitality subsections of the NHP and PGWB, respectively, after

9 years of GH treatment. A significant improvement in the overall NHP score and the energy and emotional subsections in GH-treated patients in comparison with the untreated GH-deficient group was observed by Gibney *et al.* [35] after 10 years of GH therapy.

In addition to the self-rating inventories, an evaluation of behaviour by spouses during placebo and GH replacement was made in one study, as it was thought that a family member would be less likely to be subject to a placebo effect [3]. The partners observed marked effects after treatment with GH but not after placebo (Table 1).

Results are disparate when patients with CO- and AO-GHD are compared. In an unselected cohort of patients, Attanasio *et al.* [11] observed a significant improvement in QoL, in terms of physical mobility and energy, after 18 months in patients with AO-GHD, whereas patients with CO-GHD showed no long-term changes. Murray *et al.* [12] studied a selected cohort of GH-deficient patients with the most impaired QoL. Patients with AO-GHD expressed greater distress at baseline, and those with CO-GHD showed a capacity for improvement equal to or even greater than that seen in AO-GHD.

A recent study by Stouthart *et al.* [36] addressed the question of the effect of discontinuation and restart of GH treatment on QoL in young adults with CO-GHD. They studied 22 patients (11 with IGHD and 11 with MPHD) for 1 year following discontinuation of GH and 20 patients (including nine of the original group) for 1 year after the restart of GH therapy. The number of psychological complaints and reports of depression increased only during the first 6 months of discontinuation. In the first 6 months of GH treatment anxiety decreased and QoL improved. During the 2-year discontinuation and treatment period, intra-subject levels of insulin-like growth factor I were negatively correlated with depression, fatigue, tension and anxiety and positively with vigour and memory. At the end of the treatment

Table 1. *Questionnaire responses from the partners of 36 adult patients with GHD who had been treated in a cross-over trial for 21 months with either GH or placebo. The values indicate the percentages of yes responses to the different short questions. Significance was evaluated by the χ^2 test. Reproduced from [3] with permission. Copyright 1995, The Endocrine Society.*

	Placebo	**GH**	***p* value**
More alert (%)	0.0	69.0	< 0.0001
More active (%)	3.7	51.8	< 0.001
Higher endurance (%)	3.6	60.7	< 0.0001
Less easily annoyed (%)	7.1	28.6	< 0.1
Less worried (%)	6.9	37.9	< 0.05
More extrovert (%)	3.4	37.9	< 0.01
More industrious (%)	3.3	46.7	< 0.001
More happy (%)	11.1	48.1	< 0.01
Better looks (%)	10.3	51.7	< 0.01
More satisfied with his/her occupation (%)	7.7	34.6	< 0.05
Fewer family conflicts (%)	3.4	24.1	< 0.1
Better personal relationships (%)	3.4	34.5	< 0.01

period, all psychometric parameters were similar or even improved compared with those at the start of the discontinuation period. It is concluded that 1 year of discontinuation of GH treatment leads to a decrease in QoL within 6 months, which is counteracted within 6 months after the restart of GH treatment.

Cost of illness to society

Untreated GHD clearly represents a significant health burden to the patient; however, there are also costs to society. In recent years, studies have assessed the cost of GHD to society both directly, in terms of the money spent on the resources used by patients, and indirectly, in terms of loss of productivity in the workplace. Hypopituitary patients who were not receiving GH replacement were found to use more healthcare and social resources and to have reduced productivity compared with the general population [37, 38]. Analysis of 199 adult hypopituitary patients with suspected GHD revealed a healthcare cost per individual 1.9 times higher than that of age-matched controls [37]. In addition, patients with hypopituitarism took more days of sick leave and were more likely to have drawn a disability pension compared with age- and sex-matched controls. Similarly, Hakkaart-van Roijen *et al.* [38] reported that patients with hypopituitarism took twice as many sick days, made more annual visits to general practitioners and specialists, spent more days in hospital and were more likely to be unable to carry out paid work due to health problems, compared with the general population.

More recently, the effects of GH therapy on the use of healthcare resources and QoL were evaluated in an analysis of data from 304 patients enrolled in KIMS [39]. Details of the patient's personal situation and use of social care and healthcare resources during the preceding 6 months were recorded before receiving GH and 12 months after the start of treatment using the KIMS Patient Life Situation Form (see Appendix C). After 6–12 months of GH treatment there was a significant reduction in the amount of sick leave, number of visits to the doctor and number of days in hospital. There was also a reduction in the need for assistance with daily activities, although this was only significant for men. In addition, there was a significant improvement in QoL as measured by QoL-AGHDA, and a significant increase in physical activity and patients' levels of satisfaction with physical activity after 12 months of GH replacement therapy. Interestingly, the significant decrease in the use of healthcare resources was correlated with improvements in QoL-AGHDA.

Possible mechanisms of the effects of GH on the brain and well-being

The mechanisms responsible for the influence of GH on psychological function and perceived well-being are not well understood, although several hypotheses have been suggested. These propose that GH has positive effects on body composition and exercise capacity [40], as well as normalizing extracellular water volume [6], improving left ventricular function [41] and changing brain biochemistry [42]. GH binding sites have been demonstrated in several areas of the central nervous system (CNS) of man. The most abundant are in the choroid plexus, but they are also found in the pituitary, hypothalamus and hippocampus [43]. The hippocampus is considered to play a central role in learning and memory and is a part of the limbic system, which is involved in affective behaviour. The binding sites in the choroid plexus are suggested to be the place of transport of GH across the blood–brain barrier [43]. Subcutaneous administration of GH is associated with an increase of GH in the cerebrospinal fluid (CSF) [42, 44]. Administration of GH is also accompanied by changes in the concentration of neurotransmitters and their metabolites (homovanillic acid – a metabolite of dopamine, β-endorphin, aspartate and others) in the CSF [42, 44, 45]. The monoamine system is considered to be involved in mood disorders. Changes in dopamine metabolism in the CNS induced by GH might therefore be one of the potential mechanisms for the action of GH on psychological state. Another suggested mechanism is through the effect of GH on the metabolism of thyroid hormones, with an enhanced conversion of free thyroxine to tri-iodothyronine [44, 46].

Currently, it is not clear whether any of the above, alone or in combination, constitute the key mechanism underlying the beneficial effect of GH replacement on psychological function.

Conclusions

Psychological problems, with loss of energy, emotional lability, low mood, social isolation and impairment of perceived QoL, have recently become widely recognized as a part of the GHD syndrome. Both patients with IGHD and those with MPHD display similar disturbances. More severe impairment in QoL (psychosocial distress) is observed in patients with AO-GHD than in those with CO-GHD.

The majority of studies investigating the effects of GH replacement have shown that QoL improves with treatment; however, the results are not uniform. When patients are selected for impaired QoL a clear improvement in QoL is demonstrated and it is proportional to the degree of impairment before commencing therapy. Once started, GH therapy should be continued for at least 6 months before any judgement is made regarding its efficacy in improving QoL. Long-term studies have now shown a positive effect of GH therapy over 10 years. Discontinuation of GH treatment leads to a decrease in QoL within 6 months, the effect of which is counteracted within 6 months of the restart of GH treatment. Despite extensive research into GHD and the effect of GH replacement therapy, the mechanisms responsible for the influence of GH on psychological functions and perceived well-being remain poorly understood.

References

1. Raben MS. Growth hormone. Clinical use of human growth hormone. N Engl J Med 1962;266:82–6
2. Human growth hormone (somatropin) in adults with growth hormone deficiency. National Institute for Clinical Excellence Technology Appraisal 64 2003
3. Burman P, Broman JE, Hetta J, Wiklund I, Erfurth EM, Hagg E, Karlsson FA. Quality of life in adults with growth hormone (GH) deficiency: response to treatment with recombinant human GH in a placebo-controlled 21-month trial. J Clin Endocrinol Metab 1995;80:3585–90
4. McGauley GA. Quality of life assessment before and after growth hormone treatment in adults with growth hormone deficiency. Acta Paediatr Scand Suppl 1989;356:70–2
5. McGauley GA, Cuneo RC, Salomon F, Sönksen PH. Psychological well-being before and after growth hormone treatment in adults with growth hormone deficiency. Horm Res 1990;33 (Suppl 4):52–4
6. Rosén T, Wirén L, Wilhelmsen L, Wiklund I, Bengtsson B-Å. Decreased psychological well-being in adult patients with growth hormone deficiency. Clin Endocrinol (Oxf) 1994;40:111–6
7. Wallymahmed ME, Baker GA, Humphris G, Dewey M, MacFarlane IA. The development, reliability and validity of a disease specific quality of life model for adults with growth hormone deficiency. Clin Endocrinol (Oxf) 1996;44:403–11
8. Rotnem D, Genel M, Hintz RL, Cohen DJ. Personality development in children with growth hormone deficiency. J Am Acad Child Psychiatry 1977;16:412–26
9. Dean HJ, McTaggart TL, Fish DG, Friesen HG. The educational, vocational, and marital status of growth hormone-deficient adults treated with growth hormone during childhood. Am J Dis Child 1985;139:1105–10
10. Björk S, Jönsson B, Westphal O, Levin JE. Quality of life of adults with growth hormone deficiency: a controlled study. Acta Paediatr Scand Suppl 1989; 356:55–9
11. Attanasio AF, Lamberts SW, Matranga AM, Birkett MA, Bates PC, Valk NK, Hilsted J, Bengtsson B-Å, Strasburger CJ. Adult growth hormone (GH)-deficient patients demonstrate heterogeneity between childhood onset and adult onset before and during human GH treatment. Adult Growth Hormone Deficiency Study Group. J Clin Endocrinol Metab 1997;82:82–8
12. Murray RD, Skillicorn CJ, Howell SJ, Lissett CA, Rahim A, Smethurst LE, Shalet SM. Influences on quality of life in GH deficient adults and their effect on response to treatment. Clin Endocrinol (Oxf) 1999; 51:565–73
13. Li Voon Chong JS, Groves T, Foy P, Wallymahmed ME, MacFarlane IA. Elderly people with hypothalamic–pituitary disease and untreated GH deficiency: clinical outcome, body composition, lipid profiles and quality of life after 2 years compared to controls. Clin Endocrinol (Oxf) 2002;56:175–81
14. Degerblad M, Almkvist O, Grunditz R, Hall K, Kaijser L, Knutsson E, Ringertz H, Thorén M. Physical and psychological capabilities during substitution

therapy with recombinant growth hormone in adults with growth hormone deficiency. Acta Endocrinol (Copenh) 1990;123:185–93

15. Whitehead HM, Boreham C, McIlrath EM, Sheridan B, Kennedy L, Atkinson AB, Hadden DR. Growth hormone treatment of adults with growth hormone deficiency: results of a 13-month placebo controlled cross-over study. Clin Endocrinol (Oxf) 1992;36:45–52

16. Holmes SJ, McKenna SP, Doward LC, Shalet SM. Development of a questionnaire to assess the quality of life of adults with growth hormone deficiency. Endocrinol Metab 1995;2:63–9

17. Badia X, Lucas A, Sanmarti A, Roset M, Ulied A. One-year follow-up of quality of life in adults with untreated growth hormone deficiency. Clin Endocrinol (Oxf) 1998;49:765–71

18. Wirén L, Whalley D, McKenna S, Wilhelmsen L. Application of a disease-specific, quality-of-life measure (QoL-AGHDA) in growth hormone-deficient adults and a random population sample in Sweden: validation of the measure by Rasch analysis. Clin Endocrinol (Oxf) 2000;52:143–52

19. Abs R, Bengtsson B-Å, Hernberg-Ståhl E, Monson JP, Tauber JP, Wilton P, Wüster C. GH replacement in 1034 growth hormone deficient hypopituitary adults: demographic and clinical characteristics, dosing and safety. Clin Endocrinol (Oxf) 1999;50:703–13

20. Bengtsson B-Å, Abs R, Bennmarker H, Monson JP, Feldt-Rasmussen U, Hernberg-Ståhl E, Westberg B, Wilton P, Wüster C. The effects of treatment and the individual responsiveness to growth hormone (GH) replacement therapy in 665 GH-deficient adults. KIMS Study Group and the KIMS International Board. J Clin Endocrinol Metab 1999;84:3929–35

21. Wallymahmed ME, Foy P, MacFarlane IA. The quality of life of adults with growth hormone deficiency: comparison with diabetic patients and control subjects. Clin Endocrinol (Oxf) 1999;51:333–8

22. Lynch S, Merson S, Beshyah SA, Skinner E, Sharp P, Priest RG, Johnston DG. Psychiatric morbidity in adults with hypopituitarism. J R Soc Med 1994;87:445–7

23. Simpson H, Savine R, Sönksen P, Bengtsson B-Å, Carlsson L, Christiansen JS, Clemmons D, Cohen P, Hintz R, Ho K, Mullis P, Robinson I, Strasburger C, Tanaka T, Thorner M. Growth hormone replacement therapy for adults: into the new millennium. Growth Horm IGF Res 2002;12:1–33

24. Page RC, Hammersley MS, Burke CW, Wass JA. An account of the quality of life of patients after treatment for non-functioning pituitary tumours. Clin Endocrinol (Oxf) 1997;46:401–6

25. Caroll PV, Littlewood R, Weissberger AJ, Bogalho P, McGauley G, Sönksen PH. The effects of two doses of replacement growth hormone on the biochemical, body composition and psychological profiles of growth hormone-deficient adults. Eur J Endocrinol 1997; 137:146–53

26. Mardh G, Lundin K, Borg G, Jönsson B, Lindeberg A. Growth hormone replacement therapy in adult hypopituitary patients with growth hormone deficiency: combined data from 12 European placebo-controlled clinical trials. Endocrinol Metab 1994;1 (Suppl A):43–9

27. Wirén L, Bengtsson B-Å, Johannsson G. Beneficial effects of long-term GH replacement therapy on quality of life in adults with GH deficiency. Clin Endocrinol (Oxf) 1998;48:613–20

28. Gilchrist FJ, Murray RD, Shalet SM. The effect of long-term untreated growth hormone deficiency (GHD) and 9 years of GH replacement on the quality of life (QoL) of GH-deficient adults. Clin Endocrinol (Oxf) 2002;57:363–70

29. Wallymahmed ME, Foy P, Shaw D, Hutcheon R, Edwards RH, MacFarlane IA. Quality of life, body composition and muscle strength in adult growth hormone deficiency: the influence of growth hormone replacement therapy for up to 3 years. Clin Endocrinol (Oxf) 1997;47:439–46

30. Baum HB, Katznelson L, Sherman JC, Biller BM, Hayden DL, Schoenfeld DA, Cannistraro KE, Klibanski A. Effects of physiological growth hormone (GH) therapy on cognition and quality of life in patients with adult-onset GH deficiency. J Clin Endocrinol Metab 1998;83:3184–9

31. Cuneo RC, Judd S, Wallace JD, Perry-Keene D, Burger H, Lim-Tio S, Strauss B, Stockigt J, Topliss D, Alford F, Hew L, Bode H, Conway A, Handelsman D, Dunn S, Boyages S, Cheung NW, Hurley D. The Australian multicenter trial of growth hormone (GH) treatment in GH-deficient adults. J Clin Endocrinol Metab 1998; 83:107–16

32. Murray RD, Skillicorn CJ, Howell SJ, Lissett CA, Rahim A, Shalet SM. Dose titration and patient selection increases the efficacy of GH replacement in severely GH deficient adults. Clin Endocrinol (Oxf) 1999;50:749–57

33. Holmes SJ, Shalet SM. Factors influencing the desire for long-term growth hormone replacement in adults. Clin Endocrinol (Oxf) 1995;43:151–7

34. KIMS Annual Report. 2002; Number 5:4–11

35. Gibney J, Wallace JD, Spinks T, Schnorr L, Ranicar A, Cuneo RC, Lockhart S, Burnand KG, Salomon F, Sönksen PH, Russell-Jones D. The effects of 10 years

of recombinant human growth hormone (GH) in adult GH-deficient patients. J Clin Endocrinol Metab 1999;84:2596–602

36. Stouthart PJ, Deijen JB, Roffel M, Delemarre-van de Waal HA. Quality of life of growth hormone (GH) deficient young adults during discontinuation and restart of GH therapy. Psychoneuroendocrinology 2003;28:612–26

37. Ehrnborg C, Hakkaart-Van Roijen L, Jonsson B, Rutten FF, Bengtsson B-Å, Rosén T. Cost of illness in adult patients with hypopituitarism. Pharmacoeconomics 2000;17:621–8

38. Hakkaart-van Roijen L, Beckers A, Stevenaert A, Rutten FF. The burden of illness of hypopituitary adults with growth hormone deficiency. Pharmacoeconomics 1998;14:395–403

39. Hernberg-Ståhl E, Luger A, Abs R, Bengtsson B-Å, Feldt-Rasmussen U, Wilton P, Westberg B, Monson JP. Healthcare consumption decreases in parallel with improvements in quality of life during GH replacement in hypopituitary adults with GH deficiency. J Clin Endocrinol Metab 2001;86:5277–81

40. Jørgensen JO, Pedersen SA, Thuesen L, Jørgensen J, Ingemann-Hansen T, Skakkebæk NE, Christiansen JS. Beneficial effects of growth hormone treatment in GH-deficient adults. Lancet 1989;1:1221–5

41. Caidahl K, Edén S, Bengtsson B-Å. Cardiovascular and renal effects of growth hormone. Clin Endocrinol (Oxf) 1994;40:393–400

42. Johansson JO, Larson G, Andersson M, Elmgren A, Hynsjo L, Lindahl A, Lundberg PA, Isaksson OG, Lindstedt S, Bengtsson B-Å. Treatment of growth hormone-deficient adults with recombinant human growth hormone increases the concentration of growth hormone in the cerebrospinal fluid and affects neurotransmitters. Neuroendocrinology 1995;61:57–66

43. Lai ZN, Emtner M, Roos P, Nyberg F. Characterization of putative growth hormone receptors in human choroid plexus. Brain Res 1991;546:222–6

44. Burman P, Hetta J, Wide L, Mansson JE, Ekman R, Karlsson FA. Growth hormone treatment affects brain neurotransmitters and thyroxine. Clin Endocrinol (Oxf) 1996;44:319–24

45. Burman P, Deijen JB. Quality of life and cognitive function in patients with pituitary insufficiency. Psychother Psychosom 1998;67:154–67

46. Jørgensen JO, Pedersen SA, Laurberg P, Weeke J, Skakkebæk NE, Christiansen JS. Effects of growth hormone therapy on thyroid function of growth hormone-deficient adults with and without concomitant thyroxine-substituted central hypothyroidism. J Clin Endocrinol Metab 1989;69:1127–32

20 Transition of growth hormone-deficient patients from paediatric to adult endocrinologists

William M Drake
Department of Endocrinology, St Bartholomew's Hospital, London, UK

Summary

While the benefits of growth hormone (GH) therapy in adult hypopituitary patients with GH deficiency (GHD) are well established, the role of continued GH therapy after achievement of final height in adolescent GH-deficient patients remains unclear. Preliminary data suggest that cessation of GH therapy on completion of linear growth may be associated with impairment of somatic development and adverse changes in body composition. However, the classic syndrome of adult GHD does not obviously evolve, at least over the first 12 months following discontinuation of GH. While larger studies of longer duration than those currently available are clearly needed to gather longitudinal data, large databases of outcomes research, such as KIMS – Pfizer International Metabolic Database – are likely to provide additional information on the aetiology and management of GHD in transition. For the present time, the decision of whether to continue GH treatment in adolescent patients with GHD is probably best made on an individual basis. For such patients, continuity of care is crucial. Children and adults with GHD are usually managed by physicians in separate departments, who may focus on different aspects of treatment and care. Close collaboration between paediatric and adult physicians is essential to ensure smooth transition and to minimize the drop-out rate from follow-up. Given the previous, often lengthy, period of treatment during childhood, paediatric physicians should be best placed to discuss with the patient the potential benefits of continuing GH therapy and instigate retesting of spontaneous GH secretion. Many, but not all, children with isolated idiopathic GHD will produce GH responses within the normal range if retested when adult height is achieved. Patients with multiple pituitary hormone deficits are more likely to have ongoing GHD, as are patients who have received radiotherapy to the hypothalamic–pituitary region. Quality of life does not appear to be decreased in adolescents with GHD who stop treatment, so achievement of satisfactory bone mass is likely to be the main determinant of the decision of whether to continue therapy. In the absence of clear data regarding optimum GH dosing schedules, it seems reasonable to titrate the dose in order to avoid serum concentrations of insulin-like growth factor I above the age-adjusted normal range, as is current practice in the treatment of hypopituitary adults with GHD.

Introduction

The benefits of treating severely growth hormone (GH)-deficient children with recombinant human GH, in order to facilitate linear growth, are firmly established. If therapy is commenced sufficiently early and continued for long enough, affected children achieve adult heights that are within the normal range [1]. Given that growth failure is the universal presenting feature of GH deficiency (GHD) in children, the goal of therapy has, traditionally, been entirely statural, with cessation of treatment taking place when a satisfactory adult height is attained. Indeed, for many patients, this is likely to have been predicted by the child's physician at the start of treatment. The relatively recent recognition of a characteristic clinical syndrome associated with failure of spontaneous GH secretion in adults, and the fact that many of its features are favourably influenced by treatment with GH [2, 3], raises the possibility that, for some patients, GH therapy may need to continue beyond the completion of linear growth. This, in turn, demands a critical re-evaluation of the process by which adolescent GH-deficient patients are best transferred from the care of a paediatric endocrinologist into an adult endocrine clinic. This chapter addresses some of the important issues relating to 'transition care' of GH-deficient patients and highlights some important unanswered questions.

Retesting for ongoing GHD at the completion of growth

A substantial proportion of children with isolated GHD (IGHD) will have recovered normal GH reserve by the time adult height is attained [4]. This is particularly likely in those previously diagnosed with partial GHD (i.e. peak GH, 10–20 mU/L [3.3–6.7 μg/L]) on dynamic testing or low 24-hour integrated GH secretion. Patients with multiple pituitary hormone deficits (MPHD), with or without structural pituitary or peri-pituitary disease, are more likely to have ongoing GHD [5]. Previous radiotherapy involving the hypothalamic–pituitary region is also a strong predictor of ongoing GHD [6]. However, examples clearly exist both of patients with IGHD in childhood who subsequently satisfy the criteria for severe GHD when retested as adults, and of children with MPHD who have normal GH reserve on retesting [7]. Hence, although it seems reasonable to advise patients with IGHD (particularly those with 'borderline' diagnostic results) that they are unlikely to require ongoing GH therapy into adult life, retesting of GH reserve is mandatory in all patients on completion of linear growth, as there is a possibility that GHD may persist into adulthood.

Current guidelines from a consensus meeting on the diagnosis of GHD in adults suggest that two biochemical tests of GH status are required in patients with IGHD, whereas a single GH-provocation test is sufficient in patients with MPHD [8]. This has been advised because the peak GH concentrations obtained in patients with IGHD typically vary depending on the particular test used, making the results of a single test unreliable. In contrast, measurements of peak GH concentrations in patients with MPHD are typically reliable irrespective of the test used. The insulin tolerance test (ITT) remains the 'gold standard' for testing GH reserve and has been shown to be safe and reliable when performed in experienced endocrine units, provided that there is strict adherence to the exclusion criteria [9, 10]. An alternative test in patients for whom the ITT is contraindicated (or as the second test in patients with IGHD) is the combined arginine/GH-releasing hormone test [8]. In adolescents, as in adults, a serum concentration of insulin-like growth factor I (IGF-I) below the lower end of the age-adjusted normal range is highly suggestive of GHD in patients with MPHD [7].

Effects of discontinuation of GH at final height

Although it is clear that many of the adverse pathophysiological features of the adult GHD syndrome are improved by GH replacement [2, 3], such observations do not provide sufficient basis for the continuation of GH therapy in GH-deficient adolescents once growth is complete. Nor is it satisfactory to quote data from studies in which patients with childhood-onset GHD (CO-GHD) have subsequently been treated with GH in adult life, as such studies have usually been initiated several years after the discontinuation of GH therapy. As adult patients with CO-GHD have lower serum IGF-I levels, a lower lean body mass (LBM), reduced height, less reduction in quality of life (QoL) and less marked derangement of serum lipoprotein levels than patients with adult-onset GHD (AO-GHD), it has been argued that the two should be considered as separate entities [11]. Given that the rationale for continuing GH treatment is partly to prevent adult GHD, it is appropriate to review whether withdrawal of GH therapy in this patient group is associated with adverse pathological changes.

Body composition

Observational discontinuation studies provide some evidence that withdrawal of GH therapy in adolescents who have completed their growth is associated with adverse changes in body composition [12, 13]. Although both studies were small (eight and six patients respectively), analysis of these and other, similar, studies suggests that withdrawal of GH at the completion of final height is associated with a decrease in muscle strength and an increase in fat mass [14]. However, such studies require cautious interpretation on account of the fact that a substantial proportion of patients treated with GH replacement in childhood show evidence of normal GH status by the time they achieve final height [4, 15, 16].

Vahl *et al.* [17] randomized 19 patients either to placebo or to continue with their regular paediatric weight-based GH dose, 2.0–5.0 IU/day (0.7–1.7 mg/day), for 12 months after the cessation of linear growth, followed by a further 12 months of GH therapy in all patients. No change in LBM was evident over 1 year in either group, but there was a significant increase in LBM when placebo-treated patients subsequently restarted GH (Fig. 1). Total body fat (TBF) increased significantly in the placebo-treated patients, but this was largely reversed during the open-label GH phase of the study. Interestingly, despite this change in TBF, there were no significant differences in insulin sensitivity between the two groups [18].

In a recent, preliminary, report of a UK multicentre study of similar design, 24 adolescent patients either stopped GH therapy or continued with a weight-based dosing regimen of 0.35 IU/kg/week (0.12 mg/kg/week) for 12 months [19]. In those who discontinued GH therapy, LBM remained static. In contrast, there was an increase in LBM of approximately 4% in patients who continued GH. No statistically significant change in total, truncal or percentage fat was observed in either group, although a trend towards an increase in all three measures was noted in patients who discontinued GH. Despite these increases in fat mass, there was a significant improvement in insulin sensitivity following cessation of GH, as determined by the short ITT. A similar, non-significant, trend in insulin sensitivity was observed when assessed by a homeostatic model. No changes in insulin sensitivity were noted using either method in patients remaining on GH therapy.

The results of these two studies are not completely consistent with the established adult model of hypopituitarism, in which increased central adiposity is associated with relative insulin resistance. This highlights the complexity of the role of GH in modulating physical development and insulin sensitivity in adolescence. It is possible that the anabolic actions of GH are partly mediated via an indirect effect on insulin secretion. The 'insulin antagonistic' effects of GH are postulated to be due, at least in part, to its lipolytic action, with consequent mobilization of free fatty acids. This leads to Randle cycle substrate competition between glucose and lipid fuels in the periphery, increased insulin secretion and a state of partially compensated hyperinsulinaemia [20]. If this model is correct, then a relative insulin-resistant state caused by GH action may, potentially, be advantageous to the adolescent patient because of the increased anabolism associated with higher circulating insulin concentrations. Larger studies, of longer duration, will be required to determine whether the classic body composition of adult GHD evolves in adolescent GH-deficient patients

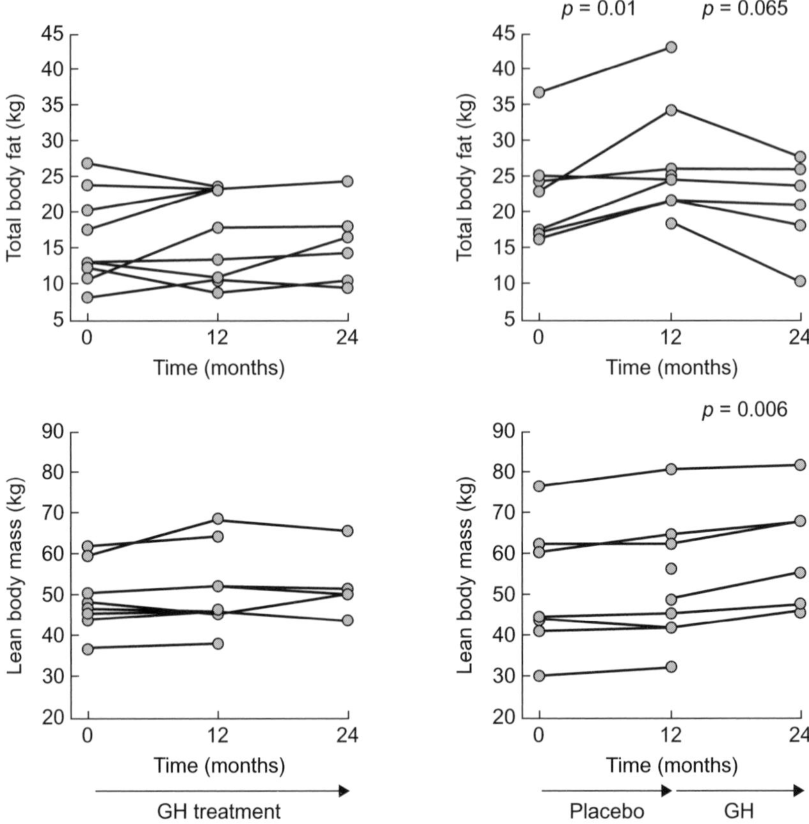

__Figure 1.__ Total body fat and lean body mass in young adults with childhood-onset GHD, assessed from dual-energy X-ray absorptiometry scans. Measurements were taken at baseline, after 12 months of GH replacement or placebo, and after a further 12 months during which both groups received GH. Reproduced from [17] with permission. Copyright 2000, The Endocrine Society.

and to define the role of GH in determining insulin sensitivity at this stage of life.

Bone mineral density (BMD)

Peak bone mass (PBM), defined as the highest level of bone mass achieved as a result of normal growth, together with subsequent age-related loss, is an important determinant of an individual's risk of osteoporosis-related fracture in later life [21, 22]. During puberty, areal bone mineral content (BMC) and BMD increase four- to sixfold over 3 years (11–14 years of age in girls and 13–16 years of age in boys) [22], such that approximately 37% of skeletal mass is acquired between pubertal stages 2 and 5 [22]. Increased gonadal steroid secretion around the time of puberty is the most important hormonal regulator of bone accretion, but the anabolic effects of GH *in vitro*, together with the beneficial effects of GH replacement on bone remodelling and BMD in adult hypopituitarism, have highlighted the possible role of GH in the attainment of PBM.

Patients with CO-GHD are relatively osteopenic compared with age-matched healthy controls [23, 24]. This is true both for patients with IGHD and those with MPHD [24], suggesting that it is the GHD *per se*, rather than inadequate/supraphysiological replacement of deficient anterior pituitary hormones, that is the cause of the low bone mass. However, cross-sectional studies using dual-energy X-ray absorptiometry should be interpreted with caution, as an important determinant of areal BMD is bone size [25] (see Chapter 13 for discussion of methods for studying bone metabolism). Hence, it is possible that the observed deficits in bone mass were due, at least in part, to a period of untreated GHD prior to the commencement of childhood therapy and/or to suboptimal replacement of GH. The latter possibility is supported by the observation that patients treated with recombinant human GH have a greater bone mass than patients with similar aetiologies of GHD treated with cadaveric GH [26].

A recent UK multicentre study examined the skeletal consequences of continuation/discontinuation of GH therapy in 24 adolescent patients treated with GH in childhood [27]. At the completion of linear growth, all of these patients had ongoing severe GHD as assessed using adult criteria. Continuation of GH at a fixed weight-based dose of 0.35 IU/kg/week (0.12 mg/kg/week) was associated with an increment in whole body BMC approximately 3% greater than that observed in patients who discontinued GH (6% rise in the patients who continued GH treatment versus 3% in those who discontinued GH). This extra increase in BMC would represent 2 years of bone loss later in life in a typical postmenopausal woman [28]. Interestingly, the 6% increase in BMC in those who continued GH approximates to that observed in previous longitudinal studies in healthy adolescents [21, 22] and parallels the change in LBM reported in the same cohort of patients [19]. The discrepancy between the groups was less marked with respect to lumbar spine BMD than whole body BMC, suggesting that GH facilitates bone accretion at both cortical and trabecular sites.

The mechanism underlying the apparent disadvantage of those patients who discontinued GH was not clearly identified. Although the fall in bone-specific alkaline phosphatase (BAP) between 0 and 6 months in those who discontinued GH is suggestive of a reduction in osteoblastic activity as the cause of reduced bone mineral accretion, the similar reduction in BAP observed between 6 and 12 months in those who continued GH would also be compatible with the decline in bone markers seen at the end of normal puberty. A larger study examining the relationship between baseline markers of bone turnover and subsequent bone mineral accretion is required to clarify this point.

In a separate 2-year study, Shalet *et al.* [29] randomized 149 young adults who had received GH treatment during childhood and discontinued treatment upon attainment of adult height to one of three groups, receiving no treatment or a GH dose of 25.0 μg/kg/day (paediatric dose) or 12.5 μg/kg/day (adult dose). Unlike the study reported above [27], however, the time since discontinuing GH therapy varied between 6 weeks and 5 years. Results showed that in the control group mean BMC increased by 5.6% over 2 years; a figure strikingly similar to the 3% observed over 1 year by Drake *et al.* [27]. In patients treated with GH, however, BMC increased by 9.5% (adult dose) and 8.1% (paediatric dose), further supporting the notion that withdrawal of GH replacement in young adult patients with GHD limits the progression towards PBM. Interestingly, marked variability in the BMC response was observed in patients treated with GH and, although not formally analysed, it is possible that the variability in time since discontinuation of GH is one source of the heterogeneity of response. This, in turn, highlights the important clinical point that certain patients may be further than others from PBM at the time of completion of linear growth (and may therefore have more to gain by continuation of GH) (Fig. 2). There is a need for further studies to establish whether a 'sabbatical' from GH therapy at final height, followed by reintroduction at a later date, has adverse consequences for bone accrual.

Markers of cardiovascular risk

In adolescent GH-deficient patients there is no evidence that discontinuation of GH results in the characteristic derangement of the lipid profile seen in patients with AO-GHD; however, it is important to note that the duration of both studies was only 12 months [17–19], and such data should be interpreted in the light of the obvious complexity of the role of GH in determining insulin sensitivity in this age group. Larger studies of longer duration will be required to determine whether this

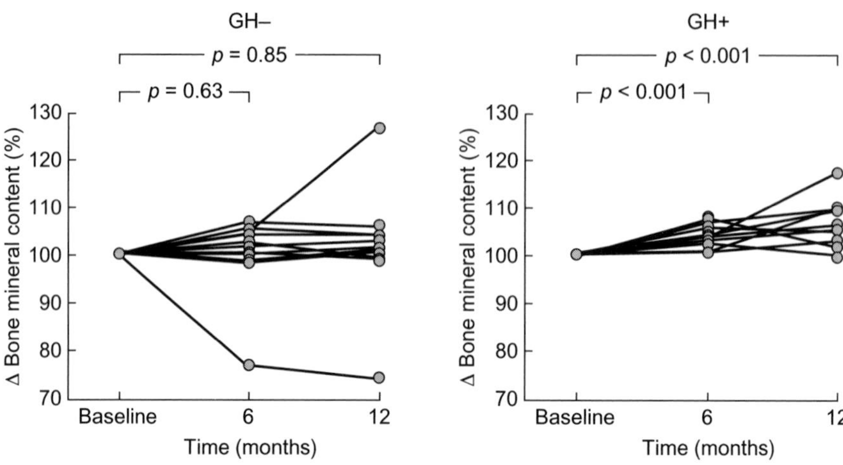

Figure 2. *Percentage change in total body bone mineral content over time in young adult patients with GHD, who continued (GH+) or discontinued (GH–) GH therapy. Measurements were taken at baseline and at 6 months and 12 months after continuing or discontinuing GH therapy. Reproduced from [27] with permission. Copyright 2003, The Endocrine Society.*

aspect of the adult GHD syndrome evolves in adolescent GH-deficient patients. No data from continuation/discontinuation studies are currently available regarding fibrinogen, plasminogen-activating inhibitor or intima–media thickness in this patient group.

In summary, there is preliminary evidence that withdrawal of GH therapy on completion of linear growth in GH-deficient adolescents may be associated with impaired somatic development and adverse changes in body composition. To date, there is little evidence that such patients are significantly disadvantaged in terms of QoL, insulin sensitivity or surrogate markers of cardiovascular risk. It is clear that the role of GH in determining insulin sensitivity in this age group and the evolution of this aspect of the adult GHD phenotype requires further clarification.

Options for GH therapy at completion of growth

In the absence of compelling data to justify widespread continuation of GH into adult life, and the lack of evidence that a delay in re-introducing therapy has deleterious consequences, several possible strategies exist. One approach would involve the seamless continuation of GH into adult life, with only a brief cessation of therapy to allow re-assessment of GH status. A second option, given that the greatest short-term benefit of GH replacement in adult life is improved well-being, would be to offer GH replacement only to those patients who demonstrate the greatest disadvantage in terms of QoL on withdrawal of GH at final height. A proportion of adult patients with GHD, particularly those with CO-GHD, report an entirely normal QoL when off treatment [11]. Hence, a period of cessation of GH would help to determine whether GH therapy is likely to be symptomatically beneficial. The practice of universal continuation of GH from childhood to adulthood would not identify such patients. In addition, compliance with therapy is likely to be improved in patients who experience a period of symptomatic GHD prior to subsequent recommencement of GH therapy. A third strategy would be to continue with GH for some years after linear growth is complete in order to facilitate the development of PBM, followed by discontinuation of therapy with subsequent re-evaluation.

Dosing strategies for the adolescent patient with GHD

The optimum dosing schedule for patients with GHD in 'transition' remains unclear. In paediatric practice, the dose of GH is usually calculated according to weight or surface area, without biochemical monitoring. This strategy, however, does not allow for inter-individual variability in GH sensitivity or residual GH secretion. Doses of GH used in paediatric patients nearing the completion of linear growth are approximately three- to sixfold greater than the average dose used for adult GH replacement, an observation consistent with the decline in normal GH secretion following the completion of puberty [30, 31]. Clearly, it is not possible to recreate normal GH physiology with a single subcutaneous injection of GH. Therefore, as with other forms of endocrine replacement therapy (such as glucocorticoids for patients with primary or secondary adrenal failure), the goal of therapy is to maximize the clinical benefit, whilst minimizing the risks of excess GH exposure. There is no biological marker in adults that is the equivalent of linear growth in a child by which to judge the efficacy of GH replacement. QoL, the main indication for GH therapy in adult hypopituitarism, is less deranged in patients with CO-GHD, and it is far from clear whether the typical adult GHD phenotype evolves in adolescent patients who discontinue GH at final height. Furthermore, symptoms of GH excess are less common in patients with CO-GHD treated with weight-based GH doses than in those with AO-GHD using similar dosing regimens. This creates the possibility that continuation of a weight-based GH dose to promote full physical maturation may be associated with asymptomatic elevation of serum IGF-I concentrations. The long-term implications of supraphysiological levels of IGF-I in this patient group are unknown. However, by analogy with acromegaly, the likely effects on insulin resistance, hypertension and left ventricular hypertrophy suggest that supraphysiological levels of IGF-I should be avoided. Recent reports, suggesting a link between circulating IGF-I levels in the upper part of the normal range with the risk of developing breast and prostate cancer in normal individuals, emphasize the need for caution in this regard [32–34].

Against this background, a number of different approaches may be taken to GH dosing in adolescent patients, with the most appropriate method depending, at least in part, on the timing of the re-initiation of GH after re-testing. If GH therapy is stopped for a period of time following completion of growth, then restarting treatment at a low dose with titration according to the serum IGF-I response (i.e. the standard practice in adults) seems most appropriate [35]. However, various other options exist if GH is continued seamlessly into adult life. A low-dose titration regimen could be instituted as soon as the decision has been made to continue treatment. However, the dose required to normalize serum IGF-I levels in adolescents who have just completed linear growth is likely to be closer to paediatric than adult doses, and achieving an appropriate maintenance dose may take some time. It may therefore be more appropriate initially to continue treatment at the paediatric dose and gradually to titrate down according to serum IGF-I levels. A further potential approach would be to continue GH at the higher paediatric dose until completion of somatic development, in order to allow maximal accrual of bone and muscle mass, prior to reduction to the conventional adult dose. Irrespective of the regimen adopted, robust age-related reference ranges for serum IGF-I and other GH-dependent markers are mandatory.

Some important unanswered questions

In adult clinical practice, most cases of GHD arise on a background of structural pituitary/peri-pituitary disease and/or its treatment. In contrast, the causes of ongoing GHD in adolescent patients treated with GH in childhood are more varied. They include pituitary/peri-pituitary tumours, abnormalities of pituitary development (e.g. transcription factor defects and septo-optic dysplasia) and external beam irradiation for intracranial/head and neck neoplasms. This means that it is unlikely that a single centre, using a single protocol, will accumulate sufficient cases to answer specific questions about, and guide treatment for, each of these groups of causes of ongoing GHD in adolescents. Large international databases, such as KIMS – Pfizer International Metabolic Database – in which data are recorded during longitudinal follow-up in a conventional clinical setting, may identify subtle differences in GH efficacy in certain rare aetiologies of GHD. KIMS may also allow early detection of important safety issues (such as tumour relapse rates) that may not be apparent from a single-centre experience.

Arrangements for handover of patients

Aside from the paucity of data regarding the merits of continuation of GH therapy in GH-deficient adolescents, and the uncertainty about optimum dosing schedules, completion of linear growth and subsequent full somatic maturation occur at a time when the patient's commitment to ongoing therapy and medical supervision may be suboptimal [36]. Furthermore, adults and children with GHD are usually managed by physicians in separate departments, with particular focus on different clinical endpoints. Thus, an adolescent patient may be required to discuss with a new physician the possibility that GH therapy may have potential advantages (cardiovascular risk, body composition, future risk of osteoporotic fracture) that are of limited immediate relevance. Under these circumstances, it is clearly imperative that adult and paediatric endocrinologist should have a close working relationship, and that each physician should have detailed knowledge of the clinical issues during the transition period that are conventionally undertaken by their adult/paediatric colleague. For example, paediatric endocrinologists should have sufficient understanding of the role of GH in determining body composition and PBM in order to introduce the possibility that GH therapy may need to continue beyond the completion of linear growth. Similarly, if transfer occurs before the completion of linear growth, adequate auxological expertise and competence in the supervision of the final stages of puberty should be available in the adult clinic. Given that the patient's care has been supervised by a paediatric physician up to the point of transition, it seems logical that the initial onus for re-testing and discussion of the potential merits of continuing with GH should lie in his/her hands. Thereafter, although the details will vary between units, it is the joint responsibility of both adult and paediatric physicians to ensure full and seamless transition. Although the paediatric endocrinologist may have a long-standing clinical relationship with the patient and his/her parents, it is clearly imperative, throughout the transition process, to respect the fact that the patient is now a legally competent adult.

Key points for seamless transition of care from paediatric to adult endocrinologist

- Paediatricians should have a working knowledge of the adult GHD syndrome in order to introduce the possibility that GH therapy may need to continue.
- Paediatricians should initiate retesting for ongoing GHD.
- Adult physicians should have knowledge and experience of the latter stages of pubertal development.
- Adequate access to densitometry and auxology in late adolescence and early adulthood.
- Access to a laboratory testing IGF-I levels using a robust reference range.
- Adolescents and young adults should have access to oncology services (if GHD has a tumour origin and in the event of recurrence/relapse).
- Liaison with the patient's family physician is necessary to ensure that the transfer of responsibility for specialist care is clearly understood.

Conclusions

Although the benefits of GH therapy in adult hypopituitary patients with clinical GHD syndrome are well established, the role of continued GH therapy beyond the completion of linear growth in adolescent GH-deficient patients remains unclear. There are preliminary data to suggest that cessation of GH once adult height is achieved may be associated with impairment of somatic development. However, the classic adult GHD body composition phenotype does not develop clearly, at least over the first 12 months following discontinuation of GH. Larger studies, of longer duration, are required in order to clarify these issues. In the meantime, the decision of whether to continue with GH into adult life is likely to be made on an individual basis. In adolescents with GHD, QoL appears to be minimally deranged and so achievement of satisfactory bone mass with full somatic maturation is likely to be the main criteria for deciding whether to continue GH therapy. In the absence of clear data regarding optimum dosing schedules, it seems reasonable to adopt the clinical practice of dose titration during transition, avoiding serum IGF-I concentrations above the age-adjusted normal range. Close collaboration between paediatric and adult physicians is necessary to ensure seamless transition and to minimize the rate of default from follow-up.

References

1. Blethen SL, Baptista J, Kuntze J, Foley T, LaFranchi S, Johanson A. Adult height in growth hormone (GH)-deficient children treated with biosynthetic GH. The Genentech Growth Study Group. J Clin Endocrinol Metab 1997;82:418–20

2. Jørgensen JO, Pedersen SA, Thuesen L, Jørgensen J, Ingemann-Hansen T, Skakkebæk NE, Christiansen JS. Beneficial effects of growth hormone treatment in GH-deficient adults. Lancet 1989;1:1221–5

3. Salomon F, Cuneo RC, Hesp R, Sönksen PH. The effects of treatment with recombinant human growth hormone on body composition and metabolism in adults with growth hormone deficiency. N Engl J Med 1989;321:1797–803

4. Tauber M, Moulin P, Pienkowski C, Jouret B, Rochiccioli P. Growth hormone (GH) retesting and auxological data in 131 GH-deficient patients after completion of treatment. J Clin Endocrinol Metab 1997;82:352–6

5. Toogood AA, Shalet SM. Diagnosis of severe growth hormone (GH) deficiency in young adults who received GH replacement therapy during childhood. Acta Paediatr Suppl 1997;423:117–20

6. Nicolson A, Toogood AA, Rahim A, Shalet SM. The prevalence of severe growth hormone deficiency in adults who received growth hormone replacement in childhood. Clin Endocrinol (Oxf) 1996;44:311–6

7. Shalet SM, Toogood A, Rahim A, Brennan BM. The diagnosis of growth hormone deficiency in children and adults. Endocr Rev 1998;19:203–23

8. Consensus guidelines for the diagnosis and treatment of adults with growth hormone deficiency: summary statement of the Growth Hormone Research Society Workshop on Adult Growth Hormone Deficiency. J Clin Endocrinol Metab 1998;83:379–81

9. Lange M, Svendsen OL, Skakkebæk NE, Müller J, Juul A, Schmiegelow M, Feldt-Rasmussen U. An audit of the insulin-tolerance test in 255 patients with pituitary disease. Eur J Endocrinol 2002;147:41–7

10. Jones SL, Trainer PJ, Perry L, Wass JA, Bessser GM, Grossman A. An audit of the insulin tolerance test in adult subjects in an acute investigation unit over one year. Clin Endocrinol (Oxf) 1994;41:123–8

11. Attanasio AF, Lamberts SW, Matranga AM, Birkett MA, Bates PC, Valk NK, Hilsted J, Bengtsson B-Å, Strasburger CJ. Adult growth hormone (GH)-deficient patients demonstrate heterogeneity between childhood onset and adult onset before and during human GH treatment. Adult Growth Hormone Deficiency Study Group. J Clin Endocrinol Metab 1997;82:82–8

12. Rutherford OM, Jones DA, Round JM, Buchanan CR, Preece MA. Changes in skeletal muscle and body composition after discontinuation of growth hormone treatment in growth hormone deficient young adults. Clin Endocrinol (Oxf) 1991;34:469–75

13. Colle M, Auzerie J. Discontinuation of growth hormone therapy in growth hormone-deficient patients: assessment of body fat mass using bioelectrical impedance. Horm Res 1993;39:192–6

14. de Boer H, van der Veen EA. Why retest young adults with childhood-onset growth hormone deficiency? J Clin Endocrinol Metab 1997;82:2032–6

15. Wacharasindhu S, Cotterill AM, Camacho-Hubner C, Besser GM, Savage MO. Normal growth hormone secretion in growth hormone insufficient children retested after completion of linear growth. Clin Endocrinol (Oxf) 1996;45:553–6

16. Johannsson G, Albertsson-Wikland K, Bengtsson B-Å. Discontinuation of growth hormone (GH) treatment: metabolic effects in GH-deficient and GH-sufficient adolescent patients compared with control subjects. Swedish Study Group for Growth Hormone Treatment in Children. J Clin Endocrinol Metab 1999;84:4516–24

17. Vahl N, Juul A, Jørgensen JO, Ørskov H, Skakkebæk NE, Christiansen JS. Continuation of growth hormone

(GH) replacement in GH-deficient patients during transition from childhood to adulthood: a two-year placebo-controlled study. J Clin Endocrinol Metab 2000;85:1874–81

18. Nørrelund H, Vahl N, Juul A, Møller N, Alberti KG, Skakkebæk NE, Christiansen JS, Jørgensen JO. Continuation of growth hormone (GH) therapy in GH-deficient patients during transition from childhood to adulthood: impact on insulin sensitivity and substrate metabolism. J Clin Endocrinol Metab 2000;85:1912–7

19. Carroll PV, Drake WM, Metcalfe KA, Maher KT, Savage MO, Dunger DB, Shaw NJ, Cheetham TD, Camacho-Hubner C, Monson JP. Growth hormone (GH) treatment is an important regulator of insulin sensitivity in the adolescent with severe GH-deficiency. The Endocrine Society's 84th Annual Meeting 2002 Jun 19–22; San Francisco, USA. P3–578

20. Randle PJ, Garland PB, Hales CN, Newsholme EA. The glucose fatty-acid cycle. Its role in insulin sensitivity and the metabolic disturbances of diabetes mellitus. Lancet 1963;1:785–9

21. Bonjour JP, Theintz G, Buchs B, Slosman D, Rizzoli R. Critical years and stages of puberty for spinal and femoral bone mass accumulation during adolescence. J Clin Endocrinol Metab 1991;73:555–63

22. Matkovic V, Jelic T, Wardlaw GM, Ilich JZ, Goel PK, Wright JK, Andon MB, Smith KT, Heaney RP. Timing of peak bone mass in Caucasian females and its implication for the prevention of osteoporosis. Inference from a cross-sectional model. J Clin Invest 1994; 93:799–808

23. Kaufman JM, Taelman P, Vermeulen A, Vandeweghe M. Bone mineral status in growth hormone-deficient males with isolated and multiple pituitary deficiencies of childhood onset. J Clin Endocrinol Metab 1992; 74:118–23

24. de Boer H, Blok GJ, van Lingen A, Teule GJ, Lips P, van der Veen EA. Consequences of childhood-onset growth hormone deficiency for adult bone mass. J Bone Miner Res 1994;9:1319–26

25. Genant HK, Engelke K, Fuerst T, Gluer CC, Grampp S, Harris ST, Jergas M, Lang T, Lu Y, Majumdar S, Mathur A, Takada M. Non-invasive assessment of bone mineral and structure: state of the art. J Bone Miner Res 1996;11:707–30

26. Saggese G, Baroncelli GI, Bertelloni S, Barsanti S. The effect of long-term growth hormone (GH) treatment on bone mineral density in children with GH deficiency. Role of GH in the attainment of peak bone mass. J Clin Endocrinol Metab 1996;81:3077–83

27. Drake WM, Carroll PV, Maher KT, Metcalfe KA, Camacho-Hubner C, Shaw NJ, Dunger DB, Cheetham TD, Savage MO, Monson JP. The effect of cessation of growth hormone (GH) therapy on bone mineral accretion in GH-deficient adolescents at the completion of linear growth. J Clin Endocrinol Metab 2003; 88:1658–63

28. Effects of hormone therapy on bone mineral density: results from the postmenopausal estrogen/progestin interventions (PEPI) trial. The Writing Group for the PEPI. JAMA 1996;276:1389–96

29. Shalet SM, Shavrikova E, Cromer M, Child CJ, Keller E, Zapletalova J, Moshang T, Blum WF, Chipman JJ, Quigley CA, Attanasio AF. Effect of growth hormone (GH) treatment on bone in postpubertal GH-deficient patients: a 2-year randomized, controlled, dose-ranging study. J Clin Endocrinol Metab 2003;88:4124–9

30. Zadik Z, Chalew SA, McCarter RJ Jr, Meistas M, Kowarski AA. The influence of age on the 24-hour integrated concentration of growth hormone in normal individuals. J Clin Endocrinol Metab 1985;60:513–6

31. Iranmanesh A, Lizarralde G, Veldhuis JD. Age and relative adiposity are specific negative determinants of the frequency and amplitude of growth hormone (GH) secretory bursts and the half-life of endogenous GH in healthy men. J Clin Endocrinol Metab 1991;73:1081–8

32. Chan JM, Stampfer MJ, Giovannucci E, Gann PH, Ma J, Wilkinson P, Hennekens CH, Pollak M. Plasma insulin-like growth factor-I and prostate cancer risk: a prospective study. Science 1998;279:563–6

33. Wolk A, Mantzoros CS, Andersson SO, Bergstrom R, Signorello LB, Lagiou P, Adami HO, Trichopoulos D. Insulin-like growth factor 1 and prostate cancer risk: a population-based, case-control study. J Natl Cancer Inst 1998;90:911–5

34. Hankinson SE, Willett WC, Colditz GA, Hunter DJ, Michaud DS, Deroo B, Rosner B, Speizer FE, Pollak M. Circulating concentrations of insulin-like growth factor-I and risk of breast cancer. Lancet 1998;351: 1393–6

35. Drake WM, Howell SJ, Monson JP, Shalet SM. Optimizing GH therapy in adults and children. Endocr Rev 2001;22:425–50

36. Monson JP. Conditions spanning paediatric and adult endocrine practice – the adult perspective. Acta Paediatr Suppl 1997;423:124–6

21 Growth hormone (GH) deficiency and GH replacement in the elderly

Antonia M Brooke and John P Monson

Department of Endocrinology, St Bartholomew's and The Royal London, Queen Mary's School of Medicine and Dentistry, University of London, London, UK

Summary

Normal ageing is associated with a progressive decline in growth hormone (GH) secretion, and several features of GH deficiency (GHD) are similar to those of normal ageing. GH-deficient patients can, however, be distinguished from the normal ageing population by dynamic testing of GH secretion and clinical features. Improvements in quality of life (QoL), body composition and lipoprotein profile have been demonstrated in hypopituitary patients aged over 60 years who received GH replacement compared with normal elderly subjects. Analysis of large numbers of patients according to sex and age in KIMS – Pfizer International Metabolic Database – has shown similar baseline clinical characteristics in patients with GHD across a range of ages, although elderly female patients had a poorer cardiovascular risk profile compared with younger female patients. The KIMS analysis also confirmed that the benefits of GH replacement, in terms of improvement in waist circumference, serum low-density lipoprotein-cholesterol and QoL, occurred in patients of all ages. Thus, in the absence of a specific contra-indication, elderly GH-deficient patients should be considered for GH replacement therapy.

Introduction

Growth hormone deficiency (GHD) in adults results in a well-recognized constellation of clinical symptoms and signs. However, normal ageing is also associated with a progressive decline in growth hormone (GH) secretion. It is therefore important to distinguish between the effects of physiological decline in serum GH with age and those of GHD associated with pituitary or peri-pituitary disease in older subjects. It is also important to establish whether GHD in older subjects can be diagnosed using standard methods and if clinical features and responses to treatment are similar to those observed in younger patients.

Normal ageing

Normal ageing is associated with a decline in GH secretion of 14% per decade of adult life after puberty [1]. This is, in part, due to an augmentation of somatostatinergic tone, as acute GH responsiveness in elderly subjects is increased by the administration of arginine [2, 3]. Several features of GHD, such as increased abdominal adiposity, reduced strength and exercise capacity, increased social isolation and impaired psychological well-being are similar to those of normal ageing. It is important to question whether acquired GHD should be distinguished from the effects of normal ageing but also whether symptoms associated with normal ageing can be improved with additional GH treatment.

Several studies have examined baseline clinical parameters and the response to additional GH in the normal ageing population. Ageing is a specific negative determinant of GH secretory burst frequency and amplitude [4]. Serum insulin-like growth factor I (IGF-I) levels have been shown to be inversely related to adiposity [1]. In normal ageing there is a reduction in lean body mass (LBM). Rudman and colleagues [5] showed, in an open trial, that 6 months of additional GH in normal elderly men, with a predictably physiologically low serum IGF-I, resulted in an increase in LBM and a reduction in adipose tissue mass.

Other placebo-controlled double-blind studies of GH treatment in normal elderly men and women have confirmed Rudman's findings on body composition, but found no change in muscle strength or maximal oxygen uptake during exercise [6–8]. In studies involving normal elderly people serum IGF-I levels increase into the young adult reference range. The long-term effects of this are not known. Studies to date in normal elderly subjects indicate that the effects of GH treatment are subtle and functional benefits have not been documented.

Diagnosis of GHD

Given the marginal effects of GH therapy in the normal elderly population, it is important to establish if GHD in older hypopituitary patients can be distinguished from normal GH secretory status in the elderly population. Up to 87% of the individual values of serum IGF-I in patients with GHD over the age of 65 years are in the age-related reference range [9], but GH is only one stimulus for hepatic IGF-I production; insulin and nutrition are also important. There are differences in GH secretion in older hypopituitary patients compared with age-matched controls. GH-deficient patients aged over 65 years have a 90% reduction in spontaneous GH secretion [10]. These patients are also distinguishable from age-matched controls on dynamic testing. The responses to insulin-induced hypoglycaemia (using the insulin tolerance test) and intravenous arginine are decreased in elderly hypopituitary patients compared with age-matched controls [11, 12] and therefore remain valuable diagnostic tools for GHD in the elderly.

Clinical features

It is important to assess whether older patients with GHD have similar clinical features and signs to those found in younger GH-deficient patients, or whether they are similar to the normal elderly population. Elderly GH-deficient patients have abnormal fat deposits, with an increase in total and regional fat mass compared with age-matched controls; however, LBM is not significantly reduced [13]. Bone turnover is reduced in GH-deficient patients, but this does not appear to impact significantly on bone mineral density (BMD), possibly because of the overriding influence of oestrogen deficiency in the female cohorts [14].

Analyses from KIMS – Pfizer International Metabolic Database – have facilitated the study of large numbers of patients according to sex and age group at baseline, prior to initiation of GH replacement and after 6 and 12 months of therapy [15, 16]. In the second KIMS study [16], clinical characteristics were studied in patients aged over 65 years (170 patients) compared with those younger than 65 years (1395 patients). The latter group was further subdivided into patients aged under 45, 45–55 and 55–65 years. Craniopharyngioma was more prevalent in patients aged under 65 years, and pituitary adenoma more common in those over 65 years. The methods used to diagnose GHD were similar in the two age groups. Mean peak stimulated serum GH was significantly lower in females over 65 years of age compared with females under 65 years of age, but values in men were similar. The IGF-I SD score (SDS) was significantly higher in females over 65 years compared with younger patients, but values in males were similar across the age groups. Patients over 65 years of age tended to have a longer duration of pituitary disease.

There were predictable differences in baseline clinical characteristics between patients aged over 65 years and younger patients (Tables 1 and 2) [16]. Mean glycosylated haemoglobin (HbA_{1C}) and

Table 1. *Baseline body mass index (BMI), waist/hip ratio, lipoprotein profiles, glycosylated haemoglobin (HbA_{1C}), systolic and diastolic blood pressure (BP), prevalence of hypertension, prevalence of diabetes mellitus and Quality of Life Assessment of GHD in Adults (QoL-AGHDA) score in male patients with GHD aged above 65 and below 65 years in KIMS. Data are shown as means ± SD; HDL, high-density lipoprotein; LDL, low-density lipoprotein.*

	Age > 65 years	**Age < 65 years**	***p* value**
BMI (kg/m^2)	28.1 ± 4.2	28.9 ± 4.9	0.18
Waist/hip ratio	0.97 ± 0.06	0.97 ± 0.09	0.35
Total cholesterol (mmol/L)	5.79 ± 1.07	5.94 ± 1.25	0.71
LDL-cholesterol (mmol/L)	3.76 ± 0.93	3.85 ± 1.17	0.95
HDL-cholesterol (mmol/L)	1.20 ± 0.36	1.15 ± 0.33	0.28
Triglycerides (mmol/L)	1.90 ± 0.92	2.23 ± 1.41	0.17
Systolic BP (mmHg)	141.3 ± 18.9	129.6 ± 17.5	< 0.0001
Diastolic BP (mmHg)	83.3 ± 10.4	80.9 ± 11.2	< 0.02
HbA_{1C} (%)	5.34 ± 0.76	5.07 ± 0.85	< 0.003
Prevalence of hypertension (%)	24.0	16.6	0.063
Prevalence of diabetes mellitus (%)	3.9	4.2	0.86
QoL-AGHDA score	7.9 ± 6.4	9.0 ± 6.6	0.19

Table 2. *Baseline body mass index (BMI), waist/hip ratio, lipoprotein profiles, glycosylated haemoglobin (HbA_{1C}), systolic and diastolic blood pressure (BP), prevalence of hypertension, prevalence of diabetes mellitus and Quality of Life Assessment of GHD in Adults (QoL-AGHDA) score in female patients with GHD aged above 65 and below 65 years in KIMS. Data are shown as means ± SD; HDL, high-density lipoprotein; LDL, low-density lipoprotein.*

	Age > 65 years	**Age < 65 years**	***p* value**
BMI (kg/m^2)	29.9 ± 5.5	28.2 ± 6.0	< 0.02
Waist/hip ratio	0.90 ± 0.07	0.86 ± 0.07	< 0.01
Total cholesterol (mmol/L)	6.70 ± 1.52	6.12 ± 1.27	< 0.01
LDL-cholesterol (mmol/L)	4.42 ± 1.41	3.85 ± 1.08	< 0.02
HDL-cholesterol (mmol/L)	1.24 ± 0.33	1.39 ± 0.38	< 0.02
Triglycerides (mmol/L)	2.27 ± 1.09	2.05 ± 1.96	< 0.02
Systolic BP (mmHg)	142.4 ± 20.7	125.7 ± 17.9	< 0.0001
Diastolic BP (mmHg)	81.0 ± 9.7	79.4 ± 10.5	0.18
HbA_{1C} (%)	5.58 ± 0.99	5.12 ± 0.90	< 0.002
Prevalence of hypertension (%)	43.1	13.6	< 0.0001
Prevalence of diabetes mellitus (%)	12.3	3.8	< 0.002
QoL-AGHDA score	10.9 ± 6.1	11.5 ± 6.8	0.47

systolic blood pressure were significantly higher in patients aged over 65 years. Mean diastolic pressure was higher in older men only (Table 1), but the prevalence of diagnosed hypertension was higher in older compared with younger women (Table 2). Older women had an increase in body mass index, waist/hip ratio, low-density lipoprotein (LDL)-cholesterol and reported diabetes mellitus, and a reduction in high-density lipoprotein-cholesterol compared with younger females (Table 2), but there were no significant differences in these measurements in males (Table 1).

Psychological well-being was assessed using the Quality of Life Assessment of GHD in Adults (QoL-AGHDA, see Appendix B) [17]. This is a GH-sensitive questionnaire, which has excellent reliability and cross-cultural comparability and is useful as a means of assessing change in QoL during GH replacement [18]. A higher score, to a maximum of 25, represents a poorer QoL. Although QoL-AGHDA was designed on the basis of interviews with middle-aged GH-deficient patients, and therefore may not focus on issues particularly relevant to the elderly, such as independence, it is still a useful means of assessing change associated with treatment. The QoL-AGHDA scores at baseline in the study population were higher in females than males, but there was no difference across the age groups.

Treatment

Many of the clinical features of GHD may be particularly relevant in the elderly. Increased fracture risk [19, 20], increased LDL-cholesterol and apolipoprotein B levels, decreased left ventricular function [21], accelerated atherogenesis [22], decreased sweating and impaired thermoregulation [23] and the psychological aspects of GHD – leading to social isolation – may all impact adversely in the older patient.

In general, patients with GHD show an increase in BMD after 12–24 months of GH replacement. The increase amounts to approximately 12% over the long term. GH replacement also lowers cholesterol and increases exercise capacity [24]. It has also been shown that GH replacement results in a reduction in the percentage of patients requiring assistance with activities of daily living and use of hospital resources over 24 months of treatment [25]. If these effects of GH replacement are evident in the elderly with GHD this would predict a very favourable impact on QoL, morbidity, and mortality from macrovascular disease and hip fractures.

Single-centre studies and analyses of the KIMS database have demonstrated improvements in QoL, body composition (reduction in fat mass and increase in LBM) and lipoprotein profiles in

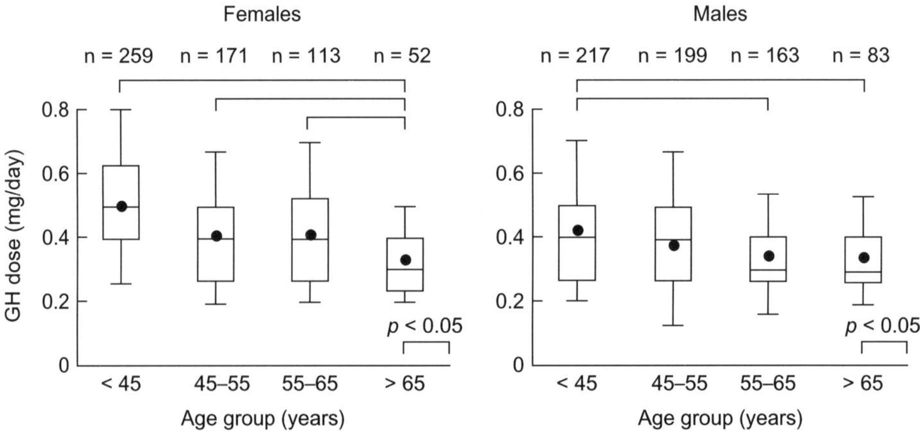

Figure 1. The dose of GH administered to patients in different age groups after 1 year of GH replacement therapy in KIMS. Data are shown as mean (black circles), median and 10th–90th percentile. Reproduced from [16] with permission from S Karger AG, Basel.

hypopituitary adults over 60 years of age given GH replacement, in comparison with normal elderly subjects [15, 26, 27]. Indeed, over 75% of elderly GH-deficient patients expressed a wish to continue GH replacement at the end of one trial [28]. In the studies of Fernholm *et al.*, [27] BMD had not changed significantly by 18 months, but markers of bone turnover were increased, and it remains possible that longer term follow-up may demonstrate a favourable effect on BMD.

A recent KIMS analysis, comparing elderly GH-deficient patients with younger GH-deficient patients treated with GH replacement for 12 months, helps to establish further whether the benefits of treatment are age related [16]. As might be expected, the GH dose required to achieve a similar IGF-I SDS was significantly lower in patients over 65 years of age compared with that in younger age groups (Fig. 1). As the baseline serum concentration of IGF-I is often in the normal range,

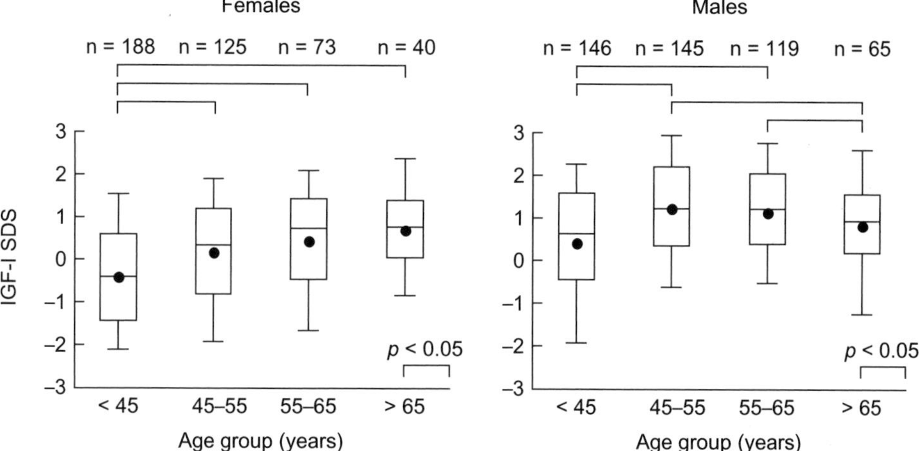

Figure 2. *IGF-I SDS in patients in different age groups after 1 year of GH replacement therapy in KIMS. Data are shown as mean (black circles), median and 10th–90th percentiles. Reproduced from [16] with permission from S Karger AG, Basel.*

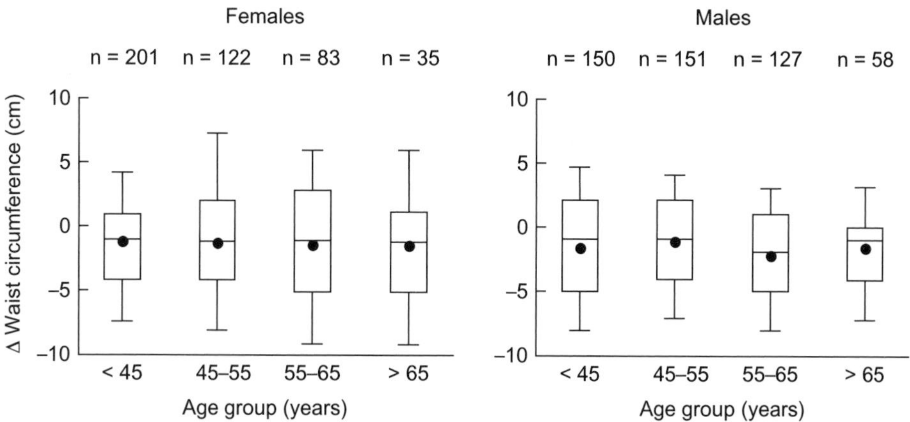

Figure 3. *Change in waist circumference in patients in different age groups after 1 year of GH replacement therapy in KIMS. Data are shown as mean (black circles), median and 10th–90th percentiles. Reproduced from [16] with permission from S Karger AG, Basel.*

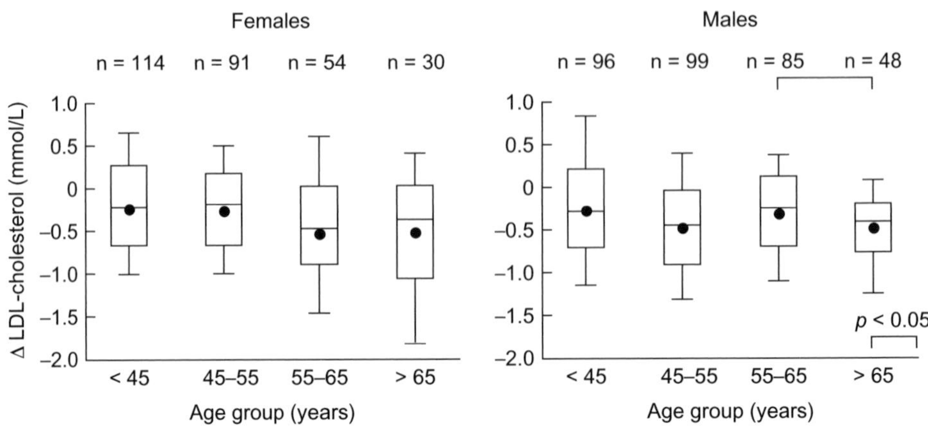

Figure 4. *Change in low-density lipoprotein (LDL)-cholesterol in patients in different age groups after 1 year of GH replacement therapy in KIMS. Data are shown as mean (black circles), median and 10th–90th percentiles. p < 0.0002 for all groups versus baseline. Reproduced from [16] with permission from S Karger AG, Basel.*

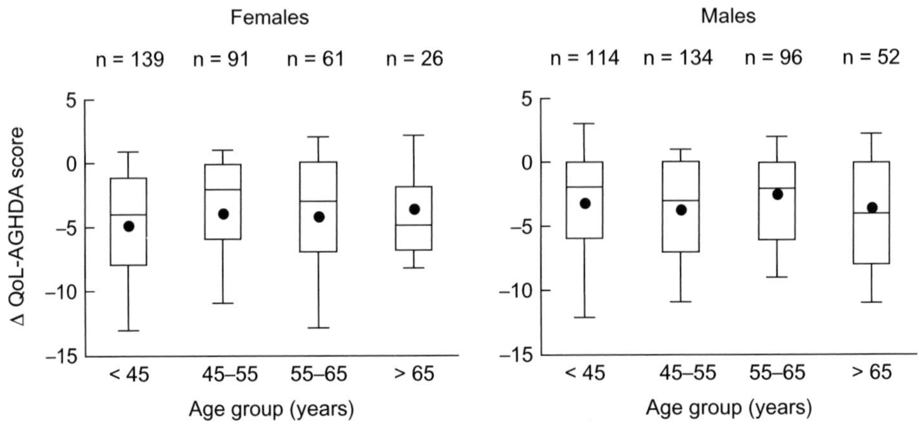

Figure 5. *Change in Quality of Life Assessment of GHD in Adults (QoL-AGHDA) scores in patients in different age groups after 1 year of GH replacement therapy in KIMS. Data are shown as mean (black circles), median and 10th–90th percentiles. Reproduced from [16] with permission from S Karger AG, Basel.*

titrating to the upper part of the reference range is more difficult. Elderly women tended to have an IGF-I SDS higher than younger females, but male patients aged 45–65 years had the highest IGF-I SDS (Fig. 2).

Waist circumference decreased in all age groups in both sexes, and there was no difference in the degree of change between men and women (Fig. 3). Serum total- and LDL-cholesterol decreased during 12 months of GH treatment in all age groups, but was greater in men aged over 65 years compared with younger men; there was no age-related variation in females (Fig. 4). In contrast to observations in the younger age groups, there was no significant increase in fasting blood glucose or HbA_{1C} in older patients. There was no significant change in systolic blood pressure across the ages ranges; however, diastolic blood pressure fell significantly in women aged less than 45 years and men aged over 65 years compared with baseline. Furthermore, the reduction in blood pressure was significantly greater in men aged over 65 years than in those under 55 years and in women aged under 55 years than in those over 65 years. Again, males and females in all the age groups demonstrated an improvement in QoL-AGHDA score over 12 months, with no significant differences across the age ranges (Fig. 5).

This extensive analysis of KIMS data provides additional evidence of the benefits of GH replacement in elderly hypopituitary subjects. Baseline clinical characteristics were qualitatively similar across the age ranges, with older women showing a greater relative degree of adverse change in cardiovascular risk factors in comparison with younger women. Qualitatively similar improvements in waist circumference and serum LDL-cholesterol and quantitatively similar improvements in QoL-AGHDA scores occurred in all age groups.

Conclusions

GHD in the elderly can be diagnosed by conventional dynamic testing, shows the same clinical features and responds to treatment in a similar way to GHD in younger patients. Elderly GH-deficient patients are clinically and biochemically distinguishable from the normal ageing population. In the absence of a specific contraindication, such as active malignancy, they should be considered for GH replacement. The long-term effects on morbidity and mortality are yet to be elucidated but age alone should not be regarded as a contraindication to GH replacement.

Acknowledgements

Antonia Brooke is supported by a clinical training fellowship from St Bartholomew's and The Royal London Charitable Foundation. The Department of Endocrinology at St Bartholomew's Hospital receives research support from Pharmacia (Pfizer) Corporation for its work on GH and growth factors.

References

1. Rudman D, Kutner MH, Rogers CM, Lubin MF, Fleming GA, Bain RP. Impaired growth hormone secretion in the adult population: relation to age and adiposity. J Clin Invest 1981;67:1361–9

2. Arvat E, Gianotti L, Grottoli S, Imbimbo BP, Lenaerts V, Deghenghi R, Camanni F, Ghigo E. Arginine and growth hormone-releasing hormone restore the blunted growth hormone-releasing activity of hexarelin in elderly subjects. J Clin Endocrinol Metab 1994;79:1440–3

3. Ghigo E, Arvat E, Rizzi G, Bellone J, Nicolosi M, Boffano GM, Mucci M, Boghen MF, Camanni F. Arginine enhances the growth hormone-releasing activity of a synthetic hexapeptide (GHRP-6) in elderly but not in young subjects after oral administration. J Endocrinol Invest 1994;17:157–62

4. Iranmanesh A, Lizarralde G, Veldhuis JD. Age and relative adiposity are specific negative determinants of the frequency and amplitude of growth hormone (GH) secretory bursts and the half-life of endogenous GH in healthy men. J Clin Endocrinol Metab 1991; 73:1081–8

5. Rudman D, Feller AG, Nagraj HS, Gergans GA, Lalitha PY, Goldberg AF, Schlenker RA, Cohn L, Rudman IW, Mattson DE. Effects of human growth hormone in men over 60 years old. N Engl J Med 1990;323:1–6

6. Blackman MR, Sorkin JD, Munzer T, Bellantoni MF, Busby-Whitehead J, Stevens TE, Jayme J, O'Connor KG, Christmas C, Tobin JD, Stewart KJ, Cottrell E, St Clair C, Pabst KM, Harman SM. Growth hormone and sex steroid administration in healthy aged women and men: a randomized controlled trial. JAMA 2002; 288:2282–92

7. Papadakis MA, Grady D, Black D, Tierney MJ, Gooding GA, Schambelan M, Grunfeld C. Growth hormone replacement in healthy older men improves body composition but not functional ability. Ann Intern Med 1996;124:708–16

8. Taaffe DR, Pruitt L, Reim J, Hintz RL, Butterfield G, Hoffman AR, Marcus R. Effect of recombinant human growth hormone on the muscle strength response to resistance exercise in elderly men. J Clin Endocrinol Metab 1994;79:1361–6

9. Toogood AA, Jones J, O'Neill PA, Thorner MO, Shalet SM. The diagnosis of severe growth hormone deficiency in elderly patients with hypothalamic–pituitary disease. Clin Endocrinol (Oxf) 1998;48:569–76

10. Toogood AA, Nass RM, Pezzoli SS, O'Neill PA, Thorner MO, Shalet SM. Preservation of growth hormone pulsatility despite pituitary pathology, surgery, and irradiation. J Clin Endocrinol Metab 1997; 82:2215–21

11. Hoffman DM, Nguyen TV, O'Sullivan AJ, Baxter RC, Ho KK. Diagnosis of growth hormone deficiency in adults. Lancet 1994;344:482–3

12. Toogood AA, O'Neill PA, Shalet SM. Beyond the somatopause: growth hormone deficiency in adults over the age of 60 years. J Clin Endocrinol Metab 1996; 81:460–5

13. Toogood AA, Adams JE, O'Neill PA, Shalet SM. Body composition in growth hormone deficient adults over the age of 60 years. Clin Endocrinol (Oxf) 1996; 45:399–405

14. Toogood AA, Adams JE, O'Neill PA, Shalet SM. Elderly patients with adult-onset growth hormone deficiency are not osteopenic. J Clin Endocrinol Metab 1997;82:1462–6

15. Monson JP, Abs R, Bengtsson B-Å, Bennmarker H, Feldt-Rasmussen U, Hernberg-Ståhl E, Thorén M, Westberg B, Wilton P, Wüster C. Growth hormone deficiency and replacement in elderly hypopituitary adults. KIMS Study Group and the KIMS International Board. Pharmacia and Upjohn International Metabolic Database. Clin Endocrinol (Oxf) 2000;53:281–9

16. Monson JP, Jönsson P. Aspects of growth hormone (GH) replacement in elderly patients with GH deficiency: data from KIMS. Horm Res 2003;60:112–20

17. McKenna SP, Doward LC, Alonso J, Kohlmann T, Niero M, Prieto L, Wirén L. The QoL-AGHDA: an instrument for the assessment of quality of life in adults with growth hormone deficiency. Qual Life Res 1999;8:373–83

18. Abs R, Bengtsson B-Å, Hernberg-Ståhl E, Monson JP, Tauber JP, Wilton P, Wüster C. GH replacement in 1034 growth hormone deficient hypopituitary adults: demographic and clinical characteristics, dosing and safety. Clin Endocrinol (Oxf) 1999;50:703–13

19. Wüster C, Abs R, Bengtsson B-Å, Bennmarker H, Feldt-Rasmussen U, Hernberg-Stähl E, Monson JP, Westberg B, Wilton P. The influence of growth hormone deficiency, growth hormone replacement therapy, and other aspects of hypopituitarism on fracture rate and bone mineral density. J Bone Miner Res 2001;16:398–405

20. Rosén T, Wilhelmsen L, Landin-Wilhelmsen K, Lappas G, Bengtsson B-Å. Increased fracture frequency in adult patients with hypopituitarism and GH deficiency. Eur J Endocrinol 1997;137:240–5

21. Longobardi S, Cuocolo A, Merola B, Di Rella F, Colao A, Nicolai E, Cardei S, Salvatore M, Lombardi G. Left ventricular function in young adults with childhood and adulthood onset growth hormone deficiency. Clin Endocrinol (Oxf) 1998;48:137–43

22. Markussis V, Beshyah SA, Fisher C, Sharp P, Nicolaides AN, Johnston DG. Detection of premature atherosclerosis by high-resolution ultrasonography in symptom-free hypopituitary adults. Lancet 1992; 340:1188–92

23. Juul A, Behrenscheer A, Tims T, Nielsen B, Halkjaer-Kristensen J, Skakkebæk NE. Impaired thermoregulation in adults with growth hormone deficiency during heat exposure and exercise. Clin Endocrinol (Oxf) 1993;38:237–44

24. Nass R, Huber RM, Klauss V, Muller OA, Schopohl J, Strasburger CJ. Effect of growth hormone (hGH) replacement therapy on physical work capacity and cardiac and pulmonary function in patients with hGH deficiency acquired in adulthood. J Clin Endocrinol Metab 1995;80:552–7

25. Hernberg-Ståhl E, Luger A, Abs R, Bengtsson B-Å, Feldt-Rasmussen U, Wilton P, Westberg B, Monson JP. Healthcare consumption decreases in parallel with improvements in quality of life during GH replacement in hypopituitary adults with GH deficiency. J Clin Endocrinol Metab 2001;86:5277–81

26. Toogood AA, Shalet SM. Growth hormone replacement therapy in the elderly with hypothalamic–pituitary disease: a dose-finding study. J Clin Endocrinol Metab 1999;84:131–6

27. Fernholm R, Bramnert M, Hagg E, Hilding A, Baylink DJ, Mohan S, Thoren M. Growth hormone replacement therapy improves body composition and increases bone metabolism in elderly patients with pituitary disease. J Clin Endocrinol Metab 2000;85:4104–12

28. Toogood AA, Shalet SM. Growth hormone deficiency in the elderly. Curr Ther Endocrinol Metab 1997; 6:645–9

22 Advanced pituitary surgery

Rudolf Fahlbusch and Lars Anker
Department of Neurosurgery, University of Erlangen-Nuremberg, Erlangen, Germany

Summary

Surgical removal is still the treatment of choice for the majority of patients with pituitary tumours. Ongoing pharmacological advances have improved the management of pituitary adenomas and give reason to believe that the number of conservatively treated patients will increase in the future. Despite the continuous improvement in the medical treatment of prolactin-, growth hormone (GH)- and thyrotrophin-secreting adenomas, neurosurgeons are still confronted with therapeutic failures for which surgery is required, such as patients who do not respond to, or who experience side-effects from, medication. Furthermore, surgery remains necessary for hormonally inactive adenomas and other tumours of the sella region.

Classic transsphenoidal and transcranial surgical approaches, which have been performed as microsurgical procedures since the introduction of the operation microscope in the early 1970s, are established as effective and safe methods. Their limitations, however, are obvious. Even in experienced hands, total removal of tumours remains dependent on their size, location and invasiveness. Reoperation, in particular, requires a high degree of anatomical information, optical visualization and mechanical guidance for safe and precise surgical procedures and improved outcomes. These are offered mainly by minimally invasive techniques, such as computer-assisted surgery incorporating navigation, endoscopy and intra-operative magnetic resonance imaging. The questions are how far will these new technical tools be able to improve the high current surgical standard, and what are their potentials and limitations?

Parasellar tumours: diagnosis and indications for 'classic' surgery

Diagnosis

Tumours of the pituitary and hypothalamic region can be classified according to clinical appearance, histological diagnosis and location. Within larger neurosurgical series, the leading group of parasellar tumours are pituitary adenomas followed by craniopharyngiomas, which together are regarded as typical pituitary tumours but of different origin (Fig. 1). In pituitary adenomas, the tumours arise from cells of the anterior lobe of the pituitary gland. The origin of craniopharyngiomas lies in embryological development; remnants of Rathke's pouch or the pituitary stalk can develop into an intra- and/or extrasellar tumour. Many other tumours can originate in this area and/or grow into this area, including those resulting from rare diseases that may present with special characteristics.

Common symptoms of these diseases are endocrinological and ophthalmological disturbances. Neurological deficits are rare. The tumour size can vary from a few millimetres, as in

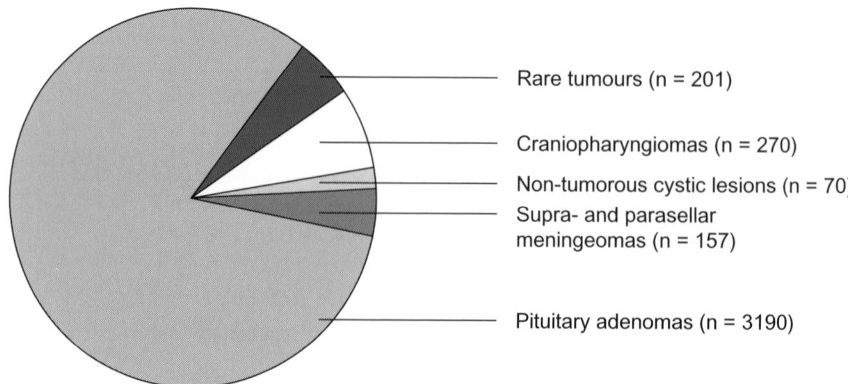

Figure 1. *Distribution of types of hypothalamic–pituitary tumours in a neurosurgical series of 3888 patients (University of Erlangen, Nuremberg Dec 1982–Dec 2002).*

microadenomas producing severe Cushing's disease, to greater than 7 cm, as in tumours that compress the hypothalamic–pituitary axis as well as causing obstruction of the foramen of Monro. Symptomatic occlusive hydrocephalus with headache and increased intracranial pressure can be life-threatening. Compression of important midline structures may be responsible for neuropsychological dysfunction, such as memory deficits and changes in personality.

Magnetic resonance imaging (MRI) is the leading imaging method, which allows for a specific diagnosis in the majority of cases; however, differential diagnosis may be especially difficult in patients with cystic tumours. MRI angiography demonstrates the position of arteries and is replacing conventional angiography. Computed tomography is the leading tool used for identifying bony structures and, especially, the calcification of tumours.

Indications for surgery

Surgery is always indicated if there is no better non-neurosurgical alternative, such as medical treatment, which is established as the treatment of choice in prolactin-producing pituitary adenomas. Radiotherapy is the first choice of treatment in ectopic pinealomas. We distinguish between symptomatic and causal treatment. In the case of hydrocephalus, symptomatic shunt operations are performed to control intracranial pressure. Causal treatment means elimination of the disease, where the goal should be selective tumour resection with preservation of anatomical structure and function. In adenomas, selective adenomectomy is performed rather than hypophysectomy. The hormonally active adenoma is resected, resulting in correction of the hormone excess and preservation of pituitary function. Indications for surgery are based on:

- endocrinological disturbances – deficiency or hypersecretion
- ophthalmological disturbances – chiasm compression and/or optomotoric nerve deficits
- vital indications, such as hydrocephalus, meningitis and rhinoliquorrhoea causing intradural air and, sometimes, in its severest form, tension pneumocephalus.

Contraindications

Contraindications to immediate surgery are severe hypothalamic disturbances, defined as continuous electrolyte and water disturbances, disturbed sleep–wake rhythm and disturbed temperature regulation, as well as caloric disturbances (obesity, cachexia).

From the neurosurgical standpoint, resectable and non-resectable tumours have to be distinguished according to the localization of the tumour and its behaviour with regard to neighbouring structures.

Table 1. Number of patients in Erlangen receiving transsphenoidal (TS), transcranial (TC) and both TS and TC surgical procedures for pituitary adenoma (Dec 1982–Dec 2002).

	Procedures		
Endocrinological classification	**TS**	**TC**	**TS and TC**
Non-secreting	1222	167	70
Prolactin secreting	558	18	6
Growth hormone secreting	716	24	15
Adrenocorticotrophin secreting (Cushing's syndrome)	414	4	1
Nelson tumour	36	4	0
Thyrotrophin secreting	25	2	0
Total	**2971**	**219**	**92**

Factors that limit total resection of the tumour are complete and general involvement or invasion of the cavernous sinus and the hypothalamus, respectively.

In these situations, primary radiotherapy is indicated in practically all cases. Postoperative radiotherapy has to be taken into consideration to control tumour remnants and, more importantly, to prevent recurrence.

Classic surgical approaches

In 90% of all hypothalamic–pituitary tumours, transsphenoidal surgery is indicated (Table 1, Fig. 2) [1, 2]. The nasal approach can be sublabial or transnasal and, in the latter cases, paraseptal or directly through the cavum nasi to the sphenoid sinus. Indications for the transsphenoidal approach include all intra- and suprasellar tumours, particularly microadenomas, but also larger tumours that have developed symmetrically into the suprasellar space [3]. Surgical complications, such as meningitis or cerebrospinal fluid (CSF) leakage are rare (both with an incidence of < 1%) [4].

In 10% of cases, transcranial surgery has to be performed (Table 1, Fig. 3), especially for large asymmetrical suprasellar tumours. In the majority of cases, a fronto-lateral or a pterional approach is sufficient. Today, trepanation itself should no longer produce cosmetic problems. For large supra- and, especially, retrosellar tumours, the bifrontal–subfrontal approach may be indicated. For tumours reaching the lateral ventricles, transventricular or transcallosal approaches may be indicated. In cases where tumours are growing retrosellarly, the lamina terminalis (the anterior wall of the third ventricle) has to be opened. This can be performed either via a pterional or a bifrontal approach.

For very extensive tumours, both approaches should be performed in two stages. In general, the transsphenoidal approach is used first, followed by the transcranial approach (Table 1).

Advanced surgical techniques

Today, surgical procedures are based on microscopic techniques, as well as on more advanced techniques, such as neuronavigation, endoscopy, ultrasound and intra-operative MRI (Tables 2, 3 and 4). These methods are improving intra-operative visualization of anatomical conditions and, to some extent, also the surgical results [5]. Traditionally, invasive procedures have been performed in pituitary surgery using the transsphenoidal approach. Tiny incisions, either sublabially or in the nostril, and a 10–15 cm long

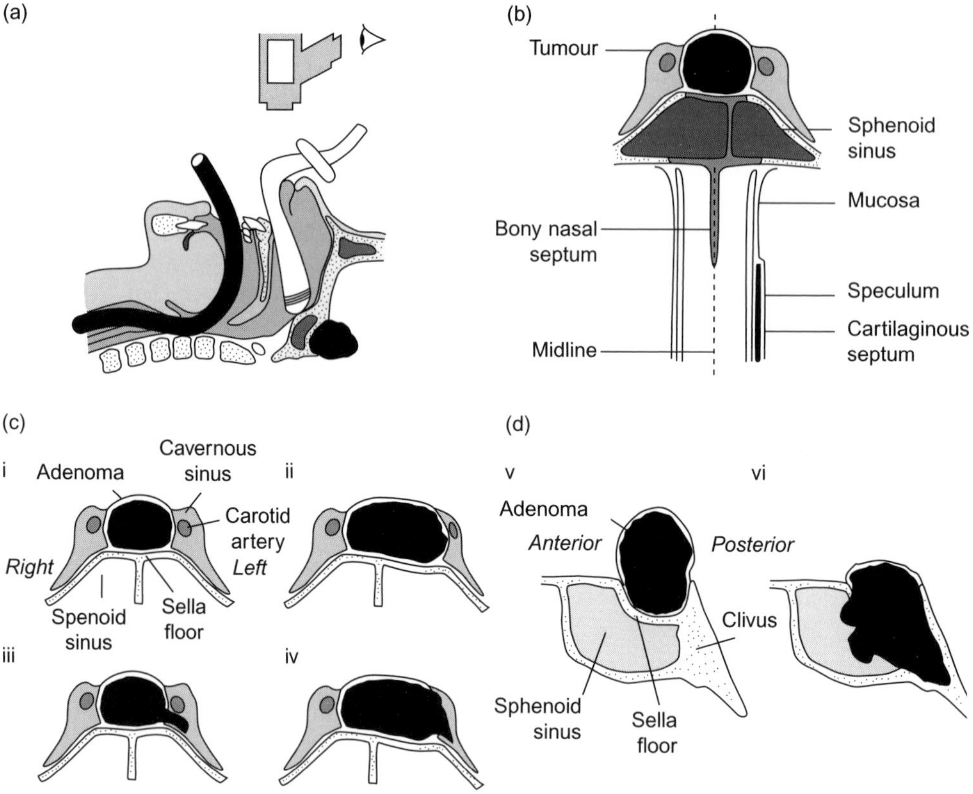

Figure 2. *Principles of the transsphenoidal approach to the sella turcica. (a) Cushing's position of patient with microscope. (b) Endonasal placement of the speculum. (c) Relationship of tumour to cavernous sinus: (i) intrasellar, (ii) compression of cavernous sinus, (iii) focal invasion of cavernous sinus, (iv) global invasion of cavernous sinus (non-resectable). (d) Extrasellar tumour extension: (v) suprasellar extension, (vi) invasion into sphenoid sinus and clivus.*

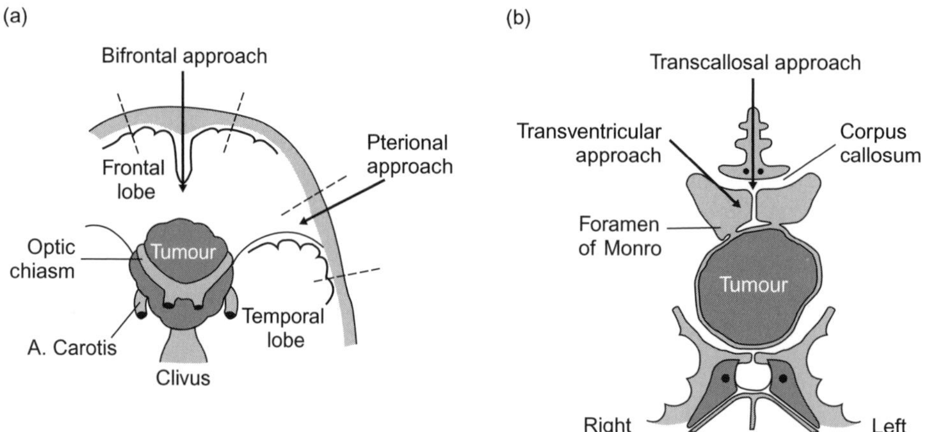

Figure 3. *Transcranial surgery: (a) the subfrontal approach via a bifrontal trepanation and the pterional approach via a fronto-lateral and fronto-temporal trepanation, and (b) the transcallosal and transventricular approaches.*

pernasal narrow tunnel approach, allow for resection of micro and giant adenomas. In some cases, anatomical landmarks are not very obvious for the inexperienced neurosurgeon or even for the expert. These difficulties arise from problems with the fusion of the virtual (MRI) and the physical (operative site) space.

Image-guided surgery is a new and important innovation of the past decade, which can also be used for didactic purposes, for virtual training of the approach, but also to guide the experienced surgeon to difficult anatomical locations.

There is no doubt that fundamental experience with endocrinological assessments and indications for surgery, together with extensive anatomical knowledge of the classic transsphenoidal approach, are preconditions for successful introduction and use of these new techniques.

Neuronavigation

Neuronavigation is the modern frameless form of stereotactic procedures, and is useful for pituitary surgery [6–8]. Target areas in the brain, such as the pituitary, can be reached via a trajectory with an accuracy of about 2 mm. Virtual planning, including (segmented) information on the tumour shape and volume, as well as on important structures such as the carotid artery in the cavernous sinus, is matched with the actual physical space and the operative field by means of a navigation microscope. The images obtained can be superimposed on the actual area of interest, for instance the sella floor, and are visible through the eye-pieces of the microscope (Fig. 4). Neuronavigation is very helpful, especially if there are variations in the course of the carotid arteries, as can occur when the vessels follow an unusually medial course, which can narrow the transverse dimension of the sella down to 6–8 mm. Furthermore, it is useful in operations for recurrent disease, where the usual anatomical landmarks have been replaced by scar tissue.

Various companies offer different navigation systems. There are pointer-related systems available, which have been devised for the localization of a structure encountered during dissection within a radiological image. We prefer microscope-based navigation systems, which

Table 2. *Neuronavigation – indications for transsphenoidal surgery*

Goals:

- Segmentation of:
  - tumour boundary
  - carotid/basilar arteries
- Trajectory entry – target zone
- Didactic/virtual training of approach

Useful for:

- Difficult relationships between tumours and arteries
  - narrow carotid arteries
  - arteries close to or surrounded by tumour
  - re-operation – loss of anatomical landmarks
- Biopsy of hidden/deep-seated tumours

Table 3. *Pure endoscopy – endoscopy-assisted surgery*

Identification of anatomical landmarks

- Pernasal approach:
  - ostium to sphenoid sinus
- Sphenoid sinus:
  - Protuberance of the carotid artery, vomer – sella – tuberculum sellae
- Intrasellar:
  - medial wall of cavernous sinus diaphragma sellae
  - suprasellar capsule
- Tumour remnants:
  - lateral sphenoid sinus
  - intra-cavernous (carotid artery) of diaphragma sellae
- Cerebrospinal fluid leak
  - suprasellar folds

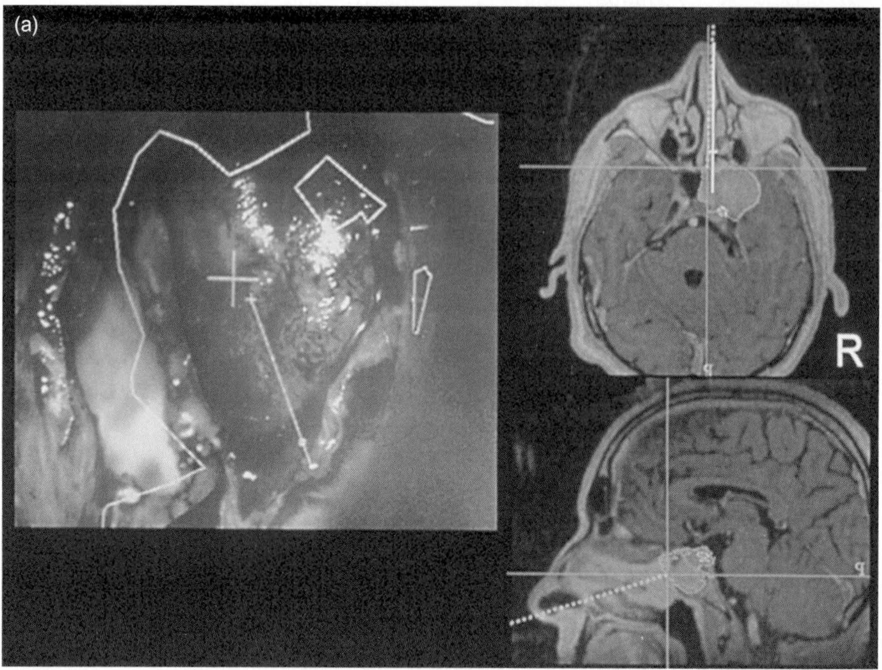

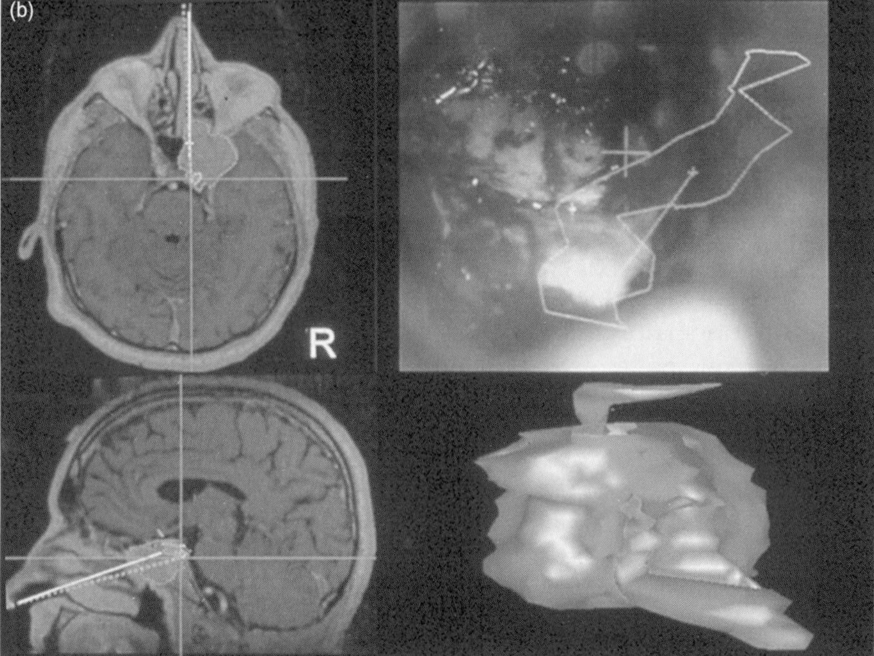

Figure 4. *Navigation: right parasellar cavernous sinus meningioma (a) before and (b) after partial removal of the tumour, with segmentation of the tumour configuration and the carotid artery. Comparison of physical space (sphenoid sinus/sella floor) and virtual space on MRI. The crosses indicate the actual position in real time.*

allow for the direct visualization of the segmented structures and, thus, are more comfortable for the surgeon.

Navigation can also be combined with endoscopy.

Endoscopy

Endoscopy, with rigid observation endoscopes of 4 mm diameter, is used to enter the sphenoid sinus via the nostril and cavum nasi at the level of the sphenoid sinus ostium. The fish-eye lens of the system offers a panoramic view (120°) of the sphenoid sinus (Fig. 5). Identification of the protuberance of the carotid arteries results in greater safety during sella exploration [9–17]. In contrast to the microscopic view, visualization 'around the corner' with a 30° lens is possible after resection of the intrasellar mass. This offers a good view of lateral structures, such as the cavernous sinus, where focally invasive tumour parts can be identified and removed (Figs 5, 6a, 6b). Whether a pure endoscopic approach is superior to microscopic procedures will be seen in the near future when three-dimensional endoscopy systems become available.

Currently, some disadvantages remain: the usefulness of endoscopes in a narrow sphenoid sinus, or in a bloody operative site, is limited and time consuming. The resolution of the optic system, combined with visualization artefacts, makes it difficult to distinguish the boundaries of the tumour from the normal pituitary gland. Furthermore, improved mechanical adaptors for the endoscope and improved direct visualization during surgery have to be developed. We have taken the first steps to improve the endoscopic transsphenoidal procedure, by using a robotic system for automatic movement of an observation microscope and neuronavigation [18]. In the near future a robotic prototype will be combined with an integrated drilling system.

Currently, comparative data on outcomes, including the extent of tumour removal, as well as endocrinological and ophthalmological results, are not available to define the efficacy of endoscopic methods. In daily practice, however, endoscope-assisted neurosurgery may be considered real progress.

Many neurosurgeons use the endoscopic pernasal approach for microscopic procedures after introducing a small Cushing speculum into the nasal cavity. This direct endonasal approach through the cavum nasi to the floor of the sphenoid sinus – using the same long and narrow tunnel as used for endoscopes – was used by Griffith and Veerapen [19], who introduced the nasal speculum into the sphenoid sinus using the beam of the microscope to visualize this region of interest. After coagulating the nasal mucosa, the bony structure of the vomer is drilled, offering an entrance into the sphenoid sinus. The direct endoscopic pernasal approach, without the microscope, offers the advantage of passing the nasal septum without elevating its mucosa so that no packing of the cavum nasi (nasal tamponade) is necessary at the end of surgery. The advantage is that inflammation induced by packing of the nasal sinuses can be avoided. This results in early recovery of normal nasal ventilation for the patient, better comfort and the feeling of being able to 'go home the next day'. An early discharge from hospital, however, would prevent the necessary postoperative surveillance of the patient, who may suffer from a potential disturbance of hormone and/or water/electrolyte balance.

Intra-operative MRI

The traditional intra-operative imaging modality is X-ray fluoroscopy, using the classic C-shaped mobile X-ray machine. This demonstrates bony structures, mainly in one (sagittal) plane. It also depicts surgical instruments introduced into the field. This technique has been enhanced by using fluoroscopy X-ray data for navigation [7]. Indirect visualization, and distinction between tumour tissue and the anterior and posterior lobes, are possible by introducing a tiny laser probe and measuring values for laser-Doppler flow in different tissues [20]. The use of ultrasound for the detection of microadenomas [21], as well as for the localization of the carotid arteries, was the first step towards the visualization of soft tissues.

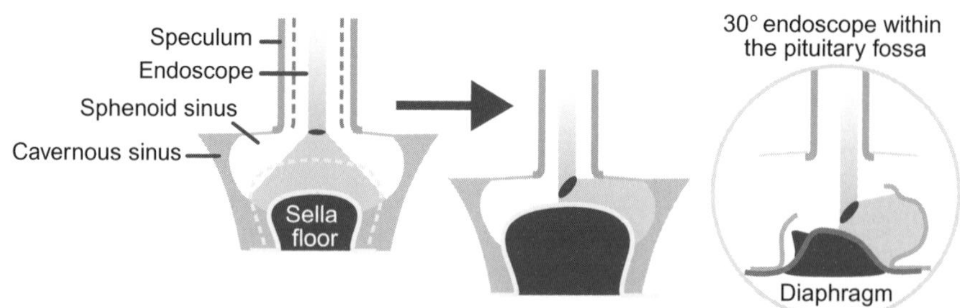

Figure 5. *Principles of endoscopy in the sphenoid sinus: visualization 'around the corner' using a rigid endoscope.*

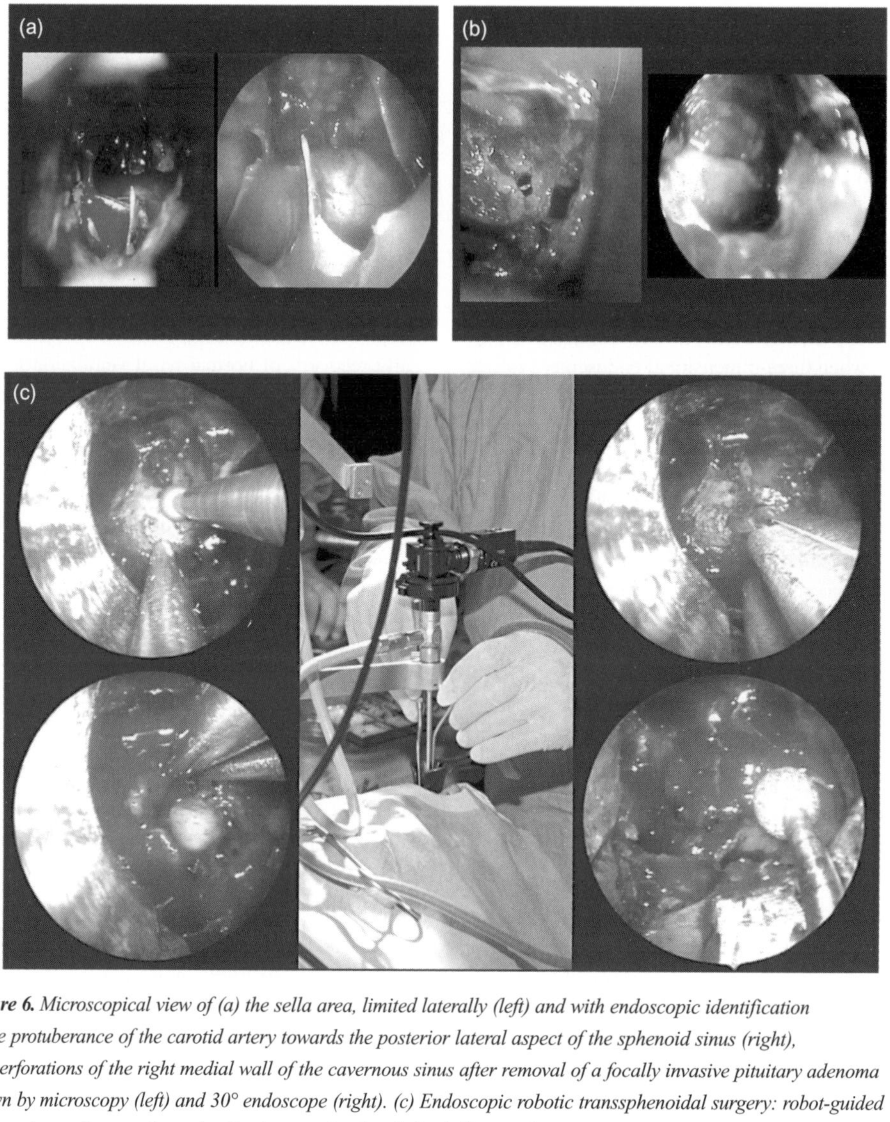

(a) (b) (c)

Figure 6. *Microscopical view of (a) the sella area, limited laterally (left) and with endoscopic identification of the protuberance of the carotid artery towards the posterior lateral aspect of the sphenoid sinus (right), (b) perforations of the right medial wall of the cavernous sinus after removal of a focally invasive pituitary adenoma shown by microscopy (left) and 30° endoscope (right). (c) Endoscopic robotic transsphenoidal surgery: robot-guided observation endoscope (centre), allowing two free hands for drilling and cutting manoeuvres.*

Tremendous progress for direct visualization of soft tissue has been made with the introduction of intra-operative MRI into neurosurgery by P Black in Boston in 1996 [22]. In Erlangen we started with a low-field 0.2 Tesla MRI scanner in early 1997 [23, 24]. For the first time this allowed the depiction of soft tumour tissue intra-operatively. We started with a so-called 'open' scanner design for diagnostic purposes (0.2 Tesla Siemens Open). The patient is positioned in the MRI scanner, which itself is located in a radiofrequency shielded operating room. The patient's head is placed on a cushion, at a distance of 1.5 m from the centre of the magnet, which is located outside the so-called 5-Gauss line. A standard transsphenoidal procedure can then be performed without disturbances caused by the magnetic field.

After tumour removal, the table is moved into the centre of the magnet and imaging is performed. After about 8 minutes of examination time using t_1 and t_2 sequences in one plane, MRI pictures allow assessment of the degree of tumour removal. This 'second look' enables the continuation of

Table 4. *Intra-operative MRI (low-field 0.15–0.4 Tesla; high-field 1.5 Tesla)*

Goals:

- Identification and further resection of tumour remnants
- Identification of displaced:
  - pituitary stalk
  - pituitary gland
  - medial wall cavernous sinus/carotid artery

'Second look':

- Further extension of:
  - bony sella opening
  - lateral cavernous sinus
  - anterior → tuberculum sellae
  - posterior → clivus
- Resection of tumour remnants
  - suprasellar – retro
  - parasellar (main locations)

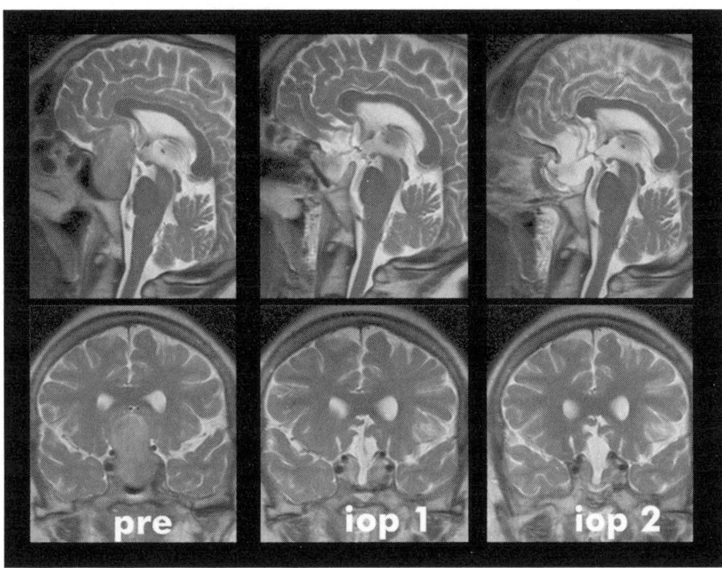

Figure 7. *Intra-operative MRI: high-field 1.5 Tesla MRI, t_2-weighted images, demonstrating a large intra- and suprasellar hormonally inactive pituitary adenoma. (iop 1) Intra-operative MRI demonstrating a small overlooked tumour remnant, hidden in an anterior fold of the suprasellar capsule diaphragm, protruding into the sella lumen. (iop 2) Complete resection after 'second look' demonstrated by MRI in the same operation session under continuous anaesthesia.*

surgery in cases where tumour remnants are still present.

In another low-field MRI system, the GE-double doughnut 0.4 Tesla MRI, the surgeon operates within the narrow gantry of the MRI but has the advantage of real-time examination, as well as a navigation-like orientation [22]. Using our system the patient is positioned on the examination table at the 5-Gauss line, where metallic surgical instruments and the magnetic resonance-compatible navigation microscope (Zeiss NC4) are used. The examination starts about 2 minutes after turning the table around and transporting it automatically into the gantry of the scanner. The first results can be obtained by an ultra early t_2-Haste sequence in 10–20 seconds. The normal examination time for preferred t_2 images is 4 minutes for coronal and sagittal sections.

Since early 2003, we have used a 1.5 Tesla MRI (Siemens Sonata). The 1.5 Tesla MRI offers an even higher quality of imaging that is comparable to pre- and postoperative MRI, and is usually performed no earlier than 2–3 months after surgery in order to avoid images with early postoperative artefacts. Using this method, tumour remnants in hidden corners, which are initially overlooked (occurring in about 30% of cases of large suprasellar tumours following transsphenoidal surgery), can be removed during the same operative session. This results in a higher rate of total removal and prevents further operations and, probably, radiotherapy.

Current applications and results

Current results in pituitary surgery, including application of modern technical tools, will be discussed for two histological tumour types: hormonally inactive adenomas and craniopharyngiomas.

Hormonally inactive tumours

Diagnosis

Morphological and immunohistochemical findings demonstrate that adenomas are a heterogeneous group of tumours. Only some of them are so-called null cell adenomas with no detected hormone activities. Other subgroups are immunohistochemically positive for gonadotrophins, luteinizing hormone and follicle-stimulating hormone, indicating a gonadotrophinoma. A smaller subgroup exhibits (silent) adrenocorticotrophin production; patients with this type of tumour are expected to develop a more rapidly growing and invasive tumour, combined with a higher chance of recurrence. They do not present with Cushing's disease. Inactive adenomas can expand to an enormous size. Giant adenomas are defined as tumours with a diameter larger than 3–4 cm and tumour growth outside the sella (middle fossa) to the anterior, posterior and lateral fossa. Patients with these tumours normally present with hypogonadism (and hyposomatotrophism) followed by secondary hypothyroidism and secondary hypocortisolism. Only a few inactive tumours are small. The majority present with compression of the chiasm. In general, transsphenoidal surgery is indicated (90% of cases); however, transcranial surgery is indicated for large and giant pituitary adenomas with asymmetrical development (10% of cases). In cases with larger extension, both approaches are used to obtain complete removal (Table 1).

Results

Up to 60% of hormonally inactive tumours can be resected totally. An additional 10–15% of patients profit from intra-operative MRI, where hidden tumour remnants can be detected and removed during the same anaesthesia. Among 44 patients with large intra- and suprasellar tumours, intra-operative MRI imaging (0.2 Tesla) allowed an ultra-early evaluation of tumour resection in 73% of the cases. Normally such an evaluation is only possible 2–3 months after surgery. A second intra-operative examination of 24 patients for suspected tumour remnants led to additional resection in 15 patients (34%) [24]. While 0.2 Tesla low-field MRI has been successfully used for suprasellar and, to some extent, intrasellar tumour resection, the 1.5 Tesla high-field MRI offers a quicker examination time and higher image quality, as well as a clear evaluation of the parasellar structures, particularly the cavernous sinus containing the carotid artery (Fig. 7). Figure 8 demonstrates all the modern modalities (intra-operative MRI, navigation, endoscopy) together in a patient with a right parasellar tumour. Patients with hormonally active tumours that are resistant to antiproliferative medical treatment, in particular, would profit from such complete and safe tumour removal.

Pituitary function remains stable in more than 90% of patients after adenoma resection. Ophthalmological disturbances resulting from compression of the chiasm normalize in 80% of cases operated on via the transsphenoidal approach. Transcranial surgery, which is generally performed for larger tumours, does not produce as good results; however, amaurosis is rarely seen today.

Craniopharyngiomas

Craniopharyngiomas originate from remnants of Rathke's pouch within the sella or from the pituitary stalk, resulting in intra- and suprasellar subdiaphragmatic tumours and in primarily suprasellar and supradiaphragmatic tumours, respectively. Some tumours can develop both sub- and supradiaphragmatically. As in pituitary adenomas, pituitary insufficiency occurs when the tumour is developing in close proximity to the pituitary gland. In contrast to adenomas, craniopharyngiomas cause central diabetes insipidus in about 25% of cases. Visual field disturbances can occur if the tumour compresses the optic nerves and the chiasm from below or above. On the other hand, about 20% of patients with suprasellar tumours do not present with endocrinological and ophthal-

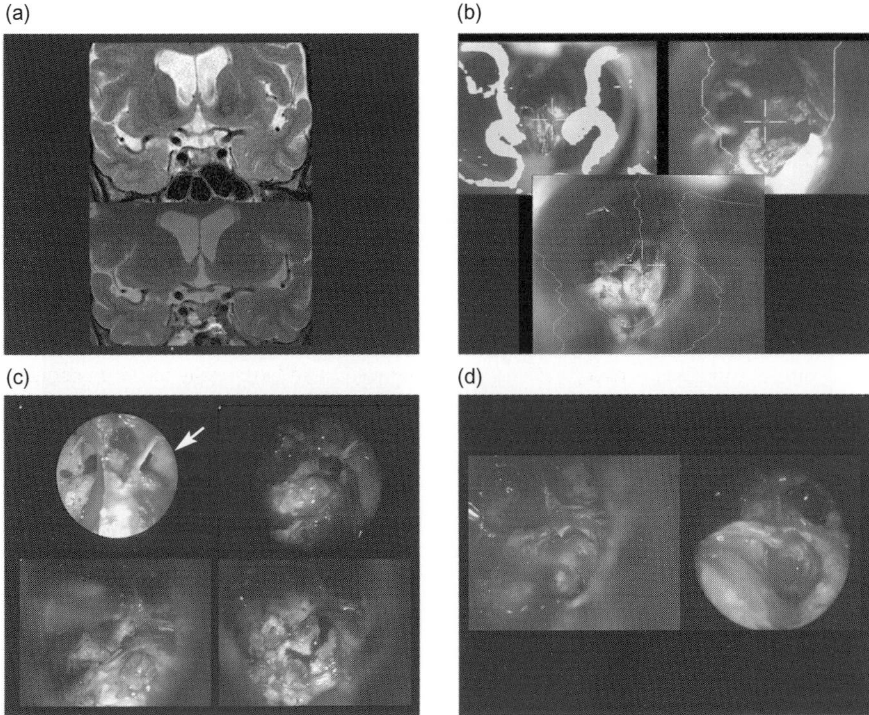

Figure 8. *(a) Removal of an intrasellar and right parasellar pituitary adenoma located around the carotid artery, compressing but not infiltrating the cavernous sinus. 1.5 Tesla MRI pre- (top) and intra-operatively (bottom) demonstrating total tumour removal. (b) Intra-operative navigation with segmentation of tumour and carotid arteries. (c) Endoscopical (top) and microscopical (bottom) view. The carotid protuberance (shown by arrow) is only seen using the endoscope.(d) Microscopical (left) and endoscopical (right) view after tumour removal from around the right carotid artery.*

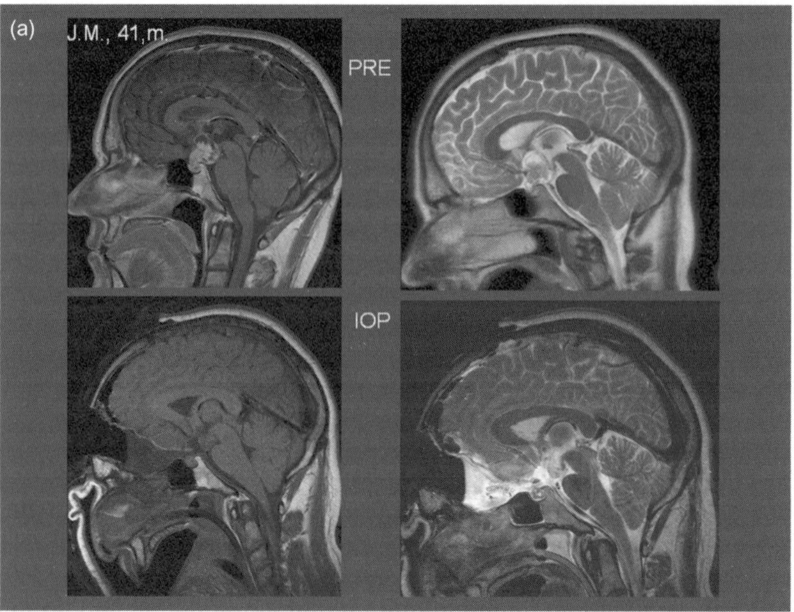

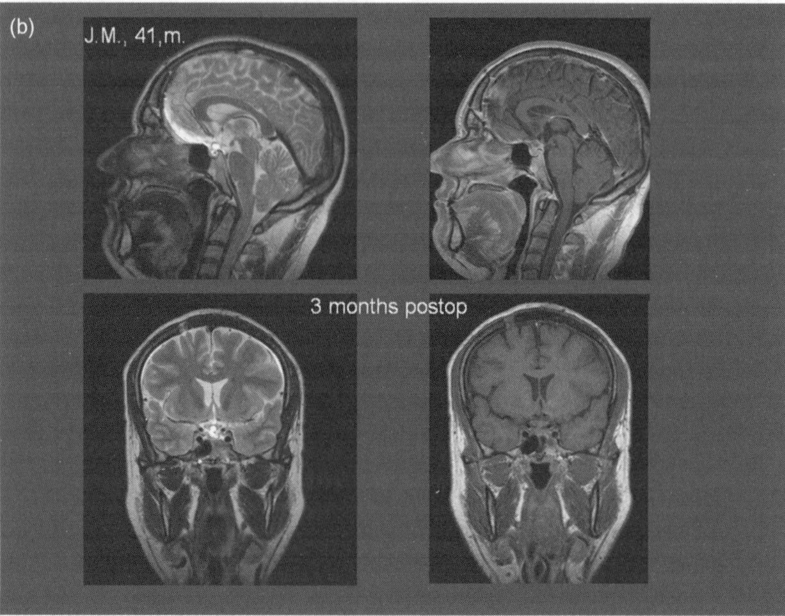

Figure 9. *Supra- and retrosellar craniopharyngioma (a) pre- and intra-operatively (IOP) and (b) 3 months after total removal.*

mological symptoms. These large tumours cause psychological symptoms and/or compression of the foramen of Monro, resulting in occlusive hydrocephalus. Neuroradiologically, many of these tumours are cystic and calcified.

Treatment

After experiencing poor results during the early years of treating craniopharyngiomas, two treatment approaches have been developed: conservative treatment, including biopsy, cyst puncture and drainage and radiotherapy, versus radical removal, if possible, in order to achieve a long-term cure. Both approaches should be applied individually, even today [5]. Transsphenoidal surgery is indicated when the tumour has developed subdiaphragmatically. Only in experienced hands can an extended transsphenoidal operation with opening of the tuberculum sellae be performed for larger supradiaphragmatic tumours. Otherwise, all of these tumours have to be operated on via transcranial approaches (Fig. 9). The pterional approach is preferred for smaller suprasellar tumours, whereas for giant craniopharyngiomas with retrosellar extension, a bifrontal–subfrontal translamina approach is chosen. Thirty per cent of all craniopharyngiomas can be resected via a transsphenoidal approach. This kind of surgery differs from normal pituitary surgery, as the majority of craniopharyngiomas develop a capsule that has to be dissected meticulously and removed totally from the pituitary stalk close to the diaphragm, which frequently results in an intra-operative CSF leak. That is why careful closure of the sella turcica with fascia, subcutaneous tissue or muscle is mandatory. This is followed by lumbar CSF drainage for some days. A similar procedure is recommended for pituitary adenomas.

Neuronavigation is helpful, especially to visualize the segmented tumour configuration and the carotid and basilar arteries through the eye-pieces of the navigation microscope. The tumour boundary is superimposed onto the area of the opened lamina terminalis and demonstrates the extent of the tumour and its actual location during surgery; however, some brain-shift occurring during surgery can limit the accuracy of assessment.

Transcranial surgery for giant tumours may yield complete removal in up to 80–85% of cases for the supra- and retrosellar tumour types. Altogether, no more than two-thirds of craniopharyngiomas can be removed by primary surgery. Limitations of surgery are infiltration of the wall of the third ventricle or the hypothalamus, intra-operative cardiovascular events and calcifications around the perforating arteries supplying the hypothalamus. Intra-operative MRI [2], performed during or at the end of tumour resection, documents the degree of resection and the presence of remnants. In addition, it shows the decompression of anatomical structures, such as the third ventricle during transcranial surgery and the pituitary gland and stalk during transsphenoidal surgery. If tumour remnants are present, resection can be continued. In cases of persistent hypothalamic disturbances, direct surgical manipulations are contraindicated. Resectable tumour remnants, visualized 2–3 months after surgery on a control MRI, offer major management problems. Treatment options at this time include (high-risk) repeat surgery, radiotherapy or observation.

Even when complete tumour removal is documented by MRI at the time of surgery, recurrences were seen in about 15% of cases over an observation period of approximately 10 years. These are thought to originate mainly from undetectable capsule remnants. These tiny remnants are not visible on intra-operative MRI [25]. Early recurrence (within months) leads to a real management challenge. In initial cases of mainly cystic tumours, puncturing the cysts may result in a definitive treatment in some patients. While performing cysto-ventricular puncture the correct placement of the catheter can be visualized using intra-operative MRI (Figs 8a, 8b). For cystic tumours, a cysto-ventricular drainage catheter can be an acceptable symptomatic treatment. When these tumours recur a combination of treatments, including radiotherapy, is needed.

Endocrinological functions normally do not improve following tumour removal, although partial improvements of individual anterior lobe functions can be seen. In contrast to pituitary adenomas, these tumours compress the pituitary gland over decades and the gland loses its original plasticity and capacity to regenerate [26].

Deterioration of pituitary function, such as partial or complete pituitary insufficiency, has to be treated with hormone replacement in order to maintain quality of life. This may include GH replacement. GH deficiency is frequently observed in patients with larger pituitary tumours, even before surgery. It does not necessarily occur after all pituitary operations. The same can be said about hypogonadism. In female patients who wish to become pregnant, amenorrhoea will often improve after removing the compressing mass from the gland. If hypogonadism does not improve or, as in rare cases, deteriorates, hormone replacement with oestrogens or testosterone, respectively, has to be performed. Hypothyroidism should be treated using thyroid hormones and secondary hypocortisolism using hydrocortisone, administered to match regular circadian cortisol secretion.

Perspectives

Early diagnosis of tumours in the hypothalamic–pituitary region is an interdisciplinary challenge, not only for endocrinologists and neurosurgeons, but also for general practitioners, who require continuous education in this field. Better imaging and, especially, image processing, will provide a morphological description of the tumour, whereas sophisticated tests of endocrinological function document the disease. Hopefully, this too will be simplified in the future. Ophthalmologists, in particular, have to bear the burden of continuous education to improve early diagnoses. Many of these tumours initially present with discrete disturbances of visual-field perception which need to be detected early. There is no doubt that medical treatment will improve, especially for hormonally active tumours; however, concepts for the successful medical treatment of Cushing's disease and of hormonally inactive tumours are still missing. On the other hand, new neurosurgical techniques will improve results on the basis of better intra-operative visualization and, in the near future, by computer-aided instrumentation. This includes the development of small intelligent instruments for enhanced visual perception and microprecision manoeuvres, as well as accurate MRI-controlled local application of biologically active, antiproliferative substances based on modern molecular biological research. In the future, areas such as the third ventricle, the hypothalamus, the lateral sphenoid sinus and, especially, the cavernous sinus which – although approached via transsphenoidal and transcranial routes today – remain difficult to reach, may be directly visualized, which will help to ensure complete tumour removal. There is no doubt that tumours of the hypothalamic–pituitary region require highly sophisticated management, consisting of interdisciplinary cooperation between doctors, pharmacologists, physicists and computer scientists with an outstanding expertise in their field. The result is a great potential for interdisciplinary research projects and cooperation between science, medicine and industry.

Acknowledgements:

The senior author thanks the following colleagues and members of the Neurosurgical Department for their continuous support: PD Dr Ch Nimsky, PD Dr O Ganslandt, Dr B von Keller (MRI, neuronavigation); Mrs Kreckel (medical technician); Dr J Kreutzer, Dr B Hofmann (neurosurgery/endocrinology); Professor W Huk (neuroradiology).

References

1. Fahlbusch R (guest editor). Surgical techniques of pituitary tumours. In: Spetzler, editor. Operative techniques in neuro-surgery. Philadelphia: W. B. Saunders 2002;5:199–251
2. Fahlbusch R, Buchfelder M, Nomikos P. Pituitary surgery. In: Melmed S, editor. The pituitary. Malden: Blackwell 2002:405–18
3. Buchfelder M, Fahlbusch R. The "classical" transsphenoidal approach for resection of pituitary tumours. Techn in Neurosurg 2002;5:210–7
4. Fahlbusch R, Buchfelder M. Surgical complications. In: Landolt AM, Vance ML, Reilly PL, editors. Pituitary adenomas: Churchill Livingstone 1996:395–408
5. Fahlbusch R, Honegger J, Paulus W, Huk W, Buchfelder M. Surgical treatment of craniopharyngiomas: experience with 168 patients. J Neurosurg 1999;90:237–50
6. Kacker A, Komisar A, Huo J, Mangiardi J. Transsphenoidal surgery utilizing computer-assisted stereotactic guidance. Rhinology 2001;39:207–10
7. Jane JA Jr, Thapar K, Alden TD, Laws ER, Jr. Fluoroscopic frameless stereotaxy for transsphenoidal surgery. Neurosurgery 2001;48:1302–8

8. Nimsky C, Ganslandt O, Kober H, Buchfelder M, Fahlbusch R. Intraoperative magnetic resonance imaging combined with neuronavigation: a new concept. Neurosurgery 2001;48:1082–91

9. Torrens MJ. Endoscopic neurosurgery. Neurosurgery Quarterly 1995;5:18–33

10. Fahlbusch R, Heigl T, Huk W, Steinmeier R. The role of endoscopy and intra-operative MRI in transsphenoidal pituitary surgery. In: Werder KV, Fahlbusch R, editors. Pituitary adenomas. Amsterdam: Elsevier 1996:237–44

11. Jho HD, Carrau RL. Endoscopic endonasal transsphenoidal surgery: experience with 50 patients. J Neurosurg 1997;87:44–51

12. Jho HD, Carrau RL, Ko Y, Daly MA. Endoscopic pituitary surgery: an early experience. Surg Neurol 1997;47:213–22

13. Cappabianca P, Alfieri A, Colao A, Cavallo LM, Fusco M, Peca C, Lombardi G, de Divitiis E. Endoscopic endonasal transsphenoidal surgery in recurrent and residual pituitary adenomas: technical note. Minim Invasive Neurosurg 2000;43:38–43

14. Nakagawa T, Asada M, Takashima T, Tomiyama K. Sellar reconstruction after endoscopic transnasal hypophysectomy. Laryngoscope 2001;111:2077–81

15. Nasseri SS, Kasperbauer JL, Strome SE, McCaffrey TV, Atkinson JL, Meyer FB. Endoscopic transnasal pituitary surgery: report on 180 cases. Am J Rhinol 2001;15:281–7

16. Kawamata T, Iseki H, Shibasaki T, Hori T. Endoscopic augmented reality navigation system for endonasal transsphenoidal surgery to treat pituitary tumors: technical note. Neurosurgery 2002;50:1393–7

17. Ohhashi G, Kamio M, Abe T, Otori N, Haruna S. Endoscopic transnasal approach to the pituitary lesions using a navigation system (InstaTrak system): technical note. Minim Invasive Neurosurg 2002;45:120–3

18. Nimsky C, Rachinger J, Iro H, Fahlbusch R. Adaptation of a hexapod-based robotic system for extended endoscopic transsphenoidal skull base surgery. Minim Invasive Neurosurg 2004 (in press)

19. Griffith HB, Veerapen R. A direct transnasal approach to the sphenoid sinus. Technical note. J Neurosurg 1987;66:140–2

20. Steinmeier R, Fahlbusch R, Powers AD, Dotterl A, Buchfelder M. Pituitary microcirculation: physiological aspects and clinical implications. A laser-Doppler flow study during transsphenoidal adenomectomy. Neurosurgery 1991;29:47–54

21. Ram Z, Shawker TH, Bradford MH, Doppman JL, Oldfield EH. Intraoperative ultrasound-directed resection of pituitary tumors. J Neurosurg 1995; 83:225–30

22. Martin CH, Schwartz R, Jolesz F, Black PM. Transsphenoidal resection of pituitary adenomas in an intraoperative MRI unit. Pituitary 1999;2:155–62

23. Steinmeier R, Fahlbusch R, Ganslandt O, Nimsky C, Buchfelder M, Kaus M, Heigl T, Lenz G, Kuth R, Huk W. Intraoperative magnetic resonance imaging with the magnetom open scanner: concepts, neurosurgical indications, and procedures: a preliminary report. Neurosurgery 1998;43:739–48

24. Fahlbusch R, Ganslandt O, Buchfelder M, Schott W, Nimsky C. Intraoperative magnetic resonance imaging during transsphenoidal surgery. J Neurosurg 2001; 95:381–90

25. Nimsky C, Ganslandt O, Hofmann B, Fahlbusch R. Limited benefit of intraoperative low-field magnetic resonance imaging in craniopharyngioma surgery. Neurosurgery 2003;53:72–80

26. Honegger J, Buchfelder M, Fahlbusch R. Surgical treatment of craniopharyngiomas: endocrinological results. J Neurosurg 1999;90:251–7

23 Adults with craniopharyngioma: a review of the literature and data from KIMS

Johan Verhelst[1] and Pat Kendall-Taylor[2]
[1]*Algemeen Ziekenhuis Middelheim, Antwerp, Belgium and* [2]*University of Newcastle, Newcastle upon Tyne, UK*

Summary

Craniopharyngioma is a rare intracranial tumour with an annual incidence of approximately 0.5–2 per million per year. The prevalence of craniopharyngioma is characterized by a peak in childhood and a second peak at 50–74 years of age. Craniopharyngioma is believed to originate from the embryonic remnants of Rathke's pouch and, although histopathologically benign, may be aggressive at the clinical level. Patients may present with a broad range of symptoms, depending on the location and size of the tumour. The present chapter reviews the current insights into diagnosis and treatment of craniopharyngioma; we also describe the demographic characteristics and evaluate the response to growth hormone (GH) therapy of a large group (n = 165) of patients with adult-onset craniopharyngioma in KIMS – Pfizer International Metabolic Database. At entry into KIMS, patients had a mean age of 41.7 years and an estimated duration of GH deficiency (GHD) of 7.5 ± 7.2 years. Over 80% of patients were overweight, with males and females similarly affected, and 47% were clinically obese. Mean waist circumferences suggested marked visceral obesity in the majority of patients. The abnormal lipid profile, characteristic of patients with GHD, was also present. Approximately 60% of patients had panhypopituitarism and only 2% had isolated GHD. Scores on the Quality of Life Assessment of GHD in Adults questionnaire showed that quality of life (QoL) is poor in males and females. With GH therapy, which over half of the patients had received for 1 year, significant improvements were seen in total and low-density lipoprotein-cholesterol levels, QoL and lean body mass. In contrast to the consistent effect of GH seen in patients with GHD not associated with craniopharyngioma, fat mass did not decrease significantly and mean weight continued to rise, predominantly due to the increase in lean body mass. Despite the lack of effect on fat mass, it is highly likely that GH therapy prevented a further increase that would otherwise have occurred. In the majority of patients with craniopharyngioma, early and adequate GH replacement therapy is important for improving QoL, and for correcting dyslipidaemia and body composition, which confer an increased risk of cardiovascular disease and mortality.

Introduction

Craniopharyngioma is the underlying pathology in 10–20% of adult patients with growth hormone deficiency (GHD). Patients with craniopharyngioma share many characteristics with patients with pituitary adenoma, but differ greatly in some aspects. For example, patients with craniopharyngioma have a 3–5 times higher mortality than other groups of patients with pituitary pathology. In this chapter we review current insights into the diagnosis and treatment of craniopharyngioma, and describe the population of craniopharyngioma patients with adult-onset (AO) disease included in KIMS – Pfizer International Metabolic Database – in 2001.

Craniopharyngioma: review of the literature

Epidemiology

Craniopharyngioma is a rare intracranial tumour, occurring as frequently in men as in women, with an annual incidence of 0.5–2 per million. Its prevalence is characterized by two distinct peaks: the first in childhood between 5 and 14 years of age, and the second in adulthood between 50 and 74 years of age [1]. Craniopharyngioma has also been described in fetuses [2]. In children, craniopharyngioma is the third most common intracranial tumour, while in adults it accounts for only 1–3% of all intracranial neoplasms.

Pathology

Craniopharyngioma is believed to originate from the embryonic remnants of Rathke's pouch and to grow slowly from birth. It can be localized along a line from the nasopharynx to the diencephalon. Most are found in the suprasellar region and pituitary stalk, a smaller number in the pituitary, and a few intraventricularly or in other nearby structures [3, 4].

Histopathologically, a craniopharyngioma is a benign tumour; however, it can behave aggressively at the clinical level. Two basic histological types exist:

- Adamantinomatous craniopharyngioma consists of a reticular epithelial mass, resembling the enamel pulp of developing teeth. Features are a palisading basal layer of small cells, which encloses a loose stellate reticular zone, and nodules of keratin. This variant easily forms cysts and calcifies
- Papillary (or squamous) craniopharyngioma is composed of simple squamous epithelium and fibrovascular islands of connective tissue. Cystic degeneration and calcification is uncommon. Papillary craniopharyngioma is less frequent (~16%) than the adamantinomatous variant and is more likely to be found in adults.

Macroscopically, craniopharyngioma typically consist of single or multiple cysts, partially calcified and filled with a turbid fluid containing cholesterol crystals, resembling 'machine oil'. About 10% are solid masses. Tumour volume can vary from a few mililitres to a very large mass that can compress surrounding brain structures. Metastases are extremely rare.

Symptoms

Patients with craniopharyngioma present with a broad range of symptoms, depending on tumour size and localization [3]. Symptoms can be caused by:

- increased intracranial pressure, leading to headaches, nausea or vomiting
- compression of the optic pathways, with visual disturbances
- pituitary hormone deficiencies resulting in growth failure and delayed puberty; partial or complete panhypopituitarism may occur
- hypothalamic dysfunction resulting in diabetes insipidus, obesity due to increased appetite, precocious puberty, neuropsychological abnormalities, loss of memory and sleep disorders
- neurological disturbances where there is involvement of adjacent brain tissue or neurological pathways.

Endocrine symptoms are dependent upon the age of presentation; endocrine dysfunction usually presents as growth failure in children, as delayed puberty in adolescents and as sexual dysfunction (amenorrhoea, impotence) in adults. Nevertheless, some patients may be asymptomatic and diagnosis may be incidental, when brain imaging is carried out for other reasons.

Diagnosis

Diagnosis of craniopharyngioma is usually made by computed tomography or magnetic resonance imaging (MRI). Differential diagnosis includes a large list of other tumours that are known to occur in the region. The suprasellar localization, calcification (present in 80–87%) and occurrence of cystic structures (present in 70–75%) are very suggestive of craniopharyngioma; in atypical cases, however, diagnosis can be difficult and is sometimes made only after surgery.

As patients with craniopharyngioma have a high risk of partial or complete hypopituitarism, endocrine testing is necessary. Detailed visual field testing should be performed, because of the high risk of compression of the optic pathways. A full neurological examination is advisable, and psychological tests may be useful.

Therapy for craniopharyngioma

Primary therapy

Conservative approach

When the craniopharyngioma is relatively small and provokes few or no symptoms, a wait-and-see approach may be adopted. There should be close clinical and endocrine follow-up, with regular imaging of the tumour.

Surgery

The primary therapy for symptomatic craniopharyngioma cases is most frequently surgical resection of the tumour (see Chapter 22). As craniopharyngiomas are usually localized in the suprasellar region, the majority of operations are done by a transcranial procedure, for which several approaches are possible (interhemispheric, transfrontal, etc.) depending on the size and localization of the mass [5]. If the tumour is in the sella or is suprasellar prechiasmatic (even if it is large), the transsphenoidal route is preferred, with the advantage of less morbidity from the procedure itself [5, 6].

The initial goal of surgery is to remove all tumour tissue. Recurrence is frequent where this is not done completely. In one study, for example, recurrence after surgery was 51% after 5 years if removal was incomplete, compared with 13% when removal was total [5]. Unfortunately, because of the large size and/or invasiveness of the tumour, complete removal can be accomplished in only half of all cases. Even when complete resolution is depicted by intraoperative low-field MRI, recurrence is not excluded [7].

Surgery that is too aggressive can result in unacceptable additional neurological, psychological or visual damage [8, 9]. The optimal surgery is therefore a delicate balance between taking out as much tumour as possible (leading to low recurrence), and minimizing additional damage (which would otherwise lead to high morbidity).

Intermittent percutaneous aspiration of large cysts or the placement of an Ommaya reservoir system can be considered whenever surgery is thought to be too risky [10].

Radiotherapy

Conventional radiotherapy is another treatment option. This procedure delivers radiation to the tumour by a three-field technique, using two opposing lateral fields, and one anterior oblique field lying in the same plane. The ideal dose range is between 53 and 60 gray (Gy), delivered as daily fractions of 1.6–1.7 Gy [11].

As a primary therapy, conventional radiotherapy is usually restricted to patients with small tumours, as tumours are not very radiosensitive and the effect on growth is slow.

Radiotherapy was found to be most useful after incomplete surgery, as it substantially reduces the subsequent risk of recurrence [11, 12].

Some authors advocate a ‘conservative’ surgical approach, based upon the risks of aggressive surgery and the efficacy of radiotherapy.

Stereotactic radiosurgery, with either a ‘gamma knife’ or multiple arcs using a conventional linear accelerator, may deliver a high dose of radiation to the tumour in one session, while delivering less radiation to the surrounding structures. This offers the advantage of minimizing late neurocognitive defects due to radiation [13, 14]. Because of the need for clear focussing on the target and the possibility of radiation damage to the optic chiasm, this technique is best suited for well-delineated tumours at least 5 mm away from the optic chiasm [15]. Reduction of the cystic component of the tumour before stereotactic surgery can be useful.

Treatment of recurrent disease

If the tumour recurs, a further attempt at surgical resection can be considered. Results have been shown to be satisfactory in 40–70% of patients, depending on the size and localization of the remnant [5]; however, a second operation carries an even higher risk of morbidity and mortality than primary surgery, and this should be weighed against the possible advantages. As when used immediately after surgery, conventional or stereotactic radiotherapy may provide good local control, and is associated with a low incidence of complications. If the recurrent tumour consists predominantly of a large cyst, intracystic administration of antimitotic agents (bleomycin) or radioisotopes (radioactive phosphorous) have been successfully employed [16, 17]. The role of these techniques as a primary treatment for craniopharyngioma remains to be established.

Endocrine treatment

Various degrees of hypopituitarism and hypothalamic dysfunction usually persist, or even increase, after surgery and/or radiotherapy. In a series of 143 patients with craniopharyngioma, 16% had diabetes insipidus and 40% panhypopituitarism at diagnosis, with corresponding figures after surgery of 59% and 43% [18]. In children, the situation is even worse [19, 20]. These patients therefore need life-long hormone substitution therapy.

The recognition of adult GHD syndrome and the availability of recombinant growth hormone (GH) since 1989 have stimulated the use of GH in all groups of patients with GHD, including those with craniopharyngioma [21]. In most of the initial studies on GH replacement therapy, 10–20% of adult patients had a diagnosis of craniopharyngioma [22–24]. In these studies, however, results for craniopharyngioma patients have not been analysed separately, making it difficult to judge whether the response of these patients to GH differed from that of other patient groups.

In addition to hypopituitarism and diabetes insipidus, obesity is a common problem in patients who have been treated for craniopharyngioma, and demands special attention. In a series of 185 children and adolescents with craniopharyngioma, 44% were obese [25]. Hypothalamic damage has been identified as an important risk factor for the development of obesity [25, 26], and a close relationship has been found between the amount of hypothalamic damage shown on MRI, and weight [27]. Furthermore, the finding of high serum leptin levels in these patients suggests that the damaged hypothalamic structures have become insensitive to leptin [28].

Prognosis

Adult craniopharyngioma patients have a high mortality rate. In one large study, mortality after 7 years was more than nine times higher than in the normal population (standardized mortality ratio [SMR], 9.28), and five times higher than in patients with pituitary adenomas (SMR, 1.70) [29]. In another study, the 10- and 15-year survival rates in adult craniopharyngioma patients were 68 and 59%, respectively, and the SMR 5.55. In this study, a multivariate survival analysis also confirmed the importance of recurrence as a negative prognostic factor [30]. Similarly, in a study of children with craniopharyngioma, the 20-year survival rate was only 60% [31]. Estimation of long-term survival is, however, confounded by the fact that it is based, for the major part, on patients who were assessed and treated with older diagnostic and surgical tools.

Currently, it remains difficult to estimate to what extent visual, neurological, psychological or metabolic sequelae after treatment directly or indirectly contribute to the increased mortality rate in craniopharyngioma patients.

The finding of excess cerebro- and cardiovascular accidents in adult craniopharyngioma patients at autopsy, suggests that an underlying metabolic problem may be responsible for the increased mortality rate [29, 30]. Obesity and untreated GHD are probably the key elements in this metabolic problem [30].

Craniopharyngioma: data from KIMS

Database

The current analysis was based on the KIMS database as on 01/09/2001, containing 4506 patients, with GHD of various aetiologies. Evaluation of baseline characteristics and GH replacement parameters was only possible in so-called 'naive' patients who had never received GH, or who had discontinued GH treatment for at least 6 months ('semi-naive') prior to enrolment in KIMS. This reduced the initial group of patients to 2857. Of these patients, 268 had received a diagnosis of craniopharyngioma with severe GHD (peak GH < 3 μg/L in a validated GH test); 165 had AO-craniopharyngioma (> 18 years at the time of diagnosis) and 103 had childhood-onset craniopharyngioma. The current analysis was limited to the 165 patients with AO-craniopharyngioma.

Epidemiology

Craniopharyngioma patients with AO disease in KIMS were aged 41.7 ± 11.9 years at entry (see Fig. 1). The estimated duration of GHD was 7.5 ± 7.2 years (median, 4.2 years). The male to female ratio was 1.14.

Previous therapy for craniopharyngioma

The majority of patients had received surgery (92 patients, 55.8%) or combined surgery and radiotherapy (60 patients, 36.4%). One patient (0.61%) received radiotherapy as primary therapy and 12 patients (7.3%) were only observed. Of the 152 patients receiving surgery, 76.3% underwent one procedure, 20.4% two procedures and 3.3% three procedures before entering KIMS. Two-thirds (69.3%) of the patients had surgery at least once by the transcranial route, whereas one-third were operated on by the transsphenoidal route.

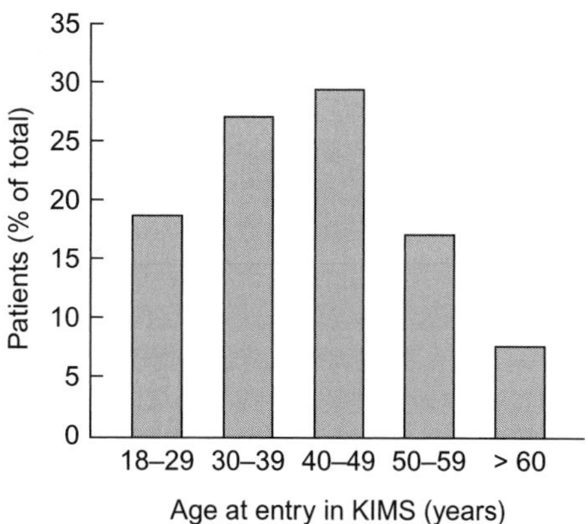

Figure 1. *Age of adult craniopharyngioma patients at entry into KIMS.*

Medical history, quality of life (QoL) and clinical examination

Co-morbidity at baseline is shown in Table 1. The most frequently observed co-morbidity was visual field deficits, which were observed in 68.0% of patients. A relatively high percentage of patients were reported to have previous fractures (27.9%). Of the patients analysed, 31.6% were smokers, 11.2% of whom smoked more than 15 cigarettes per day. The Quality of Life Assessment of GHD in Adults (QoL-AGHDA) score was equally high in men and women, with values of 10.7 ± 7.2 and 10.5 ± 5.7, indicating a poor QoL. At baseline, 16.1% of patients were unable to work because of sickness or invalidity (Fig. 2).

Table 1. *Co-morbidity in adult craniopharyngioma patients at baseline expressed as a percentage of the total patient group (n = 165).*

Co-morbidity	Percentage at baseline
Fractures	27.9
Visual field defect	68.0
Hypertension	8.5
Coronary disease	2.4
Stroke	1.8
Diabetes mellitus	1.8

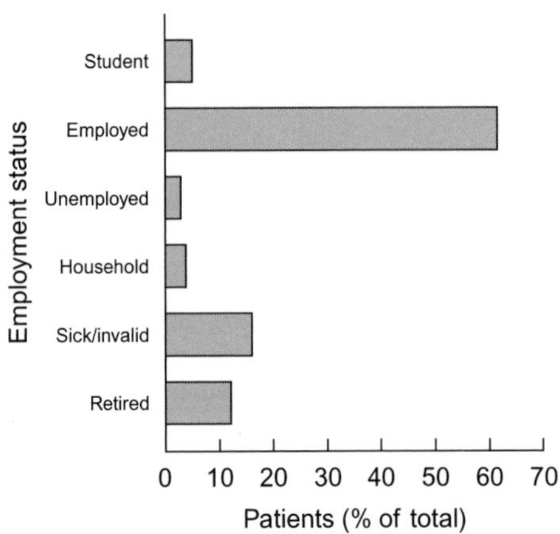

Figure 2. *Employment status in adult craniopharyngioma patients at baseline.*

The adult craniopharyngioma patients in KIMS were very obese. Their mean total body weight was 93.0 kg for men (mean height, 1.74 m) and 80.5 kg for women (mean height, 1.64 m). The mean body mass index (BMI) was 30.2 ± 6.25 kg/m^2 (normal, 18.5–25 kg/m^2), with no difference between men and women. According to World Health Organization criteria, 82.9% of patients were considered 'overweight' (BMI > 25 kg/m^2), 47.4% 'obese' (BMI > 30 kg/m^2) and 5.9% 'morbid obese' (BMI > 40 kg/m^2). In a subgroup of patients (n = 62), bioelectrical impedance (BI) analysis of body composition revealed 28.1% fat in men (normal, < 19%) and 39.3% fat in women (normal, < 30%). In men the mean waist circumference was 103.8 ± 12.9 cm (abnormal if > 94 cm, high risk if > 102 cm) and the waist to hip ratio 1.01 ± 0.17 (high risk if > 0.95). Corresponding figures for women were 96.5 ± 15.2 cm for waist (abnormal if > 80 cm, high risk if > 88 cm) and 0.88 ± 0.08 for the waist to hip ratio (high risk if > 0.85). There was thus a high prevalence of visceral obesity in both sexes.

Mean levels of systolic (125 ± 17 mmHg) and diastolic (75 ± 10 mmHg) blood pressure were within the normal range. Few patients had a blood pressure in the hypo- or hypertensive range (10th–90th percentile, 110/65 mmHg to 150/92 mmHg). At baseline, 8.5% were being treated for hypertension.

Endocrine function and diagnosis of GHD

By definition, all patients in the KIMS study had severe GHD, with a peak GH level below 3 µg/L. In 87.9% of patients, the GH peak was below 1 µg/L. Insulin-induced hypoglycaemia was the most frequently used test to diagnose GHD (66.7% of cases), followed by arginine (17.6%), glucagon (11.5%) and GH-releasing hormone (4.3%). Baseline insulin-like growth factor I (IGF-I) SD scores (SDS) in men were higher than in women: –1.30 ± 1.59 versus –2.51 ± 2.12 ($p < 0.01$).

Although all patients enrolled in KIMS are GH-deficient, few patients (1.8%) were reported to have isolated GHD. The majority of patients (58.8%) had panhypopituitarism (Fig. 3). After GH, luteinizing hormone (LH) and/or follicle-stimulating hormone (FSH) were the most frequently deficient (93.9%), followed by thyrotrophin (TSH) (90.9%) and adrenocorticotrophin (88.5%). Diabetes insipidus was reported in 62.4% of patients. As most patients had surgery before entry into KIMS, it is not known whether these deficiencies were already present when cranio-

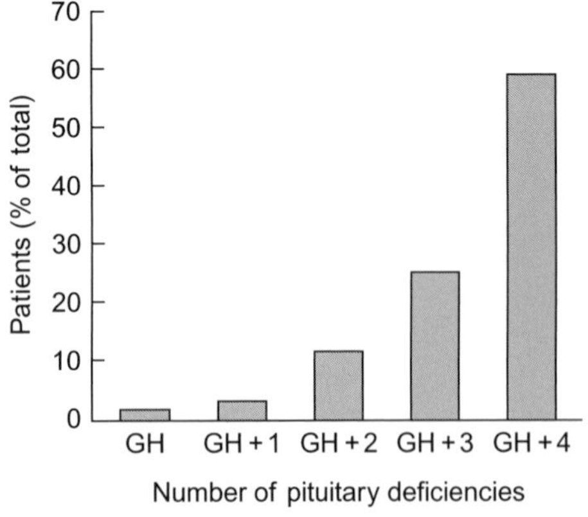

Figure 3. *Number of pituitary hormone deficiencies in adult craniopharyngioma patients at baseline.*

pharyngioma was diagnosed, or only occurred post-operatively.

Serum lipids and glucose

The characteristic abnormalities in lipid profile that are associated with GHD were also observed in this group of adult craniopharyngioma patients. Levels of total and low-density lipoprotein (LDL)-cholesterol were relatively high (6.30 ± 1.31 mmol/L and 3.92 ± 1.13 mmol/L respectively). High-density lipoprotein (HDL)-cholesterol levels were in the low range (1.17 ± 0.42 mmol/L) and triglycerides were usually elevated (2.60 ± 1.39 mmol/L).

Levels of fasting plasma glucose (mean, 4.55 ± 0.8 mmol/L) and glycosylated haemoglobin (mean, 5.1 ± 1.0%) were within normal limits in the majority of patients. At baseline, a small number of patients (1.8%) had diabetes mellitus.

Effects of GH replacement therapy

At the time that the database was frozen, a large number of patients had not reached their 1- and 2-year treatment visits (time in KIMS after starting GH replacement therapy). Data were available from 85 patients after 1 year and 62 patients after 2 years of GH replacement therapy.

A significant increase in serum IGF-I levels was observed after 1 year (+2.39 SDS, $p < 0.0001$) in patients receiving a median dose of GH of 0.27 mg/day. After this time, IGF-I levels remained stable (+2.46 SDS compared with baseline) using a similar dose of GH. As expected on the basis of previous studies, a significant improvement in QoL-AGHDA scores was reported in this group of patients: –2.27 after 1 year ($p = 0.0002$) and –3.97 after 2 years ($p < 0.0001$).

The characteristic effect of GH therapy on the lipid profile was also observed in this group of patients. Levels of total and LDL-cholesterol dropped significantly by 0.34 mmol/L ($p = 0.019$) and 0.26 mmol/L ($p = 0.039$), respectively, after 1 year and by 0.86 mmol/L ($p < 0.0001$) and 0.75 mmol/L ($p = 0.0001$), respectively, after 2 years. Levels of HDL-cholesterol and triglycerides did not change significantly.

Lean body mass (measured using BI analysis), increased significantly after both 1 (+1.65 kg [+2.87%], $p = 0.19$) and 2 (+2.72 [+4.73%], $p = 0.01$) years of GH replacement therapy; however, in contrast to the known effects of GH therapy in other groups of patients, body fat did not decrease significantly (–0.08 kg [–0.31%]). As a result of the increase in lean body mass without concomitant loss of body fat, mean weight increased (+1.65 kg after 1 year [$p = 0.078$]; +3.18 kg after 2 years [$p < 0.0004$]). Waist circumference and the waist to hip ratio did not change significantly.

Systolic and diastolic blood pressure and heart rate remained unchanged during GH replacement therapy.

Discussion

These KIMS data are unique in providing the opportunity to assess metabolic parameters and QoL in a large group of patients with AO-GHD and craniopharyngioma. The current analysis also allowed evaluation of the effects of GH replacement therapy in adult craniopharyngioma patients as distinct from other groups of patients with GHD. At baseline, we found a high degree of pituitary deficiencies, with diabetes insipidus in 62.4% and panhypopituitarism in 58.8% of patients studied. These results are consistent with data available from the literature.

The extent of weight excess was striking, with 82.9% of patients classified as overweight (BMI > 25 kg/m^2), and 47.4% as obese (BMI > 30 kg/m^2). This is in line with observations in children with craniopharyngioma [25]. These numbers contrast sharply with estimations in the normal adult European population, where about 30% have a BMI above 25 kg/m^2 and 10% above 30 kg/m^2 [32]. Interestingly, the mean BMI, of 30.2 kg/m^2, was higher than the 28.5 kg/m^2 in a group of GH-deficient patients from KIMS with various other pathologies, predominantly pituitary adenomas [33]. This suggests that craniopharyngioma patients are more prone to weight gain than patients with other types of pituitary pathologies. As expected, excess weight in this study was predominantly the result of increased fat tissue. The excess fat was most likely of visceral origin, as judged by the large waist and excess waist to hip ratio of these patients.

In this study, LDL-cholesterol was increased within the range found in other groups of patients with GHD [34]. Although it is difficult to compare results from different studies, triglyceride levels in this patient group (mean, 2.6 mmol/L) seem to be higher, on average, than those in other studies of GH-deficient patients (between 1.5 and 2.0 mmol/L) with a similar age and sex distribution [33, 35, 36]. Because of the known relationship between central obesity, decreased HDL-cholesterol and high triglyceride levels [37, 38], the more pronounced abnormality in serum triglycerides in our craniopharyngioma patients can probably be explained by their excess weight.

Nearly one-third of the patients were active smokers, which is close to the frequency in the normal population in Europe [39, 40]. Some 16% of the adult craniopharyngioma patients were sick or invalid. This is higher than the 11% reported in an earlier study of hypopituitary patients of various aetiologies, and also twice that in the average population in a European country, such as Belgium [41].

Treatment with GH induced the expected improvement in QoL, lean body mass and LDL-cholesterol levels [42], indicating that patients with craniopharyngioma respond as well as other patients with GHD. In contrast to studies with other groups of patients with GHD [22, 23, 43], no decrease in fat mass was observed after 2 years of GH therapy. From studies in children with craniopharyngioma it is known that obesity develops in the years following diagnosis and therapy [26, 44]; therefore, it is likely that GH therapy prevented the expected increase in fat mass in this group of patients, but was unable to reduce it.

Craniopharyngioma patients have a high mortality rate. We found a number of risk factors for mortality and cardiovascular disease in these patients, including obesity [45], a high waist to hip ratio [46], dyslipidaemia [47, 48] and a low QoL [49]. All of these factors were more prevalent in patients with craniopharyngioma than in the normal population, and more prevalent than in the average patient with GHD. The extent of neurological damage or other parameters, such as insulin resistance or coagulopathy, were not evaluated in this study, but are also likely to play a role in the high mortality rate of craniopharyngioma patients [42, 50, 51].

These data reinforce the importance of minimizing damage to the hypothalamus when choosing the appropriate therapy for a patient with craniopharyngioma, not focussing on surgical criteria alone for success. In addition, specific measures to prevent weight gain after treatment may be necessary in craniopharyngioma patients. As many patients with craniopharyngioma are at high risk for cardio- and cerebrovascular disease, early targeting of metabolic abnormalities is necessary. In this respect, GH replacement therapy could be an important tool.

References

1. Bunin GR, Surawicz TS, Witman PA, Preston-Martin S, Davis F, Bruner JM. The descriptive epidemiology of craniopharyngioma. J Neurosurg 1998;89:547–51

2. Arai T, Ohno K, Takada Y, Aoyagi M, Hirakawa K. Neonatal craniopharyngioma and inference of tumor inception time: case report and review of the literature. Surg Neurol 2003;60:254–9

3. Petito CK, DeGirolami U, Earle KM. Craniopharyngiomas: a clinical and pathological review. Cancer 1976;37:1944–52

4. Behari S, Banerji D, Mishra A, Sharma S, Chhabra DK, Jain VK. Intrinsic third ventricular craniopharyngiomas: report on six cases and a review of the literature. Surg Neurol 2003;60:245–52

5. Fahlbusch R, Honegger J, Paulus W, Huk W, Buchfelder M. Surgical treatment of craniopharyngiomas: experience with 168 patients. J Neurosurg 1999;90:237–50

6. Im SH, Wang KC, Kim SK, Chung YN, Kim HS, Lee CH, Cho BK. Transsphenoidal microsurgery for pediatric craniopharyngioma: special considerations regarding indications and method. Pediatr Neurosurg 2003;39:97–103

7. Nimsky C, Ganslandt O, Hofmann B, Fahlbusch R. Limited benefit of intraoperative low-field magnetic resonance imaging in craniopharyngioma surgery. Neurosurgery 2003;53:72–80

8. Vernet O, Montes JL, Farmer JP, Blundell JE, Bertrand G, Freeman CR. Long term results of multi-modality treatment of craniopharyngioma in children. J Clin Neurosci 1999;6:199–203

9. Merchant TE, Kiehna EN, Sanford RA, Mulhern RK, Thompson SJ, Wilson MW, Lustig RH, Kun LE. Craniopharyngioma: the St. Jude Children's Research Hospital experience 1984–2001. Int J Radiat Oncol Biol Phys 2002;53:533–42

10. Joki T, Oi S, Babapour B, Kaito N, Ohashi K, Ebara M, Kato M, Abe T. Neuroendoscopic placement of Ommaya reservoir into a cystic craniopharyngioma. Childs Nerv Syst 2002;18:629–33

11. Varlotto JM, Flickinger JC, Kondziolka D, Lunsford LD, Deutsch M. External beam irradiation of craniopharyngiomas: long-term analysis of tumor control and morbidity. Int J Radiat Oncol Biol Phys 2002;54:492–9

12. Habrand JL, Ganry O, Couanet D, Rouxel V, Levy-Piedbois C, Pierre-Kahn A, Kalifa C. The role of radiation therapy in the management of craniopharyngioma: a 25-year experience and review of the literature. Int J Radiat Oncol Biol Phys 1999;44:255–63

13. Selch MT, DeSalles AA, Wade M, Lee SP, Solberg TD, Wallace RE, Ford JM, Rubino G, Cabatan-Awang C, Withers HR. Initial clinical results of stereotactic radiotherapy for the treatment of craniopharyngiomas. Technol Cancer Res Treat 2002;1:51–9

14. Ulfarsson E, Lindquist C, Roberts M, Rahn T, Lindquist M, Thorén M, Lippitz B. Gamma knife radiosurgery for craniopharyngiomas: long-term results in the first Swedish patients. J Neurosurg 2002;97:613–22

15. Jackson AS, St George EJ, Hayward RJ, Plowman PN. Stereotactic radiosurgery. XVII: Recurrent intrasellar craniopharyngioma. Br J Neurosurg 2003;17:138–43

16. Alen JF, Boto GR, Lagares A, de la Lama A, Gomez PA, Lobato RD. Intratumoural bleomycin as a treatment for recurrent cystic craniopharyngioma. Case report and review of the literature. Neurocirugia (Astur) 2002; 13:479–85

17. Jiang R, Liu Z, Zhu C. Preliminary exploration of the clinical effect of bleomycin on craniopharyngiomas. Stereotact Funct Neurosurg 2002;78:84–94

18. Honegger J, Buchfelder M, Fahlbusch R. Surgical treatment of craniopharyngiomas: endocrinological results. J Neurosurg 1999;90:251–7

19. Kalapurakal JA, Goldman S, Hsieh YC, Tomita T, Marymont MH. Clinical outcome in children with recurrent craniopharyngioma after primary surgery. Cancer J 2000;6:388–93

20. de Vries L, Lazar L, Phillip M. Craniopharyngioma: presentation and endocrine sequelae in 36 children. J Pediatr Endocrinol Metab 2003;16:703–10

21. Salomon F, Cuneo RC, Hesp R, Sönksen PH. The effects of treatment with recombinant human growth hormone on body composition and metabolism in adults with growth hormone deficiency. N Engl J Med 1989; 321:1797–803.

22. Beshyah SA, Freemantle C, Shahi M, Anyaoku V, Merson S, Lynch S, Skinner E, Sharp P, Foale R, Johnston DG. Replacement treatment with biosynthetic human growth hormone in growth hormone-deficient hypopituitary adults. Clin Endocrinol (Oxf) 1995; 42:73–84

23. Verhelst J, Abs R, Vandeweghe M, Mockel J, Legros JJ, Copinschi G, Mahler C, Velkeniers B, Vanhaelst L, Van Aelst A, De Rijdt D, Stevenaert A, Beckers A. Two years of replacement therapy in adults with growth hormone deficiency. Clin Endocrinol (Oxf) 1997;47:485–94

24. Weaver JU, Monson JP, Noonan K, John WG, Edwards A, Evans KA, Cunningham J. The effect of low dose recombinant human growth hormone replacement on regional fat distribution, insulin sensitivity, and cardiovascular risk factors in hypopituitary adults. J Clin Endocrinol Metab 1995;80:153–9

25. Muller HL, Bueb K, Bartels U, Roth C, Harz K, Graf N, Korinthenberg R, Bettendorf M, Kuhl J, Gutjahr P, Sorensen N, Calaminus G. Obesity after childhood craniopharyngioma – German multicenter study on pre-operative risk factors and quality of life. Klin Padiatr 2001;213:244–9

26. Lustig RH, Post SR, Srivannaboon K, Rose SR, Danish RK, Burghen GA, Xiong X, Wu S, Merchant TE. Risk factors for the development of obesity in children surviving brain tumors. J Clin Endocrinol Metab 2003;88:611–6

27. de Vile CJ, Grant DB, Hayward RD, Kendall BE, Neville BG, Stanhope R. Obesity in childhood craniopharyngioma: relation to post-operative hypothalamic damage shown by magnetic resonance imaging. J Clin Endocrinol Metab 1996;81:2734–7

28. Roth C, Wilken B, Hanefeld F, Schroter W, Leonhardt U. Hyperphagia in children with craniopharyngioma is associated with hyperleptinaemia and a failure in the downregulation of appetite. Eur J Endocrinol 1998; 138:89–91

29. Tomlinson JW, Holden N, Hills RK, Wheatley K, Clayton RN, Bates AS, Sheppard MC, Stewart PM. Association between premature mortality and hypopituitarism. West Midlands Prospective Hypopituitary Study Group. Lancet 2001;357:425–31

30. Bülow B, Attewell R, Hagmar L, Malmstrom P, Nordström CH, Erfurth EM. Postoperative prognosis in craniopharyngioma with respect to cardiovascular mortality, survival, and tumor recurrence. J Clin Endocrinol Metab 1998;83:3897–904

31. Regine WF, Kramer S. Pediatric craniopharyngiomas: long term results of combined treatment with surgery and radiation. Int J Radiat Oncol Biol Phys 1992;24:611–7

32. Martinez JA, Kearney JM, Kafatos A, Paquet S, Martinez-Gonzalez MA. Variables independently associated with self-reported obesity in the European Union. Public Health Nutr 1999;2:125–33

33. Abs R, Bengtsson B-Å, Hernberg-Ståhl E, Monson JP, Tauber JP, Wilton P, Wüster C. GH replacement in 1034 growth hormone deficient hypopituitary adults: demographic and clinical characteristics, dosing and safety. Clin Endocrinol (Oxf) 1999;50:703–13

34. de Boer H, Blok GJ, Voerman HJ, Phillips M, Schouten JA. Serum lipid levels in growth hormone-deficient men. Metabolism 1994;43:199–203

35. Rosén T, Edén S, Larson G, Wilhelmsen L, Bengtsson B-Å. Cardiovascular risk factors in adult patients with growth hormone deficiency. Acta Endocrinol (Copenh) 1993;129:195–200

36. Cuneo RC, Salomon F, Watts GF, Hesp R, Sönksen PH. Growth hormone treatment improves serum lipids and lipoproteins in adults with growth hormone deficiency. Metabolism 1993;42:1519–23

37. Seidell JC, Cigolini M, Charzewska J, Ellsinger BM, Contaldo F. Regional obesity and serum lipids in European women born in 1948. A multicenter study. Acta Med Scand Suppl 1988;723:189–97

38. Walton C, Lees B, Crook D, Worthington M, Godsland IF, Stevenson JC. Body fat distribution, rather than overall adiposity, influences serum lipids and lipoproteins in healthy men independently of age. Am J Med 1995;99:459–64

39. Gallus S, Colombo P, Scarpino V, Zuccaro P, Apolone G, La Vecchia C. Smoking in Italy, 2002. Tumori 2002; 88:453–6

40. Fernandez E, Schiaffino A, Borras JM. Epidemiology of smoking in Europe. [Spanish] Salud Publica Mex 2002;44 (Suppl 1):S11–19

41. Hakkaart-van Roijen L, Beckers A, Stevenaert A, Rutten FF. The burden of illness of hypopituitary adults with growth hormone deficiency. Pharmacoeconomics 1998;14:395–403

42. Verhelst J, Abs R. Long-term growth hormone replacement therapy in hypopituitary adults. Drugs 2002;62:2399–412

43. Carroll PV, Christ ER, Bengtsson B-Å, Carlsson L, Christiansen JS, Clemmons D, Hintz R, Ho K, Laron Z, Sizonenko P, Sönksen PH, Tanaka T, Thorne M. Growth hormone deficiency in adulthood and the effects of growth hormone replacement: a review. Growth Hormone Research Society Scientific Committee. J Clin Endocrinol Metab 1998;83:382–95

44. Pinto G, Bussieres L, Recasens C, Souberbielle JC, Zerah M, Brauner R. Hormonal factors influencing weight and growth pattern in craniopharyngioma. Horm Res 2000;53:163–9

45. Fontaine KR, Redden DT, Wang C, Westfall AO, Allison DB. Years of life lost due to obesity. JAMA 2003;289:187–93

46. Larsson B, Svardsudd K, Welin L, Wilhelmsen L, Bjorntorp P, Tibblin G. Abdominal adipose tissue distribution, obesity, and risk of cardiovascular disease and death: 13 year follow up of participants in the study of men born in 1913. Br Med J (Clin Res Ed) 1984;288:1401–4

47. Anderson KM, Castelli WP, Levy D. Cholesterol and mortality. 30 years of follow-up from the Framingham study. JAMA 1987;257:2176–80

48. Abdu TA, Neary R, Elhadd TA, Akber M, Clayton RN. Coronary risk in growth hormone deficient hypopituitary adults: increased predicted risk is due largely to lipid profile abnormalities. Clin Endocrinol (Oxf) 2001;55:209–16

49. Tibblin G, Svardsudd K, Welin L, Erikson H, Larsson B. Quality of life as an outcome variable and a risk factor for total mortality and cardiovascular disease: a study of men born in 1913. J Hypertens Suppl 1993;11:S81–6

50. Donnet A, Schmitt A, Dufour H, Grisoli F. Neuropsychological follow-up of twenty two adult patients after surgery for craniopharyngioma. Acta Neurochir (Wien) 1999;141:1049–54

51. Hew FL, Koschmann M, Christopher M, Rantzau C, Vaag A, Ward G, Beck-Nielsen H, Alford F. Insulin resistance in growth hormone-deficient adults: defects in glucose utilization and glycogen synthase activity. J Clin Endocrinol Metab 1996;81:555–64

24 Radiotherapy for the treatment of pituitary tumours and growth hormone deficiency in irradiated patients

Dominique Maiter

Cliniques Universitaires Saint Luc, Université Catholique de Louvain, Brussels, Belgium

Summary

With recent advances in surgical and medical techniques, pituitary tumours can generally be successfully treated using a combination of surgery, drugs and external radiotherapy. Pituitary irradiation is widely used as an efficient adjuvant treatment for preventing re-growth of incompletely resected or relapsing pituitary tumours. The effects of irradiation on hormone oversecretion, however, are often incomplete and slow. In patients with malignant brain tumours, the use of high-dose radiation therapy, which is often combined with chemotherapy, may cause serious and debilitating long-term complications. Late adverse effects of cranial or craniospinal irradiation include an increased risk of secondary meningiomas and gliomas. Radiation may also potentially cause cerebrovascular and neuro-psychological changes, although age, extent of surgery, concurrent diseases, and the duration of untreated hypopituitarism may also contribute to these adverse effects. The most frequent complication following radiation therapy of pituitary adenomas is hypopituitarism. The severity of pituitary deficit varies widely, ranging from isolated growth hormone (GH) insufficiency to complete anterior panhypopituitarism. Because the risk of hypopituitarism increases over time and can occur up to 20 years after treatment, long-term endocrine surveillance of patients who have received radiation therapy for pituitary tumours is clearly important. Radiation-induced endocrine effects appear in a given order of sensitivity, with the GH axis being the most vulnerable to the late effects of radiotherapy, followed by the gonadotrophin and corticotrophin axes. Nearly all children treated for a brain tumour with radiation of 30 gray or more develop severe GH deficiency (GHD) within 2–5 years. Although adults appear to be less radiosensitive than children, severe GHD is seen in the large majority of adult patients 5–10 years after they receive irradiation for a pituitary tumour. Data from KIMS – Pfizer International Metabolic Database – show that such patients have a poorer quality of life, higher body fat mass, lower high-density lipoprotein-cholesterol levels and lower bone mineral content (BMC) than non-irradiated patients with GHD. Importantly, the KIMS data demonstrate that irradiated patients respond equally well to GH therapy as non-irradiated patients, with comparable improvements in lean body mass, fat mass and BMC and a better response with respect to lipid profile. To date, data from KIMS also show no increased rate of tumour recurrence in irradiated patients treated with GH therapy.

Introduction

Most pituitary adenomas can be successfully treated with a variable combination of surgery, medical therapy and pituitary irradiation. Transsphenoidal surgery remains the mainstay treatment for the majority of these tumours [1] (see Chapter 22), although prolactinomas are usually well controlled with dopamine agonists (e.g. bromocriptine and cabergoline) and acromegalic patients benefit from recently developed medical agents, such as long-acting somatostatin analogues (octreotide LAR, lanreotide SR and Autogel) or a growth hormone (GH) receptor antagonist (peg-visomant) [2, 3]. Radiotherapy may be used as an adjuvant treatment to prevent re-growth of incompletely resected or relapsing pituitary tumours, or to obtain long-term hormonal control of secreting adenomas, when surgery and medical treatment have failed or are no longer desirable. Patients in whom surgery is contraindicated or refused may also be good candidates for radiation therapy.

In this chapter, we will first review the general principles and different types of radiotherapy, as well as the indications and limits of these techniques in the case of pituitary tumours. Late adverse consequences of cranial irradiation will be discussed, with a special emphasis on GH deficiency (GHD). Lastly, we will review our experience derived from KIMS – Pfizer International Metabolic Database – on the efficacy of GH treatment in irradiated GH-deficient adults.

General principles and techniques of radiotherapy

High-energy ionizing radiation produces biological effects on human tissues by altering DNA synthesis and repair [4]. Most cells will be specifically affected at the time of cell division, and therefore rapidly proliferating normal or tumorous tissues will be more sensitive to radiation than slowly or non-proliferating cells. The energy of the radiation determines the depth of absorption and the intensity of molecular/atomic interactions in the target tissue. The unit of absorbed dose is the gray (Gy), defined as the absorption of one joule per kilogram. One Gy is equivalent to 100 rads or 100 centi-gray. For any given total dose, the biological effects of radiation also depend on tissue sensitivity and on the fractionation size, as high doses per fraction increase the severity of effects occurring late after radiotherapy [5]. Calculation of the biologically effective dose provides a means of expressing the effects of various irradiation treatment schedules on a specific region in a uniform way [6].

Radiotherapy can be administered either by an external beam source or via intracavity techniques or interstitial implants (brachytherapy). Pituitary adenomas, as well as other tumours of the sellar region, are now treated almost exclusively by external techniques. Injection of a radioactive isotope such as yttrium^{90} (^{90}Y) may still be used occasionally for large cyst expansions of craniopharyngiomas [7], while treatment of pituitary tumours with radioactive implants – gold^{198} or ^{90}Y – is no longer used in most centres. We will therefore focus on external radiotherapy techniques.

Fractionated conventional radiotherapy

Fractionated conventional radiotherapy remains the most frequently employed radiotherapy technique. For deep-seated benign pituitary adenomas, high-energy (4 to 6 megavolt) photons are generated by a megavoltage linear accelerator or through nuclear decay of cobalt^{60} (^{60}Co). Radiation is usually delivered to the tumour and the entire pituitary fossa with a 1–2 cm margin by a three-field technique of two opposing lateral fields and one anterior oblique field lying in the same plane. In most European and American centres, the total dose ranges between 45 and 54 Gy, delivered as daily fractions of 1.8 to 2.0 Gy, five fractions per week, for a total period of 5 to 6 weeks. By contrast, large malignant brain tumours such as gliomas or astrocytomas, require higher doses of up to 60–70 Gy. The arrangement of the radiation fields leads inevitably to the administration of relatively high doses to regions in the frontal and temporal lobes, as well as in the hypothalamus.

Stereotactic conformal radiotherapy (SCRT)

SCRT is a high-precision technique derived from conventional fractionated irradiation, which combines a precise computer-assisted three-dimensional localization of the tumour and administration of linear accelerator stereotactic radiation by multiple fixed fields (4–6) with individualized shielding of each field conforming to the shape of the tumour [8, 9]. Compared with conventional radiotherapy, this technique ensures a more accurate delivery of radiation to the target volume, together with a reduction in the volume of normal tissue irradiated. Experience with SCRT is still scarce, but preliminary results indicate that it might be suitable for the treatment of pituitary adenomas, allowing for effective tumour control with low toxicity [9].

Stereotactic radiosurgery (SRS)

SRS utilizes multiple convergent beams to deliver a high (100 Gy or more) single dose of radiation to a discrete spherical tumour volume, with a steep dose gradient between high and low dose regions, thereby minimizing damage to surrounding structures. This can be accomplished with either a multiheaded gamma-emitting ^{60}Co unit, the 'gamma knife', or with multiple arcs, using a modified conventional linear accelerator. These techniques were used initially for the treatment of vascular malformations and small benign brain lesions [10]. They are now increasingly used for other indications including brain metastases and pituitary adenomas [11, 12]. Because of the damaging effects of high single doses of radiation to normal central nervous system structures [13, 14], SRS is particularly well suited for small, spherical pituitary tumours, at least 5 mm away from the optic chiasm. In addition to normal-tissue-sparing effects, SRS might also produce a more rapid normalization of hormonal overproduction by secreting pituitary adenomas [15, 16], although this remains to be ascertained in long-term prospective trials.

Proton beam therapy

Like SRS, proton beam therapy delivers high-dose stereotactic irradiation. In this case, fast charged particles (protons) lose energy and slow down in their passage through matter, thus increasing the chance of further atomic interactions. This results in a sharp increase in the ionization events close to the end of each particle's track (the Bragg peak). The width of the Bragg peak is pre-determined by adjusting the energy of the particles, allowing a precise 'deposition' of radiation at the level of the targeted tissue. Although appealing, this technique has so far been restricted to a few specialized centres, equipped with a cyclotron [17].

Indications for radiotherapy in the management of pituitary adenomas

Prolactinomas

Irradiation of prolactinomas may reduce the size of the tumour and prolactin hypersecretion, but this effect occurs very slowly and will often remain incomplete, with prolactin levels still remaining high 10 years after therapy [18, 19]. Recent results using SRS are more encouraging, although longer follow-up is needed [12, 20]. As a consequence of this, and because most prolactinomas, even invasive tumours, usually respond well to dopamine agonist therapy [3, 21], radiation is seldom used in the management of prolactinomas. Only after trans-sphenoidal debulking is radiation used to prevent re-growth of large/invasive residual tumours in patients who respond poorly to medical therapy.

GH-secreting adenomas

Modern goals of therapy in acromegaly are not only control of tumour growth and alleviation of mass effects, but also – most importantly – normalization of GH secretion, so that normal life-expectancy can be restored [2, 22]. This means lowering random serum GH concentrations to below 2 ng/ml and serum insulin-like growth factor I (IGF-I) concentrations to within the reference range for the patient's age and gender [22, 23]. In this regard, radiotherapy is not well suited for the treatment of acromegaly. Indeed, even though adenoma growth is invariably arrested, the decline in GH secretion, and therefore clinical improvement, is very slow after irradiation. Several studies have shown that safe GH and IGF-I levels are finally obtained only after 5–10 years, and then only in a minority of patients, ranging between 0 and 40% [24–30]. Somewhat better results were reported recently by Attanasio and colleagues [31] using gamma-knife SRS, although the rate of IGF-I normalization did not exceed 23% after a median follow-up of 46 months.

Cushing's disease

Pituitary irradiation is the rational choice in patients with Cushing's disease when pituitary surgery has been unsuccessful, or is contra-indicated. In addition, it may be considered as a possible first-line therapy in children, where it has a cure rate of 80%. This high success rate is at least as good as that observed after transsphenoidal surgery [32, 33]. In adults, the cure rate is lower (30–50%); however, a further third of patients are sufficiently improved to stop additional treatment [34, 35]. The results seem to be even better after failed pituitary surgery, as one study performed in 30 adults with persistent or recurrent Cushing's disease after surgery showed a remission rate of 43% at 12 months and up to 83% at 60 months [36]. None of these patients had a relapse of their disease after remission was achieved. The maximal benefits of radiotherapy usually occur within the first 2 years of treatment. High cure rates may also be achieved with proton beam therapy [17] or SRS [37, 38]; however, this is often at the expense of a higher incidence of side-effects, especially hypopituitarism.

Non-functioning pituitary adenomas (NFPAs)

NFPAs represent the most common type of pituitary macroadenomas and are conventionally treated with surgery in the first instance. Radiotherapy may be given as an adjuvant treatment post-operatively, but there is still considerable debate about who should receive it [39]. While some centres advocate pituitary irradiation for nearly all patients operated for an NFPA [40], others recommend it only for patients who are relapsing or considered at high risk of relapsing. To date, there have been no randomized trials of surgery alone versus surgery plus radiotherapy in the management of NFPAs.

The risk of tumour re-growth following surgery without post-operative irradiation is high, averaging 20–30% at 5 years, and 50% or more at 10 years, in several series [40–44] (Table 1). In contrast, most series of patients with NFPAs

Table 1. *Tumour control in patients with a pituitary tumour treated by surgery alone or by surgery and radiotherapy, expressed either as recurrence rate or as progression-free survival (PFS) rate at 10 years.*

	Surgery alone			**Surgery and radiotherapy**		
Reference	**Number of patients**	**Recurrence (%)**	**PFS at 10 years (%)**	**Number of patients**	**Recurrence (%)**	**PFS at 10 years (%)**
Sheline [41]	29	69	14	80	11	86
Ciric *et al.* [45]	32	28		67	6	
Ebersold *et al.* [42]	42	16		50	9	
Chun *et al.* [43]	60	15		54	7	
McCollough *et al.* [46]				76	5	92
Brada *et al.* [47]				336		95
Tsang *et al.* [48]				160	12	87
Gittoes *et al.* [44]	63		47	63		93
Turner *et al.* [40]	65		56			

treated with surgery followed by radiotherapy report excellent actuarial progression-free survival rates of 90–95% at both 5 and 10 years [41–48] (Table 1). Thus, clearly, radiotherapy is effective in preventing recurrence of NFPAs and should be considered in patients with a residual tumour after surgery, and in those with a particularly aggressive or invasive macroadenoma, as cavernous sinus invasion is correlated with a higher risk of relapse [1].

On the other hand, recent progress in the management of these tumours has allowed earlier diagnosis, a more complete excision by transsphenoidal surgery and careful surveillance through modern pituitary imaging techniques. These advances reduce the risk of recurrence and the obligatory need for early complementary irradiation [39]. Data reported by Lillehei and colleagues [49] clearly show that the risk of recurrence is very low when there is no macroscopic tumour remnant on a post-operative magnetic resonance imaging (MRI) scan. To date, however, there is no clear clinical, radiological or histological parameter that could guide clinicians in assessing the likelihood of relapse [39, 50]. The use of several immunohistochemical and molecular proliferation markers, such as PCNA, Ki-67, MIB-1 or PTTG, may help to identify potentially aggressive pituitary adenomas [51] that would warrant post-operative radiotherapy.

Currently accepted indications for radiotherapy in NFPAs include large tumour remnants with suprasellar or extrasellar extension, and small intrasellar residues showing evidence of re-growth on serial MRI scans after surgery. Because NFPAs are usually large, non-spherical and in close proximity to the optic apparatus, they are not good candidates for SRS. Limited experience seems to indicate efficient tumour control in selected cases [52].

Complications of radiotherapy for pituitary adenomas

In patients with malignant brain tumours, high-dose radiation therapy, often combined with chemotherapy, may induce long-term profound and debilitating complications, such as focal brain necrosis, leukoencephalopathy and cerebral atrophy, cerebrovascular changes, visual toxicity (cataract, optic neuropathy, retinopathy, cortical blindness, glaucoma) or hearing loss [53]. Fortunately, the lower doses of radiation used for treatment of pituitary adenomas (42–55 Gy), the absence of concomitant chemotherapy and the sparing of normal brain tissue from irradiation using conformal techniques, all result in a much lower toxicity after conventional pituitary irradiation. Even damage to the optic chiasm is very uncommon, provided the total dose does not exceed 50 Gy and fractionation is used. For example, Jones [54] found no case of optic neuropathy in a series of 322 patients treated with a total dose of 45 Gy in 1.8 Gy daily fractions, while Brada *et al.* [47] found only two cases of optic pathway damage in 411 patients treated with doses up to 50 Gy in daily fractions of 2 Gy or less.

Immediate side-effects of pituitary radiotherapy are mild and include nausea, loss of appetite and fatigue, which may last for 2–3 months after treatment. A reduction in taste, olfaction and salivation are also usual and may last for up to 6 months. Focal and reversible alopecia occurs almost universally at the entry sites of radiation, while mild dermatitis is less frequent. The most significant side-effects are delayed and include hypopituitarism, secondary brain tumours, cerebrovascular alterations and neuropsychological changes.

Hypopituitarism

Hypopituitarism is by far the most frequent complication occurring after radiation therapy of pituitary adenomas (Fig. 1; Table 2). The risk increases over time [55] and hormonal deficits may occur up to 20 years following radiotherapy, thus indicating the importance of long-term endocrine surveillance of these patients [47]. The degree of pituitary involvement is also dependent on the biologically effective dose to the hypothalamic–pituitary axis (a lower dose given in multiple fractions has less deleterious effects), age (children are more sensitive than adults) and the nature of the

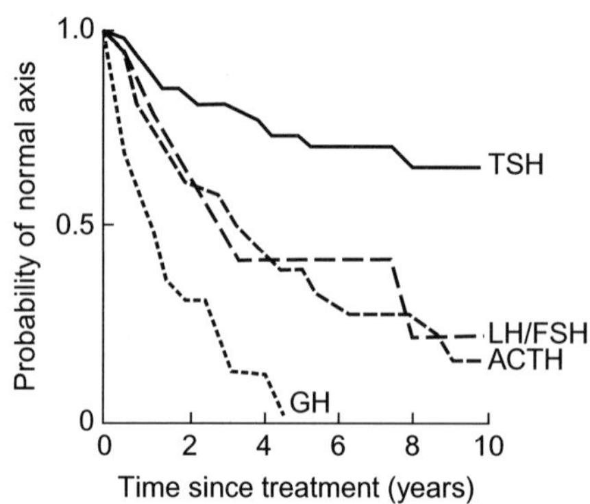

Figure 1. *Life-table analysis indicating probabilities of initially normal hypothalamic–pituitary–target gland axes remaining normal after radiotherapy for pituitary adenomas. ACTH, adrenocorticotrophin; FSH, follicle-stimulating hormone; LH, luteinizing hormone; TSH, thyrotrophin. Reproduced from [55] with permission from Oxford University Press.*

underlying disease [56]. The more disturbed the pituitary function prior to irradiation, the greater the overall incidence of hypopituitarism [39, 55, 57].

There is evidence that radiation-induced endocrine effects occur predominantly at the hypothalamic rather than the pituitary level [39, 56, 58]. Patients with pituitary adenomas treated by brachytherapy develop less hypopituitarism than do patients who undergo external irradiation [59], probably as a result of lower hypothalamic exposure to radiation. The pattern of neuroendocrine disturbances following radiotherapy (hyperprolactinaemia, delayed gonadotrophin response to gonadotrophin-releasing hormone, delayed response of thyrotrophin [TSH] to TSH-releasing hormone, impaired GH response to an insulin tolerance test [ITT] but intact somatotroph responsiveness to exogenous GH-releasing hormone [GHRH]) points to a primary

Table 2. *Observed or calculated incidences (%) of anterior pituitary hormone deficiencies after conventional radiotherapy (RT) for a pituitary adenoma or a tumour of the hypothalamic–pituitary (H–P) region.*

					Pituitary hormone deficiency			
Reference	**Number of patients**	**Treatment**	**Dose (Gy) to the H–P axis**	**Time after RT (years)**	**GH (%)**	**LH/FSH (%)**	**ACTH (%)**	**TSH (%)**
Feek *et al.*	30	RT alone	37.5	10	NA	47	30	16
[57]	16	RT + surgery	37.5	10	NA	70	54	38
Snyder *et al.*	13	RT alone	44–50	5 [2–9]	NA	50	55	15
[66]	22	RT + surgery	42–53	4.2 [2–9]	NA	67	67	55
Littley *et al.*	165	RT	37.5–42.5	5	100	91	77	42
[55]		(+ surgery in 140)		8	100	96	84	49
McCollough	11	RT alone	42–55	[2–21]	NA	NA	41	45
et al. [46]	57	RT + surgery	42–55	[2–21]	NA	NA	77	84
Tsang *et al.*	160	RT	40–50	8.3 [1–20]	NA	67	68	65
[48]		(+ surgery in 128)						
Toogood *et al.*	85	RT	37.5–45	[1–10]	100*	76	47	26
[99]		(+ surgery in 58)						
Estimated overall incidence	**559**		**37.5–55**	**5–10**	**> 95**	**73**	**63**	**50**

*100% probability of developing severe GHD 4 years after RT if the initial GH peak in an insulin tolerance test is below 30 mU/L. ACTH, adrenocorticotrophin; FSH, follicle-stimulating hormone; LH, luteinizing hormone; NA, not available; TSH, thyrotrophin.

hypothalamic defect [56]. Early or accelerated puberty may also occasionally occur after cranial irradiation in childhood [60, 61].

As will be discussed below, the GH axis is the most sensitive to the late effects of radiotherapy [62], followed by the gonadotrophin and corticotrophin axes. Prolactin levels may be slightly elevated, while the TSH axis seems to be the least sensitive to radiation damage (Fig. 1; Table 2). Mild forms of central hypothyroidism following irradiation might, however, be underestimated [63], as diagnosis usually relies on a low circulating thyroxine concentration, which is not a very sensitive marker of thyroid dysfunction. One should also remember that deficiencies may occur in any sequence, and that full endocrine testing is always required in irradiated patients.

The reason for this order of pituitary hormone sensitivity to radiation is not known. Radiation damage to the hypothalamic–pituitary region is related to both direct lesions of hypothalamic neurons and vascular alterations in the hypothalamic–pituitary axis. Differential radiosensitivity of hypothalamic neurones has been suggested and is supported by animal studies [64]. Furthermore, defects in neurotransmitter input from suprahypothalamic pathways may also participate in the impairment of anterior pituitary secretions [65].

After 5–10 years following post-operative radiotherapy for pituitary adenoma, 40–50% of patients have developed panhypopituitarism [55, 66, 67], at a speed dependent on the total and fractional doses received. Almost all patients will be GH deficient at this time, more than 70% will have gonadotrophin deficiency, about 50–60% will have secondary adrenal insufficiency and 40–50% will be overtly TSH-insufficient (Table 2). It should be noted, however, that hypopituitarism in these patients cannot be attributed to radiotherapy alone, but also results to a significant extent from the pre-existing tumour and its surgical treatment [48, 50]. Early recognition and treatment of radiation-induced pituitary deficits are of importance because several studies have now reported a twofold increase in mortality in patients with hypopituitarism, mainly as a result of cardiovascular and cerebrovascular complications [68–70].

Radiation-induced brain tumours

There is compelling evidence that cranial or craniospinal irradiation given for childhood cancer induces an increased risk of meningiomas or gliomas [71, 72]. Whether a similar risk of late secondary brain tumours occurs after irradiation for a pituitary tumour is still a matter of debate. In a long-term follow-up study of 334 patients irradiated for a pituitary adenoma, Brada *et al.* [73] observed the development of two meningiomas, two gliomas and one meningeal sarcoma, consistent with an increased risk of a secondary brain tumour of 1.9% at 20 years, about tenfold that in the normal population. Likewise, Tsang and colleagues [74] reported a 16-fold risk increase for glioma in a similar Canadian cohort. These findings have, however, not been corroborated by other studies [54, 75], and a more valid comparison with a control population of non-irradiated pituitary tumour patients remains to be made. With this caveat in mind, it is nevertheless reasonable to assume that there is a slight but definite excess risk of secondary brain tumours among individuals irradiated for a pituitary adenoma, as suggested by two recent crude meta-analyses [39, 76].

Cerebrovascular alterations

Radiation may cause accelerated atherosclerosis and thus affect all blood vessels, including cerebral arteries. The supraclinoid region of the internal carotid seems especially vulnerable in children irradiated for a chiasmatic glioma [77, 78], and several case reports implicate brain radiotherapy as a major contributing factor for the development of cerebrovascular damage [79]. Cerebrovascular complications and deaths occur more frequently in patients with a pituitary tumour treated by surgery and radiotherapy [69, 80–82], but recent studies suggest that factors other than radiation – such as age, female gender, the presence of craniopharyngioma (see Chapter 23), the extent of surgery and the duration of untreated pituitary insufficiency – probably have more important roles in explaining cerebrovascular alterations and mortality [68–70].

Neuropsychological changes

Large parts of the frontal and temporal lobes are exposed to significant irradiation, as are central areas of the brain. It is therefore a concern that conventional radiotherapy for a pituitary tumour may lead to adverse neuropsychological and cognitive consequences, as a result of micro-vascular injury or direct damage to neural or glial cells [83]. An increased prevalence of cognitive dysfunction (memory loss, difficulty with problem solving or coping with new situations), poor social adjustment and mood disorders (depression, anxiety, obsessive–compulsive disorder) has been reported in patients operated on and irradiated for a pituitary tumour, when compared with healthy controls [84–87]. Again, in addition to radiotherapy, a number of different variables, such as age, surgery, hypo-pituitarism and the underlying disease, may contribute to these late neuropsychological effects. In fact, in the few relevant studies so far, neuropsychological function was found to be similar in irradiated and non-irradiated patients [84, 86], but more research is clearly needed in this field.

Is stereotactic radiotherapy less harmful?

The previous descriptions of late complications mainly apply to conventional fractionated radio-therapy and are for the most part based on old or retrospective studies of treatments given up to 50 years ago. Recent improvements in imaging techniques, radiation equipment and radiotherapy strategies should reduce the future incidence of these complications. SRS and other highly conformal dose-delivering techniques seem to be associated with less adverse consequences on the surrounding brain structures, although extended long-term follow-up studies are still scarce. However, the incidence of hypopituitarism after stereotactic radiotherapy does not seem to be significantly lowered because high doses of radiation are still being delivered to the hypothalamic–pituitary axis [88–90]. More than 50% of these patients will develop panhypo-pituitarism over time, and the majority will become severely GH deficient [91].

Irradiation-induced GHD

Over the last few years, the characterization of a distinct GHD syndrome in adults has led to increased interest in the study of the GH axis [92]. Replacement therapy for GH-deficient adults has been shown to be valuable and is approved and recommended in many countries [92, 93]. As already mentioned, GH is the most vulnerable of all the anterior pituitary hormones to the effects of radiation on the hypothalamic–pituitary axis [62]. Following cranial irradiation, secretion of GH declines more rapidly than luteinizing hormone/follicle-stimulating hormone, adrenocorticotrophin and TSH (Fig. 1) and in some instances will be the only hormone affected. Doses as low as 18 Gy – such as those given prophylactically for acute lymphoblastic leukaemia – already impact on the somatotrophic axis [94–96], and isolated severe GHD has been observed following total body irradiation with a dose of 10 Gy [97].

Evidence suggests that nearly 100% of children irradiated for a brain tumour and receiving doses in excess of 30 Gy on the hypothalamic–pituitary structures will develop severe GHD 2–5 years later [6, 98]. Young children seem to be more radiosensitive than older children or adults [56], but severe GHD is also observed in the vast majority of adult patients, 5–10 years after they have received conventional fractionated radiotherapy for a pitu-itary tumour [55, 99] (Table 2). The mechanisms of radiation-induced GHD appear to operate mainly at the hypothalamic level, GHRH-producing neurons being very sensitive to radiation, but may also involve damage to the suprahypothalamic neuro-transmitter pathways [56, 65, 100, 101].

The biochemical diagnosis of severe adult GHD is classically based on the demonstration of a decreased GH peak response (< 3.0 ng/ml) to two pharmacological stimuli [102]. The ITT is the 'gold standard' and the most sensitive test for identifying radiation-induced GHD [103], while responses to GHRH and/or arginine stimulation are less sensitive to changes in GH secretory status [103–105]. The GH-dependent markers, IGF-I and IGF-binding protein-3 (IGFBP-3) are frequently low in irradiated GH-deficient patients, but cannot be used as reliable indices of the occurrence of radiation-induced GHD [56, 106]. The exception, perhaps, is paediatric cancer survivors, in whom severe GHD is associated with an IGF-I SD score (SDS) of less than –2 in over 95% of cases [96].

Effects of GH treatment in irradiated GH-deficient patients

There is a logical concern that the known beneficial effects of GH replacement therapy in GH-deficient adults may be attenuated in patients who have received prior cranial irradiation, as irradiation may have late adverse effects on brain structures and functions. For example, physiological GH replacement therapy induced only minor improvements in body composition, lipid profile and bone mineral density in GH-deficient adult survivors of childhood cancer previously treated by cranial irradiation [107]. We therefore recently analysed data from 1107 patients (590 males) with severe GHD in KIMS, who had previously received treatment for either a pituitary adenoma (n = 904) or a craniopharyngioma (n = 203) [108]. Among these patients, 477 (43%) had received radiotherapy at least 1 year (median, 9 years) before the onset of GH treatment.

Prior to the start of GH treatment, adult GH-deficient patients with a previous history of pituitary radiotherapy had a greater impairment in quality of life (QoL), a higher body fat mass, lower high-density lipoprotein-cholesterol levels and lower bone mineral content (BMC) than non-irradiated patients, whereas there were no differences in IGF-I SDS, body mass index, blood pressure, lean body mass (LBM) and other lipid parameters between the two groups of patients (Table 3). The observed alterations in irradiated patients may result from a longer duration of untreated GHD, or from the detrimental effects of

Table 3. *Baseline clinical and biochemical parameters in adult patients with severe GHD, having received (IRR; n = 477) or not received (N-IRR; n = 630) radiotherapy for a pituitary adenoma or a craniopharyngioma. Data are shown as mean ± SEM.*

	IRR	N-IRR	*p* value
IGF-I SDS	–1.72 ± 0.07	–1.92 ± 0.07	NS
QoL-AGHDA score*	10.4 ± 0.3	9.3 ± 0.3	< 0.02
Body mass index	29.2 ± 0.3	29.0 ± 0.2	NS
Systolic blood pressure (mmHg)	128 ± 1	130 ± 1	NS
Diastolic blood pressure (mmHg)	80 ± 1	80 ± 1	NS
Lean body mass† (kg)	56.5 ± 1.0	57.7 ± 0.9	NS
Fat mass† (kg)	27.9 ± 0.9	25.2 ± 0.9	< 0.001
Total cholesterol (mmol/L)	6.07 ± 0.06	6.02 ± 0.06	NS
HDL-cholesterol (mmol/L)	1.22 ± 0.02	1.27 ± 0.02	< 0.05
LDL-cholesterol (mmol/L)	3.86 ± 0.06	3.79 ± 0.05	NS
Bone mineral content‡ (kg)	2.95 ± 0.32	3.33 ± 0.36	< 0.01

*A lower QoL-AGHDA score means a better quality of life (QoL); †, measured by bioimpedance; ‡, measured by dual-energy X-ray absorptiometry. HDL, high-density lipoprotein; LDL, low-density lipoprotein; QoL-AGHDA, quality of life-assessment of GHD in adults. No difference was observed between the two groups regarding age at baseline evaluation, sex ratio, aetiology, previous medical history, severity of GHD and other treatment modalities [108].

radiotherapy on the brain. Page *et al.* [109] also reported more depression and emotional lability in a group of irradiated GH-deficient patients compared with patients who had undergone mastoid surgery, but the respective effects of GHD and irradiation could not be disentangled from each other. In contrast, in a small cohort of patients with hypopituitarism and GHD, using a different questionnaire, Wallymahmed and colleagues [110] could not find any significant differences in QoL scores between those who had received radiotherapy and those who had not.

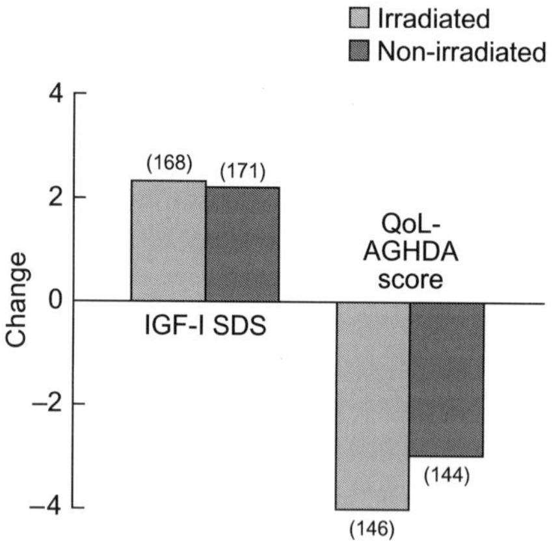

Figure 2. *Change in IGF-I SDS and Quality of Life Assessment of GHD in Adults (QoL-AGHDA) score in irradiated and non-irradiated GH-deficient adult patients after 1 year of GH treatment with a median dose of 0.40 mg/day (data from KIMS 2002). Number of patients in parentheses.*

Our recent analysis of the KIMS database also showed that adult patients who have been irradiated respond equally well to GH as patients with severe GHD who have never received pituitary irradiation [108]. Replacement therapy with a comparable daily dose of GH (median, 0.40 mg) for 1 year induced similar increases in IGF-I SDS (+2) in both irradiated and non-irradiated patients, and similar improvements in QoL (Fig. 2). LBM increased and fat mass decreased to a similar degree in both groups (Fig. 3). These positive effects of GH were maintained during the first 2 years of treatment. By the end of the second year of GH treatment, BMC had also increased in both groups. In comparison with patients who had never received radiotherapy, irradiated patients showed an even better response with respect to the lipid profile. Levels of total and low-density lipoprotein-cholesterol were reduced in both groups. However, the reduction was significantly greater in irradiated compared with non-irradiated patients (Fig. 3). This difference was maintained over the first 2 years of GH treatment. Data from KIMS also show no increased rate of tumour recurrence in irradiated patients treated

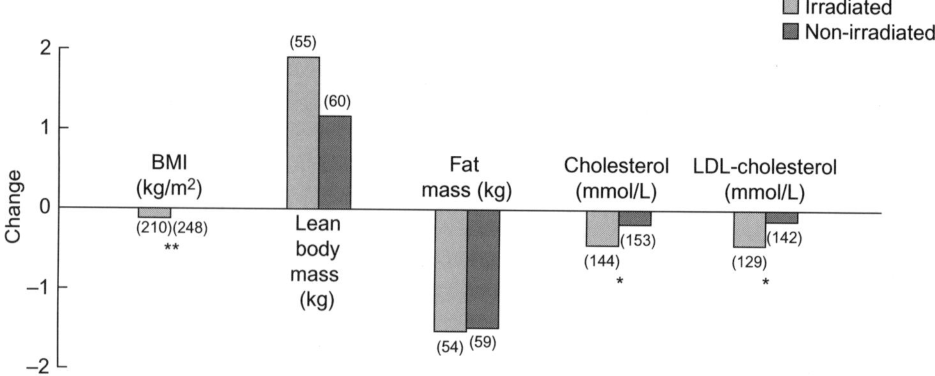

Figure 3. *Changes in body composition (measured by bioelectrical impedance analysis), lipids and body mass index (BMI) in irradiated and non-irradiated GH-deficient adult patients after 1 year of GH treatment (data from KIMS 2002). Number of patients in parentheses. LDL, low-density lipoprotein.* $^*p < 0.05$, $^{**}p < 0.01$.

with GH, but a longer follow-up is needed to clearly settle this issue.

Conclusions

Despite significant advances in the surgical and medical management of patients with pituitary tumours, external radiotherapy remains widely used as an adjuvant treatment. Pituitary irradiation is especially efficient for preventing re-growth of a tumour remnant, although its effects on hormonal overproduction are often delayed and incomplete. The most significant complication of radiotherapy is hypopituitarism. This may encompass a wide range of deficits from isolated GH insufficiency to complete anterior panhypopituitarism, which is observed in about half of all patients after a delay of 5–10 years. Other late adverse effects include a slight but definite risk of secondary brain tumours and, potentially, cerebrovascular and neuropsychological alterations. A direct link between these latter changes and pituitary irradiation is, however, not firmly established, and other confounding factors such as age, underlying disease, extent of surgery, or the duration of untreated hypopituitarism, may contribute to a significant extent. Stereotactic radiotherapy and SRS are well-suited techniques for small spherical pituitary tumours, at least 5 mm away from the optic apparatus. Although these techniques may result in less damage to the surrounding brain structures than conventional radiotherapy, they will also frequently induce pituitary hormone deficits.

Severe GHD is present after a few years in the vast majority of patients irradiated post-operatively for a pituitary tumour. Because this deficit results in well-characterized metabolic alterations in adults and seems to be associated with increased mortality, it needs to be diagnosed as early as possible, preferably using the ITT, which is the most sensitive test for detecting radiation-induced GHD. Nowadays, most of these patients will receive GH replacement therapy and, reassuringly, data recently analysed from KIMS show that prior pituitary irradiation does not compromise the well-known beneficial effects of GH in these patients.

References

1. Fahlbusch R, Buchfelder M, Nomikos P. Pituitary surgery. In: Melmed S. The pituitary. 2. Malden: Blackwell Science 2002:405–18
2. Melmed S, Casanueva FF, Cavagnini F, Chanson P, Frohman L, Grossman A, Ho K, Kleinberg D, Lamberts S, Laws E, Lombardi G, Vance ML, Werder KV, Wass J, Giustina A. Guidelines for acromegaly management. J Clin Endocrinol Metab 2002;87:4054–8
3. Verhelst J, Abs R, Maiter D, van den Bruel A, Vandeweghe M, Velkeniers B, Mockel J, Lamberigts G, Petrossians P, Coremans P, Mahler C, Stevenaert A, Verlooy J, Raftopoulos C, Beckers A. Cabergoline in the treatment of hyperprolactinemia: a study in 455 patients. J Clin Endocrinol Metab 1999;84:2518–22
4. Purdy JA. Principles of radiologic physics, dosimetry and treatment planning. In: Perez CA, Brady LW. Principles and practice of radiation oncology. Philadelphia: Lippincott-Raven 1998:253–71
5. Fowler JF. Fractionation factors for late effects in head and neck cancers. Int J Radiat Oncol Biol Phys 1992;22:219–25
6. Schmiegelow M, Lassen S, Poulsen HS, Feldt-Rasmussen U, Schmiegelow K, Hertz H, Müller J. Cranial radiotherapy of childhood brain tumours: growth hormone deficiency and its relation to the biological effective dose of irradiation in a large population based study. Clin Endocrinol (Oxf) 2000;53:191–7
7. Blackburn TP, Doughty D, Plowman PN. Stereotactic intracavitary therapy of recurrent cystic craniopharyngioma by instillation of 90yttrium. Br J Neurosurg 1999;13:359–65
8. Laing RW, Bentley RE, Nahum AE, Warrington AP, Brada M. Stereotactic radiotherapy of irregular targets: a comparison between static conformal beams and non-coplanar arcs. Radiother Oncol 1993;28:241–6
9. Jalali R, Brada M, Perks JR, Warrington AP, Traish D, Burchell L, McNair H, Thomas DG, Robinson S, Johnston DG. Stereotactic conformal radiotherapy for pituitary adenomas: technique and preliminary experience. Clin Endocrinol (Oxf) 2000;52:695–702
10. Backlund EO. Radiosurgery in intracranial tumors and vascular malformations. J Neurosurg Sci 1989;33:91–3
11. Boyd TS, Mehta MP. Stereotactic radiosurgery for brain metastases. Oncology (Huntingt) 1999;13:1397–409
12. Pollock BE, Nippoldt TB, Stafford SL, Foote RL, Abboud CF. Results of stereotactic radiosurgery in patients with hormone-producing pituitary adenomas: factors associated with endocrine normalization. J Neurosurg 2002;97:525–30

13. Sheline GE, Wara WM, Smith V. Therapeutic irradiation and brain injury. Int J Radiat Oncol Biol Phys 1980;6:1215–28

14. Leber KA, Bergloff J, Pendl G. Dose-response tolerance of the visual pathways and cranial nerves of the cavernous sinus to stereotactic radiosurgery. J Neurosurg 1998;88:43–50

15. Landolt AM, Haller D, Lomax N, Scheib S, Schubiger O, Siegfried J, Wellis G. Stereotactic radiosurgery for recurrent surgically treated acromegaly: comparison with fractionated radiotherapy. J Neurosurg 1998; 88:1002–8

16. Yoon SC, Suh TS, Jang HS, Chung SM, Kim YS, Ryu MR, Choi KH, Son HY, Kim MC, Shinn KS. Clinical results of 24 pituitary macroadenomas with linac-based stereotactic radiosurgery. Int J Radiat Oncol Biol Phys 1998;41:849–53

17. Kjellberg RN, Kliman B, Swisher B, Butler W. Proton beam therapy of Cushing's disease and Nelson's syndrome. In: Black PML, Zervas NT, Chester Ridgway E, Martin JB, editors. Secretory tumors of the pituitary gland. New York: Raven Press 1984:295–307

18. Littley MD, Shalet SM, Reid H, Beardwell CG, Sutton ML. The effect of external pituitary irradiation on elevated serum prolactin levels in patients with pituitary macroadenomas. Q J Med 1991;81:985–98

19. Tsagarakis S, Grossman A, Plowman PN, Jones AE, Touzel R, Rees LH, Wass JA, Besser GM. Megavoltage pituitary irradiation in the management of prolactinomas: long-term follow-up. Clin Endocrinol (Oxf) 1991;34:399–406

20. Landolt AM, Lomax N. Gamma knife radiosurgery for prolactinomas. J Neurosurg 2000;93 (Suppl 3):14–18

21. Colao A, Di Sarno A, Landi ML, Cirillo S, Sarnacchiaro F, Facciolli G, Pivonello R, Cataldi M, Merola B, Annunziato L, Lombardi G. Long-term and low-dose treatment with cabergoline induces macroprolactinoma shrinkage. J Clin Endocrinol Metab 1997;82:3574–9

22. Brabant G. Insulin-like growth factor I: marker for diagnosis of acromegaly and monitoring the efficacy of treatment. Eur J Endocrinol 2003;148 (Suppl 2):S15–20

23. Swearingen B, Barker FG, 2nd, Katznelson L, Biller BM, Grinspoon S, Klibanski A, Moayeri N, Black PM, Zervas NT. Long-term mortality after transsphenoidal surgery and adjunctive therapy for acromegaly. J Clin Endocrinol Metab 1998;83:3419–26

24. Barkan AL, Halasz I, Dornfeld KJ, Jaffe CA, Friberg RD, Chandler WF, Sandler HM. Pituitary irradiation is ineffective in normalizing plasma insulin-like growth factor I in patients with acromegaly. J Clin Endocrinol Metab 1997;82:3187–91

25. Thalassinos NC, Tsagarakis S, Ioannides G, Tzavara I, Papavasiliou C. Megavoltage pituitary irradiation lowers but seldom leads to safe GH levels in acromegaly: a long-term follow-up study. Eur J Endocrinol 1998; 138:160–3

26. Jaffe CA. Reevaluation of conventional pituitary irradiation in the therapy of acromegaly. Pituitary 1999;2:55–62

27. Powell JS, Wardlaw SL, Post KD, Freda PU. Outcome of radiotherapy for acromegaly using normalization of insulin-like growth factor I to define cure. J Clin Endocrinol Metab 2000;85:2068–71

28. Barrande G, Pittino-Lungo M, Coste J, Ponvert D, Bertagna X, Luton JP, Bertherat J. Hormonal and metabolic effects of radiotherapy in acromegaly: long-term results in 128 patients followed in a single center. J Clin Endocrinol Metab 2000;85:3779–85

29. Cozzi R, Barausse M, Asnaghi D, Dallabonzana D, Lodrini S, Attanasio R. Failure of radiotherapy in acromegaly. Eur J Endocrinol 2001;145:717–26

30. Epaminonda P, Porretti S, Cappiello V, Beck-Peccoz P, Faglia G, Arosio M. Efficacy of radiotherapy in normalizing serum IGF-I, acid-labile subunit (ALS) and IGFBP-3 levels in acromegaly. Clin Endocrinol (Oxf) 2001;55:183–9

31. Attanasio R, Epaminonda P, Motti E, Giugni E, Ventrella L, Cozzi R, Farabola M, Loli P, Beck-Peccoz P, Arosio M. Gamma-knife radiosurgery in acromegaly: a 4-year follow-up study. J Clin Endocrinol Metab 2003;88:3105–12

32. Devoe DJ, Miller WL, Conte FA, Kaplan SL, Grumbach MM, Rosenthal SM, Wilson CB, Gitelman SE. Long-term outcome in children and adolescents after transsphenoidal surgery for Cushing's disease. J Clin Endocrinol Metab 1997;82:3196–202

33. Jennings AS, Liddle GW, Orth DN. Results of treating childhood Cushing's disease with pituitary irradiation. N Engl J Med 1977;297:957–62

34. Howlett TA, Plowman PN, Wass JA, Rees LH, Jones AE, Besser GM. Megavoltage pituitary irradiation in the management of Cushing's disease and Nelson's syndrome: long-term follow-up. Clin Endocrinol (Oxf) 1989;31:309–23

35. Orth DN, Liddle GW. Results of treatment in 108 patients with Cushing's syndrome. N Engl J Med 1971;285:243–7

36. Estrada J, Boronat M, Mielgo M, Magallon R, Millan I, Diez S, Lucas T, Barcelo B. The long-term outcome of pituitary irradiation after unsuccessful transsphenoidal surgery in Cushing's disease. N Engl J Med 1997; 336:172–7

37. Sheehan JM, Vance ML, Sheehan JP, Ellegala DB, Laws ER Jr. Radiosurgery for Cushing's disease after failed transsphenoidal surgery. J Neurosurg 2000;93:738–42

38. Hoybye C, Grenback E, Rahn T, Degerblad M, Thorén M, Hulting AL. Adrenocorticotropic hormone-producing pituitary tumors: 12- to 22-year follow-up after treatment with stereotactic radiosurgery. Neurosurgery 2001;49:284–91

39. Plowman PN. Pituitary adenoma radiotherapy – when, who and how? Clin Endocrinol (Oxf) 1999;51:265–71

40. Turner HE, Stratton IM, Byrne JV, Adams CB, Wass JA. Audit of selected patients with nonfunctioning pituitary adenomas treated without irradiation – a follow-up study. Clin Endocrinol (Oxf) 1999;51:281–4

41. Sheline GE. Treatment of nonfunctioning chromophobe adenomas of the pituitary. Am J Roentgenol Radium Ther Nucl Med 1974;120:553–61

42. Ebersold MJ, Quast LM, Laws ER Jr, Scheithauer B, Randall RV. Long-term results in transsphenoidal removal of nonfunctioning pituitary adenomas. J Neurosurg 1986;64:713–9

43. Chun M, Masko GB, Hetelekidis S. Radiotherapy in the treatment of pituitary adenomas. Int J Radiat Oncol Biol Phys 1988;15:305–9

44. Gittoes NJ, Bates AS, Tse W, Bullivant B, Sheppard MC, Clayton RN, Stewart PM. Radiotherapy for non-function pituitary tumours. Clin Endocrinol (Oxf) 1998;48:331–7

45. Ciric I, Mikhael M, Stafford T, Lawson L, Garces R. Transsphenoidal microsurgery of pituitary macro-adenomas with long-term follow-up results. J Neurosurg 1983;59:395–401

46. McCollough WM, Marcus RB Jr, Rhoton AL Jr, Ballinger WE, Million RR. Long-term follow-up of radiotherapy for pituitary adenoma: the absence of late recurrence after greater than or equal to 4500 cGy. Int J Radiat Oncol Biol Phys 1991;21:607–14

47. Brada M, Rajan B, Traish D, Ashley S, Holmes-Sellors PJ, Nussey S, Uttley D. The long-term efficacy of conservative surgery and radiotherapy in the control of pituitary adenomas. Clin Endocrinol (Oxf) 1993;38:571–8

48. Tsang RW, Brierley JD, Panzarella T, Gospodarowicz MK, Sutcliffe SB, Simpson WJ. Radiation therapy for pituitary adenoma: treatment outcome and prognostic factors. Int J Radiat Oncol Biol Phys 1994;30:557–65

49. Lillehei KO, Kirschman DL, Kleinschmidt-DeMasters BK, Ridgway EC. Reassessment of the role of radiation therapy in the treatment of endocrine-inactive pituitary macroadenomas. Neurosurgery 1998;43:432–8

50. Boelaert K, Gittoes NJ. Radiotherapy for non-functioning pituitary adenomas. Eur J Endocrinol 2001;144:569–75

51. Thapar K, Kovacs K, Scheithauer BW, Stefaneanu L, Horvath E, Pernicone PJ, Murray D, Laws ER Jr. Proliferative activity and invasiveness among pituitary adenomas and carcinomas: an analysis using the MIB-1 antibody. Neurosurgery 1996;38:99–107

52. Hayashi M, Izawa M, Hiyama H, Nakamura S, Atsuchi S, Sato H, Nakaya K, Sasaki K, Ochiai T, Kubo O, Hori T, Takakura K. Gamma knife radiosurgery for pituitary adenomas. Stereotact Funct Neurosurg 1999;72 (Suppl 1):111–8

53. Keime-Guibert F, Napolitano M, Delattre JY. Neurological complications of radiotherapy and chemotherapy. J Neurol 1998;245:695–708

54. Jones A. Radiation oncogenesis in relation to the treatment of pituitary tumours. Clin Endocrinol (Oxf) 1991;35:379–97

55. Littley MD, Shalet SM, Beardwell CG, Ahmed SR, Applegate G, Sutton ML. Hypopituitarism following external radiotherapy for pituitary tumours in adults. Q J Med 1989;70:145–60

56. Darzy KH, Shalet SM. Pathogenesis and clinical presentation of radiation-induced hypopituitarism. In: Kleinberg DL, Clemmons DR, editors. Central and peripheral mechanisms in pituitary disease. Bristol: Bioscientifica 2002:51–69

57. Feek CM, McLelland J, Seth J, Toft AD, Irvine WJ, Padfield PL, Edwards CR. How effective is external pituitary irradiation for growth hormone-secreting pituitary tumors? Clin Endocrinol (Oxf) 1984;20:401–8

58. Blacklay A, Grossman A, Ross RJ, Savage MO, Davies PS, Plowman PN, Coy DH, Besser GM. Cranial irradiation for cerebral and nasopharyngeal tumours in children: evidence for the production of a hypothalamic defect in growth hormone release. J Endocrinol 1986;108:25–9

59. Jadresic A, Jimenez LE, Joplin GF. Long-term effect of ^{90}Y pituitary implantation in acromegaly. Acta Endocrinol (Copenh) 1987;115:301–6

60. Rappaport R, Brauner R, Czernichow P, Thibaud E, Renier D, Zucker JM, Lemerle J. Effect of hypothalamic and pituitary irradiation on pubertal development in children with cranial tumors. J Clin Endocrinol Metab 1982;54:1164–8

61. Ogilvy-Stuart AL, Clayton PE, Shalet SM. Cranial irradiation and early puberty. J Clin Endocrinol Metab 1994;78:1282–6

62. Shalet SM. Radiation and pituitary dysfunction. N Engl J Med 1993;328:131–3

63. Rose SR, Lustig RH, Pitukcheewanont P, Broome DC, Burghen GA, Li H, Hudson MM, Kun LE, Heideman RL. Diagnosis of hidden central hypothyroidism in survivors of childhood cancer. J Clin Endocrinol Metab 1999;84:4472–9

64. Robinson IC, Fairhall KM, Hendry JH, Shalet SM. Differential radiosensitivity of hypothalamo-pituitary function in the young adult rat. J Endocrinol 2001;169:519–26

65. Jorgensen EV, Schwartz ID, Hvizdala E, Barbosa J, Phuphanich S, Shulman DI, Root AW, Estrada J, Hu CS, Bercu BB. Neurotransmitter control of growth hormone secretion in children after cranial radiation therapy. J Pediatr Endocrinol 1993;6:131–42

66. Snyder PJ, Fowble BF, Schatz NJ, Savino PJ, Gennarelli TA. Hypopituitarism following radiation therapy of pituitary adenomas. Am J Med 1986;81:457–62

67. Nelson PB, Goodman ML, Flickenger JC, Richardson DW, Robinson AG. Endocrine function in patients with large pituitary tumors treated with operative decompression and radiation therapy. Neurosurgery 1989;24:398–400

68. Tomlinson JW, Holden N, Hills RK, Wheatley K, Clayton RN, Bates AS, Sheppard MC, Stewart PM. Association between premature mortality and hypopituitarism. West Midlands Prospective Hypopituitary Study Group. Lancet 2001;357:425–31

69. Brada M, Ashley S, Ford D, Traish D, Burchell L, Rajan B. Cerebrovascular mortality in patients with pituitary adenoma. Clin Endocrinol (Oxf) 2002;57:713–7

70. Erfurth EM, Bülow B, Svahn-Tapper G, Norrving B, Odh K, Mikoczy Z, Bjork J, Hagmar L. Risk factors for cerebrovascular deaths in patients operated and irradiated for pituitary tumors. J Clin Endocrinol Metab 2002;87:4892–9

71. Neglia JP, Meadows AT, Robison LL, Kim TH, Newton WA, Ruymann FB, Sather HN, Hammond GD. Second neoplasms after acute lymphoblastic leukemia in childhood. N Engl J Med 1991;325:1330–6

72. Relling MV, Rubnitz JE, Rivera GK, Boyett JM, Hancock ML, Felix CA, Kun LE, Walter AW, Evans WE, Pui CH. High incidence of secondary brain tumours after radiotherapy and antimetabolites. Lancet 1999;354:34–9

73. Brada M, Ford D, Ashley S, Bliss JM, Crowley S, Mason M, Rajan B, Traish D. Risk of second brain tumour after conservative surgery and radiotherapy for pituitary adenoma. BMJ 1992;304:1343–6

74. Tsang RW, Laperriere NJ, Simpson WJ, Brierley J, Panzarella T, Smyth HS. Glioma arising after radiation therapy for pituitary adenoma. A report of four patients and estimation of risk. Cancer 1993;72:2227–33

75. Bliss P, Kerr GR, Gregor A. Incidence of second brain tumours after pituitary irradiation in Edinburgh 1962–1990. Clin Oncol (R Coll Radiol) 1994;6:361–3

76. Erfurth EM, Bülow B, Mikoczy Z, Svahn-Tapper G, Hagmar L. Is there an increase in second brain tumours after surgery and irradiation for a pituitary tumour? Clin Endocrinol (Oxf) 2001;55:613–6

77. Kestle JR, Hoffman HJ, Mock AR. Moyamoya phenomenon after radiation for optic glioma. J Neurosurg 1993;79:32–5

78. Grill J, Couanet D, Cappelli C, Habrand JL, Rodriguez D, Sainte-Rose C, Kalifa C. Radiation-induced cerebral vasculopathy in children with neurofibromatosis and optic pathway glioma. Ann Neurol 1999;45:393–6

79. O'Connor MM, Mayberg MR. Effects of radiation on cerebral vasculature: a review. Neurosurgery 2000; 46:138–51

80. Flickinger JC, Nelson PB, Taylor FH, Robinson A. Incidence of cerebral infarction after radiotherapy for pituitary adenoma. Cancer 1989;63:2404–8

81. Bowen J, Paulsen CA. Stroke after pituitary irradiation. Stroke 1992;23:908–11

82. Brada M, Burchell L, Ashley S, Traish D. The incidence of cerebrovascular accidents in patients with pituitary adenoma. Int J Radiat Oncol Biol Phys 1999;45:693–8

83. Crossen JR, Garwood D, Glatstein E, Neuwelt EA. Neurobehavioral sequelae of cranial irradiation in adults: a review of radiation-induced encephalopathy. J Clin Oncol 1994;12:627–42

84. Grattan-Smith PJ, Morris JG, Shores EA, Batchelor J, Sparks RS. Neuropsychological abnormalities in patients with pituitary tumours. Acta Neurol Scand 1992; 86:626–31

85. Peace KA, Orme SM, Sebastian JP, Thompson AR, Barnes S, Ellis A, Belchetz PE. The effect of treatment variables on mood and social adjustment in adult patients with pituitary disease. Clin Endocrinol (Oxf) 1997;46:445–50

86. Peace KA, Orme SM, Padayatty SJ, Godfrey HP, Belchetz PE. Cognitive dysfunction in patients with pituitary tumour who have been treated with transfrontal or transsphenoidal surgery or medication. Clin Endocrinol (Oxf) 1998;49:391–6

87. Bülow B, Hagmar L, Orbaek P, Osterberg K, Erfurth EM. High incidence of mental disorders, reduced mental well-being and cognitive function in hypopituitary women with GH deficiency treated for pituitary disease. Clin Endocrinol (Oxf) 2002;56:183–93

88. Degerblad M, Rähn T, Bergstrand G, Thorén M. Long-term results of stereotactic radiosurgery to the pituitary gland in Cushing's disease. Acta Endocrinol (Copenh) 1986;112:310–4

89. Pai HH, Thornton A, Katznelson L, Finkelstein DM, Adams JA, Fullerton BC, Loeffler JS, Leibsch NJ, Klibanski A, Munzenrider JE. Hypothalamic/pituitary function following high-dose conformal radiotherapy to the base of skull: demonstration of a dose-effect relationship using dose-volume histogram analysis. Int J Radiat Oncol Biol Phys 2001;49:1079–92

90. Feigl GC, Bonelli CM, Berghold A, Mokry M. Effects of gamma knife radiosurgery of pituitary adenomas on pituitary function. J Neurosurg 2002;97:415–21

91. Degerblad M, Brismar K, Rähn T, Thorén M. The hypothalamus-pituitary function after pituitary stereotactic radiosurgery: evaluation of growth hormone deficiency. J Intern Med 2003;253:454–62

92. Carroll PV, Christ ER, Bengtsson B-Å, Carlsson L, Christiansen JS, Clemmons D, Hintz R, Ho K, Laron Z, Sizonenko P, Sönksen PH, Tanaka T, Thorne M. Growth hormone deficiency in adulthood and the effects of growth hormone replacement: a review. Growth Hormone Research Society Scientific Committee. J Clin Endocrinol Metab 1998;83:382–95

93. Drake WM, Howell SJ, Monson JP, Shalet SM. Optimizing GH therapy in adults and children. Endocr Rev 2001;22:425–50

94. Shalet SM, Beardwell CG, Pearson D, Jones PH. The effect of varying doses of cerebral irradiation on growth hormone production in childhood. Clin Endocrinol (Oxf) 1976;5:287–90

95. Brennan BM, Rahim A, Mackie EM, Eden OB, Shalet SM. Growth hormone status in adults treated for acute lymphoblastic leukaemia in childhood. Clin Endocrinol (Oxf) 1998;48:777–83

96. Adan L, Trivin C, Sainte-Rose C, Zucker JM, Hartmann O, Brauner R. GH deficiency caused by cranial irradiation during childhood: factors and markers in young adults. J Clin Endocrinol Metab 2001; 86:5245–51

97. Ogilvy-Stuart AL, Clark DJ, Wallace WH, Gibson BE, Stevens RF, Shalet SM, Donaldson MD. Endocrine deficit after fractionated total body irradiation. Arch Dis Child 1992;67:1107–10

98. Clayton PE, Shalet SM. Dose dependency of time of onset of radiation-induced growth hormone deficiency. J Pediatr 1991;118:226–8

99. Toogood AA, Ryder WD, Beardwell CG, Shalet SM. The evolution of radiation-induced growth hormone deficiency in adults is determined by the baseline growth hormone status. Clin Endocrinol (Oxf) 1995;43:97–103

100. Ahmed SR, Shalet SM. Hypothalamic growth hormone releasing factor deficiency following cranial irradiation. Clin Endocrinol (Oxf) 1984;21:483–8

101. Ogilvy-Stuart AL, Wallace WH, Shalet SM. Radiation and neuroregulatory control of growth hormone secretion. Clin Endocrinol (Oxf) 1994;41:163–8

102. Consensus guidelines for the diagnosis and treatment of adults with growth hormone deficiency: summary statement of the Growth Hormone Research Society Workshop on Adult Growth Hormone Deficiency. J Clin Endocrinol Metab 1998;83:379–81

103. Lissett CA, Saleem S, Rahim A, Brennan BM, Shalet SM. The impact of irradiation on growth hormone responsiveness to provocative agents is stimulus dependent: results in 161 individuals with radiation damage to the somatotropic axis. J Clin Endocrinol Metab 2001;86:663–8

104. Schmiegelow M, Lassen S, Poulsen HS, Feldt-Rasmussen U, Schmiegelow K, Hertz H, Müller J. Growth hormone response to a growth hormone-releasing hormone stimulation test in a population-based study following cranial irradiation of childhood brain tumors. Horm Res 2000;54:53–9

105. Darzy KH, Aimaretti G, Wieringa G, Gattamaneni HR, Ghigo E, Shalet SM. The usefulness of the combined growth hormone (GH)-releasing hormone and arginine stimulation test in the diagnosis of radiation-induced GH deficiency is dependent on the post-irradiation time interval. J Clin Endocrinol Metab 2003;88:95–102

106. Shalet SM, Toogood A, Rahim A, Brennan BM. The diagnosis of growth hormone deficiency in children and adults. Endocr Rev 1998;19:203–23

107. Murray RD, Darzy KH, Gleeson HK, Shalet SM. GH-deficient survivors of childhood cancer: GH replacement during adult life. J Clin Endocrinol Metab 2002;87:129–35

108. Maiter D, Abs R, Johannsson G, Scanlon M, Jönsson P, Kołtowska M, Wilton P. Influence of prior irradiation for pituitary adenoma or craniopharyngioma on the efficacy of growth hormone (GH) in adult GH-deficient patients. Poster presented at 84th Annual meeting of the Endocrine Society, San Francisco 2002:P1–269, 217

109. Page RC, Hammersley MS, Burke CW, Wass JA. An account of the quality of life of patients after treatment for non-functioning pituitary tumours. Clin Endocrinol (Oxf) 1997;46:401–6

110. Wallymahmed ME, Foy P, MacFarlane IA. The quality of life of adults with growth hormone deficiency: comparison with diabetic patients and control subjects. Clin Endocrinol (Oxf) 1999;51:333–8

25 Conditions with a high risk of growth hormone deficiency in adulthood

Gianluca Aimaretti, Ginevra Corneli, Valentina Gasco,
Silvia Grottoli and Ezio Ghigo
Division of Endocrinology and Metabolism, Department of Internal Medicine, University of Turin, Turin, Italy

Summary

Hypopituitarism and growth hormone deficiency (GHD) in adults should be suspected and diagnosed within an appropriate clinical context. All patients with primary hypothalamic–pituitary diseases are obviously at very high risk of developing hypopituitarism (comprising more than 80% of severe cases of GHD) both before and after treatment (neurosurgery and/or radiotherapy and/or medical therapy). Also at very high risk are patients who have been diagnosed as having congenital or acquired GHD in childhood (comprising between approximately 30 and 50% of severe cases of GHD after re-testing in adulthood). In addition, patients with other common pathological central nervous system conditions, such as traumatic brain injury, subarachnoid haemorrhage or primary brain tumours, should be considered at risk of developing hypopituitarism. GHD is usually the first and most common sign of pituitary impairment in these cases. Despite the risk of hypopituitarism, the clinical management of these conditions does not routinely include neuroendocrine evaluations. Recent studies suggest that patients with primary empty sella are also at high risk of GHD, despite the common assumption that empty sella is associated with preserved pituitary function. Unexpectedly, growth hormone insufficiency has even been demonstrated in patients with primary hyperparathyroidism; GHD would further impair bone metabolism. In conclusion, besides the obvious impairment in patients with primary hypothalamic–pituitary diseases, somatotroph function appears to be severely impaired in adulthood in a number of frequently observed clinical conditions that were not previously considered to be associated with hypopituitarism. Screening for pituitary deficits, including GHD, is therefore important during the investigation of these conditions.

Introduction

In adulthood, hypopituitarism and growth hormone deficiency (GHD) are most frequently 'acquired' as a consequence of primary hypothalamic–pituitary diseases [1–5] or represent the persistence of a congenital or acquired pituitary defect that had been diagnosed in childhood [2, 5]. In cases in which multiple pituitary deficits develop, it has been clearly demonstrated that growth hormone (GH) is usually the first of the anterior pituitary hormones to be affected [1–3]. Thus, it has been suggested that GHD can be considered as a marker that indicates the possibility of impaired pituitary function, which may subsequently evolve to include other pituitary axes resulting in secondary hypogonadism, hypoadrenalism and hypothyroidism.

Recent studies have shown that adult patients who have hypothalamic–pituitary masses and women affected by Sheehan's syndrome (see Chapter 26) are at very high risk of hypopituitarism both before and, especially, after therapy (neurosurgery and/or radiotherapy and/or medical therapy). In a large cohort of patients who underwent neurosurgery and/or radiotherapy for treatment of hypothalamic–pituitary masses, more than 69.7% had severe GHD following treatment. Thus, patients with these clinical conditions are at 'obvious' rather than high risk of hypopituitarism [2, 3, 6] (Fig. 1). It is now, therefore, widely accepted that routine evaluation of pituitary function, with particular attention to somatotroph function, is mandatory in all patients with hypothalamic–pituitary diseases, particularly after neurosurgery and/or radiotherapy. The same also applies to patients who have been diagnosed as having either congenital or acquired GHD in childhood, in order to identify patients with persistent severe GHD who will need to continue GH replacement in adulthood [5, 7]. It has been demonstrated that the majority (more than 90%) of patients with childhood-onset multiple hypopituitarism show persistent severe GHD at re-testing in adulthood [2, 8]. Among patients who have been treated with GH for isolated GHD in childhood, however, a lower percentage show persistence of severe GHD at re-testing; in our studies this is approximately 50% [9]. It is also clear that the probability of severe GHD at re-testing is essentially nil in patients with so called 'short stature due to non-classical GHD' [8]. It is essential, therefore, that pituitary function is re-tested in patients in whom some pituitary derangement has been found during childhood (Fig. 1).

In conditions that are recognized to increase the risk of GHD in adulthood, the presence of GHD should be confirmed by a severely reduced GH response to a GH-provocation test [2, 3, 5, 10–12]. In fact, the measurement of spontaneous GH secretion or of insulin-like growth factor I (IGF-I) and IGF-binding protein-3 do not distinguish between normal and GH-deficient individuals [2, 3, 13, 14]. The insulin tolerance test (ITT) is widely considered to be the gold standard for the diagnosis of adult GHD [2, 5, 10] and, in order to select only patients with severe GHD, an arbitrary cut-off point of 3 μg/L has been established, which is the first centile of the normal GH response [5]. However, the ITT is not suitable for use in patients with disorders involving seizures and those with ischaemic heart disease, in whom insulin-induced hypoglycaemia is potentially dangerous. The ITT should therefore not be performed in patients when these conditions are suspected. These limitations are particularly relevant to patients who have undergone neurosurgery or cranial radiotherapy [2, 5, 8, 10, 11].

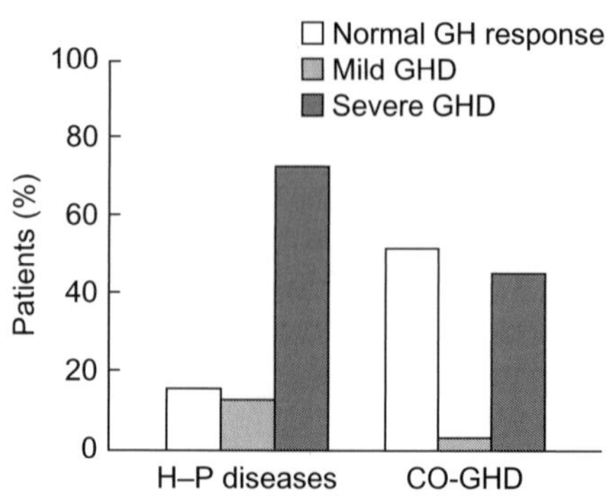

Figure 1. *Percentage of patients with adult-onset primary hypothalamic–pituitary (H–P) diseases and childhood-onset GHD (CO-GHD) who have a normal GH response, or mild or severe GHD (personal data).*

Alternative GH-provocation tests have been proposed. Among them, the combined GH-releasing hormone and arginine (GHRH + ARG) test is considered one of the best [2, 5]. This test is potent, shows good intra-individual reproducibility, has clear cut-off limits, induces no significant side-effects and does not vary significantly with age [11, 12]. The GHRH + ARG test has a high specificity (calculated in a large population of normal subjects of both sexes aged between 20 and 80 years) and high sensitivity, and a strong positive correlation with the ITT [11, 12]. This test also clearly distinguishes patients with GHD from normal individuals, provided that appropriate cut-off points are used [5, 6, 11, 12]. The cut-off point for defining GHD using the GHRH + ARG test is 16.5 μg/L, which is equivalent to the third centile in the normal population; severe GHD is defined by a peak GH response below the first centile, 9 μg/L [11, 12]. This test is a short procedure (requiring only three GH assays), thus reducing cost and improving patient compliance [15].

'Newly' recognized conditions with a high risk of GHD in adulthood

Brain injury

Recent studies have shown that hypopituitarism, with GHD as its first or isolated sign, occurs in adulthood in clinical contexts in which it has previously been considered rare or was not suspected [16–20]. Therefore, neuroendocrine evaluations have not been commonly performed in the clinical management of these patients [19, 20]. That brain injury can cause hypopituitarism is commonly stated in textbooks, and is predicted by the fragility of the anatomical structure of the infundibular–hypothalamic–pituitary area.

Traumatic brain injury

According to the literature, head trauma, or traumatic brain injury, is accompanied by varying degrees of hypopituitarism. [16, 18–20]. In old autopsy studies, it has been demonstrated that 30% of the patients who underwent a fatal head trauma showed necrosis of the anterior pituitary gland [21, 22]. Edwards and Clark [16] reviewed the topic of post-traumatic hypopituitarism in 1986, reporting that the typical patient with post-traumatic hypopituitarism was a young adult male with severe head trauma, presenting with endocrinological symptoms months or years after an accident. These patients often had temporary or permanent diabetes insipidus and symptoms such as weight loss, fatigue, faintness, loss of libido and impotence that suggest panhypopituitarism. Brain injury poses a significant risk of hypothalamic (as indicated by the high incidence of diabetes insipidus and hyperprolactinaemia) and pituitary insult. It has been proposed that trauma-mediated vascular injury to the hypothalamus may be the basis of the traumatic brain injury-mediated GHD, though pituitary lesions are also a prominent factor. The symptoms suggestive of panhypopituitarism were typically ascribed to depression or 'post-concussion syndrome' and inappropriate treatment and rehabilitation were often advised.

Following these observations, it was recommended that patients with major head injury (defined by post-traumatic amnesia of more than 24 hours), particularly those with fractures of the base of the skull or diabetes insipidus, should be closely monitored for signs and symptoms of endocrine dysfunction, and appropriate dynamic pituitary-function tests performed. Recently, Benvenga and co-workers [19] screened case reports of hypopituitarism and head trauma from the past 30 years. They found a total of 367 cases with pituitary insufficiency that could have had life-threatening consequences. Nearly three-quarters of these patients showed hypopituitarism within 1 year of the pathological event. It was emphasized that hypopituitarism impairs adaptation to stressful events and represents a negative risk factor for the prognosis of patients who have experienced head trauma. Thus, taking into account these forensic findings, it was recommended that endocrinologists, neurosurgeons and doctors involved in rehabilitation should be alerted to the possibility of hypopituitarism following traumatic brain injury, and should perform careful clinical and biochemical follow-up of these patients.

In the chronic recovery phase after injury, patients with traumatic brain injury have reported specific deficits in their general health, vitality and mental health [23], including depression and anxiety [24]. Recently, Liebermann and colleagues [20] studied the impact of hypopituitarism on the rehabilitation period following a traumatic brain injury. They found that the characteristics seen during rehabilitation in patients with traumatic brain injury were similar to those seen in adults with GHD – decreased physical strength and aerobic capacity, and a reduced sense of well-being [3–5]. They also reported a high prevalence of neuroendocrine dysfunction in patients with a history of traumatic brain injury. The frequency of GHD (15%) and low cortisol levels (46%) are striking, and may have important implications for patient health, sense of well-being and rehabilitation potential. Recently, traumatic brain injury was reported to be the cause of GHD in nearly 2% (168/8300) of patients in KIMS – Pfizer International Metabolic Database. This percentage seems low considering the previous findings; however, as mentioned above, clinical endocrinologists have only recently become more aware that traumatic brain injury may cause hypopituitarism [25].

Subarachnoid haemorrhage

That hypopituitarism and GHD may also occur after acute vascular injuries, such as subarachnoid haemorrhage secondary to rupture of a cerebral aneurysm, has recently been emphasized by Kelly *et al.* [18]. These authors found that subarachnoid haemorrhage poses a risk to the pituitary gland and stalk, given the proximity of these structures to the vessels of the circle of Willis and the potential of vasospasm of the branches to the hypophyseal vasculature. Given that the majority of patients with subarachnoid haemorrhage have persistent neurobehavioural and quality of life problems, the search for a treatable cause of these impairments, such as GHD, warrants further study. Reports on pituitary dysfunction after subarachnoid haemorrhage are very limited and have only described the direct mechanical effects of aneurysm compression of the pituitary gland. It is notable that no consistent relationship has been reported between the site of aneurysm rupture and the nature of the neurocognitive deficits that occur after subarachnoid haemorrhage. A more global neurobehavioural derangement, such as that which can occur in patients with hypopituitarism and GHD, may explain these discrepant findings in at least a proportion of patients with subarachnoid haemorrhage.

Ongoing studies

Despite the high theoretical risk and the great number of case reports describing hypopituitarism after traumatic brain injury and subarachnoid haemorrhage, there are, to our knowledge, no prospective diagnostic and therapeutic studies that have attempted to define the epidemiological importance of hypopituitarism in these clinical conditions. Therefore, under the auspices of the Italian Society of Endocrinology, and in collaboration with several Italian centres of Endocrinology and Neurosurgery, we are conducting a prospective clinical study. To date, 87 patients (27 female, 60 male) with traumatic brain injury (aged 37.9 ± 1.9 years; body mass index [BMI], 23.8 ± 0.5 kg/m^2; Glasgow coma scale range, 3–15) and 34 patients (21 female, 13 male) with subarachnoid haemorrhage (aged 51.7 ± 2.2 years; BMI, 24.9 ± 0.8 kg/m^2) have been enrolled in the study. Each patient will undergo endocrine evaluations at 3 and 12 months after the pathological event. Specifically, regarding assessment of the GH/IGF-I axis, all patients will be evaluated using the GHRH + ARG test, as well as by measuring IGF-I levels. Preliminary results are now available for the 3-month evaluation. Some degree of hypopituitarism was found in 45.9% of the patients with traumatic brain injury. Thirty-three of the patients (37.9%) were GH deficient, and this deficiency was severe in 21%, with low age-related IGF-I levels in 11.4% of severe cases (Fig. 2). No correlation was found between the peak GH response to the GHRH + ARG test and the Glasgow coma scale. Some degree of hypopituitarism was found in 50% of patients with subarachnoid haemorrhage. GHD was shown in 38.4% of patients with subarachnoid haemorrhage, and was severe in 30.7% (Fig. 2). IGF-I levels were

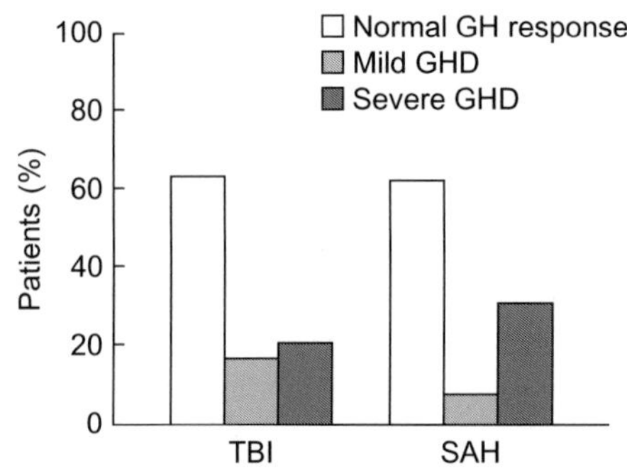

Figure 2. *Percentage of patients with normal GH response, or mild or severe GHD after traumatic brain injury (TBI) or subarachnoid haemorrhage (SAH) (personal data).*

below age-related normal limits in 8.8% of these patients. These preliminary results have to be confirmed in a larger population of patients and verified at the 12-month evaluation.

General comments

The picture that we have in front of us is impressive. Data from the USA suggest that more than 80 000 Americans are severely disabled by traumatic brain injury every year [26]. In Italy, the number of people admitted to hospital with traumatic brain injury is about 300–500/100 000 per year, with a mortality rate of 20/100 000 per year (data from the Italian Minister of Health); it is of note that 90% of the traumatic brain injuries are of medium severity. Based on previous studies and our preliminary results, it is strongly recommended that endocrine evaluation should be mandatory in the clinical management of patients who have suffered traumatic brain injury or subarachnoid haemorrhage. All of these patients should be carefully followed-up in order to disclose GHD and/or other pituitary deficiencies. In order to screen for hypopituitarism in these conditions, collaboration between neurosurgeons, endocrinologists and doctors involved in rehabilitation must be improved.

Empty sella

Empty sella may represent an idiopathic condition (primary empty sella) or may be the consequence of pituitary surgery, irradiation or drug-induced shrinkage of pituitary tumours (secondary empty sella) [27, 28]. It is generally assumed that primary empty sella is not associated with overt endocrine abnormalities, although altered pituitary function has occasionally been reported [29]. A study by Gasperi *et al.* [30] reappraised primary empty sella as a condition in which there is a high risk of developing GHD. The authors reported that more than 50% of a cohort of 51 subjects showed severe GHD, as evaluated by the ITT or the GHRH + ARG test, compared with a matched normal population [30]. This defect was similar to those observed in 'classic' pan-hypopituitary patients. Although nearly 50% of the subjects examined were obese, the authors found that the pattern of GH secretion was similar in lean and obese patients with primary empty sella, showing that obesity did not influence the response to the GH-provocation test. Thus, primary empty sella seems to represent a high-risk condition for GHD in adults. In addition, as GHD is the first anterior pituitary hormone impairment in patients with acquired hypopituitarism, these data indirectly suggest the opportunity for a periodic reassessment of pituitary function in patients with primary empty sella.

Primary hyperparathyroidism

Little is known about the effect of hypo- and hypercalcaemia on GH secretion. The effects of acute calcium excess, or deprivation, on GH secretion have produced contradictory results. Patients with primary hyperparathyroidism after parathyroidectomy have been reported to have decreased [31] or increased [32] serum GH concentrations. On the other hand, the influence of chronic hypercalcaemia on the activity of the GH/IGF-I axis is unknown [33]. Recently, Gasperi and co-workers [34] have investigated the influence of chronic hypercalcaemia due to primary hyperparathyroidism on adult somatotroph function by evaluating both spontaneous and stimulated GH secretion. The authors demonstrated that patients with primary hyperparathyroidism (without a history of previous pituitary abnormality) show a clear reduction in the GH response to a provocation test. This impaired response, even to maximal GH-stimulation, such as that with the GHRH + ARG test, is associated with a reduction in spontaneous 24-hour GH secretion, as well as, in some cases, a reduction in serum total IGF-I concentration. These data suggest that primary hyperparathyroidism may represent a further example of a metabolic condition in which GH secretion is reduced in adulthood. The real pathophysiological significance of GHD in primary hyperparathyroidism remains to be clarified, because it may represent a normal physiological reaction to the provocation test. GHD in patients with primary hyperparathyroidism is likely to be reversed by correction of the primary disease. At present, the use of GH replacement therapy should be discouraged in this subset of patients.

Proposal for hormone evaluation in patients with newly recognized conditions with a high risk of GHD in adulthood

It is proposed that all patients with 'newly' recognized conditions with a high risk of GHD in adulthood should undergo diagnostic screening, including basal measurement of morning serum cortisol, 24-hour urinary free cortisol, free tri-iodothyronine, free thyroxine, thyroid-stimulating hormone, follicle-stimulating hormone, luteinizing hormone, testosterone (in men), oestradiol-17β (in women), prolactin and IGF-I. In patients with polyuria, further investigation is needed to verify the presence of diabetes insipidus. Further investigation of various endocrine axes should be performed using provocation tests in all patients with newly recognized conditions.

It is well known that hypopituitarism, including deficits in the adrenal, thyroid and gonadal axes, can be demonstrated by basal hormone evaluations in the majority of patients; however, tests that provoke a hormone response may be needed in a minority of patients in whom basal evaluations are unclear, and in patients with GHD. As IGF-I levels – the best marker of GH status – are often normal in patients with GHD, it is necessary to use a GH-provocation test to demonstrate GHD. It is true, however, that low IGF-I levels in a patient who is at risk of hypopituitarism, and is not suffering from malnutrition, strongly predict severe GHD. The first step in diagnosing hypopituitarism is to record a detailed patient and family history.

Although the ITT is considered the gold standard test for the diagnosis of GH and adrenocorticotrophin deficiency, it is generally contraindicated in patients who have central nervous system (CNS) pathology and those at risk of cardiac ischaemia. An alternative test for use in these patients is the glucagon test. Of the tests that produce maximal GH stimulation, the GHRH + ARG test or GH-releasing peptides are most reliable. In fact, these tests are potent, reproducible and are at least as reliable as the ITT provided that they are used with cut-off limits appropriate for their higher GH-releasing potency [2, 5, 11, 35].

Routine basal hormone testing should be performed in any patient who has been hospitalized for traumatic brain injury or subarachnoid haemorrhage, and who has symptoms such as hyponatraemia and hypotension. Prospectively, all patients who have traumatic brain injury – regardless of the severity – should undergo a baseline hormone evaluation 3 and 12 months after the primary brain insult or discharge from the hospital/intensive care unit. Patients with adrenal insufficiency, diabetes insipidus or other clinical symptoms of hypopituitarism should undergo immediate testing of the rest of the pituitary axis. Patients with clinical signs or symptoms suggestive of impaired hypothalamic–pituitary function (for example, polyuria) should be investigated whenever medically warranted. Retrospectively, all patients with signs and symptoms of hypopituitarism who have experienced a moderate or severe traumatic brain injury more than 12 months before the onset of symptoms should undergo immediate hormone testing. Given the 12-month passage of time, it is unlikely that any hormone deficit is transient, so for these patients screening can be conducted in a single session.

Conclusions

In addition to conditions such as primary hypothalamic–pituitary diseases, in which there is clearly a high risk of developing hypopituitarism (in particular GHD), somatotroph function may be impaired in adulthood in a number of common conditions (CNS diseases, empty sella syndrome and primary hyperparathyroidism). Diagnostic screening of the hypothalamic–pituitary axis should be mandatory in patients with these conditions, which have only recently been recognized as being associated with a risk of hypopituitarism.

Acknowledgements

The studies reported in this paper have been supported by MIUR (Ministero Istuzione n-2003069821_004 Università e Ricerca, Rome, Italy), University of Turin and SMEM Foundation (Foundation for the study of Metabolic and Endocrine diseases, Turin, Italy).

References

1. Lamberts SW, de Herder WW, van der Lely AJ. Pituitary insufficiency. Lancet 1998;352:127–34

2. Shalet SM, Toogood A, Rahim A, Brennan BM. The diagnosis of growth hormone deficiency in children and adults. Endocr Rev 1998;19:203–23

3. de Boer H, Blok GJ, Van der Veen EA. Clinical aspects of growth hormone deficiency in adults. Endocr Rev 1995;16:63–86

4. Carroll PV, Christ ER, Bengtsson B-Å, Carlsson L, Christiansen JS, Clemmons D, Hintz R, Ho K, Laron Z, Sizonenko P, Sönksen PH, Tanaka T, Thorne M. Growth hormone deficiency in adulthood and the effects of growth hormone replacement: a review. Growth Hormone Research Society Scientific Committee. J Clin Endocrinol Metab 1998;83:382–95

5. Consensus guidelines for the diagnosis and treatment of adults with growth hormone deficiency: summary statement of the Growth Hormone Research Society Workshop on Adult Growth Hormone Deficiency. J Clin Endocrinol Metab 1998;83:379–81

6. Corneli G, Baldelli R, Di Somma C, Rovere S, Gaia D, Pellegrino M, Gasco V, Durante C, Grottoli S, Colao A, Tamburrano G, Lombardi G, Ghigo E, Aimaretti G. Occurrence of GH deficiency in adult patients who underwent neurosurgery in the hypothalamus–pituitary area for non-functioning tumour masses. Growth Horm IGF Res 2003;13:104–8

7. Consensus guidelines for the diagnosis and treatment of growth hormone (GH) deficiency in childhood and adolescence: summary statement of the GH Research Society. GH Research Society. J Clin Endocrinol Metab 2000;85:3990–3

8. Aimaretti G, Corneli G, Bellone S, Baffoni C, Camanni F, Ghigo E. Growth hormone deficiency in the transition adolescent: should treatment be continued in adult life? J Pediatr Endocrinol Metab 2001;14 (Suppl 5):1233–42

9. Aimaretti G, Baffoni C, Bellone S, Di Vito L, Corneli G, Arvat E, Benso L, Camanni F, Ghigo E. Retesting young adults with childhood-onset growth hormone (GH) deficiency with GH-releasing-hormone-plus-arginine test. J Clin Endocrinol Metab 2000;85:3693–9

10. Hoffman DM, O'Sullivan AJ, Baxter RC, Ho KK. Diagnosis of growth-hormone deficiency in adults. Lancet 1994;343:1064–8

11. Ghigo E, Aimaretti G, Arvat E, Camanni F. Growth hormone-releasing hormone combined with arginine or growth hormone secretagogues for the diagnosis of growth hormone deficiency in adults. Endocrine 2001;15:29–38

12. Aimaretti G, Corneli G, Razzore P, Bellone S, Baffoni C, Arvat E, Camanni F, Ghigo E. Comparison between insulin-induced hypoglycemia and growth hormone (GH)-releasing hormone + arginine as provocative tests for the diagnosis of GH deficiency in adults. J Clin Endocrinol Metab 1998;83:1615–8

13. Aimaretti G, Corneli G, Baldelli R, Di Somma C, Gasco V, Durante C, Ausiello L, Rovere S, Grottoli S, Tamburrano G, Ghigo E. Diagnostic reliability of a single IGF-I measurement in 237 adults with total anterior hypopituitarism and severe GH deficiency. Clin Endocrinol (Oxf) 2003;59:56–61

14. Hartman ML, Crowe BJ, Biller BM, Ho KK, Clemmons DR, Chipman JJ. Which patients do not require a GH stimulation test for the diagnosis of adult GH deficiency? J Clin Endocrinol Metab 2002;87:477–85

15. Aimaretti G, Bellone S, Baffoni C, Corneli G, Origlia C, Di Vito L, Rovere S, Arvat E, Camanni F, Ghigo E. Short procedure of GHRH plus arginine test in clinical practice. Pituitary 2001;4:129–34

16. Edwards OM, Clark JD. Post-traumatic hypopituitarism. Six cases and a review of the literature. Medicine (Baltimore) 1986;65:281–90

17. Ceballos R. Pituitary changes in head trauma (analysis of 102 consecutive cases of head injury). Ala J Med Sci 1966;3:185–98

18. Kelly DF, Gonzalo IT, Cohan P, Berman N, Swerdloff R, Wang C. Hypopituitarism following traumatic brain injury and aneurysmal subarachnoid hemorrhage: a preliminary report. J Neurosurg 2000;93:743–52

19. Benvenga S, Campenni A, Ruggeri RM, Trimarchi F. Clinical review 113: Hypopituitarism secondary to head trauma. J Clin Endocrinol Metab 2000;85:1353–61

20. Lieberman SA, Oberoi AL, Gilkison CR, Masel BE, Urban RJ. Prevalence of neuroendocrine dysfunction in patients recovering from traumatic brain injury. J Clin Endocrinol Metab 2001;86:2752–6

21. Daniel PM, Prichard MM, Treip CS. Traumatic infarction of the anterior lobe of the pituitary gland. Lancet 1959;2:927–30

22. Kornblum RN, Fisher RS. Pituitary lesions in craniocerebral injuries. Arch Pathol 1969;88:242–8

23. Colantonio A, Dawson DR, McLellan BA. Head injury in young adults: long-term outcome. Arch Phys Med Rehabil 1998;79:550–8

24. Morton MV, Wehman P. Psychosocial and emotional sequelae of individuals with traumatic brain injury: a literature review and recommendations. Brain Inj 1995;9:81–92

25. Casanueva FF, Leal-Cerro A, Keleştimur F, Kołtowska-Haggström M, Góth M. Characteristics of GH deficiency (GHD) in adult patients who suffered

traumatic brain injury (TBI), reflected in KIMS (Pharmacia International Metabolic Database). The Endocrine Society's 85th Annual Meeting 2003 Jun 19–22; Philadelphia, USA. Abstract book p384

26. Agency for health care policy and research. Rehabilitation for traumatic brain injury, summary, evidence report/technology assessment. Silver spring, MD: AHRQ Publications, 1998

27. Bergland RM, Ray BS, Torack RM. Anatomical variations in the pituitary gland and adjacent structures in 225 human autopsy cases. J Neurosurg 1968; 28:93–9

28. Kaufman B. The "empty" sella turcica – a manifestation of the intrasellar subarachnoid space. Radiology 1968;90:931–41

29. Brismar K, Efendic S. Pituitary function in the empty sella syndrome. Neuroendocrinology 1981;32:70–7

30. Gasperi M, Aimaretti G, Cecconi E, Colao A, Di Somma C, Cannavo S, Baffoni C, Cosottini M, Curto L, Trimarchi F, Lombardi G, Grasso L, Ghigo E, Martino E. Impairment of GH secretion in adults with primary empty sella. J Endocrinol Invest 2002; 25:329–33

31. Schernthaner G, Kovarik J, Prager R, Willvonseder R. Growth hormone, prolactin and insulin following arginine infusion in primary hyperparathyroidism before and after parathyroidectomy. Acta Endocrinol (Copenh) 1983;104:206–9

32. Kovacs L, Szilagyi G, Szabolcs I, Góth M. The reaction of adenohypophysis hormones in primary hyperparathyroidism and after surgical treatment. Acta Med Hung 1994;50:15–21

33. Veldhuis JD, Borges JL, Drake CR, Rogol AD. Divergent influences of calcium ions on releasing factor-stimulated anterior pituitary hormone secretion in normal man. J Clin Endocrinol Metab 1984;59:56–61

34. Gasperi M, Cecconi E, Grasso L, Bartalena L, Centoni R, Aimaretti G, Broglio F, Miccoli P, Marcocci C, Ghigo E, Martino E. GH secretion is impaired in patients with primary hyperparathyroidism. J Clin Endocrinol Metab 2002;87:1961–4

35. Popovic V, Leal A, Micic D, Koppeschaar HP, Torres E, Paramo C, Obradovic S, Dieguez C, Casanueva FF. GH-releasing hormone and GH-releasing peptide-6 for diagnostic testing in GH-deficient adults. Lancet 2000;356:1137–42

26 Sheehan's syndrome

Fahrettin Keleştimur

Department of Endocrinology, Medical School, Erciyes University, Kayseri, Turkey

Summary

Sheehan's syndrome is not uncommon in developing countries, but is relatively little known in developed countries due to improvements in obstetric care. However, in KIMS – Pfizer International Metabolic Database – Sheehan's syndrome is the sixth most frequent cause of growth hormone (GH) deficiency, with a prevalence of 3.1%. The pathogenesis of the syndrome is poorly understood, but is associated with pregnancy. Increased pituitary size during pregnancy, resulting from placental hormone-induced lactotroph hyperplasia, may make the pituitary more susceptible to ischaemia through compression of the superior hypophyseal artery. In addition, severe hypotension or shock due to postpartum haemorrhage is thought to be associated with the hypopituitarism of Sheehan's syndrome. It is important to be aware of the signs and symptoms of the syndrome so that the appropriate hormone replacement therapy can be initiated. Diagnosis, however, is problematic and patients are frequently not correctly diagnosed for many years. GH is one of the earliest hormones to become deficient in Sheehan's syndrome, and GH replacement therapy has been shown to have beneficial effects on lean body mass, lipid profiles and quality of life.

Introduction

Sheehan's syndrome was first described by Sheehan in 1937 after he had investigated pituitary damage in patients who had died in the post-partum period [1]. Sheehan's syndrome, which occurs as a result of ischaemic pituitary necrosis due to severe postpartum haemorrhage, is not commonly seen today in developed countries because of remarkable improvements in obstetric care. However, in underdeveloped and developing countries, it is probably one of the most common causes of hypopituitarism. The prevalence of Sheehan's syndrome was estimated by Sheehan about 40 years ago to be 100–200 per million women [2]. In a UK survey in 1995, only one case of Sheehan's syndrome in a database of 404 patients with pituitary disease was reported [3]. In a Swedish report of 333 patients with hypopituitarism, Sheehan's syndrome was not listed as a cause [4]. In a recent analysis of 1034 patients enrolled in KIMS – Pfizer International Metabolic Database – pituitary tumours were the most common cause of hypopituitarism, and the prevalence of Sheehan's syndrome was 3.1%, making it the sixth most frequent cause of adult growth hormone deficiency (GHD) [5]. Recent data suggest that more patients with Sheehan's syndrome are being reported from Western Europe. Even so, the lack of sufficient information provided to students at medical school means that the number of patients with Sheehan's syndrome in this area is probably underestimated.

The pathophysiology and natural history of Sheehan's syndrome is not well known. Patients present with various signs and symptoms of hypopituitarism, sometimes resulting in coma and death. For this reason, early diagnosis – before severe clinical symptoms develop due to endocrine deficiencies – is of clinical importance. This chapter discusses the pathophysiology and clinical characteristics of Sheehan's syndrome.

Pathophysiology

Sheehan's syndrome is characterized by hypopituitarism that occurs as a result of ischaemic pituitary necrosis due to severe postpartum haemorrhage. Another pregnancy-related pituitary disorder, which may result in hypopituitarism, is lymphocytic hypophysitis. Lymphocytic hypophysitis is a primary disorder of the pituitary gland and results from lymphocytic infiltration and destruction of the normal pituitary tissue. Obstetric history is critical in distinguishing between Sheehan's syndrome and lymphocytic hypophysitis. Postpartum thyroiditis, which is a variant of autoimmune thyroiditis, may present with thyroid dysfunction, and hypothyroidism may be the initial presentation. Postpartum thyroiditis is invariably associated with thyroid antibodies and its differentiation from Sheehan's syndrome is not difficult if a careful medical and obstetric history, physical examination and laboratory investigation are carried out. Although these three pregnancy-related endocrine diseases have some common features, their pathogenesis is clearly different.

The pathogenesis of Sheehan's syndrome remains poorly understood. It has long been known that the pituitary gland is enlarged during pregnancy [6–8]. Pituitary enlargement is due to diffuse and nodular hyperplasia of lactotrophs. These cells are stimulated by placental oestrogens and progesterone during pregnancy, and pituitary enlargement may be a contributory factor in the development of postpartum pituitary necrosis. This may result in a 30–100% increase in the weight of the pituitary gland, and an increase in the number of lactotrophs is evident at 1 month and continues throughout gestation [9–11]. It has been reported that pituitary growth could cause compression of the superior hypophyseal artery against the sellar diaphragm, and thereby cause mild ischaemia. Sudden changes in arterial pressure that may occur during delivery due to severe hypotension or shock due to massive haemorrhage, may cause arterial spasm in small vessels, and apoplexy [12]. Thus, an increase in pituitary volume during pregnancy may make the pituitary gland more susceptible to ischaemic necrosis after severe postpartum haemorrhage [13]. Sheehan's syndrome is therefore usually associated with massive haemorrhage and shock in the postpartum period, but it may occasionally be seen in patients who have not experienced haemorrhage [14, 15]. For this reason, it has been suggested that any female patient presenting with clinical features of pituitary hormone deficiency, with an empty sella but with no history of postpartum haemorrhage, should be evaluated for the presence of Sheehan's syndrome [15]. Although the absence of a history of postpartum haemorrhage makes the diagnosis of Sheehan's syndrome more difficult, failure to lactate, secondary amenorrhoea and loss of pubic and auxiliary hair after delivery suggest Sheehan's syndrome.

It has been speculated that autoimmunity may play a role in the development of Sheehan's syndrome; however, there are no convincing data suggesting that Sheehan's syndrome is an autoimmune disease. Some patients with Sheehan's syndrome have anti-pituitary antibodies [16–18]. Goswami *et al.* [19] evaluated autoantibodies against the pituitary (PitAb) and thyroid gland in patients with Sheehan's syndrome; 63.1% had PitAb against the 49 kDa autoantigen, neuron-specific enolase, which was a significantly higher percentage than in the controls. The percentage of patients positive for thyroid gland autoantibodies (14.2%) was similar to that seen in the control group. It seems that the presence of pituitary autoantibodies may be due to release of sequestered pituitary antigens from necrotic pituitary tissue, rather than the result of an autoimmune disorder underlying Sheehan's syndrome. On the other hand, the patients with Sheehan's syndrome had higher levels of T-lymphocytes (CD_2), including helper (CD_4) and suppressor (CD_8) cell subpopulations and B-lymphocytes (CD_{19}), when compared with normal menstruating women. An increase in serum concentrations of immunoglobulin A was also observed [20]. Further studies are needed to clarify the role of autoimmunity in the pathogenesis of Sheehan's syndrome.

An empty sella, of a relatively small size, has been reported to be a common radiological finding, and both extremes of sella size may be risk factors for the development of Sheehan's syndrome [21]. Another study found that the sella turcica in some patients with Sheehan's syndrome was significantly smaller than in the controls, and the presence of pituitary remnants was inversely correlated to the duration and extent of the disease [22]. On the other hand, an empty sella of normal size was reported as the characteristic finding in patients with Sheehan's syndrome [23]. A small sella may play a role in the development of pituitary necrosis, as an enlarged pituitary compressed in a smaller space would more easily become necrotic during ischaemia due to severe postpartum haemorrhage [22]. As the sella in most patients is of normal size, a small sella may be a contributory factor in only some patients, but does not account for the development of postpartum pituitary necrosis in all patients.

Lust *et al.* [24] presented a patient with Sheehan's syndrome who developed hypovolaemic shock and disseminated intravascular coagulation following a precipitate spontaneous vaginal delivery. Whether disseminated intravascular coagulation plays a role in the pathogenesis of postpartum pituitary necrosis remains unknown. The factors that may play a role in the pathophysiology of Sheehan's syndrome are shown in Table 1.

Table 1. *Factors that may play a role in the pathophysiology of Sheehan's syndrome.*

Enlargement of pituitary gland during pregnancy
Postpartum or peripartum vaginal haemorrhage
Small sella
Disseminated intravascular coagulation

Clinical findings

Sheehan's syndrome is rarely diagnosed in the acute postpartum period. Most patients with Sheehan's syndrome usually present months to years later, with a history of failure of postpartum lactation, failure to resume menses, fatigue, weakness, hypotension and cold intolerance. In mild forms of the disease, patients may remain undetected and receive inappropriate treatment for many years. Molitch classified Sheehan's syndrome into acute and chronic forms; however, the signs and symptoms seen in the acute form may also be seen in the chronic form. The onset may be abrupt – just after delivery – and the signs and symptoms may be severe enough to lead to the correct diagnosis [9]. On the other hand, Sheehan's syndrome may be subclinical and may only be manifest if patients are stressed [14]. One of the most remarkable findings on physical examination is the fine wrinkling around the eyes and mouth (Fig. 1). This finding is more recognizable in patients with Sheehan's syndrome than in patients with other aetiologies of hypopituitarism. It is probably due to longer-term and more severe GHD and long-term oestrogen deficiency.

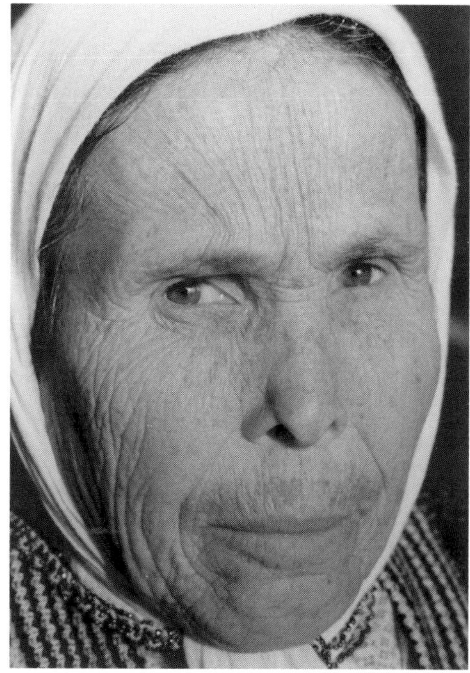

Figure 1. *Individual with Sheehan's syndrome, showing the characteristic fine wrinkling around the eyes and mouth.*

Diagnosis of Sheehan's syndrome is usually made retrospectively and, as in other types of hypopituitarism, hormonal deficiency varies from loss of a single hormone to classic panhypopituitarism. Haddock *et al.* [25] evaluated 50 patients with Sheehan's syndrome and found that 86% had panhypopituitarism, whereas 14% had selective pituitary deficiencies. Only one patient had growth hormone (GH) secretory capacity. In a study of 40 patients, 6.6% had a normal GH response to insulin-induced hypoglycaemia [26]. We have previously reported that 56.2% of patients with Sheehan's syndrome had panhypopituitarism, with the remainder having selective pituitary insufficiency; all the patients had GHD in this study [27]. As somatotrophs are situated in the lower and lateral regions of the pituitary gland and are most likely to be damaged by ischaemic necrosis, it is not surprising that GH is one of the earliest hormones lost. In another study, 59.3% of patients had complete anterior hypopituitarism, and 40.7% had partial anterior hypopituitarism [22].

Failure of lactation is the most common initial clinical finding, with most patients presenting with a history of failure of postpartum lactation, sometimes attributed to the stress of parturition. Prolactin deficiency may be suspected in a woman who is not able to breast-feed. It has been reported that failure of postpartum lactation and the prolactin response to thyrotrophin-releasing hormone (TRH) is the most sensitive screening test for detecting Sheehan's syndrome in patients with a typical obstetric history [26]. However, prolactin deficiency is not a *sine qua non* for the diagnosis of Sheehan's syndrome. Indeed, in rare cases, Sheehan's syndrome may result in hyperprolactinaemia [28].

Severe hypoglycaemia may be the presenting symptom in Sheehan's syndrome; in fact, Sheehan's syndrome has been reported as one of the most frequent causes of hypoglycaemia [29]. Therefore, Sheehan's syndrome must be considered as a possibility in the differential diagnosis of hypoglycaemia, particularly in regions where Sheehan's syndrome is common.

The clinical picture and laboratory findings of hypothyroidism due to Sheehan's syndrome are less severe than those seen in primary hypothyroidism. On the other hand, patients with Sheehan's syndrome may have normal or slightly increased secretion of thyrotrophin (TSH), as in patients with hypothalamic hypothyroidism. Thus, normal TSH levels do not exclude the diagnosis of secondary hypothyroidism [30]. Late-onset myxoedema and adrenal insufficiency resulting in death have been reported in patients with Sheehan's syndrome [31]. In rare cases, Sheehan's syndrome may also be associated with painless thyroiditis [32, 33]. This may be due to hypocortisolism developed after postpartum pituitary necrosis.

Adrenocortical insufficiency is one of the most important outcomes of Sheehan's syndrome. Sheehan [34] reported the autopsy findings of patients with postpartum hypopituitarism and found not only almost complete destruction of the anterior pituitary, but also severe atrophy of the adrenals compared with findings in normal individuals. Sudden death may therefore be due to an adrenal crisis. Sheehan's syndrome may also be characterized by isolated adrenocorticotrophin (ACTH) deficiency [35]. One of the most characteristic findings in Sheehan's syndrome is the lack of pigmentation which is due to deficiency of pro-opiomelanocortin derivatives including ACTH and β-endorphin.

Huang *et al.* [36] assessed 14 patients with postpartum haemorrhage followed by secondary amenorrhoea and agalactia in terms of their residual pituitary function. The time for patients with secondary amenorrhoea, developed after postpartum haemorrhage, to seek endocrine evaluation varied from 1 to over 30 years (mean 18 years). Seven out of 14 patients had normal basal luteinizing hormone (LH) levels and adequate LH responses to gonadotrophin-releasing hormone (GnRH) stimulation. Although all the patients had amenorrhoea, pituitary gonadotrophic function remained in some patients. The authors suggested that the amenorrhoea of patients with Sheehan's syndrome is not due simply to a dysfunction of pituitary gonadotrophs. Grimes and Brooks [37] evaluated a 38-year-old woman who had eight spontaneous pregnancies after the onset of hypopituitarism secondary to massive postpartum haemorrhage. Hormonal replacement therapy was not provided during seven pregnancies, which all terminated in spontaneous abortions. Hormone replacement therapy during the eighth pregnancy was associated with the delivery of a normal premature infant.

Pregnancy does not constitute evidence against the diagnosis of Sheehan's syndrome [37]. Laboratory procedures designed to investigate pituitary secretory reserve should be performed whenever hypopituitarism is suspected, as normal gonadotrophin levels do not exclude the diagnosis. Sheehan and Murdoch [38] have suggested that pregnancy might improve hypopituitarism by stimulating the pituitary remnant to undergo hyperplasia. Shahmanesh *et al.* [39] performed pituitary function tests in 14 patients with Sheehan's syndrome and found that pituitary function was relatively preserved for LH and follicle-stimulating hormone (FSH), but not for prolactin and GH. They suggested that the absence of a rise in prolactin following TRH stimulation may provide the most sensitive test of pituitary hypofunction in postpartum haemorrhage. Administration of gonadotrophins as replacement therapy may result in successful induction of normal cycles and ovulation [40]. Gonadotrophin production may, however, remain adequate for ovulation, and patients with Sheehan's syndrome may have successful pregnancies.

Psychiatric disorders, sometimes severe, may occur in some patients with Sheehan's syndrome, and hyponatraemic and hypoglycaemic convulsions have been reported [41, 42].

Barkan [43] reported two patients with Sheehan's syndrome in whom the diagnosis of pituitary atrophy was made *in vivo*, both biochemically and radiologically. One of the patients developed Sheehan's syndrome despite blood transfusion. Loss of pituitary tissue creates an empty space within the fossa, with subsequent herniation of the arachnoid and entry of cerebrospinal fluid into the sella – visible on computed tomography (CT) scans. Sheehan's syndrome may be characterized by an enlarged non-haemorrhagic pituitary gland with subsequent involution and pituitary insufficiency, followed by an improvement to almost normal status [42].

Atrophy of the posterior lobe of the pituitary and hypothalamic nuclei is found in over 90% of patients with Sheehan's syndrome [44, 45]. Arnaout and Ajlouni [46] investigated neurohypophyseal function by measuring the plasma vasopressin response to an osmolar challenge. They demonstrated impaired osmoregulation of vasopressin secretion in 12 of 15 patients with Sheehan's syndrome. None of the patients developed permanent diabetes insipidus. They concluded that partial diabetes insipidus seems to be much more frequent in postpartum hypopituitarism than previously believed. In rare cases, however, patients with Sheehan's syndrome may present with diabetes insipidus [47]. In another study, 8 of 14 patients presented with symptoms of severe hyponatraemia (serum sodium less than 125 mmol/L) more than 16 years after the occurrence of postpartum haemorrhage. Adrenal insufficiency is one of the most likely causes of hyponatraemia among patients with Sheehan's syndrome. The inappropriate vasopressin secretion may also cause hyponatraemia in patients with Sheehan's syndrome [36]. The clinical signs and symptoms of Sheehan's syndrome are shown in Table 2.

Diagnosis

A careful obstetric history and physical examination are very important in the diagnosis of Sheehan's syndrome. The development of modern dynamic tests of pituitary function coincided with a marked reduction in the prevalence of Sheehan's syndrome. Data regarding pituitary function tests are therefore limited. The measurement of basal hormone levels is sufficient to make a diagnosis of Sheehan's syndrome in most patients with a medical history compatible with Sheehan's syndrome. Dynamic pituitary function tests,

Table 2. Clinical signs and symptoms of Sheehan's syndrome.

Failure of lactation
Amenorrhoea
Dry and sparse hair
Weakness
Tiredness
Hypotension
Breast atrophy
Pale skin
Hypopigmentation
Wrinkling around mouth and eyes
Infertility
Symptoms and signs of hypothyroidism
Symptoms and signs of adrenocortical insufficiency
Atrophic uterus and reduced pubic hair on pelvic examination
Diabetes insipidus (about 5%)

including the insulin tolerance test to assess GH and ACTH reserve or other tests used in the diagnosis of GHD, the TRH stimulation test to assess prolactin and TSH reserve, and the GnRH stimulation test to assess LH and FSH reserve, may be needed in some patients. Jialal *et al.* [48] suggested that the absence of a prolactin response to TRH stimulation is diagnostic for Sheehan's syndrome. This finding, however, has not been supported by others [23, 28, 31]. Nevertheless, the failure of a prolactin response to a TRH challenge is very helpful and may be used as a screening test. Variability of target hormone responses to stimulation tests are closely related to the pituitary reserve.

Radiological imaging is very helpful in the diagnosis of Sheehan's syndrome. An empty or partially empty sella on CT scan or magnetic resonance imaging (MRI) is a characteristic finding of the syndrome [22, 23]. Bakiri *et al.* [22] evaluated 54 patients with Sheehan's syndrome. All the patients had a CT scan, and in 72.2% the sella turcica was completely empty, with pituitary remnants visible in the remainder. Pituitary remnants were seen more frequently in those patients with incomplete hypopituitarism and in those with a short history of the syndrome. In this study, the size of the sella turcica was determined from the CT scan using the two-dimensional measurements of height and length on their greatest axes; it was not possible to obtain measurements of width at the same level in all subjects. An empty sella of a small or normal size could be an important sign in the aetiological diagnosis of postpartum hypopituitarism. Figure 2 demonstrates an empty sella in one of our patients with Sheehan's syndrome.

An empty sella was found in 8.6% (5/58) of patients with lymphocytic hypophysitis, and is supposed to be its final stage [49]. The differential diagnosis in Sheehan's syndrome should include lymphocytic hypophysitis, which is a primary inflammatory disorder of the pituitary gland. Iwaoka [50] reported a patient with hypopituitarism associated with Hashimoto's thyroiditis and candidiasis. Although the medical history was compatible with Sheehan's syndrome, the clinical features and immunological data suggested lymphocytic hypophysitis. Iwaoka suggested that Sheehan's syndrome should be distinguished from lymphocytic hypophysitis. Lymphocytic hypophysitis is a form of autoimmune endocrine disorder and is usually associated with other autoimmune endocrine disorders. Sheehan's syndrome has not been reported to be associated with autoimmune disorders. A history of other autoimmune endocrine disorders therefore suggests lymphocytic hypophysitis. Lymphocytic hypophysitis can also be confused clinically with Sheehan's syndrome, but there is no history of obstetric haemorrhage in lymphocytic hypophysitis. The diagnosis of lymphocytic hypophysitis should be considered in women with symptoms of hypopituitarism or mass lesions of the sella during pregnancy or postpartum,

(a)

(b)

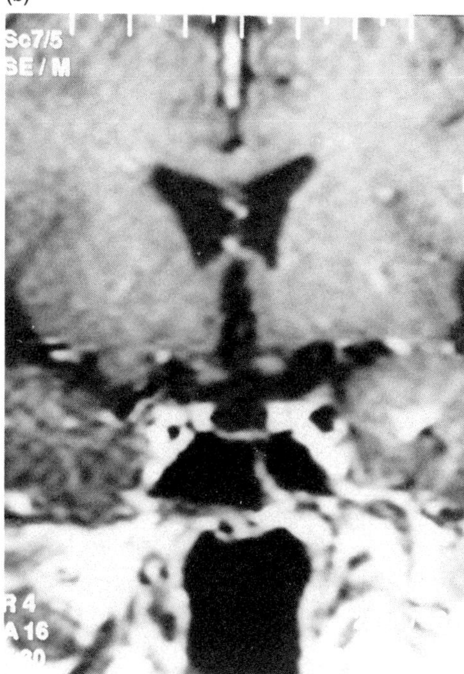

Figure 2. *Magnetic resonance imaging of (a) sagittal and (b) coronal sections of the pituitary gland in a patient with Sheehan's syndrome, demonstrating the empty sella.*

especially in the absence of a history of obstetric haemorrhage [9]. Patients with lymphocytic hypophysitis may present with the symptoms of partial or panhypopituitarism, similar to patients with Sheehan's syndrome; however, isolated anterior pituitary hormone deficiency is more frequent in lymphocytic hypophysitis. The most frequently reported isolated hormone deficiency in lymphocytic hypophysitis is ACTH deficiency; however, this is not the case in Sheehan's syndrome. Some women with lymphocytic hypophysitis may undergo spontaneous regression of the mass and a return of pituitary function [51, 52]. Some patients diagnosed as having Sheehan's syndrome in the past might really have had lymphocytic hypophysitis. The clinical signs and symptoms of lymphocytic hypophysitis are shown in Table 3.

Sheehan's syndrome may initially closely mimic hypophysitis, or the necrosis of an adenoma. Immediately after delivery complicated by severe hypotension, the patient may develop hypopituitarism, and MRI may disclose the presence of an enlarged non-haemorrhagic pituitary gland. Although MRI may reveal an

Table 3. *Clinical signs and symptoms of lymphocytic hypophysitis.*

Symptoms and signs due to mass effects: Headache Visual field defects
Galactorrhoea
Amenorrhoea
Loss of libido
Infertility
Diabetes insipidus
Isolated pituitary hormone deficiency
Most commonly adrenocorticotrophin deficiency
Symptoms and signs of hypothyroidism
Symptoms and signs of hypoadrenalism

Table 4. *Diagnosis of Sheehan's syndrome.*

- Medical/obstetric history
  - Postpartum haemorrhage?
  - Failure of postpartum lactation?
  - Failure of postpartum menses?
- Physical examination
- Laboratory investigation
  - Biochemistry
    - hypoglycaemia?
    - hyponatraemia?
  - Endocrine investigation
    - basal hormone levels (cortisol, prolactin, free T_4, TSH, FSH, LH, oestradiol, IGF-I, ACTH)
    - dynamic pituitary function tests (if necessary)
      - TSH and prolactin responses to TRH
      - FSH and LH responses to GnRH
      - Cortisol and GH responses to ITT or other tests to assess the hypothalamic–pituitary axis and GH/IGF-I axis if ITT is contraindicated
      - water deprivation – desmopressin or saline infusion test if diabetes insipidus is suspected
- Radiological investigation
  - MRI of pituitary gland

ACTH, adrenocorticotrophin; FSH, follicle-stimulating hormone; GnRH, gonadotrophin-releasing hormone; ITT, insulin tolerance test; LH, luteinizing hormone; T_4, thyroxine; TRH, thyrotrophin-releasing hormone; TSH, thyrotrophin.

enlarged pituitary mass, which is due to acute haemorrhage in the early phase of Sheehan's syndrome, the radiological hallmark of Sheehan's syndrome is an empty sella. However, an empty sella may be the final outcome in patients with lymphocytic hypophysitis [53, 54]. Table 4 shows the diagnosis of Sheehan's syndrome.

Treatment

The treatment of patients with Sheehan's syndrome is based on which pituitary hormones are deficient. ACTH deficiency is the situation most likely to require emergency treatment, and adrenal insufficiency is treated with glucocorticoids. In patients presenting with severe hypopituitarism and evidence of fluid depletion, treatment should be as for a patient with an adrenal crisis. Patients with ACTH deficiency do not demonstrate defects in mineralocorticoid secretion, and replacement with fludrocortisone is not necessary.

Hypothyroidism is treated with thyroxine (T_4), which is the treatment of choice for secondary hypothyroidism. Whenever it is suspected that TSH deficiency coexists with severe ACTH deficiency, it is important to start treatment with glucocorticoids prior to T_4, in order to prevent an acute adrenal crisis. In patients with Sheehan's syndrome, measurement of serum TSH levels is not helpful for monitoring T_4 replacement therapy. GH replacement therapy in GH-deficient patients with Sheehan's syndrome enrolled in KIMS has beneficial effects on lean body mass, lipid profile and, particularly, on quality of life. Patients with Sheehan's syndrome have more severe GHD, indicated by significantly lower levels of insulin-like growth factor I, and require higher doses of GH than GH-deficient patients without Sheehan's syndrome [55]. We have recently reported that GH replacement therapy in GH-deficient patients with Sheehan's syndrome improved cognitive function, as detected by the latency of P300 auditory event-related potentials [56].

Hypogonadism in women is associated with decreased bone density and an increased risk of osteoporosis. Although the benefits of oestrogen replacement in postmenopausal women are controversial, data support the importance of physiological oestrogen/progesterone replacement in hypogonadal premenopausal women. Gonadotrophin deficiency is manifest by partial loss of secondary sex characteristics and amenorrhoea, and the premature development of osteoporosis. Replacement therapy is therefore important, particularly in premenopausal patients with Sheehan's syndrome.

Conclusions

Sheehan's syndrome is not an uncommon cause of hypopituitarism in developing countries, and recent data suggest that it is being reported more often in western society. Its pathophysiology is still not clearly understood. Hypopituitarism in Sheehan's syndrome, which may be partial or complete, starts at an earlier age and is more severe than hypopituitarism due to other causes. Sheehan's syndrome is rarely diagnosed in the acute postpartum state. Most patients with Sheehan's syndrome usually present months to years later with a history of failure of postpartum lactation, failure to resume menses and the symptoms of secondary hypoadrenalism, hypothyroidism and GHD. Diabetes insipidus is very rare. The symptoms of hypopituitarism in mild cases may be non-specific and Sheehan's syndrome may therefore remain undetected for many years, with patients sometimes being given inappropriate long-term treatment. Delays in diagnosis may also be due to insufficient information and limited teaching in medical schools, particularly in western society. Treatment of Sheehan's syndrome is based on the appropriate replacement of deficient hormones. GH is one of the earliest hormones lost in Sheehan's syndrome, and GH replacement therapy has been shown to be beneficial.

References

1. Sheehan HL. Postpartum necrosis of the anterior pituitary. J Pathol Bact 1937;45:189–214
2. Sheehan HL. The frequency of post-partum hypopituitarism. J Obstet Gynaecol Br Commonw 1965; 72:103–11
3. Toogood A, Shalet S. GH deficiency and the degree of hypopituitarism. Clin Endocrinol (Oxf) 1995;42:443–4 (Reply)
4. Rosén T, Bengtsson B-Å. Premature mortality due to cardiovascular disease in hypopituitarism. Lancet 1990;336:285–8
5. Abs R, Bengtsson B-Å, Hernberg-Ståhl E, Monson JP, Tauber JP, Wilton P, Wüster C. GH replacement in 1034 growth hormone deficient hypopituitary adults: demographic and clinical characteristics, dosing and safety. Clin Endocrinol (Oxf) 1999;50:703–13
6. Comte L. Contriution a l'etude de l'hypophse humaine, Doctoral thesis. Lausanne, Switzerland 1898
7. Erdheim J, Stumme E. Über die schwangerschafts-veranderung der hypophuse. Beitr Z Pathol Anat Allg Pathol 1909;46:1–132
8. Goluboff LG, Ezrin C. Effect of pregnancy on the somatotroph and the prolactin cell of the human adenohypophysis. J Clin Endocrinol Metab 1969; 29:1533–8
9. Molitch ME. Pituitary diseases in pregnancy. Semin Perinatol 1998;22:457–70
10. Scheithauer BW, Sano T, Kovacs KT, Young WF Jr, Ryan N, Randall RV. The pituitary gland in pregnancy: a clinicopathologic and immunohistochemical study of 69 cases. Mayo Clin Proc 1990;65:461–74
11. Bergland RM, Ray BS, Torack RM. Anatomical variations in the pituitary gland and adjacent structures in 225 human autopsy cases. J Neurosurg 1968;28:93–9
12. Dejager S, Gerber S, Foubert L, Turpin G. Sheehan's syndrome: differential diagnosis in the acute phase. J Intern Med 1998;244:261–6
13. Daughaday WH. The anterior pituitary. In: Wilson JD, Foster DW, editors. Textbook of endocrinology. Philadelphia: W. B. Saunders 1985:568–613
14. Roberts DM. Sheehan's syndrome. Am Fam Physician 1988;37:223–7
15. Gupta D, Gaiha M, Mahajan R, Daga MK. Atypical presentation of Sheehan's syndrome without post-partum haemorrhage. J Assoc Physicians India 2001; 49:386–7

16. Engelberth O, Jezkova K, Bleha O, Malek J, Bendl J. Autoantibodies in Sheehan' syndrome. Vnitr Lek 1965;11:737–41

17. Nishiyama S, Takano T, Hidaka Y, Takada K, Iwatani Y, Amino N. A case of postpartum hypopituitarism associated with empty sella: possible relation to postpartum autoimmune hypophysitis. Endocr J 1993;40:431–8

18. Patel MC, Guneratne N, Haq N, West TE, Weetman AP, Clayton RN. Peripartum hypopituitarism and lymphocytic hypophysitis. QJM 1995;88:571–80

19. Goswami R, Kochupillai N, Crock PA, Jaleel A, Gupta N. Pituitary autoimmunity in patients with Sheehan's syndrome. J Clin Endocrinol Metab 2002; 87:4137–41

20. López-Karpovitchs X, Larrea F, Cárdenas R, Valencia X, Piedras J, Diaz-Sanchez V, Alarcon-Segovia D. Peripheral blood lymphocyte subsets and serum immunoglobulins in Sheehan's syndrome and in normal women during the menstrual cycle. Rev Invest Clin 1993;45:247–53

21. Sherif IH, Vanderley CM, Beshyah S, Bosairi S. Sella size and contents in Sheehan's syndrome. Clin Endocrinol (Oxf) 1989;30:613–8

22. Bakiri F, Bendib SE, Maoui R, Bendib A, Benmiloud M. The sella turcica in Sheehan's syndrome: computerized tomographic study in 54 patients. J Endocrinol Invest 1991;14:193–6

23. Fleckman AM, Schubart UK, Danziger A, Fleischer N. Empty sella of normal size in Sheehan's syndrome. Am J Med 1983;75:585–91

24. Lust K, McIntyre HD, Morton A. Sheehan's syndrome – acute presentation with hyponatraemia and headache. Aust NZ J Obstet Gynaecol 2001;41:348–51

25. Haddock L, Vega LA, Aguiló F, Rodriguez O. Adrenocortical, thyroidal and human growth hormone reserve in Sheehan's syndrome. Johns Hopkins Med J 1972;131:80–99

26. Özbey N, İnanç S, Aral F, Azezli A, Orhan Y, Sencer E, Molvalilar S. Clinical and laboratory evaluation of 40 patients with Sheehan's syndrome. Isr J Med Sci 1994; 30:826–9

27. Keleştimur F. GH deficiency and the degree of hypopituitarism. Clin Endocrinol (Oxf) 1995;42:443–4

28. Keleştimur F. Hyperprolactinemia in a patient with Sheehan's syndrome. South Med J 1992;85:1008–10

29. Güven M, Bayram F, Güven K, Keleştimur F. Evaluation of patients admitted with hypoglycaemia to a teaching hospital in Central Anatolia. Postgrad Med J 2000; 76:150–2

30. MacCagnan P, Oliveira JH, Castro V, Abucham J. Abnormal circadian rhythm and increased non-pulsatile secretion of thyrotrophin in Sheehan's syndrome. Clin Endocrinol (Oxf) 1999;51:439–47

31. DiZerega G, Kletzky OA, Mishell DR Jr. Diagnosis of Sheehan's syndrome using a sequential pituitary stimulation test. Am J Obstet Gynecol 1978;132: 348–53

32. Sasaki H, Shijyo H, Cugini P, Kawasaki T, Okumura M. Simultaneous occurrence of postpartum hypopituitarism (Sheehan's syndrome) and transient resolving thyrotoxicosis due to postpartum painless thyroiditis. South Med J 1992;85:660–2

33. Watanobe H, Kawabe H. Painless thyroiditis developed in a patient with Sheehan's syndrome. J Endocrinol Invest 1997;20:335–7

34. Sheehan HL. Atypical hypopituitarism. Proc Royal Soc Med 1961;54:43–8

35. Stacpoole PW, Kandell TW, Fisher WR. Primary empty sella, hyperprolactinemia, and isolated ACTH deficiency after postpartum hemorrhage. Am J Med 1983;74:905–8

36. Huang YY, Ting MK, Hsu BR, Tsai JS. Demonstration of reserved anterior pituitary function among patients with amenorrhea after postpartum hemorrhage. Gynecol Endocrinol 2000;14:99–104

37. Grimes HG, Brooks MH. Pregnancy in Sheehan's syndrome. Report of a case and review. Obstet Gynecol Surv 1980;35:481–8

38. Sheehan HL, Murdoch R. Postpartum necrosis of the anterior pituitary. Effect of subsequent pregnancy. Lancet 1938;2:123

39. Shahmanesh M, Ali Z, Pourmand M, Nourmand I. Pituitary function tests in Sheehan's syndome. Clin Endocrinol (Oxf) 1980;12:303–11

40. Çolakoglu M, Erçal T, Karslioglu S. Commencement of normal menstrual cycles after 17 years in a patient with Sheehan's syndrome. Am J Med 1987;82:578

41. Farmer TW, Flowers CA, Jr. Neurologic manifestations of postpartum pituitary insufficiency. Neurology 1955;5:212–4

42. Lavallée G, Morcos R, Palardy J, Aubé M, Gilbert D. MR of nonhemorrhagic postpartum pituitary apoplexy. Am J Neuroradiol 1995;16:1939–41

43. Barkan AL. Pituitary atrophy in patients with Sheehan's syndrome. Am J Med Sci 1989;298:38–40

44. Sheehan HL, Whitehead R. The neurohypophysis in post-partum hypopituitarism. J Pathol Bacteriol 1963; 85:145–69

45. Whitehead R. The hypothalamus in post-partum hypopituitarism. J Pathol Bacteriol 1963;86:55–67

46. Arnaout MA, Ajlouni K. Plasma vasopressin responses in postpartum hypopituitarism: impaired response to osmotic stimuli. Acta Endocrinol (Copenh) 1992; 127:494–8

47. Kan AK, Calligerous D. A case report of Sheehan syndrome presenting with diabetes insipidus. Aust NZ J Obstet Gynaecol 1998;38:224–6

48. Jialal I, Naidoo C, Norman RJ, Rajput MC, Omar MA, Joubert SM. Pituitary function in Sheehan's syndrome. Obstet Gynecol 1984;63:15–19

49. Hashimoto K, Takao T, Makino S. Lymphocytic adenohypophysitis and lymphocytic infundibuloneuro-hypophysitis. Endocr J 1997;44:1–10

50. Iwaoka T. A case of hypopituitarism associated with Hashimoto's thyroiditis and candidiasis: lymphocytic hypophysitis or Sheehan's syndrome? Endocr J 2001;48:585–90

51. Leiba S, Schindel B, Weinstein R, Lidor I, Friedman S, Matz S. Spontaneous postpartum regression of pituitary mass with return of function. JAMA 1986;255:230–2

52. McGrail KM, Beyerl BD, Black PM, Klibanski A, Zervas NT. Lymphocytic adenohypophysitis of pregnancy with complete recovery. Neurosurgery 1987;20:791–3

53. Keleştimur F. Lymphocytic hypophisitis and autoimmune thyroid disease. J Endocrinol Invest 2000;23:339–40 (Reply)

54. Ünlühizarci K, Bayram F, Çolak R, Öztürk F, Selçuklu A, Durak AC, Keleştimur F. Distinct radiological and clinical appearance of lymphocytic hypophysitis. J Clin Endocrinol Metab 2001;86:1861–4

55. Keleştimur F, Auernhammer C, Çolak R, Gomez JM, Molvalilar S, Kołtowska-Häggström M, Jönsson PJ, Góth MI. The baseline characteristics and the effects of GH replacement therapy in patients with Sheehan's syndrome as compared to non-functioning pituitary adenoma. The Endocrine Society's 85th Annual Meeting 2003 Jun 19–22; Philadelphia, USA. 589

56. Gölgeli A, Tanriverdi F, Süer C, Gökce C, Özesmi C, Bayram F, Keleştimur F. Utility of P300 auditory event-related potential latency in detecting cognitive function in growth hormone (GH)-deficient patients with Sheehan's syndrome and effects of GH replacement therapy. Eur J Endocrinol 2004;150:153–9

27 Growth hormone and the metabolic syndrome

Joop AMJL Janssen and Aart Jan van der Lely
Department of Internal Medicine, Endocrinology Section, Erasmus MC, Rotterdam, The Netherlands

Summary

Metabolic syndrome and untreated growth hormone deficiency (GHD) share several key features, including abdominal visceral obesity, insulin resistance, impaired glucose tolerance and/or type 2 diabetes mellitus, hypertension, hypertriglyceridaemia, decreased high-density lipoprotein (HDL)-cholesterol levels and increased carotid intimal thickness. The considerable overlap of clinical signs and symptoms between the two syndromes indicates commonality of the underlying endocrine disturbances. This suggests that growth hormone (GH) therapy might be appropriate for patients with metabolic syndrome, given the well-documented beneficial effects of GH therapy on the lipid profile and other cardiovascular risk factors in GH-deficient adult patients. The physiological activities of GH, insulin, and insulin-like growth factor I (IGF-I) are highly interrelated, however, particularly in relation to glucose and lipid metabolism. Compounding the complexity of these interrelationships are interactions with other hormones, such as cortisol and sex steroids, as well as the influences of non-endocrine factors such as nutrition and time of day. Furthermore, conditions prevailing in fetal and/or postnatal life may permanently alter the activities of the GH/IGF-I and hypothalamic–pituitary–adrenal axes. This chapter reviews the role of GH both in the pathophysiology and as a potential treatment of the metabolic syndrome.

Introduction

Hypercholesterolaemia, hypertension and smoking have long been considered the three main cardiovascular risk factors. In 1988, Gerard Reaven [1] postulated that resistance to insulin-mediated glucose uptake and hyperinsulinaemia are involved in the aetiology of three major related diseases: essential hypertension, coronary artery disease and type 2 diabetes mellitus. He suggested that metabolic abnormalities – each separately considered a risk factor for coronary artery disease – clustered in some individuals and identified a group at risk of adverse clinical outcomes. The key features of this syndrome as originally described by Reaven were decreased insulin-mediated glucose disposal, glucose intolerance and/or diabetes mellitus, hyperinsulinaemia, hypertriglyceridaemia, low plasma high-density lipoprotein (HDL)-cholesterol levels, and essential hypertension. Some years later, abdominal adiposity was added to this syndrome. The combination of abdominal obesity, hypertension, diabetes, and dyslipidaemia has been called the metabolic syndrome, or syndrome X [1, 2]. Figure 1 shows the changes in carbohydrate and lipid metabolism in liver, fat and muscle, which are commonly seen in individuals with the metabolic syndrome.

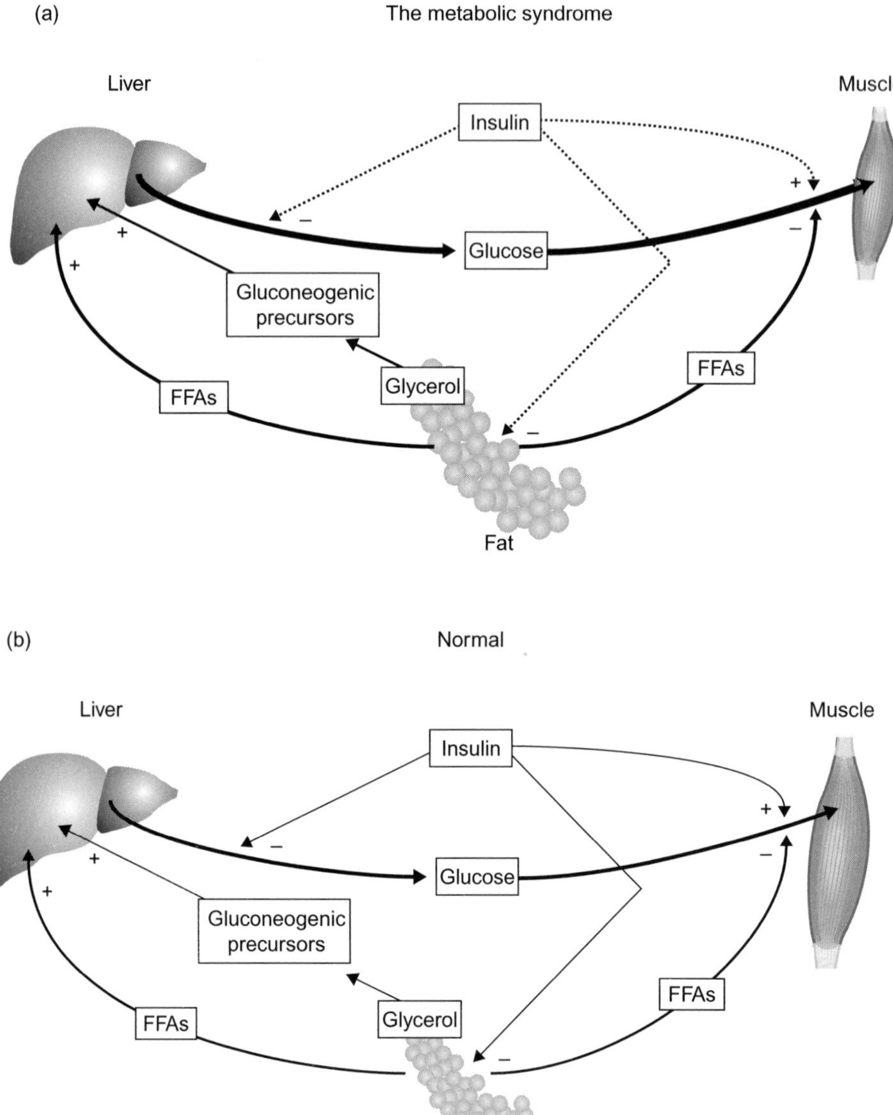

Figure 1. *(a) Schematic representation of the abnormal regulation of carbohydrate and lipid metabolism in the liver, fat and muscle of individuals with the metabolic syndrome. (b) The pattern of regulation in normal subjects is shown for comparison. Note the differences in muscle mass and fat mass between normal subjects and patients with the metabolic syndrome. The thickness of the arrows provides a qualitative index of the fluxes. The decrease in insulin action in subjects with the metabolic syndrome (dotted lines in [a]) can lead to an increased release of glucose and free fatty acids (FFAs) from the liver and adipose tissue, respectively. Both the decrease in insulin action and the increase in FFAs can contribute to decreased muscle glucose uptake and increased hepatic gluconeogenesis.*

There are striking similarities and a considerable overlap between patients with untreated growth hormone deficiency (GHD) and the metabolic syndrome [3]. Both syndromes are associated with abdominal visceral obesity, insulin resistance, impaired glucose tolerance and/or type 2 diabetes mellitus, hypertension, hypertriglyceridaemia, low HDL-cholesterol levels and increased carotid intimal thickness.

Lean body mass is decreased in adults who are deficient in growth hormone (GH) compared with those who have normal GH secretion [4, 5]. Both untreated GHD and insulin resistance seem to be associated with premature cardiovascular morbidity and mortality [3]. Recently the National Cholesterol Education Program Adult Treatment Panel III has developed criteria for the identification of the metabolic syndrome (Table 1) [6]. Not all individuals with the metabolic syndrome will develop all of the abnormalities listed in Table 1. Diagnosis of the metabolic syndrome is made when three or more of the risk determinants shown in Table 1 are present.

The interrelationships between GH, insulin, insulin-like growth factor-I (IGF-I) and nutrition

Insulin, GH and IGF-I are highly interrelated (Fig. 2). GH and insulin both stimulate hepatic IGF-I production, and IGF-I feeds back to suppress GH and insulin release. The relationships are even more complex, as GH positively regulates IGF-binding protein-3 (IGFBP-3), which is quantitatively the main IGFBP, and the associated acid-labile subunit (ALS), whereas IGFBP-1 levels are negatively regulated by insulin [7].

Another important factor may be nutrition, which is, after GH and insulin, the most important factor in regulating serum levels of IGF-I [8]. After food intake, the acute increase in glucose and amino acid concentrations in blood induces an acute increase in insulin levels. As a consequence, glucose production by the liver stops, and insulin-mediated uptake of glucose in the muscles and the liver is stimulated. The increased insulin levels also inhibit lipolysis in adipose tissue, resulting in a decrease of free fatty acids (FFAs) in the circulation. Thus, glucose becomes the main postprandial source of energy [8]. Directly after a meal, insulin also promotes the storage of glucose and lipids in the liver, adipose tissue and muscle and stimulates the conversion of amino acids into proteins in various tissues [9].

GH is mainly secreted in peaks during the night. Dietary amino acids may – like insulin – stimulate GH secretion. In contrast, a rise in glucose levels suppresses GH secretion. However, when food intake is too low to meet the needs of the body,

Table 1. *Adult Treatment Panel III criteria for identification of the metabolic syndrome. Adapted from [6] with permission.*

Abdominal obesity (waist circumference)	
Men	> 102 cm (40 in)
Women	> 88 cm (35 in)
Triglycerides	> 3.75 mmol/L (150 mg/dL)
HDL-cholesterol	
Men	< 1.0 mmol/L (< 40 mg/dL)
Women	< 1.1 mmol/L (< 50 mg/dL)
Blood pressure	≥ 130 (systolic) / ≥ 85 (diastolic) mmHg
Fasting glucose	≥ 6.1 mmol/L (≥ 110 mg/dL)

HDL, high-density lipoprotein

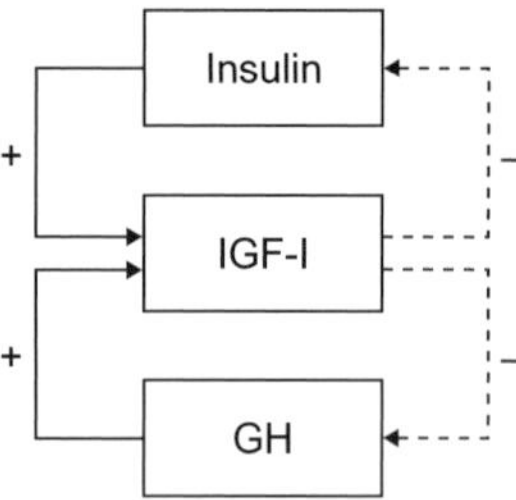

Figure 2. Relationship between GH, insulin and IGF-I. +, stimulation; –, negative feedback.

insulin secretion decreases and GH secretion increases. This induces insulin resistance and results in increased lipolysis and ketogenesis [8]. In fact, GH secretion is increased when either food intake is too low or insulin action is lacking. In both these circumstances, GH is no longer able to stimulate sufficient IGF-I synthesis. GH actions are mediated by IGF-I only in so far as they are anabolic; that is, when they are assisted by insulin and adequate food intake [8]. In other words, the anabolic effects of GH, insulin and IGF-I occur only when these hormones act in concert.

Immediately after a meal, insulin is the major stimulator, not only of uptake and storage of glucose and amino acids, but also of lipid synthesis. IGF-I increases insulin sensitivity and suppresses proteolysis. In the early postprandial period, GH, IGF-I and insulin promote anabolism, with IGF-I as the main modulator in mediating and/or supporting the effects of both insulin and GH (Fig. 2). In the late postprandial period, IGF-I reduces the GH-induced insulin resistance and stimulates lipolysis by reducing insulin secretion. This results in increased lipid oxidation. As IGF-I also reduces insulin secretion, lipolysis is no longer inhibited by insulin. In addition, IGF-I inhibits proteolysis and decreases protein oxidation. IGF-I thus plays a key role in switching the body from using glucose to using FFAs as a source of energy [8].

Could decreased GH secretion *per se* play a role in the development of the metabolic syndrome?

GH secretion is decreased in obese individuals [10]. However, in contrast to GH-deficient patients, obesity is associated with normal or even high serum IGF-I levels. In addition, prepubertal obese children are generally of normal or tall stature [11]. Decreased GH secretion therefore seems to be a consequence rather than the cause of obesity.

GH-deficient patients respond differently to over-nutrition compared with obese individuals [12]. Short-term over-nutrition in GH-deficient patients fails to normalize IGF-I, which suggests that an excess of nutrient intake is not able to override the effects of GHD [13]. Hypophysectomy in rats has been demonstrated to decrease GH receptor gene expression in adipocytes, while GH replacement restores receptor expression [14, 15]. Similarly in man, treatment of GH-deficient patients with GH results in the up-regulation of adipose tissue GH receptor gene expression [16].

GH exerts several metabolic effects either directly or indirectly on adipocytes. It has opposing effects on glucose and lipid metabolism in adipose tissue: insulin-like effects and insulin-antagonizing effects depending on the time frame (see above) [17]. The GH-mediated insulin-like effect is an acute antilipolytic action, whereas the GH-mediated insulin-antagonizing action is a long-term effect, inhibiting lipogenesis and glucose transport and increasing lipolysis [18]. The lack of the GH-mediated long-term insulin-antagonizing action on lipid and glucose metabolism may thus contribute to the development of adiposity in GH-deficient patients. IGF-I receptors are not expressed in mature adipocytes, and thus the effects of GH treatment on adipocyte functions are not directly mediated by IGF-I [19].

Long-term GH treatment is lipolytic in cultured adipocytes, and the lipolytic responses to GH seem to be the consequence of an increase in the activity of hormone-sensitive lipase, a key lipolytic enzyme [18]. In addition, GH treatment increases catecholamine-induced lipolysis *in vitro* and in hypophysectomized rats [18, 20]. Abdominal adiposity is a common finding in GHD and the metabolic syndrome, and both disorders are associated with high levels of very low-density lipoprotein (VLDL)-cholesterol and triglycerides, and reduced levels of HDL-cholesterol. In contrast, active acromegaly is associated with low serum triglyceride and low-density lipoprotein (LDL)-cholesterol levels, whereas treatment with a GH receptor antagonist increases serum triglyceride and LDL-cholesterol levels [21]. In the majority of studies, GH replacement has led to a decrease in total cholesterol, LDL-cholesterol and triglyceride levels and an increase in HDL-cholesterol. These effects are sustained for at least 3 years [22, 23]. Administration of GH up-regulates hepatic LDL-cholesterol receptors, thereby increasing the clearance of LDL by the liver [24].

Untreated GHD, like the metabolic syndrome, has been associated with hypertension [25]. The precise mechanisms underlying the development of hypertension in GHD are not fully understood. It has been reported that systemic nitric oxide (NO) formation is decreased in untreated GH-deficient patients [26]. Decreased NO formation may increase peripheral arterial resistance and thereby induce hypertension. Treatment with GH decreases peripheral arterial resistance in patients with GHD. This latter effect is probably mediated via IGF-I stimulation of endothelial NO formation [26]. Recently, an adipose-derived renin–angiotensin system has also been described [27]. Overproduction of angiotensinogen by adipose tissue may result in elevated levels of angiotensin II [28]. It has been speculated that increased local formation of angiotensin II may induce obesity-related hypertension and insulin resistance [28, 29]. Vickers *et al* [30]. have suggested that GH treatment may indirectly lower blood pressure by reducing fat mass, thereby down-regulating the activity of the adipose-derived renin–angiotensin system. In addition, GH treatment may also lower blood pressure via IGF-I-mediated down-regulation of the angiotensin II type 1 receptor [30].

Decreased serum IGF-I levels are coupled with increased sympathetic nerve activity to the muscle vascular bed in healthy ageing men [31]. In untreated GH-deficient patients, increased activity of the sympathetic nervous system in association with peripheral vascular resistance has been reported [32]. Increased sympathetic nerve activity may be another pathway by which the GH/IGF-I axis is related to blood pressure. It has been hypothesized that increased activity of the sympathetic nervous system is one of the mechanisms responsible for the development of hypertension in the metabolic syndrome [31, 33].

GH may modify glucose metabolism directly or indirectly via induction of IGF-I (see also above). Using the hyperinsulinaemic euglycaemic clamp technique, peripheral insulin resistance has been found in GH-deficient patients [34]. It has been suggested that the insulin resistance in GHD is directly related to the decreased lean body mass and increased abdominal obesity that usually characterize this condition [3]. A lowered serum IGF-I level, which also characterizes GHD, may be another factor that contributes to insulin resistance, as IGF-I has GH-independent insulin-sensitizing actions [35]. Other factors that may contribute to the insulin resistance of untreated GH-deficient patients are decreased physical activity and a decreased capillary permeability and density [36].

The increased sympathetic nerve activity discussed above may also contribute to several other aspects of the metabolic syndrome [33, 37, 38]. Reduced blood flow to skeletal muscle will attenuate glucose uptake and thus reduce insulin sensitivity. Sympathetically mediated lipolysis will increase FFAs and glycerol and thereby increase gluconeogenesis.

Is the development of the metabolic syndrome the consequence of an imbalance between cortisol and the GH/IGF-I axis?

In patients with glucose intolerance it has been reported that cortisol secretion, although normal, is inappropriately high given the enhanced central and peripheral sensitivity to glucocorticoids [39]. Rosmond and Bjorntorp [40] have previously suggested that the metabolic syndrome is due to elevated cortisol secretion. They also made the interesting suggestion that the combination of increased cortisol secretion and low GH secretion with decreased IGF-I levels may result in the metabolic syndrome [41]. GHD effectively increases cortisol production in key target tissues, including liver and adipose tissue, promoting insulin resistance and visceral adiposity [42]. Overexpression of type 1 11β-hydroxysteroid dehydrogenase (11β-HSD1), the enzyme that reduces cortisone to cortisol in liver, adipose tissue and omental adipose tissue, can stimulate glucocorticoid-induced adipocyte differentiation, which may lead to central obesity. However, cortisol action at the tissue level is partially regulated by GH [43]. GH has an important inhibitory effect on 11β-HSD1 [44]. It has been found that patients with GHD not receiving replacement therapy have higher levels of metabolites of cortisol than those receiving GH replacement therapy [44].

Lipoprotein lipase (LPL) is a main regulator of triglyceride assimilation in adipose tissue, where increased concentrations of cortisol promote lipid accumulation by increasing expression of LPL. Increased visceral adipose tissue depots and the FFAs released from these depots induce an increase in insulin resistance [45]. The increased delivery of FFAs to the liver may then add to the generation of other risk factors, such as hyperinsulinaemia, lipoprotein abnormalities and hypertension [45, 46].

GH inhibits LPL expression induced by cortisol, and increases lipolysis [43]. GH administration results in a profound reduction of visceral adipose tissue and less marked effects on other adipose tissue depots. The consequences of GH treatment are more evident in visceral than subcutaneous adipose tissues because of a higher cellularity, innervation and blood flow [43]. In summary, elevated cortisol activity and decreased GH secretion are able to induce many of the symptoms and signs of the metabolic syndrome. GH treatment may decrease cortisol activity. This may be partly explained by inhibitory activity on 11β-HSD1.

Is the metabolic syndrome due to adverse environmental conditions during fetal and postnatal life?

Increasing experimental evidence suggests that adverse environmental conditions during fetal and/or postnatal life may have long-term consequences for the development of the metabolic syndrome in adult life [47]. It has been found that people who were small or disproportionate (thin or short) at birth have high rates of coronary heart disease, high blood pressure, high cholesterol concentrations and abnormal glucose–insulin metabolism. These effects are independent of the length of gestation, suggesting that the occurrence of the metabolic syndrome is directly linked to fetal growth restriction [47]. In late gestation, GH assumes increasing importance in driving fetal growth [48]. There is evidence that the GH/IGF-I axis and the hypothalamic–pituitary–adrenal (HPA) axis may be permanently influenced by events in early life. This process has been called 'fetal programming', whereby the environmental conditions at a critical, sensitive period of early life have permanent effects on structure, physiology and metabolism in adult life. Fetal programming is likely to involve permanent changes in the 'set-points' of the endocrine systems. Studies in rats have suggested that maternal dietary restriction during gestation and lactation may permanently reduce the activity of the GH/IGF-I axis and upregulate the HPA axis in the offspring [48]. It has been found that treatment with GH (or IGF-I) alleviates obesity, hyperinsulinaemia and hypertension in rats programmed to develop the metabolic syndrome [30, 49].

Is there any evidence for beneficial effects of GH treatment in non-GH-deficient subjects with the metabolic syndrome?

The above-cited studies of Vickers *et al.* [30, 49] demonstrated that in rats programmed to develop the metabolic syndrome, GH/IGF-I treatment may improve many of the symptoms associated with this syndrome. However, whether GH treatment can also improve the metabolic syndrome in man is unknown. Some small studies have been published which suggest that GH treatment may have advantageous effects on the metabolic syndrome in man. Johannsson *et al.* [50] observed that 9 months of GH treatment reduced abdominal fat mass, improved glucose and lipid metabolism, and reduced diastolic blood pressure in middle-aged men with abdominal obesity and low to normal serum IGF-I concentrations. In another study in patients with the metabolic syndrome and elevated fasting glucose levels, the combination of GH treatment and metformin over 18 months did not induce sustained negative effects on glucose metabolism and insulin sensitivity [51]. The authors suggest that metformin may be effective in reducing the GH-induced insulin-antagonistic effects. In addition, GH in combination with metformin was more effective than metformin alone in reducing waist circumference. Whether GH-induced metabolic changes also influence cardiovascular risk in patients with the metabolic syndrome needs further investigation.

Conclusions

Metabolic syndrome and untreated GHD have several key features in common, suggesting that they share an underlying endocrine disturbance. GH therapy may therefore be an appropriate treatment for non GH-deficient subjects with the metabolic syndrome.

References

1. Reaven GM. Role of insulin resistance in human disease (syndrome X): an expanded definition. Annu Rev Med 1993;44:121–31
2. DeFronzo RA, Ferrannini E. Insulin resistance. A multifaceted syndrome responsible for NIDDM, obesity, hypertension, dyslipidemia, and atherosclerotic cardiovascular disease. Diabetes Care 1991;14:173–94
3. Johannsson G, Marin P, Johansson JO, Bengtsson B-Å Growth hormone and syndrome X. In: Smith R, Thorner MO, editors. Human growth hormone, research and clinical practice. Totowa: Humana Press 2000: 247–60
4. De Boer H, Blok GJ, Voerman HJ, De Vries PM, van der Veen EA. Body composition in adult growth hormone-deficient men, assessed by anthropometry and bioimpedance analysis. J Clin Endocrinol Metab 1992;75:833–7
5. Binnerts A, Deurenberg P, Swart GR, Wilson JH, Lamberts SW. Body composition in growth hormone-deficient adults. Am J Clin Nutr 1992;55:918–23
6. Executive summary of the third report of the National Cholesterol Education Program (NCEP) expert panel on detection, evaluation, and treatment of high blood cholesterol in adults (Adult Treatment Panel III). JAMA 2001;285:2486–97
7. Bondy CA, Underwood LE, Clemmons DR, Guler HP, Bach MA, Skarulis M. Clinical uses of insulin-like growth factor I. Ann Intern Med 1994;120:593–601
8. Froesch ER. Insulin-like growth factor: endocrine and autocrine/paracrine implications and relations to diabetes mellitus. In: Zahnd GR, Wollheim CB, editors. Contributions of physiology to the understanding of diabetes. Berlin: Springer-Verlag 1997:127–47
9. Goodman HM. Hormonal regulation of fuel metabolism. In: Goodman HM, editor. Basic medical endocrinology. Amsterdam: Elsevier 2003:291–325
10. Nam SY, Marcus C. Growth hormone and adipocyte function in obesity. Horm Res 2000;53 (Suppl 1): 87–97
11. Dietz WH, Jr., Hartung R. Changes in height velocity of obese preadolescents during weight reduction. Am J Dis Child 1985;139:705–7
12. Thissen JP, Ketelslegers JM, Underwood LE. Nutritional regulation of the insulin-like growth factors. Endocr Rev 1994;15:80–101
13. Underwood LE, Smith EP, Clemmons DR, Maes M, Maiter D, Kelelslegers JM. The productions and actions of insulin-like growth factors: their relationship to nutrition and growth. In: Tanner JM, editor. Auxology. London: Smith-Gordon 1989:235–49
14. Frick GP, Leonard JL, Goodman HM. Effect of hypophysectomy on growth hormone receptor gene expression in rat tissues. Endocrinology 1990;126: 3076–82

15. Peter MA, Winterhalter KH, Boni-Schnetzler M, Froesch ER, Zapf J. Regulation of insulin-like growth factor-I (IGF-I) and IGF-binding proteins by growth hormone in rat white adipose tissue. Endocrinology 1993;133:2624–31

16. Kamel A, Margery V, Norstedt G, Thorén M, Lindgren AC, Bronnegard M, Marcus C. Growth hormone (GH) treatment up-regulates GH receptor mRNA levels in adipocytes from patients with GH deficiency and Prader-Willi syndrome. Pediatr Res 1995;38:418–21

17. Davidson MB. Effect of growth hormone on carbohydrate and lipid metabolism. Endocr Rev 1987;8:115–31

18. Dietz J, Schwartz J. Growth hormone alters lipolysis and hormone-sensitive lipase activity in 3T3-F442A adipocytes. Metabolism 1991;40:800–6

19. Shimizu M, Torti F, Roth RA. Characterization of the insulin and insulin-like growth factor receptors and responsitivity of a fibroblast/adipocyte cell line before and after differentiation. Biochem Biophys Res Commun 1986;137:552–8

20. Yang S, Xu X, Bjorntorp P, Edén S. Additive effects of growth hormone and testosterone on lipolysis in adipocytes of hypophysectomized rats. J Endocrinol 1995;147:147–52

21. Parkinson C, Drake WM, Wieringa G, Yates AP, Besser GM, Trainer PJ. Serum lipoprotein changes following IGF-I normalization using a growth hormone receptor antagonist in acromegaly. Clin Endocrinol (Oxf) 2002;56:303–11

22. Garry P, Collins P, Devlin JG. An open 36-month study of lipid changes with growth hormone in adults: lipid changes following replacement of growth hormone in adult acquired growth hormone deficiency. Eur J Endocrinol 1996;134:61–6

23. Götherström G, Svensson J, Koranyi J, Alpsten M, Bosæus I, Bengtsson B, Johannsson G. A prospective study of 5 years of GH replacement therapy in GH-deficient adults: sustained effects on body composition, bone mass, and metabolic indices. J Clin Endocrinol Metab 2001;86:4657–65

24. Angelin B, Rudling M. Growth hormone and hepatic lipoprotein metabolism. Curr Opin Lipidol 1994; 5:160–5

25. Hew FL, O'Neal D, Kamarudin N, Alford FP, Best JD. Growth hormone deficiency and cardiovascular risk. Baillieres Clin Endocrinol Metab 1998;12:199–216

26. Boger RH, Skamira C, Bode-Boger SM, Brabant G, von zur Muhlen A, Frolich JC. Nitric oxide may mediate the hemodynamic effects of recombinant growth hormone in patients with acquired growth hormone deficiency. A double-blind, placebo-controlled study. J Clin Invest 1996;98:2706–13

27. Ailhaud G, Teboul M, Massiera F. Angiotensinogen, adipocyte differentiation and fat mass enlargement. Curr Opin Clin Nutr Metab Care 2002;5:385–9

28. Gorzelniak K, Engeli S, Janke J, Luft FC, Sharma AM. Hormonal regulation of the human adipose-tissue renin–angiotensin system: relationship to obesity and hypertension. J Hypertens 2002;20:965–73

29. Engeli S, Schling P, Gorzelniak K, Boschmann M, Janke J, Ailhaud G, Teboul M, Massiera F, Sharma AM. The adipose-tissue renin–angiotensin–aldosterone system: role in the metabolic syndrome? Int J Biochem Cell Biol 2003;35:807–25

30. Vickers MH, Ikenasio BA, Breier BH. Adult growth hormone treatment reduces hypertension and obesity induced by an adverse prenatal environment. J Endocrinol 2002;175:615–23

31. Sverrisdottir YB, Johannsson G, Jungersten L, Wallin BG, Elam M. Is the somatotropic axis related to sympathetic nerve activity in healthy ageing men? J Hypertens 2001;19:2019–24

32. Scott EM, Greenwood JP, Stoker JB, Mary DA, Gilbey SG. Sympathetic nerve hyperactivity is associated with increased peripheral vascular resistance in hypopituitary patients with growth hormone deficiency. Clin Endocrinol (Oxf) 2002;56:759–63

33. Reaven GM, Lithell H, Landsberg L. Hypertension and associated metabolic abnormalities – the role of insulin resistance and the sympathoadrenal system. N Engl J Med 1996;334:374–81

34. Johansson JO, Fowelin J, Landin K, Lager I, Bengtsson B-Å. Growth hormone-deficient adults are insulin-resistant. Metabolism 1995;44:1126–9

35. O'Connell T, Clemmons DR. IGF-I/IGF-binding protein-3 combination improves insulin resistance by GH-dependent and independent mechanisms. J Clin Endocrinol Metab 2002;87:4356–60

36. Oomen PH, Beentjes JA, Bosma E, Smit AJ, Reitsma WD, Dullaart RP. Reduced capillary permeability and capillary density in the skin of GH-deficient adults: improvement after 12 months GH replacement. Clin Endocrinol (Oxf) 2002;56:519–24

37. Brook RD, Julius S. Autonomic imbalance, hypertension, and cardiovascular risk. Am J Hypertens 2000; 13:112S–22

38. Hjemdahl P. Stress and the metabolic syndrome: an interesting but enigmatic association. Circulation 2002;106:2634–6

39. Andrews RC, Herlihy O, Livingstone DE, Andrew R, Walker BR. Abnormal cortisol metabolism and tissue sensitivity to cortisol in patients with glucose intolerance. J Clin Endocrinol Metab 2002;87: 5587–93

40. Rosmond R, Bjorntorp P. The interactions between hypothalamic–pituitary–adrenal axis activity, testosterone, insulin-like growth factor I and abdominal obesity with metabolism and blood pressure in men. Int J Obes Relat Metab Disord 1998;22:1184–96

41. Bjorntorp P, Rosmond R. Hypothalamic origin of the metabolic syndrome X. Ann NY Acad Sci 1999; 892:297–307

42. Stewart PM, Toogood AA, Tomlinson JW. Growth hormone, insulin-like growth factor-I and the cortisol–cortisone shuttle. Horm Res 2001;56 (Suppl 1):1–6

43. Bjorntorp P. The regulation of adipose tissue distribution in humans. Int J Obes Relat Metab Disord 1996; 20:291–302

44. Gelding SV, Taylor NF, Wood PJ, Noonan K, Weaver JU, Wood DF, Monson JP. The effect of growth hormone replacement therapy on cortisol–cortisone interconversion in hypopituitary adults: evidence for growth hormone modulation of extrarenal 11 beta-hydroxysteroid dehydrogenase activity. Clin Endocrinol (Oxf) 1998;48:153–62

45. Bjorntorp P. "Portal" adipose tissue as a generator of risk factors for cardiovascular disease and diabetes. Arteriosclerosis 1990;10:493–6

46. Johannsson G, Bjorntorp P, Bengtsson B-Å. Is GH therapy indicated in the metabolic syndrome? In: Monson J, editor. Growth hormone therapy. Oxford: Blackwell Science 1999: 264–81

47. Godfrey KM, Barker DJ. Fetal nutrition and adult disease. Am J Clin Nutr 2000;71:1344S–52

48. Barker DJP. Programming the baby. In: Barker DJP, editor. Mothers, babies, and disease in later life. London: BMJ Publishing Group 1994:14–36

49. Vickers MH, Ikenasio BA, Breier BH. IGF-I treatment reduces hyperphagia, obesity, and hypertension in metabolic disorders induced by fetal programming. Endocrinology 2001;142:3964–73

50. Johannsson G, Marin P, Lonn L, Ottosson M, Stenlof K, Bjorntorp P, Sjöström L, Bengtsson B-Å. Growth hormone treatment of abdominally obese men reduces abdominal fat mass, improves glucose and lipoprotein metabolism, and reduces diastolic blood pressure. J Clin Endocrinol Metab 1997;82:727–34

51. Herrmann BL, Berg C, Vogel E, Nowak T, Renzing-Koehler K, Mann K, Saller B. Effects of a combination of recombinant human growth hormone with metformin on glucose metabolism and body composition in patients with metabolic syndrome. Horm Metab Res 2004;36:54–61

28 The catabolic syndrome of prolonged critical illness

Frank Weekers and Greet Van den Berghe
Department of Intensive Care Medicine, University Hospital Leuven, Leuven, Belgium

Summary

A prolonged hypercatabolic response to an unresolving critical illness leads to profound loss of lean tissue mass. Weakness and immune dysfunction increase morbidity and compromise the survival chances of critically ill patients. As the cachexia of prolonged critical illness is associated with low concentrations of anabolic hormones such as insulin-like growth factor I (IGF-I) and testosterone, hormonal intervention to reverse catabolism was deemed to be beneficial. However, interventions with certain hormones have been shown to be ineffective in this patient group, and their indiscriminate use may even cause harm. Before considering endocrine intervention in this frail population, a detailed understanding of the pathophysiology of the neuroendocrine stress response is necessary. It is now clear that the stress response consists primarily of an actively secreting pituitary in the presence of low levels of circulating peripheral anabolic hormones such as IGF-I, testosterone and thyroid hormones. This constellation indicates, predominantly, a state of peripheral resistance to anterior pituitary hormones. From a teleological point of view these alterations make sense and may be beneficial as they presumably mediate the provision of essential substrates for the healing process while costly anabolism is postponed. However, when the disease process becomes prolonged, a uniformly reduced secretion of anterior pituitary hormones ensues, with proportionately reduced concentrations of the peripheral target hormones. This suppressed secretion has a central origin, as infused hypothalamic secretagogues are able to reactivate the anterior pituitary and restore pulsatile secretion. Reactivation of the anterior pituitary is accompanied by near normalization of the circulating levels of peripheral effector hormones, indicating at least partial recovery of sensitivity in the target tissues. Based on these findings, endocrine intervention using a combination of hypothalamic secretagogues, instead of high doses of selective peripherally active hormones, appears to be a more logical and safer strategy. Preserved feedback inhibition prevents overstimulation of these secretagogues.

Introduction

Illness or trauma is accompanied by immediate and complex changes in metabolism, which presumably contribute to survival. Within hours and during the first few days following a severe insult, patients develop a syndrome of hypermetabolism [1] consisting of such clinical manifestations as fever, tachypnoea and a hyperdynamic cardiovascular state accompanied by leukocytosis, hyperglycaemia, hyperlactataemia, lipolysis, muscle protein hypercatabolism and altered hepatic protein synthesis. The main purpose of this orchestrated response is to deliver sufficient amounts of substrates to wounded tissues so that healing can progress. When the underlying disease resolves, the stress response abates and recovery ensues.

In the modern era of intensive care, patients survive conditions that were previously lethal. Recovery from such severe insults may take weeks [2] and the prolongation of the hypermetabolic response induces a profound reduction in lean body mass (LBM), which is resistant to feeding [3]. Indeed, patients can lose up to 10% of their muscle mass per week [4] because of the proteolysis that provides substrates for vital cells in the brain, wounds and the immune system. The loss of protein is not confined to the skeletal muscle but also occurs in other organs, such as the liver, kidney and heart, reducing their cell mass and leading to impaired function [5]. Profound catabolism is thought to have a negative influence on outcome, to increase infectious complications [6], to delay the healing process and to prolong the need for intensive medical care. Extended recuperation often includes a prolonged duration of mechanical ventilatory support because of extreme muscle weakness and fatigue. Such cachectic patients often die of infections due to diminished immune competency and multiple organ failure.

As endocrine changes are invariably associated with critical illness and, in view of their role in intermediate metabolism, altered function of the anterior pituitary and its peripheral effectors may contribute to the wasting syndrome. Indeed, all critically ill patients have low serum concentrations of anabolic hormones, such as insulin-like growth factor I (IGF-I) and testosterone. As recombinant human growth hormone (GH) replacement has been used for many years in GH-deficient patients and increases LBM in this condition [7], it was thought that GH treatment may benefit the profoundly catabolic intensive care patient. The combination of active GH secretion in the presence of low peripheral IGF-I concentrations, consistently found following acute stress, was correctly interpreted as representing a state of GH resistance. Additionally, anecdotal evidence showed that GH had a reduced efficacy in generating IGF-I in patients with sepsis, again pointing to the presence of GH resistance [8]. It was assumed that this GH resistance persisted throughout the course of critical illness and that high doses of GH would thus be required in order to overcome it and to induce anabolism. After numerous studies, mostly small and non-randomized, reported positive effects of high-dose GH treatment in hypercatabolic patients [9–13] a large, multicentre, European trial investigating the effects of pharmacological doses of GH was initiated by Takala and co-workers [14] in the mid-1990s. Quite unexpectedly, this study revealed a significant increase in morbidity and mortality, the cause of which was unclear.

At the initiation of the Takala study, the neuroendocrine changes occurring during prolonged severe illness were largely unknown. Rather, as explained above, data obtained from acute catabolic states were merely extrapolated to the prolonged critical illness setting, an assumption that was clearly erroneous.

At the present time, we know that acute and prolonged critical illness are associated with completely different neuroendocrine characteristics [15, 16]. Indeed, in prolonged critical illness, somatotrophs no longer actively secrete GH. Instead, a state of relative hyposomatotrophism follows the initial stress response, in which pulsatile GH secretion is reduced to levels that are in proportion to the low IGF-I concentrations. In this chronic phase of illness, at least partial recovery of peripheral GH sensitivity occurs. Administration of pharmacological doses of GH at a time of recovered GH sensitivity may expose patients to toxic side-effects. In particular, the aggravation of insulin resistance by GH and the concomitant hyperglycaemia may have important consequences for critically ill patients [17]. The biphasic response, first described in the GH axis, is also present in the thyroid, prolactin and gonadal axes and this relative 'panhypopituitarism' could aggravate GH toxicity. In the following review, we discuss the neuroendocrine changes associated with critical illness and reappraise the current strategies to reverse hypercatabolism.

Endocrine changes associated with critical illness

The hypothalamic–anterior pituitary–peripheral hormone axes play a central role in the endocrine regulation of nearly all metabolic processes. As even partial dysfunction of the pituitary is associated with increased morbidity and mortality [18], there is a growing interest among intensivists in the neuroendocrine pathophysiology of critical illness. Until recently, it was commonly believed that the endocrine changes evoked by acute illness persisted even when the disease was prolonged, although a scientific basis for this was lacking. In the last decade it has become clear that the anterior pituitary responds biphasically to stress and that the acute and chronic (7–10 days following injury) phases of critical illness are substantially different.

Neuroendocrinology of acute illness

GH secretion is clearly enhanced in response to stress. At the same time, however, the serum concentration of its main peripheral effector molecule, IGF-I, is low [19]. In addition, the GH-dependent IGF-binding proteins (IGFBPs) and the circulating levels of GH-binding protein, presumably reflecting the functional GH receptor status, are low following acute stress [20]. These findings clearly indicate the presence of GH resistance early after injury. The finding that regular doses of GH administered to sick patients elicited a decreased anabolic response and that there is a reduction in gene expression of the GH receptor in muscle [20] and liver [21] again point to the presence of GH resistance. Concomitantly, suppressor of cytokine signalling proteins, induced by inflammation [22], negatively regulate the Janus kinase/signal transducer and activator of transcription pathway for GH signalling, thus adding to GH resistance. Enhanced clearance of IGF-I [23], also partially related to changes in IGFBPs [24, 25], contributes to its low serum levels. From a teleological point of view, this somatotrophic response following acute injury seems appropriate. Indeed, the direct lipolytic and anti-insulin effects of GH may be enhanced, thus providing metabolic substrates, such as free fatty acids and glucose to vital tissues [25], while anabolism, which is mediated largely by IGF-I and is considered to be less vital at this time, is postponed.

Hypercortisolism, driven by increased release of corticotrophin-releasing hormone and adreno-corticotrophin following illness [26], also contributes to the acute provision of energy by shifting endogenous carbohydrate, fat and protein metabolism. In addition, cortisol suppresses the endogenous inflammatory response, protecting the acutely ill patient against over-response of this system. Furthermore, cortisol improves the haemodynamic status of the stressed individual by inducing fluid retention and by its sensitizing effect on the vasopressor response to catecholamines.

Prolactin, presumed to be an immune-enhancing hormone [27], is a well-known stress hormone [28], and the elevated serum concentrations following acute stress are thought to contribute to the activated state of the immune system early in the disease process.

While the somatotrophic, adrenocortical and lactotrophic axes are clearly activated in the acute phase following injury or disease, such activation within the thyroid and gonadal axes is much more short lived. The thyroid axis responds to acute stress with a rapid drop in tri-iodothyronine (T_3) levels and an increase in reverse T_3, partially related to an alternative peripheral conversion of thyroxine (T_4) [29]. Thyrotrophin (TSH) concentrations are only transiently elevated [30] and then normalize. This normalization is considered inappropriate in the face of the low T_4 and T_3 concentrations, suggesting altered central feedback settings [31]. As thyroid hormones are implicated in the regulation of energy expenditure and protein synthesis, their low activity in acute illness could be seen as a beneficial adaptation at times when exogenous provision of substrates is reduced. Finally, despite elevated luteinizing hormone (LH) concentrations [32], Leydig cells are suppressed soon after injury or disease, resulting in low testosterone concentrations.

Thus, while the pituitary is actively secreting in the acute phase following illness, target organs become resistant, resulting in low concentrations of their peripheral effector molecules. These endocrine and metabolic responses to acute stress are probably evolutionary adaptions and are likely to be beneficial as they reduce energy and substrate consumption, drive substrates to vital tissues, postpone anabolism and modulate the immune response in order to improve survival.

Neuroendocrine changes in prolonged critical illness

When the disease process becomes prolonged, the normal defence mechanisms of the human body become insufficient and the continuing hypercatabolism leads to a profound decrease in LBM, which is thought to be detrimental. The pathophysiology underlying this catabolic response in prolonged critical illness is not clear. Severe illness and tissue damage is invariably accompanied by an inflammatory response characterized by elevated levels of pro-inflammatory cytokines – tumour necrosis factor-α (TNF-α), interleukin-1 (IL-1) and IL-6 – and counter-regulatory hormones – catecholamines, glucocorticoids, glucagon – [33] which have a profound influence on body metabolism. However, although circulating levels of these hormones are high in response to acute stress, with prolongation of the disease, serum concentrations of most of these mediators usually normalize [34] and thus are unlikely to contribute to the wasting syndrome of prolonged critical illness.

In view of their role in intermediate metabolism and the immune system, anterior pituitary hormones may have a role in the wasting syndrome associated with prolonged critical illness.

The somatotrophic axis

In contrast to the first few days following illness, a time when release of GH from somatotrophs is increased while the concentration of IGF-I is low, pulsatile release of GH is suppressed in the chronic phase (Fig. 1). Concomitantly, the non-pulsatile fraction of GH release remains somewhat elevated [35]. Together, these changes explain why serum concentrations of GH measured in a single sample may be either slightly elevated, normal or low, and underline the importance of frequent and prolonged blood sampling when studying the dynamics of hormone release from the anterior pituitary.

The finding of a strong, positive correlation between circulating IGF-I, IGFBP-3 and acid-labile subunit (ALS) on the one hand, and the pulsatile fraction of GH release on the other,

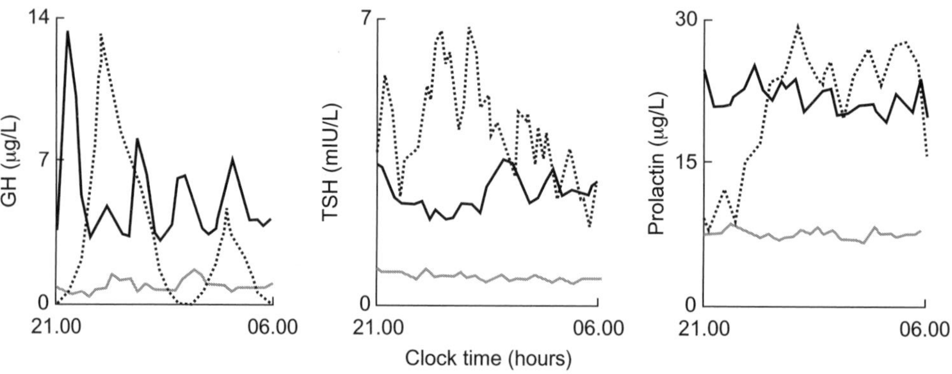

Figure 1. Nocturnal serum concentration profiles of GH, thyrotrophin (TSH) and prolactin, illustrating the differences between the initial phase (black line) and the chronic phase (grey line) of critical illness within an intensive-care setting. The dotted lines illustrate normal patterns. Adapted from [15] with permission. Copyright 1998, The Endocrine Society.

indicates that the loss of pulsatile GH release in the chronic phase of critical illness probably contributes to the low IGF-I, IGFBP-3 and ALS concentrations in this condition [36]. This conflicts with the previously presumed GH resistance, as an inverse relationship would then be expected. Moreover, a clear increase in IGF-I and GH-dependent binding protein concentrations after infusion of GH secretagogue (GHS) [35], and the presence of elevated GH-binding protein concentrations [37] indicate at least some recovery of GH responsiveness during prolonged severe illness.

The mechanism underlying this relative hyposomatotrophism is likely to be located in the hypothalamus. Indeed, the impaired GH secretion reacts robustly to the injection of GHS, thus excluding a pituitary deficiency of GH as the mechanism underlying the relative hyposomatotrophism [35, 38]. The GH release observed following the injection of GH-releasing hormone (GHRH) is less pronounced than following GHS injection. This suggests that, if reduced hypothalamic drive is responsible for the hyposomatotrophism, a deficiency of GHS is more plausible than GHRH deficiency. Reduced somatostatin tone could also explain the profound response to GHS but cannot be reconciled with the spontaneous dynamics of low-amplitude GH bursts. This (relative) hyposomatotrophism associated with prolonged critical illness is not trivial, as it has been shown to contribute to the wasting syndrome [36]. Considering GHS deficiency as a mechanism involved in the relative hyposomatotrophism during prolonged critical illness and the recovery of peripheral GH sensitivity in this phase of illness, administration of GHS may have potential in the management of feeding-resistant hypercatabolism. Another important aspect of this treatment would be its safety. Indeed, endogenous negative feedback mechanisms appear intact in the prolonged critically ill patient, which prevents overstimulation. Rather, a more individualized response to treatment is allowed, which is adjusted to the requirements of the disease process [15]. GHS infusion results in a reactivation of pulsatile GH secretion and increases IGF-I concentrations to a level above which further increases in GH secretion have little or no additional effects on IGF-I (Fig. 2). In contrast, administration of peripherally active hormones at an inappropriate dose (too high) may expose these very sick patients to toxic side-effects.

The thyrotrophic axis

As for the somatotrophic axis, circulating levels of TSH measured in a single sample are often within the low normal range, but the pulsatile fraction of TSH release is dramatically reduced during prolonged illness [15] (Fig. 1). In addition, the serum concentrations of T_4 and, particularly T_3, are low and correlate positively with the reduced pulsatile TSH release [39]. The low T_4 and T_3 levels in the face of normal or reduced TSH release suggests an altered feedback inhibition set point, impaired TSH synthesis, inadequate TSH stimulation by TSH-releasing hormone (TRH) or elevated somatostatin tone. In critically ill patients, TRH infusion increases TSH secretion and, concomitantly, peripheral thyroid hormone levels [15]. As for the somatotrophic axis, these data are consistent with a predominantly central origin of the suppressed thyroid axis, suggesting reduced TRH activity in the chronic phase of critical illness. The indirect evidence provided by dynamic clinical studies was supported by the work of Fliers *et al.* [40], confirming reduced TRH mRNA levels in the hypothalamus of patients who died after chronic critical illness compared with those who died after a road accident or an acute illness. A role for reduced GHS action in the pathophysiology of the suppressed thyroid axis has also been suggested. Indeed, pulsatile TSH release was only increased with TRH infusions when GHSs were infused concomitantly [15]. These findings were largely confirmed in a rabbit model of critical illness. In the acute phase of illness, TRH injection induced a hyper-responsive release of TSH that waned in the chronic phase [16]. We hypothesized that GHS deficiency accounts for this finding, as the full effect of TRH apparently requires sufficient endogenous GHS availability [41].

Low T_3 syndrome results not only from alterations in the pituitary, but also changes in peripheral

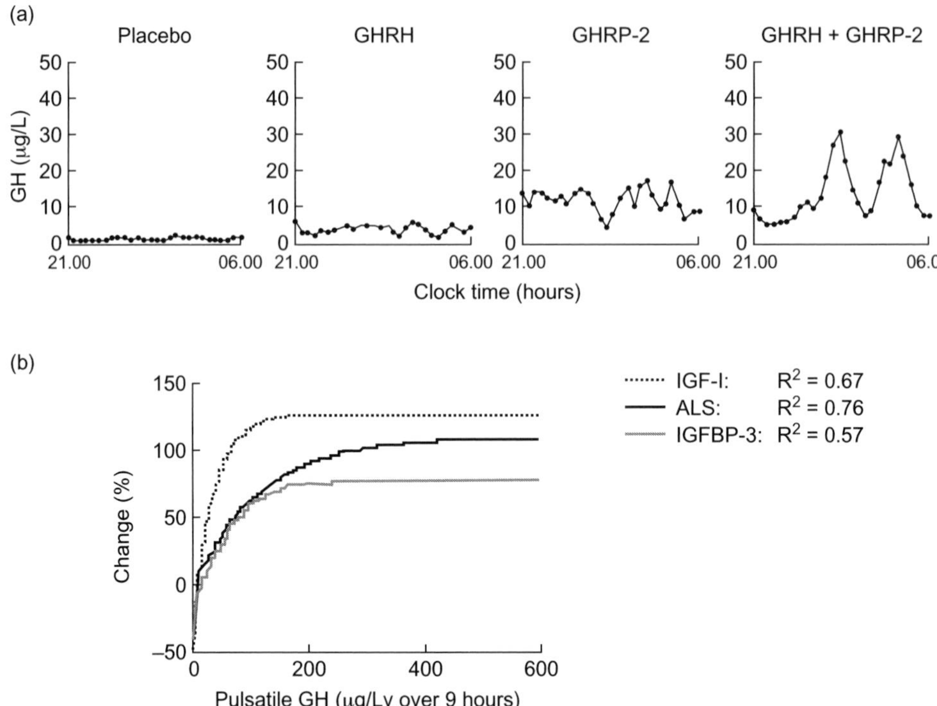

Figure 2. *(a) Nocturnal serum profiles of GH in the prolonged phase of critical illness, illustrating the effects of continuous infusion of placebo, GH-releasing hormone (GHRH; 1 μg/kg/hour), GH-releasing peptide-2 (GHRP-2; 1 μg/kg/hour), or GHRH plus GHRP-2 (1+1 μg/kg/hour). (b) Exponential regression lines have been reported between pulsatile GH secretion and the changes in circulating IGF-I, acid-labile subunit (ALS) and IGF-binding protein-3 (IGFBP-3) obtained with a 45-hour infusion of placebo, GHRP-2 or GHRH plus GHRP-2. They indicate that the parameters of GH responsiveness increase in proportion to GH secretion up to a certain point, beyond which further increase of GH secretion has apparently little or no additional effect. It is noteworthy that the latter point corresponds to a pulsatile GH secretion of approximately 200 μg/L of distribution volume (Lv) over 9 hours, or less, a value that can usually be evoked by the infusion of GHRP-2 alone. In the chronic, non-thriving, phase of critical illness, patients are clearly sensitive to GH, in contrast to the acute phase of illness, which is thought to be primarily a condition of GH resistance. Adapted from [15] with permission. Copyright 1998, The Endocrine Society.*

metabolism. Our group previously showed that the reduced T_3 levels in patients with prolonged critical illness are in part due to reduced type 1 deiodinase activity, the enzyme responsible for the peripheral conversion of T_4 to active T_3 [42]. Interestingly, the addition of GH-releasing peptide-2 (GHRP-2) to TRH infusion, not only stimulated pulsatile TSH release and circulating T_4 and T_3, but also prevented the rise in reverse T_3. This suggests an effect of GHRP-2 on deiodinase activity, either directly, or indirectly through its effect on GH and IGF-I. In our animal model, combined GHRP and TRH infusion augmented the catalytic activity of hepatic type 1 deiodinase activity and depressed the activity of the main peripheral hormone inactivator enzyme, type 3 deiodinase [43]. The low T_3 syndrome in these patients is relevant, as it has been related to hypercatabolism [36].

The gonadal and prolactin axes

Hypogonadotrophism occurs with prolonged critical illness [44]. Indeed, in men with prolonged critical illness, mean LH concentrations and pulsatile LH release have been shown to be suppressed in the face of extremely low serum testosterone concentrations. The profound hypoandrogenism appears to be the result of a combined central and peripheral defect within the male gonadal axis [45, 46]. Similar changes have been reported for the prolactin axis. Although prolactin levels acutely increase in response to stress, the pulsatile fraction of prolactin release becomes suppressed with prolongation of the disease process [16, 39], and it has been suggested that this may contribute to the immune suppression associated with prolonged critical illness.

We conclude that the anterior pituitary reacts biphasically to severe stress. In contrast to the acute phase of illness, prolonged critical illness is associated with a uniform suppression of the pituitary hormone axes. This contributes to the low serum concentrations of the respective target organ hormones. Evidence now points to a predominantly hypothalamic origin of these alterations.

Interventions to attenuate the catabolic syndrome of prolonged critical illness

As hypercatabolism has severe consequences for the critically ill patient, the quest for strategies to efficiently reverse loss of LBM has been ongoing for some time.

Parenteral nutrition has been advocated as an effective intervention to halt protein loss and muscle wasting. Older studies showed a beneficial effect of both glucose and amino acid infusions on postoperative protein sparing [47], leading to the provision of parenteral nutrition in the postoperative setting. Critically ill patients, however, are frequently underfed [48] and just increasing calorie intake or protein supply is now known to be insufficient to prevent or reverse muscle wasting in hypercatabolic patients. In fact, this strategy merely results in fat accretion [49] and enhanced, instead of reduced, nitrogen loss. In addition, a recent meta-analysis concluded that parenteral nutrition is not entirely harmless and may be associated with a higher incidence of complications, particularly in critically ill patients [50]. New nutritional formulations have therefore been studied. A high carbohydrate enteral feeding regimen has been shown to decrease muscle protein breakdown in severely burned children, probably by stimulating insulin release [51]. However, a glucose-rich parenteral feeding regimen in critically ill patients has been shown to induce hyperglycaemia, to increase carbon dioxide production and to stimulate *de novo* lipogenesis. In addition, it was unable to suppress gluconeogenesis and proteolysis [52]. The development of hyperglycaemia is particularly problematic in view of the important effects of stress hyperglycaemia on morbidity and mortality in critically ill patients [17]. Several small studies have shown that parenteral and enteral feeding formulations enriched with specific supplements, such as glutamine [53] and arginine [54], may be beneficial for certain patients, although a recent meta-analysis also suggested potentially harmful effects [55]. Therefore, we should await confirmation from large clinical trials before these new nutritional formulations enter widespread clinical use.

As a consequence of the failures encountered during the last decade with nutritional interventions, pharmacological enhancement of caloric support has been evaluated. The non-selective β-blocker, propanolol, significantly preserved LBM in severely burned children, mainly through an efficient endogenous use of amino acids that increased protein synthesis [56].

Insulin has clear anabolic actions in patients with burn injuries, and is able to improve net protein balance by increasing protein synthesis [57] or reducing protein degradation [58]. Both are thought to be related to a more efficient incorporation of amino acids into muscle. While the effect of insulin on proteolysis has been shown consistently, only extreme hyperinsulinaemia has been demonstrated to stimulate protein synthesis [59]. In liver biopsies of patients with prolonged critical illness, insulin treatment to maintain normoglycaemia did not affect expression of phosphoenolpyruvate carboxykinase, the key enzyme controlling gluconeogenesis [60]. In addition, in order for insulin to induce anabolism, it is of paramount importance that sufficient exogenous amino acids are available as, without these, insulin-stimulated protein synthesis uses amino acids derived from accelerated endogenous proteolysis [61]. Whether the anabolic effect of insulin is direct or mediated via stimulated IGF-I synthesis [62] remains to be determined.

As with insulin, infusion of IGF-I has been shown to inhibit protein breakdown and stimulate protein synthesis in the presence of sufficient amino acids [63] and improve postoperative catabolism [64]. Prolonged administration, however, resulted in reduced efficacy.

As several anterior pituitary-dependent hormones are extensively involved in the regulation of intermediate metabolism, and in view of the relative hypopituitarism associated with prolonged critical illness, it is rational to search for a role of these hormones in the treatment of catabolism. Thyroid hormones are important for protein synthesis, lipolysis, fuel utilization by muscle, and GH secretion and responsiveness. At present it is unclear whether treatment with thyroid hormones is beneficial or harmful for the critically ill patient [65]. Administration of T_3 during starvation has been shown to increase muscle wasting [66], and increased mortality was seen in animal models of sepsis [67].

Testosterone administration to men with severe burn injuries was accompanied by a significant reduction in protein catabolism, mainly through efficient intracellular amino acid handling and inhibition of muscle breakdown [68]; however, there was no effect on protein synthesis in these patients. In a small study, the synthetic androgen, oxandrolone, was shown to reduce weight loss, improve functional status and increase wound healing, and seemed to be as effective as GH therapy in the acute and recovery phase of illness [69]. Caution is warranted, however as these studies were not well controlled and did not report the potential complications of this intervention. Moreover, testosterone supplementation during illness may be associated with negative effects on the immune system [70].

The beneficial metabolic effects of recombinant human GH treatment in GH-deficient patients have been known for many years. In these patients, treatment with GH increases LBM and stimulates bone remodelling [7]. The direct effects of GH are diverse. It induces insulin insensitivity [71] and stimulates lipolysis [72], inhibits the peripheral conversion of cortisone to cortisol [73], regulates the peripheral conversion of thyroid hormones [74] and interferes with drug metabolism [75]. GH has also been shown to improve heart function in patients with heart failure [76] although it remains to be seen whether this is also applicable to patients in intensive care [77]. In addition, GH is an immune-modulating agent and enhances innate immunity [78], properties that might be beneficial in the immune-deficient critically ill patient [79].

Several small and often poorly controlled studies suggest beneficial effects of GH in catabolic patients, but very few of them have reported the potential complications. Most of these studies used relatively large doses of GH, as GH has been shown to have diminished metabolic efficacy in patients with sepsis due to GH resistance [80]. In elective colorectal surgery, a 9-day perioperative GH injection (4 and 8 U/day [1.3 and 2.6 mg/day]) improved nitrogen balance [81] and LBM even when patients had a low calorie intake [82]; however, the treatment was associated with an average retention of 4 litres of fluid. In postoperative cancer patients, whole-body net protein balance was improved following 5 days of GH treatment, whereas no effect was seen on muscle protein balance unless insulin was added [9]. In patients with sepsis, 7 days of GH treatment improved net protein synthesis [10]. Five days of GH treatment has been shown to stimulate muscle protein synthesis and to increase glutamine stores in the muscle of patients with prolonged critical illness [11]. In children with burns, GH treatment was associated with faster healing of the donor site [12] and improved protein synthesis [13]. Furthermore, there was a reduced albumin requirement, an anti-inflammatory response (reductions in C-reactive protein, TNF-α and IL-6) and only a transient increase in free fatty acids [83]. Mjaaland *et al.* [84] found that GH altered substrate utilization with increased fat oxidation, fatty acids and energy expenditure and decreased carbohydrate oxidation.

In 1999, Takala *et al.* [14] published the first prospective, double-blind, randomized, controlled trial on GH administration in a large population of long-stay intensive care patients that was of sufficient power to analyse morbidity and mortality. Prolonged critically ill and mechanically ventilated patients without sepsis were randomized to receive pharmacological doses of GH or placebo for a maximum of 3 weeks. Surprisingly, there was an excess of intensive care mortality in the GH-treated group, which persisted when analyzing in-hospital mortality. The main causes of death in patients receiving GH treatment were sepsis and multiple organ failure. Furthermore, surviving patients had longer periods of mechanical ventilation and hospitalization and higher health-care costs despite increased levels of IGF-I and a positive nitrogen balance. Hyperglycaemia was present more frequently in the GH-treated patients compared with those receiving placebo. The aetiology of the dramatic effect of GH treatment in the critically ill was not clear. It has been suggested that GH treatment may have limited glutamine release from skeletal muscle, thus reducing the supply of this amino acid for immune and gut cells. Increased intestinal permeability and impaired immune function could explain the high incidence of infections in patients treated with high-dose GH; however, this hypothesis has been questioned by findings in rats with sepsis treated with GH [85]. Furthermore, Jackson *et al.* [86] suggested that GH and IGF-I had no influence on glutamine. Additionally, as glutamine is involved in the preservation of reserves of the anti-oxidant glutathione in the liver [87], the finding that early GH treatment in rats had an anti-oxidant effect, with reduced lipid peroxidation in lung and liver, and increased tissue levels of glutathione [88], is not in favour of such a hypothesis.

In 1996, Liao *et al.* [89] reported that GH pre-treatment (by continuous infusion) followed by endotoxin injection in rats resulted in a worse outcome, with profound shock, hypertriglyceridaemia and liver and kidney failure. This effect was independent of IGF-I and presumed to be related to the priming of lymphocytes with increased release of interferon-γ. In agreement with this are reports of a worsening of acidosis associated with reduced portal vein flow and higher TNF-α levels in a septic animal model treated with GH [90].

In view of recent data on the neuroendocrine pathophysiology of prolonged critical illness, the findings of the study by Takala *et al.* [14] can be interpreted from another perspective. It is now clear that GH secretion is suppressed and GH responsiveness recovers in the prolonged phase of critical illness. Hence, the high dose of GH used in the multicentre trial was probably much too high, exposing these patients to the potentially deleterious direct effects of GH. Furthermore, the finding that multiple endocrine axes are inactivated in critical illness suggests that endocrine intervention should target the somatotrophic, thyrotrophic and gonadal axes.

Our studies have shown that infusion of GHRP-2, together with TRH, for 5 days reactivated both the somatotrophic and thyrotrophic axes in patients with prolonged critical illness. Basal and pulsatile GH release and circulating IGF-I, IGFBP-3, ALS and IGFBP-5 were all stimulated (Fig. 3). Concomitantly, secretion of TSH and T_4 and T_3 release were amplified without affecting levels of reverse T_3 [36]. Feedback inhibition loops remained active, thus preventing overstimulation. IGF-I levels increased to normal during the first 48 hours of treatment, and then stabilized. The clear reactivation of the GH and thyroid hormone axes that resulted from the administration of these hypothalamic-releasing factors was associated after 5 days with a reduction in hypercatabolism and the stimulation of anabolism. The rate of proteolysis was significantly reduced. This was predominantly related to the correction of the tertiary hypothyroidism. Osteocalcin, a surrogate marker for anabolism, increased with treatment due to improved maturation of osteoblasts, and this

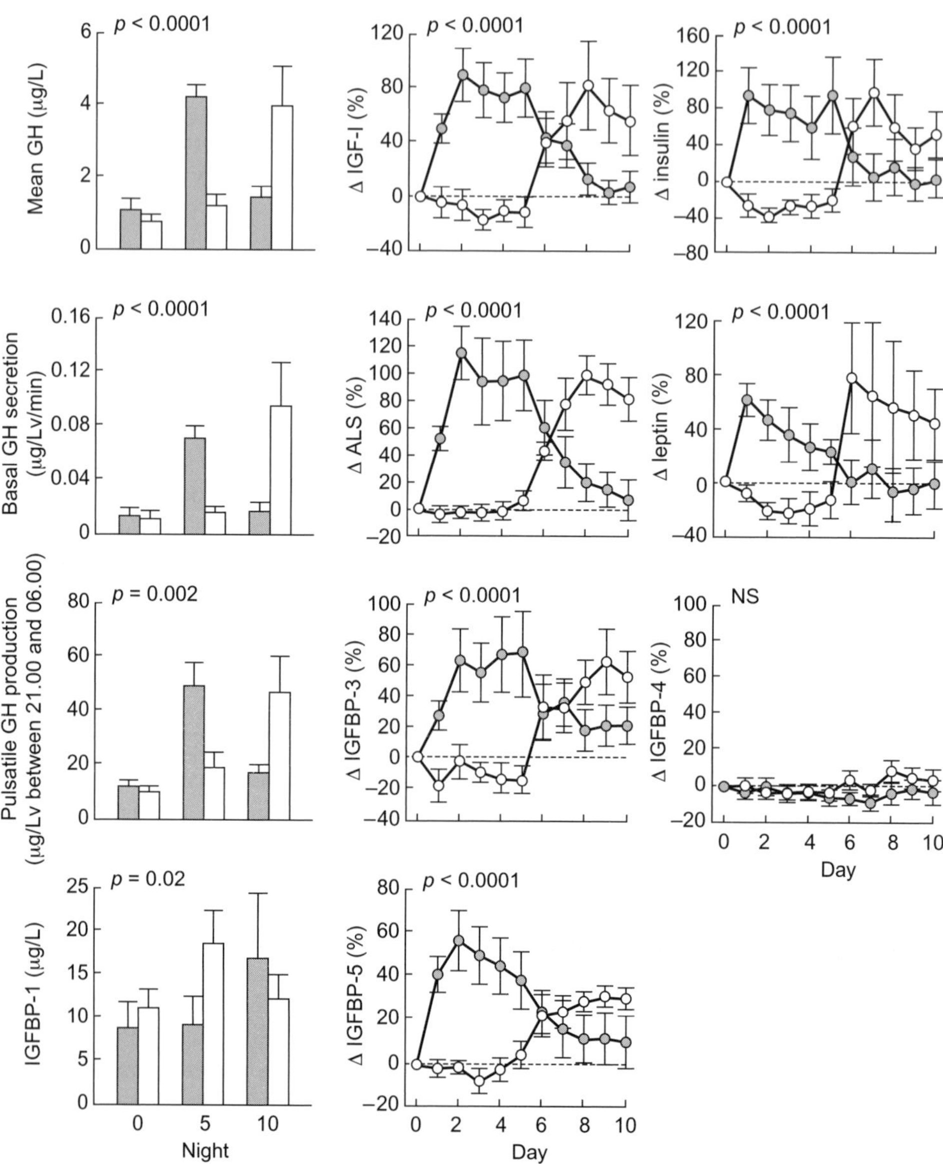

Figure 3. *Responses (mean ± SEM) of deconvolution-derived GH secretion and of serum levels of IGF-binding protein-1 (IGFBP-1) (left-hand column), IGF-I, acid-labile subunit (ALS), IGFBP-3, IGFBP-5 (centre column), and insulin, leptin and IGFBP-4 (right-hand column) to randomized treatment with either 5 days of GH-releasing peptide-2 (GHRP-2) plus thyrotrophin-releasing hormone (TRH) infusion (1+1 μg/kg/hour) followed by 5 days of placebo (grey symbols) or 5 days of placebo followed by 5 days of GHRP-2 plus TRH infusion (1+1 μg/kg/hour) (open symbols). p values indicate the level of significance of the difference in time course between the two groups. 'Night' indicates that data are taken from a nocturnal time series of serum GH concentrations obtained on nights 0, 5 and 10. 'Day' indicates that data are from single samples, taken at 6 am, on 10 consecutive days. LV, litre of distribution volume; NS, not significant. Reproduced from [36] with permission. Copyright 1999, The Endocrine Society.*

anabolic effect could be largely explained by the rise of IGF-I and GH-dependent IGFBPs. Recently, we found that co-activation of the male gonadal axis using gonadotrophin-releasing hormone, in addition to the infusion of GHRP-2 and TRH – that is, restoration of the three pituitary axes – in critically ill patients was associated with an even more pronounced anabolic effect [44].

Conclusions

Patients with critical illness face a dramatic loss of LBM when their disease process becomes prolonged. Routine intensive care interventions, such as feeding, are unable to revert this catabolic state, and delay recuperation of these patients. Changes in anterior pituitary function are invariably associated with critical illness. The acute phase is characterized by an actively secreting pituitary, whereas the peripheral tissues are resistant to the effects of anterior pituitary hormones, resulting in low concentrations of their effector molecules. It was originally assumed that this condition persisted with ongoing disease. As a result, interventions with high doses of single hormone treatment, such as GH, were deemed to be necessary in order to induce anabolism. The results of these interventions were disappointing and some of them caused severe harm.

With prolonged illness, we now know that there is a cessation in the secretion of hormones by the anterior pituitary, which causes reduced concentrations of peripheral effector hormones and contributes to the general wasting syndrome in these patients. Importantly, infusion of hypothalamic-releasing substances can reactivate the anterior pituitary, leading to an increase of peripheral effector hormones, such as IGF-I and T_3. These substances therefore hold promise for the future, as short-term reactivation of the somatotrophic, thyrotrophic and gonadal axes has been shown to be associated with improved anabolism and attenuated catabolism. Large-scale clinical studies examining the effect of hypothalamic secretagogues on the outcome of critical illness should now be initiated.

References

1. Cuthbertson D. Observations on the disturbance of metabolism produced by injury to the limbs. Q J Med 1932;25:233–46
2. Lipsett PA, Swoboda SM, Dickerson J, Ylitalo M, Gordon T, Breslow M, Campbell K, Dorman T, Pronovost P, Rosenfeld B. Survival and functional outcome after prolonged intensive care unit stay. Ann Surg 2000;231:262–8
3. Hart DW, Wolf SE, Herndon DN, Chinkes DL, Lal SO, Obeng MK, Beauford RB, Mlcak R. Energy expenditure and caloric balance after burn: increased feeding leads to fat rather than lean mass accretion. Ann Surg 2002;235:152–61
4. Gamrin L, Andersson K, Hultman E, Nilsson E, Essen P, Wernerman J. Longitudinal changes of biochemical parameters in muscle during critical illness. Metabolism 1997;46:756–62
5. Burrin DG, Britton RA, Ferrell CL. Visceral organ size and hepatocyte metabolic activity in fed and fasted rats. J Nutr 1988;118:1547–52
6. Abraham E. Host defense abnormalities after hemorrhage, trauma, and burns. Crit Care Med 1989;17:934–9
7. Binnerts A, Swart GR, Wilson JH, Hoogerbrugge N, Pols HA, Birkenhager JC, Lamberts SW. The effect of growth hormone administration in growth hormone deficient adults on bone, protein, carbohydrate and lipid homeostasis, as well as on body composition. Clin Endocrinol (Oxf) 1992;37:79–87
8. Ross RJ, Rodriguez-Arnao J, Bentham J, Coakley JH. The role of insulin, growth hormone and IGF-I as anabolic agents in the critically ill. Intensive Care Med 1993;19 (Suppl 2):S54–7
9. Berman RS, Harrison LE, Pearlstone DB, Burt M, Brennan MF. Growth hormone, alone and in combination with insulin, increases whole body and skeletal muscle protein kinetics in cancer patients after surgery. Ann Surg 1999;229:1–10
10. Koea JB, Breier BH, Douglas RG, Gluckman PD, Shaw JH. Anabolic and cardiovascular effects of recombinant human growth hormone in surgical patients with sepsis. Br J Surg 1996;83:196–202
11. Gamrin L, Essen P, Hultman E, McNurlan MA, Garlick PJ, Wernerman J. Protein-sparing effect in skeletal muscle of growth hormone treatment in critically ill patients. Ann Surg 2000;231:577–86
12. Herndon DN, Barrow RE, Kunkel KR, Broemeling L, Rutan RL. Effects of recombinant human growth hormone on donor-site healing in severely burned children. Ann Surg 1990;212:424–31

13. Gore DC, Honeycutt D, Jahoor F, Wolfe RR, Herndon DN. Effect of exogenous growth hormone on whole-body and isolated-limb protein kinetics in burned patients. Arch Surg 1991;126:38–43

14. Takala J, Ruokonen E, Webster NR, Nielsen MS, Zandstra DF, Vundelinckx G, Hinds CJ. Increased mortality associated with growth hormone treatment in critically ill adults. N Engl J Med 1999;341:785–92

15. Van den Berghe G, de Zegher F, Bouillon R. Acute and prolonged critical illness as different neuroendocrine paradigms. J Clin Endocrinol Metab 1998;83:1827–34

16. Weekers F, Van Herck E, Coopmans W, Michalaki M, Bowers CY, Veldhuis JD, Van den Berghe G. A novel *in vivo* rabbit model of hypercatabolic critical illness reveals a biphasic neuroendocrine stress response. Endocrinology 2002;143:764–74

17. Van den Berghe G, Wouters P, Weekers F, Verwaest C, Bruyninckx F, Schetz M, Vlasselaers D, Ferdinande P, Lauwers P, Bouillon R. Intensive insulin therapy in the critically ill patients. N Engl J Med 2001;345:1359–67

18. Vance ML. Hypopituitarism. N Engl J Med 1994;330:1651–62

19. Ross R, Miell J, Freeman E, Jones J, Matthews D, Preece M, Buchanan C. Critically ill patients have high basal growth hormone levels with attenuated oscillatory activity associated with low levels of insulin-like growth factor-I. Clin Endocrinol (Oxf) 1991;35:47–54

20. Hermansson M, Wickelgren RB, Hammarqvist F, Bjarnason R, Wennstrom I, Wernerman J, Carlsson B, Carlsson LM. Measurement of human growth hormone receptor messenger ribonucleic acid by a quantitative polymerase chain reaction-based assay: demonstration of reduced expression after elective surgery. J Clin Endocrinol Metab 1997;82:421–8

21. Defalque D, Brandt N, Ketelslegers JM, Thissen JP. GH insensitivity induced by endotoxin injection is associated with decreased liver GH receptors. Am J Physiol 1999;276:E565–72

22. Johnson TS, O'Leary M, Justice SK, Maamra M, Zarkesh-Esfahani SH, Furlanetto R, Preedy VR, Hinds CJ, El Nahas AM, Ross RJ. Differential expression of suppressors of cytokine signalling genes in response to nutrition and growth hormone in the septic rat. J Endocrinol 2001;169:409–15

23. Miell JP, Taylor AM, Jones J, Buchanan CR, Rennie J, Sherwood R, Leicester R, Ross RJ. Administration of human recombinant insulin-like growth factor-I to patients following major gastrointestinal surgery. Clin Endocrinol (Oxf) 1992;37:542–51

24. Cwyfan Hughes SC, Cotterill AM, Molloy AR, Cassell TB, Braude N, Hinds CJ, Wass JA, Holly JM. The induction of specific proteases for insulin-like growth factor-binding proteins following major heart surgery. J Endocrinol 1992;135:135–45

25. Van den Berghe G, de Zegher F, Bouillon R. The somatotrophic axis in critical illness: effects of growth hormone secretagogues. Growth Horm IGF Res 1998;8 (Suppl B):153–5

26. Rivier C, Vale W. Modulation of stress-induced ACTH release by corticotropin-releasing factor, catecholamines and vasopressin. Nature 1983;305:325–7

27. Bernton EW, Meltzer MS, Holaday JW. Suppression of macrophage activation and T-lymphocyte function in hypoprolactinemic mice. Science 1988;239:401–4

28. Noel GL, Suh HK, Stone JG, Frantz AG. Human prolactin and growth hormone release during surgery and other conditions of stress. J Clin Endocrinol Metab 1972;35:840–51

29. Chopra IJ, Huang TS, Beredo A, Solomon DH, Chua Teco GN, Mead JF. Evidence for an inhibitor of extrathyroidal conversion of thyroxine to 3,5,3'-triiodothyronine in sera of patients with nonthyroidal illnesses. J Clin Endocrinol Metab 1985;60:666–72

30. Michalaki M, Vagenakis AG, Makri M, Kalfarentzos F, Kyriazopoulou V. Dissociation of the early decline in serum T_3 concentration and serum IL-6 rise and TNFα in nonthyroidal illness syndrome induced by abdominal surgery. J Clin Endocrinol Metab 2001;86:4198–205

31. Bacci V, Schussler GC, Kaplan TB. The relationship between serum triiodothyronine and thyrotropin during systemic illness. J Clin Endocrinol Metab 1982; 54:1229–35

32. Wang C, Chan V, Yeung RT. Effect of surgical stress on pituitary-testicular function. Clin Endocrinol (Oxf) 1978;9:255–66

33. Bessey PQ, Watters JM, Aoki TT, Wilmore DW. Combined hormonal infusion simulates the metabolic response to injury. Ann Surg 1984;200:264–81

34. Damas P, Reuter A, Gysen P, Demonty J, Lamy M, Franchimont P. Tumor necrosis factor and interleukin-1 serum levels during severe sepsis in humans. Crit Care Med 1989;17:975–8

35. Van den Berghe G, de Zegher F, Veldhuis JD, Wouters P, Awouters M, Verbruggen W, Schetz M, Verwaest C, Lauwers P, Bouillon R, Bowers CY. The somatotropic axis in critical illness: effect of continuous growth hormone (GH)-releasing hormone and GH-releasing peptide-2 infusion. J Clin Endocrinol Metab 1997;82:590–9

36. Van den Berghe G, Wouters P, Weekers F, Mohan S, Baxter RC, Veldhuis JD, Bowers CY, Bouillon R. Reactivation of pituitary hormone release and metabolic improvement by infusion of growth hormone-releasing peptide and thyrotropin-releasing hormone in patients with protracted critical illness. J Clin Endocrinol Metab 1999;84:1311–23

37. Van den Berghe G, Baxter RC, Weekers F, Wouters P, Bowers CY, Veldhuis JD. A paradoxical gender dissociation within the growth hormone/insulin-like growth factor I axis during protracted critical illness. J Clin Endocrinol Metab 2000;85:183–92

38. Van den Berghe G, de Zegher F, Bowers CY, Wouters P, Muller P, Soetens F, Vlasselaers D, Schetz M, Verwaest C, Lauwers P, Bouillon R. Pituitary responsiveness to GH-releasing hormone, GH-releasing peptide-2 and thyrotrophin-releasing hormone in critical illness. Clin Endocrinol (Oxf) 1996;45:341–51

39. Van den Berghe G, de Zegher F, Veldhuis JD, Wouters P, Gouwy S, Stockman W, Weekers F, Schetz M, Lauwers P, Bouillon R, Bowers CY. Thyrotrophin and prolactin release in prolonged critical illness: dynamics of spontaneous secretion and effects of growth hormone-secretagogues. Clin Endocrinol (Oxf) 1997;47:599–612

40. Fliers E, Wiersinga WM, Swaab DF. Physiological and pathophysiological aspects of thyrotropin-releasing hormone gene expression in the human hypothalamus. Thyroid 1998;8:921–8

41. Van den Berghe G, Baxter RC, Weekers F, Wouters P, Bowers CY, Iranmanesh A, Veldhuis JD, Bouillon R. The combined administration of GH-releasing peptide-2 (GHRP-2), TRH and GnRH to men with prolonged critical illness evokes superior endocrine and metabolic effects compared to treatment with GHRP-2 alone. Clin Endocrinol (Oxf) 2002;56:655–69

42. Peeters RP, Wouters PJ, Kaptein E, van Toor H, Visser TJ, Van den Berghe G. Reduced activation and increased inactivation of thyroid hormone in tissues of critically ill patients. J Clin Endocrinol Metab 2003; 88:3202–11

43. Weekers F, Michalaki M, Coopmans W, Van Herck E, Veldhuis JD, Darras VM, Van den Berghe G. Endocrine and metabolic effects of growth hormone (GH) compared with GH-releasing peptide, thyrotropin-releasing hormone and insulin infusion in a rabbit model of prolonged critical illness. Endocrinology 2004;145:205–13

44. Woolf PD, Hamill RW, McDonald JV, Lee LA, Kelly M. Transient hypogonadotropic hypogonadism caused by critical illness. J Clin Endocrinol Metab 1985;60:444–50

45. Van den Berghe G, Weekers F, Baxter RC, Wouters P, Iranmanesh A, Bouillon R, Veldhuis JD. Five-day pulsatile gonadotropin-releasing hormone administration unveils combined hypothalamic–pituitary–gonadal defects underlying profound hypoandrogenism in men with prolonged critical illness. J Clin Endocrinol Metab 2001;86:3217–26

46. Van den Berghe G, de Zegher F, Lauwers P, Veldhuis JD. Luteinizing hormone secretion and hypoandrogenaemia in critically ill men: effect of dopamine. Clin Endocrinol (Oxf) 1994;41:563–9

47. Craig RP, Tweedle D, Davidson HA, Johnston ID. Intravenous glucose, aminoacids, and fat in the postoperative period. a controlled evaluation of each substrate. Lancet 1977;2:8–11

48. De Jonghe B, Appere-De-Vechi C, Fournier M, Tran B, Merrer J, Melchior JC, Outin H. A prospective survey of nutritional support practices in intensive care unit patients: what is prescribed? What is delivered? Crit Care Med 2001;29:8–12

49. Streat SJ, Beddoe AH, Hill GL. Aggressive nutritional support does not prevent protein loss despite fat gain in septic intensive care patients. J Trauma 1987;27:262–6

50. Heyland DK, MacDonald S, Keefe L, Drover JW. Total parenteral nutrition in the critically ill patient: a meta-analysis. JAMA 1998;280:2013–9

51. Hart DW, Wolf SE, Zhang XJ, Chinkes DL, Buffalo MC, Matin SI, DebRoy MA, Wolfe RR, Herndon DN. Efficacy of a high-carbohydrate diet in catabolic illness. Crit Care Med 2001;29:1318–24

52. Tappy L, Schwarz JM, Schneiter P, Cayeux C, Revelly JP, Fagerquist CK, Jequier E, Chiolero R. Effects of isoenergetic glucose-based or lipid-based parenteral nutrition on glucose metabolism, *de novo* lipogenesis, and respiratory gas exchanges in critically ill patients. Crit Care Med 1998;26:860–7

53. Houdijk AP, Rijnsburger ER, Jansen J, Wesdorp RI, Weiss JK, McCamish MA, Teerlink T, Meuwissen SG, Haarman HJ, Thijs LG, van Leeuwen PA. Randomised trial of glutamine-enriched enteral nutrition on infectious morbidity in patients with multiple trauma. Lancet 1998;352:772–6

54. Evoy D, Lieberman MD, Fahey TJ 3rd, Daly JM. Immunonutrition: the role of arginine. Nutrition 1998;14:611–7

55. Heyland DK, Novak F, Drover JW, Jain M, Su X, Suchner U. Should immunonutrition become routine in critically ill patients? A systematic review of the evidence. JAMA 2001;286:944–53

56. Herndon DN, Hart DW, Wolf SE, Chinkes DL, Wolfe RR. Reversal of catabolism by beta-blockade after severe burns. N Engl J Med 2001;345:1223–9

57. Ferrando AA, Chinkes DL, Wolf SE, Matin S, Herndon DN, Wolfe RR. A submaximal dose of insulin

promotes net skeletal muscle protein synthesis in patients with severe burns. Ann Surg 1999;229:11–18

58. Zhang XJ, Chinkes DL, Wolf SE, Wolfe RR. Insulin but not growth hormone stimulates protein anabolism in skin wound and muscle. Am J Physiol 1999; 276:E712–20

59. Hillier TA, Fryburg DA, Jahn LA, Barrett EJ. Extreme hyperinsulinemia unmasks insulin's effect to stimulate protein synthesis in the human forearm. Am J Physiol 1998;274:E1067–74

60. Mesotten D, Delhanty PJ, Vanderhoydonc F, Hardman KV, Weekers F, Baxter RC, Van den Berghe G. Regulation of insulin-like growth factor binding protein-1 during protracted critical illness. J Clin Endocrinol Metab 2002;87:5516–23

61. Zhang XJ, Chinkes DL, Irtun O, Wolfe RR. Anabolic action of insulin on skin wound protein is augmented by exogenous amino acids. Am J Physiol Endocrinol Metab 2002;282:E1308–15

62. Denver RJ, Nicoll CS. Pancreatic hormones differentially regulate insulin-like growth factor (IGF)-I and IGF-binding protein production by primary rat hepatocytes. J Endocrinol 1994;142:299–310

63. Russell-Jones DL, Umpleby AM, Hennessy TR, Bowes SB, Shojaee-Moradie F, Hopkins KD, Jackson NC, Kelly JM, Jones RH, Sönksen PH. Use of a leucine clamp to demonstrate that IGF-I actively stimulates protein synthesis in normal humans. Am J Physiol 1994;267:E591–8

64. Clemmons DR, Smith-Banks A, Underwood LE. Reversal of diet-induced catabolism by infusion of recombinant insulin-like growth factor-I in humans. J Clin Endocrinol Metab 1992;75:234–8

65. Stathatos N, Levetan C, Burman KD, Wartofsky L. The controversy of the treatment of critically ill patients with thyroid hormone. Best Pract Res Clin Endocrinol Metab 2001;15:465–78

66. Gardner DF, Kaplan MM, Stanley CA, Utiger RD. Effect of tri-iodothyronine replacement on the metabolic and pituitary responses to starvation. N Engl J Med 1979;300:579–84

67. Chopra IJ, Huang TS, Boado R, Solomon DH, Chua Teco GN. Evidence against benefit from replacement doses of thyroid hormones in nonthyroidal illness (NTI): studies using turpentine oil-injected rat. J Endocrinol Invest 1987;10:559–64

68. Ferrando AA, Sheffield-Moore M, Wolf SE, Herndon DN, Wolfe RR. Testosterone administration in severe burns ameliorates muscle catabolism. Crit Care Med 2001;29:1936–42

69. Demling RH. Comparison of the anabolic effects and complications of human growth hormone and the testosterone analog, oxandrolone, after severe burn injury. Burns 1999;25:215–21

70. Angele MK, Ayala A, Cioffi WG, Bland KI, Chaudry IH. Testosterone: the culprit for producing splenocyte immune depression after trauma hemorrhage. Am J Physiol 1998;274:C1530–6

71. Costa C, Solanes G, Visa J, Bosch F. Transgenic rabbits overexpressing growth hormone develop acromegaly and diabetes mellitus. Faseb J 1998;12:1455–60

72. Keller U, Miles JM. Growth hormone and lipids. Horm Res 1991;36 (Suppl 1):36–40

73. Stewart PM, Toogood AA, Tomlinson JW. Growth hormone, insulin-like growth factor-I and the cortisol-cortisone shuttle. Horm Res 2001;56 (Suppl 1):1–6

74. Møller J, Jørgensen JO, Møller N, Christiansen JS, Weeke J. Effects of growth hormone administration on fuel oxidation and thyroid function in normal man. Metabolism 1992;41:728–31

75. Shapiro BH, Agrawal AK, Pampori NA. Gender differences in drug metabolism regulated by growth hormone. Int J Biochem Cell Biol 1995;27:9–20

76. Cittadini A, Stromer H, Katz SE, Clark R, Moses AC, Morgan JP, Douglas PS. Differential cardiac effects of growth hormone and insulin-like growth factor-1 in the rat. A combined *in vivo* and *in vitro* evaluation. Circulation 1996;93:800–9

77. Barry MC, Mealy K, Sheehan SJ, Burke PE, Cunningham AJ, Leahy A, Bouchier Hayes D. The effects of recombinant human growth hormone on cardiopulmonary function in elective abdominal aortic aneurysm repair. Eur J Vasc Endovasc Surg 1998;16:311–9

78. Saito H, Inoue T, Fukatsu K, Ming-Tsan L, Inaba T, Fukushima R, Muto T. Growth hormone and the immune response to bacterial infection. Horm Res 1996;45:50–4

79. Edwards CK 3rd, Arkins S, Yunger LM, Blum A, Dantzer R, Kelley KW. The macrophage-activating properties of growth hormone. Cell Mol Neurobiol 1992;12:499–510

80. Dahn MS, Lange MP, Jacobs LA. Insulin-like growth factor 1 production is inhibited in human sepsis. Arch Surg 1988;123:1409–14

81. Vara-Thorbeck R, Guerrero JA, Ruiz-Requena ME, Capitan J, Rodriguez M, Rosell J, Mekinassi K, Maldonado M, Martin R. Effects of growth hormone in patients receiving total parenteral nutrition following major gastrointestinal surgery. Hepatogastroenterology 1992;39:270–2

82. Jensen MB, Kissmeyer-Nielsen P, Laurberg S. Perioperative growth hormone treatment increases nitrogen and fluid balance and results in short-term and long-term conservation of lean tissue mass. Am J Clin Nutr 1998;68:840–6

83. Jeschke MG, Barrow RE, Herndon DN. Recombinant human growth hormone treatment in pediatric burn patients and its role during the hepatic acute phase response. Crit Care Med 2000;28:1578–84

84. Mjaaland M, Unneberg K, Larsson J, Nilsson L, Revhaug A. Growth hormone after abdominal surgery attenuated forearm glutamine, alanine, 3-methylhistidine, and total amino acid efflux in patients receiving total parenteral nutrition. Ann Surg 1993; 217:413–22

85. O'Leary MJ, Ferguson CN, Rennie M, Hinds CJ, Coakley JH, Preedy VR. Effect of growth hormone on muscle and liver protein synthesis in septic rats receiving glutamine-enriched parenteral nutrition. Crit Care Med 2002;30:1099–105

86. Jackson NC, Carroll PV, Russell-Jones DL, Sönksen PH, Treacher DF, Umpleby AM. Effects of glutamine supplementation, GH, and IGF-I on glutamine metabolism in critically ill patients. Am J Physiol Endocrinol Metab 2000;278:E226–33

87. Hong RW, Rounds JD, Helton WS, Robinson MK, Wilmore DW. Glutamine preserves liver glutathione after lethal hepatic injury. Ann Surg 1992;215:114–9

88. Youn YK, Suh GJ, Jung SE, Oh SK, Demling R. Recombinant human growth hormone decreases lung and liver tissue lipid peroxidation and increases antioxidant activity after thermal injury in rats. J Burn Care Rehabil 1998;19:542–8

89. Liao W, Rudling M, Angelin B. Growth hormone potentiates the in vivo biological activities of endotoxin in the rat. Eur J Clin Invest 1996;26:254–8

90. Unneberg K, Balteskard L, Mjaaland M, Revhaug A. Growth hormone impaired compensation of hemorrhagic shock after trauma and sepsis in swine. J Trauma 1996;41:775–80

29 Safety of growth hormone replacement therapy in adults

Johan Svensson and Bengt-Åke Bengtsson
Research Centre for Endocrinology and Metabolism, Sahlgrenska University Hospital, Gothenburg, Sweden

Summary

In children, final height is often reached after 5–10 years of growth hormone (GH) treatment. In adults, GH replacement therapy will often be maintained for decades. It is essential, therefore, to establish the long-term safety aspects of the treatment, especially as untreated acromegaly is characterized by GH excess, high serum insulin-like growth factor I concentrations, and increased morbidity and mortality. Several studies, including those based on data from KIMS – Pfizer International Metabolic Database – show that long-term GH replacement in adults has an excellent safety profile. Long-term GH replacement therapy not only appears to be safe, but may even improve cardiovascular morbidity and mortality in GH-deficient adults. There are now also data showing that GH replacement in adults is safe in terms of diabetes mellitus and neoplasms.

Introduction

In the late 1950s, it was shown that growth hormone (GH) treatment increases linear bone growth in GH-deficient children [1]. Until the late 1980s, however, GH was considered to be of little importance in adult life. The introduction of recombinant human GH made it possible to study the effects of GH in adults. During the past 15 years, several studies have shown that GH replacement therapy in adults improves quality of life, bone mass, and cardiovascular risk factors [2–6]. Safety studies have also been performed; however, single centres only have access to relatively small numbers of hypopituitary patients. Therefore, studies based on data from KIMS – Pfizer International Metabolic Database – have been of profound importance in establishing that long-term GH replacement therapy in adults has an excellent safety profile in terms of type 2 diabetes mellitus, neoplasms and cardiovascular morbidity and mortality.

Fluid retention

In a recent study based on data from KIMS in Sweden, 237 patients (116 men) were included [7]. During a 3-year period of GH replacement therapy, fluid retention (oedema) was the most common side-effect, and was reported in 42 (18%) of the patients. Women received a higher mean dose of GH than men (0.41 versus 0.32 mg/day at study end), and women also experienced fluid retention more frequently than men (27% of women and 8% of men had oedema as a side-effect). In conclusion, a small proportion of hypopituitary patients have clinically detectable fluid retention during low-dose, individualized GH replacement therapy.

Insulin sensitivity

Several studies show that untreated GH deficiency (GHD) in adults is associated with insulin resistance [8, 9]. The effect of GH replacement therapy on insulin sensitivity appears to be biphasic. Short-term (< 6 months) GH replacement further decreases insulin sensitivity in adults with GHD [10]. After this initial deterioration of insulin sensitivity, however, an improvement is observed, and insulin sensitivity returns towards baseline values. In studies by O´Neal *et al.* [11] and Fowelin *et al.* [10], insulin sensitivity returned towards baseline values after 3 and 6 months of GH replacement, respectively. During long-term GH replacement, some studies report that insulin sensitivity is still lower than at baseline [12, 13], whereas other studies report unchanged insulin sensitivity compared with baseline [14, 15]. The results of one study, using the hyperinsulinaemic, euglycaemic clamp technique, suggest that the decreased baseline insulin sensitivity persists for up to at least 2 years of GH treatment [16]. However, in a study by Hwu *et al.* [17], 1 year of GH treatment normalized insulin sensitivity as measured by a modified insulin suppression test. In a study by Jørgensen *et al.* [18], insulin sensitivity was similar in patients with GHD and controls after 5 years of GH replacement therapy.

In a 5-year GH treatment trial in patients with adult-onset GHD (AO-GHD), circulating glycosylated haemoglobin levels were reduced after 5 years compared with baseline [5]. In a study by Svensson *et al.* [19], insulin sensitivity was unchanged during 7 years of GH replacement therapy, and there was even a tendency for GH replacement therapy to provide protection from the age-related decline in insulin sensitivity that was observed in matched control subjects.

Type 2 diabetes mellitus

There are few data regarding the incidence of type 2 diabetes mellitus in GH-deficient adults. An analysis was performed in 5120 patients (2706 men) included in KIMS [20]. Each patient had at least one return visit, corresponding to a total of 11 049 years of follow-up on GH replacement therapy. Twenty-six men and 17 women developed *de novo* diabetes mellitus during the follow-up (Table 1). Sixteen of the patients developed diabetes mellitus during the first year of GH replacement therapy. Mean age and body mass index (BMI) of patients who developed diabetes mellitus was 44.0 years and 34.0 kg/m^2 in women and 49.2 years and 32.8 kg/m^2 in men. The standardized incidence ratio was calculated in a Swedish cohort of 138 000 of the general population above 18 years of age followed prospectively for 3 years (Table 1) [20]. No significant sex difference was found. These data suggest that the incidence of type 2 diabetes mellitus in GH-treated hypopituitary patients with a normal BMI is similar to that in the background population. Furthermore, it is reasonable to believe that a high BMI is a risk factor for the development of type 2 diabetes mellitus in GH-deficient adults, as well as in the normal population. It is recommended that GH

Table 1. *Development of diabetes mellitus during GH replacement therapy in 5120 patients (2706 men) included in KIMS. The standardized incidence ratio (SIR) was calculated using a Swedish cohort of 138 000 of the general population above 18 years of age followed prospectively for 3 years.*

BMI	Observed cases	SIR	95% confidence interval
Below 20	0	0.0	0.0–6.4
20–25	3	0.5	0.1–1.5
25–30	10	0.9	0.4–1.7
30–35	18	3.8	2.2–6.0
Above 35	12	5.9	3.1–10.4

BMI, body mass index.

replacement is initiated with a low dose in GH-deficient adults with a high BMI, and that this dose is slowly increased based on the clinical response.

The heart

Short-term placebo-controlled studies have demonstrated that GH replacement therapy in adults has an anabolic effect on cardiac structure [21–23] and improves diastolic [24] and systolic function [21–23, 25]. A few open studies have investigated the long-term effects of GH replacement on the heart. Normalization of cardiac structure was seen during 38 months of GH replacement therapy; however, heart rate and cardiac index increased to supranormal levels [26]. In another study, including 38 young men with childhood-onset GHD followed openly for a mean period of 55 months (range, 39–69 months), GH replacement therapy increased stroke volume and maximal exercise capacity without any long-term increase in left ventricular mass [27].

In seven adults with AO-GHD, 42 months of open GH treatment increased left ventricular mass and decreased the atrial emptying index, which reflects diastolic function, as compared with healthy matched controls [28]. This study might suggest that age increases the susceptibility of patients to developing an inappropriate increment in left ventricular mass during long-term GH replacement therapy, although a higher dose of GH was given than that used today. The available data therefore suggest that low-dose individualized GH replacement therapy improves cardiac function. Combined with the increased muscle strength, this may explain the increased exercise capacity observed in GH-deficient adults after GH replacement. However, if too high a dose of GH is given, there is a risk of an inappropriate increment in left ventricular mass in elderly GH-deficient adults during long-term treatment.

Overall and cardiovascular morbidity and mortality

A retrospective study by Rosén and Bengtsson [29] showed that overall mortality was doubled in hypopituitary adults receiving routine hormone replacement, but not GH replacement, compared with the normal population. Additional retrospective studies [30, 31], and one prospective study [32], have confirmed that total mortality is increased in hypopituitary adults without GH replacement therapy. Most of these studies showed that the increased overall mortality in hypopituitary adults without GH replacement therapy was mainly due to increased cardiovascular mortality [29–32].

GH replacement therapy normalizes most of the cardiovascular risk factors observed in hypopituitary patients without GH replacement therapy. Carotid intima–media thickness is rapidly improved by GH replacement therapy [33]. In addition, GH improves the lipoprotein profile and body composition [34]. There are still, however, limited data regarding the effect of GH replacement therapy on cardiovascular morbidity and mortality. In a recent study by Svensson *et al.* [35], the number of myocardial infarctions and cerebrovascular events was increased compared with the normal population in a cohort of hypopituitary patients without GH replacement therapy, studied retrospectively. In another cohort of hypopituitary patients who received GH replacement therapy and were followed prospectively, the risk ratio for myocardial infarction was even lower than that in the normal population, whereas the risk ratio for cerebrovascular events still tended to be higher than that in the normal population [35]. This could suggest that GH replacement therapy will be effective in reducing the risk of myocardial infarction in hypopituitary adults, whereas the risk of cerebrovascular events will be less affected. Radiation-induced angiopathy has been suggested as a risk factor for stroke [36, 37]. Two previous studies have found that radiotherapy is a predictor of stroke in hypopituitary patients [30, 32]. A possible interpretation of the data by Svensson *et al.* [35] is that GH replacement therapy does not provide protection from strokes that are caused by radiation-induced angiopathy.

Bengtsson *et al.* [38] studied 1903 hypopituitary patients who had received GH for a total of 2334 patient-years within KIMS. Expected mortality was calculated from sex- and age-specific death rates in each country. Eleven of the hypopituitary patients died during GH replacement therapy (1 death/212 patient-years). The standardized mortality rate (SMR) was similar to that in the normal population. Furthermore, the mortality rate in the hypopituitary patients on GH replacement therapy in KIMS was significantly lower than that previously observed by Rosén and Bengtsson [29] in hypopituitary patients not receiving GH replacement therapy. In a study by Götherström *et al.* [5], one of 118 patients with AO-GHD died during 5 years of GH replacement therapy (approximately 1 death/600 patient-years). The recent study by Svensson *et al.* [35] showed increased overall mortality in a cohort of 1411 hypopituitary patients not receiving GH replacement, whereas in another cohort of hypopituitary patients receiving GH replacement therapy, overall mortality was similar to that in the general population. Therefore, it appears that GH replacement may reduce the increased mortality observed in hypopituitary patients.

Hypothalamic–pituitary tumours

No increase in pituitary tumour recurrence rate was found during 3.6 years of GH replacement [39]. One recurrence of craniopharyngioma was reported in a study by Attanasio *et al.* [40] of 173 patients (25.5% of the AO-GHD group had non-functional pituitary adenoma). Moreover, in the Australian Multicenter Trial, 48% of the GH group and 39% of the placebo group had hypopituitarism due to pituitary adenoma [41]. One subject in the GH group and one in the placebo group were operated on for pituitary adenoma during the study period.

In 1034 hypopituitary adults treated with GH for a total of 818 patient-years in KIMS, four patients had recurrent pituitary adenoma, one had recurrent gonadotrophinoma and one had recurrent pituitary dysgerminoma [3]. These results were compared with data from 43 clinical trials involving a total of 1145 hypopituitary adults with a similar geographic distribution. This selection included eight cases of central nervous system or pituitary tumours. Four of these occurred during administration of placebo and four during administration of GH.

In conclusion, the available data suggest that GH replacement therapy does not increase the recurrence or re-growth of hypothalamic–pituitary tumours in adults.

Other neoplasms

Retrospective trials have shown that patients with acromegaly and GH excess have an increased frequency of malignant diseases [42, 43]. The most frequent are mammary cancer and colorectal cancer, and the overall observed/expected ratio for cancer in these studies is between 1.27 and 2.5. In prospective trials, the incidence of tubular adenomas and hyperplastic colon polyps is increased, with some studies also showing higher than expected numbers of colon cancers [42, 43]. In a retrospective survey from the UK of 1362 patients with acromegaly, a lower overall cancer incidence rate was found in the patients than in the general population [44]. The colon cancer mortality rate was, however, higher than expected, with an SMR of 2.47 (confidence interval, 1.31–4.22). Furthermore, an association between serum insulin-like growth factor I levels and prostate, breast and colonic cancer risk in the general population has been demonstrated in prospective trials [45, 46].

In the retrospective study by Rosén and Bengtsson [29], mortality from malignant diseases was reduced in hypopituitary patients. In the study by Bates *et al.* [31], women had an increased mortality from malignancies. Another retrospective study by Popovic *et al.* [47] compared the rate of neoplasia in patients with non-functional and GH-producing pituitary adenomas with that in the general population. They found an increased frequency of cancer in patients with non-functional pituitary adenoma and in acromegalic patients, compared with the expected incidence in the general population. In a large retrospective Swedish study, compromising all individuals with pituitary tumours in

Table 2. Standardized incidence ratio (SIR) for different types of neoplasms during GH replacement therapy in 6428 patients (3281 men) enrolled in KIMS.

	Number of cases			
Type of neoplasm	**Observed**	**Expected**	**SIR**	**95% confidence interval**
Basal cell carcinoma	12	3.8	3.2	1.7–5.6
Prostate cancer	10	4.8	2.1	0.98–3.9
Lung cancer	10	9.2	1.09	0.5–2.0
Breast cancer	8	8.5	0.9	0.4–1.9
Cranial tumours	8	1.1	7.5	3.2–14.8
Melanoma	6	2.1	2.9	1.06–6.3
Stomach cancer	4	2.7	1.5	0.4–3.8
Bladder cancer	4	3.0	1.3	0.4–3.4
Non-Hodgkin lymphoma	3	1.9	1.6	0.3–4.7
Leukaemia	3	1.3	2.4	0.5–6.9
Pituitary carcinoma	2	0.03	76	8.5–274
Pancreas cancer	2	1.5	1.4	0.2–4.9
Carcinoid	2	0.18	11.3	1.3–40.7
Colon cancer	1	4.2	0.2	0–1.3
Rectal cancer	1	2.9	0.3	0–1.9
Corpus uteri myosarcoma	1	1.5	0.7	0–3.7
All neoplasms (secondary included)	82	64	1.3	1.0–1.6
All neoplasms but skin excluded	70	61	1.2	0.9–1.5
All *de novo* neoplasms	73	64	1.1	0.9–1.4

SIR not calculated for two cases of vocal cord cancer and single cases of kidney carcinoma, bone tumour and abnormal smear.

the Swedish Cancer Registry between 1958 and 1991, excess mortality was found from malignant tumours (after exclusion of pituitary malignancies) [48]. Some studies therefore indicate that other forms of cancer may be associated with pituitary tumours and/or their treatment.

In the recent study by Svensson *et al.* [35], 1411 hypopituitary patients who had not received GH replacement therapy were studied retrospectively. An increased risk ratio for all malignancies (fatal as well as non-fatal) was found compared with the general population. The most predominant malignancy in hypopituitary patients who were not receiving GH replacement therapy in adult life was colorectal cancer, which was increased compared with the normal population. This was not explained by GH treatment in childhood. Also, after exclusion of patients who could have received GH treatment in childhood, the increase in the risk ratio for colorectal cancer in hypopituitary patients not treated with GH replacement therapy remained highly significant compared with that in the general population [35].

Swerdlow *et al.* [49], studied young adults who had previously received long-term GH treatment in childhood. Colorectal cancer was detected in two patients, which was significantly higher than that expected in the normal population. However, in the light of the results of the study by Svensson *et al.* [35], in which an increased risk ratio for colorectal cancer was observed in hypopituitary patients not treated with GH replacement therapy, interpretation of the results of the study by Swerdlow *et al.* is difficult.

The incidence of neoplasms was evaluated in 6428 patients (3281 men) enrolled in KIMS [50]. All patients had at least one baseline visit and one return visit while on GH replacement therapy. Median age was 44.4 years and the total duration of GH replacement therapy was 14 073 years. In total, 118 neoplasms were reported in 115 patients (Table 2). There was no evidence that GH replacement therapy in patients enrolled in KIMS increased the risk of developing a malignant neoplasm. Interestingly, subanalyses showed a higher incidence of neoplasms in patients with non-functioning pituitary adenomas than in patients with idiopathic GHD, which is in line with the data reported by Popovic *et al.* [47], Nilsson *et al.* [48], and Svensson *et al.* [35] discussed above.

Conclusions

The available data suggest that long-term GH replacement therapy is safe in adult hypopituitary patients, in terms of the incidence of diabetes mellitus and neoplasms. There are several indications that long-term GH replacement therapy can, at least partly, reverse the increased total and cardiovascular mortality observed in hypopituitary patients not receiving GH replacement therapy. Long-term monitoring is, however, mandatory in terms of glucose metabolism, cardiovascular measurements and underlying neoplasia.

References

1. Raben MS. Treatment of a pituitary dwarf with human growth hormone. J Clin Endocrinol Metab 1958; 18:901–3

2. Wirén L, Bengtsson B-Å, Johannsson G. Beneficial effects of long-term GH replacement therapy on quality of life in adults with GH deficiency. Clin Endocrinol (Oxf) 1998;48:613–20

3. Abs R, Bengtsson B-Å, Hernberg-Ståhl E, Monson JP, Tauber JP, Wilton P, Wüster C. GH replacement in 1034 growth hormone deficient hypopituitary adults: demographic and clinical characteristics, dosing and safety. Clin Endocrinol (Oxf) 1999;50:703–13

4. Bengtsson B-Å, Abs R, Bennmarker H, Monson JP, Feldt-Rasmussen U, Hernberg-Ståhl E, Westberg B, Wilton P, Wüster C. The effects of treatment and the individual responsiveness to growth hormone (GH) replacement therapy in 665 GH-deficient adults. KIMS Study Group and the KIMS International Board. J Clin Endocrinol Metab 1999;84:3929–35

5. Götherström G, Svensson J, Koranyi J, Alpsten M, Bosæus I, Bengtsson B-Å, Johannsson G. A prospective study of 5 years of GH replacement therapy in GH-deficient adults: sustained effects on body composition, bone mass, and metabolic indices. J Clin Endocrinol Metab 2001;86:4657–65

6. Wüster C, Abs R, Bengtsson B-Å, Bennmarker H, Feldt-Rasmussen U, Hernberg-Ståhl E, Monson JP, Westberg B, Wilton P. The influence of growth hormone deficiency, growth hormone replacement therapy, and other aspects of hypopituitarism on fracture rate and bone mineral density. J Bone Miner Res 2001; 16:398–405

7. Svensson J, Mattsson A, Rosén T, Wirén L, Johannson G, Bengtsson B-Å, Koltowska-Häggström M. Three-years of growth hormone (GH) replacement therapy in GH-deficient adults: effects on quality of life, patient-reported outcomes and healthcare consumption. Growth Horm IGF Res 2004, in press

8. Johansson JO, Fowelin J, Landin K, Lager I, Bengtsson B-Å. Growth hormone-deficient adults are insulin-resistant. Metabolism 1995;44:1126–9

9. Hew FL, Koschmann M, Christopher M, Rantzau C, Vaag A, Ward G, Beck-Nielsen H, Alford F. Insulin resistance in growth hormone-deficient adults: defects in glucose utilization and glycogen synthase activity. J Clin Endocrinol Metab 1996;81:555–64

10. Fowelin J, Attvall S, Lager I, Bengtsson B-Å. Effects of treatment with recombinant human growth hormone on insulin sensitivity and glucose metabolism in adults with growth hormone deficiency. Metabolism 1993; 42:1443–7

11. O'Neal DN, Kalfas A, Dunning PL, Christopher MJ, Sawyer SD, Ward GM, Alford FP. The effect of 3 months of recombinant human growth hormone (GH) therapy on insulin and glucose-mediated glucose disposal and insulin secretion in GH-deficient adults: a minimal model analysis. J Clin Endocrinol Metab 1994; 79:975–83

12. Weaver JU, Monson JP, Noonan K, John WG, Edwards A, Evans KA, Cunningham J. The effect of low dose recombinant human growth hormone replacement on regional fat distribution, insulin sensitivity, and cardiovascular risk factors in hypopituitary adults. J Clin Endocrinol Metab 1995;80:153–9

13. Rosenfalck AM, Maghsoudi S, Fisker S, Jørgensen JO, Christiansen JS, Hilsted J, Vølund AA, Madsbad S. The effect of 30 months of low-dose replacement therapy with recombinant human growth hormone (rhGH) on insulin and C-peptide kinetics, insulin secretion, insulin sensitivity, glucose effectiveness, and body composition in GH-deficient adults. J Clin Endocrinol Metab 2000;85:4173–81

14. al-Shoumer KA, Gray R, Anyaoku V, Hughes C, Beshyah S, Richmond W, Johnston DG. Effects of four years' treatment with biosynthetic human growth hormone (GH) on glucose homeostasis, insulin secretion and lipid metabolism in GH-deficient adults. Clin Endocrinol (Oxf) 1998;48:795–802

15. Bülow B, Erfurth EM. A low individualized GH dose in young patients with childhood onset GH deficiency normalized serum IGF-I without significant deterioration in glucose tolerance. Clin Endocrinol (Oxf) 1999;50:45–55

16. Christopher M, Hew FL, Oakley M, Rantzau C, Alford F. Defects of insulin action and skeletal muscle glucose metabolism in growth hormone-deficient adults persist after 24 months of recombinant human growth hormone therapy. J Clin Endocrinol Metab 1998;83:1668–81

17. Hwu CM, Kwok CF, Lai TY, Shih KC, Lee TS, Hsiao LC, Lee SH, Fang VS, Ho LT. Growth hormone (GH) replacement reduces total body fat and normalizes insulin sensitivity in GH-deficient adults: a report of one-year clinical experience. J Clin Endocrinol Metab 1997;82:3285–92

18. Jørgensen JO, Vahl N, Nyholm B, Juul A, Müller J, Møller N, Schmitz O, Skakkebæk NE, Christiansen JS. Substrate metabolism and insulin sensitivity following long-term growth hormone (GH) replacement therapy in GH-deficient adults. Endocrinol Metab 1996;3:281–6

19. Svensson J, Fowelin J, Landin K, Bengtsson B-Å, Johansson JO. Effects of seven years of GH-replacement therapy on insulin sensitivity in GH-deficient adults. J Clin Endocrinol Metab 2002;87:2121–7

20. Bengtsson B-Å, Abs R, Feldt-Rasmussen U, Góth M, Monson J, Thunander M, Koltowska-Häggström M, Mattsson A, Wilton P. The risk of diabetes mellitus in hypopituitary patients on growth hormone substitution. Growth Horm IGF Res 2002;12:302–3

21. Cuneo RC, Salomon F, Wiles CM, Hesp R, Sönksen PH. Growth hormone treatment in growth hormone-deficient adults. II. Effects on exercise performance. J Appl Physiol 1991;70:695–700

22. Amato G, Carella C, Fazio S, La Montagna G, Cittadini A, Sabatini D, Marciano-Mone C, Saccà L, Bellastella A. Body composition, bone metabolism, and heart structure and function in growth hormone (GH)-deficient adults before and after GH replacement therapy at low doses. J Clin Endocrinol Metab 1993;77:1671–6

23. Caidahl K, Edén S, Bengtsson B-Å. Cardiovascular and renal effects of growth hormone. Clin Endocrinol (Oxf) 1994;40:393–400

24. Beshyah SA, Shahi M, Skinner E, Sharp P, Foale R, Johnston DG. Cardiovascular effects of growth hormone replacement therapy in hypopituitary adults. Eur J Endocrinol 1994;130:451–8

25. Fort S, Weaver J, Monson J, Mills P. The effects of low dose recombinant human growth hormone on cardiovascular structure and function in hypopituitary growth hormone-deficient adults. Endocrinol Metab 1995;2:119–26

26. Thuesen L, Jørgensen JO, Müller JR, Kristensen BO, Skakkebæk NE, Vahl N, Christiansen JS. Short and long-term cardiovascular effects of growth hormone therapy in growth hormone deficient adults. Clin Endocrinol (Oxf) 1994;41:615–20

27. ter Maaten JC, de Boer H, Kamp O, Stuurman L, van der Veen EA. Long-term effects of growth hormone (GH) replacement in men with childhood-onset GH deficiency. J Clin Endocrinol Metab 1999;84:2373–80

28. Johannsson G, Bengtsson B-Å, Andersson B, Isgaard J, Caidahl K. Long-term cardiovascular effects of growth hormone treatment in GH-deficient adults. Preliminary data in a small group of patients. Clin Endocrinol (Oxf) 1996;45:305–14

29. Rosén T, Bengtsson B-Å. Premature mortality due to cardiovascular disease in hypopituitarism. Lancet 1990;336:285–8

30. Bülow B, Hagmar L, Mikoczy Z, Nordström CH, Erfurth EM. Increased cerebrovascular mortality in patients with hypopituitarism. Clin Endocrinol (Oxf) 1997;46:75–81

31. Bates AS, Van't Hoff W, Jones PJ, Clayton RN. The effect of hypopituitarism on life expectancy. J Clin Endocrinol Metab 1996;81:1169–72

32. Tomlinson JW, Holden N, Hills RK, Wheatley K, Clayton RN, Bates AS, Sheppard MC, Stewart PM. Association between premature mortality and hypopituitarism. West Midlands Prospective Hypopituitary Study Group. Lancet 2001;357:425–31

33. Borson-Chazot F, Serusclat A, Kalfallah Y, Ducottet X, Sassolas G, Bernard S, Labrousse F, Pastene J, Sassolas A, Roux Y, Berthezene F. Decrease in carotid intima-media thickness after one year growth hormone (GH) treatment in adults with GH deficiency. J Clin Endocrinol Metab 1999;84:1329–33

34. Drake WM, Howell SJ, Monson JP, Shalet SM. Optimizing GH therapy in adults and children. Endocr Rev 2001;22:425–50

35. Svensson J, Bengtsson B-Å, Rosén T, Odén A, Johannson G. The incidence of malignant disease and cardiovascular morbidity in hypopituitary patients with or without growth hormone replacement therapy. The Endocrine Society's 85th Annual Meeting 2003; Abstract P2–344

36. Flickinger JC, Nelson PB, Taylor FH, Robinson A. Incidence of cerebral infarction after radiotherapy for pituitary adenoma. Cancer 1989;63:2404–8

37. Murros KE, Toole JF. The effect of radiation on carotid arteries. Arch Neurol 1989;46:449–55

38. Bengtsson B-Å, Koppeschaar HP, Abs R, Bennmarker H, Hernberg-Ståhl E, Westberg B, Wilton P, Monson JP, Feldt-Rasmussen U, Wüster C. Growth hormone replacement therapy is not associated with any increase in mortality. KIMS Study Group. J Clin Endocrinol Metab 1999;84:4291–2

39. Hatrick AG, Boghalo P, Bingham JB, Ayres AB, Sönksen PH, Russell-Jones DL. Does GH replacement therapy in adult GH-deficient patients result in recurrence or increase in size of pituitary tumours? Eur J Endocrinol 2002;146:807–11

40. Attanasio AF, Lamberts SW, Matranga AM, Birkett MA, Bates PC, Valk NK, Hilsted J, Bengtsson B-Å, Strasburger CJ. Adult growth hormone (GH)-deficient patients demonstrate heterogeneity between childhood onset and adult onset before and during human GH treatment. Adult Growth Hormone Deficiency Study Group. J Clin Endocrinol Metab 1997;82:82–8

41. Cuneo RC, Judd S, Wallace JD, Perry-Keene D, Burger H, Lim-Tio S, Strauss B, Stockigt J, Topliss D, Alford F, Hew L, Bode H, Conway A, Handelsman D, Dunn S, Boyages S, Cheung NW, Hurley D. The Australian Multicenter Trial of Growth Hormone (GH) Treatment in GH-Deficient Adults. J Clin Endocrinol Metab 1998;83:107–16

42. Bengtsson B-Å. Acromegaly and neoplasia. J Pediatr Endocrinol 1993;6:73–8

43. Jenkins PJ, Besser M. Clinical perspective: acromegaly and cancer: a problem. J Clin Endocrinol Metab 2001; 86:2935–41

44. Orme SM, McNally RJ, Cartwright RA, Belchetz PE. Mortality and cancer incidence in acromegaly: a retrospective cohort study. United Kingdom Acromegaly Study Group. J Clin Endocrinol Metab 1998;83:2730–4

45. Hankinson SE, Willett WC, Colditz GA, Hunter DJ, Michaud DS, Deroo B, Rosner B, Speizer FE, Pollak M. Circulating concentrations of insulin-like growth factor-I and risk of breast cancer. Lancet 1998; 351:1393–6

46. Shaneyfelt T, Husein R, Bubley G, Mantzoros CS. Hormonal predictors of prostrate cancer: a meta-analysis. J Clin Oncol 2000;18:847–53

47. Popovic V, Damjanovic S, Mimic D, Nesovic M, Djurovic M, Petakov M, Obradovic S, Zoric S, Simic M, Penezic Z, Marinkovic J. Increased incidence of neoplasia in patients with pituitary adenomas. The Pituitary Study Group. Clin Endocrinol (Oxf) 1998; 49:441–5

48. Nilsson B, Gustavsson-Kadaka E, Bengtsson B-Å, Jonsson B. Pituitary adenomas in Sweden between 1958 and 1991: incidence, survival, and mortality. J Clin Endocrinol Metab 2000;85:1420–5

49. Swerdlow AJ, Higgins CD, Adlard P, Preece MA. Risk of cancer in patients treated with human pituitary growth hormone in the UK, 1959–85: a cohort study. Lancet 2002;360:273–7

50. Wilton P, Mattsson A, Abs R, Bengtsson B-Å, Feldt-Rasmussen U, Góth M, Monson J. Neoplasms reported during growth hormone replacement in KIMS. The Endocrine Society's 85th Annual Meeting 2003; Abstract OR20–6

30 Growth hormone: the future

Mary Lee Vance
University of Virginia Health System, Charlottesville, Virginia, USA

Summary

Growth hormone (GH) is currently licensed in Europe for the treatment of GH deficiency (GHD) in adults, as well as for a variety of indications in children, including GHD, Turner syndrome, chronic renal insufficiency, Prader–Willi syndrome and, most recently, short stature in children born small for gestational age. GH therapy has beneficial effects on body composition, resulting in an increase in muscle mass and bone density, and a decrease in adiposity. Long-term GH replacement also improves muscle strength and exercise tolerance, lowers total cholesterol levels and improves quality of life in adults with GHD. The anabolic effects of GH may therefore also have beneficial effects on other conditions, such as Cushing's syndrome, obesity and insulin resistance associated with the metabolic syndrome, and disturbance in pituitary function associated with fibromyalgia; however, the effects of GH in these conditions are currently poorly understood. Careful, long-term, randomized placebo-controlled studies are required to characterize these effects. The future uses of GH are unknown, but the potentially beneficial uses of this hormone are both exciting and challenging. It is the responsibility of the scientific community to study and define the use of GH for the treatment of conditions for which GH therapy is currently considered experimental.

Introduction

Growth hormone (GH) replacement is an established and approved treatment for childhood and adult GH deficiency (GHD). GH therapy has also been shown to have beneficial effects in children with renal failure, Turner syndrome, Prader–Willi syndrome (excluding patients with sleep apnoea and respiratory problems) and, more recently, in short children born small for gestational age. Most recently in the USA, it has been licensed for the treatment of idiopathic short stature. In adults, GH also has beneficial effects on the AIDS-associated wasting syndrome [1]. GH not only increases linear growth in children but, as an anabolic hormone, also affects all aspects of metabolism including the actions of protein, lipid and carbohydrate. Numerous studies have demonstrated the beneficial effects of GH on body composition, which include an increase in muscle mass and bone density and a decrease in adipose mass, particularly intra-abdominal fat mass. Long-term GH replacement in GH-deficient adults has also been shown to improve muscle strength and exercise tolerance, lower total cholesterol, increase high-density lipoprotein (HDL)-cholesterol levels and bone density, and improve insulin sensitivity and quality of life (QoL). These beneficial effects are dose and time dependent. As GH has these anabolic actions, does it have a role in the treatment of other catabolic disorders? This question remains to be answered with appropriately designed placebo-controlled long-term studies.

The potential future of GH

GH is currently administered as a daily subcutaneous injection. A long-acting depot preparation is also available, and has been approved in the USA for the treatment of children with GHD. Studies of long-acting GH in adults with GHD are currently underway. There is interest in developing an inhaled form of GH, as exemplified by an announced collaboration between a pharmaceutical company and a drug delivery company. Other potential formulations include a transdermal system (whereby GH would be administered via a patch or gel).

Should GH be used to treat Cushing's syndrome, obesity and insulin resistance associated with the metabolic syndrome, adults with Prader–Willi syndrome, polycystic ovary syndrome, chronic fatigue syndrome, fibromyalgia, renal insufficiency and steroid-induced muscle loss, or in elderly people? Given the lack of properly designed long-term studies, the use of GH to treat such patients is not appropriate at this time; however, there is a rationale for investigating the possible use of GH in these conditions.

Cushing's syndrome and chronic steroid therapy

Excessive glucocorticoid levels, as a result of either cortisol hypersecretion or pharmacological glucocorticoid therapy for a chronic illness, exert a profound catabolic effect on protein metabolism. This results in muscle loss, weakness, loss of bone mass, cerebral atrophy, an increase in adipose mass and a deterioration in QoL and emotional well-being. The primary treatment for endogenous Cushing's syndrome is the surgical removal of an adrenocorticotrophin-producing pituitary adenoma or adrenal cortisol-producing tumour; however, those patients who do not achieve remission will require additional treatment. A further problem is that even after successful surgery, the improvement in signs and symptoms of the disorder is not immediate; it usually takes a year or more for patients to return to their pre-Cushing's state, and many patients never recover adequately.

Will GH effectively accelerate recovery following successful treatment of Cushing's syndrome, or in patients receiving chronic steroid therapy? There is no specific information regarding the effect of GH therapy in these patients. Appropriate studies are therefore needed. Patients who require long-term steroid therapy due to organ transplantation, or for conditions such as chronic obstructive pulmonary disease, asthma, rheumatoid arthritis and Crohn's disease, are also in a chronic catabolic state due to excess steroid exposure. These patients are ideal candidates for GH replacement therapy; however, long-term randomized placebo-controlled studies are needed to confirm whether they will benefit from such therapy.

Metabolic syndrome: obesity, insulin resistance and dyslipidaemia

Obesity is a significant problem in many countries; in the USA, approximately 60% of adults are overweight, and approximately 30% are obese. Unfortunately, increasing numbers of children are also obese. Abdominal obesity, hyperlipidaemia and insulin resistance are associated with an increased risk of developing cardiovascular disease, particularly coronary artery disease. Is GH a potentially beneficial therapy? Although GH does not promote weight loss, it has beneficial effects on body composition in adults with GHD (a decrease in adipose mass, with a preferential reduction in intra-abdominal adipose mass), which suggests that GH therapy may be beneficial in obesity, the metabolic syndrome and in adults with Prader–Willi syndrome. GH replacement also lowers total cholesterol levels, raises HDL-cholesterol levels and improves insulin sensitivity in adults with GHD. There is, therefore, a rationale for conducting long-term randomized placebo-controlled studies in obese patients to determine the effect of GH on intra-abdominal adipose mass, serum lipids, insulin sensitivity and the risk of premature cardiovascular disease.

Polycystic ovary syndrome

Polycystic ovary syndrome is the most common cause of infertility and is estimated to occur in 5–10% of women of reproductive age. Although the pathophysiological cause of this disorder is controversial and not precisely defined, a common feature is obesity and insulin resistance, also characteristic of the metabolic syndrome. Treatment with insulin-sensitizing agents, such as metformin, has been shown to improve ovulation and conception rates. Obese women with polycystic ovary syndrome are likely to have a variant of the metabolic syndrome. These patients may therefore benefit from GH therapy, either alone or in conjunction with an insulin-sensitizing medication, to reduce insulin resistance, improve ovulation and fertility rates, improve body composition and reduce the development of risk factors for premature coronary artery disease. Again, however, randomized placebo-controlled trials will be needed to document a possible use in these patients.

Chronic fatigue syndrome

Chronic fatigue syndrome is characterized by symptoms of weakness, fatigue and an inability to perform normal activities, which have an unidentifiable cause. As with many poorly understood syndromes, the aetiology is often attributed to 'psychosomatic illness', as occurred with Crohn's disease several years ago. Crohn's disease is now known to be an organic disorder that can be successfully treated with medication. The fact that medical science has not yet determined the aetiology of chronic fatigue syndrome does not negate the importance of trying to alleviate the symptoms. Is GH secretion diminished in this group of patients and is GH an effective treatment? This is not yet known and it will be necessary to conduct appropriate tests for GHD and long-term, double-blind placebo-controlled studies to address this question.

Fibromyalgia

Fibromyalgia is a debilitating chronic condition that is characterized by chronic pain, muscle weakness, 'trigger point' pain and an inability to function normally. Treatment with analgesics, often narcotics, is required. At least one study has demonstrated a reduced GH response to a stimulation test in patients with fibromyalgia. While there is no obvious reason for impaired GH secretion, the observation of a decreased response to a GH stimulation test suggests some disturbance in pituitary function. It is possible that this is a consequence of the narcotics used to control the pain, as long-term narcotic medication may induce gonadotrophin insufficiency [2, 3]. Again, it remains to be determined whether there is a role for GH therapy in this disorder.

Renal insufficiency

GH improves growth velocity in short children with chronic renal failure before and after renal transplantation. In the short term (6 months), GH also has an anabolic effect in adults undergoing haemodialysis, resulting in an increase in lean body mass, including left ventricular mass (without a change in cardiac function), a decrease in fat mass, an increase in serum albumin levels and an increase in hand grip strength. Renal failure is a severe catabolic condition that also causes bone loss as a consequence of secondary hyperparathyroidism. This is a chronic condition in which GH therapy is potentially beneficial in the long term and should be studied rigorously.

Ageing

Since the first study that reported the beneficial effects of GH administration on body composition by Rudman and colleagues in 1990 [4], there has been an 'explosion' of Internet web sites supporting the use of GH or oral amino acid preparations that claim to increase GH production and retard the effects of ageing. Properly conducted placebo-controlled short-term studies of GH administration in elderly adults have demonstrated the expected changes in body composition (increase in muscle mass, decrease in fat mass); however, there were no beneficial effects on muscle strength or exercise tolerance. Contrary to expectations, oral amino acid preparations have not been shown to increase GH production consistently. Intravenous administration of L-arginine produces a transient increase in serum GH levels, lasting less than 30 minutes [5]. Branched-chain amino acids are components of animal and other proteins, and thus are components of a balanced diet, but there is no evidence that an ingested protein containing branched-chain amino acids substantially increases GH production or retards progression of the effects of ageing. Regardless of the current scientific evidence, however, GH and oral amino acid preparations are being used as anti-ageing treatments. These activities underscore two things:

- the use of unproven agents based on the desire to retard ageing
- the susceptibility of the public to unproven claims.

These problems can only be overcome by long-term (e.g. 10–20 or more years) placebo-controlled studies of GH treatment beginning in healthy 40-year-old adults.

Challenges

The conditions described above may benefit from GH treatment, and the challenge is to address these issues in a proper scientific fashion. This requires appropriately designed, long-term, placebo-controlled studies that include outcome measures, such as body composition, bone density, functional measures of strength and endurance, QoL and the impact of GH on the use of medical resources, including the cost–benefit ratio. The ultimate benefits of GH treatment will need to be demonstrated using these measures, together with the effects of GH on longevity. The use of GH for the treatment of many chronic conditions presents an exciting challenge for the scientific community and should be pursued.

References

1. Nemechek PM, Polsky B, Gottlieb MS. Treatment guidelines for HIV-associated wasting. Mayo Clin Proc 2000;75:386–94

2. Abs R, Verhelst J, Maeyaert J, Van Buyten JP, Opsomer F, Adriaensen H, Verlooy J, Van Havenbergh T, Smet M, Van Acker K. Endocrine consequences of long-term intrathecal administration of opioids. J Clin Endocrinol Metab 2000;85:2215–22

3. Daniell HW. Narcotic-induced hypogonadism during therapy for heroin addiction. J Addict Dis 2002;21:47–53

4. Rudman D, Feller AG, Nagraj HS, Gergans GA, Lalitha PY, Goldberg AF, Schlenker RA, Cohn L, Rudman IW, Mattson DE. Effects of human growth hormone in men over 60 years old. N Eng J Med 1990;323:1–6.

5. Hartman ML, Crowe BJ, Biller BM, Ho KK, Clemmons DR, Chipman JJ. Which patients do not require a GH stimulation test for the diagnosis of adult GH deficiency? J Clin Endocrinol Metab 2002;87:477–85

Subject index

Appendices

Contents

Appendices reproduced with permission.

The Psychological General Well-Being Schedule

This section of the quality of life assessment asks you questions about how you have been feeling and how things have been going for you, DURING THE PAST MONTH. For each question please tick [✓] the answer which best applies to you. Please answer <u>all</u> questions.

1. How have you been feeling in general? (DURING THE PAST MONTH)

   5 ❑ In excellent spirits
   4 ❑ In very good spirits
   3 ❑ In good spirits mostly
   2 ❑ I have been up and down in spirits a lot
   1 ❑ In low spirits mostly
   0 ❑ In very low spirits

2. How often were you bothered by any illness, bodily disorder, aches or pains? (DURING THE PAST MONTH)

   0 ❑ Every day
   1 ❑ Almost every day
   2 ❑ About half of the time
   3 ❑ Now and then, but less than half the time
   4 ❑ Rarely
   5 ❑ None of the time

3. Did you feel depressed? (DURING THE PAST MONTH)

   0 ❑ Yes – to the point that I felt like taking my life
   1 ❑ Yes – to the point that I did not care about anything
   2 ❑ Yes – very depressed almost every day
   3 ❑ Yes – quite depressed several times
   4 ❑ Yes – a little depressed now and then
   5 ❑ No – never felt depressed at all

4. Have you been in firm control of your behaviour, thoughts, emotions, or feelings? (DURING THE PAST MONTH)

   5 ❑ Yes, definitely so
   4 ❑ Yes, for the most part
   3 ❑ Generally so
   2 ❑ Not too well
   1 ❑ No, and I am somewhat disturbed
   0 ❑ No, and I am very disturbed

5. Have you been bothered by nervousness or your "nerves"? (DURING THE PAST MONTH)

   0 ❑ Extremely so – to the point where I could not work or take care of things
   1 ❑ Very much so
   2 ❑ Quite a bit
   3 ❑ Some – enough to bother me
   4 ❑ A little
   5 ❑ Not at all

6. How much energy, pep, or vitality did you have or feel? (DURING THE PAST MONTH)

   5 ❑ Very full of energy – lots of pep
   4 ❑ Fairly energetic most of the time
   3 ❑ My energy level varied quite a bit
   2 ❑ Generally low in energy or pep
   1 ❑ Very low in energy or pep most of the time
   0 ❑ No energy or pep at all – I felt drained, sapped

7. I felt downhearted and blue
(DURING THE PAST MONTH)

- 5 ☐ None of the time
- 4 ☐ A little of the time
- 3 ☐ Some of the time
- 2 ☐ A good bit of the time
- 1 ☐ Most of the time
- 0 ☐ All of the time

8. Were you generally tense or did you feel any tension?
(DURING THE PAST MONTH)

- 0 ☐ Yes – extremely tense, most or all of the time
- 1 ☐ Yes – very tense most of the time
- 2 ☐ Not generally tense, but did feel fairly tense a few times
- 3 ☐ I felt a little tense a few times
- 4 ☐ My general tension level was quite low
- 5 ☐ I never felt tense or any tension at all

9. How happy, satisfied, or pleased have you been with your personal life?
(DURING THE PAST MONTH)

- 5 ☐ Extremely happy – could not have been more satisfied or pleased
- 4 ☐ Very happy most of the time
- 3 ☐ Generally satisfied – pleased
- 2 ☐ Sometimes fairly happy, sometimes fairly unhappy
- 1 ☐ Generally dissatisfied or unhappy
- 0 ☐ Very dissatisfied or unhappy most or all of the time

10. Did you feel healthy enough to carry out things you like to do or had to do?
(DURING THE PAST MONTH)

- 5 ☐ Yes – definitely so
- 4 ☐ For the most part
- 3 ☐ Health problems limited me in some important ways
- 2 ☐ I was only healthy enough to take care of myself
- 1 ☐ I needed some help in taking care of myself
- 0 ☐ I needed someone to help me with most or all of the things I had to do

11. Have you felt so sad, discouraged, hopeless, or had so many problems that you wondered if anything was worthwhile? (DURING THE PAST MONTH)

- 0 ☐ Extremely so – to the point that I have just about given up
- 1 ☐ Very much so
- 2 ☐ Quite a bit
- 3 ☐ Some – enough to bother me
- 4 ☐ A little bit
- 5 ☐ Not at all

12. I woke up feeling fresh and rested
(DURING THE PAST MONTH)

- 0 ☐ None of the time
- 1 ☐ A little of the time
- 2 ☐ Some of the time
- 3 ☐ A good bit of the time
- 4 ☐ Most of the time
- 5 ☐ All of the time

13. Have you been concerned, worried, or had any fears about your health? (DURING THE PAST MONTH)

0 ❑ Extremely so
1 ❑ Very much so
2 ❑ Quite a bit
3 ❑ Some, but not a lot
4 ❑ Practically never
5 ❑ Not at all

14. Have you had any reason to wonder if you were losing your mind, or losing control over the way you act, talk, think, feel or of your memory? (DURING THE PAST MONTH)

5 ❑ Not at all
4 ❑ Only a little
3 ❑ Some – but not enough to be concerned or worried about
2 ❑ Some and I have been a little concerned
1 ❑ Some and I am quite concerned
0 ❑ Yes, very much so and I am very concerned

15. My daily life was full of things that were interesting to me (DURING THE PAST MONTH)

0 ❑ None of the time
1 ❑ A little of the time
2 ❑ Some of the time
3 ❑ A good bit of the time
4 ❑ Most of the time
5 ❑ All of the time

16. Did you feel active, vigorous, or dull, sluggish? (DURING THE PAST MONTH)

5 ❑ Very active, vigorous every day
4 ❑ Mostly active, vigorous – never really dull, sluggish
3 ❑ Fairly active, vigorous – seldom dull, sluggish
2 ❑ Fairly dull, sluggish – seldom active, vigorous
1 ❑ Mostly dull, sluggish – never really active, vigorous
0 ❑ Very dull, sluggish every day

17. Have you been anxious, worried, or upset? (DURING THE PAST MONTH)

0 ❑ Extremely so – to the point of being sick or almost sick
1 ❑ Very much so
2 ❑ Quite a bit
3 ❑ Some – enough to bother me
4 ❑ A little bit
5 ❑ Not at all

18. I was emotionally stable and sure of myself (DURING THE PAST MONTH)

0 ❑ None of the time
1 ❑ A little of the time
2 ❑ Some of the time
3 ❑ A good bit of the time
4 ❑ Most of the time
5 ❑ All of the time

19. Did you feel relaxed, at ease or high strung, tight, or keyed-up? (DURING THE PAST MONTH)

5 ❑ Felt relaxed and at ease the whole month

4 ❑ Felt relaxed and at ease most of the time

3 ❑ Generally felt relaxed but at times felt fairly high strung

2 ❑ Generally felt high strung but at times felt fairly relaxed

1 ❑ Felt high strung, tight, or keyed-up most of the time

0 ❑ Felt high strung, tight, or keyed up the whole month

20. I felt cheerful, light-hearted (DURING THE PAST MONTH)

0 ❑ None of the time

1 ❑ A little of the time

2 ❑ Some of the time

3 ❑ A good bit of the time

4 ❑ Most of the time

5 ❑ All of the time

21. I felt tired, worn out, used up, or exhausted (DURING THE PAST MONTH)

5 ❑ None of the time

4 ❑ A little of the time

3 ❑ Some of the time

2 ❑ A good bit of the time

1 ❑ Most of the time

0 ❑ All of the time

22. Have you been under or felt you were under any strain, stress or pressure? (DURING THE PAST MONTH)

0 ❑ Yes – almost more than I could bear or stand

1 ❑ Yes – quite a bit of pressure

2 ❑ Yes, some – more than usual

3 ❑ Yes, some – but about usual

4 ❑ Yes – a little

5 ❑ Not at all

Quality of Life Assessment of Growth Hormone Deficiency in Adults

LISTED BELOW ARE SOME STATEMENTS that people may make about themselves. Read the list carefully and put a tick in the box marked YES if the statement applies to you. Tick the box marked NO if it does not apply to you.

> Please answer every item.
> If you are not sure whether to answer YES or NO,
> tick whichever answer you think is most true in general.

	YES	NO
I have to struggle to finish jobs	❑	❑
I feel a strong need to sleep during the day	❑	❑
I often feel lonely even when I am with other people	❑	❑
I have to read things several times before they sink in	❑	❑

	YES	NO
It is difficult for me to make friends	❑	❑
It takes a lot of effort for me to do simple tasks	❑	❑
I have difficulty controlling my emotions	❑	❑
I often lose track of what I want to say	❑	❑

	YES	NO
I lack confidence	❑	❑
I have to push myself to do things	❑	❑
I often feel very tense	❑	❑

	YES	NO
I feel as if I let people down	❑	❑
I find it hard to mix with people	❑	❑
I feel worn out even when I've not done anything	❑	❑

	YES	NO
There are times when I feel very low	❑	❑
I avoid responsibilities if possible	❑	❑
I avoid mixing with people I don't know well	❑	❑

	YES	NO
I feel as if I'm a burden to people	❑	❑
I often forget what people have said to me	❑	❑
I find it difficult to plan ahead	❑	❑
I am easily irritated by other people	❑	❑

	YES	NO
I often feel too tired to do the things I ought to do	❑	❑
I have to force myself to do all the things that need doing	❑	❑
I often have to force myself to stay awake	❑	❑
My memory lets me down	❑	❑

Now please go back to the first question and make sure that you have answered 'YES' or 'NO' to every question, on all two pages of the questionnaire.
Thank you for your help.

Patient Life Situation Form

This questionnaire aims to find out about your personal and social situation. Please answer all questions and tick the relevant box.

1 What is your **present** marital status?

- ☐ Unmarried = not living in a partnership now or previously
- ☐ Married/Cohabiting = living in a partnership
- ☐ Widow/er = not living in a partnership
- ☐ Divorced/Separated = not living in a partnership

2 Do you have any children? (own and/or spouse's children in other relationship, also include adopted children)

☐ No ☐ Yes

If yes, how many? ______________

How many children are living at home? ______________

3 With whom do you live presently?

- ☐ Alone
- ☐ Spouse/Partner
- ☐ Parents

Other, please specify

____

4 How many years of formal education have you had? (i.e. time at school and in higher education)

- ☐ <5 e.g. primary education only
- ☐ 5–9 e.g. junior school
- ☐ 10–13 e.g. secondary school – 6th form
- ☐ >13 further education e.g. diploma/degree

5 What is your professional/vocational training?

____
(i.e. secretary, carpenter)

6 What type of employment are you in now?

_______________ (year)

(If you are working and studying part-time, tick both the full and part-time boxes)

- ☐ Full-time as:

  ____

  (specify)

  Please indicate if you are employed as a:

  - ☐ professional and/or non-manual salaried employee
  - ☐ manual wage earner
  - ☐ self-employed

- ☐ Part-time as:

  ____

  (specify)

  Please indicate if you are employed as a:

  - ☐ professional and/or non-manual salaried employee
  - ☐ manual wage earner
  - ☐ self-employed

- ☐ Unemployed
  (Looking for job)
- ☐ Student
  (Or under professional/vocational training)
- ☐ Running family home full-time
  (Do not tick this box if you are retired, on sickness/ disability pension or unemployed, and therefore can take care of home)
- ☐ Sickness/Disability pension

  Reason: ______________________________
- ☐ Retired – early

  Reason: ______________________________
- ☐ Retired – normal

7 Do you need any assistance with your daily life activities?
(Tick whichever activities you normally/usually need assistance with)

☐ No ☐ Yes

If yes, please specify with what:

☐ Errands/shopping

☐ Housekeeping

☐ Grooming and dressing

☐ Personal hygiene

☐ Other, specify

____

Questions 8–10. Please ensure that the first time you fill in the form you give the information asked for, **based on the last six months prior to the visit**. At future visits you should give the information based on the time period since you last completed the form. **Do not forget to check your patient diary!**

8 How many days of sick-leave have you taken since the last visit?

__________ full days

__________ part days

9 If you have been hospitalized since the last visit, state the number of days.
(As an in-patient)

__________ days

Specify reason and clinic/hospital:

____

____

10 How many times have you visited your general practitioner or other physician since the last visit?

__________ times

11 Are you physically active in your leisure time?

(Put a cross on the line below to describe your physical activity during the past two weeks)

Totally inactive — Extremely active

12 Are you satisfied with your physical activity in your leisure time?

(Put a cross on the line below to describe your satisfaction with your physical activity during the past two weeks)

Totally dissatisfied — Completely satisfied

13 Do you feel any change in yourself since you started your GH treatment?

(Do not complete this question if you have not yet started your Genotropin treatment)

- ☐ Yes, I feel much improved
- ☐ Yes, I feel a little improved
- ☐ No, I feel no change
- ☐ Yes, I feel a little worse
- ☐ Yes, I feel much worse

Aetiology of growth hormone deficiency (KIMS classification list)

Idiopathic

1.1 Idiopathic GHD

Congenital

Genetic cause of GHD

2.1.1.1 GH-gene-defect (Type 1A dominant or recessive)

2.1.1.2 GH-gene-defect (specify)

2.1.1.3 GHRH-gene-defect (specify)

2.1.1.9 Other genetic cause of GHD (specify)

Central malformation

2.1.2.1 Septo-optic dysplasia

2.1.2.2 Empty sella syndrome (including pituitary aplasia)

2.1.2.3 Solitary central maxillary incisor syndrome

2.1.2.4 Mid-line palatal cleft

2.1.2.5 Arachnoid cyst

2.1.2.6 Congenital hydrocephalus

2.1.2.9 Other central malformation (specify)

Complex syndrome with congenital GHD

2.1.3.1 Fanconi pancytopenia

2.1.3.2 Rieger syndrome

2.1.3.3 EEC syndrome (Ectrodactyly-Ectodermal Dyplasia-Clefting syndrome)

2.1.3.9 Other complex syndrome with congenital GHD (specify)

Prenatal infection

2.1.4.1 Rubella

2.1.4.9 Other than rubella prenatal infection (specify)

Bio-inactive GH syndrome

2.1.5.1 Kowarski type

2.1.5.9 Other than Kowarski type bio-inactive GH syndrome (specify)

Functional GHD

2.1.6.1 GH-receptor defect (Laron Type)

2.1.6.2 GH-receptor/postreceptor defect (specify)

2.1.6.3 IGF resistance (specify)

2.1.6.9 Other functional GHD (specify)

2.1.9 Congenital unknown

Acquired

	Tumors of the pituitary/hypothalamic area	
2.2.1.1	Craniopharyngioma	
2.2.1.2	Germ cell tumors (specify: dysgerminoma, pinealoma)	
2.2.1.3	Hamartoma	
	Adenoma	
2.2.1.4.1		Non-secreting
2.2.1.4.2		ACTH
2.2.1.4.3		GH
2.2.1.4.4		Prolactin
2.2.1.4.5		Gonadotropin
2.2.1.4.6		TSH
2.2.1.4.7		Co-secreting (specify)
2.2.1.4.9	Other adenoma (specify)	
2.2.1.5	Cyst (specify: Rathke's, epidermoid, dermoid)	
2.2.1.6	Glioma	
2.2.1.7	Meningioma	
2.2.1.8	Schwannoma	
2.2.1.10	Chordoma	
2.2.1.11	Primary pituitary carcinoma	
2.2.1.12	Sarcoma	
2.2.1.13	Metastatic carcinoma	
2.2.1.14	Hematologic metastases	
2.2.1.9	Other tumors of pituitary/hypothalamic area (specify)	
	Cranial tumors distant from the pituitary/hypothalamic area	
2.2.2.1	Astrocytoma	
2.2.2.2	Ependymoma	
2.2.2.3	Glioma	
2.2.3.4	Medulloblastoma	
2.2.2.5	Nasopharyngeal tumour	
2.2.2.9	Other cranial tumors distant from the pituitary/hypothalamic area (specify)	
	Treatment for malignancy outside the cranium	
	Leukemia	
2.2.3.1.1		Lymphatic leukemia
2.2.3.1.2		Myeloid leukemia
2.2.3.1.3		Aplastic leukemia

2.2.3.1.9 Other leukemia (specify)

Lymphoma

2.2.3.2.1 Hodgkin lymphoma

2.2.3.2.2 Non-Hodgkin lymphoma

2.2.3.2.9 Other lymphoma (specify)

Solid tumor

2.2.3.3 Solid tumor (specify)

Other causes of acquired GHD

2.2.4.1.1 Perinatal head trauma

2.2.4.1.2 Traumatic brain injury

2.2.4.2 CNS infection (specify: meningitis, encephalitis, septic cavernous sinus)

2.2.4.3 Hydrocephalus

2.2.4.4 Granulomatous diseases (specify: sarcoidosis, tuberculosis, syphilis, fungal)

2.2.4.5 Langerhans cell histiocytosis (histiocytosis X, eosinophilic granuloma, Hand-Schüller-Christian disease)

2.2.4.6.1 Infarction (apoplexy)

2.2.4.6.2 Postpartum necrosis (Sheehan's syndrome)

2.2.4.6.4 Aneurysm

2.2.4.6.5 Sickle cell anemia

2.2.4.6.6 Thalassemia

2.2.4.6.9 Other vascular (specify)

2.2.4.7 Lymphocytic hypophysitis

2.2.4.8 Hemochromatosis

2.2.4.9 Other (specify)

References

1. Dupuy HJ. The Psychological General Well-Being (PGWB) Index. In: Wegner NK, editor. Association of QoL in clinical trials of cardiovascular therapies. Le Jaco Publications 1984:170–83

2. Hunt SM, McKenna SP, Doward LC. Preliminary report on the development of a disease-specific instrument for assessing quality of life of adults with growth hormone deficiency. Acta Endocrinol (Copenh) 1993;128 (Suppl 2): 37–40

3. McKenna SP, Doward LC. Quality-of-Life Assessment of Adults with Growth Hormone Deficiency. Implications for drug therapy. Pharmacoeconomics 1994;6:434–41

4. Holmes SJ, McKenna SP, Doward LC, Hunt SM, Shalet SM. Development of a questionnaire to assess the quality of life of adults with growth hormone deficiency. Endocrinol Metab 1995;2:63–9

5. Doward LC. The development of the AGHDA. A measure to assess quality of life of adults with growth hormone deficiency. Qual Life Res 1995;4:420–1

6. McKenna S, Doward L. Measuring quality of life in adults with growth hormone deficiency. Clin Endocrinol (Oxf) 1996;45:507–8

7. McKenna S, Koppeschaar H, Zelissen P, Snel Y. The impact of replacement GH on quality of life of patients; results of a clinical trial in The Netherlands. Endocrinol Metab 1997;4 (Suppl B):167

8. Badia X, Lucas A, Sanmartí A, Roset M, Ulied A. One-year follow-up of quality of life in adults with untreated growth hormone deficiency. Clin Endocrinol (Oxf) 1998;49:765–71

9. McKenna SP, Doward LC, Alonso J, Kohlmann T, Niero M, Prieto L, Wirén L. The QoL-AGHDA: an instrument for the assessment of quality of life in adults with growth hormone deficiency. Qual Life Res 1999;8:373–83

10. Wirén L, Whalley D, McKenna S, Wilhelmsen L. Application of a disease-specific, quality-of-life measure (QoL-AGHDA) in growth hormone-deficient adults and a random population sample in Sweden: validation of the measure by Rasch analysis. Clin Endocrinol (Oxf) 2000;52:143–52

11. Hernberg-Ståhl E, Luger A, Abs R, Bengtsson B-Å, Feldt-Rasmussen U, Wilton P, Westberg B, Monson JP. Healthcare consumption decreases in parallel with improvements in quality of life during GH replacement in hypopituitary adults with GH deficiency. J Clin Endocrinol Metab 2001;86:5277–81